T0335491

Sparse Image and Signal Processing
Wavelets and Related Geometric Multiscale Analysis
Second Edition

This thoroughly updated new edition presents state-of-the-art sparse and multiscale image and signal processing. It covers linear multiscale geometric transforms, such as wavelet, ridgelet, or curvelet transforms, and nonlinear multiscale transforms based on the median and mathematical morphology operators. Along with an up-to-the-minute description of required computation, it covers the latest results in inverse problem solving and regularization, sparse signal decomposition, blind source separation, inpainting, and compressed sensing. New chapters and sections cover multiscale geometric transforms for three-dimensional data (data cubes), data on the sphere (geolocated data), dictionary learning, and nonnegative matrix factorization.

The authors wed theory and practice in examining applications in areas such as astronomy, including recent results from the European Space Agency's Herschel mission, biology, fusion physics, cold dark matter simulation, medical MRI, digital media, and forensics. MATLAB® and IDL code, available online at www.SparseSignalRecipes.info, accompany these methods and all applications.

Jean-Luc Starck is Senior Scientist at the Institute of Research into the Fundamental Laws of the Universe, Commissariat à l'Énergie Atomique de Saclay, France. His research interests include cosmology, weak lensing data, and statistical methods such as wavelets and other sparse representations of data. He has published more than 200 papers in astrophysics, cosmology, signal processing, and applied mathematics, and is also the author of three books.

Fionn Murtagh has served in the Space Science Department of the European Space Agency for twelve years. He is a Fellow of both the International Association for Pattern Recognition and the British Computer Society, as well as an elected member of the Royal Irish Academy and of Academia Europaea. He is a member of the editorial boards of many journals and has been editor-in-chief of *The Computer Journal* for more than ten years.

Jalal M. Fadili has been a full professor at Institut Universitaire de France since October 2013. His research interests include signal and image processing, statistics, optimization theory, and low-complexity regularization. He is a member of the editorial boards of several journals.

SPARSE IMAGE AND SIGNAL PROCESSING

Wavelets and Related Geometric Multiscale Analysis
Second Edition

Jean-Luc Starck
Centre d'études de Saclay

Fionn Murtagh
Goldsmiths University of London and University of Derby

Jalal Fadili
Ecole Nationale Supérieure d'Ingénieurs de Caen

CAMBRIDGE
UNIVERSITY PRESS

CAMBRIDGE
UNIVERSITY PRESS

Shaftesbury Road, Cambridge CB2 8EA, United Kingdom

One Liberty Plaza, 20th Floor, New York, NY 10006, USA

477 Williamstown Road, Port Melbourne, VIC 3207, Australia

314–321, 3rd Floor, Plot 3, Splendor Forum, Jasola District Centre, New Delhi – 110025, India

103 Penang Road, #05–06/07, Visioncrest Commercial, Singapore 238467

Cambridge University Press is part of Cambridge University Press & Assessment,
a department of the University of Cambridge.

We share the University's mission to contribute to society through the pursuit of
education, learning and research at the highest international levels of excellence.

www.cambridge.org
Information on this title: www.cambridge.org/9781107088061

First published 2015

A catalogue record for this publication is available from the British Library

Library of Congress Cataloging-in-Publication data
Starck, J.-L. (Jean-Luc), 1965– author.
Sparse image and signal processing : wavelets and related geometric multiscale
analysis / Jean-Luc Starck (Centre d'études de Saclay), Fionn Murtagh (Royal
Holloway, University of London), Jalal Fadili (Ecole Nationale Supérieure
d'Ingénieurs de Caen). – Second edition.
   pages   cm
Includes bibliographical references and index.
ISBN 978-1-107-08806-1 (hardback : alk. paper)   1. Transformations (Mathematics)
2. Signal processing.   3. Image processing.   4. Sparse matrices.   5.Wavelets
(Mathematics)   I.Murtagh, Fionn, author.   II. Fadili, Jalal M., 1973– author.
III. Title.
QA601.S785   2015
621.36 7–dc23   2015021268

ISBN   978-1-107-08806-1   Hardback

Contents

Color plates follow page 124

List of Acronyms

1-D, 2-D, 3-D	one-, two-, three-dimensional
AAC	Advanced Audio Coding
ADMM	Alternating-Direction Method of Multipliers
AIC	Akaike Information Criterion
BCR	Block-Coordinate Relaxation
BIC	Bayesian Information Criterion
BP	Basis Pursuit
BPDN	Basis Pursuit DeNoising
BSS	Blind Source Separation
BSE	Back Scattered Electron
BT	Beamlet Transform
CCD	Charge Coupled Device
CeCILL	CEA CNRS INRIA Logiciel Libre
CIF	Common Intermediate Format
CMB	Cosmic Microwave Background
CTS	Curvelet Transform on the Sphere
CurveletG1, G2	first, second generation curvelet
CS	Compressed Sensing
CWT	Continuous Wavelet Transform
dB	Decibel
DCT	Discrete Cosine Transform
DCTG1, DCTG2	Discrete Curvelet Transform, first/second Generation
DR	Douglas-Rachford
DRT	Discrete Ridgelet Transform
DWT	Discrete Wavelet Transform
ECP	Equidistant Coordinate Partition
EEG	ElectroEncephaloGraphy
EFICA	Efficient Fast Independent Component Analysis
EM	Expectation Maximization
ERS	European Remote Sensing
ESO	European Southern Observatory

ESA	European Space Agency
FB	Forward-Backward
FCT	Fast Curvelet Transform
FDCT	Fast Discrete Curvelet Transform
FDR	False Discovery Rate
FFT	Fast Fourier Transform
FIR	Finite Impulse Response
FISTA	Fast Iterative Shrinkage-Thresholding Algorithm
FITS	Flexible Image Transport System
fMRI	functional Magnetic Resonance Imaging
FOCUSS	FOcal Underdetermined System Solver
FSS	Fast Slant Stack
FWER	Family-Wise Error Rate
FWHM	Full Width at Half Maximum
GCV	Generalized Cross-Validation
GFB	Generalized Forward-Backward
GLESP	Gauss-Legendre Sky Pixelization
GMCA	Generalized Morphological Component Analysis
GUI	Graphical User Interface
HALS	Hierarchical Alternating Least Squares
HEALPix	Hierarchical Equal Area isoLatitude Pixelization
HSD	Hybrid Steepest Descent
HTM	Hierarchical Triangular Mesh
ICF	Inertial Confinement Fusion
ICA	Independent Component Analysis
IDL	Interactive Data Language
IFFT	Inverse FFT
IHT	Iterative Hard Thresholding
iid	Independently and Identically Distributed
IRAS	Infrared Astronomical Satellite
IRLS	Iterative Reweighted Least-Squares
ISO	Infrared Space Observatory
IST	Iterative Soft Thresholding
ISTA	Iterative Soft Thresholding Algorithm
ITZ	Interfacial Transition Zone
IUWT	Isotropic Undecimated Wavelet (starlet) Transform
JADE	Joint Approximate Diagonalization of Eigen-matrices
JPEG	Joint Photographic Experts Group
KL	Kullback-Leibler
KL	Kurdyka-Łojasiewicz
LARS	Least Angle Regression
LAT	Large Area Telescope
lhs	lefthand side
LoG	Laplacian of Gaussian
LP	Linear Programming
LR-FCT	Low Redundancy Fast Curvelet Transform

lsc	lower semi-continuous
MAD	Median Absolute Deviation
MAP	Maximum a Posteriori
MCA	Morphological Component Analysis
MDL	Minimum Description Length
MGA	Multiscale Geometric Analysis
MI	Mutual Information
ML	Maximum Likelihood
MM	Majorization-Minimization
MMT	Multiscale Median Transform
MMV	Multiple Measurements Vector
MOLA	Mars Orbiter Laser Altimeter
MOM	Mean of Max
MP	Matching Pursuit
Mpc	Mega parsecs
MP3	MPEG-1 Audio Layer 3
MPEG	Moving Picture Experts Group
MPI	Message Passing Interface
MR	Magnetic Resonance
MRF	Markov Random Field
MSE	Mean Square Error
MS-VST	Multiscale Variance Stabilization Transform
NLA	Nonlinear Approximation
NASA	National Aeronautics and Space Administration
NMF	Nonnegative Matrix Factorization
NOAA	National Oceanic and Atmospheric Administration
NP	Non-Polynomial
NRMSE	Normalized Root Mean Square Error
OFRT	Orthonormal Finite Ridgelet Transform
OSCIR	Observatory Spectrometer and Camera for the Infrared
OWT	Orthogonal Wavelet Transform
PACS	Photodetector Array Camera and Spectrometer
PCA	Principal Components Analysis
PCTS	Pyramidal Curvelet Transform on the Sphere
PDE	Partial Differential Equation
PDF	Probability Density Function
PMT	Pyramidal Median Transform
PNG	Portable Network Graphics
POCS	Projections Onto Convex Sets
PPFT	Pseudo-Polar Fourier transform
PSF	Point Spread Funcation
PSNR	Peak Signal to Noise Ratio
PTF	Parseval Tight Frame
PWT	Partially decimated Wavelet Transform
PWTS	Pyramidal Wavelet Transform on the Sphere
QMF	Quadrature Mirror Filter

rhs	righthand side
RIC	Restricted Isometry Constant
RIP	Restricted Isometry Property
RNA	Relative Newton Algorithm
RTS	Ridgelet Transform on the Sphere
SAR	Synthetic Aperture Radar
SBT	Spherical Bessel Transform
SDR	Source-to-Distortion Ratio
SeaWiFS	Sea-viewing Wide Field-of-view Sensor
SEM	Scanning Electron Microscope
SFB	Spherical Fourier-Bessel
SNR	Signal-to-Noise Ratio
s.t.	subject to
SSRT	Slant Stack Radon Transform
STFT	Short-Time Fourier Transform
SURE	Stein Unbiased Risk Estimator
USFFT	Unequi-Spaced FFT
UWT	Undecimated Wavelet Transform
UWTS	Undecimated Wavelet Transform on the Sphere
VST	Variance Stabilizing Transform
WMAP	Wilkinson Microwave Anisotropy Probe
WT	Wavelet Transform
TV	Total Variation

Notation

Functions and signals

$f(t)$	Continuous-time function, $t \in \mathbb{R}$.
$f(\mathbf{t})$ or $f(t_1, \ldots, t_d)$	d-D continuous-time function, $\mathbf{t} \in \mathbb{R}^d$.
$f[k]$	Discrete-time signal, $k \in \mathbb{Z}$, or kth entry of a finite dimensional vector.
$f[\mathbf{k}]$ or $f[k, l, \ldots]$	d-D discrete-time signal, $\mathbf{k} \in \mathbb{Z}^d$.
$\bar{f}$	Time-reversed version of f as a function $(\bar{f}(t) = f(-t), \forall t \in \mathbb{R})$ or signal $(\bar{f}[k] = f[-k], \forall k \in \mathbb{Z})$.
$\hat{f}$	Fourier transform of f.
f^*	Complex conjugate of a function or signal.
$H(z)$	z-transform of a discrete filter h.
lhs $= O(\text{rhs})$	lhs is of order rhs; there exists a constant $C > 0$ such that lhs $\leq C$rhs.
lhs $\sim$ rhs	lhs is equivalent to rhs; lhs $= O(\text{rhs})$ and rhs $= O(\text{lhs})$.
$\mathbf{1}_{\{\text{condition}\}}$	1 if condition is met, and zero otherwise.
$L_2(\Omega)$	Space of square-integrable functions on a continuous domain Ω.
$\ell_2(\Omega)$	Space of square-summable signals on a discrete domain Ω.
$\Gamma_0(\mathcal{H})$	Class of proper lower-semicontinuous convex functions from $\mathcal{H}$ to $\mathbb{R} \cup \{+\infty\}$.

Operators on signals or functions

$[\cdot]_{\downarrow 2}$	Down-sampling or decimation by a factor two.
$[\cdot]_{\downarrow 2^e}$	Down-sampling by a factor two that keeps even samples.
$[\cdot]_{\downarrow 2^o}$	Down-sampling by a factor two that keeps odd samples.
$\breve{}$ or $[\cdot]_{\uparrow 2}$	Up-sampling by a factor two (i.e. zero-insertion between each two samples).
$[\cdot]_{\uparrow 2^e}$	Even-sample zero-insertion.
$[\cdot]_{\uparrow 2^o}$	Odd-sample zero-insertion.

$[\cdot]_{\downarrow 2,2}$	Down-sampling or decimation by a factor two in each direction of a 2D image.
$*$	Continuous convolution.
$\star$	Discrete convolution.
$\bullet$	Composition (arbitrary).
∂F	Subdiffential of F.
∇F	Gradient of F
prox_F	Proximity operator of F.
$\mathrm{SoftThresh}_\lambda$	Soft-thresholding with threshold λ.
$\mathrm{HardThresh}_\lambda$	Hard-thresholding with threshold λ.

Sets

$\mathrm{dom}(F)$	Domain of function F.
$\mathrm{ri}(\mathcal{C})$	Relative interior of set $\mathcal{C}$.
$\iota_\mathcal{C}$	Indicator function of set $\mathcal{C}$.
$\mathrm{P}_\mathcal{C}$	Orthogonal projector on $\mathcal{C}$.

Matrices, linear operators, and norms

Bold capital symbols	Matrices or linear operators (e.g. $\mathbf{M}$).
$.^\mathrm{T}$	Transpose of a vector or a matrix.
$\mathbf{M}^*$	Adjoint of $\mathbf{M}$.
Gram matrix of $\mathbf{M}$	$\mathbf{M}^*\mathbf{M}$ or $\mathbf{M}^\mathrm{T}\mathbf{M}$.
$\mathbf{M}[i, j]$	Entry at ith row and jth column of a matrix $\mathbf{M}$.
$\det(\mathbf{M})$	Determinant of a matrix $\mathbf{M}$.
$\mathrm{rank}(\mathbf{M})$	Rank of a matrix $\mathbf{M}$.
$\mathrm{diag}(\mathbf{M})$	Diagonal matrix with the same diagonal elements as its argument $\mathbf{M}$.
$\mathrm{Diag}(x)$	Diagonal matrix whose diagonal elements are the vector x.
$\mathrm{trace}(\mathbf{M})$	Trace of a square matrix $\mathbf{M}$.
$\mathrm{Im}(\mathbf{M})$	Range of $\mathbf{M}$.
$\ker(\mathbf{M})$	Kernel of $\mathbf{M}$.
$\mathrm{vect}(\mathbf{M})$	Stacks the columns of $\mathbf{M}$ in a long column vector.
$\mathbf{M}^+$	Moore-Penrose pseudo-inverse of $\mathbf{M}$.
$\mathbf{I}$	Identity operator or identity matrix of appropriate dimension. $\mathbf{I}_n$ if the dimension is not clear from the context.
$\langle \cdot, \cdot \rangle$	Euclidian inner product.
$\|\cdot\|$	Associated norm.
$\|\cdot\|_p$	$p \geq 1$, ℓ_p-norm of a signal.
$\|\cdot\|_0$	ℓ_0 quasi-norm of a signal; number of non-zero elements.
$\|\cdot\|_\mathrm{TV}$	Discrete total variation (semi)norm.
$\overline{\nabla}$	Discrete gradient of an image.
$\overline{\mathrm{div}}$	Discrete divergence operator (adjoint of $\overline{\nabla}$).
$\vert\!\vert\!\vert \cdot \vert\!\vert\!\vert$	Spectral norm for linear operators.
$\|\cdot\|_\mathrm{F}$	Frobenius norm of a matrix.

$\otimes$	Tensor product.
$\odot$	Entrywise (Hadamard) product.

Random variables and vectors

$\varepsilon \sim \mathcal{N}(\mu, \boldsymbol{\Sigma})$	ε is normally distributed with mean μ and covariance $\boldsymbol{\Sigma}$.
$\varepsilon \sim \mathcal{N}(\mu, \sigma^2)$	ε is additive white Gaussian with mean μ and variance σ^2.
$\varepsilon \sim \mathcal{P}(\lambda)$	ε is Poisson distributed with intensity (mean) λ.
$\mathbb{E}[.]$	Expectation operator.
$\text{Var}[.]$	Variance operator.
$\phi(\varepsilon; \mu, \sigma^2)$	Normal probability density function of mean μ and variance σ^2.
$\Phi(\varepsilon; \mu, \sigma^2)$	Normal cumulative distribution of mean μ and variance σ^2.

Foreword

Often, nowadays, one addresses the public understanding of mathematics and rigor by pointing to important applications and how they underpin a great deal of science and engineering. In this context, multiple resolution methods in image and signal processing, as discussed in depth in this book, are important. Results of such methods are often visual. Results too can often be presented to the layperson in an easily understood way. In addition to those aspects that speak powerfully in favor of the methods presented here, the following is worth noting. Among the most cited articles in statistics and signal processing, one finds works in the general area of what we cover in this book.

The methods discussed in this book are essential underpinnings of data analysis and are of relevance to multimedia data processing and to image, video, and signal processing. The methods discussed here feature very crucially in statistics, in mathematical methods, and in computational techniques.

Domains of application are incredibly wide, including imaging and signal processing in biology, medicine, and the life sciences generally; astronomy, physics, and the natural sciences; seismology and land use studies as indicative subdomains from geology and geography in the earth sciences; materials science, metrology, and other areas of mechanical and civil engineering; image and video compression, analysis, and synthesis for movie and television; and so on.

There is a weakness, though, in regard to well-written available works in this area: the very rigor of the methods also means that the ideas can be very deep. When separated from the means to apply and to experiment with the methods, the theory and underpinnings can require a great deal of background knowledge and diligence, and study too, in order to grasp the essential material.

Our aim in this book is to provide an essential bridge between theoretical background and easily applicable experimentation. We have an additional aim, namely that coverage is as extensive as can be, given the dynamic and broad field with which we are dealing.

Our approach, which is wedded to theory and practice, is based on a great deal of practical engagement across many application areas. Very varied applications are used for illustration and discussion in this book. This is natural, given how ubiquitous the wavelet and other multiresolution transforms have become. These transforms have become essential building blocks for addressing problems across most of data, signal, image, and indeed information handling and processing. We can characterize our approach as premised on an *embedded systems* view of how and where wavelets and multiresolution methods are to be used.

Each chapter has a section titled "Guided Numerical Experiments" complementing the accompanying description. In fact, these sections independently provide the reader with a set of recipes for a quick and easy trial and assessment of the methods presented. Our bridging of theory and practice uses openly accessible and freely available, as well as very widely used, Matlab toolboxes. In addition, IDL is used, and all code described and used here is freely available.

The scripts that we discuss in this book are available online (www .SparseSignalRecipes.info) together with the sample images used. In this form the software code is succinct and easily shown in the text of the book. The code caters to all commonly used platforms: Windows, Macintosh, Linux, and other Unix systems.

In this book we exemplify the theme of *reproducible research*. Reproducibility is at the heart of the scientific method and all successful technology development. In theoretical disciplines, the gold standard has been set by mathematics, where formal proof in principle allows anyone to reproduce the cognitive steps leading to verification of a theorem. In experimental disciplines, such as biology, physics, or chemistry, for a result to be well established, particular attention is paid to experiment replication. Computational science is a much younger field than mathematics, but already of great importance. By reproducibility of research here it is recognized that the outcome of a research project is not just the publication, but rather the entire environment used to reproduce the results presented, including data, software, and documentation. An inspiring early example was Don Knuth's seminal notion of literate programming that he developed in the 1980s in order to ensure trust or even understanding for software code and algorithms. In the late 1980s Jon Claerbout, at Stanford, used the Unix Make tool to guarantee automatic rebuilding of all results in a paper. He imposed on his group the discipline that all research books and publications originating from his group be completely reproducible.

In computational science a paradigmatic end product is a figure in a paper. Unfortunately it is rare that the reader can attempt to rebuild the authors' complex system in an attempt to understand what the authors might have done over months or years. By providing software and data sets coupled to the figures in this book, we enable the reader to reproduce what we have here.

This book provides both a means to access the state of the art in theory and to experiment through the software provided. By applying in practice the many cutting-edge signal processing approaches described here, the reader will gain a great deal of understanding. As a work of reference we believe that this book will remain invaluable for a long time to come.

The book is aimed at graduate-level study, advanced undergraduate level, and self-study. Its readership includes whoever has a professional interest in image and signal processing, to begin with. Additionally the reader is a domain specialist in data analysis in any of a very wide swath of applications who wants to adopt innovative approaches in his or her field. A further class of reader is interested in learning all there is to know about the potential of multiscale methods and also in having a very complete overview of the most recent perspectives in this area. Another class of reader is undoubtedly the student, an advanced undergraduate project student, for example, or a PhD student, who needs to grasp theory and application-oriented understanding quickly and decisively in quite varied application fields, as well as in statistics, industrially oriented mathematics, electrical engineering, and elsewhere.

The central themes of this book are *scale*, *sparsity*, and *morphological diversity*. The term *sparsity* implies a form of parsimony. *Scale* is synonymous with *resolution*. *Morphological diversity* implies use of the most appropriate morphological building blocks.

Colleagues we would like to acknowledge include Bedros Afeyan, Nabila Aghanim, Albert Bijaoui, Emmanuel Candès, Christophe Chesneau, David Donoho, Miki Elad, Olivier Forni, Gabriel Peyré, Bo Zhang, Simon Beckouche, Gitta Kutyniok, Julien Girard, and Hugh Garsden. We would like to particularly acknowledge Jérôme Bobin and Jeremy Rapin who contributed to the blind source separation chapter. We acknowledge joint analysis work with the following, relating to images in Chapter 1: Will Aicken, Kurt Birkle, P.A.M. Basheer, Adrian Long and and Paul Walsh. For their contributions to the new chapter on 3-D analysis, we would like to acknowledge François Lanusse and Arnaud Woiselle. François Lanusse is also thanked for joint analysis work in regard to wavelets on the ball or sphere. The cover was designed by Aurélie Bordenave (www.aurel-illus.com). We thank her for this work.

The following covers the major changes in this second edition. Chapter 5, formerly titled "The Ridgelet and Curvelet Transforms," has been renamed "Multiscale Geometric Transforms." Chapter 3 elaborates further on the starlet wavelet transform.

Chapter 7 is a greatly rewritten state-of-the-art description of required computation. Research has been very active in this area, since the first edition. This chapter has been reorganized and rewritten in order to take account of this. It has been organized such that the reader starts with problems, and therefore the associated algorithms, that are the most simple and then progresses to those that are more sophisticated and complex. Algorithms are focused on, over and above theory. As elsewhere, Matlab code that implements these algorithms is made available.

Chapter 9 contains new work on nonnegative matrix factorization. Chapter 11 relating to three-dimensional data is new. It covers 3-D wavelets, 3-D ridgelets and beamlets, and 3-D curvelets. An application to inpainting of magnetic resonance imaging (MRI) data of the brain is described. Chapter 12 covers new work for data on the sphere, as typifies geolocated data. This chapter includes new applications in fusion physics and, in cosmology, for the cold dark matter simulation.

Chapter 13, on compressed sensing covers the recent evolution of theory in this domain. It has also been updated in regard to the European Space Agency's Herschel mission. Recent results on real data — a compressed sensing study on Herschel data of the galaxy, NGC6946 – are presented.

1

Introduction to the World of Sparsity

We first explore recent developments in multiresolution analysis. Essential terminology will be introduced in the scope of our general overview. This includes coverage of: sparsity and sampling; best dictionary; overcomplete representation and redundancy; compressed sensing and sparse representation; and morphological diversity.

Then we describe a range of applications of visualization, filtering, feature detection, and image grading. Applications range over Earth observation and astronomy; medicine; civil engineering and materials science; and image databases generally.

1.1 SPARSE REPRESENTATION

1.1.1 Introduction

In the last decade sparsity has emerged as one of the leading concepts in a wide range of signal processing applications (restoration, feature extraction, source separation, compression, to name only a few). Sparsity has long been an attractive theoretical and practical signal property in many areas of applied mathematics (such as computational harmonic analysis, statistical estimation, theoretical signal processing).

Recently, researchers spanning a wide range of viewpoints have advocated the use of overcomplete signal representations. Such representations differ from the more traditional basis representations because they offer a wider range of generating elements (called *atoms*). Indeed, the attractiveness of redundant signal representations relies on their ability to *economically* (or compactly) represent a large class of signals. Potentially, this wider range allows more flexibility in signal representation and adaptivity to its *morphological* content, and entails more effectiveness in many signal processing tasks (restoration, separation, compression, estimation). Neuroscience also underlined the role of overcompleteness. Indeed, the mammalian visual system has been shown to be probably in need of overcomplete representation (Field 1999; Hyvärinen and Hoyer 2001; Olshausen and Field 1996a; Simoncelli and Olshausen 2001). In that setting, overcomplete *sparse coding* may lead to more effective (sparser) codes.

The interest in sparsity has arisen owing to the new sampling theory, *compressed sensing* (also called compressive sensing or compressive sampling), which provides an alternative to the well-known Shannon sampling theory (Candès and Tao 2006; Donoho 2006a; Candès et al. 2006b). Compressed sensing uses the prior knowledge that signals are sparse, while Shannon theory was designed for frequency band-limited signals. By establishing a direct link between sampling and sparsity, compressed sensing has had a huge impact in many scientific fields such as coding and information theory, signal and image acquisition and processing, medical imaging, geophysical and astronomical data analysis. Compressed sensing acts today as wavelets did two decades ago, linking together researchers from different fields. A further aspect which has contributed to the success of compressed sensing is that some traditional inverse problems like tomographic image reconstruction can be understood as a compressed sensing problem (Candès et al. 2006b; Lustig et al. 2007). Such ill-posed problems need to be regularized, and many different approaches have been proposed in the last 30 years (Tikhonov regularization, Markov random fields, total variation, wavelets, and so on). But compressed sensing gives strong theoretical support for methods which seek a sparse solution, since such a solution may be (under certain conditions) the exact one. Similar results have not been demonstrated with any other regularization method. These reasons explain why, just a few years after seminal compressed sensing papers were published, many hundred papers have already appeared in this field (see, e.g., the compressed sensing resources web site http://www.compressedsensing.com).

By emphasizing so rigorously the importance of sparsity, compressed sensing has also cast light on all work related to sparse data representation (such as the wavelet transform, curvelet transform, etc.). Indeed, a signal is generally not sparse in direct space (i.e. pixel space), but it can be very sparse after being decomposed on a specific set of functions.

1.1.2 What Is Sparsity?

Strictly sparse signals/images

A signal x, considered as a vector in a finite dimensional subspace of $\mathbb{R}^N$, $x = [x[1], \ldots, x[N]]$, is strictly or exactly sparse if most of its entries are equal to zero; i.e. if its support $\Lambda(x) = \{1 \leq i \leq N \mid x[i] \neq 0\}$ is of cardinality $k \ll N$. A k-sparse signal is a signal where exactly k samples have a nonzero value.

If a signal is not sparse, it may be *sparsified* in an appropriate transform domain. For instance, if x is a sine, it is clearly not sparse but its Fourier transform is extremely sparse (actually 1-sparse). Another example is a piecewise constant image away from edges of finite length which has a sparse gradient.

More generally, we can model a signal x as the linear combination of T elementary waveforms, also called *signal atoms*, such that

$$x = \Phi\alpha = \sum_{i=1}^{T} \alpha[i]\varphi_i, \tag{1.1}$$

where $\alpha[i]$ are called the representation coefficients of x in the *dictionary* $\Phi = [\varphi_1, \ldots, \varphi_T]$ (the $N \times T$ matrix whose columns are the atoms φ_i in general normalized to a unit ℓ_2-norm, i.e. $\forall i \in \{1, \ldots, T\}$, $\|\varphi_i\|^2 = \sum_{n=1}^{N} |\varphi_i[n]|^2 = 1$).

Signals or images x that are sparse in $\mathbf{\Phi}$ are those that can be written *exactly* as a superposition of a small fraction of the atoms in the family $(\varphi_i)_i$.

Compressible signals/images

Signals and images of practical interest are not in general strictly sparse. Instead, they may be *compressible* or *weakly sparse* in the sense that the sorted magnitudes $|\alpha_{(i)}|$ of the representation coefficients $\alpha = \mathbf{\Phi}^{\mathrm{T}} x$ decay quickly according to the power law

$$|\alpha_{(i)}| \leq Ci^{-1/s} , \quad i = 1, \ldots, T ,$$

and the nonlinear approximation error of x from its k-largest coefficients (denoted x_k) decays as

$$\|x - x_k\| \leq C(2/s - 1)^{-1/2} k^{1/2 - 1/s} , \quad s < 2 .$$

In words, one can neglect all but perhaps a small fraction of the coefficients without much loss. Thus x can be well-approximated as k-sparse.

Smooth signals and piecewise smooth signals exhibit this property in the wavelet domain (Mallat 2008). Owing to recent advances in harmonic analysis, many redundant systems, like the undecimated wavelet transform, curvelet, contourlet, and so on, have been shown to be very effective in sparsely representing images. As popular examples, one may think of wavelets for smooth images with isotropic singularities (Mallat 1989, 2008), bandlets (Le Pennec and Mallat 2005; Peyré and Mallat 2007; Mallat and Peyré 2008), grouplets (Mallat 2009) or curvelets for representing piecewise smooth C^2 images away from C^2 contours (Candès and Donoho 2001; Candès et al. 2006a), wave atoms or local DCT (Discrete Cosine Transform) to represent locally oscillating textures (Demanet and Ying 2007; Mallat 2008), etc. Compressibility of signals and images forms the foundation of transform coding which is the backbone of popular compression standards in audio (MP3, AAC), imaging (JPEG, JPEG-2000), and video (MPEG).

Figure 1.1 shows the histogram of an image in both the original domain (i.e. $\mathbf{\Phi} = \mathbf{I}$, $\mathbf{I}$ is the identity operator, hence $\alpha = x$) and the curvelet domain. We can see immediately that these two histograms are very different. The second one presents a typical sparse behavior (unimodal, sharply peaked with heavy tails), where most of the coefficients are close to zero and few of them are in the tail of the distribution.

Throughout the book, with a slight abuse of terminology, we may call signals and images sparse, both those that are strictly sparse and those that are compressible.

1.1.3 Sparsity Terminology

Atom

As explained in the previous section, an atom is an elementary signal-representing template. Examples might include sinusoids, monomials, wavelets, and Gaussians. Using a collection of atoms as building blocks, one can construct more complex waveforms by linear superposition.

Dictionary

A dictionary $\mathbf{\Phi}$ is an indexed collection of atoms $(\varphi_\gamma)_{\gamma \in \Gamma}$, where Γ is a countable set; that is, its cardinality $|\Gamma| = T$. The interpretation of the index γ depends on the dictionary; frequency for the Fourier dictionary (i.e., sinusoids), position for the Dirac dictionary (also known as standard unit vector basis or Kronecker basis),

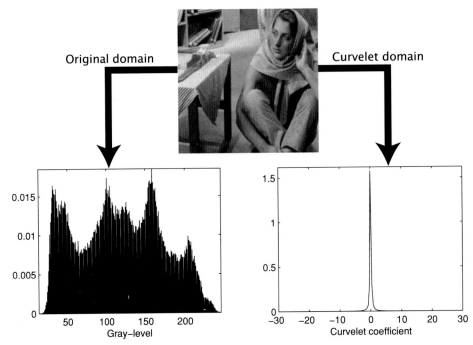

Figure 1.1. Histogram of an image in (left) the original (pixel) domain and (right) the curvelet domain.

position-scale for the wavelet dictionary, translation-duration-frequency for cosine packets, and position-scale-orientation for the curvelet dictionary in two dimensions. In discrete-time finite-length signal processing, a dictionary is viewed as an $N \times T$ matrix whose columns are the atoms, and the atoms are considered as column vectors. When the dictionary has more columns than rows, $T > N$, it is called *overcomplete* or *redundant*. The overcomplete case is the setting where $x = \Phi\alpha$ amounts to an underdetermined system of linear equations.

Analysis and synthesis

Given a dictionary, one has to distinguish between analysis and synthesis operations. Analysis is the operation which associates with each signal x a vector of coefficients α attached to atom: $\alpha = \Phi^{\mathrm{T}} x^1$. Synthesis is the operation of reconstructing x by superposing atoms: $x = \Phi\alpha$. Analysis and synthesis are different linear operations. In the overcomplete case, Φ is not invertible and the reconstruction is not unique (see also Section 8.2 for further details).

1.1.4 Best Dictionary

Obviously, the best dictionary is the one which leads to the sparsest representation. Hence we could imagine having a huge dictionary (i.e., $T \gg N$), but we would be faced with prohibitive computation time cost for calculating the α coefficients. Therefore there is a trade-off between the complexity of our analysis (i.e., the size of the dictionary) and the computation time. Some specific dictionaries have the advantage of having fast operators and are very good candidates for analyzing the data. The

Fourier dictionary is certainly the most well-known, but many others have been proposed in the literature such as wavelets (Mallat 2008), ridgelets (Candès and Donoho 1999), curvelets (Candès and Donoho 2002; Candès et al. 2006a; Starck et al. 2002), bandlets (Le Pennec and Mallat 2005), contourlets (Do and Vetterli 2005), to name but a few. We will present some of them in the chapters to follow and show how to use them for many inverse problems such as denoising or deconvolution.

1.2 FROM FOURIER TO WAVELETS

The Fourier transform is well suited only to the study of stationary signals where all frequencies have an infinite coherence time, or, otherwise expressed, the signal's statistical properties do not change over time. Fourier analysis is based on global information which is not adequate for the study of compact or local patterns.

As is well known, Fourier analysis uses basis functions consisting of sine and cosine functions. Their frequency content is time-independent. Hence the description of the signal provided by Fourier analysis is purely in the frequency domain. Music, or the voice, however, imparts information in both the time and the frequency domain. The windowed Fourier transform, and the wavelet transform, aim at an analysis of both time and frequency. A short, informal introduction to these different methods can be found in Bentley and McDonnell (1994) and further material is covered in Chui (1992); Cohen (2003); Mallat (2008).

For nonstationary analysis, a windowed Fourier transform (short-time Fourier transform, STFT) can be used. Gabor (1946) introduced a local Fourier analysis, taking into account a sliding Gaussian window. Such approaches provide tools for investigating time as well as frequency. Stationarity is assumed within the window. The smaller the window size, the better the time-resolution. However the smaller the window size also, the more the number of discrete frequencies which can be represented in the frequency domain will be reduced, and therefore the more weakened will be the discrimination potential among frequencies. The choice of window thus leads to an uncertainty trade-off.

The STFT transform, for a continuous-time signal $s(t)$, a window g around time-point τ, and frequency ω, is

$$\text{STFT}(\tau, \omega) = \int_{-\infty}^{+\infty} s(t)g(t - \tau)e^{-j\omega t}dt \ . \tag{1.2}$$

Considering

$$k_{\tau,\omega}(t) = g(t - \tau)e^{-j\omega t} \tag{1.3}$$

as a new basis, and rewriting this with window size, a, inversely proportional to the frequency, ω, and with positional parameter b replacing τ, as

$$k_{b,a}(t) = \frac{1}{\sqrt{a}}\psi^*\left(\frac{t - b}{a}\right) \tag{1.4}$$

yields the continuous wavelet transform (CWT), where ψ^* is the complex conjugate of ψ. In the STFT, the basis functions are windowed sinusoids, whereas in the continuous wavelet transform they are scaled versions of a so-called mother function ψ.

In the early 1980s, the wavelet transform was studied theoretically in geophysics and mathematics by Morlet, Grossman and Meyer. In the late 1980s, links with digital signal processing were pursued by Daubechies and Mallat, thereby putting wavelets firmly into the application domain.

A wavelet mother function can take many forms, subject to some admissibility constraints. The best choice of mother function for a particular application is not given a priori.

From the basic wavelet formulation, one can distinguish (Mallat 2008) between: (1) the continuous wavelet transform, described above; (2) the discrete wavelet transform, which discretizes the continuous transform, but which does not in general have an exact analytical reconstruction formula; and within discrete transforms, distinction can be made between (3) redundant versus nonredundant (e.g., pyramidal) transforms; and (4) orthonormal versus other bases of wavelets. The wavelet transform provides a decomposition of the original data, allowing operations to be performed on the wavelet coefficients and then the data reconstituted.

1.3 FROM WAVELETS TO OVERCOMPLETE REPRESENTATIONS

1.3.1 The Blessing of Overcomplete Representations

As discussed earlier, there are different wavelet transform algorithms which correspond to different wavelet dictionaries. When the dictionary is overcomplete, $T > N$, the number of coefficients is larger than the number of signal samples. Because of the redundancy, there is no unique way to reconstruct x from the coefficients α. For compression applications, we obviously prefer to avoid this redundancy which would require us to encode a greater number of coefficients. But for other applications such as image restoration, it will be shown that redundant wavelet transforms outperform orthogonal wavelets. Redundancy here is welcome, and as long as we have fast analysis and synthesis algorithms, we prefer to analyze the data with overcomplete representations.

If wavelets are well designed for representing isotropic features, ridgelets or curvelets lead to sparser representation for anisotropic structures. Both ridgelet and curvelet dictionaries are overcomplete. Hence, as we will see throughout this book, we can use different transforms, overcomplete or otherwise, to represent our data:

■ The Fourier transform for stationary signals.
■ The windowed Fourier transform (or a local cosine transform) for locally stationary signals.
■ The isotropic undecimated wavelet transform for isotropic features. This wavelet transform is well adapted to the detection of isotropic features such as the clumpy structures we referred to above.
■ The anisotropic biorthogonal wavelet transform. We expect the biorthogonal wavelet transform to be optimal for detecting mildly anisotropic features.
■ The ridgelet transform was developed to process images that include ridge elements, and so provides a good representation of perfectly straight edges.

■ The curvelet transform allows us to approximate curved singularities with few coefficients and then provides a good representation of curvilinear structures.

Therefore, when we choose one transform rather than another, we introduce in fact a prior on what is in the data. The analysis is optimal when the most appropriate decomposition to our data is chosen.

1.3.2 Toward Morphological Diversity

The morphological diversity concept was introduced in order to model a signal as a sum of a mixture, each component of the mixture being sparse in a given dictionary (Starck et al. 2004b; Elad et al. 2005; Starck et al. 2005b). The idea is that a single transformation may not always represent an image well, especially if the image contains structures with different spatial morphologies. For instance, if an image is composed of edges and texture, or alignments and Gaussians, we will show how we can analyze our data with a large dictionary, and still have fast decomposition. What we do is that we choose the dictionary as a combination of several subdictionaries, and each subdictionary has a fast transformation/reconstruction. Chapter 8 will describe the morphological diversity concept in full detail.

1.3.3 Compressed Sensing: The Link between Sparsity and Sampling

Compressed sensing is based on a nonlinear sampling theorem, showing that an N-sample signal x with exactly k nonzero components can be recovered perfectly from order $k \log N$ incoherent measurements. Therefore the number of measurements required for exact reconstruction is much smaller than the number of signal samples, and is directly related to the sparsity level of x. In addition to the sparsity of the signal, compressed sensing requires that the measurements be incoherent. Incoherent measurements means that the information contained in the signal is spread out in the domain in which it is acquired, just as a Dirac in the time domain is spread out in the frequency domain. Compressed sensing is a very active domain of research and applications. We will describe it in more detail in Chapter 13.

1.3.4 Applications of Sparse Representations

We briefly motivate the varied applications that will be discussed in the following chapters.

The human visual interpretation system does a good job at taking scales of a phenomenon or scene into account simultaneously. A wavelet or other multiscale transform may help us with visualizing image or other data. A decomposition into different resolution scales may open up, or lay bare, faint phenomena which are part of what is under investigation.

In capturing a view of multilayered reality in an image, we are also picking up noise at different levels. Therefore, in trying to specify what is noise in an image, we may find it effective to look for noise on a range of resolution levels. Such a strategy has proven quite successful in practice.

Noise, of course, is pivotal for the effective operation, or even selection, of analysis methods. Image deblurring, or deconvolution or restoration, would be trivially solved, were it not for the difficulties posed by noise. Image compression would also be easy, were it not for the presence of what is by definition noncompressible, that is, noise.

In all of these areas, efficiency and effectiveness (or quality of the result) are important. Various application fields come immediately to mind: astronomy, remote sensing, medicine, industrial vision, and so on.

All told, there are many and varied applications for the methods described in this book. Based on the description of many applications, we aim to arm the reader well for tackling other similar applications. Clearly this objective holds too for tackling new and challenging applications.

1.4 NOVEL APPLICATIONS OF THE WAVELET AND CURVELET TRANSFORMS

To provide an overview of the potential of the methods to be discussed in later chapters, the remainder of the present chapter is an appetizer.

1.4.1 Edge Detection from Earth Observation Images

Our first application (Figs. 1.2 and 1.3) in this section relates to Earth observation. The European Remote Sensing, Synthetic Aperture Radar (SAR) image of the Gulf

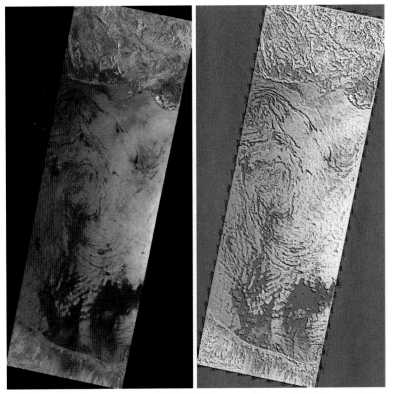

Figure 1.2. (left) SAR image of Gulf of Oman region and (right) resolution-scale information superimposed.

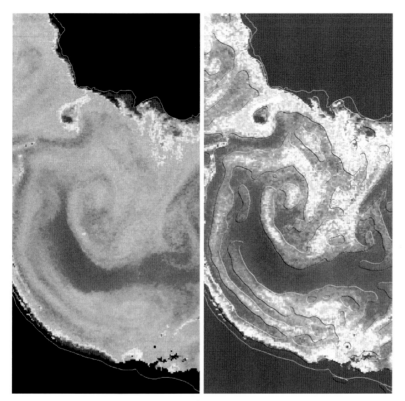

Figure 1.3. (left) SeaWiFS image of the Gulf of Oman region and (right) resolution-scale information superimposed. (See *color plates*.)

of Oman contains several spiral features. The Sea-viewing Wide Field-of-view Sensor (SeaWiFS) image is coincident with this SAR image.

There is some nice correspondence between the two images. The spirals are visible in the SAR image as a result of biological matter on the surface which forms into slicks when there are circulatory patterns set up due to eddies. The slicks show up against the normal sea surface background due to reduction in backscatter from the surface. The biological content of the slicks causes the sea surface to become less rough, hence providing less surface area to reflect back emitted radar from the SAR sensor. The benefit of SAR is its all weather capability, i.e. even when SeaWiFS is cloud covered, SAR will still give signals back from the sea surface. Returns from the sea surface however are affected by wind speed over the surface and this explains the large black patches. The patches result from a drop in the wind at these locations, leading to reduced roughness of the surface.

Motivation for us was to know how successful SeaWiFS feature (spiral) detection routines would be in highlighting the spirals in this type of image, bearing in mind the other features and artifacts. Multiresolution transforms could be employed in this context, as a form of reducing the background signal to highlight the spirals.

Figure 1.2 shows an original SAR image, followed by a superimposition of resolution scale information on the original image. The right hand image is given by:

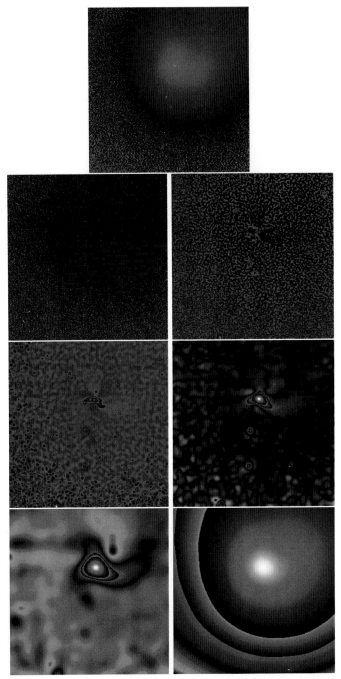

Figure 1.4. (top) Original comet image. Then, successively, wavelet scales 1, 2, 3, 4, 5 and the smooth subband are shown. The starlet transform is used. The images are false color coded to show the faint contrast. (See *color plates*.)

original image plus 100 times the resolution scale 3 image plus 20 times the resolution scale 4 image.

In Fig. 1.3 the corresponding SeaWiFS image is shown. The weighting used here for the right hand image is: original image times 0.0005 plus resolution scale 5 image.

In both cases, the analysis was based on the starlet transform, to be discussed in Section 3.5.

1.4.2 Wavelet Visualization of a Comet

Figure 1.4 shows periodic comet P/Swift-Tuttle observed with the 1.2m telescope at Calar Alto Observatory in Spain in October and November 1992. Irregularity of nucleus is indicative of the presence of jets in the coma (see resolution scales 4 and 5 of the wavelet transform, where these jets can be clearly seen). The starlet, or B_3 spline à trous wavelet, transform was used.

1.4.3 Filtering an Echocardiograph Image

Figure 1.5 shows an echocardiograph image. We see in this noninvasive ultrasound image a cross section of the heart showing blood pools and tissue. The heavy speckle, typical of ultrasound images, makes interpretation difficult. For the filtered image in Fig. 1.5, wavelet scales 4 and 5 were retained, and here we see the sum of these two images. Again, the starlet transform was used.

In Fig. 1.6, a superimposition of the original image is shown with resolution level information. This is done in order to show up edge or boundary information, and simultaneously to relate this to the original image values for validation purposes. In Fig. 1.6, the left image is: the original image plus 500 times the second derivative of the fourth resolution scale image resulting from the starlet transform algorithm. The

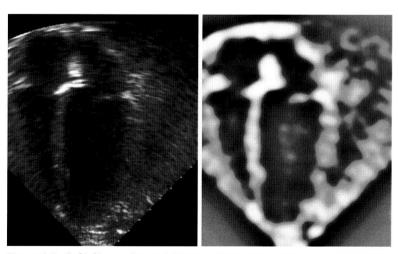

Figure 1.5. (left) Chocardiograph image, with typical textual annotation (date, location, patient, etc.) removed. (right) Wavelet filtered image. (See *color plates*.)

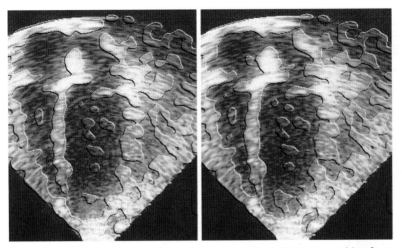

Figure 1.6. Superimposed on the echocardiograph are images resulting from the fourth resolution scale of a wavelet transform.

right image in Fig. 1.6 is the original image plus 50,000 times the logarithm of the second derivative of the fourth resolution scale.

1.4.4 Curvelet Moments for Image Grading and Retrieval

1.4.4.1 Image Grading as a Content-Based Image Retrieval Problem

Physical sieves are used to classify crushed stone based on size and granularity. Then mixes of aggregate are used. We directly address the problem of classifying the mixtures, and we assess the algorithmic potential of this approach which has considerable industrial importance.

The success of content-based image finding and retrieval is most marked when the user's requirements are very specific. An example of a specific application domain is the grading of engineering materials. Civil engineering construction *aggregate* sizing is carried out in the industrial context by passing the material over sieves or screens of particular sizes. Aggregate is a three-dimensional material (two-dimensional images are shown) and as such need not necessarily meet the screen aperture size in all directions so as to pass through that screen. The British Standard and other specifications suggest that any single size aggregate may contain a percentage of larger and smaller sizes, the magnitude of this percentage depending on the use to which the aggregate is to be put. An ability to measure the size and shape characteristics of an aggregate or mix of aggregate, ideally quickly, is desirable to enable the most efficient use to be made of the aggregate and binder available. This area of application is an ideal one for image content-based matching and retrieval, in support of automated grading. Compliance with mixture specification is tested by means of match against an image database of standard images, leading to an automated "virtual sieve."

In Murtagh and Starck (2008), we do not seek to discriminate as such between particles of varying sizes and granularities, but rather to directly classify mixtures. Our work shows the extent to which we can successfully address this more practical and operational problem. As a "virtual sieve" this classification of mixtures is far more powerful than physical sieving which can only handle individual components in the mixtures.

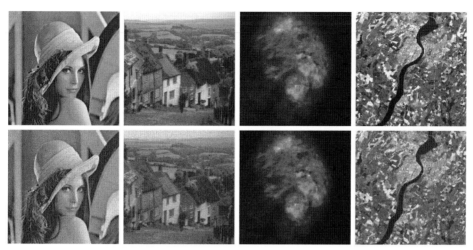

Figure 1.7. (top row) Four images used and (bottom row) each with added Gaussian noise of standard deviation 20.

1.4.4.2 Assessments of Higher Order Wavelet and Curvelet Moments

We took four images with a good quantity of curved edgelike structure for two reasons: firstly, due to a similar mix of smooth, but noisy in appearance, and edge-like regions in our construction images; and secondly, in order to test the curvelet as well as the wavelet transforms. To each image we added three realizations of Gaussian noise of standard deviation 10, and three realizations of Gaussian noise of standard deviation 20. Thus for each of our four images, we had seven realizations of it. In all, we used these 28 images.

Examples are shown in Fig. 1.7. The images used were all of dimensions 512×512. The images were the widely used test images Lena and Landscape, a mammogram, and a satellite view of the city of Derry and River Foyle in Northern Ireland. We expect the effect of the added noise to make the image increasingly smooth at the more low (i.e., smooth) levels in the multiresolution transform.

Each of the 28 images are characterized by the following:

- For each of five wavelet scales resulting from the starlet transform, we determined the second-, third-, and fourth-order moments at each scale (hence variance, skewness and kurtosis). So each image had 15 features.
- For each of 19 bands resulting from the curvelet transform, we again determined the second-, third-, and fourth-order moments at each band (hence variance, skewness and kurtosis). So each image had 57 features.

The most relevant features, which we sought in a global context using a simultaneous analysis of the images and the features provided by correspondence analysis (Murtagh 2005), gave the following outcome. The most relevant features relate to the curvelet transform. Firstly band 12 and secondly band 16 are at issue. In both cases it is a matter of the fourth order moment. See Murtagh and Starck (2008) for details.

1.4.4.3 Image Grading

The image grading problem related to construction materials, and involving discrimination of aggregate mixes, is exemplified in Fig. 1.8. The data capture conditions

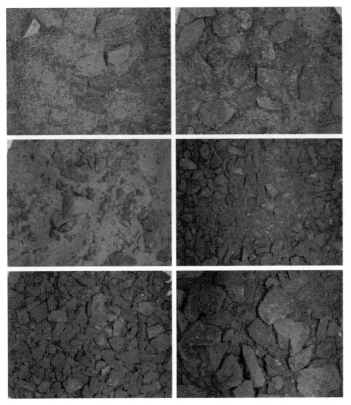

Figure 1.8. Sample images from classes 1 through 6, in sequence
from the upper left.

included (1) constant height of camera above the scene imaged, and (2) a constant
and soft lighting resulting from two bar lamps, again at fixed height and orientation. It may be noted that some of the variables we use, in particular the variance,
would ordinarily require prior image normalization. This was expressly not done in
this work on account of the relatively homogeneous image data capture conditions.
In an operational environment such a standardized image capture context would be
used.

Our training data consisted of 12 classes of 50 images, and we selected 3 classes
(classes 2, 4 and 9, spanning the 12 classes), each of 100 images, as test data. We
used 5 wavelet scales from the starlet transform, and for each scale we determined
the wavelet coefficients' variance, kurtosis and skewness. Similarly, using the curvelet
transform with 19 bands, for each band we determined the curvelet coefficients' variance, kurtosis and skewness. In all, based on the properties of the coefficients, we used
72 features. Our training set comprised three classes, each of 50 images. Our test set
comprised three classes, each of 100 images.

Our features are diverse in value, and require some form of normalization. A
correspondence analysis was carried out on 900 images, each characterized by 72
features. One important aim was to map the data, both images and features, into a

Euclidean space as a preliminary step prior to using k-nearest neighbors discriminant analysis (or supervised classification).

The most relevant features were found to be the following indicating a strong predominance of higher-order moments – the fourth-order moment in particular – and higher-order moments derived from the curvelet transform:

- wavelet scale 5, fourth-order moment
- curvelet band 1, second-order moment
- curvelet band 7, third- and fourth-order moments
- curvelet band 8, fourth-order moment
- curvelet band 11, fourth-order moment
- curvelet band 12, fourth-order moment
- curvelet band 16, fourth-order moment
- curvelet band 19, second- and fourth-order moments

Our results confirm some other studies also pointing to the importance of higher-order moments as features (Starck et al. 2004a, 2005c).

1.5 SUMMARY

The appropriate sparse representation has much to offer in very diverse application areas. Such a representation may come close to providing insightful and revealing answers to issues raised by our images, and to the application-specific problems that the images represent. More often in practice there are further actions to be undertaken by the analyst based on the processing provided for by the sparse representation. Sparse representations now occupy a central role in all of image and signal processing, and in all application domains.

2

The Wavelet Transform

2.1 INTRODUCTION

In this chapter, we start with the continuous wavelet transform followed by implementations of it using the Morlet and the Mexican hat wavelets. The Haar wavelet
is then discussed. With the continuous transform we seek all possible, practical,
resolution-related information. The Morlet wavelet, with many oscillations, is good
for oscillatory data. When the data is not very oscillatory, then the less oscillatory
Mexican hat wavelet is more appropriate.

We then move to the discrete wavelet transform. Multiresolution analysis
expresses well how we need to consider the direct, original (sample) domain, and
the frequency, or Fourier domain. Pyramidal data structures are used for practical
reasons, including computational, and storage size. An example is the biorthogonal
wavelet transform, used in the JPEG-2000 image storage and compression standard.
The Feauveau wavelet transform is another computationally and storage efficient
scheme that uses a different, non-dyadic decomposition. We next look at the lifting
scheme which is a very versatile algorithmic framework. Finally wavelet packets are
described.

A section on Guided Numerical Experiments in Matlab ends the chapter.

2.2 THE CONTINUOUS WAVELET TRANSFORM

2.2.1 Definition

The continuous wavelet transform uses a single function $\psi(t)$ and all its dilated
and shifted versions to analyze functions. The Morlet-Grossmann definition (Grossmann et al. 1989) of the continuous wavelet transform (CWT) for a one-dimensional
(1-D) real-valued function $f(t) \in L_2(\mathbb{R})$, the space of all square-integrable functions,
is:

$$W(a,b) = \frac{1}{\sqrt{a}} \int_{-\infty}^{+\infty} f(t) \psi^* \left(\frac{t-b}{a} \right) dt = f * \bar{\psi}_a(b) , \qquad (2.1)$$

with $\bar{\psi}_a(t) = \frac{1}{\sqrt{a}} \psi^* \left(\frac{-t}{a} \right)$, and where:

- $W(a, b)$ is the wavelet coefficient of the function $f(t)$,
- $\psi(t)$ is the analyzing wavelet and $\psi^*(t)$ its complex conjugate,
- $a \in \mathbb{R}^+ \setminus \{0\}$ is the scale parameter,
- $b \in \mathbb{R}$ is the position parameter.

In the Fourier domain, we have:

$$\hat{W}(a, \nu) = \sqrt{a} \hat{f}(\nu) \hat{\psi}^*(a\nu) . \tag{2.2}$$

When the scale a varies, the filter $\hat{\psi}^*(a\nu)$ is only reduced or dilated while keeping the same pattern.

2.2.2 Properties

The continuous wavelet transform (CWT) is characterized by the following three properties:

(i) CWT is a linear transformation, for any scalar ρ_1 and ρ_2,

$$\text{if } f(t) = \rho_1 f_1(t) + \rho_2 f_2(t) \text{ then } W_f(a, b) = \rho_1 W_{f_1}(a, b) + \rho_2 W_{f_2}(a, b) .$$

(ii) CWT is covariant under translation:

$$\text{if } f_0(t) = f(t - t_0) \text{ then } W_{f_0}(a, b) = W_f(a, b - t_0) .$$

(iii) CWT is covariant under dilation:

$$\text{if } f_s(t) = f(st) \text{ then } W_{f_s}(a, b) = \frac{1}{\sqrt{s}} W_f(sa, sb) .$$

The last property makes the wavelet transform very suitable for analyzing hierarchical structures. It is like a mathematical microscope with properties that do not depend on the magnification.

2.2.3 The Inverse Transform

Consider now a function $W(a, b)$ which is the wavelet transform of a given function $f(t)$. It has been shown (Grossmann and Morlet 1984) that $f(t)$ can be recovered using the inverse formula:

$$f(t) = \frac{1}{C_\chi} \int_0^{+\infty} \int_{-\infty}^{+\infty} \frac{1}{\sqrt{a}} W(a, b) \chi \left(\frac{t - b}{a} \right) \frac{da.db}{a^2} , \tag{2.3}$$

where

$$C_\chi = \int_0^{+\infty} \frac{\hat{\psi}^*(\nu) \hat{\chi}(\nu)}{\nu} d\nu = \int_{-\infty}^0 \frac{\hat{\psi}^*(\nu) \hat{\chi}(\nu)}{\nu} d\nu . \tag{2.4}$$

Reconstruction is only possible if C_χ is finite (admissibility condition) which implies that $\hat{\psi}(0) = 0$, i.e. the mean of the wavelet function is 0. The wavelet is said to

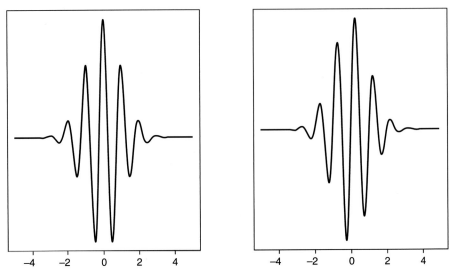

Figure 2.1. Morlet's wavelet: real part on the left and imaginary part on the right.

have a zero moment property, and appears to have a band-pass profile. Generally, the function $\chi(t) = \psi(t)$, but other choices can enhance certain features for some applications, and χ is not necessarily a wavelet function. For example, we will show in the next chapter (Section 3.6) how to reconstruct a signal from its wavelet coefficients using non-negative functions.

2.3 EXAMPLES OF WAVELET FUNCTIONS

2.3.1 Morlet's Wavelet

The wavelet defined by Morlet (Coupinot et al. 1992; Goupillaud et al. 1985) is given in the Fourier domain as

$$\hat{\psi}(\nu) = e^{-2\pi^2(\nu - \nu_0)^2} . \tag{2.5}$$

By taking the inverse Fourier transform it is straightforward to obtain the complex wavelet whose real and imaginary parts are

$$\Re(\psi(t)) = \frac{1}{\sqrt{2\pi}} e^{-\frac{t^2}{2}} \cos(2\pi \nu_0 t)$$

$$\Im(\psi(t)) = \frac{1}{\sqrt{2\pi}} e^{-\frac{t^2}{2}} \sin(2\pi \nu_0 t) ,$$

where ν_0 is a constant. Morlet's transform is not admissible. For ν_0 greater than approximately 0.8 the mean of the wavelet function is very small, so that approximate reconstruction is satisfactory. Figure 2.1 shows these two functions.

2.3.2 Mexican Hat

The Mexican hat used, for example, by Murenzi (1988) is in one dimension:

$$\psi(t) = (1 - t^2) e^{-\frac{t^2}{2}} \tag{2.6}$$

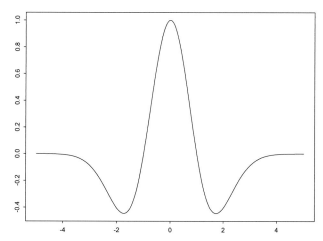

Figure 2.2. Mexican hat wavelet.

This wavelet is, up to the minus sign, the second derivative of a Gaussian (see Figure 2.2).

The lower part of Figure 2.3 shows the CWT of a 1-D signal (top plot of Figure 2.3) computed using the Mexican hat wavelet with the CWT algorithm described in Section 2.4. This diagram is called a *scalogram*. Its y-axis represents the scale, and its x-axis represents the position parameter b. Note how the singularities

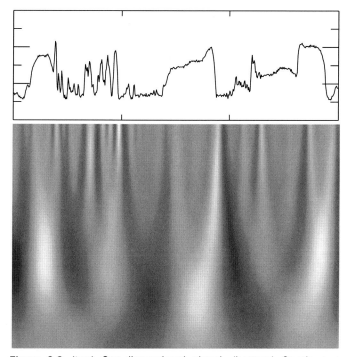

Figure 2.3. (top) One-dimensional signal. (bottom) Continuous wavelet transform (CWT) computed with the Mexican hat wavelet; the *y* axis represents the scale and the *x* axis represents the position parameter *b*.

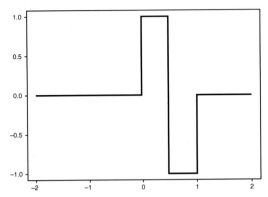

Figure 2.4. Haar wavelet.

of the signal define cones of large wavelet coefficients that converge to the location of the singularities as the scale gets finer.

2.3.3 Haar Wavelet

Parametrizing the continuous wavelet transform by scale and location, and relating the choice of a and b to fixed a_0 and b_0 (and requiring b to be proportional to a), we have (Mallat 2008):

$$\psi_{m,n}(t) = a_0^{-m/2}\psi\left(a_0^{-m}(t - nb_0a_0^m)\right). \tag{2.7}$$

The Haar wavelet transform is given by $a_0 = 2$ and $b_0 = 1$. The compact support of $\psi_{m,n}$ is then $[2^m n, 2^m(n+1)]$.

As far back as 1910, Haar (1910) described the following function as providing an orthonormal basis of $L_2(\mathbb{R})$. The analyzing wavelet in continuous time is a piecewise constant function (Figure 2.4),

$$\psi(t) = \begin{cases} 1 & \text{if } 0 \le t < \frac{1}{2} \\ -1 & \text{if } \frac{1}{2} \le t < 1 \\ 0 & \text{otherwise}. \end{cases} \tag{2.8}$$

Two Haar wavelets of the same scale (i.e. value of m) never overlap, so we have inner product $\langle \psi_{m,n}, \psi_{m,n'} \rangle = \delta_{n,n'}$, where $\delta_{n,n'}$ is the Kronecker delta. Overlapping supports are possible if the two wavelets have different scales, e.g. $\psi_{1,1}$ and $\psi_{3,0}$ (see Daubechies (1992, pages 10–11)). However, if $m < m'$, then the support of $\psi_{m,n}$ lies wholly in the region where $\psi_{m',n'}$ is constant. It follows that $\langle \psi_{m,n}, \psi_{m',n'} \rangle$ is proportional to the integral of $\psi_{m,n}$, that is, zero.

Application of this transform to data smoothing and periodicity detection is considered in Scargle (1993), and to turbulence in fluid mechanics in Meneveau (1991). A clear introduction to the Haar wavelet transform is provided in particular in the first part of the two-part survey in Stollnitz et al. (1995).

Relative to other orthonormal wavelet transforms, the Haar wavelet lacks smoothness; and although the Haar wavelet is compact in original space, it decays slowly in Fourier space.

2.4 CONTINUOUS WAVELET TRANSFORM ALGORITHM

In practice, to compute the CWT of sampled signal $X[n] = f(nT_s)$ (T_s is the sampling period), we need to discretize the scale-space, and the CWT is computed for scales between a_{min} and a_{max} with a step Δ_a. a_{min} must be chosen large enough to discretize properly the wavelet function, and a_{max} is limited by the number N of samples in the sampled signal X. For the example shown in Figure 2.3 (i.e. Mexican hat wavelet transform), a_{min} was set to 0.66 and since the dilated Mexican hat wavelet at scale a is approximately supported in $[-4a, 4a]$, we choose $a_{max} = \frac{N}{8}$. The number of scales J is defined as the number of voices per octave multiplied by the number of octaves. The number of octaves is the integral part of $\log_2\left(\frac{a_{max}}{a_{min}}\right)$. The number of voices per octave is generally chosen equal to 12, which guarantees a good resolution in scale and the possibility to reconstruct the signal from its wavelet coefficients. We then have $J = 12 \log_2\left(\frac{a_{max}}{a_{min}}\right)$, and $\Delta_a = \frac{a_{max}-a_{min}}{J-1}$.

The CWT algorithm follows.

Algorithm 1 Discretized CWT algorithm

Task: Compute CWT of a discrete finite-length signal X.
Parameters: Wavelet ψ, a_{min}, a_{max} and number of voices/octave. These values depend on both ψ and the number of samples N.
Initialization: $J =$ voices/octave $\log_2\left(\frac{a_{max}}{a_{min}}\right)$, $\Delta_a = \frac{a_{max}-a_{min}}{J-1}$.
for $a = a_{min}$ to a_{max} with step Δ_a **do**

1. Compute $\psi_a = \psi\left(\frac{x}{a}\right)/\sqrt{a}$.
2. Convolve the data X with $\bar{\psi}_a$ to get $W(a, .)$, see expression (2.1). The convolution product can be carried out either in the original domain or in the Fourier domain.
3. $a = a + \Delta_a$.

Output: $W(.,.)$ the discretized CWT of X.

If discrete computations where periodic boundary conditions are assumed, the discrete convolution $\bar{\psi}_a \star X$ can be performed in the Fourier domain:

$$\bar{\psi}_a \star X = \text{IFFT}(\text{FFT}(\bar{\psi}_a)\text{FFT}(X)),$$

where FFT and IFFT denote respectively the Fast Fourier Transform and its inverse. In this case, if the number of voices/octave is set to 12, it is easy to check that the computation of the CWT requires $O(12N(\log_2 N)^2)$ operations (Rioul and Duhamel 1992). If the convolution is done in the original (sample) domain, we can choose other ways to deal with the boundaries. For instance, we may prefer to consider mirror reflexive boundary conditions (i.e. for $n = 0, \ldots, N-1$ we have $X[-n] = X[n]$ and $X[N + n] = X[N - 1 - n]$).

The choice of the wavelet function is left to the user. As described above, the only constraint is to have a function with a zero mean (admissibility condition). Hence, a large class of functions verifies it and we can adapt the analyzing tool, i.e. the wavelet, to the data. For oscillating data such as audio signals or seismic data, we will prefer a wavelet function which oscillates like the Morlet wavelet. For other kinds of data such as spectra, it is better to choose a wavelet function with minimum oscillation and the Mexican hat would certainly be a good choice. The wavelet function can also be complex, in which case the wavelet transform will be complex. Both the modulus and the phase will carry information about the data.

Here, we have considered only 1-D data. In higher dimension, we can apply exactly the same approach as above. For 2-D images for example, the wavelet function will be defined as a function of five parameters – position $\mathbf{b} = (b_1, b_2) \in \mathbb{R}^2$, scale in the two directions $\mathbf{a} = (a_1, a_2) \in \mathbb{R} \setminus \{0\} \times \mathbb{R} \setminus \{0\}$ and orientation $\theta \in [0, 2\pi)$ – and the wavelet transform of an image will be defined in a five-dimensional space. But the required memory and the computation time would not be acceptable in most applications. Considering an "isotropic" (i.e. $a_1 = a_2 = a$) wavelet reduces the dimensionality significantly to only three. An even more efficient approach is the (bi-)orthogonal wavelet transform algorithm.

2.5 THE DISCRETE WAVELET TRANSFORM

In the discrete case, the wavelet function is sampled at discrete mesh-points using not Dirac sampling distributions but rather a smoothing function, ϕ. Inner products with the wavelets can be performed in the original domain or in the Fourier domain, the former in preference when the support of the wavelet function is small (i.e., it is nonzero on a limited number of grid points).

For processing classical (regularly sampled) signals, sampling is carried out in accordance with Shannon's well-known theorem (Shannon 1948). The discrete wavelet transform (DWT) can be derived from this theorem if the signal under consideration is band-limited. If we are considering images, we can note that the frequency band is always limited by the size of the camera aperture.

A digital analysis is made possible by the discretization of expression (2.1), with some careful considerations given to the modification of the wavelet pattern due to dilation. Usually the wavelet function $\psi(t)$ has no cut-off frequency and it is necessary to suppress the values outside the frequency band in order to avoid aliasing effects. It is possible to work in the Fourier domain, computing the transform scale-by-scale. The number of elements for a scale can be reduced, if the frequency bandwidth is also reduced. This is possible only for a wavelet which also has a cut-off frequency within the Nyquist band. The decomposition proposed by Littlewood and Paley (1931) provides a very nice illustration of the scale-by-scale reduction of elements. This decomposition is based on an iterative dichotomy of the frequency band. The associated wavelet is well localized in the Fourier domain where a reasonable analysis is possible. This is not the case, however, in the original domain. The search for a discrete transform which is well localized in both domains leads to multiresolution analysis.

2.5.1 Multiresolution Analysis

Multiresolution analysis (Mallat 1989) results from the sequence of embedded closed subspaces generated by interpolations at different scales. In formula (2.1), $a = 2^j$ for increasing integer values of j. From the function, $f(t)$, a ladder of approximation subspaces is constructed with the embeddings

$$\ldots \subset V_3 \subset V_2 \subset V_1 \subset V_0 \ldots \qquad (2.9)$$

such that, if $f(t) \in V_j$ then $f(2t) \in V_{j+1}$.

The function $f(t)$ is projected at each level j onto the subspace V_j. This projection is defined by the approximation coefficient $c_j[l]$, the inner product of $f(t)$ with the dilated-scaled and translated version of the scaling function $\phi(t)$:

$$c_j[l] = \langle f, \phi_{j,l} \rangle = \langle f, 2^{-j}\phi(2^{-j}. - l) \rangle . \qquad (2.10)$$

$\phi(t)$ is a scaling function which satisfies the property

$$\frac{1}{2}\phi\left(\frac{t}{2}\right) = \sum_k h[k]\phi(t - k) , \qquad (2.11)$$

or equivalently in the Fourier domain

$$\hat{\phi}(2\nu) = \hat{h}(\nu)\hat{\phi}(\nu) , \qquad (2.12)$$

where $\hat{h}(\nu)$ is the Fourier transform of the discrete filter h

$$\hat{h}(\nu) = \sum_k h[k]e^{-2\pi i k\nu} . \qquad (2.13)$$

Expression (2.11) allows the direct computation of the coefficients c_{j+1} from c_j. Starting from c_0, we compute all the coefficients $(c_j[l])_{j>0,l}$, without directly computing any other inner product:

$$c_{j+1}[l] = \sum_k h[k - 2l]c_j[k] . \qquad (2.14)$$

At each level j, the number of inner products is divided by 2. Step-by-step the signal is smoothed and information is lost. The remaining information (details) can be recovered from the subspace W_{j+1}, the orthogonal complement of V_{j+1} in V_j. This subspace can be generated from a suitable wavelet function $\psi(t)$ by translation and dilation:

$$\frac{1}{2}\psi\left(\frac{t}{2}\right) = \sum_k g[k]\phi(t - k) , \qquad (2.15)$$

or by taking the Fourier transform of both sides

$$\hat{\psi}(2\nu) = \hat{g}(\nu)\hat{\phi}(\nu) , \qquad (2.16)$$

where $\hat{g}(\nu) = \sum_k g[k]e^{-2\pi i k\nu}$.

The wavelet coefficients are computed as the inner products

$$w_{j+1}[l] = \langle f, \psi_{j+1,l} \rangle = \langle f, 2^{-(j+1)}\psi(2^{-(j+1)}. - l) \rangle$$
$$= \sum_k g[k - 2l]c_j[k] . \qquad (2.17)$$

Furthermore, if the notation $[\cdot]_{\downarrow 2}$ stands for the decimation by a factor 2 (i.e. only even samples are kept), and $\bar{h}[l] = h[-l]$, we can write:

$$c_{j+1} = [\bar{h} \star c_j]_{\downarrow 2}$$
$$w_{j+1} = [\bar{g} \star c_j]_{\downarrow 2} . \tag{2.18}$$

We recall that $\star$ denotes discrete convolution.

With this analysis, we have built the first part of a filter bank (Smith and Barnwell 1988). In order to recover the original data, we can use the properties of orthogonal wavelets, but the theory has been generalized to biorthogonal wavelet bases by introducing the filters $\tilde{h}$ and $\tilde{g}$ (Cohen et al. 1992), defined to be dual to h and g such that $(h, g, \tilde{h}, \tilde{g})$ is a perfect reconstruction filter bank. The reconstruction of the signal is then performed by

$$c_j[l] = 2 \sum_k (\tilde{h}[k + 2l]c_{j+1}[k] + \tilde{g}[k + 2l]w_{j+1}[k])$$
$$= 2(\tilde{h} \star \check{c}_{j+1} + \tilde{g} \star \check{w}_{j+1})[l] , \tag{2.19}$$

where $\check{c}_{j+1}$ is the zero-interpolation of c_{j+1} defined by zero insertions

$$\check{c}_{j+1}[l] = [c_{j+1}]_{\uparrow 2}[l] = \begin{cases} c_{j+1}[m] & \text{if } l = 2m \\ 0 & \text{otherwise} \end{cases} ,$$

and the filters $\tilde{h}$ and $\tilde{g}$ must verify the biorthogonal conditions of dealiasing and exact reconstruction (Vetterli 1986):

- *Dealiasing*:

$$\hat{h}^* \left(\nu + \frac{1}{2} \right) \hat{\tilde{h}}(\nu) + \hat{g}^* \left(\nu + \frac{1}{2} \right) \hat{\tilde{g}}(\nu) = 0 . \tag{2.20}$$

- *Exact reconstruction*:

$$\hat{h}^*(\nu)\hat{\tilde{h}}(\nu) + \hat{g}^*(\nu)\hat{\tilde{g}}(\nu) = 1 , \tag{2.21}$$

or equivalently, in the z-transform domain:

$$H(-z^{-1})\tilde{H}(z) + G(-z^{-1})\tilde{G}(z) = 0$$
$$H(z^{-1})\tilde{H}(z) + G(z^{-1})\tilde{G}(z) = 1 .$$

Note that in terms of filter banks, the biorthogonal wavelet transform becomes orthogonal when $h = \tilde{h}$ and $g = \tilde{g}$, in which case h is a conjugate mirror filter.

2.5.2 Fast Pyramidal Algorithm

In the decomposition (2.18), c_{j+1} and w_{j+1} are computed by successively convolving c_j with the filters $\bar{h}$ (low pass) and $\bar{g}$ (high pass). Each resulting channel is then downsampled (decimated) by suppression of one sample out of two. The high frequency channel w_{j+1} is left, and the process is iterated with the low frequency part c_{j+1}. This is displayed in the upper part of Figure 2.5. In the reconstruction or synthesis side, the coefficients are up-sampled by inserting a 0 between each sample, and then convolved with the dual filters $\tilde{h}$ and $\tilde{g}$, the resulting coefficients are summed

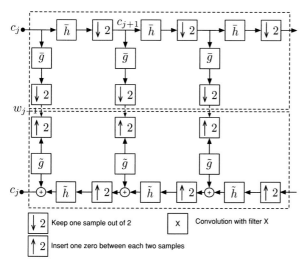

Figure 2.5. Fast pyramidal algorithm associated with the biorthogonal wavelet transform. (top) Fast analysis transform with a cascade of filtering with $\bar{h}$ and $\bar{g}$ followed by factor 2 subsampling. (bottom) Fast inverse transform by progressively inserting zeros and filtering with dual filters $\tilde{h}$ and $\tilde{g}$.

and the result is multiplied by 2. The procedure is iterated up to the smallest scale as depicted in the lower part of Figure 2.5.

Compared to the CWT, we have far fewer scales, because we consider only *dyadic scales*, i.e. scales a_j which are a power of two of the initial scale a_0 ($a_j = 2^j a_0$). Therefore, for a discrete signal $X[n]$ with N samples, one would typically use $J = \log_2 N$ scales, the indexing here is such that, $j = 1$ corresponds to the finest scale (high frequencies). The algorithm is the following.

Algorithm 2 1-D DWT algorithm

Task: Compute DWT of discrete finite-length signal X.
Parameters: Filters $h, \tilde{h}$.
Initialization: $c_0 = X$, $J = \log_2 N$.
for $j = 0$ to $J - 1$ **do**

  ■ Compute $c_{j+1} = \bar{h} \star c_j$, down-sample by a factor 2.
  ■ Compute $w_{j+1} = \bar{g} \star c_j$, down-sample by a factor 2.

Output: $\mathcal{W} = \{w_1, \ldots, w_J, c_J\}$ the DWT of X.

The biorthogonal discrete wavelet transform (DWT) is also computationally very efficient, requiring $O(N)$ operations for data with N samples as compared to $O(N \log N)$ of the FFT. Among the most used filters are certainly the 7/9 filters (by default in the JPEG 2000 compression standard), which are given in Table 2.1. In the literature, the filter bank can be given such that it is normalized either to a unit mass $\sum_l h[l] = 1$, or to a unit ℓ_2-norm $\|h\|_2^2 = \sum_l h[l]^2 = 1$.

Table 2.1. 7/9 filter bank (normalized to a unit mass)

h	g	$\tilde{h}$	$\tilde{g}$
0	0.02674875741	0.02674875741	0
−0.04563588155	0.0168641184	−0.0168641184	0.04563588155
−0.02877176311	−0.0782232665	−0.0782232665	−0.02877176311
0.295635881557	−0.26686411844	0.26686411844	−0.295635881557
0.557543526229	0.60294901823	0.60294901823	0.557543526229
0.295635881557	−0.26686411844	0.26686411844	−0.295635881557
−0.02877176311	−0.0782232665	−0.0782232665	−0.02877176311
−0.04563588155	0.0168641184	−0.0168641184	0.04563588155
0	0.02674875741	0.02674875741	0

Orthogonal wavelets correspond to the restricted case where

$$\hat{g}(v) = e^{-2\pi i v} \hat{h}^* \left(v + \frac{1}{2} \right) , \tag{2.22}$$

$$\hat{\tilde{h}}(v) = \hat{h}(v) \quad \text{and} \quad \hat{\tilde{g}}(v) = \hat{g}(v) . \tag{2.23}$$

Hence the exact reconstruction condition (2.21) simplifies to

$$| \hat{h}(v) |^2 + \left| \hat{h} \left(v + \frac{1}{2} \right) \right|^2 = 1 . \tag{2.24}$$

Such a pair of filters h and g is known as a pair of quadrature mirror filters (QMF). It can be easily verified that this choice satisfies the two basic exact reconstruction conditions (2.20)–(2.21). Daubechies wavelets are the solutions of minimum support size. For biorthogonal wavelets (Cohen et al. 1992; Meyer 1993) we have the relations

$$\hat{g}(v) = e^{-2\pi i v} \hat{\tilde{h}}^* \left(v + \frac{1}{2} \right) \quad \text{and} \quad \hat{\tilde{g}}(v) = e^{-2\pi i v} \hat{h}^* \left(v + \frac{1}{2} \right) \tag{2.25}$$

and

$$\hat{h}(v)\hat{\tilde{h}}(v) + \hat{h}^* \left(v + \frac{1}{2} \right) \hat{\tilde{h}}^* \left(v + \frac{1}{2} \right) = 1 , \tag{2.26}$$

or equivalently in the sample domain

$$g[l] = (-1)^{1-l} \tilde{h}[1-l] \quad \text{and} \quad \tilde{g}[l] = (-1)^{1-l} h[1-l] .$$

This satisfies also relations (2.20) and (2.21). A large class of compactly supported wavelet functions can be derived. Many sets of filters have been proposed, especially for coding. It has been shown (Daubechies 1988) that the choice of these filters must be guided by the regularity of the scaling and the wavelet functions.

2.5.3 Two-Dimensional Decimated Wavelet Transform

The above DWT algorithm can be extended to any dimension by *separable* (tensor) products of a scaling function ϕ and a wavelet ψ. For instance, the two-dimensional algorithm is based on separate variables leading to prioritizing of horizontal, vertical

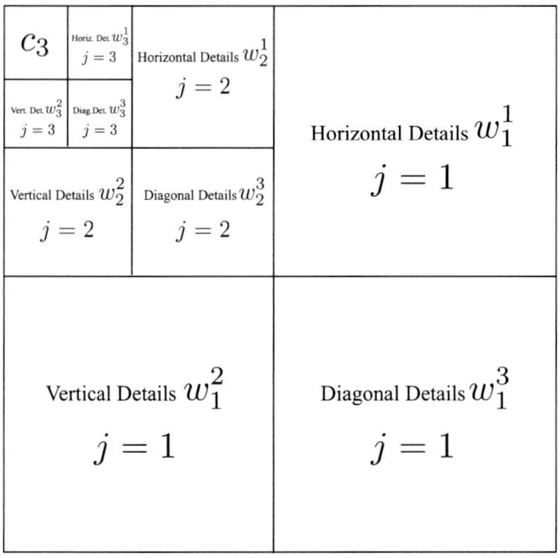

Figure 2.6. Discrete wavelet transform representation of an image with corresponding horizontal, vertical, diagonal and approximation subbands.

and diagonal directions. The scaling function is defined by $\phi(t_1, t_2) = \phi(t_1)\phi(t_2)$, and the passage from one resolution to the next is achieved by

$$c_{j+1}[k, l] = \sum_{m,n} h[m - 2k]h[n - 2l]c_j[m, n]$$

$$= [\bar{h}\bar{h} \star c_j]_{\downarrow 2,2}[k, l] , \tag{2.27}$$

where $[.]_{\downarrow 2,2}$ stands for the decimation by factor 2 along both x- and y-axes (i.e. only even pixels are kept) and $c_j \star h_1 h_2$ is the 2-D discrete convolution of c_j by the separable filter $h_1 h_2$ (i.e. convolution first along the columns by h_1 and then convolution along the rows by h_2).

The detail coefficient images are obtained from three wavelets:

- vertical wavelet : $\psi^1(t_1, t_2) = \phi(t_1)\psi(t_2)$,
- horizontal wavelet: $\psi^2(t_1, t_2) = \psi(t_1)\phi(t_2)$,
- diagonal wavelet: $\psi^3(t_1, t_2) = \psi(t_1)\psi(t_2)$,

which leads to three wavelet subimages (subbands) at each resolution level (see Figure 2.6):

$$w_{j+1}^1[k, l] = \sum_{m,n} g[m - 2k]h[n - 2l]c_j[m, n] = [\bar{g}\bar{h} \star c_j]_{\downarrow 2,2}[k, l]$$

$$w_{j+1}^2[k, l] = \sum_{m,n} h[m - 2k]g[n - 2l]c_j[m, n] = [\bar{h}\bar{g} \star c_j]_{\downarrow 2,2}[k, l]$$

$$w_{j+1}^3[k, l] = \sum_{m,n} g[m - 2k]g[n - 2l]c_j[m, n] = [\bar{g}\bar{g} \star c_j]_{\downarrow 2,2}[k, l] .$$

For 3-D data, seven wavelet subcubes are created at each resolution level, corresponding to an analysis in seven directions.

For a discrete $N \times N$ image X, the algorithm is the following.

Algorithm 3 2-D DWT algorithm

Task: Compute DWT of a discrete image X.
Parameters: Filters $h, \tilde{h}$.
Initialization: $c_0 = X$, $J = \log_2 N$.
for $j = 0$ to $J - 1$ **do**

- Compute $c_{j+1} = \tilde{h}\tilde{h} \star c_j$, down-sample by a factor 2 in each dimension.
- Compute $w_{j+1}^1 = \tilde{g}\tilde{h} \star c_j$, down-sample by a factor 2 in each dimension.
- Compute $w_{j+1}^2 = \tilde{h}\tilde{g} \star c_j$, down-sample by a factor 2 in each dimension.
- Compute $w_{j+1}^3 = \tilde{g}\tilde{g} \star c_j$, down-sample by a factor 2 in each dimension.

Output: $\mathcal{W} = \{w_1^1, w_1^2, w_1^3, \ldots, w_J^1, w_J^2, w_J^3, c_J\}$ the 2-D DWT of X.

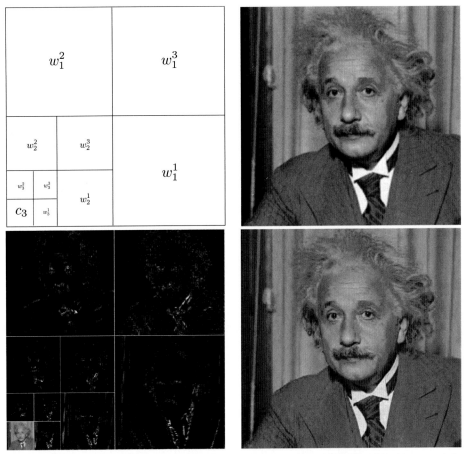

Figure 2.7. The image Einstein (top right), its DWT decomposition (schematic – top left, and coefficients – bottom left). The bottom right image is the result of the compression-decompression JPEG 2000 algorithm, employing the 7/9 DWT, using a compression ratio of 40.

The reconstruction is obtained by

$$c_j = 4\left(\tilde{h}\tilde{h} \star \check{c}_{j+1} + \tilde{g}\tilde{h} \star \check{w}^1_{j+1} + \tilde{h}\tilde{g} \star \check{w}^2_{j+1} + \tilde{g}\tilde{g} \star \check{w}^3_{j+1}\right) \qquad (2.28)$$

in a similar way to the 1-D case, and with the proper generalization to 2-D.

Figure 2.7 shows the image Einstein (top right), the schematic separation of the wavelet decomposition bands (top left), and the actual DWT coefficients (bottom left), using the 7/9 filters (Antonini et al. 1992). The application of the DWT to image compression, using the 7/9 filters (Antonini et al. 1992) leads to impressive results, compared to previous methods like JPEG. The inclusion of the wavelet transform in JPEG 2000, the recent still-picture compression standard, testifies to this lasting and significant impact. Figure 2.7, bottom right, shows the decompressed image for a compression ratio of 40, and as can be seen the result is near-perfect.

2.6 NONDYADIC RESOLUTION FACTOR

Feauveau (1990) introduced *quincunx* analysis, based on Adelson's work (Adelson et al. 1987). This analysis is not dyadic and allows an image decomposition with a resolution factor equal to $\sqrt{2}$.

The advantage is that only one non-separable wavelet is needed. At each step, the image is undersampled by two in one direction (first and second direction alternatively). This sub-sampling is made by keeping one pixel out of two, alternatively even and odd. The following conditions must be satisfied by the filters:

$$\hat{h}\left(v_1 + \frac{1}{2}, v_2 + \frac{1}{2}\right)\hat{\tilde{h}}(v_1, v_2) + \hat{g}\left(v_1 + \frac{1}{2}, v_2 + \frac{1}{2}\right)\hat{\tilde{g}}(v_1, v_2) = 0\,,$$

$$\hat{h}(v_1, v_2)\hat{\tilde{h}}(v_1, v_2) + \hat{g}(v_1, v_2)\hat{\tilde{g}}(v_1, v_2) = 1\,.$$

Using this method, we have only one wavelet image at each scale, and not three as in the previous separable DWT algorithm. Figure 2.8 shows the organization of the wavelet subimages and the smoothed image. For more effectively visualizing the entire transformation, coefficients are reorganized in a compact way. Figure 2.10 summarizes this reorganization. The low pass filter h is centered at the samples denoted by crosses, which provides the image at the lower resolution, while the high pass filter g is centered at the samples indicated by circles which allows the wavelet coefficients to be obtained. The shift due to the filter g is made during down-sampling.

Figure 2.9 shows the non-zero coefficients of the 2-D low-pass filter h and its dual $\tilde{h}$ used in the Feauveau wavelet transform. Figure 2.10 displays the overall flowchart of the Feauveau quincunx decomposition algorithm. Figure 2.11 exemplifies such a wavelet transform on the Lena image.

In Van De Ville et al. (2005), the authors introduced new semi-orthogonal 2-D wavelet bases for the quincunx subsampling scheme. But unlike the traditional

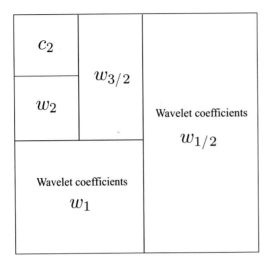

c_2

$w_{3/2}$

w_2

Wavelet coefficients

$w_{1/2}$

Wavelet coefficients

w_1

Figure 2.8. Feauveau's wavelet transform representation of an image.

```
            a
         f  b  f
      j  g  c  g  c
   f  g  i  d  i  g  f
a  b  c  d  e  d  c  b  a
   f  g  i  d  i  g  f
      j  g  c  g  c
         f  b  f
            a
```

	h	$\tilde{h}$
a	0.001671	—
b	−0.002108	−0.005704
c	−0.019555	−0.007192
d	0.139756	0.164931
e	0.687859	0.586315
f	0.006687	—
g	−0.006324	−0.017113
i	−0.052486	−0.014385
j	0.010030	—

Figure 2.9. Coefficients of the nonseparable two-dimensional low pass filter h and its dual $\tilde{h}$ used in Feauveau wavelet transform.

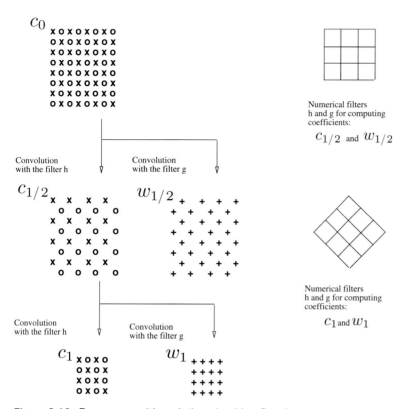

Figure 2.10. Feauveau multiresolution algorithm flowchart.

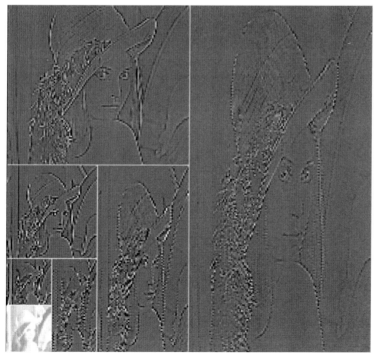

Figure 2.11. Wavelet transform of "Lena" by Feauveau's algorithm.

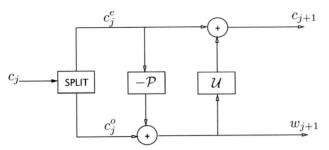

Figure 2.12. The lifting scheme, forward direction.

design which is based on the McClellan transform, those authors exploited the scaling relations of the 2-D isotropic polyharmonic B-splines.

2.7 THE LIFTING SCHEME

A lifting is an elementary modification of perfect reconstruction filters, which is used to improve the wavelet properties. The lifting scheme (Sweldens and Schröder 1996) is a flexible technique that has been used in several different settings, for easy construction and implementation of traditional wavelets (Sweldens and Schröder 1996), and for the construction of wavelets on arbitrary domains such as bounded regions of $\mathbb{R}^d$ – second generation wavelets (Sweldens 1997); or surfaces – spherical wavelets (Schröder and Sweldens 1995). To optimize the approximation and compression of signals and images, the lifting scheme has also been widely used to construct adaptive wavelet bases with signal-dependent liftings. For example, short wavelets are needed in the neighborhood of singularities, but long wavelets with more vanishing moments improve the approximation of regular regions.

The principle of the lifting scheme is to compute the difference between a true coefficient and its prediction:

$$w_{j+1}[l] = c_j[2l+1] - \mathcal{P}(c_j[2l-2L], \ldots, c_j[2l-2], c_j[2l],$$
$$c_j[2l+2], \ldots, c_j[2l+2L]) . \tag{2.29}$$

A sample at an odd location $2l+1$ is then predicted using samples at even locations.

Computing the wavelet transform using the lifting scheme consists of several stages. The idea is to first compute a trivial wavelet transform (the Lazy wavelet) and then improve its properties using alternating lifting and dual lifting steps. The transformation is carried out in three steps (see Figure 2.12):

(i) *Split:* This corresponds to Lazy wavelets which splits the signal into even and odd indexed samples:

$$c_j^e[l] = c_j[2l] ,$$
$$c_j^o[l] = c_j[2l+1] . \tag{2.30}$$

(ii) *Predict:* Calculate the wavelet coefficient $w_{j+1}[l]$ as the prediction error of $c_j^o[l]$ from $c_j^e[l]$ using the prediction operator $\mathcal{P}$:

$$w_{j+1}[l] = c_j^o[l] - \mathcal{P}(c_j^e)[l] . \tag{2.31}$$

(iii) *Update:* The coarse approximation c_{j+1} of the signal is obtained by using $c_j^e[l]$ and $w_{j+1}[l]$ and the update operator $\mathcal{U}$:

$$c_{j+1}[l] = c_j^e[l] + \mathcal{U}(w_{j+1})[l] \,. \tag{2.32}$$

The lifting steps are easily inverted by:

$$c_j[2l] = c_j^e[l] = c_{j+1}[l] - \mathcal{U}(w_{j+1})[l] \,,$$
$$c_j[2l+1] = c_j^o[l] = w_{j+1}[l] + \mathcal{P}(c_j^e)[l] \,. \tag{2.33}$$

2.7.1 Examples of Wavelet Transforms via Lifting

We here provide some examples of wavelet transforms via the lifting scheme.

2.7.1.1 Haar Wavelet via Lifting

The Haar wavelet transform can be implemented via the lifting scheme by taking the prediction operator as the identity, and an update operator which halves the difference. The transform becomes:

$$w_{j+1}[l] = c_j^o[l] - c_j^e[l] \,,$$
$$c_{j+1}[l] = c_j^e[l] + \frac{w_{j+1}[l]}{2} \,.$$

All computations can be done in place.

2.7.1.2 Linear Wavelets via Lifting

The identity predictor used above is appropriate when the signal is (piecewise) constant. In the same vein, one can use a linear predictor which is effective when the signal is linear or piecewise linear. The predictor and update operators now become:

$$\mathcal{P}(c_j^e)[l] = \frac{1}{2}\left(c_j^e[l] + c_j^e[l+1]\right) \,,$$
$$\mathcal{U}(w_{j+1})[l] = \frac{1}{4}\left(w_{j+1}[l-1] + w_{j+1}[l]\right) \,.$$

It is easy to verify that:

$$c_{j+1}[l] = -\frac{1}{8}c_j[2l-2] + \frac{1}{4}c_j[2l-1] + \frac{3}{4}c_j[2l] + \frac{1}{4}c_j[2l+1] - \frac{1}{8}c_j[2l+2] \,,$$

which is the biorthogonal Cohen-Daubechies-Feauveau (Cohen et al. 1992) wavelet transform.

The lifting factorization of the popular 7/9 filter pair leads to the following implementation (Daubechies and Sweldens 1998):

$$
\begin{aligned}
s^{(0)}[l] &= c_j[2l] \\
d^{(0)}[l] &= c_j[2l+1] \\
d^{(1)}[l] &= d^{(0)}[l] + \alpha\left(s^{(0)}[l] + s^{(0)}\right)[l+1] \\
s^{(1)}[l] &= s^{(0)}[l] + \beta\left(d^{(1)}[l] + d^{(1)}[l-1]\right) \\
d^{(2)}[l] &= d^{(1)}[l] + \gamma\left(s^{(1)}[l] + s^{(1)}[l+1]\right) \\
s^{(2)}[l] &= s^{(1)}[l] + \delta\left(d^{(2)}[l] + d^{(2)}[l-1]\right) \\
c_{j+1}[l] &= u s^{(2)}[l] \\
w_{j+1}[l] &= \frac{d^{(2)}[l]}{u} \, ,
\end{aligned}
\tag{2.34}
$$

with

$$
\begin{aligned}
\alpha &= -1.586134342 \\
\beta &= -0.05298011854 \\
\gamma &= 0.8829110762 \\
\delta &= 0.4435068522 \\
u &= 1.149604398 \, .
\end{aligned}
\tag{2.35}
$$

Every wavelet transform can be written via lifting.

2.8 WAVELET PACKETS

2.8.1 One-Dimensional Wavelet Packets

Wavelet packets were introduced in Coifman et al. (1992) as a generalization of wavelets in the sense that instead of dividing only the approximation space, as in the standard orthogonal wavelet transform, the detail spaces are also divided.

Let the sequence of functions be defined recursively as follows:

$$
\begin{aligned}
\psi^{2p}\left(2^{-(j+1)}t\right) &= 2\sum_{l\in\mathbb{Z}} h[l]\psi^p\left(2^{-j}t - l\right) \\
\psi^{2p+1}\left(2^{-(j+1)}t\right) &= 2\sum_{l\in\mathbb{Z}} g[l]\psi^p\left(2^{-j}t - l\right) ,
\end{aligned}
\tag{2.36}
$$

or equivalently in the Fourier domain:

$$
\begin{aligned}
\hat{\psi}^{2p}\left(2^{(j+1)}v\right) &= \hat{h}(2^j v)\hat{\psi}^p(2^j v) \\
\hat{\psi}^{2p+1}\left(2^{(j+1)}v\right) &= \hat{g}(2^j v)\hat{\psi}^p(2^j v) ,
\end{aligned}
\tag{2.37}
$$

for $j \geq 0$ and $p = 0, \ldots, 2^j - 1$, where h and g are the conjugate pair of QMF. At the first scale, the functions ψ^0 and ψ^1 can be respectively identified with the scaling and the wavelet functions ϕ and ψ, with their classical properties as defined in Section 2.5.1.

The collection of translated, dilated and scaled functions $\psi_{j,l}^p = 2^{-j}\psi^p(2^{-j}\cdot -l)^1$ makes up what we call the (multiscale) wavelet packets associated with the QMF pair, h and g. $j \geq 0$ is the scale index, $p = 0, \ldots, 2^j - 1$ can be identified with a frequency index and l is the position index. These are natural parameters for the function $\psi_{j,l}^p$ which is roughly centered at $2^j l$, has a support 2^j and oscillates p times.

2.8.2 Wavelet Packet Binary Tree

The recursive splitting of vector spaces is represented in a full binary tree. With each node (j, p), with $j \in \mathbb{N}$ and $p = 0, \ldots, 2^j - 1$, we associate a space V_j^p with the orthonormal basis $\{2^{j/2}\psi_{j,l}^p\}_{l\in\mathbb{Z}}$. Since the splitting relation creates two orthogonal bases, it is easy to verify that $V_j^p = V_{j+1}^{2p} \oplus V_{j+1}^{2p+1}$ where $\oplus$ denotes the sum of orthogonal complements.

This recursive splitting of wavelet packets can also be interpreted in the Fourier domain. In fact, wavelet packets generate a recursive dyadic partition of the frequency axis. This is formed by starting at $j = 0$, and segmenting the frequency axis in two intervals of equal lengths (which would correspond to application of h and g if they were perfect low pass and high pass filters). At level $j + 1$, the procedure is repeated on each of the dyadic intervals at j by splitting it into two equal pieces and so on. Each of these intervals at a node (j, p) is roughly the support of $|\hat{\psi}_{j,l}^p|$. The recursive wavelet packet spectral partition is illustrated in Figure 2.13.

The wavelet packet representation is overcomplete or redundant. That is, there are many subsets of wavelet packets which constitute orthonormal bases for the original space V_0 (typically more than $2^{2^{J-1}}$ for a binary tree of depth J). This collection of orthobases is often called a library of wavelet packet bases. For instance, the wavelet packet library contains the wavelet basis as illustrated in the top of Figure 2.13.

We denote as $\mathcal{B} = \{\psi_{j,l}^p\}_{(j,p)\in\mathcal{T},l\in\mathbb{Z}}$ any of these wavelet packet bases, and the tree $\mathcal{T}$, for which the collection of nodes (j, p) are the leaves, the associated binary tree. $\mathcal{T}$ is a subtree of the full wavelet packet binary tree. Each basis $\mathcal{B}$ corresponds to a particular dyadic covering of the frequency axis. Two examples are given in Figure 2.13.

2.8.3 Fast Wavelet Packet Transform

Any square-summable signal f can be decomposed into a family of wavelet packets. At each node (j, p), the wavelet packet coefficients $w_j^p[l]$ of f in the subspace V_j^p at position l are given by the inner product

$$w_j^p[l] = \langle \psi_{j,l}^p, f \rangle. \tag{2.38}$$

In the same vein as in expressions (2.14)–(2.17), but now using (2.36), it is straightforward to get the recursive relations between the wavelet packet coefficients:

$$w_{j+1}^{2p}[l] = \sum_k h[k - 2l]w_j^p[k] = [\bar{h} \star w_j^p]_{\downarrow 2}[l]$$

$$w_{j+1}^{2p+1}[l] = \sum_k g[k - 2l]w_j^p[k] = [\bar{g} \star w_j^p]_{\downarrow 2}[l]. \tag{2.39}$$

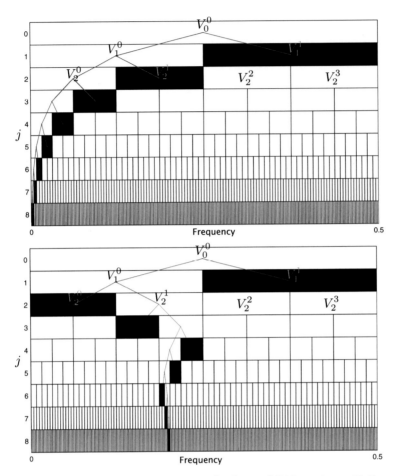

Figure 2.13. 1-D wavelet packets organized as a full binary tree with the corresponding recursive partition of the frequency axis. (top) The tree $\mathcal{T}$ for the wavelet basis, and the black rectangles correspond to its frequency axis dyadic cover. (bottom) Another example of tree $\mathcal{T}$.

For the reconstruction, using the perfect, i.e. exact, reconstruction relation of QMF pairs, we obtain:

$$w_j^p[l] = 2 \sum_k \left(h[k+2l] w_{j+1}^{2p}[k] + g[k+2l] w_{j+1}^{2p+1}[k] \right)$$

$$= 2 \left(h \star \breve{w}_{j+1}^{2p} + g \star \breve{w}_{j+1}^{2p+1} \right)[l]. \tag{2.40}$$

As in the case of the DWT, recursion (2.39) gives us a fast pyramidal algorithm to compute the whole set of wavelet packet coefficients. This is displayed in the upper part of Figure 2.14. The reconstruction or synthesis corresponding to (2.40) is depicted in the lower part of Figure 2.14. For a discrete signal of N equally spaced samples, the wavelet packet forward transform and the reconstruction require $O(N \log N)$ operations.

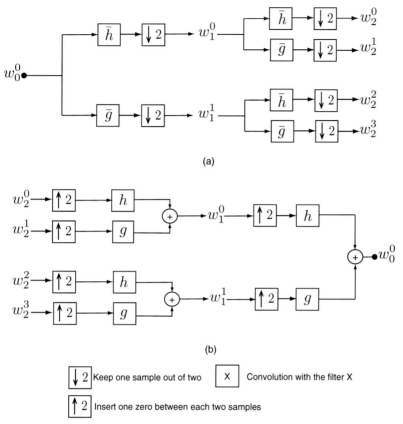

(a)

(b)

$\downarrow 2$	Keep one sample out of two
X	Convolution with the filter X
$\uparrow 2$	Insert one zero between each two samples

Figure 2.14. 1-D wavelet packet transform: (a) forward transform, (b) reconstruction.

2.8.4 Best Wavelet Packet Basis

The wavelet packet implies a large library of bases $\mathcal{B}$; i.e. the wavelet packet dictionary is a union of orthobases. Within this family, the best basis for a particular signal f is the one that will be best adapted to its time-frequency content. Coifman and Wickerhauser (1992) proposed to cast this best basis search as an optimization problem that will minimize some additive information cost function. Although wavelet packet bases form a large library, they are organized in a full binary tree, where each subtree $\mathcal{T}$ corresponds to a specific dyadic covering of the frequency axis. Thus, the optimization problem over bases amounts to an optimization over all recursive dyadic partitions of the frequency axis. Doing this by brute force is however computationally prohibitive, requiring us to explore more than $2^{2^{J-1}}$ trees $\mathcal{T}$. The construction of the best basis can be accomplished much more efficiently in $O(N \log N)$ computation using the fast bottom-up algorithm introduced by Coifman and Wickerhauser (1992). This fast algorithm exploits the tree structure of the wavelet packet dictionary and requires to recursively compare the cost function of the child nodes to that of their parent nodes. See Coifman and Wickerhauser (1992) for details.

2.8.5 Two-Dimensional Wavelet Packets

The wavelet packets can be extended to any dimension by separable (tensor) products. In 2-D, this leads to wavelet packets that are associated with quadtrees, and with octrees in 3-D. For instance, in 2-D, wavelet packets are obtained by tensor products of the functions $\psi^p_{j,k}$ and $\psi^q_{j,l}$. The recursive relations between the wavelet packet coefficients are given by

$$w^{2p,2q}_{j+1}[k,l] = [\bar{h}\bar{h} \star w^{p,q}_{j+1}]_{\downarrow 2,2}[k,l]$$

$$w^{2p+1,2q}_{j+1}[k,l] = [\bar{g}\bar{h} \star w^{p,q}_{j+1}]_{\downarrow 2,2}[k,l]$$

$$w^{2p,2q+1}_{j+1}[k,l] = [\bar{h}\bar{g} \star w^{p,q}_{j+1}]_{\downarrow 2,2}[k,l]$$

$$w^{2p+1,2q+1}_{j+1}[k,l] = [\bar{g}\bar{g} \star w^{p,q}_{j+1}]_{\downarrow 2,2}[k,l] \,,$$

and the reconstruction is obtained from

$$w^{p,q}_{j+1} = 4\big(hh \star \breve{w}^{2p,2q}_{j+1} + gh \star \breve{w}^{2p+1,2q}_{j+1} + hg \star \breve{w}^{2p,2q+1}_{j+1} + hg \star \breve{w}^{2p+1,2q+1}_{j+1}\big)[k,l] \,.$$

2.9 GUIDED NUMERICAL EXPERIMENTS

2.9.1 Software

In the pedagogical numerical experiments of several chapters in this book, we have chosen the WaveLab toolbox (Buckheit and Donoho 1995). WaveLab contains a fairly complete offering and a unified set of wavelet and time-frequency tools. It is based on the Matlab quantitative computing and interactive visualization environment. WaveLab is installed as a Matlab toolbox, and has been available on-line in some version since 1993. The latest version is WaveLab850 consisting of over 1200 files including programs, data, documentation and scripts, which can be freely retrieved from a link at this book's web site (http://www.SparseSignalRecipes.info; http://www-stat.stanford.edu/~wavelab). Versions are provided for Unix, Linux, Macintosh and Windows platforms. WaveLab has become one of the most widely used wavelet toolboxes, and users often see it as a general piece of free software that is competitive with commercial packages.

2.9.2 Continuous Wavelet Transform of a One-Dimensional Piecewise Smooth Signal

The following Matlab code uses WaveLab routines (if not automatically loaded on start-up, then load with: WavePath) to produce Figure 2.15.

```
N        = 4096; % signal length.
nvoice   = 12;   % Number of voices/octave.
amin     = 0.66; % Minimum scale.
wavsupp  = 8;    % Mexican hat wavelet support.
octave   = floor(log2(amin*wavsupp)); % octave is such that the
                      % number of scales = log2(N) - octave.
WaveName = 'Sombrero'; % Mexican hat wavelet.
```

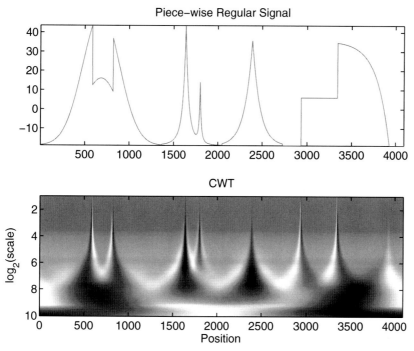

Figure 2.15. (bottom) CWT of (top) a 1-D piecewise smooth signal. This figure is generated by the Matlab code given in Section 2.9.2.

```
% Create signal.
x = MakeSignal('Piece-Regular',N);
subplot(211); plot(x); set(gca,'FontSize',14);
title(sprintf('Piece-wise Regular Signal'));axis tight

% Compute CWT with Mexican hat wavelet.
cwt = CWT_Wavelet(x,nvoice,WaveName,octave,4);

% display CWT
subplot(212);
ImageCWT(fliplr(cwt),'Individual','gray','log',octave,4);
set(gca,'FontSize',14);
xlabel('Position');ylabel('log_2(scale)');title('CWT')
```

2.9.3 Nonlinear Approximation by Discrete Wavelet Transform

The goal of this code is to illustrate the properties of the DWT (here with the 7/9 biorthogonal pair) for approximating an image from its m best – largest in magnitude – coefficients. It is well established that the nonlinear approximation error decays like $m^{-\alpha}$, where α depends on the regularity of the image. For example, bounded variation images and piecewise regular images have a nonlinear approximation from their wavelet coefficients that exhibits a decay rate like m^{-1}

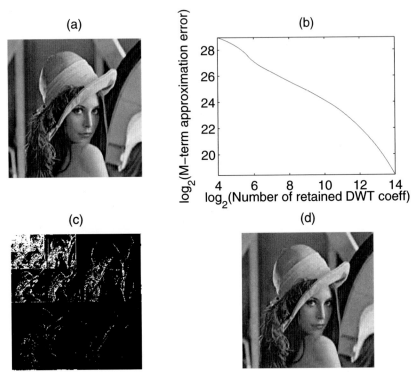

Figure 2.16. (a) Original "Lena" image. (b) Best *m*-term nonlinear approximation error. (c) Ten percent largest DWT coefficients. (d) Reconstruction from these 10 percent largest DWT coefficients: relative error, 0.0503.

(Cohen et al. 1999). This is for instance the case for Lena as can be seen from Figure 2.16(b). The reconstruction from the largest 10% of the coefficients is displayed in Figure 2.16(d).

```
% Read image;
img = ReadImage('Lenna');  % Image Lena called 'Lenna' in WaveLab.
[N,J] = quadlength(img);
subplot(221);imagesc(img);axis image;axis off;colormap('gray')
set(gca,'FontSize',14);
title('(a)');

% Coarsest decomposition scale.
coarsest = 3;

% Generate 7/9 Biorthonormal CMF Filter Pairs.
[qmf,dqmf] = MakeBSFilter('CDF',[4 4]);

% Compute biorthogonal DWT of image.
wc = FWT2_PB(img,coarsest,qmf,dqmf);
```

```
% Plot NLA error.
swc   = sort(abs(wc(:)),1,'descend');
wcerr = flipud(cumsum(flipud(swc).^2));
subplot(222);plot(log2(1:N*N),log2(wcerr));
set(gca,'XTick',[0:2:log2(N*N)]);
axis([4 14 log2(wcerr(2^14)) log2(wcerr(2^4))]);
set(gca,'FontSize',14);
xlabel('log_2(Number of retained DWT coeff)');
ylabel('log_2(m-term approximation error)');
title('(b)');

% Keep only 10% of coefficients.
thd = swc(floor(N*N/10));
ll  = wc(1:coarsest,1:coarsest);
wct = wc .* (abs(wc) >= thd);
wct(1:coarsest,1:coarsest) = ll;
subplot(223);imagesc(wct~=0);axis image;axis off
set(gca,'FontSize',14);
title('(c)');

% Reconstruct from remaining 10% DWT coefficients.
imr = IWT2_PB(wct,coarsest,qmf,dqmf);
subplot(224);imagesc(imr);axis image;axis off
set(gca,'FontSize',14);
title('(d)');
```

2.9.4 Nonlinear Approximation by Wavelet Packets

Figure 2.17 shows the nonlinear approximation of Lena from its 10% largest coefficients in the best orthobasis, selected from the wavelet packet quadtree using the Coifman-Wickerhauser algorithm. The result is also compared to the orthogonal DWT. The code used to generate this figure is the following.

```
% Read image;
img = ReadImage('Lenna');
[N,J] = quadlength(img);
subplot(311);imagesc(img);axis image;axis off;colormap('gray')
set(gca,'FontSize',14);
title('(a)');

% Deepest decomposition scale.
deepest = 5;
coarsest = J - deepest;

% Generate Symmlet 4 CMF Filter.
qmf = MakeONFilter('Symmlet',4);
```

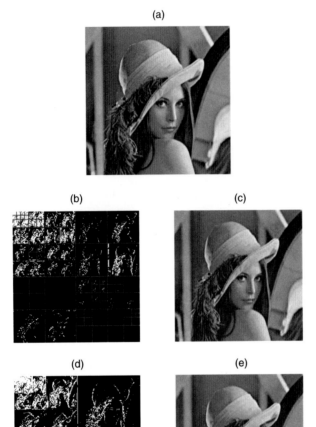

Figure 2.17. (a) Original "Lena" image. (b) Ten percent largest wavelet packet coefficients in the best orthobasis, with corresponding spatial partition. (c) Reconstruction from the 10 percent largest wavelet packet coefficients: relative error = 0.041. (d) Ten percent largest DWT coefficients. (e) Reconstruction from the 10 percent largest DWT coefficients: relative error, 0.043.

```
% Compute stat tree.
stats = Calc2dStatTree('WP',img - mean(img(:)),deepest,qmf,
                       'Entropy',[]);

% Coifman-Wickerhauser best orthobasis algorithm.
bob   = Best2dBasis(stats,deepest);
wpc   = FPT2_WP(bob,img,qmf);
```

```
% Sort and threshold the WP best orthobasis coefficients.
swpc = sort(abs(wpc(:)),1,'descend');
thd  = swpc(floor(N*N/10));
ll   = wpc(1:coarsest,1:coarsest);
wpct = wpc .* (abs(wpc) > thd);
wpct(1:coarsest,1:coarsest) = ll;

% Display retained coeffs in the best orthobasis with
% the corresponding partition.
subplot(346);imagesc(wpct~=0);axis image;axis off;
ax = axis;hold on
Plot2dPartition(bob,'b',ax,deepest);
set(gca,'FontSize',14);
title('(b)');

% Reconstruct and display.
imwpr = IPT2_WP(bob,wpct,qmf);
subplot(347);imagesc(imwpr);axis image;axis off;
set(gca,'FontSize',14);
title('(c)');

% Compute orthogonal DWT of image.
wc = FWT2_PO(img,coarsest,qmf);
% Sort, threshold and reconstruct.
swc = sort(abs(wc(:)),1,'descend');
thd = swc(floor(N*N/10));
ll  = wc(1:coarsest,1:coarsest);
wct = wc .* (abs(wc) > thd);
wct(1:coarsest,1:coarsest) = ll;

% Display retained DWT coeffs.
subplot(3,4,10);imagesc(wct~=0);axis image;axis off;
set(gca,'FontSize',14);
title('(d)');

% Reconstruct and display.
imdwtr = IWT2_PO(wct,coarsest,qmf);
subplot(3,4,11);imagesc(imdwtr);axis image;axis off;
set(gca,'FontSize',14);
title('(e)');
```

2.10 SUMMARY

We have used the continuous wavelet transform as the basic schema from which various discrete wavelet transforms can be related. We have seen how wavelet filtering is carried out. A number of examples demonstrated the usefulness of filtering data in this way. In particular, the JPEG 2000 still image compression format uses a discrete wavelet approach. Matlab code is used to illustrate the algorithms that are discussed.

3

Redundant Wavelet Transform

3.1 INTRODUCTION

Multiresolution transforms have two major uses: compression, and what we may call pattern or feature analysis. The latter includes signal restoration (denoising, deconvolution or deblurring); and object finding and measuring. The best filter bank or multiresolution schema is likely to be different depending on the application.

In this chapter we begin with the general undecimated wavelet transform. We then look at a transform that is partially decimated and partially not, with potential storage economy.

The complex wavelet transform produces real and imaginary wavelet coefficients. This transform has a limited redundancy and provides approximate shift invariance and directional selectivity. Near shift invariance in turn can lead to more limited artifacts when carrying out image denoising.

The *starlet transform* is introduced and described as an undecimated isotropic wavelet transform. This transform has been described in the past as the B_3-spline à trous wavelet transform.

We then discuss the principles of designing wavelet filters. In particular, since we are dealing with redundant wavelet transforms, we design non-orthogonal filter banks.

There follows a description of the pyramidal wavelet transform both in original and Fourier domains. The wavelet transform is consolidated into a storage-efficient pyramidal representation.

Before proceeding, we define a central notion used in the rest of the book: *frames*. An operator $\mathbf{F}$ from a Hilbert space $\mathcal{H}$ to $\mathcal{K}$ is the frame synthesis operator associated with a frame of $\mathcal{K}$ if its adjoint, i.e. the analysis operator $\mathbf{F}^*$, satisfies the generalized Parseval relation with lower and upper bounds a_1 and a_2:

$$a_1 \|u\|^2 \leq \left\| \mathbf{F}^* u \right\|^2 \leq a_2 \|u\|^2 \quad 0 < a_1 \leq a_2 < +\infty . \tag{3.1}$$

The frame is tight when $a_1 = a_2 = a$, in which case $\mathbf{FF}^* = a\mathbf{I}$, where $\mathbf{I}$ is the identity. When $a_1 = a_2 = a = 1$ we have the Parseval relation. See Christensen (2002) for a comprehensive account of frames.

3.2 THE UNDECIMATED WAVELET TRANSFORM

3.2.1 One-Dimensional Undecimated Wavelet Transform

While the biorthogonal wavelet transform leads to successful implementation in image compression, results are far from optimal for other applications such as restoration (e.g. denoising or deconvolution), detection, or more generally, analysis of data. This is mainly due to the loss of the translation-invariance property in the DWT, leading to a large number of artifacts when an image is reconstructed after modification of its wavelet coefficients.

For this reason, physicists and astronomers have generally preferred to continue working with the continuous wavelet transform (Slezak et al. 1993; Antoine and Murenzi 1994; Arneodo et al. 1995), even if the price to be paid is (i) a considerable amount of redundancy in the transformation (i.e. there are many more coefficients in the transformed data than in the input data) and (ii) there is no reconstruction operator (i.e. an image cannot be reconstructed from its coefficients). For some applications like fractal analysis, these drawbacks have no impact because there is no need to apply a reconstruction and storage is available to support the redundancy. For other applications where reconstruction is needed, some researchers have chosen an intermediate approach, keeping the filter bank construction giving fast and dyadic algorithms, but eliminating the decimation step in the orthogonal wavelet transform (Dutilleux 1987; Holschneider et al. 1989; Bijaoui and Giudicelli 1991): $c_1 = \bar{h} \star c_0$ and $w_1 = \bar{g} \star c_0$. By separating even and odd samples in c_1, we get c_1^e and c^o, where $c_1^e = [c_1]_{\downarrow 2^e}$ and $c_1^o = [c_1]_{\downarrow 2^o}$, and $[\cdot]_{\downarrow 2^e}$ (respectively, $[\cdot]_{\downarrow 2^o}$) corresponds to down-sampling that keeps only even (respectively, odd) samples. Both parts together allow us to reconstruct perfectly c_0 by recombining odd and even samples into c_1. From the exact reconstruction condition (2.21), we get

$$c_0 = \tilde{h} \star c_1 + \tilde{g} \star w_1 . \tag{3.2}$$

For the passage to the next resolution, both c_1^e and c_1^o are decomposed, leading after the splitting into even and odd samples to four coarse arrays associated with c_2. All of the four coefficient sets can again be decomposed in order to obtain the third decomposition level, and so on.

Figure 3.1(a) shows the one-dimensional (1-D) undecimated wavelet transform (UWT) decomposition. The decimation step is not applied and both w_1 and c_1 have the same size as c_0. c_1 is then split into c_1^e (even samples) and c_1^o (odd samples), and the same decomposition is applied to both c_1^e and c_1^o. c_1^e produces $c_{2,1}$ and $w_{2,1}$, while c_1^o produces $c_{2,2}$ and $w_{2,2}$. $w_2 = \{w_{2,1}, w_{2,1}\}$ contains the wavelet coefficients at the second scale, and is also of the same size as c_0. Figure 3.1(b) shows the 1-D UWT reconstruction.

It is clear that this approach is much more complicated than the decimated biorthogonal wavelet transform. There exists, however, a very efficient way to implement it, called the *à trous* algorithm, where this French term means "with holes" (Holschneider et al. 1989; Shensa 1992). Thus $c_{j+1}[l]$ and $w_{j+1}[l]$ can be expressed

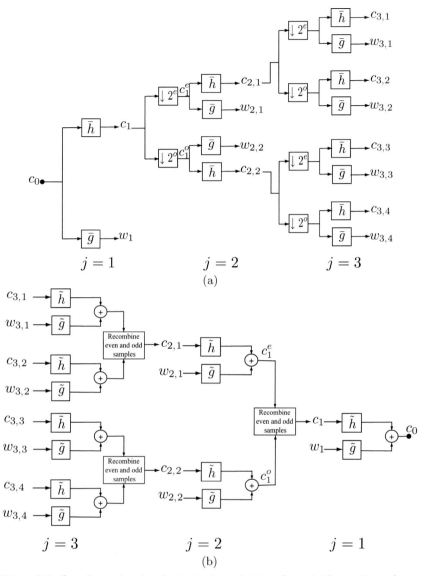

Figure 3.1. One-dimensional undecimated wavelet transform: (a) forward transform, (b) reconstruction.

as

$$c_{j+1}[l] = (\bar{h}^{(j)} \star c_j)[l] = \sum_k h[k]c_j[l + 2^j k]$$

$$w_{j+1}[l] = (\bar{g}^{(j)} \star c_j)[l] = \sum_k g[k]c_j[l + 2^j k], \tag{3.3}$$

where $h^{(j)}[l] = h[l]$ if $l/2^j$ is an integer and 0 otherwise. For example, we have

$$h^{(1)} = [\dots, h[-2], 0, h[-1], 0, h[0], 0, h[1], 0, h[2], \dots].$$

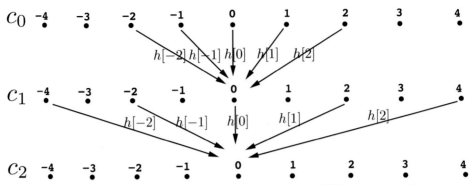

Figure 3.2. Passage from c_1 to c_1, and from c_1 to c_2 with the UWT à trous algorithm.

Algorithm 4 1-D UWT Algorithm

Task: Compute 1-D UWT of a discrete N-sample signal X.
Parameters: Filters $h, \tilde{h}$.
Initialization: $c_0 = X$, $J = \log_2 N$.
for $j = 0$ **to** $J - 1$ **do**
$\quad$ Compute $c_{j+1}[l] = (\bar{h}^{(j)} \star c_j)[l] = \sum_k h[k]c_j[l + 2^j k]$.
$\quad$ Compute $w_{j+1}[l] = (\bar{g}^{(j)} \star c_j)[l] = \sum_k g[k]c_j[l + 2^j k]$.
Output: $\mathcal{W} = \{w_1, w_2, \ldots, w_J, c_J\}$ the 1-D UWT of X.

The reconstruction of c_j is obtained as

$$c_j[l] = \left(\tilde{h}^{(j)} \star c_{j+1}\right)[l] + \left(\tilde{g}^{(j)} \star w_{j+1}\right)[l] . \tag{3.4}$$

The filter bank $(h, g, \tilde{h}, \tilde{g})$ needs only to verify the exact reconstruction condition (2.21). The dealiasing condition (2.20) is not required because there is no decimation. This provides us with a higher degree of freedom when designing the synthesis prototype filter bank as we will see in Section 3.6.

Figure 3.2 shows the passage from one resolution to the next one by the à trous algorithm. The à trous algorithm can be extended to 2-D by tensor product to yield

$$\begin{aligned}
c_{j+1}[k, l] &= (\bar{h}^{(j)}\bar{h}^{(j)} \star c_j)[k, l] \\
w^1_{j+1}[k, l] &= (\bar{g}^{(j)}\bar{h}^{(j)} \star c_j)[k, l] \\
w^2_{j+1}[k, l] &= (\bar{h}^{(j)}\bar{g}^{(j)} \star c_j)[k, l] \\
w^3_{j+1}[k, l] &= (\bar{g}^{(j)}\bar{g}^{(j)} \star c_j)[k, l] .
\end{aligned} \tag{3.5}$$

where $hg \star c$ is the convolution of c by the separable filter hg (i.e. convolution first along the columns by h and then convolution along the rows by g). At each scale, we have three wavelet images, w^1, w^2, w^3, and each has the same size as the original image. The redundancy factor is therefore $3J + 1$.

For an $N \times N$ discrete image X, the algorithm is the following.

Algorithm 5 2-D UWT Algorithm

Task: Compute UWT of $N \times N$-pixel image X.
Parameters: Filters $h, \tilde{h}$.
Initialization: $c_0 = X$, $J = \log_2 N$.
for $j = 0$ to $J - 1$ **do**

1. Compute $c_{j+1}[k, l] = (\bar{h}^{(j)} \bar{h}^{(j)} \star c_j)[k, l]$.
2. Compute $w_{j+1}^1[k, l] = (\bar{g}^{(j)} \bar{h}^{(j)} \star c_j)[k, l]$.
3. Compute $w_{j+1}^2[k, l] = (\bar{h}^{(j)} \bar{g}^{(j)} \star c_j)[k, l]$.
4. Compute $w_{j+1}^3[k, l] = (\bar{g}^{(j)} \bar{g}^{(j)} \star c_j)[k, l]$.

Output: $\mathcal{W} = \{w_1^1, w_1^2, w_1^3, \ldots, w_J^1, w_J^2, w_J^3, c_J\}$ the 2-D UWT of X.

Figure 3.3 shows the UWT of the "Einstein" image using five resolution levels. Figures 3.3(1v), 3.3(1h), and 3.3(1d) correspond to the vertical, horizontal and diagonal coefficients of the first resolution level, respectively. This transformation contains 16 bands, each one being of the same size as the original image. The redundancy factor is therefore equal to 16.

3.3 PARTIALLY DECIMATED WAVELET TRANSFORM

The UWT is highly redundant with a redundancy factor for images of $3J + 1$, where J is the number of resolution levels. This means that for an $N \times N$ image and using six resolution levels, we need to store $19N^2$ real values in memory. When dealing with very large images, this may not be acceptable in some applications for practical reasons arising from a computation time constraint or available memory space. In such cases, a compromise can be found by not decimating one or two coarse scales, while decimating the others.

We will denote $\text{PWT}^{(j_u)}$ the wavelet transform where only the first j_u resolution levels are undecimated. For j_u equal to 0, $\text{PWT}^{(j_u)}$ corresponds to the biorthogonal or orthogonal wavelet transform (OWT). Similarly, for j_u equal to J, $\text{PWT}^{(J)}$ corresponds to the UWT. In general, it is easy to see that $\text{PWT}^{(j_u)}$ leads to a redundancy factor $j_u + 1$ in 1-D and $3j_u + 1$ in 2-D. For example, $\text{PWT}^{(1)}$ yields a redundancy factor of 4 in 2-D.

For the passage from a resolution j to the next one, it will require the same operations as for the UWT when $j \leq j_u$. Denoting $j' = \min(j, j_u)$, (3.5) becomes

$$
\begin{aligned}
c_{j+1}[k, l] &= \left(\bar{h}^{(j')} \bar{h}^{(j')} \star c_j\right)[k, l], \\
w_{j+1}^1[k, l] &= \left(\bar{g}^{(j')} \bar{h}^{(j')} \star c_j\right)[k, l], \\
w_{j+1}^2[k, l] &= \left(\bar{h}^{(j')} \bar{g}^{(j')} \star c_j\right)[k, l], \\
w_{j+1}^3[k, l] &= \left(\bar{g}^{(j')} \bar{g}^{(j')} \star c_j\right)[k, l].
\end{aligned}
\tag{3.6}
$$

After the j_u scale, the number of holes in the filters $\bar{h}$ and $\bar{g}$ remains unchanged.

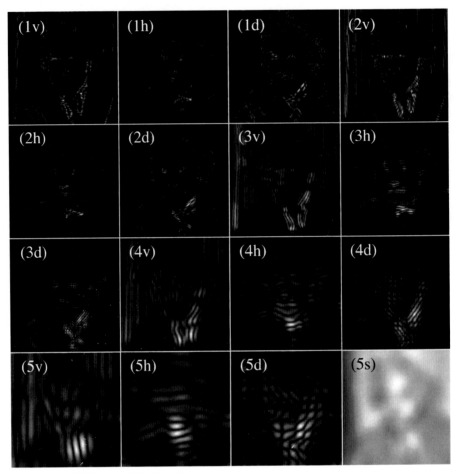

Figure 3.3. UWT of the "Einstein" image.

To demonstrate the improvement brought by using the partially decimated wavelet transform (PWT) over UWT, we show a denoising experiment where PWT is used with varying j_u. The same image, "Einstein", and the same noise properties (zero-mean additive white Gaussian), were used. For each denoised image the peak signal-to-noise ratio (PSNR) between the original image X and the denoised one $\tilde{X}$ was computed, as presented in Table 3.1. The PSNR is classically defined as

$$\text{PSNR} = 20 \log_{10} \frac{N|\max_{k,l} X[k,l] - \min_{k,l} X[k,l]|}{\sqrt{\sum_{k,l} (\tilde{X}[k,l] - X[k,l])^2}} \text{ dB} \qquad (3.7)$$

where N^2 is the number of pixels.

Table 3.1. PSNR versus j_u in the $\text{PWT}^{(j_u)}$ for the Denoising of the Image "Einstein"

	$\text{PWT}^{(0)}$	$\text{PWT}^{(1)}$	$\text{PWT}^{(2)}$	$\text{PWT}^{(3)}$	$\text{PWT}^{(4)}$
PSNR (dB)	29.34	30.66	31.35	31.67	31.77

The gain in PSNR when using the UWT ($j_u = 4$) instead of the biorthogonal wavelet transform is 2.43 dB. Using a single undecimated scale, i.e. PWT$^{(1)}$, leads to a PSNR increase of more than 1 dB, while requiring far less redundancy.

3.4 THE DUAL-TREE COMPLEX WAVELET TRANSFORM

In this section, we describe this transform only in the 2-D case. In order to obtain near translation invariance and directional selectivity with only one undecimated scale, an additional refinement can be introduced to the PWT$^{(1)}$ by considering two pairs of odd- and even-length biorthogonal linear-phase filters (h^o, g^o) and (h^e, g^e) instead of one. This transform is called the *Dual-Tree Complex Wavelet Transform* (Kingsbury 1998, 1999; Selesnick et al. 2005). The filters are real but complex numbers are derived from the dual-tree wavelet coefficients. As depicted in Figure 3.4, at the first scale an undecimated wavelet transform is first computed on the image c_0 using the filter pair (h^o, g^o), which results in four subbands, each one of the same size as c_0 (i.e. the redundancy factor is equal to 4). Then the scaling (smooth) coefficients c_1 are split into four parts to extract four trees:

1. $c_1^A = [c_1]_{\downarrow 2^e \downarrow 2^e}$: coefficients at even row index and even column index;
2. $c_1^B = [c_1]_{\downarrow 2^e \downarrow 2^o}$: coefficients at odd row index and even column index;
3. $c_1^C = [c_1]_{\downarrow 2^o \downarrow 2^e}$: coefficients at even row index and odd column index;
4. $c_1^D = [c_1]_{\downarrow 2^o \downarrow 2^o}$: coefficients at odd row index and odd column index.

These four images $c_1^A, c_1^B, c_1^C, c_1^D$ are decomposed, using the decimated wavelet transform, by separable product of the odd and even-length filter pairs.

Tree $\mathcal{T}$	A	B	C	D
c_{j+1}	$\bar{h}^e \bar{h}^e$	$\bar{h}^e \bar{h}^o$	$\bar{h}^o \bar{h}^e$	$\bar{h}^o \bar{h}^o$
$w^1_{j+1,\mathcal{T}}$	$\bar{g}^e \bar{h}^e$	$\bar{g}^e \bar{h}^o$	$\bar{g}^o \bar{h}^e$	$\bar{g}^o \bar{h}^o$
$w^2_{j+1,\mathcal{T}}$	$\bar{h}^e \bar{g}^e$	$\bar{h}^e \bar{g}^o$	$\bar{h}^o \bar{g}^e$	$\bar{h}^o \bar{g}^o$
$w^3_{j+1,\mathcal{T}}$	$\bar{g}^e \bar{g}^e$	$\bar{g}^e \bar{g}^o$	$\bar{g}^o \bar{g}^e$	$\bar{g}^o \bar{g}^o$

For each subband, the wavelet coefficients $w^q_{j,A}, w^q_{j,B}, w^q_{j,C}, w^q_{j,D}$, $q \in \{1, 2, 3\}$, are combined to form real and imaginary parts of complex wavelet coefficients:

$$w^q_{j,+}[k, l] = \left(w^q_{j,A}[k, l] - w^q_{j,D}[k, l]\right) + i\left(w^q_{j,B}[k, l] + w^q_{j,C}[k, l]\right)$$
$$w^q_{j,-}[k, l] = \left(w^q_{j,A}[k, l] + w^q_{j,D}[k, l]\right) + i\left(w^q_{j,B}[k, l] - w^q_{j,C}[k, l]\right) .$$

$$(3.8)$$

Therefore the three detail subbands lead to six complex subbands. Thus, in addition to near translation invariance, the dual tree complex transform has a better directional selectivity compared to the three-orientation of the separable real wavelet transform. This is achieved while maintaining a reasonable redundancy (4 in 2-D and 2^d in d-D), and allowing fast finite impulse response filter bank based transform and reconstruction. The fast dual-tree complex wavelet transform and reconstruction algorithms are pictorially detailed in Figure 3.4 and Figure 3.5.

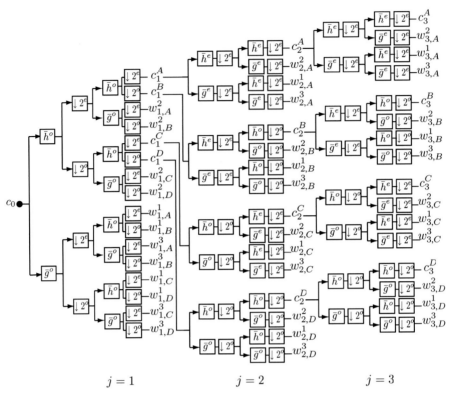

Figure 3.4. First three levels of the 2-D dual-tree complex wavelet transform.

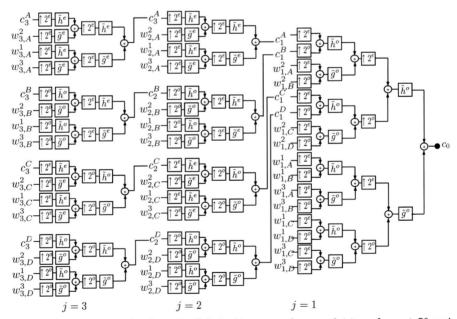

Figure 3.5. Reconstruction from the 2-D dual-tree complex wavelet transform. $\uparrow 2^e$ and $\uparrow 2^o$ are respectively even- and odd-sample zero-insertion. Note that a vector w that has been separated into its even samples $w^e = [w]_{\downarrow 2^e}$ and odd samples $w^o = [w]_{\downarrow 2^o}$, is recovered by $w = [w^e]_{\uparrow 2^e} + [w^o]_{\uparrow 2^o}$.

Algorithm 6 2-D Dual-Tree Complex Wavelet Transform Algorithm

---

Task: Compute dual-tree complex wavelet transform of $N \times N$ image X.
Parameters: Filters h^o, h^e, g^o, g^e.
Initialization: $c_0 = X$, $J = \log_2 N$.

1. Compute the one-scale undecimated wavelet $\mathcal{W} = \{w_1^1, w_1^2, w_1^3, c_1\}$:

$$c_1 = \bar{h}^{(0)} \bar{h}^{(0)} \star c_0$$

$$w_1^1 = \bar{g}^{(0)} \bar{h}^{(0)} \star c_0$$

$$w_1^2 = \bar{h}^{(0)} \bar{g}^{(0)} \star c_0$$

$$w_1^3 = \bar{g}^{(0)} \bar{g}^{(0)} \star c_0 \ .$$

2. Down-sample c_1 along rows and columns to initialize the trees:

$$c_1^A = [c_1]_{\downarrow 2^e \downarrow 2^e}$$

$$c_1^B = [c_1]_{\downarrow 2^e \downarrow 2^o}$$

$$c_1^C = [c_1]_{\downarrow 2^o \downarrow 2^e}$$

$$c_1^D = [c_1]_{\downarrow 2^o \downarrow 2^o} \ .$$

3. Compute the 2-D DWT of c_1^A with the filter pair (h^e, g^e). Get the coefficients $\{c_J^A, w_{j,A}^q\}_{2 \leq j \leq J, q \in \{1,2,3\}}$.
4. Compute the 2-D DWT of c_1^B with the filter pair (h^e, g^o). Get the coefficients $\{c_J^B, w_{j,B}^q\}_{2 \leq j \leq J, q \in \{1,2,3\}}$.
5. Compute the 2-D DWT of c_1^C with the filter pair (h^o, g^e). Get the coefficients $\{c_J^C, w_{j,C}^q\}_{2 \leq j \leq J, q \in \{1,2,3\}}$.
6. Compute the 2-D DWT of c_1^D with the filter pair (h^o, g^o). Get the coefficients $\{c_J^D, w_{j,D}^q\}_{2 \leq j \leq J, q \in \{1,2,3\}}$.
7. Form the wavelet complex coefficients $w_{j,+}^q$ and $w_{j,-}^q$ according to equation (3.8).

Output: $\mathcal{W} = \{c_J^T, w_{j,+}^q, w_{j,-}^q\}_{1 \leq j \leq J, q \in \{1,2,3\}}$ the 2-D dual-tree complex wavelet transform of X.

3.5 ISOTROPIC UNDECIMATED WAVELET TRANSFORM: STARLET TRANSFORM

The Isotropic Undecimated Wavelet Transform (IUWT) algorithm is well known in the astronomical domain because it is well adapted to astronomical data where objects are more or less isotropic in most cases (Starck and Murtagh 1994; Starck and Murtagh 2006). For this reason, and also because there is often confusion between the UWT and IUWT, we call it the *starlet wavelet transform*.

Requirements for a good analysis of such data are as follows:

■ Filters must be symmetric ($\bar{h} = h$, and $\bar{g} = g$).
■ In 2-D or higher dimension, h, g, ψ, ϕ must be nearly isotropic.

Filters do not need to be orthogonal or biorthogonal and this lack of need for orthogonality or biorthogonality is beneficial for design freedom. For computational reasons, we also prefer to have separability; $h[k, l] = h[k]_{1-D}h_{1-D}[l]$. Separability is not a required condition, but it allows us to have fast computation, which is important for large-scale data sets.

This has motivated the following choice for the analysis scaling and wavelet functions (Starck and Murtagh 2006):

$$\phi_{1-D}(t) = \frac{1}{12}(|t-2|^3 - 4|t-1|^3 + 6|t|^3 - 4|t+1|^3 + |t+2|^3)$$

$$\phi(t_1, t_2) = \phi_{1-D}(t_1)\phi_{1-D}(t_2) \tag{3.9}$$

$$\frac{1}{4}\psi\left(\frac{t_1}{2}, \frac{t_2}{2}\right) = \phi(t_1, t_2) - \frac{1}{4}\phi\left(\frac{t_1}{2}, \frac{t_2}{2}\right),$$

where $\phi_{1-D}(t)$ is the 1-D B-spline of order 3 (i.e., B_3-spline), and the wavelet function is defined as the difference between two resolutions. The related pair of filters (h, g) is defined by

$$h_{1-D}[k] = [1, 4, 6, 4, 1]/16, \quad k = -2, \ldots, 2,$$

$$h[k, l] = h_{1-D}[k]\, h_{1-D}[l], \tag{3.10}$$

$$g[k, l] = \delta[k, l] - h[k, l],$$

where δ is defined as $\delta[0, 0] = 1$ and $\delta[k, l] = 0$ for all $(k, l) \neq (0, 0)$.

The following useful properties characterize any pair of even-symmetric analysis FIR (finite impulse response) filters $(h, g = \delta - h)$ such as those of (3.10):

Property 1 *For any pair of even symmetric filters h and g such that $g = \delta - h$, the following holds:*

(i) *This FIR filter bank implements a frame decomposition, and perfect reconstruction using FIR filters is possible.*
(ii) *This FIR filter bank can not implement a tight frame decomposition.*

See Starck et al. (2007) for a proof. Figure 3.6 shows the cubic spline scaling function ϕ_{1-D} and the wavelet ψ_{1-D}, respectively.

From the structure of g, it is easily seen that the wavelet coefficients are obtained just by taking the difference between two resolutions:

$$w_{j+1}[k, l] = c_j[k, l] - c_{j+1}[k, l] \tag{3.11}$$

where $c_{j+1}[k, l] = (\bar{h}^{(j)}\bar{h}^{(j)} \star c_j)[k, l]$. The use of the B_3-spline leads to a discrete convolution with the 5×5 2-D FIR:

$$\frac{1}{256}\begin{pmatrix} 1 & 4 & 6 & 4 & 1 \\ 4 & 16 & 24 & 16 & 4 \\ 6 & 24 & 36 & 24 & 6 \\ 4 & 16 & 24 & 16 & 4 \\ 1 & 4 & 6 & 4 & 1 \end{pmatrix} = \frac{1}{16}\begin{pmatrix} 1 \\ 4 \\ 6 \\ 4 \\ 1 \end{pmatrix}(1, 4, 6, 4, 1)/16.$$

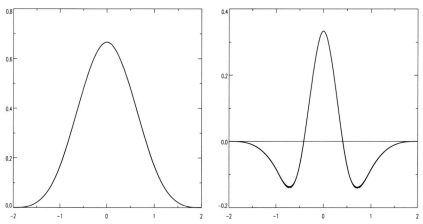

Figure 3.6. (left) The cubic spline function ϕ_{1-D}; (right) the wavelet ψ_{1-D} defined in (3.10). The ψ_{1-D} is defined as the difference between two resolutions.

But owing to separability, it is of course faster to compute the convolution first on rows, and then on the resulting columns (or vice versa).

At each scale j, we obtain one subband w_j (and not three as in the separable UWT) which has the same number of pixels as the input image.

A summary of the starlet algorithm is as follows.

Algorithm 7 2-D Starlet Transform Algorithm

Task: Compute the 2-D starlet transform of an $N \times N$ image X.
Initialization: $c_0 = X$, $J = \log_2 N$, $h_{1-D}[k] = [1, 4, 6, 4, 1]/16$, $k = -2, \ldots, 2$.
for $j = 0$ to $J - 1$ **do**

    1. **for** Each row $l = 0$ to $N - 1$ **do**

        • Carry out a 1-D discrete convolution of the image c_j with periodic or reflexive boundary conditions, using the 1-D filter h_{1-D}. The convolution is an interlaced one, where the $h_{1-D}^{(j)}$ filter's sample values have a gap (growing with level, j) between them of 2^j samples, giving rise to the name à trous ("with holes").

$$v[l, \cdot] = h_{1-D}^{(j)} \star c_j[l, \cdot] \,.$$

    2. **for** Each column $k = 0$ to $N - 1$ **do**

        • Carry out a 1-D discrete convolution of v, using 1-D filter h_{1-D}:

$$c_{j+1}[\cdot, k] = h_{1-D}^{(j)} \star v[\cdot, k] \,.$$

    3. From the smooth subband c_j, compute the IUWT detail coefficients,

$$w_{j+1} = c_j - c_{j+1} \,.$$

Output: $\mathcal{W} = \{w_1, \ldots, w_J, c_J\}$ the starlet transform of X.

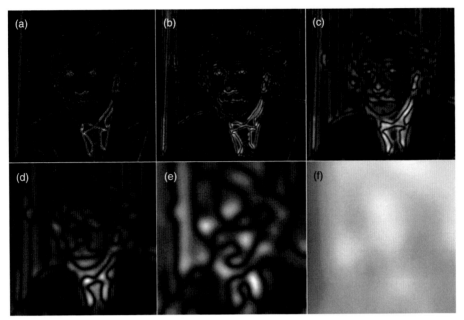

Figure 3.7. Starlet transform of the "Einstein" image. The addition of these six images reproduce exactly the original image.

It is easy to see that the reconstruction is obtained by a simple co-addition of all wavelet scales and the final smooth subband, namely

$$c_0[k, l] = c_J[k, l] + \sum_{j=1}^{J} w_j[k, l] ; \tag{3.12}$$

that is, the synthesis filters are $\tilde{h} = \delta$ and $\tilde{g} = \delta$, which are indeed FIR as expected from Property 1(i). This wavelet transformation is very well adapted to the analysis of images which contain isotropic objects such as in astronomy (Starck and Murtagh 2006) or in biology (Genovesio and Olivo-Marin 2003). This construction has a close relation with the Laplacian pyramidal construction introduced by Burt and Adelson (1983) (see also Section 3.7).

Figure 3.7 shows the IUWT, or starlet transform, of the image "Einstein" at five resolution levels. The transformation consists of five detail subbands and the smooth one, each one being of the same size as the original image. The redundancy factor is therefore equal to 6 and $J + 1$ in general for J decomposition levels. The simple addition of these six images reproduces exactly the original image.

Relation between the UWT and the Starlet Transform

Since the dealiasing filter bank condition is not required any more in the UWT decomposition, we can build the standard three-directional undecimated filter bank using the "Astro" filter bank ($h_{1-D} = [1, 4, 6, 4, 1]/16$, $g_{1-D} = \delta - h_{1-D} = [-1, -4, 10, -4, -1]/16$ and $\tilde{h}_{1-D} = \tilde{g}_{1-D} = \delta$). In two dimensions, this filter bank leads to a wavelet transform with three orientations w_j^1, w_j^2, w_j^3 at each scale j, but with the same reconstruction property as for the IUWT, i.e. the sum of all scales

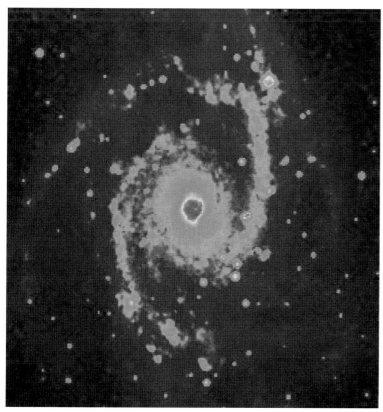

Figure 3.8. Galaxy NGC 2997. The false colors correspond to an artificial color map. (See *color plates*.)

reproduces the original image:

$$c_0[k, l] = c_J[k, l] + \sum_{j=1}^{J} \sum_{d=1}^{3} w_j^q[k, l] . \tag{3.13}$$

Indeed, a straightforward calculation immediately shows that (Starck et al. 2007)

$$w_j^1 + w_j^2 + w_j^3 = c_j - c_{j+1} . \tag{3.14}$$

Therefore, the sum of the three directions reproduces the IUWT detail subband at scale j. Figure 3.9 shows the UWT of the galaxy NGC 2997 displayed in Figure 3.8. When we add the three directional wavelet bands at a given scale, we recover exactly the starlet scale. When we add all bands, we recover exactly the original image. The relation between the two undecimated transforms is clear.

3.6 NONORTHOGONAL FILTER BANK DESIGN

3.6.1 Positive Reconstruction Filters

Because the transform is nonsubsampled, there are many ways to reconstruct the original image from its wavelet transform[1]. For a given filter bank (h, g), any synthesis filter bank $(\tilde{h}, \tilde{g})$ that satisfies the reconstruction condition (2.21) leads to an exact

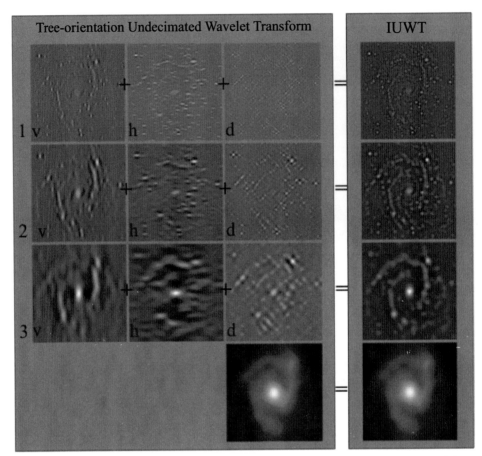

Figure 3.9. UWT of the galaxy NGC 2997 using the "Astro" filter bank. The addition of three detail subbands at a given scale is exactly the wavelet subband of the IUWT. Addition of all subbands reproduces exactly the original image.

reconstruction. For instance, for isotropic h, if we choose $\tilde{h} = h$ (the synthesis scaling function $\tilde{\phi} = \phi$) we obtain a filter $\tilde{g}$ defined by (Starck et al. 2007):

$$\tilde{g} = \delta + h .$$

Again, as expected from Property 1, the analysis filter bank $(h, g = \delta - h)$ implements a (non-tight) frame decomposition for FIR symmetric h, where $\tilde{h} = h$ and $\tilde{g} = \delta + h$ are also FIR filters. For instance, if $h_{1-D} = [1, 4, 6, 4, 1]/16$, then $\tilde{g}_{1-D} = [1, 4, 22, 4, 1]/16$. That is, $\tilde{g}_{1-D}$ *is positive*. This means that $\tilde{g}$ is no longer related to a wavelet function. The 1-D detail synthesis function related to $\tilde{g}_{1-D}$ is defined by

$$\frac{1}{2}\tilde{\psi}_{1-D}\left(\frac{t}{2}\right) = \phi_{1-D}(t) + \frac{1}{2}\phi_{1-D}\left(\frac{t}{2}\right) . \tag{3.15}$$

Note that by choosing $\tilde{\phi}_{1-D} = \phi_{1-D}$, any synthesis function $\tilde{\psi}_{1-D}$ that satisfies

$$\hat{\tilde{\psi}}_{1-D}(2\nu)\hat{\psi}_{1-D}(2\nu) = \hat{\phi}^2_{1-D}(\nu) - \hat{\phi}^2_{1-D}(2\nu) \tag{3.16}$$

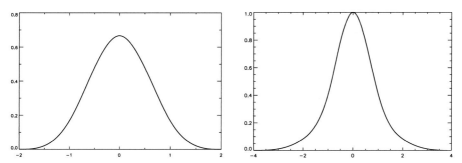

Figure 3.10. (left) $\hat{\tilde{\phi}}_{1-D}$ the 1-D synthesis scaling function and (right) $\tilde{\psi}_{1-D}$ the 1-D detail synthesis function.

leads to an exact reconstruction (Mallat 2008) and $\hat{\tilde{\psi}}_{1-D}(0)$ can take any value. The synthesis function $\tilde{\psi}_{1-D}$ does not need to verify the admissibility condition (i.e., to have a zero mean).

Figure 3.10 shows the two functions $\tilde{\phi}_{1-D} \ (= \phi_{1-D})$ and $\tilde{\psi}_{1-D}$ used in the reconstruction in 1-D, corresponding to the synthesis filters $\tilde{h}_{1-D} = h_{1-D}$ and $\tilde{g}_{1-D} = \delta + h_{1-D}$. Figure 3.11 shows the backprojection of a wavelet coefficient in 2-D (all wavelet coefficients are set to zero, except one), when the non-zero coefficient belongs to different subbands. We can see that the detail synthesis functions are indeed positive.

3.6.2 Reconstruction from the Haar Undecimated Coefficients

The 1-D Haar filters $(h_{1-D} = \tilde{h}_{1-D} = [1/2, 1/2], g_{1-D} = \tilde{g}_{1-D} = [-1/2, 1/2])$ are not considered to be good filters in practice because of their lack of smoothness. They are, however, very useful in many situations such as denoising where their simplicity allows us to derive analytical or semi-analytical detection levels even when the noise does not follow a Gaussian distribution. This will be at the heart of Section 6.5.

Adopting the same design approach as before, we can reconstruct a signal from its Haar wavelet coefficients, choosing a smooth scaling function. For instance, if $\tilde{h}_{1-D} = [1, 4, 6, 4, 1]/16$, it is easy to derive that the z transforms of these three filters are, respectively,

$$H(z) = \frac{1 + z^{-1}}{2}, \quad G(z) = \frac{z^{-1} - 1}{2}, \quad \tilde{H}(z) = \frac{z^2 + 4z + 6 + 4z^{-1} + z^{-2}}{16} . \quad (3.17)$$

From the exact reconstruction condition (2.21), we obtain

$$\tilde{G}(z) = \frac{1 - \tilde{H}(z)H(z^{-1})}{G(z^{-1})} . \quad (3.18)$$

In the case of the spline filter bank, this yields after some rearrangement (where we use simple convolution properties of splines),

$$\tilde{G}(z) = -2 \frac{1 - z^3 \left(\frac{1+z^{-1}}{2}\right)^5}{1 - z^{-1}} = z^3 \frac{1 + 6z^{-1} + 16z^{-2} - 6z^{-3} - z^{-4}}{16} , \quad (3.19)$$

which is the z-transform of the corresponding filter $\tilde{g}_{1-D} = [1, 6, 16, -6, -1]/16$.

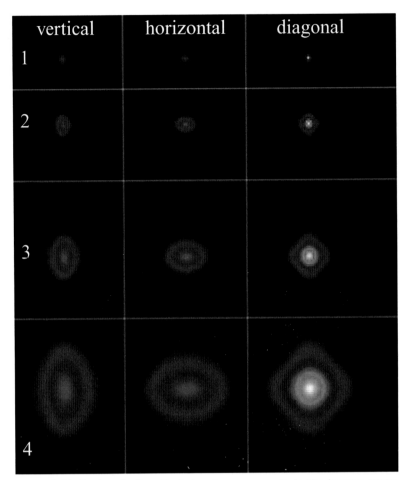

Figure 3.11. Backprojection: Each image corresponds to the inverse transform of one wavelet coefficient. All these reconstructed images are positive (no negative values). From left to right, the coefficient belongs to the vertical, horizontal, and diagonal direction. From top to bottom, the scale index increases. (See *color plates*.)

The Haar analysis filters fulfill the following property:

Property 2 *Haar analysis filters can implement a tight frame expansion (more precisely, one scale of the Haar wavelet UWT does). Moreover, perfect reconstruction with FIR synthesis filters is possible.*

Figure 3.12 (top) depicts the coarsest scale and a wavelet scale of the Haar transform when the input signal is the Dirac pulse $\delta[k]$. Figure 3.12 (bottom left) portrays the backprojection of a Dirac at the coarsest scale (all coefficients are set to zero), and Figure 3.12 (bottom right) shows the backprojection of a Haar wavelet coefficient. Since the synthesis filters are regular, the backprojection of a Dirac does not produce any block staircase-like artifact.

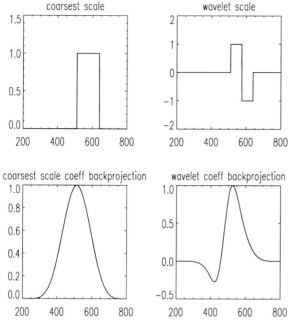

Figure 3.12. 1-D Haar undecimated transform. (top) Coarsest scale (smooth subband) and a wavelet scale when the signal is $\delta[k]$. (bottom left) Backprojection of a single coefficient at the coarsest scale. (bottom right) Backprojection of a single Haar wavelet coefficient.

Alternatives are feasible. For example, the filter bank, $h_{1-\mathrm{D}} = [1/2, -1/2]$, $g_{1-\mathrm{D}} = [-1/4, 1/2, -1/4]$, $\tilde{h}_{1-\mathrm{D}} = [1, 3, 3, 1]/8$, and $\tilde{g}_{1-\mathrm{D}} = [1, 6, 1]/4$, leads also to an interesting solution where the synthesis filters are both positive.

3.6.3 Starlet Transform: Second Generation

A particular case is obtained when $\hat{\tilde{\phi}}_{1-\mathrm{D}} = \hat{\phi}_{1-\mathrm{D}}$ and $\hat{\psi}_{1-\mathrm{D}}(2\nu) = (\hat{\phi}^2_{1-\mathrm{D}}(\nu) - \hat{\phi}^2_{1-\mathrm{D}}(2\nu))/(\hat{\phi}_{1-\mathrm{D}}(\nu))$, which leads to a filter $g_{1-\mathrm{D}}$ equal to $\delta - h_{1-\mathrm{D}} \star h_{1-\mathrm{D}}$. In this case, the synthesis function $\tilde{\psi}_{1-\mathrm{D}}$ is defined by $\frac{1}{2}\tilde{\psi}_{1-\mathrm{D}}(\frac{t}{2}) = \phi_{1-\mathrm{D}}(t)$ and the filter $\tilde{g}_{1-\mathrm{D}} = \delta$ is the solution to (2.21).

We end up with a synthesis scheme where only the smooth part is convolved during the reconstruction. Furthermore, for a symmetric FIR filter $h_{1-\mathrm{D}}$, it can be easily shown that this filter bank fulfills the statements of Property 1.

Deriving h from a spline scaling function, for instance B_1 ($h_1 = [1, 2, 1]/4$) or B_3 ($h_3 = [1, 4, 6, 4, 1]/16$) (note that $h_3 = h_1 \star h_1$), since $h_{1-\mathrm{D}}$ is even-symmetric (i.e., $H(z) = H(z^{-1})$), the z-transform of $g_{1-\mathrm{D}}$ is then

$$G(z) = 1 - H^2(z) = 1 - z^4 \left(\frac{1 + z^{-1}}{2}\right)^8$$

$$= \frac{1}{256}(-z^4 - 8z^3 - 28z^2 - 56z + 186 - 56z^{-1} - 28z^{-2} - 8z^{-3} - z^{-4}), \quad (3.20)$$

which is the z-transform of the filter

$$g_{1-D} = [-1, -8, -28, -56, 186, -56, -28, -8, -1]/256 \, .$$

We get the following filter bank:

$$h_{1-D} = h_3 = \tilde{h} = [1, 4, 6, 4, 1]/16$$

$$g_{1-D} = \delta - h \star h = [-1, -8, -28, -56, 186, -56, -28, -8, -1]/256 \quad (3.21)$$

$$\tilde{g}_{1-D} = \delta \, .$$

Algorithm 8 Starlet Second-Generation Transform Algorithm

Task: Compute the 1-D starlet transform of a signal X, with N entries.
Initialization: $c_0 = X$, $J = \log_2 N$, $h_{1-D}[k] = [1, 4, 6, 4, 1]/16$, $k = -2, \ldots, 2$.
for $j = 0$ to $J - 1$ **do**

> 1. Carry out a 1-D discrete convolution of c_j with periodic or reflexive boundary conditions, using the 1-D filter h_{1-D}. The convolution is an interlaced one, where the $h_{1-D}^{(j)}$ filter's sample values have a gap (growing with level, j) between them of 2^j samples, giving rise to the name à trous ("with holes").
>
> $$c_{j+1}[\cdot] = h_{1-D}^{(j)} \star c_j[\cdot] \, .$$
>
> 2. Carry out the same convolution on $c_{j+1}[k]$, and we obtain v.
>
> $$v[\cdot] = h_{1-D}^{(j)} \star c_{j+1}[\cdot] \, .$$
>
> 3. From the smooth subband c_j, compute the IUWT detail coefficients,
>
> $$w_{j+1} = c_j - v \, .$$

Output: $\mathcal{W} = \{w_1, \ldots, w_J, c_J\}$ the starlet transform second generation of X.

As in the standard starlet transform, extension to 2-D is trivial. We just replace the convolution with h_{1D} by a convolution with the filter h_{2D}, which is performed efficiently by using the separability.

With this filter bank, there is a no convolution with the filter $\tilde{g}_{1-D}$ during the reconstruction. Only the low-pass synthesis filter $\tilde{h}_{1-D}$ is used. The reconstruction formula is

$$c_j[l] = \left(h_{1-D}^{(j)} \star c_{j+1} \right)[l] + w_{j+1}[l] \, , \quad (3.22)$$

and denoting $L^j = h^{(0)} \star \cdots \star h^{(j-1)}$ and $L^0 = \delta$, we have

$$c_0[l] = (L^J \star c_J)[l] + \sum_{j=1}^{J} (L^{j-1} \star w_j)[l] \, . \quad (3.23)$$

Each wavelet scale is convolved with a low-pass filter.

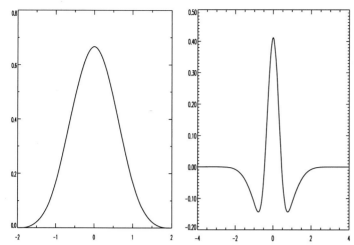

Figure 3.13. (left) The ϕ_{1-D} analysis scaling function and (right) the ψ_{1-D} analysis wavelet function. The synthesis functions $\tilde{\phi}_{1-D}$ are the same as those in Figure 3.10.

Algorithm 9 Starlet Second-Generation Reconstruction Algorithm

---

Task: Reconstruct a N signal from its second-generation starlet transform, $\mathcal{W} = \{w_1, \ldots, w_J, c_J\}$.

Initialization: $c_0 = X$, $J = \log_2 N, h_{1-D}[k] = [1, 4, 6, 4, 1]/16,\ \ k = -2, \ldots, 2$.

for $j = J - 1$ **to** 0 **do**

1. Carry out a 1-D discrete convolution of c_{j+1} with periodic or reflexive boundary conditions, using the 1-D filter h_{1-D}. The convolution is an interlaced one, where the $h_{1-D}^{(j)}$ filter's sample values have a gap (growing with level, j) between them of 2^j samples, giving rise to the name à trous ("with holes").

$$v[\cdot] = h_{1-D}^{(j)} \star c_{j+1}[\cdot] \, .$$

2. Coadd the smooth subband v with the wavelet band.

$$c_j = v + w_j \, .$$

Output: c_0 the reconstruction from $\mathcal{W}$.

As for the transformation, the 2-D extension consists just in replacing the convolution by h_{1D} with a convolution by h_{2D}.

Figure 3.13 shows the analysis scaling and wavelet functions. The synthesis functions $\tilde{\phi}_{1-D}$ and $\tilde{\psi}_{1-D}$ are the same as those in Figure 3.10.

In 2-D, similarly, the second-generation starlet transform leads to the representation of an image $X[k, l]$:

$$X[k, l] = \sum_{m,n} \phi_{j,k,l}^{(1)}(m, n)c_J[m, n] + \sum_{j=1}^{J} \sum_{m,n} \phi_{j,k,l}^{(2)}(m, n)w_j[m, n] \, , \qquad (3.24)$$

where $\phi^{(1)}_{j,k,l}(m,n) = 2^{-2j}\tilde{\phi}_{1-\mathrm{D}}(2^{-j}(k-m))\tilde{\phi}_{1-\mathrm{D}}(2^{-j}(l-n))$,   and $\phi^{(2)}_{j,k,l}(m,n) = 2^{-2j}\tilde{\psi}_{1-\mathrm{D}}(2^{-j}(k-m))\tilde{\psi}_{1-\mathrm{D}}(2^{-j}(l-n))$.

$\phi^{(1)}$ and $\phi^{(2)}$ are positive, and w_j are zero mean 2-D wavelet coefficients.

3.6.4 Iterative Reconstruction

Denoting $\mathbf{T}_W$ the undecimated wavelet transform operator and $\mathbf{R}_W$ the reconstruction operator, and using the exact reconstruction formula we have the relation: $w = \mathbf{T}_W\mathbf{R}_W w$, where w is the vector storing the wavelet coefficients of a discrete signal or image X (i.e., $w = \mathbf{T}_W X$). But we lose one fundamental property of the (bi-)orthogonal WT. The relation $\alpha = \mathbf{T}_W\mathbf{R}_W\alpha$ is not true for any vector α.

For example, if we set all wavelet coefficients to zero except one at a coarse scale, there is no image such that its UWT would produce a Dirac at a coarse scale. Another way to understand this point is to consider a given undecimated scale in the Fourier domain. Indeed, wavelet coefficients w_j at scale j obtained using the wavelet transform operator will contain information only localized at a given frequency band. But any modification of the coefficients at this scale, such as a thresholding $w_t = \mathrm{Thresh}_t(w)$, where Thresh_t is the hard thresholding operator (see Chapter 6) with threshold t, will introduce some frequency components that should not exist at this scale j, and we have $w_t \neq \mathbf{T}_W\mathbf{R}_W w_t$.

3.6.4.1 Reconstruction from a Subset of Coefficients

Without loss of generality, we consider hereafter the case of 1-D signals. If only a subset of coefficients (e.g., after thresholding) is different from zero, we would like to reconstruct a signal $\tilde{X}$ such that its wavelet transform reproduces the non-zero wavelet coefficients in w_t. This can be cast as an inverse problem. Let $\mathcal{M}$ be the *multiresolution support* of w_t that contains the indices where w_t is different from zero. We want to solve the following convex optimization problem:

$$\min_X \|\mathbf{M}(w_t - \mathbf{T}_W X)\|_2^2 \,,$$

where $\mathbf{M}$ corresponds to the multiresolution support $\mathcal{M}$ (i.e., $\mathbf{M}$ is a diagonal matrix whose ith diagonal element $\mathbf{M}[i,i] = 1$ if $i \in \mathcal{M}$, and zero otherwise). The above problem corresponds to a least-square inversion of a linear problem[2]. A solution can be obtained iteratively through gradient-descent or the Landweber scheme (Starck et al. 1995, 1998):

$$X^{(n+1)} = X^{(n)} + \mu \mathbf{T}_W^{\mathrm{T}} \mathbf{M}\left(w_t - \mathbf{T}_W X^{(n)}\right) \,,$$

where $\mu \in (0, 2/\|\mathbf{T}_W\|^2)$ is the descent stepsize, and $\|\mathbf{T}_W\|$ is the frame upper bound. In practice, this iteration is rather implemented as

$$X^{(n+1)} = X^{(n)} + \mathbf{R}_W \mathbf{M}\left(w_t - \mathbf{T}_W X^{(n)}\right) \,. \tag{3.25}$$

Note that if the wavelet transform implements a tight frame, then $\mathbf{R}_W$ is indeed $\mathbf{T}_W^{\mathrm{T}}$ up to a constant.

If the solution is known to be positive, the positivity constraint can be accounted for, which gives the following iteration:

$$X^{(n+1)} = \mathrm{P}_{\mathcal{P}_+} \left(X^{(n)} + \mathbf{R}_W \mathbf{M} \left(w_t - \mathbf{T}_W X^{(n)} \right) \right) , \tag{3.26}$$

where $\mathrm{P}_{\mathcal{P}_+}$ is the projection on the positive orthant $\mathcal{P}_+$. The last iterative scheme can also be interpreted as an alternating projection onto a convex sets (POCS) algorithm (Starck et al. 2007). It has proven very effective at many tasks such as image approximation and restoration when using the UWT (Starck et al. 2007).

3.6.5 Sparse Positive Decomposition

In some scientific fields, many images can be modeled as a sum of positive features; for instance, stars and galaxies in astronomy or cells in biology, which are more or less isotropic. The previous representation, based on the starlet transform, is well adapted to the representation of isotropic objects, but does not introduce any prior relative to the positivity of the features contained in our image. A positive and sparse modeling of such images is similar to equation (3.27):

$$Y = \Phi\alpha + N + B . \tag{3.27}$$

All coefficients in α are now positive, and all atoms in the dictionary Φ are positive functions. Such a decomposition normally requires computationally intensive algorithms such as Matching Pursuit (Mallat and Zhang 1993). The second-generation starlet transform offers us a new way to perform such a decomposition (Starck et al. 2011). Indeed, we have seen in section 3.6.3 that, using a specific filter bank, we can decompose an image Y on a positive dictionary Φ (see Figure 3.10) and obtain a set of coefficients $\alpha^{(Y)}$, where $\alpha^{(Y)} = \mathbf{W}Y = \{w_1, \ldots, w_J, c_J\}$, $\mathbf{W}$ being the second-generation starlet wavelet transform operator. α Coefficients are positive and negative, and are obtained using the standard second-generation starlet wavelet transform algorithm. Hence, by thresholding all negative (respectively, positive) coefficients, the reconstruction is always positive (respectively, negative), since Φ contains only positive atoms.

Hence, we would like to have a sparse set of positive coefficients $\tilde{\alpha}$ that verify $\Phi\tilde{\alpha} = Y$. But in order to take into account the background and the noise, we need to define the constraint in the wavelet space (i.e., $\mathbf{W}\Phi\tilde{\alpha} = \mathbf{W}Y = \alpha^{(Y)}$), and this constraint must be applied only to the subset of coefficients in $\alpha^{(Y)}$ that are larger than the detection level. Therefore, to get a sparse positive decomposition on Φ, we need to minimize

$$\tilde{\alpha} = \min_{\alpha} \parallel \alpha \parallel_1 \quad \text{s.t.} \quad M\mathbf{W}\Phi\alpha = M\alpha^{(Y)} , \tag{3.28}$$

where M is the multiresolution support defined in the previous section (i.e., $M_j[k, l] = 1$ if a significant coefficient is detected at scale j and at position (k, l), and zero otherwise). The background can also be removed by setting $M_{J+1}[k, l] = 0$ for all (k, l).

It was shown that such optimization problems can be efficiently solved through an iterative soft thresholding (IST) algorithm (Figueiredo and Nowak 2003; Starck et al. 2004b; Combettes and Wajs 2005) (full details relative to this algorithm are given in

Chapter 7). The algorithm 10, based on the IST, allows us to take into account the noise modeling through the multiresolution support and force the coefficients to be all positive.

Algorithm 10 Sparse Positive Decomposition Algorithm

Task: Compute the sparse positive decomposition of a signal Y, with N entries.
Parameters: The data Y, the second-generation starlet transform $\mathbf{W}$, the number of iterations N_{iter}.
Initialization:

- Taking the second-generation starlet wavelet transform of the data Y, we obtain $\alpha^{(Y)} = \mathbf{W}Y$.
- From a given noise model, determine the multiresolution support M.
- The first threshold, $\lambda^{(0)} = MAX(\alpha^{(Y)})$,
- Initial solution $\tilde{\alpha}^{(0)} = 0$.

Main iteration:
for $i = 1$ **to** N_{iter} **do**

- Reconstruct the image $\tilde{Y}^{(i)}$ from $\tilde{\alpha}^{(i)}$.

$$\tilde{Y}^{(i)} = \mathbf{\Phi}\tilde{\alpha}^{(i)} \ .$$

- Take the second-generation starlet wavelet transform of the data $\tilde{Y}^{(i)}$.

$$\alpha^{\tilde{Y}^{(i)}} = \mathbf{W}\mathbf{\Phi}\tilde{\alpha}^{(i)} \ .$$

- Compute the significant residual $r^{(i)}$.

$$r^{(i)} = M\big(\alpha^{(Y)} - \alpha^{\tilde{Y}^{(i)}}\big) = M\left(\alpha^{(Y)} - \mathbf{W}\mathbf{\Phi}\tilde{\alpha}^{(i)}\right)$$

- Update $\lambda^{(i)}$.

$$\lambda^{(i)} = \lambda^{(0)}(1 - i/N_{\text{iter}})$$

- Update the solution by adding the residual, applying a soft thresholding on positive coefficients using the threshold level $\lambda^{(i)}$, and setting all negative coefficients to zero.

$$\tilde{\alpha}^{(i+1)} = \big(\tilde{\alpha}^{(i)} + r^{(i)} - \lambda^{(i)}\big)_+$$
$$= \big(\tilde{\alpha}^{(i)} + M\left(\alpha^{(Y)} - \mathbf{W}\mathbf{\Phi}\tilde{\alpha}^{(i)}\right) - \lambda^{(i)}\big)_+$$

Output: $\tilde{\alpha} = \tilde{\alpha}^{(N_{\text{iter}})}$ the positive sparse decomposition of Y.

The threshold parameter $\lambda^{(i)}$ decreases with the iteration number, and it plays a role similar to the cooling parameter of the simulated annealing techniques, (i.e., it allows the solution to escape from local minima).

Example 1 *Sparse Positive Decomposition of NGC2997*

Figure 3.14 shows the positive starlet decomposition, using 100 iterations, and can be compared to Figure 3.9.

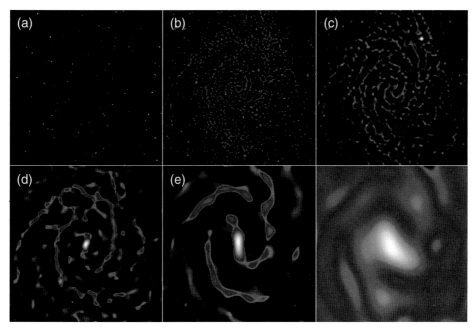

Figure 3.14. Positive starlet decomposition of the galaxy NGC2997 with six scales. (See *color plates.*)

Example 2 *Sparse Positive Starlet Decomposition of a Simulated Image*

The next example compares the standard starlet transform to the positive starlet decomposition (PSD) on a simulated image.

Figure 3.15 shows, respectively, from top to bottom and left to right, (a) the original simulated image, (b) the noisy data, (c) the reconstruction from the PSD coefficients, and (d) the residual between the noisy data and the PSD reconstructed image (i.e., image b − image c). Hence, the PSD reconstructed image gives a very good approximation of the original image. No structures can be be seen in the residual, and all sources are well detected.

The first PSD scale does not contain any non-zero coefficient. Figure 3.16 (top) shows the first four scales of the wavelet transform, and Figure 3.16 (bottom) the first four scales of the PSD.

3.7 PYRAMIDAL WAVELET TRANSFORM

3.7.1 The Laplacian Pyramid

The Laplacian pyramid was developed by Burt and Adelson (1983) in order to compress images. The term *Laplacian* was used by these authors for the difference between two successive levels in a pyramid, defined itself in turn by repeatedly applying a low-pass (smoothing) filtering operation. After the filtering, only one sample out of two is kept. The number of samples decreases by a factor 2 at each scale. The difference between images is obtained by expanding (or interpolating) one of the pair of images in the sequence associated with the pyramid.

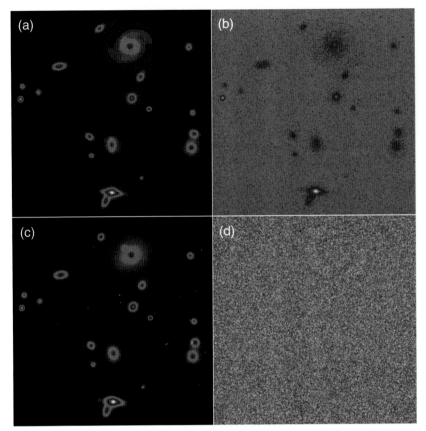

Figure 3.15. Top left and right, original simulated image and the same image contaminated by a Gaussian noise. Bottom left and right, reconstructed image for the positive starlet coefficients of the noisy image using 50 iterations, and residual (i.e., noisy image − reconstructed image). (See *color plates*.)

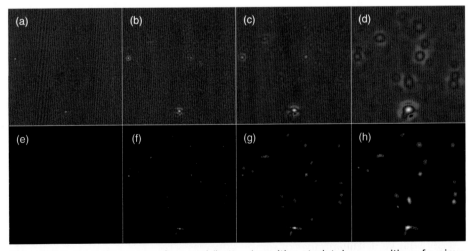

Figure 3.16. (top) Starlet transform and (bottom) positive starlet decomposition of a simulated astronomical image. (See *color plates*.)

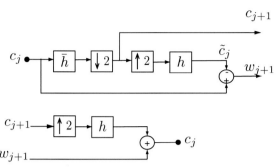

Figure 3.17. Laplacian pyramid transform. (top) Analysis, passage from c_j to the detail and smooth coefficients w_{j+1} and c_{j+1}. (bottom) Usual reconstruction.

The 1-D Laplacian pyramid transform and its usual inverse are depicted in Figure 3.17. First, the scaling coefficients are computed by discrete convolution and down-sampling (see Figure 3.17 (top)):

$$c_{j+1}[l] = \sum_k h[k - 2l] c_j[k] = [\bar{h} \star c_j]_{\downarrow 2}[l] . \tag{3.29}$$

Then the detail coefficients w_{j+1} are computed as the difference:

$$w_{j+1}[l] = c_j[l] - \tilde{c}_j[l] , \tag{3.30}$$

where $\tilde{c}_j$ is the prediction obtained by zero-interpolation and discrete convolution:

$$\tilde{c}_j[l] = 2 \sum_k h[l - 2k] c_{j+1}[k] = 2(h \star \check{c}_{j+1})[l] . \tag{3.31}$$

The scaling coefficients c_j are reconstructed from c_{j+1} and w_{j+1} as illustrated in Figure 3.17 (bottom) that is,

$$c_j[l] = 2(h \star \check{c}_{j+1})[l] + w_{j+1}[l] . \tag{3.32}$$

In two dimensions, the method is similar. The convolution is carried out by keeping one sample out of two in the two directions. We have:

$$c_{j+1}[k, l] = \sum_m \sum_n h[m - 2k, n - 2l] c_j[m, n] = [\bar{h} \star c_j]_{\downarrow 2 \downarrow 2}[k, l]$$
$$w_{j+1}[k, l] = c_j[k, l] - \tilde{c}_j[k, l] , \tag{3.33}$$

and $\tilde{c}_j$ is the prediction

$$\tilde{c}_j[k, l] = 4 \sum_m \sum_n h[m - 2k, n - 2l] c_{j+1}[m, n] = 4(h \star \check{c}_{j+1})[k, l] \tag{3.34}$$

The number of samples in c_{j+1} is divided by four, and w_{j+1} has as many samples as c_j. Therefore, the redundancy factor of the Laplacian pyramid in 2-D is $\sum_{j=0}^{J} 4^{-j} \approx 4/3$.

3.7.2 Scaling Functions with a Frequency Cutoff

3.7.2.1 Analysis

We start with the set of 1-D coarse samples $c_0[l] = \langle f, \phi(\cdot - l) \rangle$. If $\phi(t)$ has a cut-off frequency $v_c \leq \frac{1}{2}$ (Starck and Bijaoui 1994; Starck et al. 1994), the data are correctly sampled. The scaling coefficients at resolution $j = 1$ are

$$c_1[l] = \left\langle f, \frac{1}{2}\phi\left(\frac{1}{2}\cdot -l\right)\right\rangle, \tag{3.35}$$

and we can compute the c_1 from c_0 in the Fourier domain as

$$\hat{c}_{j+1}(v) = \hat{c}_j(v)\hat{h}^*(2^j v), \tag{3.36}$$

where $\hat{h}(v)$ is the Fourier transform of h obtained from equation (2.12):

$$\hat{h}(v) = \begin{cases} \frac{\hat{\phi}(2v)}{\hat{\phi}(v)} & \text{if } |v| < v_c \\ 0 & \text{if } v_c \leq |v| < \frac{1}{2}, \end{cases} \tag{3.37}$$

and $\hat{h}(v)$ is periodic of period 1:

$$\forall v \in [-1/2, 1/2), \quad \forall n \in \mathbb{Z} \quad \hat{h}(v+n) = \hat{h}(v). \tag{3.38}$$

Expression (3.36) is nothing but the Fourier transform of (3.3). The cutoff frequency is reduced by a factor 2 at each step, allowing a reduction of the number of samples by this factor.

The wavelet coefficients at scale $j + 1$ are

$$w_{j+1}[l] = \langle f, 2^{-(j+1)}\psi(2^{-(j+1)}\cdot - l)\rangle. \tag{3.39}$$

Taking the Fourier transform of equation (3.3), they can be computed directly from c_j in the Fourier domain by

$$\hat{w}_{j+1}(v) = \hat{c}_j(v)\hat{g}^*(2^j v), \tag{3.40}$$

where g has the 1-periodic Fourier transform:

$$\hat{g}(v) = \begin{cases} \frac{\hat{\psi}(2v)}{\hat{\phi}(v)} & \text{if } |v| < v_c \\ 1 & \text{if } v_c \leq |v| < \frac{1}{2}. \end{cases} \tag{3.41}$$

The frequency band is also reduced by a factor 2 at each step. Applying the sampling theorem, we can build a pyramid of $N + \frac{N}{2} + \cdots + 1 \approx 2N$ coefficients if the discrete signal has N samples. In 2-D, it is easy to see that the number of coefficients is $\frac{4}{3}N^2$ for images of $N \times N$ pixels.

The B-spline functions are compact in the original domain. They correspond to the autoconvolution of a square function. In the Fourier domain, we have

$$\hat{B}_n(v) = \left(\frac{\sin \pi v}{\pi v}\right)^{n+1} \tag{3.42}$$

$B_3(t)$ is a set of 4 polynomials of degree 3. We choose the scaling function ϕ which has a B_3-spline profile in the Fourier domain:

$$\hat{\phi}(v) = \frac{3}{2}B_3(4v). \tag{3.43}$$

Taking the inverse Fourier transform, we get

$$\phi(t) = \frac{3}{8} \left(\frac{\sin \frac{\pi t}{4}}{\frac{\pi t}{4}} \right)^4 . \tag{3.44}$$

This function is quite similar to a Gaussian and vanishes rapidly as t increases. For 2-D, the scaling function is defined by $\hat{\phi}(v_1, v_2) = \frac{3}{2} B_3(4r)$, with $r = \sqrt{v_1^2 + v_2^2}$. This is an isotropic function.

The 2-D pyramidal wavelet transform algorithm implemented in the Fourier domain with J scales is the following:

Algorithm 11 2-D Pyramidal Wavelet Transform Algorithm in the Fourier Domain

---

Task: Compute the pyramidal WT in the Fourier domain of an $N \times N$ image X.
Parameters: $\hat{\phi} = B_3$-spline.
Initialization: From the scaling function ϕ, compute ψ, $\hat{h}$ and $\hat{g}$ numerically; set $c_0 = X$ and $J = \log_2 N$.
Compute the 2-D FFT of X, name the resulting complex image $\hat{c}_0$.
for $j = 0$ to $J - 1$ **do**

1. Compute $\hat{w}_{j+1}(v_1, v_2) = \hat{c}_j(v_1, v_2) \hat{g}(2^j v_1, 2^j v_2)$.
2. The 2-D inverse FFT of $\hat{w}_{j+1}$ gives the wavelet coefficients w_{j+1}.
3. Compute $\hat{c}_{j+1}(v_1, v_2) = \hat{c}_j(v_1, v_2) \hat{h}(2^j v_1, 2^j v_2)$. The frequency band is reduced by a factor 2.

Compute the 2-D inverse FFT of $\hat{c}_J$ to get c_J.
Output: $\mathcal{W} = \{w_1, \ldots, w_J, c_J\}$ the 2-D pyramidal WT of X.

If the wavelet function is the difference between two resolutions, that is,

$$\hat{\psi}(2v) = \hat{\phi}(v) - \hat{\phi}(2v) , \tag{3.45}$$

which corresponds to

$$\hat{g}(v) = 1 - \hat{h}(v) , \tag{3.46}$$

then the Fourier transform of the wavelet coefficients $\hat{w}_j(v)$ can be computed as $\hat{c}_{j-1}(v) - \hat{c}_j(v)$.

In Figure 3.18 the Fourier transform of the scaling function derived from the B_3-spline (see equation (3.43)), and the corresponding wavelet function Fourier transform (equation (3.45)) are plotted.

3.7.2.2 Reconstruction

If the wavelet function is chosen as in equation (3.45), a trivial reconstruction from $\mathcal{W} = \{w_1, \ldots, w_J, c_J\}$ is given by

$$\hat{c}_0(v) = \hat{c}_J(v) + \sum_{j=1}^{J} \hat{w}_j(v) . \tag{3.47}$$

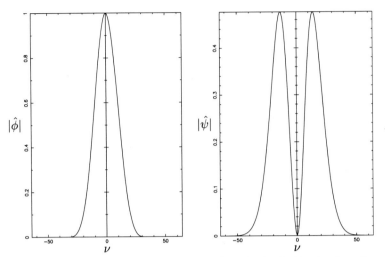

Figure 3.18. Analysis scaling and wavelet function in the Fourier domain: (left) scaling function Fourier transform $\hat{\phi}$; (right) wavelet function Fourier transform $\hat{\psi}$.

But this is a particular case, and other alternative wavelet functions can be chosen. The reconstruction can be made scale-by-scale, starting from the lowest resolution, and designing appropriate dual synthesis filters $(\tilde{h}, \tilde{g})$. From equations (3.36) and (3.40), we seek the scaling coefficients c_j knowing c_{j+1}, w_{j+1}, h and g. This can be cast as a weighted least-squares problem written in the Fourier domain as

$$
\min_{\hat{c}_j(v)} \hat{p}_h(2^j v)|\hat{c}_{j+1}(v) - \hat{h}^*(2^j v)\hat{c}_j(v)|^2 \tag{3.48}
$$
$$
+ \hat{p}_g(2^j v)|\hat{w}_{j+1}(v) - \hat{g}^*(2^j v)\hat{c}_j(v)|^2 ,
$$

for all v within the Nyquist band. $\hat{p}_h(v)$ and $\hat{p}_g(v)$ are weight functions which will give a general form solution to dual synthesis filters. Differentiating the convex objective (3.48) with respect to $\hat{c}_j(v)$, we get

$$
\hat{c}_j(v) = \hat{c}_{j+1}(v)\hat{\tilde{h}}(2^j v) + \hat{w}_{j+1}(v)\hat{\tilde{g}}(2^j v) , \tag{3.49}
$$

where the dual synthesis filters have the expressions

$$
\hat{\tilde{h}}(v) = \frac{\hat{p}_h(v)\hat{h}(v)}{\hat{p}_h(v)|\hat{h}(v)|^2 + \hat{p}_g(v)|\hat{g}(v)|^2} , \tag{3.50}
$$

$$
\hat{\tilde{g}}(v) = \frac{\hat{p}_g(v)\hat{g}(v)}{\hat{p}_h(v)|\hat{h}(v)|^2 + \hat{p}_g(v)|\hat{g}(v)|^2} . \tag{3.51}
$$

It is easy to see that these filters satisfy the exact reconstruction condition (2.21). In fact, equations (3.50) and (3.51) give the general form solution to equation (2.21). In this analysis, the Shannon sampling condition is always satisfied. No aliasing exists, so that the dealiasing condition (2.20) is not necessary.

The denominator of equations (3.50) and (3.51) reduces to a simplified form if we choose

$$
\hat{g}(v) = \sqrt{1 - |\hat{h}(v)|^2} .
$$

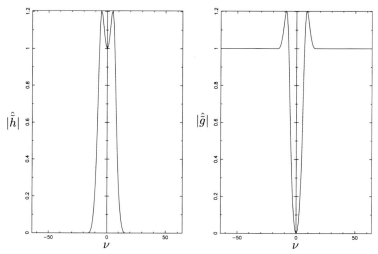

Figure 3.19. Dual synthesis filters in Fourier domain: (left) $\hat{\tilde{h}}$; (right) $\hat{\tilde{g}}$.

This corresponds to the case where the magnitude of the wavelet function in the Fourier domain is the difference between that of two resolutions:

$$|\hat{\psi}(2\nu)|^2 = |\hat{\phi}(\nu)|^2 - |\hat{\phi}(2\nu)|^2 \,. \tag{3.52}$$

The Fourier transforms of the dual synthesis filters $(\tilde{h}, \tilde{g})$ corresponding to the scaling and wavelet function of Figure 3.18 are plotted in Figure 3.19.

Finally, the reconstruction algorithm is summarized as follows.

Algorithm 12 2-D Pyramidal Wavelet Transform Reconstruction Algorithm in Fourier Domain

---

Task: Compute the inverse 2-D pyramidal wavelet transform in Fourier domain of $\mathcal{W} = \{w_1, \ldots, w_J, c_J\}$, the pyramidal WT of an $N \times N$ image X.

Parameters: $\hat{\phi} = \mathrm{B}_3$-spline.

Initialization: From the scaling function ϕ, compute ψ, $\hat{\tilde{h}}$ and $\hat{\tilde{g}}$ numerically; $J = \log_2 N$.

Compute the 2-D FFT of c_J, name the resulting complex image $\hat{c}_J$.

for $j = J$ to 1, with step=-1 **do**

1. Compute the 2-D FFT of the wavelet coefficients at scale j, $\hat{w}_j$.
2. Multiply the wavelet coefficients $\hat{w}_j(\nu_1, \nu_2)$ by $\hat{\tilde{g}}(2^j\nu_1, 2^j\nu_2)$.
3. Multiply the scaling coefficients $\hat{c}_j(\nu_1, \nu_2)$ by $\hat{\tilde{h}}(2^j\nu_1, 2^j\nu_2)$.
4. Compute $\hat{c}_{j-1} = \hat{w}_j\hat{\tilde{g}} + \hat{c}_j\hat{\tilde{h}}$.

Take the 2-D inverse FFT of $\hat{c}_0$ to get c_0.

Output: $c_0 = X$, the reconstruction from $\mathcal{W}$.

The use of a scaling function with a cutoff frequency allows a reduction of sampling at each scale, and limits the computational load and the memory storage.

3.7.3 Other Pyramidal Wavelet Constructions

There are other pyramidal wavelet constructions. For instance, the steerable wavelet transform (Simoncelli et al. 1992) allows us to choose the number of directions in the multiscale decomposition, and the redundancy is proportional to this number. Do and Vetterli (2003a) studied the Laplacian pyramid using frame theory, and showed that the Laplacian pyramid with orthogonal filters is a tight frame, and thus the reconstruction using the dual synthesis filters is optimal and has a simple structure that is symmetric with respect to the forward transform. We note also the work of Unser and his collaborators on pyramidal wavelets using splines (Unser et al. 1993; Unser 1999; Brigger et al. 1999).

3.8 GUIDED NUMERICAL EXPERIMENTS

3.8.1 Denoising by UWT

One of the main applications of redundant transforms is restoration and in particular denoising. There are numerous methods for the removal of additive noise from an image, and the wavelet-based methods draw special interest because of their theoretical underpinning, their success in practice, and their fast implementation. We here anticipate Chapter 6, devoted to denoising, and describe a few ingredients necessary to carry out this experiment. Hard thresholding consists of killing (setting to 0) all wavelet coefficients having a negligible value compared to noise, and in this way removing nonsignificant wavelet coefficients (Starck and Bijaoui 1994; Donoho and Johnstone 1995). At scale j this operation is accomplished by

$$\tilde{w}_j[k,l] = \text{HardThresh}_{t_j}(w_j[k,l]) = \begin{cases} w_j[k,l] & \text{if } |w_j[k,l]| \geq t_j \\ 0 & \text{otherwise} \end{cases}, \quad (3.53)$$

$w_j[k,l]$ is the wavelet coefficient at scale j and at spatial position (k,l). In the case of Gaussian noise, t_j can be directly derived from the noise standard deviation σ, $t_j = \tau \sigma_j$, where σ_j is the noise standard deviation at scale j, and τ is a constant generally chosen between 3 and 5. If the analysis filter is normalized to a unit ℓ_2 norm, we have $\sigma_j = \sigma$ for all j, while if the filter is normalized to a unit mass (i.e. $\sum_l h[l] = 1$), one can verify that $\sigma_j = \sigma/2^j$.

Denoting again $\mathbf{T}_W$ and $\mathbf{R}_W$ the wavelet transform and reconstruction operators (we have $\mathbf{R}_W = \mathbf{T}_W^{-1}$ for an orthogonal transform), denoising an image X by thresholding with threshold parameter τ amounts to

$$\tilde{X} = \mathbf{R}_W \text{HardThresh}_\tau(\mathbf{T}_W X). \quad (3.54)$$

Hence, simple wavelet nonlinear denoising based on hard thresholding consists of taking the wavelet transform of the signal, hard thresholding, and applying the inverse wavelet transform[3]. We return to this topic in more detail in Chapter 6.

To illustrate the denoising idea using wavelets, we added to the image "Einstein" a white, zero mean Gaussian noise with a standard deviation equal to 20. Figure 3.20 shows the noisy image, the denoised image using the UWT and the one denoised using the DWT. In both examples, τ was chosen equal to 4 at the finest scale and to 3 at other scales. As can easily be seen, the undecimated transform leads to a much

(a)   (b)

(c)   (d)

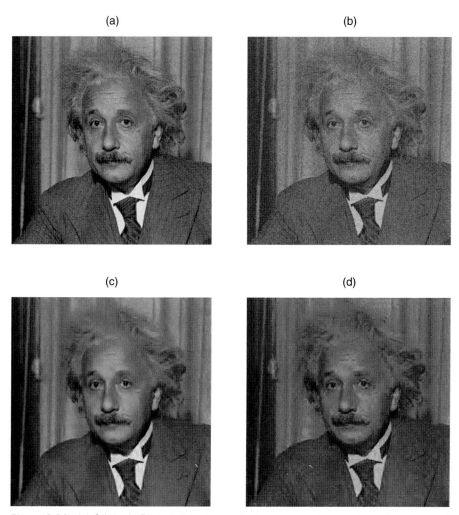

Figure 3.20. (a) Original "Einstein" image and (b) its noisy version with noise standard deviation $\sigma_n = 20$. (c) Denoised image by the UWT (PSNR = 29.6 dB). (d) Denoised image by the orthogonal DWT transform (PSNR = 27.8 dB).

better denoising result with far fewer Gibbs-like artifacts in the neighborhood of contours. The Matlab code used to produce this figure follows:

```
% Read image;
img = double(imread('einstein.bmp'));
[N,J] = quadlength(img);
% Add white Gaussian noise.
imn = img + 20*randn(size(img));

% Coarsest decomposition scale.
coarsest = 2;
```

```
% Generate Symmlet 4 CMF Filter.
qmf = MakeONFilter('Symmlet',4);

% Compute UWT and DWT of noisy image.
uwc = FWT2_TI(imn,coarsest,qmf);
wc  = FWT2_PO(imn,coarsest,qmf);

% Estimate noise std from diagonal band at finest scale.
hh = uwc(2*N+1:3*N,:);
sigma = MAD(hh(:));

% Hard-threshold UWT coeffs: finest scale at 4*sigma
% and other scales at 3*sigma.
% Finest:
uwc(1:3*N,:)        = HardThresh(uwc(1:3*N,:),4*sigma);
% Other scales:
uwc(3*N+1:end-N,:) = HardThresh(uwc(3*N+1:end-N,:),3*sigma);

% Hard-threshold DWT coeffs:
ll  = wc(1:coarsest,1:coarsest);
% Finest vertical:
wc(N/2+1:N,1:N/2)   = HardThresh(wc(N/2+1:N,1:N/2),4*sigma);
% Finest horizontal:
wc(1:N/2,N/2+1:N)   = HardThresh(wc(1:N/2,N/2+1:N),4*sigma);
% Finest diagonal:
wc(N/2+1:N,N/2+1:N) = HardThresh(wc(N/2+1:N,N/2+1:N),4*sigma);
% Other scales:
wc(1:N/2,1:N/2)     = HardThresh(wc(1:N/2,1:N/2),3*sigma);
wc(1:coarsest,1:coarsest) = ll;

% Reconstruct.
imdenuwt = IWT2_TI(uwc,coarsest,qmf);
imdendwt = IWT2_PO(wc,coarsest,qmf);

% Display.
subplot(221)
imagesc(img);axis image;axis off
set(gca,'FontSize',14);
title('(a)');
subplot(222)
imagesc(imn);axis image;axis off
set(gca,'FontSize',14);
title('(b)');
subplot(223)
imagesc(imdenuwt);axis image;axis off
set(gca,'FontSize',14);
title('(c)');
```

```
subplot(224)
imagesc(imdendwt);axis image;axis off
set(gca,'FontSize',14);
title('(d)');
colormap('gray')
```

3.8.2 Dynamic Range Compression using the IDL Starlet Transform

In this section we discuss IDL code. For support of FITS (Flexible Image Transport System) format, and other operations, the IDL Astronomical User Library, http://idlastro.gsfc.nasa.gov, can be used. This is linked to at the book's web address, http://www.SparseSignalRecipes.info.

Since some features in an image may be hard to detect by the human eye due to low contrast, we often process the image before visualization. Histogram equalization is one of the most well known methods for contrast enhancement. Images with a high dynamic range are also difficult to analyze. For example, astronomers generally visualize their images using a logarithmic look-up table conversion.

Wavelets can be used to compress the dynamic range at all scales, and therefore allow us to clearly see some very faint features. For instance, the wavelet-log representation consists of replacing $w_j[k, l]$ by $\text{sign}(w_j[k, l]) \log(|w_j[k, l]|)$, leading to the alternative image

$$X[k, l] = \log(c_J[k, l]) + \sum_{j=1}^{J} \text{sign}(w_j[k, l]) \log(|w_j[k, l]| + \epsilon) , \qquad (3.55)$$

where ϵ is a small number (e.g., $\epsilon = 10^{-3}$).

Figure 3.21 shows a Hale-Bopp comet image (top left) and an ophthalmic medical image (top right), their histogram equalization (middle row), and their wavelet-log representation (bottom). Jets clearly appear in the last representation of Hale-Bopp comet image, and many more features are distinguishable in the wavelet log representation of the ophthalmic medical image.

```
; Example of Starlet Transform
; Read an image of a Galaxy
n = float( read_png('ngc2997.png'))

; Compute its starlet wavelet transform with six scales
W = star2d(n ,nscale=6)

; visualize the different wavelet scales
for j=0,5 do begin tvscl, W[*,*,j] & wait, 2 & end

; Dynamic Range Compression
; Apply the dynamic range compression to the comet image
```

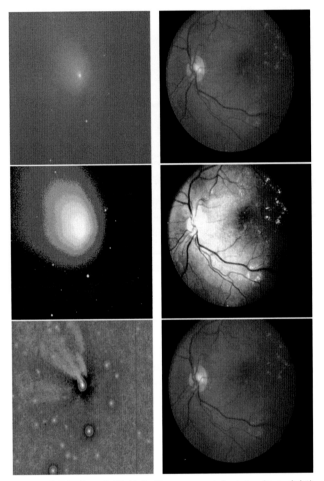

Figure 3.21. (top left) Hale-Bopp comet image. (top right) Ophthalmic medical image. (middle) Histogram equalization results. (bottom) Wavelet-log representations.

```
; To read the FITS format, the IDL Astronomical User Library must
; be installed (http://idlastro.gsfc.nasa.gov).
h = readfits('HaleBopp256.fits')

; Apply the dynamic range compression of h, using five scales,
; visualize it.
tvscl, star2d_drc(h,nscale=5, eps=0.1)

; Apply the dynamic range compression of the ophthalmic image, using
; five scales, and visualize it.
o = float( read_png('opthalmic.png'))
tvscl, star2d_drc(o,nscale=5)
```

3.9 SUMMARY

In this chapter we have focused on effective and efficient discrete redundant wavelet transform algorithms. Effectiveness is for such goals as denoising (restoration in general), faint feature detection or pattern analysis. So scientific, medical or forensic imaging applications are paramount. Efficiency is primarily computational but we also pay attention to storage needs.

4

Nonlinear Multiscale Transforms

4.1 INTRODUCTION

Some problems related to the wavelet transform may impact on their use in certain applications. This motivates the development of other multiscale representations. Such problems include the following:

1. *Negative values*: By definition, the wavelet mean is zero. Every time we have a positive structure at a scale, we have negative values surrounding it. These negative values often create artifacts during the restoration process, or complicate the analysis.
2. *Point artifacts*: For example, cosmic ray hits in optical astronomy can "pollute" all the scales of the wavelet transform, because their pixel values are huge compared to other pixel values related to the signal of interest. The wavelet transform is non-robust relative to such real or detector faults.
3. *Integer values*: The discrete wavelet transform (DWT) produces floating values which are not easy to handle for lossless image compression.

Section 4.2 introduces the decimated nonlinear multiscale transform, in particular using the lifting scheme approach, which generalizes the standard filter bank decomposition. Using the lifting scheme, nonlinearity can be introduced in a straightforward way, allowing us to perform an integer wavelet transform, or a wavelet transform on an irregularly sampled grid. In Section 4.3 multiscale transforms based on mathematical morphology are explored. Section 4.4 presents the median-based multiscale representations which handle outliers well in the data (non-Gaussian noise, pixels with high intensity values, etc.).

4.2 DECIMATED NONLINEAR TRANSFORM

4.2.1 Integer Wavelet Transform

When the input data consist of integer values, the (bi-)orthogonal wavelet transform is not necessarily integer-valued. For lossless coding and compression, it is useful to have a wavelet transform which maps integer values to integers. We can build an integer version of every wavelet transform (Calderbank et al. 1998). For instance, denoting $\lfloor t \rfloor$ as the largest integer not exceeding t, the integer Haar transform (also called "S" transform) can be calculated by

$$w_{j+1}[l] = c_j^o[l] - c_j^e[l]$$

$$c_{j+1}[l] = c_j^e[l] + \left\lfloor \frac{w_{j+1}[l]}{2} \right\rfloor , \tag{4.1}$$

where, as in the previous chapter, superscripts o and e represent odd and even indexed values. The reconstruction is trivially given by

$$c_j^e[l] = c_j[2l] = c_{j+1}[l] - \left\lfloor \frac{w_{j+1}[l]}{2} \right\rfloor$$

$$c_j^o[l] = c_j[2l+1] = w_{j+1}[l] + c_j[2l] . \tag{4.2}$$

More generally, the lifting operators for an integer version of the wavelet transform are

$$\mathcal{P}(c_j^e[l]) = \left\lfloor \sum_k p[k]c_j^e[l-k] + \frac{1}{2} \right\rfloor$$

$$\mathcal{U}(w_{j+1}[l]) = \left\lfloor \sum_k u[k]w_{j+1}[l-k] + \frac{1}{2} \right\rfloor , \tag{4.3}$$

where p and u are appropriate filters associated with primal and dual lifting steps.

For instance, the linear integer wavelet transform[1] is given by

$$w_{j+1}[l] = c_j^o[l] - \left\lfloor \frac{1}{2}(c_j^e[l] + c_j^e[l+1]) + \frac{1}{2} \right\rfloor$$

$$c_{j+1}[l] = c_j^e[l] + \left\lfloor \frac{1}{4}(w_{j+1}[l-1] + w_{j+1}[l]) + \frac{1}{2} \right\rfloor . \tag{4.4}$$

More filters can be found in Calderbank et al. (1998). In lossless compression of integer-valued digital images, even if there is no filter that consistently performs better than all other filters on all images, it has been observed that the linear integer wavelet transform generally performs better than integer wavelet transforms using other filters (Calderbank et al. 1998).

4.2.2 Wavelet Transform on Irregular Grid

A wavelet transform on irregularly sampled data can be performed by introducing weighted inner products (Sweldens and Schröder 1996; Daubechies et al. 1999), assuming that we are given weighted averages of some unknown function f over the interval:

$$c_0[l] = \frac{1}{\Upsilon_{0,l}} \int_{t_l}^{t_{l+1}} \varpi(t) f(t) dt . \tag{4.5}$$

where $[t_l, t_{l+1}]$ defines an interval, $\varpi(t)$ is a positive weighting function, and $\Upsilon_{0,l}$ is

$$\Upsilon_{0,l} = \int\limits_{t_l}^{t_{l+1}} \varpi(t)dt \; . \tag{4.6}$$

In its simplest form, $\varpi(t)$ can take the value 1 when a sample at position t is available, and 0 otherwise. If error measurements are also available, $\varpi(t)$ can be derived from them.

In the case of the Haar wavelet, this leads to the unbalanced Haar transform which is obtained by Sweldens and Schröder (1996):

$$\Upsilon_{j+1,l} = \Upsilon_{j,2l} + \Upsilon_{j,2l+1}$$
$$w_{j+1}[l] = c_j^o[l] - c_j^e[l] \tag{4.7}$$
$$c_{j+1}[l] = c_j^e[l] + \frac{\Upsilon_{j,2l+1}}{\Upsilon_{j+1,l}} w_{j+1}[l] \; .$$

This transform can be defined for other wavelets in a similar way. See Sweldens and Schröder (1996) for more details.

4.2.3 Adaptive Wavelet Transform

Adaptivity can be introduced in the wavelet transform by reversing the order of the predict and the update steps in the lifting scheme (Claypoole et al. 2003). When the update operator is first applied, the prediction is based on the low-pass coefficients that are computed as in the standard wavelet transform. In the update-first approach, as illustrated in Figure 4.1, the detail coefficients are not in the loop for calculating the coefficients at a coarser scale. Hence, we can start the prediction process at the coarser scale, and work from coarse to fine scales. The idea is now to make the predictor data dependent. The prediction operator is chosen, based on the local properties of the data at a coarser scale. If an edge is detected, the order of the predictor is reduced, while if the data are smooth, a larger order is preferred (Piella and Heijmans 2002; Heijmans et al. 2005, 2006).

4.3 MULTISCALE TRANSFORM AND MATHEMATICAL MORPHOLOGY

4.3.1 Mathematical Morphology

Mathematical morphology is a theory for the analysis of geometrical structures in images based on set theory, topology, integral geometry and lattice algebra. Mathematical morphology was originally developed by Matheron (1967, 1975) for binary images treated as sets. It was later extended to more complex structures including grayscale images as a special case, based on complete lattices (Serra 1982). Arising from this theoretical framework, Matheron and Serra formulated a theory of morphological nonlinear filtering. Mathematical morphology is based on two operators: the *infimum* (denoted $\wedge$) and the *supremum* (denoted $\vee$). The basic morphological

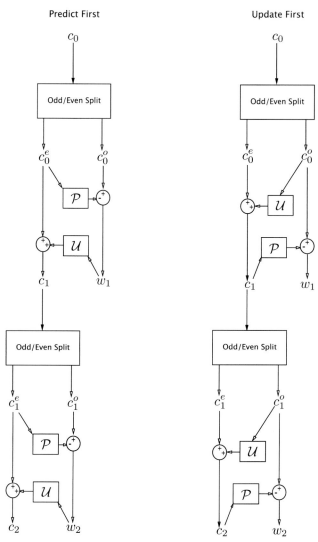

Figure 4.1. The lifting scheme with two iterations: (left) predict-first approach; (right) update-first approach.

transformations are erosion, dilation, opening and closing. For grayscale images, they can be defined in the following way:

■ *Dilation* consists of replacing each pixel of an image f by the supremum[2] of its neighbors within the structuring element $\mathcal{B}$:

$$\mathcal{D}_\mathcal{B}(f) = \Xi_{\mathbf{b} \in \mathcal{B}} f_{\mathbf{b}} \, ,$$

where the translated image $f_{\mathbf{b}}(\mathbf{t}) = f(\mathbf{t} - \mathbf{b}) = f(t_1 - b_1, t_2 - b_2)$, and the structuring element $\mathcal{B}$ has a shape usually chosen according to some a priori knowledge about the geometry of relevant and irrelevant image structures.

The dilation is commonly known as "fill", "expand", or "grow". It can be used to fill "holes" of size equal to or smaller than the structuring element. Used with binary images, where each pixel is either 1 or 0, dilation is similar to convolution. At each pixel of the image, the origin of the structuring element is overlaid. If the image pixel is non-zero, each pixel of the structuring element is added to the result using the "or" logical operator.

■ *Erosion* consists of replacing each pixel of an image by the infimum[3] of its neighbors within the structuring element $\mathcal{B}$:

$$\mathscr{E}_{\mathcal{B}}(f) = \bigwedge_{\mathbf{b} \in \mathcal{B}} f_{-\mathbf{b}} \, ,$$

where the translated image $f_{-\mathbf{b}}(\mathbf{t}) = f(\mathbf{t} + \mathbf{b}) = f(t_1 + b_1, t_2 + b_2)$.

Erosion is the dual of dilation. It does to the background what dilation does to the foreground. This operator is commonly known as "shrink" or "reduce". It can be used to remove islands smaller than the structuring element. At each pixel of the image, the origin of the structuring element is overlaid. If each nonzero element of the structuring element is contained in the image, the output pixel is set to one. Otherwise, it is set to zero.

■ *Opening* is defined as an erosion with the structuring element $\mathcal{B}$ followed by a dilation with the reflected[4] structuring element $\tilde{\mathcal{B}}$:

$$\mathcal{O}_{\mathcal{B}}(f) = \mathscr{D}_{\tilde{\mathcal{B}}}(\mathscr{E}_{\mathcal{B}}(f)) \, .$$

■ *Closing* consists of a dilation with the structuring element $\mathcal{B}$ followed by an erosion with the reflected structuring element $\tilde{\mathcal{B}}$:

$$\mathscr{C}_{\mathcal{B}}(f) = \mathscr{E}_{\tilde{\mathcal{B}}}(\mathscr{D}_{\mathcal{B}}(f)) \, .$$

In a more general way, *opening* and *closing* refer to morphological filters which respect some specific properties (Serra 1982; Breen et al. 2000; Soille 2003). Such morphological filters were used for removing "cirruslike" emission from far-infrared extragalactic Infrared Astronomical Satellite (IRAS) fields (Appleton et al. 1993), and for astronomical image compression (Huang and Bijaoui 1991).

4.3.2 Lifting Scheme and Mathematical Morphology

A nonredundant multiscale morphological transform can easily be built via the lifting scheme, by introducing morphological operators. For example, the Haar morphological transform, also called the *G transform*, is

$$\begin{aligned} w_{j+1}[l] &= c_j^o[l] - \mathcal{P}(c_j^e[l]) \\ c_{j+1}[l] &= c_j^e[l] + \mathcal{U}(w_{j+1}[l]) \, , \end{aligned} \tag{4.8}$$

where

$$\begin{aligned} \mathcal{P}(c_j^e[l]) &= c_j[2l] \\ \mathcal{U}(w_{j+1}[l]) &= 0 \wedge w_{j+1}[l] \, . \end{aligned} \tag{4.9}$$

It is easy to verify that

$$
\begin{aligned}
w_{j+1}[l] &= c_j[2l+1] - c_j[2l] \\
c_{j+1}[l] &= c_j[2l] + (0 \wedge (c_j[2l+1] - c_j[2l])) \\
&= c_j[2l] \wedge c_j[2l+1] .
\end{aligned}
\tag{4.10}
$$

4.3.3 Pyramidal Transform

A decimation can be introduced in order to produce a pyramidal transform similar to the Laplacian pyramid described in Section 3.7.1, but by using morphological filters instead of the linear filters in Figure 3.17. We now introduce two operators $\beta^{\downarrow}$, and $\beta^{\uparrow}$: $\beta^{\downarrow}$ (analysis operator) consists of filtering first the image and then decimating it, and $\beta^{\uparrow}$ (prediction operator) consists of interpolating the data. In the analysis side of the transform, (3.29)–(3.30) generalize to

$$
\begin{aligned}
c_{j+1}[l] &= \beta^{\downarrow}(c_j)[l] \\
w_{j+1}[l] &= c_j - \beta^{\uparrow}(c_{j+1})[l] .
\end{aligned}
\tag{4.11}
$$

Analogously to (3.32), the reconstruction is obtained by:

$$
c_j[l] = w_{j+1}[l] + \beta^{\uparrow}(c_{j+1})[l] .
\tag{4.12}
$$

In this scheme, $\beta^{\downarrow}$ and $\beta^{\uparrow}$ can be either linear or nonlinear.

An example of the operators $\beta^{\downarrow}$ and $\beta^{\uparrow}$ is:

$$
\begin{aligned}
\beta^{\downarrow}(c_j)[l] &= c_j[2l] \wedge c_j[2l+1] \\
\beta^{\uparrow}(c_j)[2l] &= \beta^{\uparrow}(c_j)[2l+1] = c_{j+1}[l] .
\end{aligned}
\tag{4.13}
$$

A second example is given by:

$$
\begin{aligned}
\beta^{\downarrow}(c_j)[l] &= c_j[2l] \wedge c_j[2l+1] \\
\beta^{\uparrow}(c_j)[2l] &= c_{j+1}[2l] \\
\beta^{\uparrow}(c_j)[2l+1] &= \frac{1}{2}(c_{j+1}[l] + c_{j+1}[l+1]) ,
\end{aligned}
\tag{4.14}
$$

which leads to a morphological analysis operator, and a linear synthesis operator. It is easy to verify that this pyramidal transform has the same redundancy factor as the Laplacian pyramid of Burt and Adelson.

4.3.4 Undecimated Multiscale Morphological Transform

Mathematical morphology has, up to now, been considered as another way to analyze data, in competition with linear methods. But from a multiscale point of view (Starck et al. 1998; Goutsias and Heijmans 2000; Heijmans and Goutsias 2000), mathematical morphology or linear methods are just filters allowing us to go from a given resolution to a coarser one, and the multiscale coefficients are then analyzed in the same way.

By choosing a set of structuring elements $\mathcal{B}_j$ having a size increasing with j, we can define an undecimated morphological multiscale transform by

$$c_{j+1}[l] = \mathcal{M}_j(c_j)[l]$$
$$w_{j+1}[l] = c_j[l] - c_{j+1}[l] \, , \tag{4.15}$$

where $\mathcal{M}_j$ is a morphological filter (closing, opening, etc.) using the structuring element $\mathcal{B}_j$. An example of $\mathcal{B}_j$ is a box of size $(2^j + 1) \times (2^j + 1)$. Since the detail coefficients w_{j+1} are obtained by calculating a simple difference between the scaling coefficients c_j and c_{j+1}, the reconstruction is straightforward, and is identical to that of the starlet transform (see Section 3.5). An exact reconstruction of c_0 is then given by

$$c_0[l] = c_J[l] + \sum_{j=1}^{J} w_j[l] \, , \tag{4.16}$$

where J is the number of scales used in the analysis step. Each scale has the same number of samples as the original data. The redundancy factor is therefore $J + 1$ as for the starlet transform.

4.4 MULTIRESOLUTION BASED ON THE MEDIAN TRANSFORM

4.4.1 Multiscale Median Transform

The search for new multiresolution tools has been motivated so far by problems related to the wavelet transform. It would be more desirable that a point structure (represented as an isolated or outlier sample in a signal or image) be present only at the first (finest) scale. It would also be desirable that a positive structure in the signal or image does not create negative values in the coefficient domain. We will see how such an algorithm can be arrived at, using nonlinear filters such as the median filter.

The median filter is nonlinear, and offers advantages for robust smoothing (i.e. the effects of outlier sample values are mitigated). In 2-D, denote the median filtered version of a discrete image f, with a square $L \times L$ neighborhood, as Med(f, L). Let $L = 2s + 1$; initially $s = 1$. The iteration counter will be denoted by j, and J is the user-specified number of resolution scales. The multiscale median transform (MMT) algorithm (Starck et al. 1996) is as follows.

Algorithm 13 2-D Multiscale Median Transform Algorithm

Task: Compute the 2-D multiscale median transform of an $N \times N$ image X.
Initialization: $c_0 = X$, $J = \log_2 N$, and $s = 2$.
for $j = 0$ to $J - 1$ **do**

1. Compute $c_{j+1} = \text{Med}(c_j, 2s + 1)$.
2. Compute the multiscale median coefficients: $w_{j+1} = c_j - c_{j+1}$.
3. $s \leftarrow 2s$.

Output: $\mathcal{W} = \{w_1, \ldots, w_J, c_J\}$ the pyramidal median transform of X.

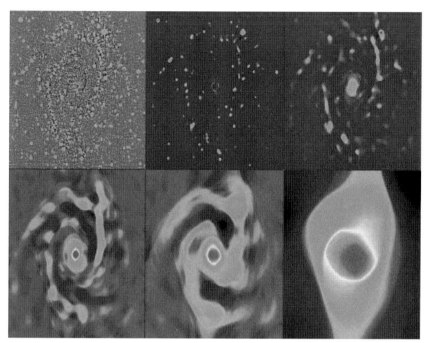

Figure 4.2. Multiscale median transform of the galaxy NGC 2997 (see Figure 3.8). (See *color plates*.)

A straightforward reconstruction formula of the original image from $\mathcal{W}$ is

$$c_0 = c_J + \sum_{j=1}^{J} w_j . \qquad (4.17)$$

In the preceding algorithm, the set of resolution levels associated with s leads to a dyadic analysis. Other possibilities involving intermediate scales (e.g. $s \longleftarrow \sqrt{2}s$) can also be considered.

The multiresolution coefficient values, w_j, are evidently not necessarily of zero mean, and so the potential artifact-creation difficulties related to this aspect of wavelet transforms do not arise. Note, of course, that values of w can be negative.

For input integer image values, this transform can be carried out in integer arithmetic only which may lead to computational savings.

Figure 4.2 shows the multiscale decomposition of the galaxy NGC 2997 (see Figure 3.8) by the multiscale median transform, with 5 scales (detail coefficients $(w_j)_{1 \leq j \leq 5}$ in the first 5 panels, and the scaling coefficients c_5 in the last panel). Summing the six images reproduce exactly the original image. We can see that even the brightest stars do not "pollute" the largest scales (for $j \geq 4$). This would not be true with a traditional linear wavelet transform. Another point to note is that there is no negative ring around the stars in the first scales. This point is of great importance, as discussed in the next example.

Figure 4.4 shows the comparison between the starlet transform (on the left) and the MMT (on the right) of the input signal displayed in Figure 4.3. In these diagrams,

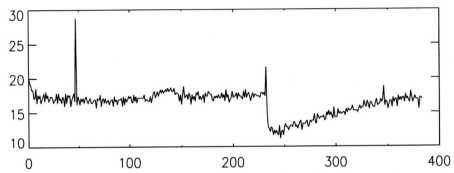

Figure 4.3. Example of a signal obtained with the ISOCAM infrared camera. A source is observed between samples 120 to 150. Cosmic ray impacts appear around samples 50 and 230. The latter cosmic ray source has introduced a variation in the detector gain. Owing to this kind of cosmic ray impact (glitch), sources are not easy to identify.

the ordinate axis is the resolution level and the abscissa axis is the time. The data were obtained with an infrared camera, on board the Infrared Space Observatory (ISO) satellite. A faint source is observed between samples 120 to 150. Cosmic ray impacts appear around samples 50 and 230. The second cosmic ray impact has introduced a variation in the detector gain. Due to this kind of cosmic ray impact (glitch), sources are not easy to identify. Owing to robustness of the MMT to outliers (glitch spikes here), the glitch and the source are clearly separated in the MMT while they merge in the starlet transform.

Computational requirements of the MMT are high, and these can be reduced by decimation: one sample out of two is retained at each scale. Here the transform kernel does not change from one iteration to the next, but the signal or image to which this transform is applied does. This pyramidal algorithm is examined next.

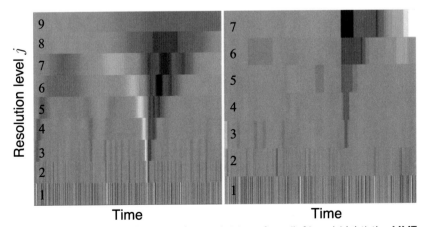

Figure 4.4. Comparison between the starlet transform (left) and (right) the MMT of the signal from Figure 4.3. We note that the separation between the source and the glitch is improved using the MMT. (See *color plates*.)

4.4.2 Pyramidal Median Transform

The pyramidal median transform (PMT) (Starck et al. 1996) of a discrete $N \times N$ image X is obtained by the following algorithm:

Algorithm 14 2-D Pyramidal Median Transform Algorithm

Task: Compute the 2-D pyramidal median transform of an $N \times N$ image X.
Initialization: $c_0 = X$, $J = \log_2 N$, and $s = 2$.
for $j = 0$ to $J - 1$ **do**

1. Compute $c_{j+1} = [\text{Med}(c_j, 2s + 1)]_{\downarrow 2,2}$.
2. Compute $\tilde{c}_{j+1} =$ interpolation of c_{j+1} to the size of c_j.
3. Compute the pyramidal median coefficients: $w_{j+1} = c_j - \tilde{c}_{j+1}$.

Output: $\mathcal{W} = \{w_1, \ldots, w_J, c_J\}$ the pyramidal median transform of X.

Here the kernel or mask of size $(2s + 1) \times (2s + 1)$ remains the same during the iterations. However, the image itself, to which this kernel is applied, becomes smaller. In regard to computation time, in step 1 of Algorithm 14, we do not have to compute the median for all pixels and then decimate; rather, it is sufficient to compute the median for the pixels to be left after decimation. This makes the transform four times faster.

For the reconstruction, we use the following algorithm based on B-spline interpolation:

Algorithm 15 2-D Inverse Pyramidal Median Transform Algorithm

---

Task: Reconstruct an $N \times N$ image from its 2-D pyramidal median transform, $\mathcal{W} = \{w_1, \ldots, w_J, c_J\}$.
Initialization: $J = \log_2 N$, and $s = 2$.
for $j = J - 1$ to 1 **do**

1. Interpolate c_j to determine the next resolution image (of twice the size of c_j in each direction). Call the interpolated image $\tilde{c}_j$.
2. Compute $c_{j-1} = w_j + \tilde{c}_j$.

Output: c_0 the reconstruction from $\mathcal{W}$.

This reconstruction procedure takes account of the pyramidal sequence of images containing the multiresolution transform coefficients, w_j. The PMT has been used for the compression of astronomical data (Starck et al. 1996; Louys et al. 1999) and of optical readout biomolecular sensory data (Stoschek 2003).

4.4.3 Merging Wavelets and the Multiscale Median Transform

One of the advantages of the PWT over the MMT is the ability to have robust noise estimation in the different scales, while the advantage of the MMT is a better separation of the structures in the scales. Using the MMT, a strong structure (like a bright star, cosmic ray hit, etc.) will not be spread over all scales as when using a wavelet transform. In fact, when there is no signal in a given region, a wavelet transform would be better, and if a strong signal appears, it is the MMT that we would like to use. So the idea naturally arises to try to merge both transforms, and to adapt the analysis at each position and at each scale, depending on the amplitude of the coefficient we measure (Starck 2002).

A possible algorithm to perform this on a 2-D image X is the following:

Algorithm 16 2-D Median-Wavelet Transform Algorithm

Task: Compute the 2-D Median-Wavelet transform of an $N \times N$ image X.

Initialization: $c_0 = X$, $J = \log_2 N$, $s = 2$, and $\tau = 5$.

for $j = 0$ to $J - 1$ **do**

1. Compute $c_{j+1} = \mathrm{Med}(c_j, 2s + 1)]$. This step is similar to that used in the MMT: it is a median smoothing with a window size depending on the scale j.
2. Compute $w_{j+1} = c_{j+1} - c_j$. m_{j+1} coefficients corresponding to median coefficients between two consecutive scales.
3. Detect in w_{j+1} the significant coefficients:

$$|w_{j+1}| > \tau \mathrm{MAD}(w_{j+1})/0.6745 \,,$$

   where MAD stands for the median absolute deviation used as an estimator of the noise standard deviation; see equation (6.9), and τ a threshold chosen large enough to avoid false detections, for instance $\tau = 5$.
4. Set to zero all significant coefficients in w_{j+1}.
5. Compute $c'_j = w_{j+1} + c_{j+1}$. Hence, c'_j is a version of c_j, but without the detected significant structures.
6. Compute the 2-D starlet transform of c'_j with $j + 1$ scales. We get $\mathcal{W} = \{w'_1, \ldots, w'_{j+1}, c'_{j+1}\}$.
7. Set $c_{j+1} = c'_{j+1}$. Therefore, c_{j+1} is smoothed with wavelets, but strong features have been extracted with the median.
8. Compute the median-wavelet coefficients: $w_{j+1} = c_j - c_{j+1}$.
9. $s = 2s$.

Output: $\mathcal{W} = \{w_1, \ldots, w_J, c_J\}$ the median-wavelet transform of X.

In this algorithm, the linear filtering involved in the wavelet transform isnot applied to the strong features contained in the image. Indeed, significant pixel values are detected at step 3, and are replaced by the median in step 5. Regions containing no bright object are treated as if the wavelet transform were used. The threshold parameter τ used in step 3 must be large enough in order to be sure that noise is not filtered by the median ($\tau = 5$ seems high enough in practice). Since this transform merges the wavelet transform and the MMT, we call it the Med-WT transform. Med-WT is computationally slower than the MMT, but this algorithm shares the advantages of the MMT without suffering its drawbacks. The reconstruction is the same as

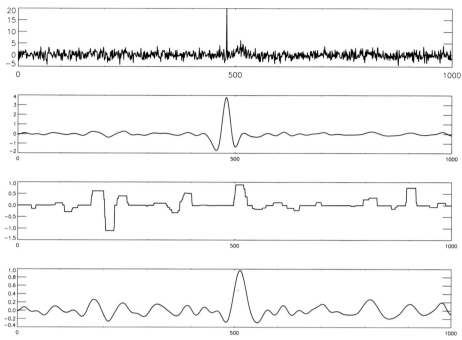

Figure 4.5. Comparison between the starlet transform, the MMT and Med-WT. From top to bottom, the figure shows a signal which contains a Gaussian ($\sigma = 10$) centered at position 512, a "glitch" at position 480, and additive Gaussian noise; the fourth scale of the starlet transform; the fourth scale of the MMT; and the fourth scale of the Med-WT transform, respectively.

for the MMT. The same approach can be used to combine the PMT and the wavelet transform (Starck 2002).

4.5 GUIDED NUMERICAL EXPERIMENTS

4.5.1 Starlet, Multiscale Median Transform, and Median-Wavelet Transform in IDL

The goal of this code is to show the difference between the starlet transform, the MMT and the Med-WT transform. We create a signal which contains a Gaussian (of standard deviation $= 10$) centered at position 512, a "glitch" at sample 480, and additive white Gaussian noise. Figure 4.5 (top) shows this signal. The Gaussian feature is hard to distinguish from the noise. The second plot in Figure 4.5 shows the fourth scale of the 1D starlet transform. The Gaussian cannot be detected because of the glitch effect. Even if the glitch is a single-spike structure, it appears strongly at scale $j = 4$, because of the high contrast between the glitch and the Gaussian. On the third plot, we can see that the glitch has no effect on the fourth scale of the MMT. The Gaussian remains difficult to detect because of other features due to the noise which have similar amplitudes. The last plot presents the fourth scale of the

Med-WT transform. Here we have the advantages of the wavelet transform, i.e. linear smoothing of noise, but also the advantages of the MMT. Hence, the glitch appears only at the first scale, and does not contaminate the others. As a consequence, we can now clearly detect the Gaussian.

```
; Create a signal of size 1024, containing a Gaussian
; (sigma=10) centered at position x=512,
idim = 1024
sigma = 10.
ind = indgen((1024)
x = findgen(idim) - idim/2.
g = EXP(-(x)^2 /(2.*SIGMA^2)) * 3

; Add a "glitch" at x=480
g[480] = 200

; Add noise to the data
g = g + randomn(seed, idim)

; Use 6 scales
ns=6
; Compute the starlet 1D Wavelet Transform
w1 = star1d(g, nscale=ns)

; Compute the Multiscale Median Transform
w2 = umt1d(g, nscale=ns)

; Compute the Median-Wavelet Transform
w3 = umt1d(g, /wt, nscale=ns)

; Plot the scale j=4 for the three decompositions
j=4
!p.background=255
tekcolor
!p.multi = [0,1,4]
plot, g < 20 , xcharsize=1.5, ycharsize = 1.5, yminor=1, $
      xticks=2, xminor=5,thick=2, xrange=[0,1000], col=0
plot, w1[*,j], yminor=1, xticks=2, xminor=5, $
      thick=2, xrange=[0,1000], col=0
plot, w2[*,j], yminor=1, xticks=2, xminor=5, $
      thick=2, xrange=[0,1000], col=0
plot, w3[*,j] , yminor=1, xticks=2, xminor=5, $
      thick=2, xrange=[0,1000], col=0
!p.multi = 0
```

4.6 SUMMARY

The multiscale median transform is well-suited to all applications where image reconstruction from a subset of coefficients is needed (e.g. restoration, compression, partial reconstruction). The suppression of subsets of coefficients leads to fewer artifacts in the reconstructed image, because often the visual artifacts are due to the shape of the wavelet function (the negative "moat", in particular, surrounding objects).

Other morphological tools can be used to perform a similar transform such as opening (a set of erosions followed by the same number of dilations). However we found results to be better with the median filter. In the median-based transform, coefficients can be positive or negative. For some applications, it would be useful to have a decomposition into multiresolution coefficients which are all positive. This can be provided by mathematical morphology.

The median based multiscale transforms present the advantage to be very robust to strong isolated singularities. These singularities can be due to non-white noise, or from the observed data such as stars in astronomical images. In such cases, the median-based multiscale transform is an appropriate tool to separate these singularities from the rest of the signal. This is the reason too for the success of the PMT for compression of astronomical images (Starck et al. 1996; Louys et al. 1999).

Nonlinear multiresolution transforms are complementary to the wavelet transform. According to the application, one or other is more suitable. Finally we point to the work of Donoho (2000) on a median-based pyramidal transform, in which a decimation of 3 is used, instead of the standard dyadic scheme, in order to preserve the independence of the coefficients.

5

Multiscale Geometric Transforms

5.1 INTRODUCTION

The ridgelet and curvelet transforms generalize the wavelet transform. Firstly they incorporate angular alignment information, and then in addition length of the alignment is covered. As with all of these transforms, multiple scales are supported. The motivation for these transforms is to build up an image from edge-related building blocks. Furthermore, as in previous chapters, the efficiency of computing these transforms is an important practical aspect.

In this chapter we consider the ridgelet transform and a number of algorithms for its implementation. Then we proceed to the curvelet transform and algorithms for it.

5.2 BACKGROUND AND EXAMPLE

Wavelets rely on a dictionary of roughly isotropic elements occurring at all scales and locations. They do not describe well highly anisotropic elements, and contain only a fixed number of directional elements, independent of scale. Despite the fact that they have had wide impact in image processing, they fail to efficiently represent objects with highly anisotropic elements such as lines or curvilinear structures (e.g. edges). The reason is that wavelets are nongeometrical and do not exploit the regularity of the edge curve. Following this reasoning, new constructions have been proposed such as ridgelets (Candès and Donoho 1999) and curvelets (Candès and Donoho 2001, 2002; Starck et al. 2002).

Ridgelets and curvelets are special members of the family of multiscale orientation-selective transforms, which have recently led to a flurry of research activity in the field of computational and applied harmonic analysis. Many other constructions belonging to this family have been investigated, and go by the name of contourlets (Do and Vetterli 2003b), directionlets (Velisavljevic et al. 2006), platelets (Willett and Nowak 2003), bandlets (Le Pennec and Mallat 2005; Peyré and Mallat 2007), grouplets (Mallat 2009), shearlets (Labate et al. 2005), dual-tree complex wavelet transform (Kingsbury 1998; Selesnick et al. 2005) (see Section 3.4), and other complex directional wavelet transforms (Fernandes et al. 2003; van Spaen-donck et al. 2003; Fernandes et al. 2004).

The ridgelet and the curvelet (Candès and Donoho 1999, 2002) transforms were developed as an answer to the weakness of the separable wavelet transform in sparsely representing what appears to be simple building-block atoms in an image, that is, lines, curves and edges. Curvelets and ridgelets take the form of basis elements which exhibit high directional sensitivity and are highly anisotropic (Donoho and Duncan 2000; Candès and Donoho 2002; Starck et al. 2002).

These very recent geometric image representations are built on ideas of multi-scale analysis and geometry. They have had considerable success in a wide range of image processing applications including denoising (Starck et al. 2002; Saevarsson et al. 2003; Hennenfent and Herrmann 2006), deconvolution (Starck et al. 2003c; Fadili and Starck 2006), contrast enhancement (Starck et al. 2003b), texture analysis (Starck et al. 2005b; Arivazhagan et al. 2006), detection (Jin et al. 2005), watermark-ing (Zhang et al. 2006), component separation (Starck et al. 2004b), inpainting (Elad et al. 2005; Fadili et al. 2009b) and blind source separation (Bobin et al. 2006, 2007a). Curvelets have also proven useful in diverse fields beyond the traditional image processing application. Let us cite for example seismic imaging (Hennenfent and Herrmann 2006; Herrmann et al. 2008; Douma and de Hoop 2007), astronomical imaging (Starck et al. 2003a, 2006; Lambert et al. 2006), scientific computing and analysis of partial differential equations (Candès and Demanet 2003, 2005). Another reason for the success of ridgelets and curvelets is the availability of fast transform algorithms which are available in noncommercial software packages.

Continuing at this informal level of discussion we will rely on an example to illustrate the fundamental difference between the wavelet and ridgelet approaches. Consider an image which contains a vertical band embedded in an additive white Gaussian noise with large standard deviation. Figure 5.1 (top left) represents such an image. The parameters are as follows: the pixel width of the band is 20 and the signal-to-noise ratio (SNR) is set to be 0.1 (-20 dB). Note that it is not possible to distinguish the band by eye. The image denoised by thresholding the undecimated wavelet coefficients does not reveal the presence of the vertical band as shown in Figure 5.1 (bottom left). Roughly speaking, wavelet coefficients correspond to averages over approximately isotropic neighborhoods (at different scales) and those wavelets clearly do not correlate very well with the very elongated structure (pattern) of the object to be detected.

We now turn our attention towards procedures of a very different nature which are based on line measurements. To be more specific, consider an *ideal* procedure which consists of integrating the image intensity over columns; that is, along the orientation of our object. We use the adjective "ideal" to emphasize the important fact that this method of integration requires a priori knowledge about the geometry of our object. This method of analysis gives of course an improved SNR for our linear functional which is better correlated with the object in question: see Figure 5.1 (top right).

This example will make our point. Unlike wavelet transforms, the ridgelet transform processes data by first computing integrals over lines at all orientations and locations. We will explain in the next section how the ridgelet transform further processes those line integrals. For now, we apply naive thresholding of the ridgelet

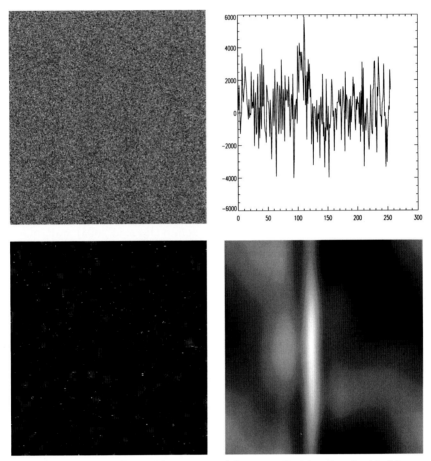

Figure 5.1. (top left) Original image containing a vertical band embedded in an additive white Gaussian noise with relatively large amplitude. (top right) Row sums illustrating the hardly visible vertical band. (bottom left) Recovered image by thresholding the undecimated wavelet coefficients. (bottom right) Recovered image by thresholding the ridgelet coefficients.

coefficients and "invert" the ridgelet transform; the bottom right panel of Figure 5.1 shows the recovered image. The qualitative difference with the wavelet approach is striking. We observe that this transform allows the detection of our object even in situations where it is overwhelmed by the noise.

In this chapter, we describe in detail the ridgelet and curvelet transforms, and emphasize efficient ways to implement the corresponding discrete analysis and synthesis algorithms.

5.3 RIDGELETS

5.3.1 The Continuous Ridgelet Transform

The two-dimensional (2-D) continuous ridgelet transform in $\mathbb{R}^2$ can be defined as follows (Candès 1999). We pick a smooth univariate function $\psi : \mathbb{R} \to \mathbb{R}$ with sufficient

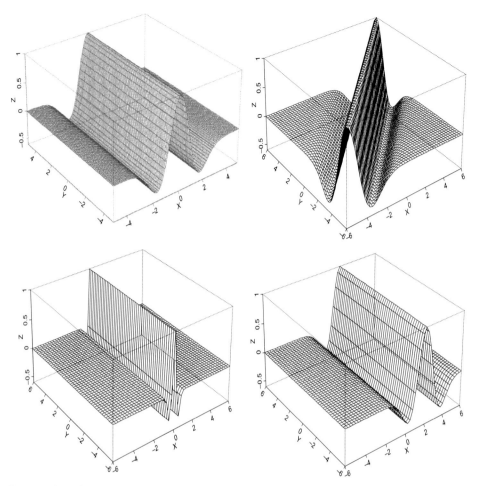

Figure 5.2. A few examples of ridgelets. The second, third and fourth graphs are obtained after simple geometric manipulations of the first ridgelet, namely rotation, rescaling, and shifting.

decay and satisfying the admissibility condition

$$\int |\hat{\psi}(v)|^2/|v|^2 \, dv < \infty \,, \tag{5.1}$$

which holds if, say, ψ has a vanishing mean $\int \psi(t)dt = 0$. We will suppose a special normalization about ψ so that $\int_0^\infty |\hat{\psi}(v)|^2 v^{-2} dv = 1$.

For each scale $a > 0$, each position $b \in \mathbb{R}$ and each orientation $\theta \in [0, 2\pi)$, we define the bivariate *ridgelet* $\psi_{a,b,\theta} : \mathbb{R}^2 \to \mathbb{R}$ by

$$\psi_{a,b,\theta}(\mathbf{t}) = \psi_{a,b,\theta}(t_1, t_2) = a^{-1/2} \cdot \psi((t_1 \cos\theta + t_2 \sin\theta - b)/a) \,, \tag{5.2}$$

where $\mathbf{t} = (t_1, t_2) \in \mathbb{R}^2$. A ridgelet is constant along lines $t_1 \cos\theta + t_2 \sin\theta = \text{const}$. Transverse to these ridges it is a wavelet. Figure 5.2 depicts a few examples of ridgelets. The second to fourth panels are obtained after simple geometric manipulations of the ridgelet (left panel), namely rotation, rescaling, and shifting.

Given an integrable bivariate function $f(\mathbf{t})$, we define its ridgelet coefficients by

$$\mathcal{R}_f(a, b, \theta) := \langle f, \psi_{a,b,\theta} \rangle = \int_{\mathbb{R}^2} f(\mathbf{t}) \psi_{a,b,\theta}^*(\mathbf{t}) d\mathbf{t}.$$

We have the exact reconstruction formula

$$f(\mathbf{t}) = \int_0^{2\pi} \int_{-\infty}^{\infty} \int_0^{\infty} \mathcal{R}_f(a, b, \theta) \psi_{a,b,\theta}(\mathbf{t}) \frac{da}{a^3} db \frac{d\theta}{4\pi} \tag{5.3}$$

valid almost everywhere for functions which are both integrable and square integrable. This formula is stable and one can prove a Parseval relation (Candès and Donoho 1999),

$$\|f\|_2^2 = \int_0^{2\pi} \int_{-\infty}^{\infty} \int_0^{\infty} |\mathcal{R}_f(a, b, \theta)|^2 \frac{da}{a^3} db \frac{d\theta}{4\pi} \,,$$

In a nutshell, this is an invariance principle where the energy of the original data equals that of the transformed data.

Ridgelet analysis may be constructed as wavelet analysis in the Radon domain. The rationale behind this is that the Radon transform translates singularities along lines into point singularities, for which the wavelet transform is known to provide a sparse representation. Recall that the Radon transform $\mathbf{R}(f)$ of an image f is the collection of line integrals indexed by $(\theta, \tau) \in [0, 2\pi) \times \mathbb{R}$ given by

$$\mathbf{R}(f)(\theta, \tau) = \int_{\mathbb{R}^2} f(t_1, t_2) \delta(t_1 \cos \theta + t_2 \sin \theta - \tau) \, dt_1 dt_2 \,, \tag{5.4}$$

where δ is the Dirac distribution. Then the ridgelet transform is precisely the application of a 1-D wavelet transform to the slices of the Radon transform where the angular variable θ is constant and t is varying. Thus, the basic strategy for calculating the continuous ridgelet transform is first to compute the Radon transform $\mathbf{R}(f)(\theta, \tau)$ and second to apply a 1-D wavelet transform to the slices $\mathbf{R}(f)(\theta, \cdot)$. Several discrete ridgelet transforms (DRTs) have been proposed, and we will describe three of them in this section, based on different implementations of the Radon transform.

5.3.2 The Rectopolar Ridgelet Transform

A fast implementation of the Radon transform can be proposed in the Fourier domain, based on the projection-slice theorem. First the 2-D fast Fourier transform (FFT) of the given $N \times N$ discrete image is computed. Then the resulting image in the frequency domain is to be used to evaluate the frequency values in a polar grid of rays passing through the origin and spread uniformly in angle. This conversion from Cartesian to polar grid could be obtained by interpolation, and this process is well known as gridding in tomography. Given the polar grid samples, the number of rays corresponds to the number of projections, and the number of samples on each ray

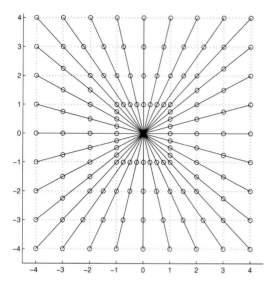

Figure 5.3. Illustration of the pseudo-polar grid in the frequency domain for an $N \times N$ image ($N = 9$).

corresponds to the number of shifts per such angle. Applying an inverse 1-D FFT for each ray, the Radon projections are obtained.

The previously described process is known to be inaccurate due to the sensitivity to the interpolation involved. This implies that for better accuracy, the first 2-D FFT employed should be done with high redundancy.

An alternative solution for the Fourier-based Radon transform exists, where the polar grid is replaced with a pseudo-polar one. The geometry of this new grid is illustrated in Figure 5.3. Concentric circles of linearly growing radius in the polar grid are replaced by concentric squares of linearly growing sides. The rays are spread uniformly not in angle but in slope. These two changes give a grid vaguely resembling the polar one, but for this grid a direct FFT can be implemented with no interpolation. When applying now a 1-D FFT for the rays, we get a variant of the Radon transform, where the projection angles are not spaced uniformly.

For the pseudo-polar FFT to be stable, it was shown that it should contain at least twice as many samples, compared to the original image we started with. A by-product of this construction is the fact that the transform is organized as a 2-D array with rows containing the projections as a function of the angle. Thus, processing the Radon transform in one axis is easily implemented. More detail can be found in the work of Starck et al. (2002).

One-Dimensional Wavelet Transform

To complete the ridgelet transform, we must take a 1-D wavelet transform (1-D WT) along the radial variable in the Radon domain. We now discuss the choice of the 1-D WT.

In Chapters 2 and 3, we have shown that compactly-supported wavelets can lead to many visual artifacts when used in conjunction with nonlinear processing, such as hard-thresholding of individual wavelet coefficients, particularly for decimated wavelet schemes used at critical sampling. Also, because of the lack of localization of such compactly-supported wavelets in the frequency domain, fluctuations in coarse-scale wavelet coefficients can introduce fine-scale fluctuations. A frequency-domain approach must be taken, where the discrete Fourier transform is obtained from the inverse Radon transform. These considerations lead us to use a band-limited wavelet, whose support is compact in the Fourier domain rather than the time-domain (Starck et al. 2002). In Starck et al. (2002), the redundant wavelet transform of Section 3.7.2 was used. We recall this wavelet transform algorithm briefly for the reader's convenience. It is based on a scaling function ϕ such that $\hat{\phi}$ vanishes outside of the interval $[-\nu_c, \nu_c]$. We define the Fourier transform of the scaling function as a renormalized B_3-spline (cf. equation (3.43)),

$$\hat{\phi}(\nu) = \frac{3}{2}B_3(4\nu) \,,$$

and $\hat{\psi}$ as the difference between two consecutive resolutions, as in equation (3.45):

$$\hat{\psi}(2\nu) = \hat{\phi}(\nu) - \hat{\phi}(2\nu) \,.$$

See Section 3.7.2 in Chapter 3 for details.

This 1-D WT transform enjoys the following useful properties:

- The wavelet coefficients are directly calculated in the Fourier domain. In the context of the ridgelet transform, this allows avoiding the computation of the 1-D inverse Fourier transform along each radial line.
- Each subband is sampled above the Nyquist rate, hence, avoiding aliasing – a phenomenon typically encountered by critically sampled orthogonal wavelet transforms (Simoncelli et al. 1992).
- The reconstruction is trivial. The wavelet coefficients simply need to be co-added to reconstruct the input signal at any given point. In our application, this implies that the ridgelet coefficients simply need to be co-added to reconstruct the Fourier coefficients of the image.

This wavelet transform introduces an extra redundancy factor. However, we note that the goal in this implementation is not data compression or efficient coding. Rather, this implementation is to be useful to the practitioner whose focus is on data analysis and restoration, for which it is well known that overcompleteness can provide substantial advantages as we argued in Chapter 1.

Assembling all above ingredients together gives the flowchart of the discrete ridgelet transform (DRT) depicted in Figure 5.4. The DRT of an image of size $N \times N$ is an image of size $2N \times 2N$, yielding a redundancy factor equal to 4.

We note that, because this transform is made of a chain of steps, each one of which is invertible, the whole transform is invertible, and so has the exact reconstruction property. For the same reason, the reconstruction is stable under perturbations of the coefficients.

Last but not least, this discrete transform is computationally attractive. The algorithm we presented here has low complexity since it runs in $O(N^2 \log N)$ operations for an $N \times N$ image.

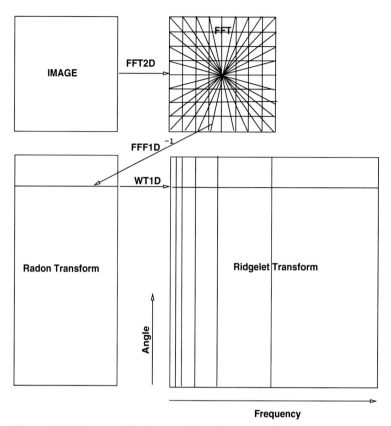

Figure 5.4. Discrete ridgelet transform flowchart of an image ($N \times N$). Each of the 2N radial lines in the Fourier domain is processed separately. The 1-D inverse FFT is calculated along each radial line followed by a 1-D nonorthogonal wavelet transform. In practice, the 1-D wavelet coefficients are directly calculated in the Fourier domain.

5.3.3 The Orthonormal Finite Ridgelet Transform

The orthonormal finite ridgelet transform (OFRT) was proposed (Do and Vetterli 2003c) for image compression and denoising. This transform is based on the finite Radon transform (Matus and Flusser 1993) and a 1-D orthogonal wavelet transform. It is not redundant and invertible. It would have been a great alternative to the previously described ridgelet transform if the OFRT were not based on an awkward definition of a line. In fact, a line in the OFRT is defined algebraically rather than geometrically, and so the points on a "line" can be arbitrarily and randomly spread out in the spatial domain. Figure 5.5 shows the inverse transform of a single ridgelet coefficient (all coefficients but one set to zero) by the FFT-based ridgelet transform (left) and by the OFRT (right). It is clear that the inverse of a single OFRT coefficient is nothing like a ridge function.

Because of this specific definition of a line, the thresholding of the OFRT coefficients produces strong artifacts. Figure 5.6 shows a part of the original image Boat, and its reconstruction after hard thresholding the OFRT of the noise-free Boat. The

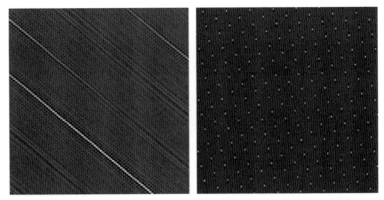

Figure 5.5. Inverse transform of a single ridgelet coefficient (left) by the FFT-based ridgelet transform and (right) by the OFRT.

resulting image is not smoothed as one would expect, but rather noise has been added to the noise-free image as part of the filtering!

Finally, the OFRT presents another limitation: the image size must be a prime number. This last point is however not too restrictive, because we generally use a spatial partitioning when processing the data, and a prime number block size can be used. The OFRT is interesting from the conceptual point of view, but still requires work before it can be used for real applications such as denoising.

5.3.4 The Fast Slant Stack Ridgelet Transform

The fast slant stack (FSS) (Averbuch et al. 2001) is a Radon transform of data on a Cartesian grid, which is algebraically exact and geometrically more accurate and faithful than the previously described methods. The backprojection of a point in Radon space is exactly a ridge function in the spatial domain (see Figure 5.7). The transformation of an $N \times N$ image yields a $2N \times 2N$ image. N line integrals with angle between $[-\frac{\pi}{4}, \frac{\pi}{4}]$ are calculated from the zero padded image along the vertical

Figure 5.6. (left) Part of original noise-free "Boat" image and (right) reconstruction after hard thresholding its OFRT coefficients.

Figure 5.7. Inverse Radon transform of Dirac at four different locations in the Radon domain using the FSS algorithm.

axis, and N line integrals with angle between $[\frac{\pi}{4}, \frac{3\pi}{4}]$ are computed by zero padding the image on the horizontal axis. For a given angle inside $[-\frac{\pi}{4}, \frac{\pi}{4}]$, $2N$ line integrals are calculated by first shearing the zero-padded image, and then integrating the pixel values along all horizontal lines (respectively, vertical lines for angles in $[\frac{\pi}{4}, \frac{3\pi}{4}]$). The shearing is performed one column at a time (respectively, one row at a time) by using the 1-D FFT. Figure 5.8 shows an example of the image shearing step with two different angles ($5\frac{\pi}{4}$ and $-\frac{\pi}{4}$). A DRT based on the FSS transform was proposed by Donoho and Flesia (2002). The connection between the FSS and the Linogram was investigated by Averbuch et al. (2001). An FSS algorithm was also proposed by Averbuch et al. (2001), based on the 2-D fast pseudo-polar Fourier transform which

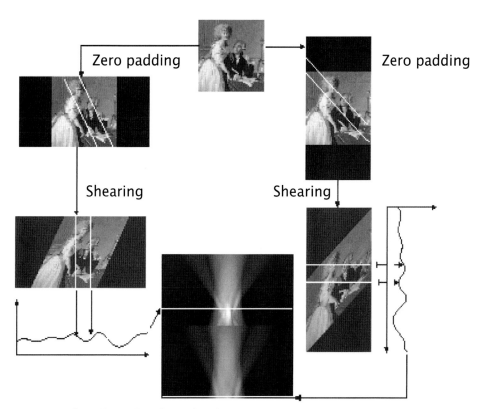

Figure 5.8. Slant Stack Transform of an image.

Figure 5.9. (left) Example of a ridgelet obtained by the Fast Slant Stack implementation. (right) Its FFT superimposed on the DRT frequency tiling.

evaluates the 2-D Fourier transform on a non-Cartesian (pseudo-polar) grid, operating in $O(N^2 \log N)$ operations.

Figure 5.9 (left) exemplifies a ridgelet in the spatial domain obtained from the DRT based on FSS implementation. Its Fourier transform is shown in Figure 5.9 (right) superimposed on the DRT frequency tiling (Donoho and Flesia 2002). The Fourier transform of the discrete ridgelet lives in an angular wedge. More precisely, the Fourier transform of a discrete ridgelet at scale j lives within a dyadic square of size $\sim 2^j$.

5.3.5 Local Ridgelet Transforms

The ridgelet transform is optimal for finding global lines of the size of the image. To detect line segments, a partitioning must be introduced (Candès and Donoho 1999). The image can be decomposed into overlapping blocks of side-length B pixels in such a way that the overlap between two vertically adjacent blocks is a rectangular array of size B by B/2; we use overlap to avoid blocking artifacts. For an $N \times N$ image, we count $2N/B$ such blocks in each direction, and thus the redundancy factor grows by a factor of 4.

The partitioning introduces redundancy, since a pixel belongs to 4 neighboring blocks. We present two competing strategies to perform the analysis and synthesis:

(i) The block values are weighted by a spatial window (analysis) in such a way that the co-addition of all blocks reproduces exactly the original pixel value (synthesis).

(ii) The block values are those of the image pixel values (analysis) but are weighted when the image is reconstructed (synthesis).

Experiments have shown that the second approach leads to better results especially for restoration problems; see Starck et al. (2002) for details.

A pixel value, $f[k, l]$ belongs to four blocks, namely, $\mathcal{B}_{b_1, b_2}[k_1, l_1]$ (with $b_1 = 2k/\mathsf{B}$ and $b_2 = 2l/\mathsf{B}$), $\mathcal{B}_{b_1+1, b_2}[k_2, l_1]$, $\mathcal{B}_{b_1, b_2+1}[k_1, l_2]$ and $\mathcal{B}_{b_1+1, b_2+1}[k_2, l_2]$, such that $k_1 = \mathsf{B}/2 + k \mod \mathsf{B}/2$, $l_1 = \mathsf{B}/2 + l \mod \mathsf{B}/2$, $k_2 = k_1 - \mathsf{B}/2$ and $l_2 = l_1 - \mathsf{B}/2$. We compute a pixel value, $f[k, l]$ in the following way:

$$f_1 = \varpi(2k_2/\mathsf{B})\mathcal{B}_{b_1, b_2}[k_1, l_1] + \varpi(1 - 2k_2/\mathsf{B})\mathcal{B}_{b_1+1, b_2}[k_2, l_1]$$
$$f_2 = \varpi(2k_2/\mathsf{B}]\mathcal{B}_{b_1, b_2+1}[k_1, l_2] + \varpi(1 - 2k_2/\mathsf{B})\mathcal{B}_{b_1+1, b_2+1}[k_2, l_2]$$
$$f[k, l] = \varpi(2l_2/\mathsf{B})f_1 + \varpi(1 - 2l_2/\mathsf{B})f_2 , \tag{5.5}$$

where $\varpi(t) = \cos^2(\pi t/2)$ is the window. Of course, one might select any other smooth, nonincreasing function satisfying $\varpi(0) = 1$, $\varpi(1) = 0$, with a derivative $\varpi'(0) = 0$ and obeying the symmetry property $\varpi(t) + \varpi(1 - t) = 1$.

5.3.6 Sparse Representation by Ridgelets

The continuous ridgelet transform provides optimally sparse representation of smooth functions that may exhibit linear singularities. As a prototype function, consider the mutilated function

$$f(t_1, t_2) = \mathbf{1}_{\{t_1 \cos\theta + t_2 \sin\theta - b > 0\}} g(t_1, t_2) ,$$

where g is compactly supported, belonging to the Sobolev space $W_2^s, s > 0^1$. f is a smooth function away from singularity along the line $t_1 \cos\theta + t_2 \sin\theta - b = 0$. It was proved by Candès (2001) that the ridgelet coefficient sequence of f is as sparse as if it were without singularity. For instance, the m-term approximation – that is, the nonlinear approximation of f by keeping only the m largest coefficients in magnitude in the ridgelet series – achieves the rate of order m^{-s} in squared L_2 error (Candès 2001; Candès and Donoho 1999). This is much better than the wavelet representation which has only a rate $O(m^{-1})$, $\forall s$. In summary, the ridgelet system provides sparse representation for piecewise smooth images away from global straight edges.

We have seen previously that there are various DRTs, i.e. expansions with a countable discrete collection of generating elements. The ones we discussed here correspond to frames. The preceding sparsity of the continuous ridgelets suggests that a DRT can be made to give a sparse representation of discrete images with singularities along (discrete) lines.

5.4 CURVELETS

5.4.1 The First-Generation Curvelet Transform

In image processing, edges are curved rather than straight lines and ridgelets are not able to effectively represent such images. However, one can still deploy the ridgelet machinery in a localized way, at fine scales, where curved edges are almost straight lines (as illustrated in Figure 5.10). This is the idea underlying the first generation curvelets (termed here *CurveletG1*) (Candès and Donoho 2002).

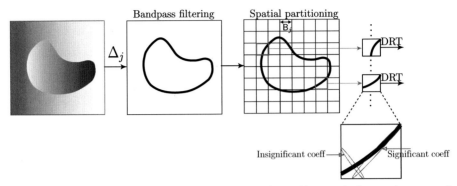

Figure 5.10. Local ridgelet transform on bandpass filtered image. At fine scales, curved edges are almost straight lines.

5.4.1.1 First-Generation Curvelets Construction

The CurveletG1 transform (Candès and Donoho 2002; Donoho and Duncan 2000; Starck et al. 2002) opens the possibility to analyze an image with different block sizes but with a single transform. The idea is to first decompose the image into a set of wavelet bands, and to analyze each band by a local ridgelet transform as illustrated in Figure 5.10. The block size can be changed at each scale level. Roughly speaking, different levels of the multiscale ridgelet pyramid are used to represent different subbands of a filter bank output. At the same time, this subband decomposition imposes a relationship between the width and length of the *important* frame elements so that they are anisotropic and obey approximately the *parabolic scaling law* width $\approx$ length^2.

The first generation discrete curvelet transform (DCTG1) of a continuum function (i.e. a function of a continuous variable) $f(\mathbf{t})$ makes use of a dyadic sequence of scales, and a bank of filters with the property that the bandpass filter Δ_j is concentrated near the frequencies $[2^{2j}, 2^{2j+2}]$, that is,

$$\Delta_j(f) = \Psi_{2j} * f, \quad \widehat{\Psi}_{2j}(\mathbf{v}) = \widehat{\Psi}(2^{-2j}\mathbf{v}) .$$

In wavelet theory, one uses a decomposition into dyadic subbands $[2^j, 2^{j+1}]$. In contrast, the subbands used in the discrete curvelet transform of continuum functions have the nonstandard form $[2^{2j}, 2^{2j+2}]$. This nonstandard feature of the DCTG1 is worth remembering (this is where the approximate parabolic scaling law comes into play).

The DCTG1 decomposition is the sequence of the following steps:

- *Subband Decomposition.* The object f is decomposed into subbands.
- *Smooth Partitioning.* Each subband is smoothly windowed into "squares" of an appropriate scale (of side-length $\sim 2^{-j}$).
- *Ridgelet Analysis.* Each square is analyzed via the DRT.

In this definition, the two dyadic subbands $[2^{2j}, 2^{2j+1}]$ and $[2^{2j+1}, 2^{2j+2}]$ are merged before applying the ridgelet transform.

5.4.1.2 Digital Implementation

It seems that the starlet, or isotropic à trous wavelet, transform (see Section 3.5) is especially well-adapted to the needs of the digital curvelet transform. The algorithm decomposes a discrete $N \times N$ image $f[k, l]$ as a superposition of the form

$$f[k, l] = c_J[k, l] + \sum_{j=1}^{J} w_j[k, l],$$

where c_J is the coarse or smooth version of the original image f and w_j represents the details of f at resolution level j. Thus, the algorithm outputs $J + 1$ subband arrays each of size $N \times N$.

A sketch of the DCTG1 algorithm is as follows:

Algorithm 17 First Generation Discrete Curvelet Transform

Task: Compute the DCTG1 of an $N \times N$ image f, using one of the DRT implementations of Section 5.3.2.

Parameters: Number of resolution levels J, minimum block size B_{min}.

Apply the starlet transform to f, and get the set $\mathcal{W} = \{w_1, \ldots, w_J, c_J\}$.

Set $B_1 = B_{min}$,

for $j = 1, \ldots, J$ **do**

    1. Partition the subband w_j with a block size B_j and apply the DRT to each block: we get the curvelet coefficients α_j.

    2. **if** j modulo $2 = 1$ **then**

        $B_{j+1} = 2B_j$,

    3. **else**

        $B_{j+1} = B_j$.

    4. **end if**

Output: $\mathcal{C} = \{\alpha_1, \alpha_2, \alpha_3, \ldots, \alpha_J, c_J\}$ the DCTG1 of f.

The side length of the localizing windows is doubled *at every other* dyadic subband, hence maintaining the fundamental property of the curvelet transform which says that elements of length about $2^{-j/2}$ serve for the analysis and synthesis of the jth subband $[2^j, 2^{j+1}]$. Note also that the coarse description of the image c_J is left intact. In the results shown in this chapter, we used the default value $B_{min} = 16$ pixels in our implementation. Figure 5.11 gives an overview of the organization of the DCTG1 algorithm.

This implementation of the DCTG1 is also redundant. The redundancy factor is equal to $16J + 1$ whenever J scales are employed. The DCTG1 algorithm enjoys exact reconstruction and stability, as each step of the analysis transform in Algorithm 17 is itself invertible. We leave as a simple exercise to show that the computational complexity of the DCTG1 algorithm we described here based on the DRT of Figure 5.4 is $O(N^2 (\log N)^2)$ for an $N \times N$ image. Figure 5.12 shows a few curvelets at different scales, orientations and locations.

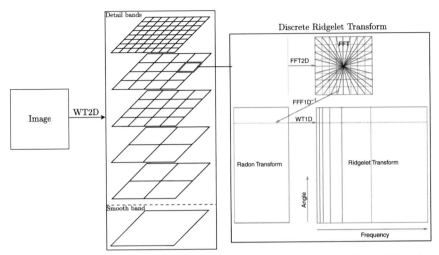

Figure 5.11. DCTG1 flowchart. The figure illustrates the decomposition of the original image into subbands followed by the spatial partitioning of each subband. The ridgelet transform is then applied to each block.

5.4.1.3 Sparse Representation by First Generation Curvelets

The CurveletG1 elements can form either a frame or a tight frame for $L_2(\mathbb{R}^2)$ (Candès and Donoho 2002), depending on the 2-D WT used and the DRT implementation (rectopolar or FSS Radon transform). The frame elements are anisotropic by construction and become successively more anisotropic at progressively higher scales. These curvelets also exhibit directional sensitivity and display oscillatory components across the "ridge." A central motivation leading to the curvelet construction was the problem of nonadaptively representing piecewise smooth (e.g. C^2) images f which have discontinuity along a C^2 curve. Such a model is the so-called cartoon model of (nontextured) images. With the CurveletG1 tight frame construction, it was shown in Candès and Donoho (2002) that for such f, the m-term nonlinear

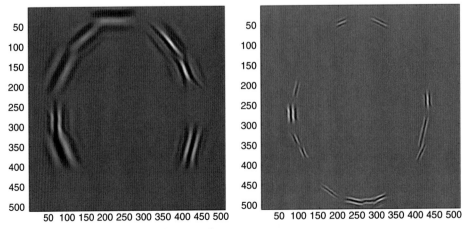

Figure 5.12. A few first-generation curvelets.

approximations f_m of f obey, for each $\kappa > 0$,

$$\| f - f_m \|_2^2 \leq C_\kappa m^{-2+\kappa}, \quad m \to +\infty .$$

The m-term approximations in the CurveletG1 are almost rate optimal, much better than m-term Fourier or wavelet approximations for such images; see Mallat (2008).

5.4.2 The Second-Generation Curvelet Transform

Despite these interesting properties, the CurveletG1 construction presents some drawbacks. First, the construction involves a complicated seven-index structure among which we have parameters for scale, location and orientation. In addition, the parabolic scaling ratio width $\approx$ length^2 is not completely true (see Section 5.4.1.1). In fact, CurveletG1 assumes a wide range of aspect ratios. These facts make mathematical and quantitative analysis especially delicate. Second, the spatial partitioning of the CurveletG1 transform uses overlapping windows to avoid blocking effects. This leads to an increase of the redundancy of the DCTG1. The computational cost of the DCTG1 algorithm may also be a limitation for large-scale data, especially if the FSS-based DRT implementation is used.

In contrast, the second-generation curvelets, CurveletG2 (Candès and Donoho 2004; Candès et al. 2006a), exhibit a much simpler and natural indexing structure with three parameters: scale, orientation (angle) and location – hence simplifying mathematical analysis. The CurveletG2 transform also implements a tight frame expansion (Candès and Donoho 2004) and has a much lower redundancy. Unlike the DCTG1, the discrete CurveletG2 implementation will not use ridgelets yielding a faster algorithm (Candès and Donoho 2004; Candès et al. 2006a).

5.4.2.1 Second-Generation Curvelet Construction
Continuous coronization
The second-generation curvelets are defined at scale 2^{-j}, orientation θ_ℓ and position $\mathbf{t}_\mathbf{k}^{j,\ell} = R_{\theta_\ell}^{-1}(2^{-j}k, 2^{-j/2}l)$ by translation and rotation of a mother curvelet φ_j as

$$\varphi_{j,\ell,\mathbf{k}}(\mathbf{t}) = \varphi_{j,\ell,\mathbf{k}}(t_1, t_2) = \varphi_j \left(R_{\theta_\ell} \left(\mathbf{t} - \mathbf{t}_\mathbf{k}^{j,\ell} \right) \right) , \tag{5.6}$$

where R_{θ_ℓ} is the rotation by θ_ℓ radians. θ_ℓ is the equi-spaced sequence of rotation angles $\theta_\ell = 2\pi 2^{-\lfloor j/2 \rfloor} \ell$, with integer ℓ such that $0 \leq \theta_\ell \leq 2\pi$ (note that the number of orientations varies as $1/\sqrt{\text{scale}}$). $\mathbf{k} = (k, l) \in \mathbb{Z}^2$ is the sequence of translation parameters. The waveform φ_j is defined by means of its Fourier transform $\hat{\varphi}_j(\boldsymbol{\nu})$, written in polar coordinates (r, θ) in the Fourier domain:

$$\hat{\varphi}_j(r, \theta) = 2^{-3j/4} \hat{\varpi}(2^{-j}r) \hat{\upsilon} \left(\frac{2^{\lfloor j/2 \rfloor} \theta}{2\pi} \right) . \tag{5.7}$$

The support of $\hat{\varphi}_j$ is a polar *parabolic wedge* defined by the support of $\hat{\varpi}$ and $\hat{\upsilon}$, respectively the radial and angular windows (both smooth, nonnegative and real-valued), applied with scale-dependent window widths in each direction. $\hat{\varpi}$ and $\hat{\upsilon}$ must also satisfy the partition of unity property (Candès et al. 2006a). See the frequency tiling in Figure 5.13(a).

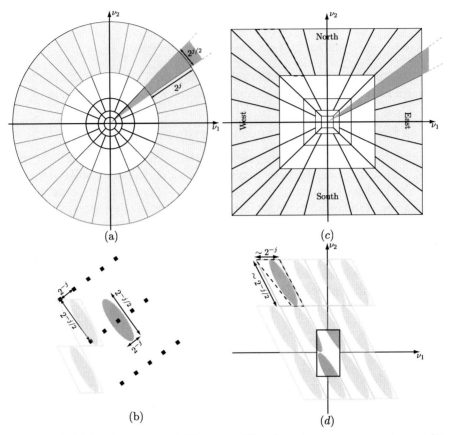

Figure 5.13. (a) Continuous curvelet frequency tiling. The gray area represents a wedge obtained as the product of the radial window (annulus shown in lighter color) and the angular window (darker color). (b) The Cartesian grid in space associated with the construction in (a) whose spacing also obeys the parabolic scaling by duality. (c) Discrete curvelet frequency tiling. The window $\hat{u}_{j,\ell}$ isolates the frequency near the trapezoidal wedge such as the ones shown in gray. (d) The wrapping transformation. The dashed line shows the same trapezoidal wedge as in (b). The parallelogram contains this wedge and hence the support of the curvelet. After periodization, the wrapped Fourier samples can be collected in the rectangle centered at the origin. (See *color plates*.)

In continuous frequency ν, the CurveletG2 coefficients of the 2-D function $f(\mathbf{t})$ are defined as the inner product

$$\alpha_{j,\ell,\mathbf{k}} := \langle f, \varphi_{j,\ell,\mathbf{k}} \rangle = \int_{\mathbb{R}^2} \hat{f}(\boldsymbol{\nu})\hat{\varphi}_j(R_{\theta_\ell}\boldsymbol{\nu})e^{i\mathbf{t}_{\mathbf{k}}^{j,\ell}\cdot\boldsymbol{\nu}}d\boldsymbol{\nu} . \tag{5.8}$$

This construction implies a few properties:

(i)   the CurveletG2 defines a tight frame of $L_2(\mathbb{R}^2)$;

(ii) the effective length and width of these curvelets obey the parabolic scaling relation $(2^{-j} = \text{width}) = (\text{length} = 2^{-j/2})^2$;

(iii) the curvelets exhibit an oscillating behavior in the direction perpendicular to their orientation.

Curvelets as just constructed are complex-valued. It is easy to obtain real-valued curvelets by working on the symmetrized version $\hat{\varphi}_j(r, \theta) + \hat{\varphi}_j(r, \theta + \pi)$.

Discrete coronization.

The discrete transform takes as input data defined on a Cartesian grid and outputs a collection of coefficients. The continuous-space definition of the CurveletG2 uses coronae and rotations that are not especially adapted to Cartesian arrays. It is then convenient to replace these concepts by their Cartesian counterparts. That is, concentric squares (instead of concentric circles) and shears (instead of rotations). See Figure 5.13(c).

The Cartesian equivalent to the radial window $\hat{\varpi}_j(\nu) = \hat{\varpi}(2^{-j}\nu)$ would be a bandpass frequency-localized window which can be derived from the difference low-pass windows:

$$\hat{\varpi}_j(\nu) = \sqrt{\hat{h}_{j+1}^2(\nu) - \hat{h}_j^2(\nu)}, \forall j \geq 0, \quad \text{and} \quad \hat{\varpi}_0(\nu) = \hat{h}(\nu_1)\hat{h}(\nu_2) , \tag{5.9}$$

where $\hat{h}_j$ is separable,

$$\hat{h}_j(\nu) = \hat{h}_{1-\mathrm{D}}(2^{-j}\nu_1)\hat{h}_{1-\mathrm{D}}(2^{-j}\nu_2) ,$$

and $h_{1-\mathrm{D}}$ is a 1-D low-pass filter. Another possible choice is to select these windows inspired by the construction of Meyer wavelets (Meyer 1993; Candès and Donoho 2004). See Candès et al. (2006a) for more details of the construction of the Cartesian version of $\hat{\varpi}_j$.

Let us now examine the angular localization. Each Cartesian corona has four quadrants: east, north, west and south. Each quadrant is separated into $2^{\lfloor j/2 \rfloor}$ orientations (wedges) with the same areas. Take for example the east quadrant ($-\pi/4 \leq \theta_\ell < \pi/4$). For the west quadrant, we would proceed by symmetry around the origin, and for the north and south quadrants by exchanging the roles of ν_1 and ν_2. Define the angular window for the ℓth direction as

$$\hat{v}_{j,\ell}(\nu) = \hat{v}\left(2^{\lfloor j/2 \rfloor}\frac{\nu_2 - \nu_1 \tan \theta_\ell}{\nu_1}\right) , \tag{5.10}$$

with the sequence of equispaced slopes (and not angles) $\tan \theta_\ell = 2^{-\lfloor j/2 \rfloor}\ell$, for $\ell = -2^{\lfloor j/2 \rfloor}, \ldots, 2^{\lfloor j/2 \rfloor} - 1$. We can now define the window which is the Cartesian analog of $\hat{\varphi}_j$ above,

$$\hat{u}_{j,\ell}(\nu) = \hat{\varpi}_j(\nu)\hat{v}_{j,\ell}(\nu) = \hat{\varpi}_j(\nu)\hat{v}_{j,0}(S_{\theta_\ell}\nu) , \tag{5.11}$$

where S_{θ_ℓ} is the shear matrix:

$$S_{\theta_\ell} = \begin{pmatrix} 1 & 0 \\ -\tan \theta_\ell & 1 \end{pmatrix} .$$

From this definition, it can be seen that $\hat{u}_{j,\ell}$ is supported near the trapezoidal wedge $\{\nu = (\nu_1, \nu_2) \mid 2^j \leq \nu_1 \leq 2^{j+1}, -2^{-j/2} \leq \nu_2/\nu_1 - \tan \theta_\ell \leq 2^{-j/2}\}$. The collection of $\hat{u}_{j,\ell}$

gives rise to the frequency tiling shown in Figure 5.13(c). From $\hat{u}_{j,\ell}(\boldsymbol{\nu})$, the digital CurveletG2 construction suggests Cartesian curvelets that are translated and sheared versions of a mother Cartesian curvelet $\hat{\varphi}_j^D(\boldsymbol{\nu}) = \hat{u}_{j,0}(\boldsymbol{\nu})$, where

$$\varphi_{j,\ell,\mathbf{k}}^D(\mathbf{t}) = 2^{3j/4}\varphi_j^D\left(S_{\theta_\ell}^{\mathrm{T}}\mathbf{t} - \mathbf{m}\right),\qquad(5.12)$$

and $\mathbf{m} = (2^{-j}k, 2^{-j/2}l)$.

5.4.2.2 Digital Implementation

The goal here is to find a digital implementation of the Second Generation Discrete Curvelet Transform (DCTG2), whose coefficients are now given by

$$\alpha_{j,\ell,\mathbf{k}} := \langle f, \varphi_{j,\ell,\mathbf{k}}^D \rangle = \int_{\mathbb{R}^2} \hat{f}(\boldsymbol{\nu})\hat{\varphi}_j^D\left(S_{\theta_\ell}^{-1}\boldsymbol{\nu}\right)e^{iS_{\theta_\ell}^{-\mathrm{T}}\mathbf{m}\cdot\boldsymbol{\nu}}d\boldsymbol{\nu}\,.\qquad(5.13)$$

This suggests the following steps to evaluate this formula with discrete data:

  (i) compute the 2-D FFT to get $\hat{f}$;
 (ii) form the windowed frequency data $\hat{f}\hat{u}_{j,\ell}$;
(iii) apply the the inverse Fourier transform.

But the last step necessitates evaluating the FFT at the sheared grid $S_{\theta_\ell}^{-\mathrm{T}}\mathbf{m}$, for which the classical FFT algorithm is not valid. Two implementations were then proposed (Candès et al. 2006a), essentially differing in their way of handling the grid:

- A tilted grid mostly aligned with the axes of $\hat{u}_{j,\ell}(\boldsymbol{\nu})$ which leads to the unequispaced FFT (USFFT)-based DCTG2. This implementation uses a nonstandard interpolation. Furthermore, the inverse transform uses conjugate gradient iteration to invert the interpolation step. This will have the drawback of a higher computational burden compared to the wrapping-based implementation that we will discuss hereafter. We will not elaborate more on the USFFT implementation as we do not use it in practice. The interested reader may refer to Candès et al. (2006a) for further details and analysis.
- A grid aligned with the input Cartesian grid which leads to the wrapping-based DCTG2.

The wrapping-based DCTG2 makes for a simpler choice of the spatial grid to translate the curvelets. The curvelet coefficients are essentially the same as in (5.13), except that $S_{\theta_\ell}^{-\mathrm{T}}\mathbf{m}$ is replaced by $\mathbf{m}$ with values on a rectangular grid. But again a difficulty arises because the window $\hat{u}_{j,\ell}$ does not fit in a rectangle of size $2^j \times 2^{j/2}$ to which an inverse FFT could be applied. The *wrapping* trick consists of periodizing the windowed frequency data $\hat{f}\hat{u}_{j,\ell}$, and re-indexing the samples array by wrapping around a $\sim 2^j \times 2^{j/2}$ rectangle centered at the origin. See Figure 5.13(d) to get the gist of the wrapping idea.

The wrapping-based DCTG2 algorithm can be summarized as follows:

Algorithm 18 Second-Generation Discrete Curvelet Transform via Wrapping

---

Task: Compute the DCTG2 of an $N \times N$ image f.
Parameters: Coarsest decomposition scale, curvelets or wavelets at the finest scale.
Apply the 2-D FFT and obtain Fourier coefficients $\hat{f}$.
for each scale j and orientation ℓ **do**

     1. Form the product $\hat{f}\hat{u}_{j,\ell}$.
     2. Wrap this product around the origin.
     3. Apply the inverse 2-D FFT to the wrapped data to get discrete DCTG2 coefficients $\alpha_{j,\ell,\mathbf{k}}$.

Output: $\mathcal{C} = (\alpha_{j,\ell,\mathbf{k}})_{j,\ell,\mathbf{k}}$ the DCTG2 of f.

The DCTG2 implementation can assign either wavelets or curvelets at the finest scale. In the Curvelab (2005), the default choice is set to wavelets at the finest scale, but this can be easily modified directly in the code.

The computational complexity of the wrapping-based DCTG2 analysis and reconstruction algorithms is that of the FFT, $O(N^2 \log N)$, and in practice, the computation time is that of 6 to 10 2-D FFTs (Candès et al. 2006a). This is a faster algorithm compared to the DCTG1.

The DCTG2 fast algorithm has helped to make the use of the curvelet transform more attractive in many applicative fields. The DCTG2 by wrapping, as it is implemented in the Curvelab (2005), has reasonable redundancy, at most ~ 7.8 (much higher in 3-D) if curvelets are used at the finest scale. This redundancy can even be reduced down to 4 (and 8 in 3-D) if we replace in this implementation the Meyer wavelet construction, which introduces a redundancy factor of 4, by another wavelet pyramidal construction, similar to the one presented in Section 5.3.2 which has a redundancy less than 2 in any dimension. Our experiments have shown that this modification does not modify the results in denoising experiments. DCTG2 redundancy is anyway much smaller than the redundancy of the DCTG1 which is $16J + 1$. As stated above in Section 5.4.2.1, the DCTG2 coefficients are complex-valued, but a real-valued DCTG2 with the same redundancy factor can be easily obtained by properly combining the pair of coefficients at orientations θ_ℓ and $\theta_\ell + \pi$.

The DCTG2 with wrapping implements an equal-norm Parseval tight frame. In other words, the frame operator $\mathbf{\Phi}_C \mathbf{\Phi}_C^* = \mathbf{I}$, where $\mathbf{\Phi}_C$ is the curvelet dictionary, and the DCTG2 atoms all have the same nonunit ℓ_2-norm. Simple calculations show that the ℓ_2-norm of the curvelets is actually $1/\sqrt{\text{redundancy of the frame}}$. Normalization has an important impact for many purposes such as denoising and inverse problems as we will see in the following chapters.

The DCTG2 can be extended to higher dimensions (Ying et al. 2005). In the same vein as wavelets on the interval (Mallat 2008), the DCGT2 has been recently adapted to handle image boundaries by mirror extension instead of periodization (Demanet and Ying 2005). The latter modification can have immediate implications in image

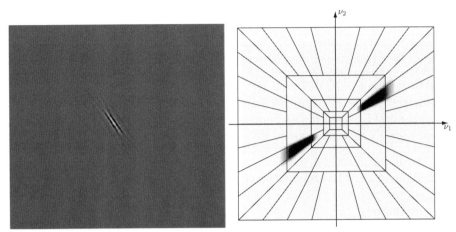

Figure 5.14. An example of a second-generation real curvelet. (left) Curvelet in spatial domain. (right) Its Fourier transform.

processing applications where the contrast difference at opposite image boundaries may be an issue.

We would like to make a connection with other multiscale directional transforms directly linked to curvelets. The contourlets' tight frame of Do and Vetterli (2003b) implements the CurveletG2 idea directly on a discrete grid using a perfect reconstruction filter bank procedure. In Lu and Do (2003), the authors proposed a modification of the contourlets with a directional filter bank that provides a frequency partitioning which is close to the curvelets but with no redundancy. Durand (2007) introduced families of nonadaptive directional wavelets with various frequency tilings, including that of curvelets. Such families are nonredundant and form orthonormal bases for $L_2(\mathbb{R}^2)$, and have an implementation derived from a single nonseparable filter bank structure with nonuniform sampling.

5.4.2.3 Sparse Representation by Second-Generation Curvelets

Consider again the $C^2 - C^2$ class of images (i.e., piecewise C^2 smoothness except at discontinuities along C^2 edges). It is known that the optimal m-term nonlinear squared approximation error rate for such images is $O(m^{-2})$ (Korostelev and Tsybakov 1993; Mallat 2008). Candès and Donoho (2004) have shown that with the CurveletG2 tight frame construction, the m-term nonlinear squared approximation error of $C^2 - C^2$ images obey

$$\|f - f_m\|_2^2 \leq C m^{-2} (\log m)^3 .$$

This is a near-optimal rate (up to the $(\log m)^3$ factor) which holds uniformly over the $C^2 - C^2$ class of functions. This is a remarkable result since the CurveletG2 representation is nonadaptive in the sense that no prior knowledge nor pre-estimation of the image geometry is required. However, the simplicity due to the nonadaptivity of curvelets has a cost: curvelet approximations lose their near optimal properties when the image is composed of edges which are not exactly C^2. Additionally, if the edges are C^κ-regular with $\kappa > 2$, then the curvelet convergence rate exponents remain 2. Other adaptive geometric representations such as bandlets are specifically designed to reach the optimal decay rate $O(m^{-\kappa})$ (Le Pennec and Mallat 2005; Peyré and Mallat 2007).

5.4.3 Contourlets and Shearlets

Other transforms have been proposed to build a decomposition with a frequency tiling similar to the curvelet representation. The contourlet transform (Do and Vetterli 2003b) consists of applying first a Laplacian pyramid (Burt and Adelson 1983), followed by a direction filter bank (Bamberger and Smith 1992) at each scale. The number of directions per scale has to be a power of two, but we can have different numbers of direction through the scales. The contourlet transform is computationally efficient, all operations are done using filter banks, and the redundancy is small (33%), due to the Laplacian pyramid. This low redundancy has, however, a cost – the loss of the translation invariance property in the analysis – which limits its interest for restoration applications. For this reason, an undecimated contourlet transform was proposed (Da Cunha et al. 2006), where both the Laplacian filter bank and the directional filter bank are nonsubsampled. The redundancy is therefore much higher, since each contourlet band has the same size as the original image, but it was shown that denoising results were much better (Da Cunha et al. 2006). The contourlet transform can be seen as a discrete filter-bank version of the curvelet decomposition. A Matlab toolbox that implements the contourlet transform and the nonsubsampled contourlet transform can be downloaded from Matlab Central (www.mathworks.com/matlabcentral/).

Based on the concept of composite wavelets (Guo et al. 2004), the shearlet theory has been proposed (Labate et al. 2005; Guo et al. 2006; Guo and Labate 2007; Kutyniok and Lim 2011); see also the survey (Kutyniok et al. 2012a). It can be seen as a theoretical justification for contourlets (Easley et al. 2008). Several distinct numerical implementations of the Discrete Shearlet Transform exist, based either on a Fourier implementation or a spatial domain implementation. The Fourier-based implementation developed in (Easley et al. 2008) has the following steps:

- Apply the Laplacian pyramid scheme.
- Compute the pseudo-polar Fourier transform (PPFT) on each band of the Laplacian decomposition.
- Apply a directional band-pass filtering in the Fourier space.
- Apply an inverse two-dimensional FFT or use the inverse PPFT from the previous step on each directional band.

Kutyniok et al. (2012b) propose another approach based on a weighted pseudo-polar transform, followed by a windowing and an inverse FFT for each direction. This transform is associated with band-limited tight shearlet frames, thereby allowing the adjoint frame operator for reconstruction (Davenport et al. 2012).

Several spatial domain shearlet transforms have also been developed (Easley et al. 2008; Lim 2010; Kutyniok and Sauer 2009; Han et al. 2011; Kutyniok et al. 2014). Easley et al. (2008) utilizes directional filters, which are obtained as approximations of the inverse Fourier transforms of digitized band-limited window functions. In Lim (2010), the use of separable shearlet generators allows a fast transform. The most efficient digitalization of the shearlet transform was derived in Lim (2013) and Kutyniok et al. (2014) by utilizing non-separable compactly supported shearlet generators, which best approximate the classical band-limited generators. Shearlet codes are available at the webpages www.math.uh.edu/~dlabate (Easley et al. 2008) and www.ShearLab.org (Lim 2010; Kutyniok et al. 2012b, 2014).

5.5 CURVELETS AND CONTRAST ENHANCEMENT

Because some features are hardly detectable by eye in an image, we often transform it before display. Histogram equalization is one of the most well-known methods for contrast enhancement. Such an approach is generally useful for images with a poor intensity distribution. Since edges play a fundamental role in image understanding, a way to enhance the contrast is to enhance the edges. The very common approach is to add to the image a fraction of its Laplacian; the so-called sharpening method in image processing. However, with such a procedure, only features at the finest scale are enhanced (linearly) and noise may be unreasonably amplified.

Since the curvelet transform is well adapted to represent images containing edges, it is a good candidate for edge enhancement (Starck et al. 2003b). In order to enhance edges in an image, each of its curvelet coefficients can be modified by multiplying it by an appropriately chosen continuous enhancement function $\mathscr{E}$. Such a function must be even-symmetric to enhance the coefficients independently of their sign. In Starck et al. (2003b), the following choice was proposed:

$$\mathscr{E}(t;\sigma) := \begin{cases} 1 & \text{if } t < \tau\sigma \\ \frac{t-\tau\sigma}{\tau\sigma}\left(\frac{\mu}{\tau\sigma}\right)^{\gamma} + \frac{2\tau\sigma-t}{\tau\sigma} & \text{if } t < 2\tau\sigma \\ \left(\frac{\mu}{t}\right)^{\gamma} & \text{if } 2\tau\sigma \leq t < \mu \\ \left(\frac{\mu}{t}\right)^{\varrho} & \text{if } t \geq \mu \end{cases} \quad \forall t \geq 0,$$

where σ is the noise standard deviation. Four parameters are involved: γ, ϱ, μ and τ. γ determines the degree of nonlinearity in the nonlinear rescaling of the luminance, and must be in $[0, 1]$. $\varrho \geq 0$ introduces dynamic range compression. Using a nonzero ϱ will enhance the faintest edges and soften the strongest edges at the same time. τ is a normalization parameter, and a value of τ typically larger than 3 ensures that a coefficient with amplitude less than 3σ will be left untouched, i.e. the noise will not be amplified. The parameter μ is the value under which the coefficient is enhanced. It appears then natural to make the value of this parameter depend on the curvelet subband at scale j and orientation ℓ. Two options to automatically set this parameter are advocated:

- Variable μ can be derived from the noise standard deviation σ as $\mu = \tau_\mu \sigma$ using an extra parameter τ_μ. The advantage is that τ_μ has an intuitive meaning and is independent of the curvelet coefficient values, and therefore is easier to set. For instance, using $\tau = 3$ and $\tau_\mu = 10$ amplifies all coefficients with a SNR between 3 and 10.
- Variable μ can also be derived from the maximum curvelet coefficient at subband (j, ℓ) $\alpha_{j,\ell}^{\max} = \max_{\mathbf{k}} |\alpha_{j,\ell,\mathbf{k}}|$, i.e. $\mu = \rho\alpha_{j,\ell}^{\max}$, with $0 \leq \rho < 1$. Choosing for instance $\tau = 3$ and $\rho = 0.5$ will enhance all coefficients with an absolute value between 3σ and half the maximum absolute value of the subband.

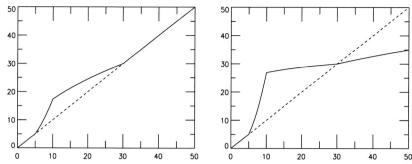

Figure 5.15. Enhanced coefficient versus original coefficient with $\sigma = 1$. Left, parameters are $(\gamma, \varrho, \mu, \tau) = (0.5, 0, 30, 3)$. Right, parameters are $(\gamma, \varrho, \mu, \tau) = (0.5, 0.6, 30, 3)$.

The first choice allows the user to define the coefficients to be amplified as a function of their signal to noise ratio, while the second one gives an easy alternative independent of the range of the original coefficients. Figure 5.15 exemplifies the obtained curve of $\mathscr{E}(t; \sigma)$ for two sets of parameters; $\sigma = 1$ in these plots.

To summarize, the curvelet-domain enhancement algorithm for grayscale is as follows:

Algorithm 19 Curvelet-Domain Contrast Enhancement

Task: Enhance the contrast of a discrete image f.
Parameters: Coarsest scale J, parameters $(\gamma, \varrho, \rho, \tau)$.

■ Estimate the noise standard deviation σ in the input image f.
■ Compute the curvelet transform of f to get $(\alpha_{j,\ell,\mathbf{k}})_{j,\ell,\mathbf{k}}$.
■ Compute the noise standard deviation $\sigma_{j,\ell}$ at each subband (j, ℓ) by multiplying σ by the ℓ_2-norm of the curvelet at subband (j, ℓ); see the end of Section 5.4.2.2. (If the ℓ_2 norms are not known in closed form, they can be estimated in practice by taking the transform of a Dirac image, and then computing the ℓ_2 norm of each subband.)

for Each scale j and orientation ℓ **do**

    1. Compute the maximum of the subband: $\alpha_{j,\ell}^{\max} = \max_{\mathbf{k}} |\alpha_{j,\ell,\mathbf{k}}|$.
    2. Compute the modified coefficient: $\tilde{\alpha}_{j,\ell,\mathbf{k}} = \alpha_{j,\ell,\mathbf{k}}\mathscr{E}(|\alpha_{j,\ell,\mathbf{k}}|; \sigma_{j,\ell})$.

■ Reconstruct the enhanced image $\tilde{f}$ from the modified curvelet coefficients.

Output: Contrast-enhanced image $\tilde{f}$.

For color images, the contrast enhancement approach can be applied according to the following steps:

■ Convert the original color image to the Luv color space.
■ Compute the curvelet transform of the L, u and v color components. Get the curvelet coefficients $(\alpha_{j,\ell,\mathbf{k}}^{L}, \alpha_{j,\ell,\mathbf{k}}^{u}, \alpha_{j,\ell,\mathbf{k}}^{v})_{j,\ell,\mathbf{k}}$.

Figure 5.16. (left) Grayscale image. (right) Curvelet enhanced image.

- Compute the magnitude of the "color" curvelet coefficient as $a_{j,\ell,\mathbf{k}} = \sqrt{(\alpha^L_{j,\ell,\mathbf{k}})^2 + (\alpha^u_{j,\ell,\mathbf{k}})^2 + (\alpha^v_{j,\ell,\mathbf{k}})^2}$.
- Compute the modified coefficients

$$\left(\tilde{\alpha}^L_{j,\ell,\mathbf{k}}, \tilde{\alpha}^u_{j,\ell,\mathbf{k}}, \tilde{\alpha}^v_{j,\ell,\mathbf{k}}\right)$$
$$= \left(\alpha^L_{j,\ell,\mathbf{k}}\mathscr{E}(|a_{j,\ell,\mathbf{k}}|; \sigma_{j,\ell}), \alpha^u_{j,\ell,\mathbf{k}}\mathscr{E}(|a_{j,\ell,\mathbf{k}}|; \sigma_{j,\ell}), \alpha^v_{j,\ell,\mathbf{k}}\mathscr{E}(|a_{j,\ell,\mathbf{k}}|; \sigma_{j,\ell})\right).$$

- Compute the inverse curvelet transform of each of $\tilde{\alpha}^L_{j,\ell,\mathbf{k}}, \tilde{\alpha}^u_{j,\ell,\mathbf{k}}$ and $\tilde{\alpha}^v_{j,\ell,\mathbf{k}}$.
- Convert from Luv to the original color space.

It may happen that the values in the enhanced color components can be larger than the authorized dynamic range (in general 255), and it may be necessary to incorporate a final step to this method, which is a gain/offset selection applied uniformly to the three color components, as described by Jobson et al. (1997).

Figure 5.16 shows the results for the enhancement of a grayscale satellite image of Marseille port. The parameters used were $(\gamma, \varrho, \rho, \tau) = (0.5, 0, 0.5, 3)$.

Figure 5.17 shows respectively a part of the Saturn image, the histogram equalized image, the enhanced image based on the (Laplacian) sharpening method, and the curvelet multiscale edge enhanced image (with parameters $(\gamma, \varrho, \rho, \tau) = (0.5, 0, 0.5, 3)$). The curvelet multiscale edge enhanced image reveals much better the rings and edges of Saturn while controlling the noise.

5.6 GUIDED NUMERICAL EXPERIMENTS

5.6.1 Software

The pedagogical numerical experiments of this chapter are conducted using both WaveLab and CurveLab toolboxes. The WaveLab toolbox was introduced in Section 2.9.1 of Chapter 2. CurveLab is a collection of C files, Mex Matlab code and Matlab routines that implement the second generation curvelet transform.

Figure 5.17. (top left) Saturn image and (top right) its histogram equalization. (bottom left) Saturn image enhancement by the (Laplacian) sharpening method and (bottom right) using the curvelet transform.

CurveLab is available for download at http://www.curvelet.org, and this is linked to from the book's software site, http://www.SparseSignalRecipes.info.

5.6.2 Sparse Representation using DCTG2

The following Matlab code uses WaveLab and CurveLab to illustrate how the DCTG2 is able to sparsely represent the "Barbara" image and produces Figure 5.18. It also compares the DCTG2 to the undecimated wavelet transform (UWT).

```
% Read image;
img = fliplr(rot90(ReadImage('Barbara'),-1));
[N,J] = quadlength(img);
subplot(221);imagesc(img);axis image;axis off;colormap('gray')
set(gca,'FontSize',14);
title('(a)');
```

(a)   (b)

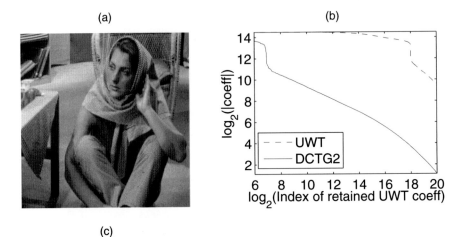

(c)

Figure 5.18. (a) Original "Barbara" image. (b) The DCTG2 and UWT coefficients in decreasing order of magnitude. (c) Reconstruction from the 2 percent DCTG2 largest coefficients.

```
% Coarsest decomposition scale.
coarsest = 2;

% Generate Symmlet 4 CMF Filter.
qmf = MakeONFilter('Symmlet',4);

% Compute UWT and DWT of noisy image.
uwc = FWT2_TI(img,coarsest,qmf);

% Plot sorted UWT coeffs.
swc  = sort(abs(uwc(:)),1,'descend');
subplot(222);plot(log2(1:(3*(J-coarsest)+1)*N*N),log2(swc),'--');
set(gca,'FontSize',14,'XTick',[0:2:log2((3*(J-coarsest)+1)*N*N)]);
xlabel('log_2(Index of retained DWT coeff)');ylabel('log_2(|coeff])');
title('(b)');
```

```
% Take DCTG2 transform.
C = fdct_wrapping(img,1,J-coarsest);

% DCTG2 implements a Parseval tight frame
% and the curvelets have l_2 norm  = 1/sqrt(redundancy).
Cvec = C{1}{1}(:);
nb=prod(size(C{1}{1}));
for j=2:length(C)
  for w=1:length(C{j})
    nb=nb+prod(size(C{j}{w}));
    Cvec = [Cvec;C{j}{w}(:)];
  end
end
E = N/sqrt(nb);

% Plot sorted UWT coeffs.
sC   = sort(abs(Cvec(:)/E),1,'descend');
subplot(222);hold on;plot(log2(1:nb),log2(sC));hold off;
axis([6 20 log2(sC(2^20)) log2(swc(2^6))]);
legend('UWT','DCTG2','Location','Best');
title('(b)');

% Keep only 2% of DCTG2 coefficients.
thd = sC(floor(nb*0.02));
Ct = C;
for j=2:length(C)
  for w = 1:length(C{j})
    Ct{j}{w} = C{j}{w}.* (abs(C{j}{w}) >= thd*E);
  end
end

% Take inverse curvelet transform
imrdctg2 = real(ifdct_wrapping(Ct,1,J-coarsest));

subplot(223)
imagesc(imrdctg2);axis image;axis off
set(gca,'FontSize',14);
title('(c)');
```

Figure 5.18(b) depicts both the DCTG2 and UWT coefficients in decreasing order of magnitude. This image contains many highly anisotropic structures. The superiority of DCTG2 over UWT is then obvious. The reconstruction from the 2% DCTG2 largest coefficients is given in Figure 5.18(c). The difference with the original image is visually weak.

(a)   (b)

(c)   (d)

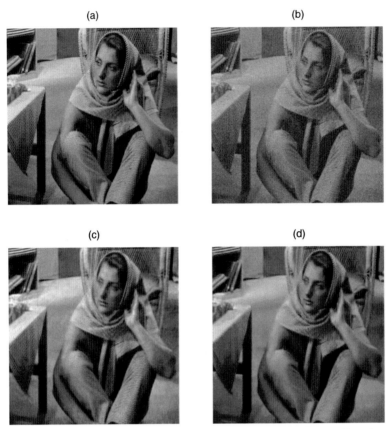

Figure 5.19. (a) Original "Barbara" image and (b) its noisy version with noise standard deviation $\sigma = 20$. (c) Denoised image by the DCTG2 (PSNR = 28.2 dB). (d) Denoised image by the UWT (PSNR = 26.5 dB).

5.6.3 Denoising using DCTG2

Suppose that we want to restore a piecewise regular image (away from regular contours) contaminated by additive white Gaussian noise of standard deviation σ. A simple strategy based on hard thresholding DCTG2 coefficients yields an estimator that achieves a mean square error (MSE) almost of the order $O(\sigma^{4/3})$ uniformly over the $C^2 - C^2$ class of functions (Candès and Donoho 2002). This is the optimal rate of convergence as the minimax rate for that class scales as $\sigma^{4/3}$ (Candès and Donoho 2002). Comparatively, wavelet thresholding methods only achieve a MSE $O(\sigma)$ and no better. We also note that the statistical optimality of the curvelet thresholding extends to a large class of ill-posed linear inverse problems (Candès and Donoho 2002).

In the experiment of Figure 5.19, we added Gaussian white noise with $\sigma = 20$ to the "Barbara" image. The denoising performance is measured in terms of PSNR as defined in (3.7) in Chapter 3. The code to generate this figure is as follows.

```
% Read image;
img = fliplr(rot90(ReadImage('Barbara'),-1));
[N,J] = quadlength(img);
% Add AWGN.
imn = img + 20*randn(size(img));

% Coarsest decomposition scale.
coarsest = 2;

% Generate Symmlet 4 CMF Filter.
qmf = MakeONFilter('Symmlet',4);

% Compute UWT of noisy image.
uwc = FWT2_TI(imn,coarsest,qmf);

% Estimate noise std from diagonal band at finest scale.
hh = uwc(2*N+1:3*N,:);
sigma = MAD(hh(:));

% Hard-threshold UWT coeffs: finest scale at 4*sigma and
% other scales at 3*sigma.
% Finest:
uwc(1:3*N,:)       = HardThresh(uwc(1:3*N,:),4*sigma);
% Other scales:
uwc(3*N+1:end-N,:) = HardThresh(uwc(3*N+1:end-N,:),3*sigma);

% Reconstruct.
imdenuwt = IWT2_TI(uwc,coarsest,qmf);

% Take DCTG2 transform.
C = fdct_wrapping(imn,1,J-coarsest);

% DCTG2 implements a Parseval tight frame
% and the curvelets have l_2 norm  = 1/sqrt(redundancy).
nb=prod(size(C{1}{1}));
for j=2:length(C)
  for w=1:length(C{j})
    nb=nb+prod(size(C{j}{w}));
  end
end
E = N/sqrt(nb);

% Hard-threshold UWT coeffs: finest scale at 4*sigma and
% other scales at 3*sigma.
Ct = C;
```

```
for j=2:length(C)
  thresh = 3*sigma + sigma*(j == length(C));
  for w=1:length(C{j})
    Ct{j}{w} = C{j}{w}.* (abs(C{j}{w}) > thresh*E);
  end
end

% Take inverse curvelet transform
imdendctg2 = real(ifdct_wrapping(Ct,1,J-coarsest));

% Display.
subplot(221)
imagesc(img);axis image;axis off;colormap('gray')
set(gca,'FontSize',14);
title('(a)');
subplot(222)
imagesc(imn);axis image;axis off
set(gca,'FontSize',14);
title('(b)');
subplot(223)
imagesc(imdendctg2);axis image;axis off
set(gca,'FontSize',14);
title('(c)');
subplot(224)
imagesc(imdenuwt);axis image;axis off
set(gca,'FontSize',14);
title('(d)');
```

Figure 5.19(c) and Figure 5.19(d) show the restored images by the DCTG2 and the UWT, respectively. Contours and stripes on the trousers and scarf are much better recovered with the DCTG2.

5.7 SUMMARY

In this chapter we have gone beyond point symmetric or other compact features to model alignments and curved shapes in images. The ridgelet and curvelet transforms are used for this. We have shown curvelet efficiency in a range of case studies. Considerable attention has been paid to fast and practical aspects and algorithms.

Concerning the contrast enhancement, our conclusions are as follows:

(i) The curvelet enhancement function takes very good account of the image geometry to enhance the edges, while avoiding noise amplification.

(ii) As evidenced by the experiments with the curvelet transform, there is better detection of noisy contours than with other methods.

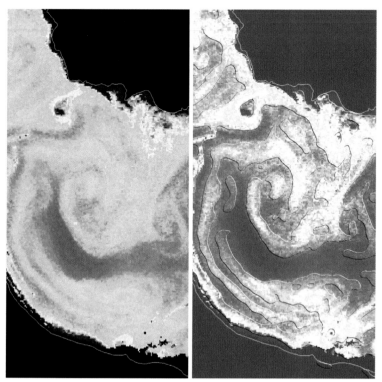

Figure 1.3. (left) SeaWiFS image of the Gulf of Oman region and (right) resolution-scale information superimposed.

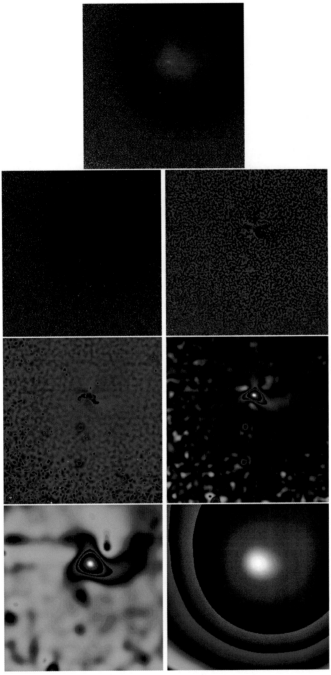

Figure 1.4. (top) Original comet image. Then, successively, wavelet scales 1, 2, 3, 4, 5 and the smooth subband are shown. The starlet transform is used. The images are false color coded to show the faint contrast.

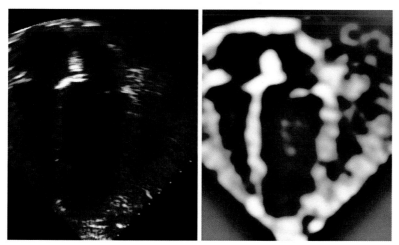

Figure 1.5. (left) chocardiograph image, with typical textual annotation (date, location, patient, etc.) removed. (right) Wavelet filtered image.

Figure 3.8. Galaxy NGC 2997. The false colors correspond to an artificial color map.

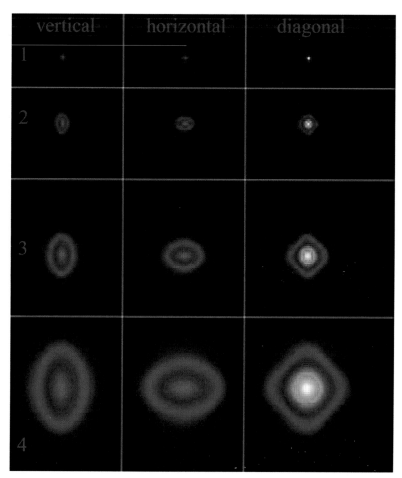

Figure 3.11. Backprojection: Each image corresponds to the inverse transform of one wavelet coefficient. All these reconstructed images are positive (no negative values). From left to right, the coefficient belongs to the vertical, horizontal, and diagonal direction. From top to bottom, the scale index increases.

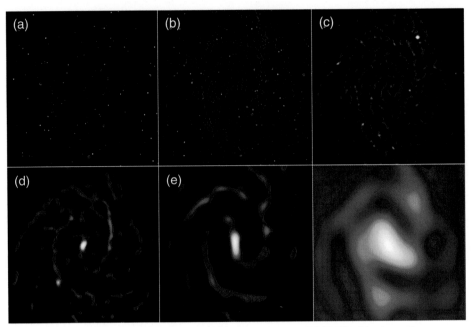

Figure 3.14. Positive starlet decomposition of the galaxy NGC2997 with six scales.

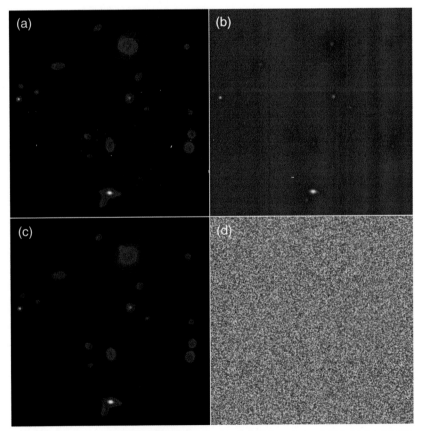

Figure 3.15. Top left and right, original simulated image and the same image contaminated by a Gaussian noise. Bottom left and right, reconstructed image for the positive starlet coefficients of the noisy image using 50 iterations, and residual (i.e., noisy image − reconstructed image).

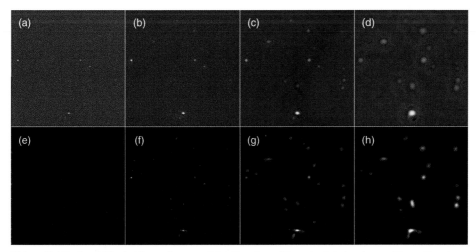

Figure 3.16. (top) Starlet transform and (bottom) positive starlet decomposition of a simulated astronomical image.

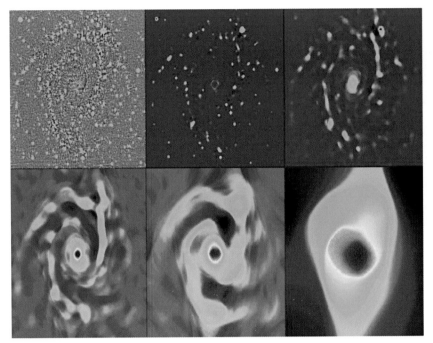

Figure 4.2. Multiscale median transform of the galaxy NGC 2997 (see Figure 3.8).

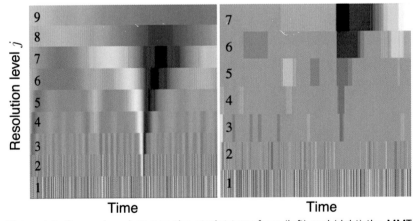

Figure 4.4. Comparison between the starlet transform (left) and (right) the MMT of the signal from Figure 4.3. We note that the separation between the source and the glitch is improved using the MMT.

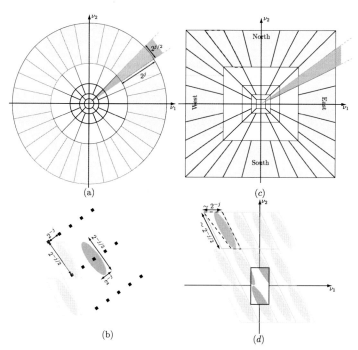

Figure 5.13. (a) Continuous curvelet frequency tiling. The gray area represents a wedge obtained as the product of the radial window (annulus shown in lighter color) and the angular window (darker color). (b) The Cartesian grid in space associated with the construction in (a) whose spacing also obeys the parabolic scaling by duality. (c) Discrete curvelet frequency tiling. The window $\hat{u}_{j,\ell}$ isolates the frequency near the trapezoidal wedge such as the ones shown in gray. (d) The wrapping transformation. The dashed line shows the same trapezoidal wedge as in (b). The parallelogram contains this wedge and hence the support of the curvelet. After periodization, the wrapped Fourier samples can be collected in the rectangle centered at the origin.

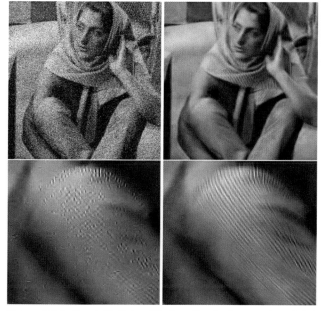

Figure 6.11. (top left) Noisy "Barbara" color image. (top right) Denoised image using the curvelet transform. (bottom) Details of the denoised images are shown on the left (UWT) and right (curvelet transform).

Figure 9.8. Inpainting color images. (top left) Original "Barbara" color image (left) and (top right) a zoom on the scarf. (middle) Masked image – 90 percent of the color pixels are missing. (bottom) Inpainted image using the adaptive GMCA algorithm.

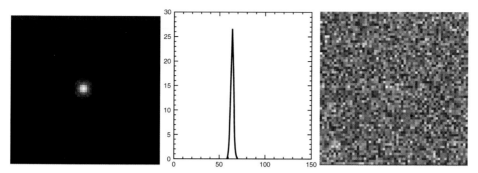

Figure 11.3. Simulated time-varying source. From left to right, simulated source, temporal flux, and co-added image along the time axis of noisy data.

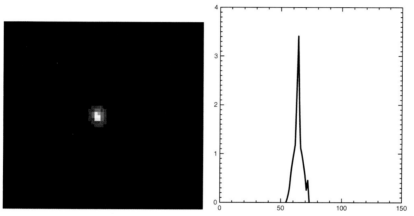

Figure 11.4. Recovered time-varying source after 2-D–1-D MS-VST denoising. One frame of the denoised cube (left) and flux per frame (right).

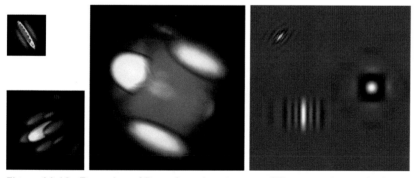

Figure 11.12. Examples of BeamCurvelet atoms at different scales and orientations. These are 3-D density plots: the values near zero are transparent, and the opacity grows with the absolute value of the voxels. Positive values are red/yellow, and negative values are blue/purple. The right map is a slice of a cube containing these three atoms in the same position as on the left. The top left atom has an arbitrary direction, the bottom left is in the slice, and the right one is normal to the slice.

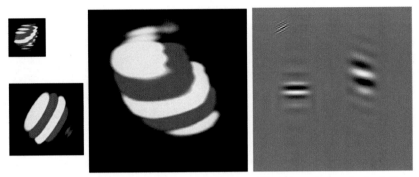

Figure 11.14. Examples of RidCurvelet atoms at different scales and orientation. The rendering is similar to that of Figure 11.12. The right plot is a slice from a cube containing the three atoms shown here.

Figure 11.15. (left to right) A 3-D view of the cube containing pieces of shells and a spring-shaped filament, a slice of the previous cube, and finally a slice from the noisy cube.

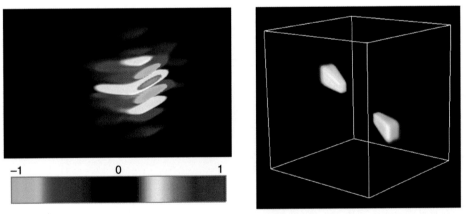

Figure 11.20. (left) Volume rendering of a 3-D curvelet atom in the spatial domain corresponding to our implementation, cut by a vertical plane to see its inner structure. (right) The magnitude of its Fourier transform. The colorbar scale is valid only for the left image.

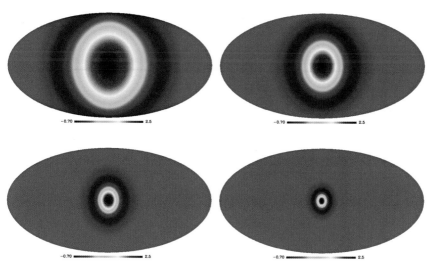

Figure 12.3. Mexican hat on the sphere for the dilation parameter equal to $a = \{1, 2, 4, 8\}$.

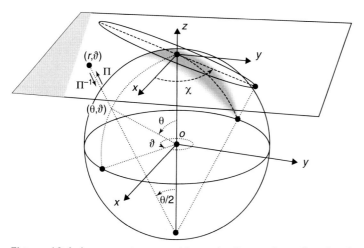

Figure 12.4. Inverse stereographic projections of a directional wavelet on the sphere.

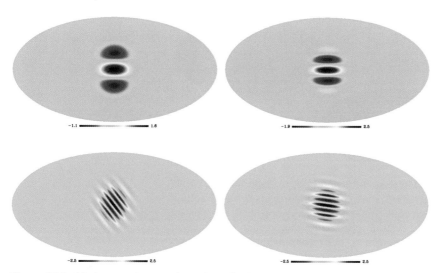

Figure 12.6. Morlet wavelets on the sphere for the parameter **k** equal to (2,0), (4,0), (6,6) et (9,1).

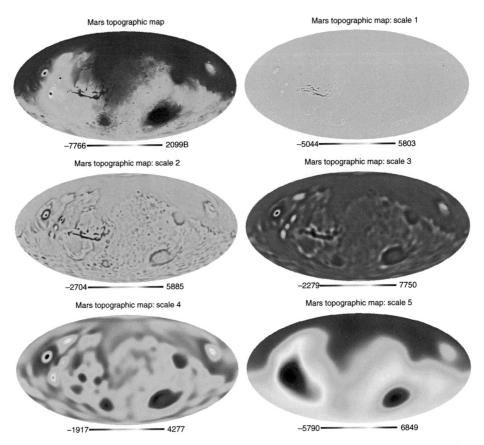

Figure 12.8. Mars topographic map and its UWTS (four wavelet detail scales and the scaling (smooth) band).

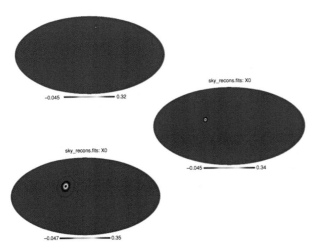

Figure 12.10. Reconstruction from a single wavelet coefficient at different scales. Each map is obtained by setting all wavelet coefficients to zero but one, and by applying an inverse UWTS. Depending on the position and scale of the nonzero coefficient, the reconstructed map shows an isotropic feature at different scales and positions.

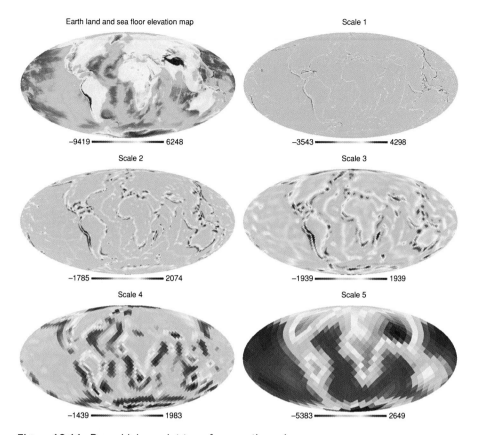

Figure 12.11. Pyramidal wavelet transform on the sphere.

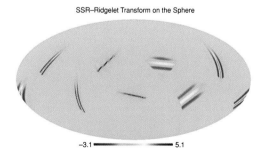

Figure 12.13. Ridgelet atoms on the sphere obtained by reconstruction from a few ridgelet coefficient at different scales and orientations.

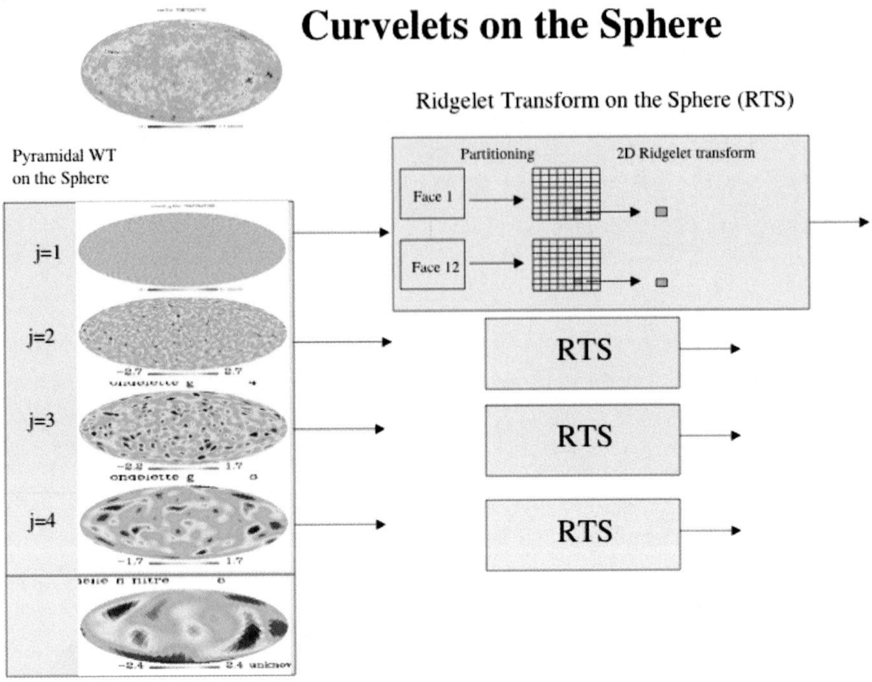

Curvelets on the Sphere

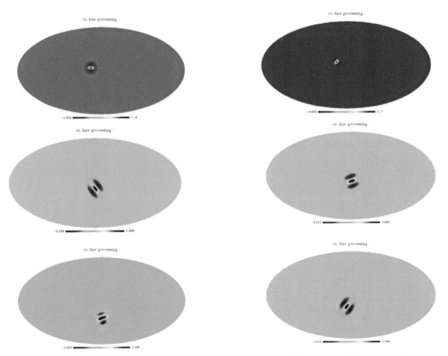

Ridgelet Transform on the Sphere (RTS)

Pyramidal WT
on the Sphere

Partitioning   2D Ridgelet transform

Face 1

Face 12

j=1

j=2

onaelette g

j=3

onaelette g

j=4

sene n ntre   o

RTS

RTS

RTS

Figure 12.14. Flow graph of the curvelet transform on the sphere.

Figure 12.15. Reconstruction from a single curvelet coefficient at different scales and orientations.

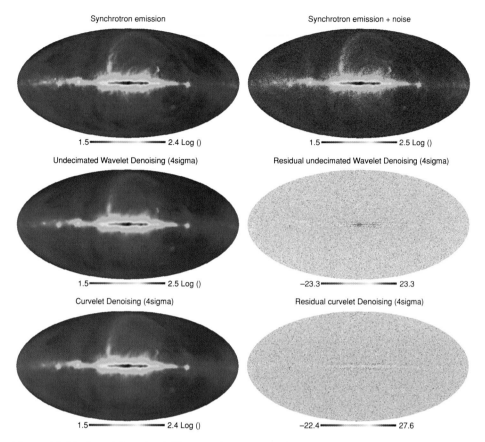

Figure 12.16. Denoising. (top) Simulated synchrotron image and same image with additive Gaussian noise (i.e., simulated data). (middle) Undecimated wavelet filtering and residual. (bottom) Pyramidal curvelet filtering and residual.

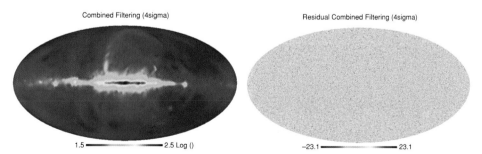

Figure 12.17. Combined denoising (using both wavelets and curvelets) and residuals.

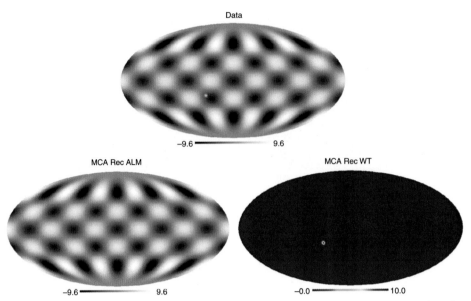

Figure 12.18. Simple toy experiment with MCA on the sphere. (top) Linear combination of a spherical harmonic function and a localized Gaussian-like function on the sphere. (bottom) Resulting separated components obtained using the proposed MCA on the sphere.

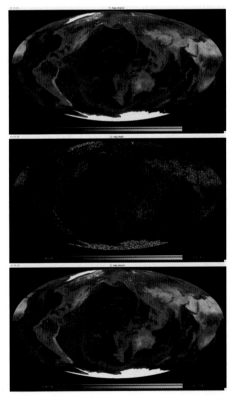

Figure 12.19. Application of the proposed MCA-inpainting algorithm on the sphere. (top) Original satellite view of the Earth. (middle) Incomplete map retaining 40 percent of the original pixels. (bottom) Inpainted map.

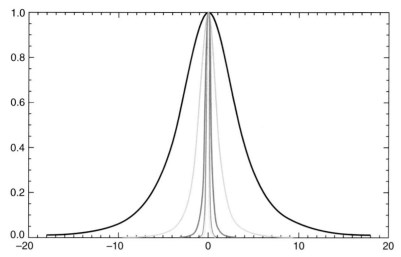

Figure 12.20. Normalized profile of the PSF for different energy bands as a function of the angle in degree. <u>Black:</u> 50 MeV – 82 MeV. <u>Cyan:</u> 220 MeV – 360 MeV. <u>Orange:</u> 960 MeV – 1.6 GeV. <u>Blue:</u> 4.2 GeV – 6.9 GeV. <u>Green:</u> 19 GeV – 31 GeV.

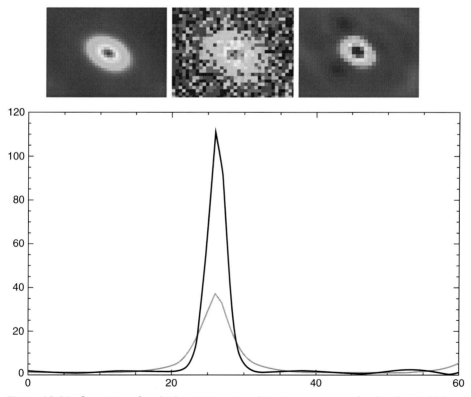

Figure 12.21. Spectrum of a single gamma-ray point source recovered using the multichannel MS-VSTS deconvolution algorithm. <u>Top:</u> Single gamma-ray point source on simulated (blurred) Fermi data (energy band: 360 MeV – 589 MeV) (<u>left:</u> simulated blurred source; <u>middle:</u> blurred noisy source; <u>right:</u> deconvolved source). <u>Bottom:</u> Spectrum profile of the center of the point source (<u>cyan:</u> simulated spectrum; <u>black:</u> restored spectrum from the deconvolved source.

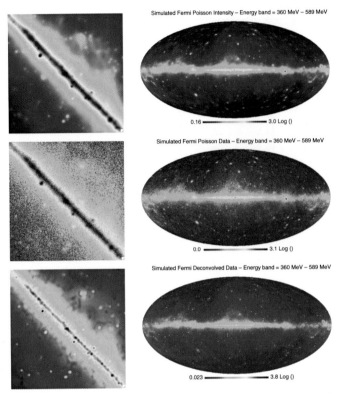

Simulated Fermi Poisson Intensity – Energy band = 360 MeV – 589 MeV

0.16 ━━━━ 3.0 Log ()

Simulated Fermi Poisson Data – Energy band = 360 MeV – 589 MeV

0.0 ━━━━ 3.1 Log ()

Simulated Fermi Deconvolved Data – Energy band = 360 MeV – 589 MeV

0.023 ━━━━ 3.8 Log ()

Figure 12.22. Result of the deconvolution algorithm in the 360 MeV – 589 MeV energy band. The left images are single HEALPix faces covering the galactic plane. <u>Top Left:</u> Simulated Fermi Poisson intensity. <u>Top Right:</u> Simulated Fermi noisy data. <u>Bottom:</u> Fermi data deconvolved with multichannel MS-VSTS.

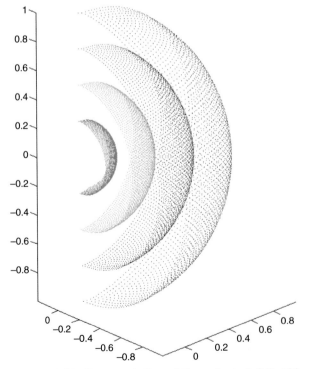

Figure 12.23. Representation of the spherical 3-D grid for the discrete spherical Fourier-Bessel transform ($R = 1$ and $N_{max} = 4$)

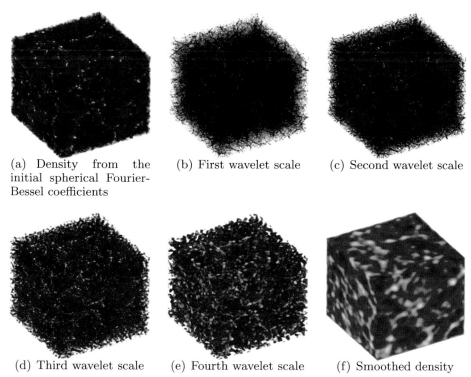

(a) Density from the initial spherical Fourier-Bessel coefficients

(b) First wavelet scale

(c) Second wavelet scale

(d) Third wavelet scale

(e) Fourth wavelet scale

(f) Smoothed density

Figure 12.26. Isotropic undecimated spherical 3-D wavelet decomposition of a density field. Only a cube at the center of the spherical field is displayed.

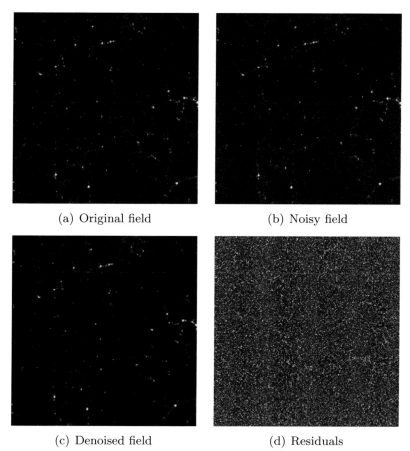

(a) Original field

(b) Noisy field

(c) Denoised field

(d) Residuals

Figure 12.27. Isotropic undecimated spherical 3-D wavelet hard-thresholding applied to a test density field.

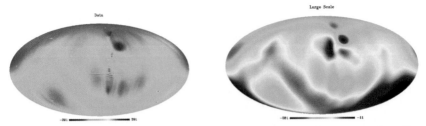

Figure 12.28. (left) Surface structures of ICF spherical shells measured on the nanometer scale are a superposition of global-scale variations, isolated bumps and scratches, as well as artifacts that look like interference patterns on intermediate scales. (right) Coarsest scale of the undecimated isotropic wavelet transform of the surface measurements of an ICF target.

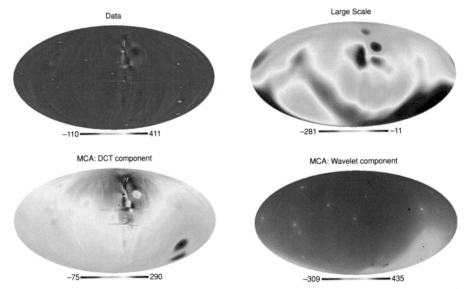

Figure 12.29. (top) Spherical map obtained by subtracting the coarse-scale map of Fig. 12.28 (right) from the initial map of Fig. 12.28 (left). (bottom) Component maps separated by the MCA method on the sphere: (left) interference patterns and measurement artifacts were caught by the local cosine functions on the sphere. whereas (right) the isolated bumps were caught using the undecimated wavelet on the sphere. Adding back the coarse scale of Fig. 12.28 (right) to the latter map results in a clean map of the surface structures of an ICF spherical shell with the interference patterns and artifacts removed.

Figure 12.30. (left) CMB data map provided by the Wilkinson microwave anisotropy probe (WMAP) team. Areas of significant foreground contamination in the galactic region and at the locations of strong radio point sources have been masked out. (right) Map obtained by applying the MCA-inpainting algorithm on the sphere to the former incomplete WMAP CMB data map.

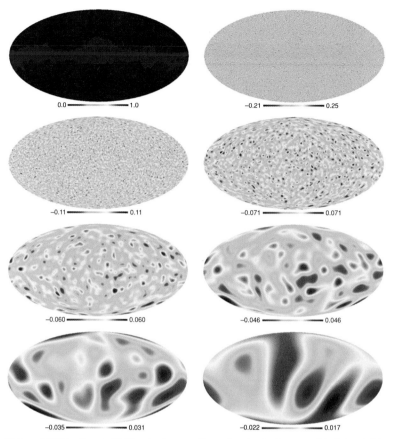

Figure 12.31. (top left) Masked area. From top to bottom and left to right, the seven wavelet scales of the inpainted map. From the visual point of view, the initially masked area cannot be distinguished any more in the wavelet scales of the inpainted map.

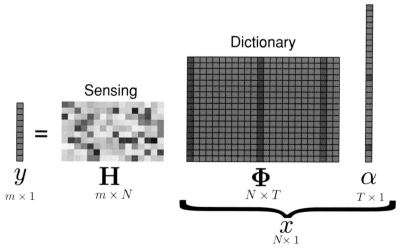

Figure 13.1. The compressed or compressive sensing paradigm. Each row of **H** is a question asked of the signal.

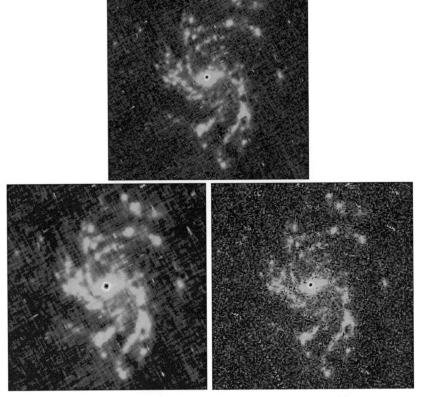

Figure 13.4. Map estimations of NGC 6946: top, reference map without any compression; bottom left, ESA pipeline using the averaging solution; and bottom right, CS solution. All maps have the same scale.

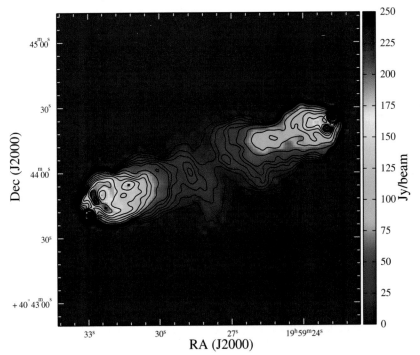

Figure 14.1. Color scale: reconstructed 512×512 image of Cygnus A at 151 MHz (with resolution 2.8″ and a pixel size of 1″). Contour levels from a 327.5 MHz Cyg A VLA image at 2.5″ angular resolution and a pixel size of 0.5″. Most of the recovered features in the image were reconstructed using sparsity regularization corresponding to real structures observed at higher frequencies.

6

Sparsity and Noise Removal

6.1 INTRODUCTION

In this chapter, we are interested in recovering X of N equally-spaced samples acquired on a regular d-dimensional grid ($d = 1$ for 1-D signals and $d = 2$ for 2-D images), from its noisy measurements Y:

$$Y[k] = X[k] \odot \varepsilon[k] \qquad k = 1, \ldots, N, \tag{6.1}$$

where ε is the contaminating noise, and $\odot$ is any composition of two arguments (e.g. $+$ for additive noise, $\times$ for multiplicative noise, etc.). This ill-posed problem is known as denoising, and is a long-standing problem in signal and image processing. Denoising can be efficiently attacked under the umbrella of sparse representations. Indeed, if the sought after signal is known to be sparse (or compressible) in some transform domain (such as those discussed in the previous chapters), it is legitimate to assume that essentially only a few large coefficients will contain information about the underlying signal, while small values can be attributed to the noise which contaminates all transform coefficients. The classical modus operandi is then to first apply the transform analysis operator (denoted $\mathbf{T}$) to the noisy data Y, then apply a nonlinear estimation rule $\mathcal{D}$ to the coefficients (each coefficient individually or as a group of coefficients), and finally compute the inverse transform (denoted $\mathbf{R}$) to get an estimate $\tilde{X}$. In brief,

$$\tilde{X} = \mathbf{R}\mathcal{D}\,(\mathbf{T}Y)\,. \tag{6.2}$$

This approach has already proven to be very successful on both practical and theoretical sides (Starck and Murtagh 2006; Härdle et al. 1998; Johnstone 1999, 2002). In particular, it is well established that the quality of the estimation is closely linked to the sparsity of the sequence of coefficients representing X in the transform domain. To make this precise, suppose that the noise in (6.1) is additive white Gaussian with variance σ^2, i.e. $\varepsilon[k] \sim \mathcal{N}(0, \sigma^2)$, $\forall k$. Assume also that the transform corresponds to an orthonormal basis, and $\mathcal{D}$ is the hard thresholding operator (see (6.12) below).

Donoho and Johnstone (1994) have shown that if the m-term nonlinear approximation error of X in the transform decays as

$$\|X - X_m\|^2 \leq Cm^{-\kappa} \, ,$$

then there is a constant $C' > 0$ such that

$$\mathbb{E}(\|X - \tilde{X}\|^2) \leq C' \sigma^{\frac{2\kappa}{\kappa+1}} \, .$$

See also Korostelev and Tsybakov (1993) for similar results on geometrical 2-D image denoising. This clearly underlies the central role of sparsity in the performance of denoising.

In this chapter, we will first describe popular term-by-term denoising techniques as well as an efficient non-Bayesian block thresholding methods to remove white Gaussian noise. Then we will discuss how to deal with more complex types of noise beyond the classical additive white noise model mostly considered in the literature. In particular, we will show that the Haar wavelet transform has very useful properties for the case of Poisson noise. In the case of Poisson noise with very low-count regime (photon-limited imaging), we introduce the Multiscale Variance Stabilization Transform (MS-VST), which allows us to remove Poisson noise with different multiscale representations such as wavelets, ridgelets and curvelets.

6.1.0.1 The Coefficient Sequence

We here give unified notation that will be used throughout the rest of the chapter, and will cover all the transforms that we have described in the previous chapters. Let $\mathbf{\Phi}$ be a dictionary whose columns are $(\varphi_{j,\ell,\mathbf{k}})_{j,\ell,\mathbf{k}}$, a collection of atoms. The notation of the indices is that of multiscale transforms considered so far (wavelet, curvelet, etc.), generally corresponding to frames or orthobases. Here, j and $\mathbf{k} = (k_1, \dots, k_d)$ are respectively the scale and position parameters, and d is the dimension of the data. ℓ is a generic integer indexing for example the orientation which may be scale-dependent. For example, in 2-D, we have one orientation for the starlet, three for the separable wavelet transform, and $\sim 2^{j/2}$ for the second generation curvelet transform.

Set $\alpha_{j,\ell,\mathbf{k}} := \langle X, \varphi_{j,\ell,\mathbf{k}} \rangle$ as the unknown frame coefficients of the true data X, $\beta_{j,\ell,\mathbf{k}} := \langle Y, \varphi_{j,\ell,\mathbf{k}} \rangle$ are the observed coefficients, and $\eta_{j,\ell,\mathbf{k}}$ is the noise sequence in the transform domain.

6.2 TERM-BY-TERM NONLINEAR DENOISING

Term-by-term denoising corresponds to the case where the operator $\mathcal{D}$ in (6.2) is applied to each coefficient *individually*, independently of the rest of the coefficients.

6.2.1 Thresholding as Hypothesis Testing

To get a denoised version of X, one has to decide which transform coefficients $\beta_{j,\ell,\mathbf{k}}$ are to be kept (due to useful signal, i.e. significant), and which are to be zeroed (due essentially to noise fluctuations, i.e. insignificant). This decision can be cast as binary hypothesis testing carried out individually in a coefficient-by-coefficient manner. For each coefficient $\beta_{j,\ell,\mathbf{k}}$, we test the following hypothesis:

$$H_0 : \alpha_{j,\ell,\mathbf{k}} = 0 \quad \text{against} \quad H_1 : \alpha_{j,\ell,\mathbf{k}} \neq 0 \,, \tag{6.3}$$

where H_0 is the null hypothesis and H_1 is the alternative. For wavelets and curvelets, H_0 can also be interpreted as saying that the data X are locally constant at scale j, orientation ℓ and around position $\mathbf{k}$, i.e. $\alpha_{j,\ell,\mathbf{k}} = 0$ (indeed, wavelet or curvelet coefficients computed from locally homogeneous parts of the data are zero-valued for sufficiently regular wavelets and curvelets).

Rejection of hypothesis H_0 depends on the double-sided p-value of each coefficient:

$$p = \mathscr{P}(U > |\beta_{j,\ell,\mathbf{k}}| \| H_0) + \mathscr{P}(U < -|\beta_{j,\ell,\mathbf{k}}| \| H_0) \,. \tag{6.4}$$

Given a type 1 error level, α, if $p > \alpha$ the null hypothesis is not excluded. Although non-zero, the value of the coefficient could be due to noise. On the other hand, if $p \leq \alpha$, the coefficient value is likely not to be due to the noise alone, and so the null hypothesis is rejected. In this case, a significant coefficient has been detected.

A key step to put equation (6.4) into practice is to specify the distribution of the coefficient $\beta_{j,\ell,\mathbf{k}}$ under the null hypothesis H_0. This is the challenging part of thresholding by hypothesis testing as it requires study of the distribution of $\eta_{j,\ell,\mathbf{k}}$ under the null hypothesis, which also amounts to investigating how the distribution of the noise ε in the original domain translates into the transform domain. We first consider in the following subsection the additive Gaussian case.

6.2.1.1 Additive Gaussian Noise

Assume that $\eta_{j,\ell,\mathbf{k}}$ is additive zero-mean Gaussian, with subband dependent standard deviation $\sigma_{j,\ell}$, or equivalently,

$$\beta_{j,\ell,\mathbf{k}} \sim \mathcal{N}(\alpha_{j,\ell,\mathbf{k}}, \sigma_{j,\ell}^2) \,. \tag{6.5}$$

This is typically the case when a zero-mean white Gaussian noise in the original domain, ε, is transformed into a zero-mean colored Gaussian process whose covariance is dictated by the Gram matrix of the dictionary Φ.

Thus, the double-symmetric p-value in (6.4) is given by

$$p = 2 \frac{1}{\sqrt{2\pi}\sigma_{j,\ell}} \int_{|\beta_{j,\ell,\mathbf{k}}|}^{+\infty} e^{-t^2/2\sigma_{j,\ell}^2} dt = 2(1 - \Phi(|\beta_{j,\ell,\mathbf{k}}|/\sigma_{j,\ell})) \,, \tag{6.6}$$

where $\Phi(.)$ is the standard normal cumulative distribution function.

Equivalently, for a given type 1 error level α, one can compute the critical threshold level as

$$\tau = \Phi^{-1}(1 - \alpha/2) \,, \tag{6.7}$$

and then threshold the coefficients $\beta_{j,\ell,\mathbf{k}}$ with threshold $\tau\sigma_{j,\ell}$ by declaring

$$\begin{aligned} &\text{if } |\beta_{j,\ell,\mathbf{k}}| \geq \tau\sigma_{j,\ell} \quad \text{then } \beta_{j,\ell,\mathbf{k}} \text{ is significant} \,, \\ &\text{if } |\beta_{j,\ell,\mathbf{k}}| < \tau\sigma_{j,\ell} \quad \text{then } \beta_{j,\ell,\mathbf{k}} \text{ is not significant} \,. \end{aligned} \tag{6.8}$$

Often τ is chosen as 3, which corresponds to $\alpha = 0.0027$.

6.2.1.2 Noise Level Estimation

The final step before applying equation (6.6) is to know the values of σ and $\sigma_{j,\ell}$ at each level and orientation, or to estimate them from the observed noisy data. For a stationary additive Gaussian noise ε, this can be done quite easily. For other noise models, the picture becomes less clear, although appropriate strategies can be developed for some noise models as we will see later for the Poisson case.

Variable ε is additive white Gaussian

To estimate σ, the usual standard deviation of the data values is clearly not a good estimator, unless the underlying signal X is reasonably flat. Donoho and Johnstone (1994) considered estimating σ in the orthogonal wavelet domain and suggested a robust estimator that is based only on the wavelet coefficients of the noisy data Y at the finest resolution level. The reason is that the wavelet coefficients of Y at the finest scale tend to consist mostly of noise, while the wavelet coefficients of X at that scale are very sparse and can be viewed as outliers. Donoho and Johnstone (1994) proposed the estimator

$$\tilde{\sigma} = \mathrm{MAD}(w_1)/0.6745 = \mathrm{median}(|w_1 - \mathrm{median}(w_1)|)/0.6745 \,, \qquad (6.9)$$

where MAD stands for the median absolute deviation, and w_1 are the orthogonal wavelet coefficients of Y at the finest scale. For 2-D images, the above estimator is to be applied with the diagonal subband of the 2-D separable orthogonal wavelet transform.

We now turn to the estimation of $\sigma_{j,\ell}$. As the noise is additive, we have $\eta_{j,\ell,\mathbf{k}} := \langle \varepsilon, \varphi_{j,\ell,\mathbf{k}} \rangle$, and it is easy to see that

$$\tilde{\sigma}_{j,\ell} = \tilde{\sigma} \|\varphi_{j,\ell,\mathbf{k}}\| \,. \qquad (6.10)$$

If the atoms in the dictionary $\boldsymbol{\Phi}$ all have equal unit ℓ_2-norm, then obviously $\tilde{\sigma}_{j,\ell} = \tilde{\sigma}, \forall(j, \ell)$. This formula is also easily implemented if the ℓ_2-norms were known analytically, as is the case for the curvelet tight frame (see Section 5.4.2.2). But if these norms are not known in closed form, they can be estimated in practice by taking the transform of a Dirac, and then computing the ℓ_2-norm of each subband.

An alternative obvious approach to estimate $\sigma_{j,\ell}$ consists of simulating a data set containing only white Gaussian noise with standard deviation equal to 1, and taking the transform of this noise. An estimator of $\sigma_{j,\ell}$ is obtained as the standard deviation of the coefficients in the subband (j, ℓ).

Variable ε is additive colored Gaussian

Suppose now that the noise in the original domain is Gaussian but correlated. If its spectral density function happens to be known, and if the transform atoms $\varphi_{j,\ell,\mathbf{k}}$ correspond to a bank of bandpass filters (as is the case for wavelets and second generation curvelets), the standard deviation $\sigma_{j,\ell}$ can be calculated explicitly from the noise spectral density function and the Fourier transform of the atoms $\varphi_{j,\ell,\mathbf{k}}$ (Papoulis 1984),

$$\sigma_{j,\ell}^2 = \int S(\boldsymbol{\nu}) |\hat{\varphi}_{j,\ell,\mathbf{k}}(\boldsymbol{\nu})|^2 d\boldsymbol{\nu} \,,$$

where $S(\nu)$ is the spectral density of ε. In the other cases where the spectral density function is not known, we follow the idea of Johnstone and Silverman (1997) who proposed to estimate $\sigma_{j,\ell}$ independently at each scale and orientation using again the MAD estimator (6.9) and assuming that $\alpha_{j,\ell,\mathbf{k}}$ are sparse in Φ at each (j, ℓ):

$$\tilde{\sigma}_{j,\ell} = \mathrm{MAD}(\beta_{j,\ell,\cdot})/0.6745 . \tag{6.11}$$

6.2.1.3 Multiple Hypotheses Correction

The individual binary hypothesis testing discussed above can face serious problems because of the large numbers of coefficients (hypotheses) being tested simultaneously. In other words, if the type 1 error is controlled at an individual level, the chance of keeping erroneously a coefficient is extremely high as the number of false detections increases with the number of hypotheses being tested simultaneously.

Therefore, if one desires to have control over global statistical error rates, multiple hypothesis testing should be corrected for. For example, the Bonferroni correction consists of comparing the p-value of each coefficient to $\alpha/($total number of tested coefficients at subband $(j, \ell))$. The Bonferroni correction controls the probability of erroneously rejecting even one of the true null hypotheses, i.e., the familywise error rate (FWER). It is however too over-conservative entailing a dissipation of detection power. To mitigate this limitation, it is better to use the Benjamini and Hochberg (1995) procedure to control the False Discovery Rate (FDR), i.e., the average fraction of false detections over the total number of detections. The control of FDR has the following advantages over that of FWER: (1) it usually has greater detection power and (2) it can easily handle correlated data (Benjamini and Yekutieli 2001). The latter point allows FDR control when the noise is not independent (e.g., when ε is additive white Gaussian and the transform is redundant). Minimaxity of FDR has also been studied in various settings: see Abramovich et al. (2006) and Donoho and Jin (2006).

6.2.2 Hard and Soft Thresholding

6.2.2.1 Definition

Many thresholding or shrinkage rules for the operator $\mathcal{D}$ have been proposed in the last decade. Among them, hard and soft thresholding are certainly the most well known.

Hard thresholding (Starck and Bijaoui 1994; Donoho et al. 1995) consists of setting to zero all coefficients whose magnitude is less than a threshold $t_{j,\ell}$:

$$\tilde{\beta}_{j,\ell,\mathbf{k}} = \mathrm{HardThresh}_{t_{j,\ell}}(\beta_{j,\ell,\mathbf{k}}) = \begin{cases} \beta_{j,\ell,\mathbf{k}} & \text{if } |\beta_{j,\ell,\mathbf{k}}| \geq t_{j,\ell} \\ 0 & \text{otherwise} \end{cases} . \tag{6.12}$$

Hard thresholding (discontinuous function) is a keep-or-kill procedure. Note that the binary decision rule (6.8) is hard thresholding.

Soft thresholding (Weaver et al. 1991; Donoho 1995a) is defined as the kill-or-shrink rule:

$$\tilde{\beta}_{j,\ell,\mathbf{k}} = \begin{cases} \mathrm{sign}(\beta_{j,\ell,\mathbf{k}})(|\beta_{j,\ell,\mathbf{k}}| - t_{j,\ell}) & \text{if } |\beta_{j,\ell,\mathbf{k}}| \geq t_{j,\ell} \\ 0 & \text{otherwise} \end{cases} . \tag{6.13}$$

The coefficients above the threshold are shrunk toward the origin. This can be written in the compact form

$$\tilde{\beta}_{j,\ell,\mathbf{k}} = \text{SoftThresh}_{t_{j,\ell}}(\beta_{j,\ell,\mathbf{k}}) = \text{sign}(\beta_{j,\ell,\mathbf{k}})(|\beta_{j,\ell,\mathbf{k}}| - t_{j,\ell})_+ , \qquad (6.14)$$

where $(\cdot)_+ = \max(\cdot, 0)$. Soft thresholding is a continuous function.

6.2.2.2 Thresholding as a Minimization Problem

Suppose that $\boldsymbol{\Phi}$ is orthonormal. In this case, the analysis operator $\mathbf{T} = \boldsymbol{\Phi}^T$ and $\mathbf{R} = \boldsymbol{\Phi} = \mathbf{T}^{-1}$. It can be proved that equation (6.2) is the unique closed form solution to the following minimization problems when $\mathcal{D}$ is hard or soft thresholding with a threshold t:

$$\tilde{\alpha} = \underset{\alpha}{\arg\min} \ \|Y - \boldsymbol{\Phi}\alpha\|^2 + t^2 \|\alpha\|_0 \quad \textbf{Hard thresholding} \qquad (6.15)$$

$$\tilde{\alpha} = \underset{\alpha}{\arg\min} \ \tfrac{1}{2} \|Y - \boldsymbol{\Phi}\alpha\|^2 + t \|\alpha\|_1 \quad \textbf{Soft thresholding} \qquad (6.16)$$

where α is the vector storing the coefficients $\alpha_{j,\ell,\mathbf{k}}$, $\|\alpha\|_0$ and $\|\alpha\|_1$ are respectively the ℓ_0 pseudo-norm and the ℓ_1-norm of α. The former counts the number of non-zero elements in the vector α, and the second is the sum of its absolute values. In statistical terminology, problems (6.15)–(6.16) correspond to penalized least-squares estimators, where the penalty function is the ℓ_0 or ℓ_1 norm.

For the orthogonal wavelet transform, hard thresholding is known to result in a larger variance estimate, while soft thresholding with the same threshold level creates undesirable bias because even large coefficients lying out of noise are shrunk. In practice, hard thresholding is generally preferred to soft thresholding. However soft thresholding orthogonal wavelet coefficients can be better than hard thresholding if used with a threshold twice smaller (e.g., 1.5σ for soft thresholding if 3σ for hard thresholding); see Mallat (2008). For redundant transforms, hard thresholding is clearly better.

6.2.2.3 Other Thresholding-Shrinkage Rules

Many authors have proposed alternative thresholding-shrinkage operators $\mathcal{D}$. These include firm thresholding (Gao and Bruce 1997), mixture of soft and hard thresholding (Fan 1997), the non-negative garrote thresholding (Gao 1998), the SCAD (smoothly clipped absolute deviation) thresholding rule (Antoniadis and Fan 2001), and shrinkage rules obtained by using ℓ_p-norm penalties in (6.16) (Antoniadis and Fan 2001). It is worth noting that some of these thresholding-shrinkage rules can be directly linked to a penalized least-squares formulation as in the previous section (Antoniadis and Fan 2001; Nikolova 2000), and see also Section 7.3.2.2 for a general treatment in the case of convex penalties.

Although not discussed further here, various univariate (i.e. term-by-term) shrinkage estimators based on penalized maximum likelihood framework have also been proposed. These estimators differ in the form of the prior imposed on the transform coefficient – essentially orthogonal wavelets in the cited references – which is designed to capture the sparsity of the expansion. See the comprehensive overviews provided in Antoniadis et al. (2001); Fadili and Boubchir (2005).

6.2.2.4 On the Choice of the Threshold

There is a variety of methods to choose the threshold value in equations (6.12)–(6.14) in the case of additive Gaussian noise. These thresholds can be either global or subband-dependent. The former means that the same threshold t is used for all levels j and orientations ℓ.

The hypothesis testing framework of Section 6.2.1 is a first way of setting the threshold(s) by controlling the error rates either at individual or global levels. In orthogonal wavelet denoising with white noise, Donoho and Johnstone (1994) proposed the minimax threshold, which is derived to minimize the constant term in an upper bound of the mean square error (MSE) risk involved in estimating a function depending on an oracle.

For orthogonal transforms again with white noise, Donoho and Johnstone (1994) proposed the simple formula of the so-called universal threshold $t = \sigma\sqrt{2\log N}$ (global) or $t_{j,\ell} = \sigma\sqrt{2\log N_{j,\ell}}$ (subband-dependent), where N is the total number of samples, and $N_{j,\ell}$ is the number of coefficients at scale j and orientation ℓ. The idea is to ensure that every coefficient, whose underlying true value is zero, will be estimated as zero with high probability. Indeed, traditional arguments from the concentration of the maximum of N independent and identically distributed Gaussian variables $\varepsilon[k] \sim \mathcal{N}(0, 1)$ tell us that as $N \to \infty$,

$$\mathcal{P}\left(\max_{1 \leq k \leq N} |\varepsilon[k]| > \sqrt{b \log N}\right) \sim \frac{\sqrt{2}}{N^{b/2-1}\sqrt{b\pi \log N}}.$$

For $b = 2$, this probability vanishes at the rate $1/\sqrt{\pi \log N}$. However, as this threshold is based on a worst-case scenario, it can be pessimistic in practice resulting in smooth estimates. Refinements of this threshold can be found in Antoniadis and Fan (2001).

The generalized cross-validation criterion (GCV) has been adopted for objectively choosing the threshold parameter in wavelet-domain soft thresholding, for both white (Jansen et al. 1997) and correlated Gaussian noise (Jansen and Bultheel 1998). GCV attempts to provide a data-driven estimate of the threshold which minimizes the unobservable MSE. Despite its simplicity and good performance in practice, the GCV-based choice cannot work for any thresholding rule. Coifman and Donoho (1995) introduced a scheme to choose a threshold value $t_{j,\ell}$ by employing Stein's unbiased risk estimator, SURE (Stein 1981) to get an unbiased estimate of the MSE. However this approach has serious drawbacks in low sparsity regimes.

6.2.3 Orthogonal versus Overcomplete Transforms

The hard thresholding and soft thresholding introduced in Section 6.2.2 are the exact solutions to equations (6.15) and (6.16) only when the transform is orthonormal. But when it is redundant or overcomplete, this is no longer valid. We describe in the following two schemes that use regularization to solve the denoising problem with redundant transforms.

6.2.3.1 Sparse Reconstruction from the Multiresolution Support
Multiresolution Support

We define the *multiresolution support* (Starck et al. 1995), which is determined by the set of detected significant coefficients at each scale j, orientation ℓ and location

k, as

$$\mathcal{M} := \{(j, \ell, \mathbf{k}) \mid \text{if } \beta_{j,\ell,\mathbf{k}} \text{ is declared significant}\} . \tag{6.17}$$

The multiresolution support is obtained from the noisy data Y by computing the forward transform coefficients $\beta_{j,\ell,\mathbf{k}} := \mathbf{T}Y$, applying hard thresholding (using a threshold policy described above), and recording the coordinates of the retained coefficients.

Iterative reconstruction

The goal is to reconstruct an estimate $\tilde{X}$, known to be sparsely represented in the dictionary $\mathbf{\Phi}$ (regularization), such that its significant transform coefficients $\mathbf{T}\tilde{X}$ are close to those of Y (fidelity to data). Formally, this amounts to solving the constrained convex optimization problem

$$\min_X \|\mathbf{T}X\|_1, \qquad \text{s.t.} \qquad X \in \mathcal{C} , \tag{6.18}$$

where $\mathcal{C}$ is a closed convex set of constraints including the linear data-fidelity constraints

$$|(\mathbf{T}(X - Y))_{j,\ell,\mathbf{k}}| \leq e_{j,\ell}, \forall (j, \ell, \mathbf{k}) \in \mathcal{M} . \tag{6.19}$$

Other constraints can be used as well, such as positivity. Note that in equation (6.18), the ℓ_1 norm was used as a convex relaxation of the ideal ℓ_0 sparsity penalty. In words, the constraints (6.19) mean that we seek a solution whose coefficients $(\mathbf{T}\tilde{X})_{j,\ell,\mathbf{k}}$, restricted to the multiresolution support, are within $e_{j,\ell}$ of the noisy coefficients $\beta_{j,\ell,\mathbf{k}}$. This constraint allows then to preserve any pattern which is detected as significant by the transform. An advocated choice in practice is $e_{j,\ell} = \sigma_{j,\ell}/2$.

Other regularization penalties can be used in place of the ℓ_1-norm of the transform coefficients. For instance, if the solution is known to have a sparse gradient, a qualifying alternative to equation (6.18) would be (Malgouyres 2002a; Candès and Guo 2002; Durand and Froment 2003):

$$\min_X \|X\|_{\mathrm{TV}}, \qquad \text{s.t.} \qquad X \in \mathcal{C} , \tag{6.20}$$

where $\| \cdot \|_{\mathrm{TV}}$ is the discrete Total Variation seminorm, that is, an edge-preserving penalization term defined as the Euclidean norm of the discrete gradient field of an image:

$$\|X\|_{\mathrm{TV}} = \sum_{k,l} |(\overline{\nabla}X)[k, l]| , \tag{6.21}$$

where, for a vector field $\zeta \in \mathbb{R}^2$, $|\zeta| = \sqrt{\zeta^{\mathrm{T}}\zeta}$. The reader may refer to Chambolle (2004) for a possible discretization of the TV seminorm. TV regularization is however known to produce staircasing artifacts that are not desirable in some applications such as astronomical or biological imaging.

Finding a solution to equation (6.18) amounts to solving a convex optimization problem which can be cast as a linear programming (LP) problem and solved using interior-point methods. However, the computational complexity of the LP solver increases dramatically with the size of the problem. A much more effective alternative is the versatile splitting framework that will be developed in detail in Chapter 7.

Here, we discuss yet another approach that has been proposed in Starck et al. (2001) based on an adaptation of the hybrid steepest descent (HSD) algorithm (Yamada 2001) to nonsmooth functionals. HSD allows minimizing smooth convex functionals over the intersection of fixed point sets of nonexpansive mappings. It is much faster than LP, and in the problem of the form (6.18), nonexpansive mappings have closed forms (Zhang et al. 2008b).

The denoising method described here can be seen as a particular instance of the combined filtering method detailed in Section 8.3.

6.2.3.2 Penalized Estimator

Let us now go back to solving equation (6.16) when Φ is redundant. For the sake of simplicity, we assume a global parameter t, but it is not difficult to generalize the discussion to a subband dependent set of parameters $t_{j,\ell}$. This minimization problem has no closed form solution and iterative algorithms must be used.

For example, if the dictionary $\Phi = [\Phi_1 \Phi_2 \cdots \Phi_L]$ is built as a union of L orthonormal transforms, the block-coordinate relaxation (BCR) algorithm was proposed by Sardy et al. (2000) as an effective numerical solver. This algorithm breaks the coefficient vector α into L parts, each referring to an orthonormal transform in Φ. The BCR algorithm addresses one set of representation coefficients at a time (say, α_l), assuming all the others as fixed, and applies soft thresholding with threshold t to the marginal residuals $Y - \sum_{l' \neq l} \Phi_{l'} \alpha_{l'}$. This process is repeated by iteratively cycling through the set of coefficients.

For a general dictionary Φ, the sparse recovery problem (6.16) is a special instance of (7.4) considered in Chapter 7. It can be solved effectively using iterative thresholding as detailed in Algorithms 25 or 26. The reader can easily verify that equation (6.2) with soft thresholding can be viewed as the first iteration of Algorithm 25[1] (Elad 2006).

6.3 BLOCK NONLINEAR DENOISING

The term-by-term thresholding achieves a degree of trade-off between variance and bias contribution to the MSE risk. However, this trade-off is not optimal; it removes too many terms from the observed coefficient expansion, with the consequence that the estimator is too biased and has a sub-optimal MSE convergence rate. One way to increase estimation precision is by exploiting information about neighboring coefficients. In other words, the observed transform coefficients tend to form clusters that could be thresholded in blocks (or groups) rather than individually. This would allow threshold decisions to be made more accurately and permit convergence rates to be improved. Such a procedure has been introduced in Hall et al. (1998, 1999) who studied wavelet shrinkage methods based on block thresholding for 1-D data.

In this approach, the procedure first divides the wavelet coefficients at each resolution level into non-overlapping blocks and then keeps all the coefficients within a block if the magnitude of the sum of the squared empirical coefficients within that block is greater than a fixed threshold. The original procedure developed by Hall et al. (1998, 1999) is defined with the block size $(\log N)^2$ (N is the number of samples). BlockShrink of Cai (2002) is the optimal version of this procedure. It uses a different block size, $\log N$, and enjoys a number of practical and theoretical advantages. Other block thresholding rules have been developed. Among them, there is BlockJS of Cai (1999, 2002) which combines the James-Stein rule (Stein 1981) with the wavelet methodology.

In the following, we describe a generalization of Stein block thresholding to any dimension d, with a particular emphasis on 2-D images $d = 2$. We provide a simple, fast and practical procedure. The choice of the threshold parameter is also discussed and its optimal value is stated for some noise models such as the (not necessarily independent and identically distributed) Gaussian case. The procedure is valid for transforms with isotropic subbands (e.g., the wavelet transform), and also for anisotropic transforms such as the curvelet transform. Here, we only stress the practical aspects and the reader who is interested in the theoretical properties of this block-shrinkage estimator may refer to Chesneau et al. (2010) for more detailed study.

A sample bibliography of the many transform-domain block-type image denoising algorithms include Portilla et al. (2003); Sendur and Selesnick (2002); Pizurica et al. (2002); Luisier et al. (2007); Chaux et al. (2008); Yu et al. (2008), to cite a few, which are amongst the most effective. Most proposed approaches use orthodox Bayesian machinery and assume different forms of multivariate priors over blocks of neighboring coefficients and even interscale dependency.

6.3.1 The Observation Model

Suppose that we observe a multidimensional sequence of coefficients $(\beta_{j,\ell,\mathbf{k}})_{j,\ell,\mathbf{k}}$ defined by

$$\beta_{j,\ell,\mathbf{k}} = \alpha_{j,\ell,\mathbf{k}} + \eta_{j,\ell,\mathbf{k}}, \quad j = 0, \ldots, J-1, \quad \ell \in \mathcal{B}_j, \quad \mathbf{k} \in \mathcal{D}_j, \tag{6.22}$$

where

- $J = \lfloor (\log_2 N)/d \rfloor$ is the maximal number of scales, d the dimension of the data and N is the total number of samples
- $\mathcal{B}_j = \{1, \ldots, \lfloor c_* 2^{\upsilon j} \rfloor\}$ is the set of subbands at scale j, with $c_* \geq 1$, $\upsilon \in [0, 1]$
- $\mathcal{D}_j = \prod_{i=1}^{d} \{0, \ldots, \lfloor 2^{\mu_i j} \rfloor - 1\}$ is the set of locations at scale j and subband ℓ
- $(\mu_i)_{i=1,\ldots,d}$ are parameters that reflect the anisotropy of the subbands. Set $d_* = \sum_{i=1}^{d} \mu_i$

To illustrate the meaning of these parameters, let us see how they specialize in some popular transforms for $d = 2$. For example, with the separable two-dimensional wavelet transform, we have $\upsilon = 0$, $c^* = 3$, and $\mu_1 = \mu_2 = 1$; see Fig. 6.1 (top). Thus, as expected, we get three isotropic subbands at each scale. For the two-dimensional second generation curvelet transform developed in Section 5.4.2, we have $\upsilon = 1/2$, $\mu_1 = 1$ and $\mu_2 = 1/2$ which corresponds to the parabolic scaling of curvelets; see Fig. 6.1 (bottom). Other transforms fall within the scope of this setting (e.g., starlet, ridgelet, etc.).

Let $L = \lfloor (\log N/d)^{1/d} \rfloor$ be the block length, $j_0 = \lfloor (1/\min_{i=1,\ldots,d} \mu_i) \log_2 L \rfloor$ is the coarsest decomposition scale, and $J_* = \lfloor (1/(d_* + \upsilon))(\log_2 N)/d \rfloor$. For any scale $j \in \{j_0, \ldots, J_*\}$, let

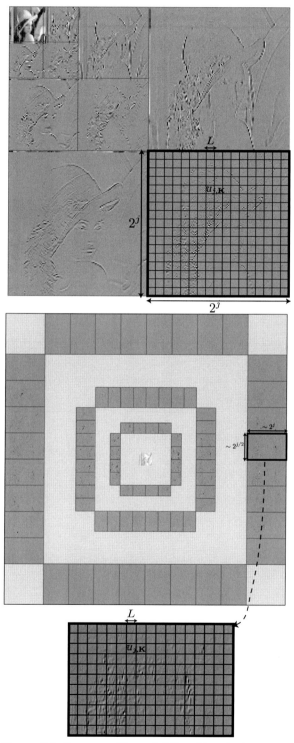

Figure 6.1. Decomposition of 2-D subbands into non-overlapping blocks of size $L \times L$. (top) Case of the orthogonal wavelet transform. (bottom) Case of the second generation curvelet transform. See text for more details.

- $\mathcal{A}_j = \prod_{i=1}^{d}\{1,\ldots,\lfloor 2^{\mu_i j}L^{-1}\rfloor\}$ be the set indexing the blocks at scale j
- For each block index $\mathbf{K} = (K_1,\ldots,K_d) \in \mathcal{A}_j$, $\mathcal{U}_{j,\mathbf{K}} = \{\mathbf{k} \in \mathcal{D}_j;\ (K_1-1)L \leq k_1 \leq K_1 L - 1,\ldots,(K_d - 1)L \leq k_d \leq K_d L - 1\}$ is the set indexing the positions of coefficients within the $\mathbf{K}$th block $\mathcal{U}_{j,\mathbf{K}}$.

6.3.2 Assumptions on the Noise

The class of noises covered by the block thresholding procedure we are about to describe are those that satisfy the following two assumptions. Suppose that there exist $\lambda_* > 0, Q_1 > 0$ and $Q_2 > 0$ independent of N such that

(A1) $\sup_{j\in\{0,\ldots,J-1\}} \sup_{\ell\in\mathcal{B}_j} 2^{-jd_*} \sum_{\mathbf{k}\in\mathcal{D}_j} \mathbb{E}(\eta_{j,\ell,\mathbf{k}}^2) \leq Q_1$.
(A1)

$$\sum_{j=j_0}^{J_*} \sum_{\ell\in\mathcal{B}_j} \sum_{\mathbf{K}\in\mathcal{A}_j} \sum_{\mathbf{k}\in\mathcal{U}_{j,\mathbf{K}}} \mathbb{E}\left(\eta_{j,\ell,\mathbf{k}}^2 \mathbf{1}_{\left\{\sum_{\mathbf{k}\in\mathcal{U}_{j,\mathbf{K}}} \eta_{j,\ell,\mathbf{k}}^2 > \lambda_* L^d/4\right\}}\right) \leq Q_2 .$$

where $\mathbb{E}(.)$ is the expectation operator.

Although they may appear somewhat abstract, assumptions (A1) and (A2) are satisfied for a wide class of noise models on the sequence $(\eta_{j,\ell,\mathbf{k}})_{j,\ell,\mathbf{k}}$ (not necessarily independent or identically distributed). Examples of noise models satisfying these conditions in practice will be given in Section 6.3.4.

6.3.3 Multidimensional Block Thresholding Estimator

From Section 6.3.1, recall the definitions of L, j_0, J_*, $\mathcal{A}_j$ and $\mathcal{U}_{j,\mathbf{K}}$. We estimate $\alpha = (\alpha_{j,\ell,\mathbf{k}})_{j,\ell,\mathbf{k}}$ by $\tilde{\alpha} = (\tilde{\alpha}_{j,\ell,\mathbf{k}})_{j,\ell,\mathbf{k}}$ where, for any $\mathbf{k} \in \mathcal{U}_{j,\mathbf{K}}$ in the block $\mathbf{K} \in \mathcal{A}_j$ and orientation $\ell \in \mathcal{B}_j$,

$$\tilde{\alpha}_{j,\ell,\mathbf{k}} = \begin{cases} \beta_{j,\ell,\mathbf{k}}, & \text{if } j \in \{0,\ldots,j_0-1\}, \\ \beta_{j,\ell,\mathbf{k}}\left(1 - \dfrac{\lambda_* \sigma_{j,\ell}^2}{\frac{1}{L^d}\sum_{\mathbf{k}\in\mathcal{U}_{j,\mathbf{K}}} \beta_{j,\ell,\mathbf{k}}^2}\right)_+, & \text{if } j \in \{j_0,\ldots,J_*\}, \\ 0, & \text{if } j \in \mathbb{N} - \{0,\ldots,J_*\}. \end{cases} \tag{6.23}$$

$\sigma_{j,\ell}$ is the standard deviation of the noise at scale j and orientation ℓ. In this definition, λ_* denotes the threshold involved in (A1) and (A2). Thus, at the coarsest scales $j \in \{0,\ldots,j_0\}$, the observed coefficients $(\beta_{j,\ell,\mathbf{k}})_{\mathbf{k}\in\mathcal{U}_{j,\mathbf{K}}}$ are left intact as usual. For each block $\mathcal{U}_{j,\mathbf{K}}$ in the scales $j \in \{j_0,\ldots,J-1\}$, if the mean energy within the block $\sum_{\mathbf{k}\in\mathcal{U}_{j,\mathbf{K}}} \beta_{j,\ell,\mathbf{k}}^2/L^d$ is larger than $\lambda_*\sigma_{j,\ell}^2$ then $\beta_{j,\mathbf{k}}$ is shrunk by the amount $\beta_{j,\ell,\mathbf{k}}(\lambda_*\sigma_{j,\ell}^2)/(\frac{1}{L^d}\sum_{\mathbf{k}\in\mathcal{U}_{j,\mathbf{K}}} \beta_{j,\ell,\mathbf{k}}^2)$; otherwise, $\alpha_{j,\ell,\mathbf{k}}$ is estimated by zero. In fact, $((1/L^d)\sum_{\mathbf{k}\in\mathcal{U}_{j,\mathbf{K}}} \beta_{j,\ell,\mathbf{k}}^2)/(\sigma_{j,\ell}^2)$ can be interpreted as a local measure of signal-to-noise ratio in the block $\mathcal{U}_{j,\mathbf{K}}$. Such a block thresholding originates from the James-Stein rule introduced in Stein (1981). As far as the choice of the threshold parameter λ_* is concerned, this is discussed next.

6.3.4 On the Choice of the Threshold

The choice of the threshold λ_* is crucial for good performance of the block thresholding estimator. We here emphasize the main practical ideas. To get the optimal behavior of block thresholding, it is enough to determine λ_* such that (A1) and (A2) are satisfied. In the following, we first provide the explicit expression of λ_* in the situation of an additive Gaussian noise sequence $(\eta_{j,\ell,\mathbf{k}})_{j,\ell,\mathbf{k}}$ not necessarily white. This result is then refined in the case of white Gaussian noise.

Case of frames

We suppose that, for any $j \in \{0, \ldots, J-1\}$ and any $\ell \in \mathcal{B}_j$, $(\eta_{j,\ell,\mathbf{k}})_{\mathbf{k}}$ is a zero-mean Gaussian process with standard deviation $\sigma_{j,\ell}$ at scale j and orientation ℓ. It was shown in Chesneau et al. (2010) that assumption (A2) can be reexpressed using the covariance of the noise in the coefficient domain. Denote such a covariance $\Sigma_{j,\ell,\mathbf{k},\mathbf{k}'} = \mathbb{E}(\eta_{j,\ell,\mathbf{k}}\eta_{j,\ell,\mathbf{k}'})$, then (A2) is satisfied if

$$|\Sigma_{j,\ell,\mathbf{k},\mathbf{k}'}| \leq C a_{||\mathbf{k}-\mathbf{k}'||} \,,$$

where $(a_\mathbf{u})_{\mathbf{u}\in\mathbb{N}}$ is a positive summable sequence; i.e. $\sum_{\mathbf{u}\in\mathbb{N}^d} a_{||\mathbf{u}||} < Q_4$. In a nutshell, this means that assumption (A2) is fulfilled as soon as the noise in the coefficient domain is not too much correlated. For example, with an additive white Gaussian noise in the original domain, with both wavelets and curvelets, this statement holds true and (A2) is verified (Chesneau et al. 2010). This result is useful as it establishes that the block denoising procedure and its optimal performance apply to the case of frames where a bounded zero-mean white Gaussian noise in the original domain is transformed into a bounded zero-mean colored Gaussian process whose covariance structure is given by the Gram matrix of the frame.

To apply the block thresholding procedure, it was also shown in Chesneau et al. (2010) that the threshold $\lambda_* = 4((2CQ_4)^{1/2} + 3^{1/4})^2$ preserves the optimal properties of the estimator, where C and Q_4 are the constants introduced above, which are independent of the number of samples N.

Case of orthobases

When $(\eta_{j,\ell,\mathbf{k}})_{j,\ell,\mathbf{k}}$ reduces to an additive white Gaussian noise, as is the case when the noise in the original domain is an additive white Gaussian noise and the transform is orthonormal (e.g., orthogonal wavelet transform), it was proved in Chesneau et al. (2010) that the best performance of block thresholding is achieved when λ_* is the root of $\lambda - \log \lambda = 3$, that is, $\lambda_* = 4.50524....$ In fact, it was shown in Chesneau et al. (2010) that this threshold works very well in practice even with redundant transforms that correspond to tight frames for which the threshold $\lambda_* \approx 4.50524$ is not rigorously valid. Only a minor improvement can be gained by taking the higher threshold $\lambda = 4((2CQ_4)^{1/2} + 3^{1/4})^2$ given for frames. This is a very useful and easy rule in practice.

6.4 BEYOND ADDITIVE GAUSSIAN NOISE

6.4.1 Multiplicative Noise

In various active imaging systems, such as synthetic aperture radar, laser or ultrasound imaging, the data representing the underlying unknown signal X is corrupted with multiplicative noise. A commonly used and realistic observation model is

$$Y[k] = X[k]\,\varepsilon[k]\,, \tag{6.24}$$

where the multiplicative noise ε follows a Gamma distribution with parameter K,

$$\text{pdf}(\varepsilon[k]) = \frac{K^K \varepsilon[k]^{K-1} \exp(-K\varepsilon[k])}{(K-1)!}. \tag{6.25}$$

A large variety of methods – see Achim et al. (2001, 2003); Durand et al. (2010) and references therein – rely on converting the multiplicative noise into additive noise using the log stabilizing transform

$$Y_S[k] = \log Y[k] = \log X[k] + \log \varepsilon[k] = \log X[k] + \epsilon[k]\,, \tag{6.26}$$

where the probability density function (pdf) of $\epsilon[k]$ reads

$$\text{pdf}(\epsilon[k]) = \frac{K^K e^{K(\epsilon[k]-e^{\epsilon[k]})}}{(K-1)!}. \tag{6.27}$$

One can prove that the mean and the variance of $\epsilon[k]$ are respectively

$$\psi_0(K) - \log K \quad \text{and} \quad \psi_1(K)\,, \tag{6.28}$$

where $\psi_n(z) = \left(\frac{d}{dz}\right)^{n+1} \log \Gamma(z)$ is the polygamma function (Abramowitz and Stegun 1972). The noise $\epsilon[k]$ is not zero-mean nor Gaussian, but tends to Gaussian with variance $\psi_1(K)$ as K gets large. This asymptotic Gaussian behavior is even better when the stabilized data Y_S are transformed in some multiscale transform domain (see Fig. 6.2). The rationale behind this is the central limit theorem. In this situation, denoising methods designed for additive white Gaussian noise such as those described in the previous sections will perform well by taking the logarithm of the input data (6.26), applying one's favorite denoiser to the log-data, and transforming back the result using an exponential function. A remaining subtlety is that the noise

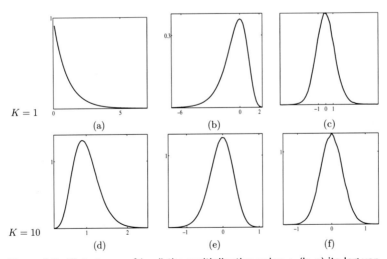

Figure 6.2. Histograms of (a–d) the multiplicative noise ε, (b–e) its log version ϵ, and (c–f) the wavelet coefficients of ϵ. Panels (a–c) correspond to $K = 1$ and (d–f) to $K = 10$.

ϵ in the log-transformed data has a non-zero mean $\psi_0(K) - \log K$. This introduces a bias which must be corrected for by removing this mean value before taking the exponential.

6.4.2 Poisson Noise and the Anscombe Transform

In many acquisition devices (photodetectors in cameras, computerized tomography, etc.), the noise stems from fluctuations of a counting process. In such a case, the Poisson distribution is an appropriate noise model. That is, each observation $Y[k] \sim \mathcal{P}(X[k])$, $\forall k$, where $X[k]$ is the underlying signal (so-called Poisson intensity). The difficulty is that now the variance of the noise is equal to its mean $X[k]$, i.e. signal-dependent. The Anscombe variance-stabilizing transform (VST) $\mathcal{A}$ (Anscombe 1948)

$$Y_S[k] = \mathcal{A}(Y[k]) = 2\sqrt{Y[k] + \frac{3}{8}} \qquad (6.29)$$

acts as if the stabilized data arose from a Gaussian white noise model $Y_S[k] \sim \mathcal{N}(2\sqrt{X[k]}, 1)$, with the proviso that the intensity $X[k]$ is large. After the Anscombe VST, we are again brought to the additive white Gaussian noise. One can apply one's favorite denoiser to Y_S and take the inverse Anscombe VST to get an estimate of X.

6.4.3 Mixed Gaussian and Poisson Noise

The arrival of photons, and their expression by electron counts, on CCD (charge coupled device) detectors may be modeled by a Poisson distribution. In addition, there is additive Gaussian read-out noise. The Anscombe transformation (6.29) has been extended (Murtagh et al. 1995) to take this combined noise into account. Consider the signal kth sample, $Y[k]$, as a sum of a Gaussian variable, $\varepsilon[k] \sim \mathcal{N}(\mu, \sigma^2)$; and a Poisson variable, $\xi[k] \sim \mathcal{P}(X[k])$. That is, $Y[k] = \varepsilon[k] + g_0\xi[k]$ where g_0 is the CCD detector gain.

The generalization of the Anscombe VST to the mixed Poisson-Gaussian noise is

$$Y_S[k] = \mathcal{A}_{\text{MPG}}(Y[k]) = \frac{2}{g_0}\sqrt{g_0 Y[k] + \frac{3}{8}g_0^2 + \sigma^2 - g_0\mu} \,. \qquad (6.30)$$

Taking $g_0 = 1$, $\sigma = 0$ and $\mu = 0$, this reduces to the Anscombe VST (6.29).

It was shown in Murtagh et al. (1995) that $Y_S[k] \sim \mathcal{N}(2\sqrt{X[k]}/g_0, 1)$, but this is only valid for a sufficiently large number of counts $X[k]$. The necessary average number of counts is about 20 if bias is to be avoided. Note that errors related to small values carry the risk of removing real objects, but not of amplifying noise. For Poisson intensities under this threshold acceptable number of counts, the Anscombe VST looses control over the bias. In this case, an alternative approach to variance stabilization is needed. Solutions based on the Haar transform and the multiscale variance stabilization transform (MS-VST) will be discussed in Sections 6.5 and 6.6.

6.5 POISSON NOISE AND THE HAAR TRANSFORM

Several authors (Kolaczyk 1997; Kolaczyk and Dixon 2000; Timmermann and Nowak 1999; Nowak and Baraniuk 1999; Bijaoui and Jammal 2001; Fryźlewicz and Nason 2004) have suggested independently that the Haar wavelet transform is very well suited for treating data with Poisson noise. Since a Haar wavelet coefficient is just the difference between two random variables following a Poisson distribution, it is easier to derive mathematical tools to remove the Poisson noise than with any other wavelet method.

An isotropic wavelet transform seems more adapted to more regular data (such as in astronomical or biomedical images). However, there is a trade-off to be made between an algorithm which optimally represents the information, and another which furnishes a reliable way to treat the noise. The approach used for noise removal differs depending on the authors. In Nowak and Baraniuk (1999), a type of Wiener filter was implemented. Timmermann and Nowak (1999) used a Bayesian approach with an a priori model on the original signal, and Kolaczyk and Dixon (2000) and Bijaoui and Jammal (2001) derived different thresholds resulting from the pdf of the wavelet coefficients. The Fisz transform (Fryźlewicz and Nason 2004) is a Haar wavelet transform-based VST used to "Gaussianize" the noise. Then the standard wavelet thresholding can be applied to the transformed signal. After the thresholding, the inverse Fisz transform has to be applied. Poisson denoising has also been formulated as a penalized maximum likelihood (ML) estimation problem (Sardy et al. 2004; Willet and Nowak 2007) within wavelet, wedgelet and platelet dictionaries. Wedgelet (platelet-) based methods are generally more effective than wavelet-based estimators in denoising piecewise constant (smooth) images with smooth contours.

6.5.1 Haar Coefficients of Poisson Noise

Kolaczyk (1997) proposed the Haar transform for gamma-ray burst detection in 1-D signals, and extended his method to 2-D images (Kolaczyk and Dixon 2000). The reason why the Haar transform (see Section 2.3.3) is used is essentially simplicity of the pdf of the Haar coefficients, hence providing a resilient mathematical tool for noise removal. Indeed, a Haar wavelet coefficient of Poisson counts can be viewed as the difference of two independent Poisson random variables $Y[k] \sim \mathcal{P}(X[k])$ and $Y[k'] \sim \mathcal{P}(X[k'])$, whose pdf is

$$\text{pdf}(Y[k] - Y[k'] = n) = e^{-(X[k]+X[k'])}(X[k]/X[k'])^{-n/2}I_n(2\sqrt{X[k]X[k']}) \,,$$

where $I_n(z)$ is the modified Bessel function of the first kind (Abramowitz and Stegun 1972).

Based on this formula, for 1-D data, Kolaczyk (1997) arrived at the detection threshold for scale j equal to

$$t_j = 2^{-(j+2)/2} \left(2\log N_j + \sqrt{(4\log N_j)^2 + 8\log N_j \lambda_j} \right) \qquad (6.31)$$

where $N_j = N/2^j$, N is the number of samples, and λ_j is the background rate per bin in the N_jth bin. This procedure can be generalized to any dimension d by replacing $2^{-(j+2)/2}$ by $2^{-(jd+2)/2}$ in the preceding threshold.

6.5.2 Biorthogonal Haar Coefficients of Poisson Noise

The Haar wavelet provides us with a manageable form of the detection threshold. But due to the lack of continuity of Haar filters, its estimate can be highly irregular with strong "staircasing" artifacts when decimation is involved. On the other hand, smoother wavelets do not yield closed forms of the pdf of wavelet coefficients of Poisson noise.

To solve this dilemma between distribution manageability and reconstruction regularity, Zhang et al. (2008a) propose to use the biorthogonal Haar wavelet transform. Its implementation filter bank is given by

$$h = 2^{-s}[1, 1], \qquad\qquad g = 2^{-s}r[\tfrac{1}{8}, \tfrac{1}{8}, -1, 1, -\tfrac{1}{8}, -\tfrac{1}{8}],$$
$$\tilde{h} = 2^{s-1}r[-\tfrac{1}{8}, \tfrac{1}{8}, 1, 1, \tfrac{1}{8}, -\tfrac{1}{8}], \quad \tilde{g} = 2^{s-1}[1, -1],$$

where s and $r = (1 + 2^{-5})^{-1/2}$ are normalizing factors, (h, g) and $(\tilde{h}, \tilde{g})$ are respectively the analysis and synthesis filter banks. For comparison, the non-normalized Haar filter bank is $(h = 2^{-s}[1, 1], g = 2^{-s}[-1, 1], \tilde{h} = 2^{s-1}[1, 1], \tilde{g} = 2^{s-1}[1, -1])$. This biorthogonal Haar filter bank has an unusual normalization. The motivation behind this is to ensure that the biorthogonal Haar coefficients will have the same variance as the Haar ones at each scale. Let us mention that to correct for the introduction of the factor r, the biorthogonal Haar coefficients must be multiplied by r^{-1} at each stage of the reconstruction. While the synthesis Haar scaling function is discontinuous, the one associated with the biorthogonal Haar is almost Lipschitz (Rioul and Duhamel 1992). Hence, the biorthogonal Haar reconstruction will be smoother.

Owing to the above normalization trick, it was shown in Zhang et al. (2008a) that the p-values of biorthogonal Haar coefficients (p_{BH}) are well approximated by those of Haar (p_H) for high-intensity settings or large scales; for low-intensity settings, they showed that p_{BH} is essentially upper-bounded by p_H. In plain terms, this suggests that one can apply the Haar-based threshold levels to biorthogonal Haar coefficients and still have comparable control over the false positive rate. The thresholds are explicitly given as (Zhang et al. 2008a)

$$t_j = 2^{-sjd-1} \left(2\tau_{\alpha/2} + \sqrt{\tau_{\alpha/2}^4 + 4\lambda_j \tau_{\alpha/2}^2} \right) \tag{6.32}$$

where $\tau_{\alpha/2} = \Phi^{-1}(1 - \alpha/2)$. Note that taking $s = 1/2$ and $\tau_{\alpha/2} = \sqrt{2 \log N_j}$ (universal threshold), we obtain the threshold value (6.31) of the normalized Haar filter bank. Thresholding the biorthogonal Haar wavelet coefficients allows benefiting from the regularity of the filter bank to gain a smooth estimate while always maintaining simplicity of the thresholds.

6.6 POISSON NOISE WITH LOW COUNTS

6.6.1 VST of a Filtered Poisson Process

As before, let $Y[k]$ be independent $\sim \mathcal{P}(X[k])$, $\forall k$, and set $Z[k] := \sum_i h[i]Y[k-i]$ as the filtered process obtained by convolving Y with a discrete filter h. Denote $\tau_n := \sum_k (h[k])^n$ for $n = 1, 2, \ldots$.

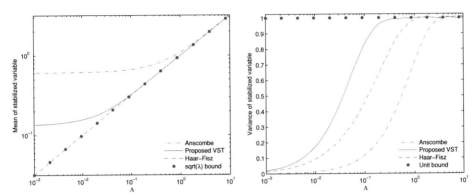

Figure 6.3. Behavior of the expectation of (left) $Y_S[k]$ and (right) the variance of $Y_S[k]$ as a function of the underlying intensity Λ, for the Anscombe VST, Haar-Fisz VST, and our VST with a low-pass filter h as the B_3-spline filter (see Section 3.6).

We have argued that the Anscombe VST performs poorly in low count settings. But, if the filter h acts as an "averaging" kernel (more generally a low-pass filter), one can reasonably expect that stabilizing $Z[k]$ would be more beneficial, since the SNR measured at the output of h is expected to be higher.

For the sake of simplicity, assume the local homogeneity assumption, $X[k - i] = \Lambda$ for all i within the support of h. It has been shown in Zhang et al. (2008b) that for a filter h, the transform $Y_S[k] = b \, \text{sign}(Y[k] + e)\sqrt{|Y[k] + e|}$ with b and e defined as

$$ e = \frac{7\tau_2}{8\tau_1} - \frac{\tau_3}{2\tau_2}, \quad b = 2\sqrt{\frac{|\tau_1|}{\tau_2}}, \tag{6.33}$$

is a second order accurate VST, with asymptotic unit variance. More precisely $Y_S[k] - b\sqrt{|\tau_1|X[k]} \sim \mathcal{N}(0, 1)$. By second-order accurate, we mean that the error term in the variance of the stabilized variable $Y_S[k]$ decreases rapidly as $O(X[k]^{-2})$. From (6.33), it is obvious that when $h = \delta$, we obtain the classical Anscombe VST parameters $b = 2$ and $e = 3/8$.

Figure 6.3 shows the estimates of the expectation (left) and the variance (right) of $Y_S[k]$ obtained from $2 \cdot 10^5$ Poisson noise realizations of $Y[k]$, plotted as a function of the intensity Λ for both Anscombe (dashed-dotted line), Haar-Fisz (Fryźlewicz and Nason 2004) (dashed line) and our VST (solid line). The theoretical bounds (i.e. 1 for the variance and $\sqrt{\Lambda}$ for the expectation) are also plotted with filled circles. It can be seen that for increasing intensity, the expectation and the variance stick to the theoretical bounds at different rates depending on the VST used. Quantitatively, Poisson variables transformed using the Anscombe VST can be reasonably considered to be unbiased and stabilized for $\Lambda \gtrsim 10$, using Haar-Fisz for $\Lambda \gtrsim 1$, and using our VST (after low-pass filtering with h) for $\Lambda \gtrsim 0.1$.

6.6.2 Multiscale Variance Stabilization Transform with the Starlet Transform

6.6.2.1 One-Dimensional Case

Recall from Section 3.5 that the starlet transform uses the filter bank $(h, g = \delta - h, \tilde{h} = \delta, \tilde{g} = \delta)$ where h is typically a symmetric low-pass filter such as the B_3-spline filter. The variance stabilizing transform can be applied on the c_js resulting in the

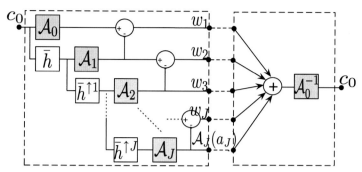

Figure 6.4. Diagrams of the MS-VST in 1-D. MS-VST combined with the starlet transform.

stabilization procedure shown in the right part of (6.34) (Zhang et al. 2008b):

$$\text{starlet}\begin{cases} c_j = \bar{h}^{\uparrow j-1} \star c_{j-1} \\ w_j = c_{j-1} - c_j \end{cases} \xRightarrow{\substack{\text{MS-VST} \\ + \\ \text{starlet}}} \begin{cases} c_j = \bar{h}^{\uparrow j-1} \star c_{j-1} \\ w_j = \mathcal{A}_{j-1}(c_{j-1}) - \mathcal{A}_j(c_j) \end{cases}. \quad (6.34)$$

Note that the filtering step on c_{j-1} can be rewritten as a filtering on $c_0 := Y$, i.e., $c_j = h^{(j)} \star c_0$, where $h^{(j)} = \bar{h}^{j-1} \star \cdots \star \bar{h}^1 \star \bar{h}$ for $j \geq 1$ and $h^{(0)} = \delta$. $\mathcal{A}_j$ is the VST operator at scale j:

$$\mathcal{A}_j(c_j) = b^{(j)}\sqrt{|c_j + e^{(j)}|}. \quad (6.35)$$

Let us define $\tau_n^{(j)} := \sum_i (h^{(j)}[i])^n$. Then according to (6.33), the constants $b^{(j)}$ and $e^{(j)}$ associated with $h^{(j)}$ should be set to:

$$e^{(j)} = \frac{7\tau_2^{(j)}}{8\tau_1^{(j)}} - \frac{\tau_3^{(j)}}{2\tau_2^{(j)}}, \quad b^{(j)} = 2\sqrt{\frac{\tau_1^{(j)}}{\tau_2^{(j)}}}. \quad (6.36)$$

The variance stabilization constants $b^{(j)}$ and $e^{(j)}$ only depend on the filter h and the scale level j. They can all be precomputed once for any given h. Since these constants are scale-dependent, so is the VST, hence the name MS-VST.

This stabilization procedure is invertible via the closed form

$$c_0 = \mathcal{A}_0^{-1}\left[\mathcal{A}_J(c_J) + \sum_{j=1}^{J} w_j\right]. \quad (6.37)$$

The decomposition scheme and the inversion of MS-VST+starlet are also illustrated in Fig. 6.4.

It was shown in Zhang et al. (2008b) that MS-VST detail coefficients are asymptotically Gaussian under the local homogeneity assumption:

$$w_j[k] \sim \mathcal{N}(0, \sigma_j^2), \quad \sigma_j^2 = \frac{\tau_2^{(j-1)}}{4\tau_1^{(j-1)2}} + \frac{\tau_2^{(j)}}{4\tau_1^{(j)2}} - \frac{\langle h^{(j-1)}, h^{(j)}\rangle}{2\tau_1^{(j-1)}\tau_1^{(j)}}. \quad (6.38)$$

The good news is that we are again brought to additive white Gaussian noise with an intensity-independent variance which relies solely on the filter h and the current

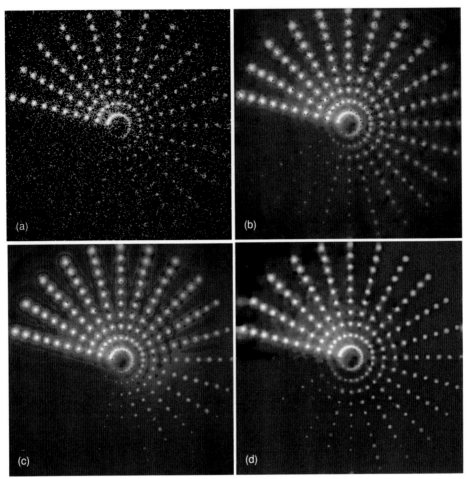

Figure 6.5. (a) Noisy. Denoised based on (b) MS-VST+starlet, (c) Anscombe VST, (d) Haar-Fisz VST.

scale. One can then apply one's favorite thresholding or shrinkage rule described above in the Gaussian case, using the expression of σ_j given in equation (6.38).

6.6.2.2 Extension to the Multidimensional Case

The filter bank in d-dimensions $(d > 1)$ becomes $(h_{d\mathrm{D}}, g_{d\mathrm{D}} = \delta - h_{d\mathrm{D}}, \tilde{h}_{d\mathrm{D}} = \delta, \tilde{g}_{d\mathrm{D}} = \delta)$ where $h_{d\mathrm{D}} = \otimes_{i=1}^{d} h$ ($\otimes$ denotes the tensor product). The MS-VST decomposition scheme remains the same as in equation (6.34). The complexity for pre-computing $b^{(j)}$, $e^{(j)}$, $\tau_k^{(j)}$ and the stabilized variance remain the same as in the 1-D case.

Figure 6.5(a) shows a set of Gaussian-like sources of different sizes and different intensities corrupted with Poisson noise. Each object along any radial branch has the same integrated intensity and has a more and more extended support as we go farther from the center. The integrated intensity reduces as the branches turn in the clockwise direction. Denoising such an image is highly challenging. Figures 6.5(b) to 6.5(d) show respectively the denoising results using the MS-VST+starlet, the Anscombe

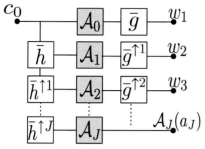

Figure 6.6. MS-VST combined with the standard UWT. The decomposition part is shown and no direct inversion exists.

VST, and the Haar-Fisz VST. Cycle spinning (i.e., translated versions of the input data) was used for the Haar-Fisz VST in order to not bias the comparison of estimators in favor of other approaches. As revealed by this figure, all estimators perform comparatively well at high intensity levels (center of the image). However, as expected, the relative merits (sensitivity) of the MS-VST estimator become increasingly salient as we go farther from the center, and as the branches turn clockwise. That is, the MS-VST estimator outperforms its competitors as the intensity becomes low. Most sources were detected by the MS-VST starlet estimator even for very low counts situations (see the last branches clockwise in (d) and compare to (b)). The Haar-Fisz VST also proves relatively sensitive. However, it still exhibits a clear staircasing artifact despite cycle spinning. Cycle spinning has the drawback of making the Haar-Fisz transform very slow compared to the MS-VST approach (typically 100–1000 times slower for 512×512 images).

6.6.3 Multiscale Variance Stabilization Transform with Undecimated Wavelets

6.6.3.1 One-Dimensional Case

The MS-VST can also be used to stabilize the wavelet coefficients of a standard separable UWT (Zhang et al. 2008b). In the same vein as equation (6.34), we can apply the VST on the approximation coefficients c_j, leading to the following scheme (see also the block diagram of Fig. 6.6):

$$
\text{UWT} \begin{cases} c_j = \bar{h}^{\uparrow j-1} \star c_{j-1} \\ w_j = \bar{g}^{\uparrow j-1} \star a_{j-1} \end{cases} \implies \begin{array}{c} \text{MS-VST} \\ + \\ \text{UWT} \end{array} \begin{cases} c_j = \bar{h}^{\uparrow j-1} \star c_{j-1} \\ w_j = \bar{g}^{\uparrow j-1} \star \mathcal{A}_{j-1}(c_{j-1}) \end{cases} \quad (6.39)
$$

where $\mathcal{A}_j(c_j) = b^{(j)}\text{sign}(c_j + e^{(j)})\sqrt{|c_j + e^{(j)}|}$, and $b^{(j)}$ and $e^{(j)}$ are defined as in (6.36).

Asymptotic normality of MS-VST+UWT detail coefficients was also proved by Zhang et al. (2008b) with an asymptotic variance that does not depend on the underlying intensity:

$$
w_j[k] \sim \mathcal{N}(0, \sigma_j^2) , \quad (6.40)
$$

where

$$\sigma_j^2 = \frac{1}{\tau_2^{(j-1)}} \sum_{m,n} \bar{g}^{(j-1)}[m]\bar{g}^{(j-1)}[n] \sum_k h^{(j-1)}[k]h^{(j-1)}[k+m-n] .$$

6.6.3.2 Extension to the Multidimensional Case

The scheme (6.39) can be extended straightforwardly to higher dimensional cases, and the asymptotic result above holds true. For example, in the 2-D case, the UWT is given by the left part of equation (6.41) and the version combined with the MS-VST is given on the right:

$$\text{UWT} \begin{cases} c_j = \bar{h}^{j-1}\bar{h}^{j-1} \star c_{j-1} \\ w_j^1 = \bar{g}^{j-1}\bar{h}^{j-1} \star c_{j-1} \\ w_j^2 = \bar{h}^{j-1}\bar{g}^{j-1} \star c_{j-1} \\ w_j^3 = \bar{g}^{j-1}\bar{g}^{j-1} \star c_{j-1} \end{cases} \implies \begin{matrix} \text{MS-VST} \\ + \\ \text{UWT} \end{matrix} \begin{cases} c_j = \bar{h}^{\uparrow j-1}\bar{h}^{\uparrow j-1} \star c_{j-1} \\ w_j^1 = \bar{g}^{\uparrow j-1}\bar{h}^{\uparrow j-1} \star \mathcal{A}_{j-1}(c_{j-1}) \\ w_j^2 = \bar{h}^{\uparrow j-1}\bar{g}^{\uparrow j-1} \star \mathcal{A}_{j-1}(c_{j-1}) \\ w_j^3 = \bar{g}^{\uparrow j-1}\bar{g}^{\uparrow j-1} \star \mathcal{A}_{j-1}(c_{j-1}) \end{cases} .$$

$$(6.41)$$

where $hg \star c$ is the convolution of c by the separable filter hg, i.e., convolution first along the rows by h and then along the columns by g. The complexity of precomputing the constants $b^{(j)}, e^{(j)}, \tau_k^{(j)}$ and σ_j remains the same as in the 1-D case.

6.6.3.3 Iterative Reconstruction

Following the detection step, we have to invert the MS-VST scheme to reconstruct the estimate of the underlying intensity. However, this is not straightforward for the standard UWT case, as there is no closed form reconstruction formula available. The formal reason is that the convolution (by $\bar{g}^{\uparrow j-1}$) operator and the nonlinear variance stabilizing operator $\mathcal{A}_{j-1}$ do not commute in (6.39). Even for the MS-VST+starlet case, although explicit inversion is possible (by equation (6.37)), it can not guarantee positive reconstruction (the Poisson intensity is non-negative by definition). A projection onto the positive orthant may be applied once the MS-VST+starlet is inverted, but this could entail a loss of important structures in the estimate. To circumvent these difficulties, it was proposed in Zhang et al. (2008b) to reformulate the reconstruction as a sparsity-promoting convex optimization problem, and solve it iteratively.

We again define the multiresolution support $\mathcal{M}$ which is determined by the set of detected significant coefficients at each scale j and location $\mathbf{k}$, and $\mathbf{M}$ as the associated binary mask matrix acting on wavelet coefficients, whose diagonal elements indicate whether a coefficient is retained in $\mathcal{M}$ or not. We denote $\mathbf{T}_W$ as the wavelet transform (starlet or separable), and $\mathbf{R}_W$ its inverse. Therefore our reconstruction is formulated as a constrained sparsity-promoting minimization problem over the transform coefficients w,

$$\min_w \|w\|_1 \quad \text{s.t.} \quad \begin{cases} w_j[\mathbf{k}] = (\mathbf{T}_W Y)_j[\mathbf{k}], \, \forall \, (j, \mathbf{k}) \in \mathcal{M} \\ \text{and } \mathbf{R}_W w \geq 0 \end{cases}, \quad (6.42)$$

and the intensity estimate $\tilde{X}$ is reconstructed as $\tilde{X} = \mathbf{R}_W \tilde{w}$, where $\tilde{w}$ is a minimizer of equation (6.42). Using again an adaptation of the hybrid steepest descent (HSD) algorithm (Yamada 2001) to solve equation (6.42), the main steps of our minimization scheme can be summarized as follows:

Inputs: Noisy data Y; a low-pass filter h; multiresolution support $\mathcal{M}$ from the detection step; number of iterations $N_{\max}$.
Initialization: $w_Y = \mathbf{T}_W Y$ and $w^{(0)} = \mathbf{M} w_Y$,
for $t = 1$ **to** $N_{\max}$ **do**

  - $\tilde{w} = \mathbf{M} w_Y + (\mathbf{I} - \mathbf{M}) w^{(t-1)}$.
  - $w^{(t)} = \mathbf{T}_W \, \mathrm{P}_{\mathcal{P}_+} (\mathbf{R}_W \, \mathrm{SoftThresh}_{\gamma_t}(\tilde{w}))$,
  - Update the step $\gamma_t = (N_{\max} - t)/(N_{\max} - 1)$.

Output: $\tilde{X} = \mathbf{R}_W w^{(N_{\max})}$.

$\mathrm{P}_{\mathcal{P}_+}$ is the projector onto the positive orthant $\mathcal{P}_+$. A careful convergence analysis of this algorithm is provided in Zhang et al. (2008b).

In summary, MS-VST with wavelets for Poisson denoising in low counts involves the following three main steps:

Algorithm 20 MS-VST+Wavelet Poisson denoising

Task: Poisson denoising of a noisy image of counts Y using the MS-VST+Wavelet transform.

1. **Transformation:** Compute the MS-VST+starlet or MS-VST+UWT using equation (6.34) or equation (6.39).
2. **Detection:** Detect significant detail coefficients and get the multiresolution support $\mathcal{M}$. We benefit from the asymptotic Gaussianity of the stabilized coefficients. The significant coefficients can be detected by hypothesis testing, corrected (or not) for multiple testing and dependencies; see Section 6.2.1.
3. **Reconstruction:** Use the multiresolution support $\mathcal{M}$ in the above algorithm to get the estimate $\tilde{X}$.

6.6.4 Multiscale Variance Stabilization Transform with Ridgelets

As explained in Chapter 5, the ridgelet transform is a wavelet transform applied to the slices of the Radon transform. Since a Radon coefficient is obtained from integration of the pixel values along a line, the noise in the Radon domain follows also a Poisson distribution. Thus, we can apply the 1-D MS-VST+UWT methodology of Section 6.6.3 to the slices of the Radon transform, and get the ridgelet multiresolution support $\mathcal{M} := \{(j, \theta_\ell, k) |$ the stabilized ridgelet coefficient at scale j, projection angle θ_ℓ and location k is significant$\}$. $\mathcal{M}$ being available, we can formulate a constrained ℓ_1-minimization problem in exactly the same way as in the wavelet case, which is then

Figure 6.7. Poisson denoising of smooth ridges (image size: 256 × 256). (top left) Intensity image (the peak intensities of the 9 vertical ridges vary progressively from 0.1 to 0.5; the inclined ridge has a maximum intensity of 0.3; background = 0.05); (top right) Poisson noisy image. (bottom left) Anscombe VST-based denoised image (UWT with 7/9 filter bank and $J = 4$). (bottom right) MS-VST+Ridgelet ($N_{max} = 10$ iterations).

solved by HSD iterations. Hence, the ridgelet Poisson denoising algorithm consists of the following steps:

Algorithm 21 MS-VST+Ridgelet Poisson Denoising

Task: Poisson denoising of a noisy image of counts Y using the MS-VST+Ridgelet transform.

- **Transformation:** Compute the Radon transform of Y.
- **Detection:** For each Radon slice, apply the 1-D MS-VST+UWT to get the stabilized ridgelet coefficients. The significant coefficients are then detected to get the ridgelet multiresolution support $\mathcal{M}$.
- **Reconstruction:** Apply the HSD iterative reconstruction with the ridgelet multiresolution support to get the final estimate $\tilde{X}$.

We simulated an image with smooth ridges shown in Fig. 6.7 (top left). The peak intensities of the vertical ridges vary progressively from 0.1 to 0.5; the inclined ridge has a maximum intensity of 0.3; the background level is 0.05. A Poisson-count image is shown in Fig. 6.7 (upper right). The image denoised by first applying the Anscombe VST, and then hard thresholding the UWT coefficients (using the 7/9 filter bank (Mallat 2008)) is depicted in Fig. 6.7 (bottom left). The one denoised using the MS-VST+Ridgelet is shown in Fig. 6.7 (bottom right). Due to the very low-count setting, the Anscombe VST-based estimate is highly biased. One can also see how sparsity of the transform affects the performance of denoising: wavelets are less adapted to line-like objects while the ridges are much better preserved in the ridgelet-based estimate.

6.6.5 Multiscale Variance Stabilization Transform with Curvelets

The first step in the first generation curvelet transform (see Section 5.4.1.1) is the starlet transform. Therefore, we can stabilize each resolution level in the same way as described in Section 6.6.2. We then apply the local ridgelet transform on each stabilized wavelet band. Significant Gaussianized curvelet coefficients are detected from which the curvelet multiresolution support $\mathcal{M}$ is derived. Finally, in the same vein as for the wavelet and ridgelet cases, a constrained ℓ_1-minimization problem similar to (6.42) is solved in terms of the curvelet coefficients using the HSD algorithm, before reconstructing the estimate. The sketch of the Poisson curvelet denoising algorithm is as follows:

Algorithm 22 MS-VST+Curvelet Poisson Denoising

Task: Poisson denoising of a noisy image of counts Y using the MS-VST+Curvelet transform.
Parameters: Number of resolution levels J, minimum block size B_{min}.
• Compute the MS-VST+starlet with J scales to get the stabilized wavelet subbands w_j.
• Set $\mathsf{B}_1 = \mathsf{B}_{min}$
for $j = 1$ to J **do**

    1. Partition the subband w_j with blocks of side-length B_j.
    2. Apply the digital ridgelet transform to each block to obtain the stabilized curvelet coefficients w_j.
    3. Detect the significant stabilized curvelet coefficients to obtain $\mathcal{M}$.
    4. **if** j modulo $2 = 1$ **then**
        $\mathsf{B}_{j+1} = 2\mathsf{B}_j$
    5. **else**
        $\mathsf{B}_{j+1} = \mathsf{B}_j$
    6. **end if**

Reconstruction: Apply the HSD iterative reconstruction with the curvelet multiresolution support to get the final estimate $\tilde{X}$.

Figure 6.8 compares the denoising methods on a biomedical image of fluorescent tubulin filaments (the image is available on the ImageJ site http://rsb.info.nih.gov/ij). Figure 6.8 (top) shows the original image and its noisy version. Figure 6.8 (bottom)

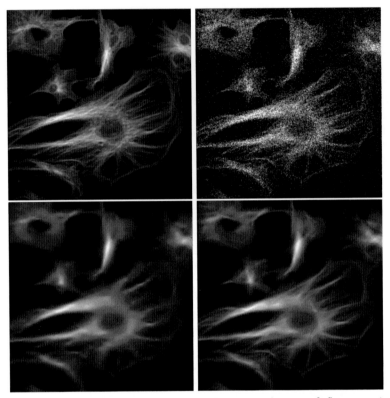

Figure 6.8. Poisson denoising of a microscopy image of fluorescent tubulins (image size: 256×256). (top left) Intensity image (intensity $\in$ $[0.53, 16.93]$). (top right) Poisson noisy image. (bottom left) Anscombe VST-based denoised image (UWT, 7/9 filter bank, $J = 4$). (bottom right) Denoised image by MS-VST+Curvelet ($J = 4$, $N_{max} = 5$ iterations).

shows the denoising using the Anscombe VST followed by hard thresholding UWT coefficients, and the MS-VST+Curvelet. As expected, preservation of geometrical structure is clearly better with the curvelet-based MS-VST.

6.7 GUIDED NUMERICAL EXPERIMENTS

A Matlab toolbox is available for download (http://www.SparseSignalRecipes.info). This toolbox is a collection of Matlab functions, scripts and datasets for image denoising. It requires at least WaveLab (see Section 2.9.1) to run. The toolbox implements term-by-term hard and soft thresholding as well as block Stein thresholding with several transforms (orthogonal discrete wavelet transform (DWT), undecimated discrete wavelet transform (UDWT), and second-generation discrete curvelet transform (DCTG2)). It contains scripts to reproduce the guided numerical experiment described below and others not included here. It has been used under Unix Solaris, Linux, MacOS X, Windows (Cygwin) under Matlab 6.x and Matlab 7.x. The toolbox is distributed under the CeCILL open source license (CeCILL Free Software License).

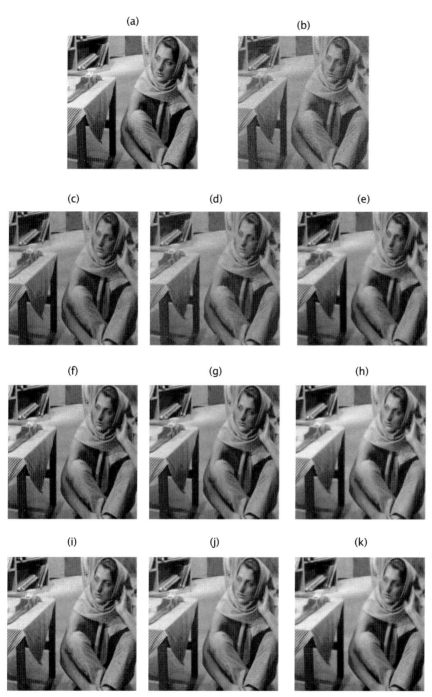

Figure 6.9. Visual comparison of term-by-term (hard and soft) and block threshold-ing on "Barbara" 512×512. (a) Original. (b) Noisy $\sigma = 20$. (c, f, i) Block denois-ing (threshold $\lambda_* = 4.50524$) with respectively, DWT (PSNR = 28.04 dB), UDWT (PSNR = 29.01 dB) and DCTG2 (PSNR = 30 dB). (d, g, j) term-by-term hard thresh-olding (threshold = 3σ) with respectively DWT (PSNR = 25.6 dB), UDWT (PSNR = 27.3 dB) and DCTG2 (PSNR = 28.93 dB). (e, h, k) Term-by-term soft threshold-ing (threshold = $\sqrt{3}\sigma$) with respectively DWT (PSNR = 26.03 dB), UDWT (PSNR = 26.84 dB) and DCTG2 (PSNR = 28.24 dB).

(a)   (b)

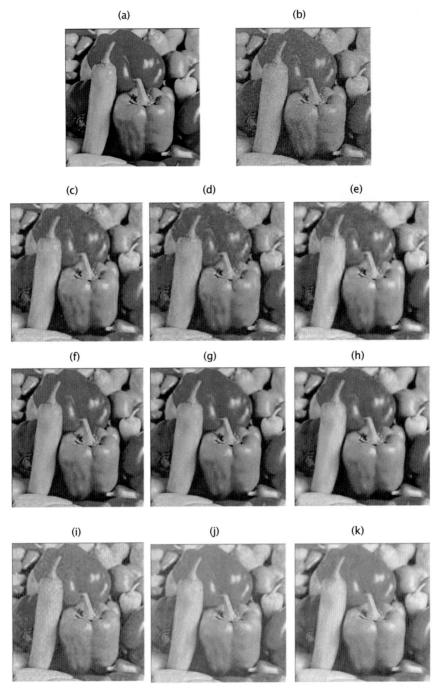

(c)   (d)   (e)

(f)   (g)   (h)

(i)   (j)   (k)

Figure 6.10. Visual comparison of term-by-term (hard and soft) and block thresholding on "Peppers" 256×256. (a) Original. (b) Noisy $\sigma = 20$. (c, f, i) Block denoising (threshold $\lambda_* = 4.50524$) with respectively DWT (PSNR = 28.56 dB), UDWT (PSNR = 29.72 dB) and DCTG2 (PSNR = 29.25 dB). (d, g, j) Term-by-term hard thresholding (threshold = 3σ) with respectively DWT (PSNR = 26.85 dB), UDWT (PSNR = 29.3 dB) and DCTG2 (PSNR = 28.81 dB). (e, h, k) Term-by-term soft thresholding (threshold = $\sqrt{3}\sigma$) with respectively DWT (PSNR = 26.87 dB), UDWT (PSNR = 27.79 dB) and DCTG2 (PSNR = 27.84 dB).

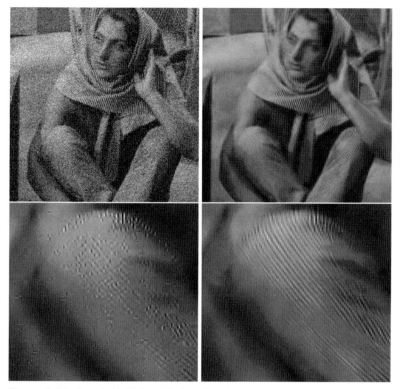

Figure 6.11. (top left) Noisy "Barbara" color image. (top right) Denoised image using the curvelet transform. (bottom) Details of the denoised images are shown on the left (UWT) and right (curvelet transform). (See *color plates*.)

6.7.1 Block Denoising

In this experiment, which can be reproduced by running the script `Scripts/blockgenfigvisual.m` in the toolbox, term-by-term (hard and soft) thresholding and block thresholding are applied with three different transforms: DWT, UDWT and DCTG2. The results on "Barbara" and "Peppers" are displayed in Fig. 6.9 and Fig. 6.10. Block denoising is systematically better than individual thresholding. Owing to block shrinkage, even the orthogonal DWT becomes competitive with redundant transforms. As discussed at the end of Section 6.2.2.2, for the DWT, soft thresholding with a threshold $\sqrt{3}\sigma$ is better than hard thresholding 3σ. This is not valid with redundant transforms such as the UDWT or the DCTG2. Note that the additional computational burden of block shrinkage compared to individual thresholding is marginal: respectively 0.1s, 1s and 0.7s for the DWT, UDWT and DCTG2 with 512×512 images, and less than 0.03s, 0.2s and 0.1 for 256×256 images. The algorithms were run under Matlab with an Intel Xeon Core Duo 3GHz CPU, 8GB RAM.

6.7.2 Denoising Color Images

In a wavelet based denoising scenario, color RGB images are generally mapped into the YUV color space, and each YUV color band is then denoised independently from the others. Figure 6.11, upper left, shows the noisy "Barbara" RGB color image and, upper right, the restored image after applying a hard thresholding in the curvelet domain independently in each of the three YUV color bands. Details of the denoised images are shown in the bottom left panel (using the UWT) and right panel (using the curvelet transform).

6.8 SUMMARY

In this chapter, several denoising methods based on sparse representations were described, under various noise models. We emphasized term-by-term and block thresholding and shrinkage. We also considered in detail the cases of additive Gaussian (white or colored), multiplicative and Poisson noise. We finally discussed a few numerical experiments some of which can be reproduced based on a toolbox which implements several algorithms described in the chapter.

Suppose now that we want to recover the signal from observations degraded by a linear transformation and corrupted by noise. This is a natural extension to the denoising problem considered in this chapter. We have briefly touched on this question in Section 6.2.3. For instance, can thresholding/shrinkage be used as a building block for solving efficiently more general inverse problems? This will be developed in detail in the next chapters.

7

Linear Inverse Problems

7.1 INTRODUCTION

Many problems in signal and image processing can be cast as inverting the system

$$y = \mathbf{H}x_0 \bullet \varepsilon \tag{7.1}$$

where $x_0 \in \mathbb{R}^N$ is the original object to recover (we treat an image or higher dimensional data by vectorizing it in a one-dimensional (1-D) vector), $y \in \mathbb{R}^m$ is the vector of noisy observations (or measurements), ε is the unknown noise/error term, and $\bullet$ translates the way the noise contaminates the data (e.g., "+" for additive noise). This noise/error can be either a stochastic measurement noise induced by the sensor (e.g., additive Gaussian noise, Poisson noise, or mixed Gaussian and Poisson) or a deterministic perturbation due, for example, to an imperfect forward model. $\mathbf{H} : \mathbb{R}^N \to \mathbb{R}^m$ is a linear operator that is typically ill behaved since it models an acquisition process that encounters the loss of information. Typical cases covered by the above degradation model are as follows:

- *Deconvolution*: $\mathbf{H}$ is the convolution by a blurring kernel, and y lacks the high-frequency content of x_0.
- *Superresolution*: $\mathbf{H}$ is the convolution by a blurring kernel of width s followed by a subsampling by a factor s. The number of measurements is typically $m = N/s$.
- *Inpainting*: $\mathbf{H}$ is a pixelwise multiplication by a binary mask; 1 for the pixels to be kept and 0 otherwise.
- *Decoding in compressed sensing*: See Chapter 13 for details. $\mathbf{H}$ is an $m \times N$ sensing matrix that only takes $m \ll N$ (random) linear measurements of the input signal or image x_0. The latter is supposed to be sparse in some dictionary $\mathbf{\Phi}$. See Section 8.2 for further explanation of dictionaries and related terminology.

Inverting (7.1) is generally an ill-posed problem in the sense of Hadamard. In order to regularize such an inversion, and thus reduce the space of candidate solutions, one has to incorporate some prior knowledge on the typical structure of the original signal or image x_0. This prior information accounts typically for the "smoothness" class of the solution and can range from the uniform smoothness assumption to more complex knowledge of the geometrical structures of x_0.

Linear inverse problems are among the most active fields in signal and image processing, and there has been a flurry of research activity on the subject. Stochastic approaches with maximum likelihood estimators or within a Bayesian framework have been extensively studied such as, for example, Markov random fields (Jeng and Woods 1991; Geman et al. 1993; Jalobeanu 2001). In order to confine candidate solutions to some particular functional spaces, several variational approaches have been developed to address inverse problems either with linear (Tikhonov 1963) or nonlinear edge-preserving regularization (e.g., potential functions on the total variation semi-norm) (Geman and Reynolds 1992; Rudin et al. 1992; Blanc-Féraud and Barlaud 1996; Charbonnier et al. 1997; Aubert and Vese 1997; Chambolle 2004).

Wavelet-based deconvolution methods have received considerable attention over the last decade. Donoho (1995b) and Starck and Bijaoui (1994) provided the first discussion of wavelet thresholding in linear inverse problems. Donoho (1995b) introduced the wavelet-vaguelet decomposition; see also Johnstone (2004). The approach was refined in Khalifa et al. (2003) and Neelamani et al. (2004). In Starck and Murtagh (1994) and Starck et al. (1995), regularization from the wavelet multiresolution support was proposed.

However, the complex structures of natural signals and images require tools in order to make use of their intricate redundancies. To capture this complexity, we have witnessed a great deal of investigation where researchers spanning a wide range of viewpoints have advocated the use of sparsity and overcomplete representations in inverse problems. Such redundant representations differ from the more traditional orthobasis representation because they offer a wider range of generating atoms forming the dictionary $\mathbf{\Phi}$; potentially, this wider range allows more flexibility in signal representation and adaptivity to its morphological content, and hence more effectiveness at tasks like compression and restoration. This is closely tied to the concept of *morphological diversity* thoroughly developed in Chapter 8.

Sparsity-based regularization methods have recently received considerable attention, either by adopting a Bayesian expectation-maximization framework (Figueiredo and Nowak 2003; Figueiredo et al. 2007a; Bioucas-Dias 2006), by introducing surrogate functionals (Daubechies et al. 2004), or using a convex analysis framework (Combettes and Wajs 2005; Chaux et al. 2007; Fadili et al. 2009b; Fadili and Starck 2006). Sparse regularization is also at the heart of the decoding step in the compressed sensing paradigm: see Chapter 13 for more details. In Section 8.4, we described a combined deconvolution method with a sparse regularization on the wavelet and curvelet coefficients in order to benefit from the advantages of both transforms.

The development of sparse representations in inverse problems is facing major challenges both theoretically and practically. These problems include the design of fast optimization algorithms to handle large-scale data and to solve real-life ill-posed problems. In this chapter, we formalize all these optimization problems within a unified framework of convex optimization theory and invoke tools from convex analysis and proximal splitting (Rockafellar 1970; Lemaréchal and Hiriart-Urruty 1996; Bauschke and Combettes 2011). We describe fast iterative and provably convergent algorithms. The chapter stresses mainly practical aspects and most the-oretical issues are deliberately omitted to make the chapter accessible to a large readership. With non-differentiable sparsity-promoting penalties, the proposed algorithms amount to iterative thresholding. Furthermore, the computational burden of these algorithms is essentially invested in applications of fast implicit operators associated with the involved dictionary $\mathbf{\Phi}$ and the linear operator $\mathbf{H}$, and their respective adjoints.

7.2 SPARSITY-REGULARIZED LINEAR INVERSE PROBLEMS

Starting from the degradation model expressed by (7.1), this chapter focuses on several optimization problems involved in linear inverse problems where the solution is assumed to be sparsely represented in a dictionary $\mathbf{\Phi}$.

When attempting to find sparse solutions to linear inverse problems, the goal in general is the composite and structured minimization problem

$$\min_{x \in \mathbb{R}^N} D(\mathbf{H}x, y) + \sum_{k=1}^{l} R_k(x) , \tag{P}$$

where $D : \mathbb{R}^m \times \mathbb{R}^m$ is a function measuring the consistency or fidelity to the observed data y, and R_k are functions that encode the priors one wants to impose on the object to recover x_0. Unless stated otherwise, we consider that $D(\cdot, y)$, $\forall y$, and R_k, $\forall k$, are lower semi-continuous (see Section 7.3 for definition) convex functions, are not infinite everywhere, but are not necessarily smooth. We also assume that the whole objective in the expression labeled (P) is not infinite everywhere. R_1 is typically a convex sparsity-promoting penalty. The other terms R_k may be designed for instance to force the solutions to satisfy additional constraints (e.g., positivity, box constraints). Each constraint can be stated implicitly by taking the corresponding R_k as the indicator function (see equation (7.14) for its definition) of some closed convex set reflecting that constraint.

Let us show how problem (P) covers both types of sparsity priors encountered in the literature (see Sections 7.5 and 7.4.8 for details).

7.2.1 Synthesis-Sparsity Problems

Suppose we are seeking a sparse set of coefficients α and a solution signal or image is synthesized from these representation coefficients as $x = \mathbf{\Phi}\alpha$, where $\mathbf{\Phi} \in \mathbb{R}^{N \times T}$. Such a prior is called a *synthesis sparsity prior*. The ℓ_1-norm decoder known as Basis Pursuit (BP) – see Chen et al. (1999) and equation (8.2) – reads

$$\min_{\alpha \in \mathbb{R}^T} \|\alpha\|_1 \quad \text{s.t.} \quad y = \mathbf{H}\mathbf{\Phi}\alpha = \mathbf{F}\alpha . \tag{7.2}$$

This is a particular instance of (P) where $l = 1$,

$$R_1(x) = \min_{\alpha \in \mathbb{R}^T} \|\alpha\|_1 \quad \text{s.t.} \quad x = \mathbf{\Phi}\alpha , \tag{7.3}$$

and $D(\mathbf{H}\cdot, y)$ is the indicator function of the affine subspace $\{x \in \mathbb{R}^N | y = \mathbf{H}x\}$.

When the observation y is subject to noise or perturbations, the equality constraint must be relaxed to a noise-aware variant. Problem (P) becomes typically Basis Pursuit DeNoising (BPDN) in its penalized form (Chen et al. 1999) when

$$\min_{\alpha \in \mathbb{R}^T} \frac{1}{2} \|y - \mathbf{F}\alpha\|^2 + \lambda \|\alpha\|_1, \quad \lambda > 0 \tag{7.4}$$

which is also known as the Lasso in the statistics literature after Tibshirani (1996); in fact this appeared there in an ℓ_1-constrained form:

$$\min_{\alpha \in \mathbb{R}^T} \frac{1}{2} \|y - \mathbf{F}\alpha\|^2 \quad \text{s.t.} \quad \|\alpha\|_1 \leq \rho. \tag{7.5}$$

Equation (7.4) is again an instance of (P) with $D(\mathbf{H}x, y) = \frac{1}{2} \|y - \mathbf{H}x\|^2$ and R_1 is, up to a multiplication by λ, as in equation (7.3). Similarly equation (7.5) is also a special case of (P) with $D(\mathbf{H}x, y) = \frac{1}{2} \|y - \mathbf{H}x\|^2$ and R_1 is the indicator function of the closed convex set $\{\mathbf{\Phi}\alpha | \|\alpha\|_1 \leq \rho\}$. BPDN/Lasso have received, and continue to receive, considerable attention, both on the theoretical and applied sides, in signal and image processing, statistics, and machine learning.

Formulations (7.4) and (7.5) are equivalent[1] to the constrained form

$$\min_{\alpha \in \mathbb{R}^T} \|\alpha\|_1 \quad \text{s.t.} \quad \|y - \mathbf{F}\alpha\| \leq \sigma, \tag{7.6}$$

which is a specialization of (P) with R_1 as in equation (7.3), and $D(\mathbf{H}\cdot, y)$ is the indicator function of the closed convex set $\{x \in \mathbb{R}^N | \|y - \mathbf{H}x\| \leq \sigma\}$. This is a completely nonsmooth optimization problem that has received less interest than equation (7.4), and is more challenging to solve; for example, second-order cone programming (Candès et al. 2006c), probing the Pareto curve (Van Den Berg and Friedlander 2008), smoothing the dual problem and using the Nesterov scheme (Becker et al. 2011), and, more recently, primal-dual splitting algorithms (see Section 7.5).

The Dantzig selector (Candès and Tao 2007) corresponds to

$$\min_{\alpha \in \mathbb{R}^T} \|\alpha\|_1 \quad \text{s.t.} \quad \|\mathbf{F}^T(y - \mathbf{F}\alpha)\| \leq \delta. \tag{7.7}$$

This is again equation (P) for R_1 as in equation (7.3), and $D(\mathbf{H}\cdot, y)$ is the indicator function of $\{x \in \mathbb{R}^N | \|\mathbf{F}^T(y - \mathbf{H}x)\|_\infty \leq \delta\}$.

7.2.2 Analysis-Sparsity Problems

In the *analysis sparsity prior*, one seeks a signal or image x whose coefficients $\mathbf{\Phi}^T x$ are sparse. Clearly, analysis sparse signals x are those such that $(\mathbf{\Phi}^T x)[i] = 0$, for $i \in I$, and I is termed the co-support of x; hence the name *co-sparse model* recently introduced in Nam et al. (2013). One of the most popular sparsity analysis priors is the total variation regularization (Rudin et al. 1992).

The ℓ_1-analysis prior version of equations (7.2), (7.4), (7.5), (7.6), and (7.7) reads respectively,

$$\min_{x \in \mathbb{R}^N} \|\mathbf{\Phi}^T x\|_1 \quad \text{s.t.} \quad y = \mathbf{H}x \tag{7.8}$$

$$\min_{x \in \mathbb{R}^N} \frac{1}{2} \|y - \mathbf{H}x\|^2 + \lambda \|\mathbf{\Phi}^T x\|_1 \tag{7.9}$$

$$\min_{x \in \mathbb{R}^N} \frac{1}{2} \|y - \mathbf{H}x\|^2 \quad \text{s.t.} \quad \|\mathbf{\Phi}^T x\|_1 \leq \rho \tag{7.10}$$

$$\min_{x \in \mathbb{R}^N} \|\mathbf{\Phi}^T x\|_1 \quad \text{s.t.} \quad \|y - \mathbf{H}x\| \leq \sigma \tag{7.11}$$

$$\min_{x \in \mathbb{R}^N} \|\mathbf{\Phi}^T x\|_1 \quad \text{s.t.} \quad \|\mathbf{H}^T(y - \mathbf{H}x)\|_\infty \leq \delta . \tag{7.12}$$

We leave as an exercise to the reader to make the necessary identification of each of these problems to (P).

7.2.3 Analysis- versus Synthesis-Sparsity

There are several natural questions that arise when looking at problems with a synthesis-type sparsity prior on the one hand, and those with an analysis-type prior on the other hand: is there a relation, if any, between the synthesis-type solutions recovered as $\mathbf{\Phi}\alpha^\star$ and the analysis-type ones? When do these two priors give the same answer? The practitioner may also be interested in knowing which type of prior is more devised for a certain application. Investigating the practical and theoretical relationships between these two types of priors has been recently the subject of active work. For example, see Elad et al. (2007); Candès et al. (2008); Selesnick and Figueiredo (2009); Nam et al. (2013) and Vaiter et al. (2013b). In this section we give some clues that we discuss informally.

For orthogonal $\mathbf{\Phi}$, by a simple change variable, the solutions to synthesis and analysis formulations are obviously the same. In the overcomplete (redundant) or rank-deficient setting, analysis- and synthesis-prior formulations are fundamentally different. Indeed, in the synthesis prior any solution $x^\star$ is confined to the column space of the dictionary $\mathbf{\Phi}$, whereas in the analysis formulation, the solutions $x^\star$ are allowed to be arbitrary vectors in $\mathbb{R}^N$. Furthermore, for redundant $\mathbf{\Phi}$, there are much fewer unknowns in the analysis formulation, hence leading to a simpler optimization problem. As opposed to the analysis approach, the synthesis approach has a constructive form that provides an explicit description of the signals it represents and, as such, can benefit from higher redundancy to synthesize rich and complex signals. On the other hand, in the analysis approach, we can ask a signal or image to be simultaneously orthogonal to many columns of $\mathbf{\Phi}$. This might become impossible with a highly redundant dictionary.

Problems with analysis-sparsity prior can be converted to ones having a synthesis-prior flavor when $\mathbf{\Phi}$ is a frame. This is achieved by operating the change of variable $\alpha = \mathbf{\Phi}^T x := \mathbf{T}x$, or equivalently to $x = \mathbf{T}^+\alpha$ with the constraint $\mathbf{T}\mathbf{T}^+\alpha = \alpha$ that is, $\alpha \in \text{Im}(\mathbf{T})$, where $\mathbf{T}^+ = (\mathbf{\Phi}\mathbf{T})^{-1}\mathbf{\Phi}$. An instructive example is when the frame corresponds to a Parseval tight frame (i.e. $\mathbf{\Phi}\mathbf{T} = \mathbf{I}$), as is the case for many dictionaries introduced in the previous chapters (with an appropriate normalization). In such a case, the change of variable becomes $x = \mathbf{\Phi}\alpha$ with constraint $\mathbf{T}\mathbf{\Phi}\alpha = \alpha$. For example, minimizing equation (7.9) with such $\mathbf{\Phi}$ is equivalent to

$$\min_{\alpha \in \mathbb{R}^T} \frac{1}{2} \|y - \mathbf{H}\alpha\|^2 + \lambda \|\alpha\|_1 \quad \text{s.t.} \quad \alpha \in \text{Im}(\mathbf{T}) . \tag{7.13}$$

Roughly speaking, with tight frames, analysis-sparsity problems are equivalent to constrained synthesis-like ones. The converse is, however, not true. Moreover, since $\text{Im}(\mathbf{T})$ is much smaller than the ambient space $\mathbb{R}^T$, α is "very" constrained unlike in the synthesis-type prior where α is allowed to be any vector in $\mathbb{R}^T$.

Choosing between the two priors is a much more delicate and intricate question than it appears at first glance. In fact, since the two priors promote different types of signals (in fact, union of subspaces), one cannot just advocate one over another without knowing the context. From a theoretical point of view, the recovery guarantees for the two priors are also different in general. For instance, for total variation, the jump set of a piecewise signal is barely stable even to small perturbations of the observations. This is true even for a simple denoising problem, which results in the so-called staircasing effect of total variation. For synthesis ℓ_1, the support recovery is more resilient to noise.

From the practitioner viewpoint, the choice of analysis versus synthesis is problem dependent. If the signal has a strictly k-sparse synthesis representation in $\mathbf{\Phi}$, the synthesis approach should be better, since it really operates on the coefficients α to make them as sparse as possible. On the contrary, if the solution is positive, it will hardly be represented with very few atoms in dictionaries such as wavelets or curvelets since all atoms have a zero mean (except coarsest scale atoms). In this case, which may be closer to some real-life applications, analysis-based priors may be better.

7.3 BASICS OF CONVEX ANALYSIS AND PROXIMAL CALCULUS

7.3.1 Basics of Convex Analysis

In this section we provide only some basic prerequisites from convex analysis that are necessary for our exposition. A comprehensive account can be found in Rockafellar (1970) and Lemaréchal and Hiriart-Urruty (1996).

Let $\mathcal{H}$ be a finite-dimensional real vector space (typically $\mathbb{R}^N$ or $\mathbb{R}^T$ throughout) equipped with the inner product $\langle ., . \rangle$ and associated norm $\|.\|$. Let $\mathbf{I}$ be the identity operator on $\mathcal{H}$. The operator spectral norm of the linear operator $\mathbf{A} : \mathcal{H} \to \mathcal{K}$, where $\mathcal{K}$ is a finite-dimensional real vector space, is denoted $\|\mathbf{A}\| = \sup_{x \in \mathcal{H}} \frac{\|\mathbf{A}x\|}{\|x\|}$. For $p \geq 1$, $\|x\|_p = (\sum_i |x[i]|^p)^{1/p}$ is the the ℓ_p-norm with the usual adaptation for the case $p = +\infty$, $\|x\|_\infty = \max_i |x[i]|$. Denote by $\mathbb{B}_p^\rho$ the (closed) ℓ_p-ball of radius $\rho > 0$ centered at the origin.

A real-valued function $F : \mathcal{H} \to (-\infty, +\infty]$ is coercive if $\lim_{\|x\| \to +\infty} F(x) = +\infty$. The domain of F is defined by $\text{dom } F = \{x \in \mathcal{H} \mid F(x) < +\infty\}$, and F is proper if $\text{dom } F \neq \emptyset$. We say that F is lower semi-continuous (lsc) if $\liminf_{x \to x_0} F(x) \geq F(x_0)$. Lower semi-continuity is weaker than continuity, and plays an important role for the existence of solutions in minimization problems. $\Gamma_0(\mathcal{H})$ is the class of all proper lsc convex functions from $\mathcal{H}$ to $(-\infty, +\infty]$.

Let C be a nonempty convex subset of $\mathcal{H}$. $\mathrm{ri}(C)$ denotes its relative interior (i.e. its interior for the topology relative to its affine hull), and the latter is the smallest affine manifold containing C. For instance, the relative interior of a point on the real line is empty, but its relative interior is itself. The indicator function ι_C of C is

$$\iota_C(x) = \begin{cases} 0, & \text{if } x \in C, \\ +\infty, & \text{otherwise}. \end{cases} \tag{7.14}$$

The conjugate of a function $F \in \Gamma_0(\mathcal{H})$ is F^* defined by

$$F^*(u) = \sup_{x \in \mathrm{dom}\, F} \langle u, x \rangle - F(x), \tag{7.15}$$

and we have $F^* \in \Gamma_0(\mathcal{H})$ and the bi-conjugate $F^{**} = F$. For instance, a result that we use intensively is that the conjugate of the ℓ_p-norm is the indicator function of the unit ball B_q^1, where $1/p + 1/q = 1$.

The subdifferential of a function $F \in \Gamma_0(\mathcal{H})$ at $x \in \mathcal{H}$ is the set-valued map ∂F from $\mathcal{H}$ into subsets of $\mathcal{H}$:

$$\partial F(x) = \{u \in \mathcal{H} | \forall z \in \mathcal{H}, F(z) \geq F(x) + \langle u, z - x \rangle\}. \tag{7.16}$$

An element u of $\partial F(x)$ is called a subgradient. If F is differentiable at x, its only subgradient is its gradient (i.e. $\partial F(x) = \{\nabla F(x)\}$ (Rockafellar 1970)). An everywhere differentiable function has a Lipschitz β-continuous gradient, $\beta \geq 0$, if

$$\|\nabla F(x) - \nabla F(z)\| \leq \beta \|x - z\|, \quad \forall (x, z) \in \mathcal{H}^2.$$

A function is strictly convex when the inequality in equation (7.16) holds as a strict inequality for $z \neq x$ (Lemaréchal and Hiriart-Urruty 1996). A function F is strongly convex with modulus $c > 0$ if and only if

$$F(z) \geq F(x) + \langle u, z - x \rangle + \frac{c}{2} \|z - x\|^2, \quad \forall z \in \mathcal{H}. \tag{7.17}$$

$x^\star$ is a global minimizer of $F \in \Gamma_0(\mathcal{H})$ over $\mathcal{H}$ if and only if

$$0 \in \partial F(x^\star), \tag{7.18}$$

see (Rockafellar 1970). The minimum is unique if F is strictly convex.

7.3.2 Proximal Calculus

7.3.2.1 Definition and Basic Properties

Armed with these ingredients from convex analysis, we are now ready to define the notion of a proximity operator, which plays a central role in the chapter. It was introduced in Moreau (1962) as a generalization of the projection operator onto a closed convex set.

Definition 1 (Proximity operator (Moreau 1962)) *Let $F \in \Gamma_0(\mathcal{H})$. Then, for every $\alpha \in \mathcal{H}$, the function $z \mapsto \frac{1}{2} \|\alpha - z\|^2 + F(z)$ achieves its infimum at a unique point denoted by $\mathrm{prox}_F(\alpha)$. The uniquely valued operator $\mathrm{prox}_F : \mathcal{H} \to \mathcal{H}$ thus defined is the proximity operator of F.*

When $F = \iota_C$ for a closed convex set C, prox_F is the projector onto C. Another example of a proximity operator that has been extensively used throughout this book is the one associated with $F(\alpha) = \lambda \|\alpha\|_1$ for $\alpha \in \mathbb{R}^T$, which turns out to be soft-thresholding with threshold λ. See equation (7.21). Throughout, we say that a function F is *simple* if its proximity operator is either known in closed form or can be efficiently computed to high accuracy.

We next record some calculus rules of proximity operators that are useful in the sequel. They are not difficult to prove, and one may refer to, for example, Moreau (1963, 1965) and Bauschke and Combettes (2011).

Property 3

> (i) $\forall z \in \mathcal{H}$, $\mathrm{prox}_{F(\cdot-z)}(\alpha) = z + \mathrm{prox}_F(\alpha - z)$.
> (ii) $\forall z \in \mathcal{H}, \forall \rho \in (-\infty, \infty)$, $\mathrm{prox}_{F(\rho\cdot)}(\alpha) = \mathrm{prox}_{\rho^2 F}(\rho\alpha)/\rho$.
> (iii) $\forall z \in \mathcal{H}, \forall \rho > 0, \tau \in \mathbb{R}$, let $G(\alpha) = F(\alpha) + \rho\|\alpha\|^2 + \langle \alpha, z \rangle + \tau$. Then $\mathrm{prox}_G = \mathrm{prox}_{F/(1+\rho)}((\alpha-z)/(\rho+1))$.
> (iv) *Separability: let $\{F_i\}_{1 \le i \le n}$ be a family of functions in $\Gamma_0(\mathcal{H})$, and F defined on $\mathcal{H}^n$ with $F(\alpha_1, \ldots, \alpha_n) = \sum_{i=1}^n F_i(\alpha_i)$. Then $\mathrm{prox}_F(\alpha) = (\mathrm{prox}_{F_i}(\alpha_i))_{1 \le i \le n}$.*

The following result, known as Moreau's identity, relates the proximity operator of F and that of its conjugate F^*. Let $F \in \Gamma_0(\mathcal{H})$; then for any $\alpha \in \mathcal{H}$

$$\mathrm{prox}_{\rho F^*}(\alpha) + \rho\, \mathrm{prox}_{F/\rho}(\alpha/\rho) = \alpha, \forall\, 0 < \rho < +\infty. \tag{7.19}$$

The first proof of this result dates back to Moreau (1965) for $\rho = 1$, and other ones are in Rockafellar (1970) and Combettes and Wajs (2005). From equation (7.19), we conclude that

$$\mathrm{prox}_{F^*} = \mathbf{I} - \mathrm{prox}_F.$$

7.3.2.2 Proximity Operator of Convex Sparsity Penalties

In the following, we consider a family of simple penalties (i.e. whose proximity operator takes an appealing closed form). Such penalties are typical of those arising to promote sparsity. Consider the additive penalty:

$$J(\alpha) = \sum_{i=1}^T \psi_i(\alpha[i]),$$

where we assume that $\forall 1 \le i \le T$:

> (i) $\psi_i \in \Gamma_0(\mathbb{R})$.
> (ii) ψ_i is even-symmetric, non-negative, non-decreasing on $[0, +\infty)$.
> (iii) ψ_i is continuous on $\mathbb{R}$, with $\psi_i(0) = 0$.
> (iv) ψ_i differentiable on $(0, +\infty)$, but is not necessarily smooth at 0 and admits a positive right derivative at zero: $\psi'_{i+}(0) = \lim_{t\downarrow 0} \frac{\psi(t)}{t} \ge 0$.

Under assumptions (i)–(iv), we have from Property 3(iv) that

$$\mathrm{prox}_{\lambda J}(\alpha) = (\mathrm{prox}_{\lambda\psi_i}(\alpha[i]))_{1 \le i \le T}, \quad \lambda > 0,$$

where $\widetilde{\alpha}[i] := \text{prox}_{\lambda \psi_i}(\alpha[i])$ has exactly one continuous and odd-symmetric solution:

$$\tilde{\alpha}[i] = \begin{cases} 0 & \text{if } |\alpha[i]| \leq \lambda \psi'_{i+}(0) \,, \\ \alpha[i] - \lambda \psi'_i(\widetilde{\alpha}[i]) & \text{if } |\alpha[i]| > \lambda \psi'_{i+}(0) \,. \end{cases} \tag{7.20}$$

The proof can be found in Fadili and Starck (2009). Similar results to (7.20) appear under different forms in several papers, including Nikolova (2000); Antoniadis and Fan (2001); Fadili and Bullmore (2005); Combettes and Pesquet (2007b); Fadili et al. (2009b). Some of these works deal even with non-convex penalties; see Section 7.6.1 and the discussion at the end of Section 6.2.2.

Example 1 *Among many penalty functions* ψ_i *that are within the scope of* (7.20), *we have:*

- $\psi_i : t \in \mathbb{R} \mapsto \lambda |t|^p$, $p \geq 1$. *For instance, for the popular case* $p = 1$, *this corresponds to* $J(\alpha) = \lambda \|\alpha\|_1$, *whose proxmity operator is given by soft-thresholding:*

$$\text{prox}_{\lambda \|\cdot\|_1}(\alpha) = \text{SoftThresh}_\lambda(\alpha) = \left(\left(1 - \frac{\lambda}{|\alpha[i]|} \right)_+ \alpha[i] \right)_{1 \leq i \leq T} , \tag{7.21}$$

  where $(\cdot)_+ = \max(\cdot, 0)$. *See equation* (6.14).
- *Huber's function:*

$$\psi_i : t \in \mathbb{R} \mapsto \begin{cases} t^2/2 & \text{if } |t| \leq \lambda \,, \\ \lambda |t| - \lambda^2/2 & \text{otherwise} \,. \end{cases}$$

  Observe that Huber's function is known in the optimization community as the Moreau envelope of index λ *of the* ℓ_1 *norm.*
- *Robust penalty in Nia and Huo (2009): for* $0 < \delta < \pi/2$

$$\psi_i : t \in \mathbb{R} \mapsto \begin{cases} -\log \cos(\delta t/\lambda) & \text{if } |t| < \lambda \,, \\ \delta \tan(\delta)(|t/\lambda| - 1) - \log \cos(\delta) & \text{otherwise} \,. \end{cases}$$

These functions are plotted in the left panel of Fig. 7.1, and the corresponding proximity operators obtained from equation (7.20) are depicted on the right. Additional examples can be found in the robust statistics literature (Huber 1981), and others are given in Combettes and Pesquet (2007b).

The main benefit of the separability of the penalty function J is to allow the proximity operator computation problem to be separable in each coordinate. However, the same reasoning holds if the penalty is separable in blocks/groups. To make things clearer, consider the example of the group-sparsity penalty, also known as the weighted $\ell_1 - \ell_2$ norm,

$$J(\alpha) = \sum_{b=1}^{B} \lambda_b \|\alpha[\mathcal{I}_b]\|, \lambda_b > 0 \,\forall 1 \leq b \leq B \,, \tag{7.22}$$

where $(\mathcal{I}_b)_{1 \leq b \leq B}$ is a non-overlapping partition of the coefficient index set $\mathcal{I} = \{1, \ldots, T\}$ into B blocks; i.e., $\bigcup_{b=1}^{B} \mathcal{I}_b = \mathcal{I}, \mathcal{I}_b \cap \mathcal{I}_{b'} = \emptyset, \,\forall b \neq b'$. This sparsity measure has appeared in many papers including the group-Lasso (Kim et al. 2006;

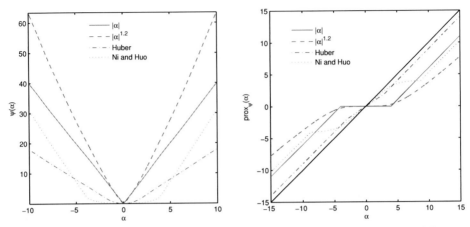

Figure 7.1. Examples of penalties ψ_i (left) and associated proximity operators (right).

Yuan and Lin 2006; Chesneau and Hebiri 2008; Meier et al. 2008) or model-based compressed sensing (Baraniuk et al. 2010). Using subdifferential calculus and Property 3(iv), it can be shown that

$$\text{prox}_{\sum_{b=1}^{B} \lambda_b \|\cdot[\mathcal{I}_b]\|}(\alpha) = \left(\alpha[\mathcal{I}_b] \left(1 - \frac{\lambda_b}{\|\alpha[\mathcal{I}_b]\|} \right)_+ \right)_{1 \leq b \leq B}. \tag{7.23}$$

7.3.2.3 Projector on the ℓ_p-ball

For $p \geq 1$ and $\rho > 0$, recall that $\mathbb{B}_p^\rho$ is the closed ℓ_p-ball of radius ρ. We here detail how to compute $P_{\mathbb{B}_p^\rho}$, the projector, onto $\mathbb{B}_p^\rho$.

- $p = 2$: we have

$$P_{\mathbb{B}_2^\rho}(\alpha) = \begin{cases} \alpha & \text{if } \|\alpha\| \leq \rho, \\ \alpha \rho / \|\alpha\| & \text{otherwise}. \end{cases} \tag{7.24}$$

- $p = \infty$: $P_{B_\rho^\infty}$ takes the simple form

$$P_{\mathbb{B}_\infty^\rho}(\alpha) = \left(\frac{\alpha[i]}{\max(|\alpha[i]|/\rho, 1)} \right)_{1 \leq i \leq T}. \tag{7.25}$$

- $p = 1$: if $\|\alpha\|_1 \leq \rho$, then obviously $P_{\mathbb{B}_1^\rho}(\alpha) = \alpha$. Otherwise, the projector onto $P_{\mathbb{B}_1^\rho}$ can be computed through soft-thresholding (7.21) and coefficient sorting as in Duchi et al. (2008); den Berg et al. (2008); Candès et al. (2006c) and Daubechies et al. (2008). Indeed, since the constraint is active, the Lagrange multiplier $\lambda > 0$. If it were known, then $P_{\mathbb{B}_1^\rho}(\alpha) = \text{SoftThresh}_\lambda(\alpha)$. It then follows that

$$\|\text{SoftThresh}_\lambda(\alpha)\|_1 = \sum_{i:|\alpha[i]| \geq \lambda} (|\alpha[i]| - \lambda).$$

Clearly, the function $\lambda \in]0, \|\alpha\|_\infty] \mapsto \|\text{SoftThresh}_\lambda(\alpha)\|_1$ is a piecewise affine and decreasing function with breakpoints at $\alpha_{(i)}$, the ordered entries in ascending magnitude of α. Now since the constraint is active, to get the Lagrange multiplier $\lambda(\rho)$, it is sufficient to locate the abscissa at which this piecewise affine function equals ρ. Define $\tilde{\alpha}_i = \sum_{j=i+1}^{T-1} \alpha_{(j)}$ as the cumulated ordered magnitudes. One can check immediately that the value of $\lambda(\rho)$ is

$$\lambda(\rho) = \alpha_{(j)} + (\alpha_{(j+1)} - \alpha_{(j)})\frac{\tilde{\alpha}_{j+1} - \rho}{\tilde{\alpha}_{j+1} - \tilde{\alpha}_j}\,, \tag{7.26}$$

where j is such that $\tilde{\alpha}_{j+1} \le \rho < \tilde{\alpha}_j$. The sorting step can be done in $O(T \log T)$ time. An improved approach replaces sorting with a median search-like procedure whose expected complexity is linear in T. This has been developed independently in Duchi et al. (2008) and den Berg et al. (2008).

It is worth pointing out that a similar procedure can be deduced for the projection on the ball associated with the weighted $\ell_1 - \ell_2$ norm in equation (7.22), by now sorting the values of $(\|\alpha[\mathcal{I}_b]\|)_{1 \le b \le B}$.

■ For the other values $2 < q < +\infty$, the projector cannot be computed analytically but only iteratively by solving the Karush-Kuhn-Tucker equations using the Newton method (Jacques et al. 2009).

7.3.2.4 Affine Subspace Projector

Let $\mathbf{F}$ be a linear operator as above. Let y be in the range of $\mathbf{F}$. The goal here is to compute the projector on the affine subspace $\mathcal{C} = \{\alpha \in \mathbb{R}^T | \mathbf{F}\alpha = y\}$. We have

$$P_\mathcal{C}(\alpha) = \alpha + \mathbf{F}^+ (y - \mathbf{F}\alpha)\,. \tag{7.27}$$

To see this, it is sufficient to check the sufficient and necessary properties of a projection: $\mathbf{F} P_\mathcal{C}(\alpha) \in \mathcal{C}$ and $\langle P_\mathcal{C}(\alpha) - \alpha, z - P_\mathcal{C}(\alpha) \rangle \ge 0, \forall z \in \mathcal{C}$.

7.3.2.5 Pre-Composition with an Affine Operator

Let $\mathbf{F}$ be a linear operator. In this section, we provide an important result on the proximity operator of the pre-composition of $F \in \Gamma_0(\mathcal{H})$ with the affine mapping $\mathbf{A} : \mathcal{H} \to \mathcal{K}, \alpha \mapsto \mathbf{F}\alpha - y$; i.e., solve

$$\min_{z \in \mathcal{H}} \frac{1}{2}\|\alpha - z\|^2 + F(\mathbf{A}z)\,. \tag{7.28}$$

Solving this problem efficiently will be useful at several stages in the rest of the chapter. First, if $\mathbf{F}$ is orthonormal, it is easily seen from equation (7.28) and Property 3(i) that

$$\text{prox}_{F \circ \mathbf{A}}(\alpha) = \mathbf{F}^{\mathrm{T}}(y + \text{prox}_F(\mathbf{F}\alpha - y))\,. \tag{7.29}$$

Otherwise, we distinguish three situations.

(i) $\mathbf{F}$ is a tight frame with constant c. Then $F \circ \mathbf{A} \in \Gamma_0(\mathcal{H})$ and

$$\text{prox}_{F \circ \mathbf{A}}(\alpha) = \alpha + c^{-1}\mathbf{F}^{\mathrm{T}}(\text{prox}_{cF} -\mathbf{I})(\mathbf{F}\alpha - y)\,. \tag{7.30}$$

(ii) $\mathbf{F}$ is a general frame with lower and upper bounds c_1 and c_2. Thus $F \circ \mathbf{A} \in \Gamma_0(\mathcal{H})$. Define the scheme described in Algorithm 23.

Algorithm 23 Iterative scheme to compute the proximity operator of precomposition with an affine operator

---

Initialization: choose some $u^{(0)} \in \mathrm{dom}(F^*)$ and set $\mathsf{p}^{(0)} = \alpha - \mathbf{F}^-\mathbf{T}u^{(0)}, \mu \in]0, 2/c_2[$.
Main iteration:
for $t = 0$ **to** $N_{\mathrm{iter}} - 1$ **do**

$$u^{(t+1)} = \mu(\mathbf{I} - \mathrm{prox}_{\mu^{-1}F})(\mu^{-1}u^{(t)} + \mathbf{A}\mathsf{p}^{(t)}) ,$$
$$\mathsf{p}^{(t+1)} = \alpha - \mathbf{F}^\mathsf{T}u^{(t+1)} . \tag{7.31}$$

Output: Estimate of $\mathrm{prox}_{F \circ \mathbf{A}}(\alpha)$: $\mathsf{p}^{(N_{\mathrm{iter}})}$.

Then $\mathsf{p}^{(t)}$ converges linearly to $\mathrm{prox}_{F \circ \mathbf{A}}(\alpha)$, and the best convergence rate is attained for $\mu \equiv 2/(c_1 + c_2)$:

$$\left\| \mathsf{p}^{(t)} - \mathrm{prox}_{F \circ \mathbf{A}}(\alpha) \right\|^2 \leq \frac{c_2}{c_1}\left(\frac{c_2 - c_1}{c_2 + c_1}\right)^{2t} \left\| \mathsf{p}^{(0)} - \mathrm{prox}_{F \circ \mathbf{A}}(\alpha) \right\|^2 . \tag{7.32}$$

(iii) For all other cases, suppose that $\mathrm{Im}(\mathbf{F}) \cap \mathrm{ri}(\mathrm{dom}\, F)) \neq \emptyset$. Apply Algorithm 23. Then $\mathsf{p}^{(t)}$ converges to $\mathrm{prox}_{F \circ \mathbf{A}}(\alpha)$ at the rate $O(1/t)$, i.e., $\exists C > 0$, such that

$$\left\| \mathsf{p}^{(t)} - \mathrm{prox}_{F \circ \mathbf{A}}(\alpha) \right\|^2 \leq C/t . \tag{7.33}$$

A complete proof is given in Fadili and Starck (2009) using the Fenchel-Rockafellar duality, the forward-backward scheme to be discussed in Section 7.4.2, as well as the rules in Property 3 and (7.19). Note that the case of tight frames was proved differently in Combettes and Pesquet (2007a).

When $\mathbf{F}$ corresponds to a frame, the convergence rate (7.32) of the forward-backward iteration depends clearly on the redundancy of the frame. The higher the redundancy, the slower the convergence. More precisely, the number of necessary iterations to obtain a solution up to the accuracy ϵ on the iterates is $O(\frac{c_2}{c_1}\log \epsilon^{-1})$. For the general case (iii) where $\mathbf{F}$ is not a frame, the convergence rate to the proximity operator is only $O(1/t)$ (Fadili and Starck 2009), hence necessitating as many as $O(1/\epsilon)$ iterations to reach an ϵ convergence tolerance.

Accelerated first-order algorithm
Instead of Algorithm 23, cases (ii) and (iii) of Section 7.3.2.5 can be solved using an accelerated first-order method inspired by the work of Nesterov (2005, 2007) or Beck and Teboulle (2009). For instance, the Fast Iterative Shrinkage-Thresholding Algorithm (FISTA) type (Beck and Teboulle 2009) accelerated scheme to be used instead of Algorithm 23 is summarized in Algorithm 24. If $\mathbf{F}$ is not a frame, break Algorithm 24 applies with $c_1 = 0$.

This algorithm enjoys the following convergence rates. See Fadili and Starck (2009) for a proof. Generally,

$$\left\| \mathsf{p}^{(t)} - \mathrm{prox}_{F \circ \mathbf{A}}(\alpha) \right\|^2 = O(1/t^2) . \tag{7.35}$$

Algorithm 24 Accelerated scheme to compute the proximity operator of pre-composition with an affine operator

---

Initialization: $u^{(0)} \in \text{dom}(F^*), \theta_1 = 1, \xi^{(1)} = u^{(0)}, \mu = 1/c_2$.
Main iteration:
for $t = 1$ **to** N_{iter} **do**

$$u^{(t+1)} = \mu(\mathbf{I} - \text{prox}_{\mu^{-1}F})\left(\mu^{-1}\xi^{(t)} + \mathbf{A}\left(\alpha - \mathbf{F}^{\mathrm{T}}\xi^{(t)}\right)\right),$$

$$\theta_{t+1} = \frac{1 + \sqrt{1 + 4\theta_t^2}}{2}, \tag{7.34}$$

$$\xi^{(t+1)} = u^{(t)} + \left(\frac{\theta_t - 1}{\theta_{t+1}}\right)\left(u^{(t)} - u^{(t-1)}\right).$$

Output: Estimate of $\text{prox}_{F \circ \mathbf{A}}(\alpha)$: $\alpha - \mathbf{F}^{\mathrm{T}}u^{(N_{\text{iter}})}$.

If $\mathbf{F}$ is a frame (nontight), then the convergence becomes linear, i.e., $\forall\, t \geq 1$

$$\left\|\mathsf{p}^{(t)} - \text{prox}_{F \circ \mathbf{A}}(\alpha)\right\|^2 = O(\rho^t) \tag{7.36}$$

for $\rho \in [0, 1[$.

7.4 PROXIMAL SPLITTING FRAMEWORK

Recall from (P) that our goal is the minimization of functions of the form $F = D(\mathbf{H}\cdot, y) + \sum_k R_k$. We assume that the set of minimizers of (P) is nonempty. From the minimality condition and Definition 1 of the proximity operator, $x^\star$ is a global minimizer of (P) if and only if

$$0 \in \partial F(x^\star)$$
$$\Longleftrightarrow 0 \in \partial(\gamma F)(x^\star), \ \forall \gamma > 0$$
$$\Longleftrightarrow x^\star - x^\star \in \partial(\gamma F)(x^\star)$$
$$\Longleftrightarrow x^\star = \text{prox}_{\gamma F}(x^\star), \tag{7.37}$$

where $\gamma > 0$ is known as the proximal step size. The proximal-type algorithm constructed as

$$x^{(t+1)} = \text{prox}_{\gamma F}\left(x^{(t)}\right)$$

is a fundamental algorithm for finding a global minimum of F. In Martinet (1972), it was proved that $x^{(t)}$ converges to a global minimizer of (P). The main difficulty with the method is that $\text{prox}_{\gamma F}$ may be hard to compute in general, depending on the function F. This is the case in most inverse problems arising in image and signal processing.

7.4.1 The Gist of Splitting

Suppose that the invidual functions D and R_k enjoy some remarkable specific properties (e.g. they are differentiable or simple). Splitting methods for problem (equation label) (P) are algorithms that do not attempt to evaluate the proximity operator $\mathrm{prox}_{\gamma F}$ of the combined function F, but instead perform a sequence of calculations involving separately the specific properties of the individual functions D and R_k involved in the summand. Some of the splitting algorithms even achieve full decomposition by isolating the actions of the involved linear operators (e.g., **H**). All the individual quantities are easier to evaluate by assumption, and this turns out to be true in many situations such as those we have already discussed in equations (7.2), (7.4), (7.6), and (7.7), in both their synthesis- and analysis-prior forms. Among the most well-known splitting algorithms in the signal and image processing community are the alternating projection onto convex sets (POCS) and the projected gradient descent scheme.

Splitting algorithms have generated an extensive literature (see, e.g., Eckstein (1989); Bauschke and Combettes (2011); Combettes and Pesquet (2011) and references therein). In the last decade, there has been revitalized and intensive work on these algorithms because of their ability to solve large-scale general convex minimization problems, in particular those appearing in sparsity regularized inverse problems. The goal in this chapter is by no means to give an exhaustive list and description of these algorithms. Rather, we focus on the most important and widely used classes pertaining to the targeted applications and problems in sparsity.

To ease the exposition in the rest of the section, we first focus on the synthesis-sparsity prior, in which case (P) reads

$$\min_{\alpha \in \mathbb{R}^T} D(\mathbf{F}\alpha, y) + \sum_{k=1}^{l} J_k(\alpha) , \tag{7.38}$$

where the regularizing penalties $J_k \in \Gamma_0(\mathbb{R}^T)$. For $l = 1$, (7.38) is equivalent to (P) with the correspondence

$$R_1(x) = \min_{\alpha} J_1(\alpha) \quad \text{s.t.} \quad x = \mathbf{\Phi}\alpha ,$$

see the examples, equations (7.2), (7.4)–(7.7). We recall that we assume that the set of minimizers of equation (7.38) is nonempty.

Leaving the details to the corresponding subsections, we provide in Table 7.1 a bird's eye view of the proximal splitting algorithms presented in this chapter. For each algorithm, we give the structured problem (specialization of (7.38)) to which it applies.

7.4.2 Forward-Backward

Forward-backward (FB) splitting (Gabay 1983; Tseng 1991; Combettes and Wajs 2005) is essentially a generalization of the classical gradient projection method for constrained convex optimization and inherits restrictions similar to those methods. FB applies in the following setting.

Table 7.1. Summary of which splitting algorithm applies to a given class of problems. We recall that a function is said to be simple if its proximity operator is either known in closed form or can be efficiently computed to high accuracy

Splitting algorithm	Objective	Assumptions
Forward-backward	$D(\mathbf{F}\cdot, y) + J_1$	J_1 simple, $\nabla D(\cdot, y)$ Lipschitz
FISTA	$D(\mathbf{F}\cdot, y) + J_1$	J_1 simple, $\nabla D(\cdot, y)$ Lipschitz
Douglas-Rachford	$D(\mathbf{F}\cdot, y) + J_1$	J_1 and $D(\mathbf{F}\cdot, y)$ simple
ADMM	$D(\mathbf{F}\cdot, y) + J_1$	J_1 and $D(\cdot, y)$ simple, $\mathbf{F}^{\mathsf{T}}\mathbf{F}$ invertible
GFB	$D(\mathbf{F}\cdot, y) + \sum_{k=1}^{l} J_k$	J_k simple, $\nabla D(\cdot, y)$ Lipschitz
Primal-dual	$D(\mathbf{F}\cdot, y) + J_1 + \sum_{k=2}^{l} G_k \circ \mathbf{A}_k$	J_1 and G_k simple, $\mathbf{A}_k$ linear, $\nabla D(\cdot, y)$ Lipschitz

Setting 1 *Solve equation* (7.38) *with* $l = 1, J_1$ *is simple, and* $D(\cdot, y)$ *is differentiable and its gradient is* β-*Lipschitz continuous.*

The relaxed form of FB splitting uses the recursion

$$
\begin{cases}
\mu \in]0, \frac{2}{\beta \|\mathbf{F}\|^2}[, \tau_t \in [0, \kappa], \kappa = \frac{4 - \mu \beta \|\mathbf{F}\|^2}{2} \in]1, 2[, \sum_{t \in \mathbb{N}} \tau_t (\kappa - \tau_t) = +\infty, \\
\alpha^{(t+1)} = \alpha^{(t)} + \tau_t \left(\mathrm{prox}_{\mu J_1} \left(\alpha^{(t)} - \mu \mathbf{F}^{\mathsf{T}} \nabla D(\mathbf{F}\alpha^{(t)}, y) \right) - \alpha^{(t)} \right).
\end{cases}
\tag{7.39}
$$

The widely used version is applied when the relaxation parameter is set to $\tau_t \equiv 1$. But this parameter may enhance convergence performance in practice. The step size μ can be made iteration dependent, but at the cost of more technicalities in the choice of μ_t and τ_t.

In the language of numerical analysis, the gradient descent step within the parentheses is the forward step, and application of the proximity operator of J_1 is the backward step. This iteration is probably one of the most popular ones used in the image and signal processing community. For instance, if we specialize J_1 to the indicator function of a closed convex set, say $\mathcal{C}$, iteration (7.39) amounts to the well-known projected gradient descent.

If we take $J_1(\alpha) = \|\alpha\|_p^p$ $(p \geq 1)$, and $D(\mathbf{F}\alpha, y) = \frac{1}{2} \|y - \mathbf{F}\alpha\|^2$, recursion (7.39) without relaxation has been recently rediscovered by several authors under different frameworks: using surrogate functionals in Daubechies et al. (2004) for $J_1(\alpha) = \|\alpha\|_p^p$, $1 \leq p < 2$, or using an expectation-maximization interpretation (Figueiredo and Nowak 2003). Combettes and Wajs (2005) were the first to revitalize the elegant and general framework of FB splitting that can be specialized to nonsmooth sparsity-promoting regularized problems with differentiable data fidelity. The careful reader may have recognized that the unrelaxed FB iteration (together woth Moreau identity (7.19)) was already applied to solve the Fenchel-Rockafellar dual problem of (7.28) to get (7.31).

Iteration (7.39) converges to a global minimizer $\alpha^\star$; see, e.g., (Combettes and Wajs 2005). Moreover, for $\tau_t \equiv 1$, $(D(\mathbf{F}\alpha^{(t)}, y) + R(\alpha^{(t)})) - (D(\mathbf{F}\alpha^{(t)}, y) + R(\alpha^{(t)}))$ is known to converge at the sublinear rate $O(1/t)$ (Nesterov 2007; Bredies and Lorenz

2008; Beck and Teboulle 2009) in the general case. If the objective function is strongly convex, then the convergence on the objective becomes globally linear, which also entails linear convergence of the iterates $\alpha^{(t)}$ themselves.

7.4.3 Accelerated/Inertial Forward-Backward

It is, however, known from complexity arguments in the sense of Nemirovsky and Yudin (1983) that for the completely smooth convex case, the optimal objective convergence rate of any first-order scheme is $O(1/t^2)$. For the composite class of problems in Setting 1, accelerated versions of FB have been proposed to achieve such a convergence rate (Nesterov 2007; Beck and Teboulle 2009; Tseng 2008). The most popular in the sparsity field is certainly the one due to Beck and Teboulle (2009), known as FISTA, which builds upon the work of Nesterov (1983). In this accelerated version, FB is modified by incorporating an *inertial* step, which gives the following iteration:

$$\begin{cases} \mu \in]0, \frac{1}{\beta\|\mathbf{F}\|^2}], \theta_1 = 1, \xi^{(1)} = \alpha^{(0)}, \\ \alpha^{(t+1)} = \text{prox}_{\mu J_1}\left(\xi^{(t)} - \mu\mathbf{F}^{\mathrm{T}}\nabla D\left(\mathbf{F}\xi^{(t)}, y\right)\right), \\ \theta_{t+1} = \frac{1+\sqrt{1+4\theta_t^2}}{2}, \\ \xi^{(t+1)} = \alpha^{(t)} + \left(\frac{\theta_t-1}{\theta_{t+1}}\right)\left(\alpha^{(t)} - \alpha^{(t-1)}\right). \end{cases} \tag{7.40}$$

Recursion (7.40) is such that $\left(D(\mathbf{F}\alpha^{(t)}, y) + R(\alpha^{(t)})\right) - \left(D(\mathbf{F}\alpha^{(t)}, y) + R(\alpha^{(t)})\right)$ converges at the rate $O(1/t^2)$ as predicted. However, there is no guarantee on the convergence of the iterates themselves in general, unless the objective is strongly convex, in which case the convergence is linear. This was an open problem until the very recent work of Chambolle and Dossal (2014). There, the authors proved that, with the choice $\theta_t = \frac{t+a-1}{a}$, for $a > 2$, $\alpha^{(t)}$ converges to a global minimizer while maintaining the $O(1/t^2)$ on the objective.

We draw the reader's attention to the fact that equation (7.34) is nothing but an application of equation (7.40) to solving the Fenchel-Rockafellar dual of equation (7.28).

7.4.4 Douglas-Rachford

One regularizer $l = 1$

Smoothness of $D(\cdot, y)$ is a prerequisite to applying FB or FISTA. We now turn to the following completely nonsmooth setting.

Setting 2 *Solve equation (7.38) with $l = 1$ and J_1 and $D(\mathbf{F}\cdot, y)$ are simple. Assume that $\text{ri}(\text{dom } D(\mathbf{F}\cdot, y)) \cap \text{ri}(\text{dom } J_1) \neq \emptyset$.*

The last assumption is crucial to application of the subdifferential sum rule. Simplicity of $D(\mathbf{F}\cdot, y)$ holds true if, for instance, $D(\cdot, y)$ is simple and $\mathbf{F}$ is a tight frame; see equation (7.30).

The Douglas-Rachford (DR) splitting scheme, which dates back to Lions and Mercier (1979), is very well suited to solving problems in this setting. The most general form of the DR scheme may be expressed via the recursion

$$
\begin{cases}
\gamma > 0, \tau_t \in [0, 2], \sum_{t \in \mathbb{N}} \tau_t(2 - \tau_t) = +\infty, \\
z^{(t+1)} = \left(1 - \frac{\tau_t}{2}\right) z^{(t)} + \frac{\tau_t}{2} \operatorname{rprox}_{\gamma J_1} \left(\operatorname{rprox}_{\gamma D(\mathbf{F} \cdot, y)} \left(z^{(t)}\right)\right), \\
\alpha^{(t+1)} = \operatorname{prox}_{\gamma D(\mathbf{F} \cdot, y)} \left(z^{(t+1)}\right),
\end{cases}
\tag{7.41}
$$

where the reflection operator $\operatorname{rprox}_{\gamma F}(\alpha) := 2 \operatorname{prox}_{\gamma F}(\alpha) - \alpha$. Since the set of minimizers is nonempty, $z^{(t)}$ converges to $\bar{z}$, where $\bar{z}$ belongs to the set of fixed points of $\operatorname{rprox}_{\gamma J_1} \circ \operatorname{rprox}_{\gamma D(\mathbf{F} \cdot, y)}$. Moreover, $\alpha^{(t)}$ converges to a global minimizer $\alpha^{\star 2}$.

Observe that the DR scheme is not symmetric, and changing the order of the functions, though this does not change the convergence guarantees, can have an important practical impact. Think, for instance, of the case of a constraint (i.e. where J_1 is the indicator function of closed convex set). See Section 7.5.3 for detailed examples.

The DR splitting has been brought to light in the image and signal processing literature recently by Combettes and Pesquet (2007a). Since then, it has been used to solve constrained inverse problems by Dupé et al. (2009); Chaux et al. (2009); Durand et al. (2010) and Starck et al. (2013).

Arbitrary number of regularizers
Consider now the following setting.

Setting 3 *Solve equation (7.38) with $l \geq 1$, all J_k, $k = 1, \ldots, l$, and $D(\mathbf{F} \cdot, y)$ are simple. Assume that* $\operatorname{ri}(\operatorname{dom} D(\mathbf{F} \cdot, y)) \cap \operatorname{ri}(\operatorname{dom} J_1) \cap \cdots \cap \operatorname{ri}(\operatorname{dom} J_l) \neq \emptyset$.

To extend the DR scheme to this setting, the key is to introduce auxiliary variables and bring back the problem to the sum of two simple functions in the product space $\mathbb{R}^{T(l+1)}$. Indeed, Setting 3 is equivalent to solving

$$
\min_{(\alpha_1, \ldots, \alpha_{l+1}) \in \mathbb{R}^{T(l+1)}} G(\alpha_1, \ldots, \alpha_{l+1}) + \iota_S(\alpha_1, \ldots, \alpha_{l+1})
\tag{7.42}
$$

where

$$
G(\alpha_1, \ldots, \alpha_{l+1}) := D(\mathbf{F}\alpha_1, y) + \sum_{k=1}^{l} J_k(\alpha_k) \text{ and}
\tag{7.43}
$$

$$
S := \{(\alpha_1, \ldots, \alpha_{l+1}) \in \mathbb{R}^{T(l+1)} | \alpha_1 = \alpha_2 = \cdots = \alpha_{l+1}\}.
\tag{7.44}
$$

This has a similar form to the problem in Setting 2. To apply DR, we need to compute the projector on S and the proximity operator of G. The projector on S is

$$
P_S(\alpha_1, \ldots, \alpha_{l+1}) = \left(\frac{1}{l+1} \sum_{k=1}^{l+1} \alpha_k, \ldots, \frac{1}{l+1} \sum_{k=1}^{l+1} \alpha_k\right).
$$

From the separability rule in Property 3(iv), the proximity operator of G is

$$
\operatorname{prox}_{\gamma G}(\alpha_1, \ldots, \alpha_{l+1}) = \left(\operatorname{prox}_{D(\mathbf{F} \cdot, y)}(\alpha_1), \operatorname{prox}_{J_1}(\alpha_2), \ldots, \operatorname{prox}_{J_l}(\alpha_{l+1})\right).
$$

With these two expressions at hand, it is straightforward to check that the DR scheme to solve the problem in Setting 3 reads

$$
\begin{cases}
\gamma > 0, \ \tau_t \in [0, 2], \ \sum_{t \in \mathbb{N}} \tau_t (2 - \tau_t) = +\infty \,, \\
z_1^{(t+1)} = z_1^{(t)} + \tau_t \left(\text{prox}_{\gamma D(\mathbf{F} \cdot, y)} \left(2\alpha^{(t)} - z_1^{(t)} \right) - \alpha^{(t)} \right) \\
z_k^{(t+1)} = z_k^{(t)} + \tau_t \left(\text{prox}_{\gamma J_{k-1}} \left(2\alpha^{(t)} - z_k^{(t)} \right) - \alpha^{(t)} \right), \ k = 2, \ldots, l+1 \,, \\
\alpha^{(t+1)} = \frac{1}{l+1} \sum_{k=1}^{l+1} z_k^{(t+1)} \,.
\end{cases}
\tag{7.45}
$$

Clearly, the DR scheme with the product space trick yields an iteration in which one performs independent parallel proximal steps on each of the simple functions and then computes the next iterate $\alpha^{(t)}$ by essentially averaging the results. The sequence $\alpha^{(t)}$ converges to a global solution of the problem in Setting 3.

Splitting the linear operator

In the above versions of DR, it was supposed that $D(\mathbf{F} \cdot, y)$ is simple. Consider now the following situation.

Setting 4 *Solve equation* (7.38) *with* $l = 1$ *and* J_1 *and* $D(\cdot, y)$ *are simple. Assume that* $\text{ri}(\text{dom } D(\mathbf{F} \cdot, y)) \cap \text{ri}(\text{dom } J_1) \neq \emptyset$.

By introducing an auxiliary variable, the problem in Setting 4 is equivalent to

$$
\min_{\alpha, u = \mathbf{F}\alpha} D(u, y) + J_1(\alpha) \iff \min_{\alpha, u} D(u, y) + J_1(\alpha) + \iota_{\text{ker}((-\mathbf{F} \ \mathbf{I}))}(\alpha, u) \,. \tag{7.46}
$$

By separability (Property 3(iv)), we have

$$
\text{prox}_{\gamma(D(\cdot, y) + J_1)}(\alpha, u) = \begin{pmatrix} \text{prox}_{\gamma J_1}(\alpha) \\ \text{prox}_{\gamma D(\cdot, y)}(u) \end{pmatrix} \,.
$$

Moreover,

$$
\mathrm{P}_{\text{ker}((-\mathbf{F} \ \mathbf{I}))}(\alpha, u) = \begin{pmatrix} \alpha \\ u \end{pmatrix} - \begin{pmatrix} -\mathbf{F}^{\mathrm{T}} \\ \mathbf{I} \end{pmatrix} \left(\mathbf{I} + \mathbf{F}\mathbf{F}^{\mathrm{T}} \right)^{-1} (u - \mathbf{F}\alpha) \,.
$$

With these two expressions at hand, one can apply the DR algorithm to solve for α and u. Note that the projector necessitates inverting $\mathbf{I} + \mathbf{F}\mathbf{F}^{\mathrm{T}}$, which turns out to be easy for some cases of interest (e.g., deconvolution or inpainting with a tight frame dictionary).

This idea of introducing auxiliary variables has been proposed in Briceño-Arias et al. (2010) and Dupé et al. (2011). It also generalizes easily to the case of $l \geq 2$ regularizers by introducing as many auxiliary variables as necessary. We leave this as an exercise to the interested reader.

7.4.5 Alternating-Direction Method of Multipliers, ADMM

In this section, we turn to a scheme that also allows one to split the action of the linear operator $\mathbf{F}$ under some assumptions.

One regularizer $l = 1$

Consider the following setting.

Setting 5 *Solve equation (7.38) with $l = 1$, J_1 and $D(\cdot, y)$ are simple, and $\mathbf{F}^T\mathbf{F}$ is invertible. Assume that $\mathrm{ri}(\mathrm{dom}\, D(\cdot, y)) \cap \mathbf{F}(\mathrm{ri}(\mathrm{dom}\, J_1)) \neq \emptyset$.*

This problem is equivalent to

$$\min_{\alpha, u = \mathbf{F}\alpha}\ D(u, y) + J_1(\alpha)\,. \tag{7.47}$$

The alternating-direction method of multipliers (ADMM) consists of minimizing the augmented Lagrangian

$$L(\alpha, u, w) := D(u, y) + J_1(\alpha) + \langle w/\gamma, \mathbf{F}\alpha - u \rangle + \frac{1}{2\gamma}\|\mathbf{F}\alpha - u\|^2\,, \quad \gamma > 0$$

over α, then over u, and then applying a proximal maximization step with respect to the Lagrange multiplier w. This gives the following ADMM iteration (in the nonrelaxed form for simplicity).

$$\begin{cases} \gamma > 0, \\ \alpha^{(t+1)} = \underset{\alpha \in \mathbb{R}^T}{\mathrm{argmin}}\ J_1(\alpha) + \langle w^{(t)}/\gamma, \mathbf{F}\alpha \rangle + \frac{1}{2\gamma}\left\|\mathbf{F}\alpha - u^{(t)}\right\|^2 \\ u^{(t+1)} = \mathrm{prox}_{\gamma D(\cdot, y)}\left(\mathbf{F}\alpha^{(t+1)} + w^{(t)}\right) \\ w^{(t+1)} = w^{(t)} + \mathbf{F}\alpha^{(t+1)} - u^{(t+1)}\,. \end{cases} \tag{7.48}$$

Observe that by the full rank assumption on $\mathbf{F}$, the update of $\alpha^{(t+1)}$ is well defined and single-valued.

Gabay (1983) showed that ADMM is equivalent to the DR splitting applied to the Fenchel-Rockafellar dual of the problem in Setting 5. Convergence properties of ADMM have been investigated by several authors (Fortin and Glowinski 1983; Gabay and Mercier 1976; Glowinski and Tallec 1989; Eckstein and Bertsekas 1992). A recent class of algorithms called Bregman iterative methods has attracted considerable interest for solving ℓ_1-regularized problems like BP (7.2). For BP and related problems, the split Bregman method (Goldstein and Osher 2009) is in fact ADMM.

Arbitrary number of regularizers
We now turn to the following setting.

Setting 6 *Solve equation (7.38) with $l \geq 1$, all J_k, $k = 1, \ldots, l$, and $D(\cdot, y)$ are simple. Assume that $\exists \alpha \in \bigcap_{k=1}^{l} \mathrm{ri}(\mathrm{dom}\, J_k)$ such that $\mathbf{F}\alpha \in \mathrm{ri}(\mathrm{dom}\, D(\cdot, y))$.*

The key is again to rewrite this problem appropriately. More precisely, the problem in Setting 6 is equivalent to

$$\min_{(u, z_1, \ldots, z_l) \in \mathbb{R}^m \times \mathbb{R}^{Tl}}\ G(u, z_1, \ldots, z_l) \quad \text{s.t.} \quad \mathbf{A}\alpha = \begin{pmatrix} u \\ z_1 \\ \vdots \\ z_l \end{pmatrix}, \tag{7.49}$$

where

$$G(u, z_1, \ldots, z_l) := D(u, y) + \sum_{k=1}^{l} J_k(z_k) \text{ and } \mathbf{A} = \begin{pmatrix} \mathbf{F} \\ \mathbf{I} \\ \vdots \\ \mathbf{I} \end{pmatrix}. \tag{7.50}$$

Such a reformulation was proposed by Afonso et al. (2011) for inverse imaging problems. It has a flavor of equation (7.47), where one of the functions, in fact J_1, has become the zero function. Thus (6) can be solved by ADMM, giving the following recursion:

$$
\begin{cases}
\gamma > 0, \\
\alpha^{(t+1)} = (\mathbf{F}^{\mathrm{T}}\mathbf{F} + l\mathbf{I})^{-1}\big(\mathbf{F}^{\mathrm{T}}(u^{(t)} - w^{(t)}) + \sum_{k=1}^{l}(z_k^{(t)} - \omega_k^{(t)})\big) \\
u^{(t+1)} = \mathrm{prox}_{\gamma D(\cdot, y)}\big(\mathbf{F}\alpha^{(t+1)} + w^{(t)}\big) \\
z_k^{(t+1)} = \mathrm{prox}_{\gamma J_k}\big(\alpha^{(t+1)} + \omega^{(t)}\big), k = 2, \ldots, l+1, \\
w^{(t+1)} = w^{(t)} + \mathbf{F}\alpha^{(t+1)} - u^{(t+1)} \\
\omega_k^{(t+1)} = \omega_k^{(t)} + \alpha^{(t+1)} - z_k^{(t+1)}, k = 2, \ldots, l+1.
\end{cases}
\tag{7.51}
$$

Observe that the full rank assumption on $\mathbf{F}$ is no longer needed since $\mathbf{A}$ is by definition full rank. One now has, however, to invert $\mathbf{F}^{\mathrm{T}}\mathbf{F} + l\mathbf{I}$, for any given $l \geq 1$. This is hopefully possible for many cases of interest in imaging (e.g., deconvolution or inpainting with a tight frame dictionary). One can also note that reformulation (7.49) and iteration (7.51) give yet another decomposition and ADMM algorithm to solve the problem in Setting 5 (i.e., $l = 1$).

7.4.6 Generalized Forward-Backward

Although the FB method has the advantage that only the proximal operator of J_1 needs to be evaluated, its main limitation is that it does not apply to $l \geq 2$ regularizers. Let us now focus on the following setting.

Setting 7 *Solve equation (7.38) with $l \geq 1$, all J_k are simple, $k = 1, \ldots, l$, and $D(\cdot, y)$ is differentiable and its gradient is β-Lipschitz continuous. Assume that $\bigcap_{k=1}^{l} \mathrm{ri}(\mathrm{dom}\, J_k)) \neq \emptyset$.*

A Generalized Forward-Backward (GFB) algorithm was designed precisely to solve problems of the type in Setting 7; see Raguet et al. (2013) for a convergence proof. The GFB recursion reads

$$
\begin{cases}
\mu \in]0, \frac{2}{\beta\|\mathbf{F}\|^2}[, \tau_t \in [0, \kappa], \kappa = \frac{4 - \mu\beta\|\mathbf{F}\|^2}{2} \in]1, 2[, \sum_{t \in \mathbb{N}} \tau_t(\kappa - \tau_t) = +\infty, \\
z_k^{(t+1)} = z_k^{(t)} + \tau_t\big(\mathrm{prox}_{l\mu J_1}\big(2\alpha^{(t)} - z_k^{(t)} - \mu\mathbf{F}^{\mathrm{T}}\nabla D(\mathbf{F}\alpha^{(t)}, y)\big) - \alpha^{(t)}\big), \\
\hspace{6cm} k = 1, \ldots, l, \\
\alpha^{(t+1)} = \frac{1}{l}\sum_{k=1}^{l} z_k^{(t+1)}.
\end{cases}
\tag{7.52}
$$

The GFB algorithm is provably convergent. It can be viewed as a hybridization of the FB and DR algorithms on the product space. Indeed, for $l = 1$, we have $\alpha^{(t)} = z_1^{(t)}$, and the update equation (7.52) becomes that of FB in equation (7.39). If we set $D(\cdot, y) = 0$, the update of the auxiliary variables $(z_k^{(t)})_k$ is exactly equation (7.45) (i.e., DR on the product space).

7.4.7 Primal-Dual Splitting

In all previous algorithms, a matrix inversion is involved whenever a linear operator pre-composes a regularizer, unless the operator corresponds to a tight frame. We
argued that such a matrix inversion can be done efficiently under certain circumstances. In this section, we discuss a class of algorithms that achieves full splitting,
including the linear operators, and where no matrix inversion is necessary. This is the
primal-dual proximal splitting family, which is able to solve the most general class of
composite convex problems. These algorithms allow one to solve problems involving
a mixture of sums and linear compositions of simple and smooth functions. By relying
on the classical Kuhn-Tucker theory, several authors have independently and concur-
rently developed (and revitalized) primal-dual algorithms (Chen and Teboulle 1994;
Tseng 1997; Chambolle and Pock 2011; Briceño-Arias and Combettes 2011; Combettes and Pesquet 2012; Condat 2013; Vũ 2013; Komodakis and Pesquet 2015) to
solve problems with increasing level of complexity. We here focus on one algorithm
that allows one to solve the following class of problems, which is sufficiently large for
the purpose of this chapter.

Setting 8 *Solve equation* (7.38) *where* $D(\cdot, y)$ *is differentiable and its gradient is* β-
Lipschitz continuous, J_1 *is simple, and* $J_{k+1} = G_k \circ \mathbf{A}_k$, $k = 1, \ldots, l - 1$, *where* G_k *is*
lsc convex and simple, and $\mathbf{A}_k$ *are linear operators. Assume that* $\exists \alpha \in \mathrm{ri}(\mathrm{dom}\, J_1)$ *such*
that $\mathbf{A}_k \alpha \, \mathrm{ri}(\mathrm{dom}\, J_k))$, $\forall k = 1, \ldots, l - 1$.

A primal-dual algorithm to solve problems in Setting 8 was developed in (Vũ
2013; Condat 2013). The corresponding recursion reads

$$
\begin{cases}
\mu > 0 \text{ and } \nu > 0 \quad \text{s.t.} \quad 1 - \mu\nu \sum_{k=2}^{l} \|\mathbf{A}_k\|^2 > \mu\beta \|\mathbf{F}\|^2 / 2 , \\
\tau_t \in [\epsilon, 1], \epsilon \in]0, 1[, \\
p^{(t+1)} = \mathrm{prox}_{\mu J_1} \left(\alpha^{(t)} - \mu\left(\sum_{k=1}^{l-1} \mathbf{A}_k^{\mathrm{T}} u_k^{(t)} + \mathbf{F}^{\mathrm{T}} \nabla D(\mathbf{F}\alpha^{(t)}, y) \right) \right) , \\
q_k^{(t+1)} = \mathrm{prox}_{\nu G_k^*} \left(u_k^{(t)} + \nu \mathbf{A}_k \left(2p^{(t+1)} - \alpha^{(t)} \right) \right), k = 1, \ldots, l - 1 , \\
\alpha^{(t+1)} = \tau_t p^{(t+1)} + (1 - \tau_t)\alpha^{(t)} , \\
u_k^{(t+1)} = \tau_t q_k^{(t+1)} + (1 - \tau_t)u_k^{(t)}, k = 1, \ldots, l - 1 .
\end{cases}
\tag{7.53}
$$

The sequence of iterates $(\alpha^{(t)}, u_1^{(t)}, \ldots, u_{l-1}^{(t)})$ is guaranteed to converge to a primal-
dual optimal pair $(\alpha^\star, u_1^\star, \ldots, u_l^\star)$, and in particular $\alpha^\star$ is a global minimizer to the
problem in Setting 8.

It can be seen that the scheme (7.53) is reminiscent of the forward-backward,
where a descent is applied to the primal variable and an ascent to the dual ones.
Moreover, it encompasses several algorithms as special cases. In particular, when
$l = 1$, one recovers the FB splitting algorithm, equation (7.39). When $l = 2$ and
$D(\cdot, y) = 0$, iterations (7.53) reduce to the relaxed Arrow-Hurwicz algorithm revitalized by (Chambolle and Pock 2011).

The scheme (7.53) can be easily adapted to solve problems where $D(\cdot, y)$ in
Setting 8 is not smooth, but simple. The idea is to consider the smooth part as the
zero function and to transfer $D(\cdot, y)$ as an additional J_{l+1} function whose associated
linear operator is $\mathbf{F}$. We leave this as an exercise to the interested reader.

7.4.8 Problems with Analysis-Sparsity Prior

Problems with analysis-sparsity priors specialize (P) to

$$\min_{x \in \mathbb{R}^N} D(\mathbf{H}x, y) + J_1(\mathbf{\Phi}^{\mathsf{T}} x) + \sum_{k=2}^{l} R_k(x) \tag{7.54}$$

where J_1 is typically promoting sparsity (e.g. ℓ_1 norm), and the R_k terms encode some other prior on x (e.g. positivity, bound constraints, etc). It is immediately apparent that the examples in equations (7.8)-(7.12) are particular instances of equation (7.54) with $l = 1$ and $J_1 = \|\cdot\|_1$.

We recall again that the set of minimizers of equation (7.54) is assumed nonempty. In the following, we distinguish two settings, one in which $D(\cdot, y)$ is differentiable and the second is where it is simple. We only focus on primal-dual splitting, but some other algorithms such as GFB or ADMM can also be efficiently used in certain cases, depending on the properties of the operators $\mathbf{H}$ and $\mathbf{\Phi}^{\mathsf{T}}$.

Observe that in the case where $D(\cdot, y)$ is strongly convex and $\mathbf{H} = \mathbf{I}$ (i.e., denoising), problem (7.54) can be solved efficiently by applying the FB (7.39) or FISTA (7.40) to its Fenchel-Rockafellar dual. This is exactly what we have done in Section 7.3.2.5. We do not elaborate on this and the interested reader may refer to Fadili and Starck (2009) and Combettes et al. (2010).

Setting 9 *Solve equation (7.54) where $D(\cdot, y)$ is differentiable and its gradient is β-Lipschitz continuous, and J_1 and R_k are simple. Assume that $\exists x \in \bigcap_{k=2}^{l} \mathrm{ri}(\mathrm{dom}\, R_k)$ such that $\mathbf{\Phi}^{\mathsf{T}} x \in \mathrm{ri}(\mathrm{dom}\, J_1)$.*

The primal-dual proximal splitting algorithm used in equation (7.53) to solve Setting 8, can be used to solve the problem in Setting 9. The correponding recursion then reads[3]

$$\begin{cases} \mu > 0 \text{ and } \nu > 0 \quad \text{s.t.} \quad 1 - \mu\nu((l-1) + \|\mathbf{\Phi}\|^2) > \mu\beta\|\mathbf{H}\|^2/2, \\ \tau_t \in [\epsilon, 1], \epsilon \in]0, 1[, \\ p^{(t+1)} = x^{(t)} - \mu\left(\mathbf{\Phi} u_1^{(t)} + \sum_{k=2}^{l} u_k^{(t)} + \mathbf{H}^{\mathsf{T}}\nabla D(\mathbf{H}x^{(t)}, y)\right), \\ q_1^{(t+1)} = \mathrm{prox}_{\nu J_1^*}\left(u_1^{(t)} + \nu\mathbf{\Phi}^{\mathsf{T}}\left(2p^{(t+1)} - x^{(t)}\right)\right), \\ q_k^{(t+1)} = \mathrm{prox}_{\nu R_k^*}\left(u_k^{(t)} + \nu\left(2p^{(t+1)} - x^{(t)}\right)\right), k = 2, \dots, l, \\ x^{(t+1)} = \tau_t p^{(t+1)} + (1 - \tau_t)x^{(t)}, \\ u_k^{(t+1)} = \tau_t q_k^{(t+1)} + (1 - \tau_t)u_k^{(t)}, k = 1, \dots, l. \end{cases} \tag{7.55}$$

Again, the sequence of iterates $(x^{(t)}, u_1^{(t)}, \dots, u_l^{(t)})$ converges to primal-dual optimal points $(x^\star, u_1^\star, \dots, u_l^\star)$, and in particular $x^\star$ is a global minimizer of the problem in Setting 9.

Let us now turn to the nonsmooth case that corresponds to the following setting.

Setting 10 *Solve equation (7.54) where $D(\cdot, y)$, and J_1 and R_k are all simple. Assume that $\exists x \in \bigcap_{k=2}^{l} \mathrm{ri}(\mathrm{dom}\, R_k)$ such that $\mathbf{\Phi}^{\mathsf{T}} x \in \mathrm{ri}(\mathrm{dom}\, J_1)$ and $\mathbf{H}x \in \mathrm{ri}(\mathrm{dom}\, D(\cdot, y))$.*

The primal-dual proximal splitting algorithm to solve Setting 10 is now[4]

$$
\begin{cases}
\mu > 0 \text{ and } \nu > 0 \quad \text{s.t.} \quad \mu\nu((l-1) + \|\mathbf{H}\|^2 + \|\mathbf{\Phi}\|^2) < 1, \\
\tau_t \in [\epsilon, 1], \epsilon \in]0, 1[, \\
p^{(t+1)} = x^{(t)} - \mu\left(\mathbf{H}^{\mathrm{T}}u_1^{(t)} + \mathbf{\Phi}u_2^{(t)} + \sum_{k=2}^l u_{k+1}^{(t)}\right), \\
q_1^{(t+1)} = \mathrm{prox}_{\nu D^*(\cdot, y)}\left(u_1^{(t)} + \nu\mathbf{H}\left(2p^{(t+1)} - x^{(t)}\right)\right), \\
q_2^{(t+1)} = \mathrm{prox}_{\nu J_1^*}\left(u_1^{(t)} + \nu\mathbf{\Phi}^{\mathrm{T}}\left(2p^{(t+1)} - x^{(t)}\right)\right), \\
q_{k+1}^{(t+1)} = \mathrm{prox}_{\nu R_k^*}\left(u_k^{(t)} + \nu\left(2p^{(t+1)} - x^{(t)}\right)\right), k = 2, \ldots, l, \\
x^{(t+1)} = \tau_t p^{(t+1)} + (1 - \tau_t)x^{(t)}, \\
u_k^{(t+1)} = \tau_t q_k^{(t+1)} + (1 - \tau_t)u_k^{(t)}, k = 1, \ldots, l+1 .
\end{cases}
\tag{7.56}
$$

The sequence $(x^{(t)}, u_1^{(t)}, \ldots, u_{l+1}^{(t)})$ converges to primal-dual optimal points $(x^\star, u_1^\star, \ldots, u_l^\star)$, where $x^\star$ is a global minimizer to the problem in Setting 10.

7.4.9 Robustness to Errors

A distinctive property of the splitting iterations, equations (7.39), (7.41), (7.45), (7.48), (7.51), (7.52), (7.53), (7.55), and (7.56), is their robustness to errors that may occur when computing the different operators involved (i.e., proximity and gradient operators). The typical condition on these errors to ensure convergence is to be summable. This offers a principled way to ensure convergence even if the output of these operators cannot be computed exactly.

7.5 SELECTED PROBLEMS AND ALGORITHMS

We now provide examples of the algorithms introduced in the previous section on problems in equations (7.2) and (7.4)–(7.7), and their analysis counterparts in equations (7.8)–(7.12).

7.5.1 BPDN/Lasso in Penalized Form

7.5.1.1 Synthesis-sparsity prior

We begin with the BPDN/Lasso problem, equation (7.4). We recall that this falls within Setting 1 with $D(\cdot, y) = \frac{1}{2}\|\cdot - y\|^2$, $l = 1$ and $J_1 = \lambda\|\cdot\|_1$. This problem has a nonempty compact set of solutions by coercivity of J_1, and all minimizers are global by convexity. $D(\mathbf{F}\cdot, y)$ is differentiable whose gradient is Lipschitz continuous with constant upper bounded by $\|\mathbf{H}\|^2\|\mathbf{\Phi}\|^2$. Thus, problem (7.4) fulfills the necessary prerequisite to apply the FB iteration, equation (7.39). This is summarized in Algorithm 25. It uses soft-thresholding, equation (7.21), which is the proximity operator of $\lambda\|\cdot\|_1$; hence the name Iterative Soft-Thresholding Algorithm (ISTA), which is widely used in the literature (in fact for $\tau_t \equiv 1$). A similar algorithm can be written for problem (7.5) by just replacing soft-thresholding with the projector on the ℓ_1-ball given in Section 7.3.2.3.

Algorithm 25 Iterative Soft-Thresholding Algorithm (ISTA) to solve (7.4)

Initialization: choose some $\alpha^{(0)}$, $\mu \in]0, \frac{2}{\|\mathbf{H}\|^2\|\mathbf{\Phi}\|^2}[$, $\tau_t \in [0, \kappa]$, $\kappa = \frac{4-\mu\beta\|\mathbf{H}\|^2\|\mathbf{\Phi}\|^2}{2} \in$
$]1, 2[$, $\sum_{t\in\mathbb{N}} \tau_t(\kappa - \tau_t) = +\infty$.
Main iteration:
for $t = 0$ **to** $N_{\text{iter}} - 1$ **do**

1. *Gradient descent:* $\alpha^{(t+1/2)} = \alpha^{(t)} + \mu\mathbf{\Phi}^{\mathrm{T}}\mathbf{H}^{\mathrm{T}}\left(y - \mathbf{H}\mathbf{\Phi}\alpha^{(t)}\right)$.
2. *Soft-thresholding:*

$$\alpha^{(t+1)} = \alpha^{(t)} + \tau_t\left(\text{SoftThresh}_{\mu\lambda}\left(\alpha^{(t+1/2)}\right) - \alpha^{(t)}\right).$$

Output: $\alpha^{(N_{\text{iter}})}$.

In general, in its nonrelaxed form ($\tau_t \equiv 1$), ISTA has a sublinear $O(1/t)$ convergence rate on the objective. In the same vein as in Section 7.4.2, we can also solve equation (7.4) using the accelerated/inertial FISTA version, equation (7.40), which is known to have a sublinear but $O(1/t^2)$ convergence rate on the iterates. Algorithm 26 details the FISTA steps to solve the BPDN/Lasso, equation (7.4).

Algorithm 26 Fast Iterative Soft-Thresholding Algorithm (FISTA) to solve equation (7.4)

Initialization: choose some $\alpha^{(0)}$, $\mu \in]0, \frac{1}{\|\mathbf{H}\|^2\|\mathbf{\Phi}\|^2}]$, $\theta_1 = 1$, $\xi^{(1)} = \alpha^{(0)}$.
Main iteration:
for $t = 0$ **to** $N_{\text{iter}} - 1$ **do**

1. *Gradient descent:* $\alpha^{(t+1/2)} = \xi^{(t)} + \mu\mathbf{\Phi}^{\mathrm{T}}\mathbf{H}^{\mathrm{T}}\left(y - \mathbf{H}\mathbf{\Phi}\xi^{(t)}\right)$.
2. *Soft-thresholding:* $\alpha^{(t+1)} = \text{SoftThresh}_{\mu\lambda}\left(\alpha^{(t+1/2)}\right)$.
3. *Intertial parameter:* $\theta_{t+1} = \frac{1+\sqrt{1+4\theta_t^2}}{2}$.
4. *Intertial step:* $\xi^{(t+1)} = \alpha^{(t)} + \left(\frac{\theta_t-1}{\theta_{t+1}}\right)\left(\alpha^{(t)} - \alpha^{(t-1)}\right)$.

Output: $\alpha^{(N_{\text{iter}})}$.

7.5.1.2 Analysis-sparsity prior

We now turn to the generalized analysis BPDN/Lasso problem, equation (7.9). This is a particular case of equation (7.54) with $D(\cdot, y) = \frac{1}{2}\|\cdot - y\|^2$ and $J_1 = \lambda\|\cdot\|_1$. It can be shown that this problem has a nonempty compact set of solutions if $\ker(\mathbf{\Phi}^{\mathrm{T}}) \cap \ker(\mathbf{H}) = \{0\}$. Problem (7.9) falls within the scope of several of the settings we described in Section 7.4:

■ Setting 9: since $D(\cdot, y)$ is indeed smooth with a 1-Lipschitz gradient and J_1 is simple. One can then apply recursion (7.55).
■ Setting 10: since $D(\cdot, y)$ is also simple, whose proximity operator at a point z is $(\mathbf{I} + \mathbf{H}^{\mathrm{T}}\mathbf{H})^{-1}(\mathbf{H}^{\mathrm{T}}y + z)$. In this case, iteration (7.56) applies, though this would necessitate one to invert $\mathbf{I} + \mathbf{H}^{\mathrm{T}}\mathbf{H}$, which can be efficiently implemented in some cases (e.g., deconvolution, inpainting, etc.).

■ Setting 7: by introducing an auxiliary variable $u = \mathbf{\Phi}^T x$, and minimizing with respect to (x, u), one can check that equation (7.9) is reformulated in a form amenable to this setting with $J_1(u) = \lambda \|u\|_1$ and the additional function $R_2(x, u) = \iota_{\ker([-\mathbf{\Phi}^T \; \mathbf{I}])}(x, u)$ for which GFB algorithm (7.52) applies. This would necessitate computing the projection onto $\ker([-\mathbf{\Phi}^T \; \mathbf{I}])$, which involves inverting $\mathbf{I} + \mathbf{\Phi}\mathbf{\Phi}^T$, or by the matrix inversion lemma, $\mathbf{I} + \mathbf{\Phi}^T\mathbf{\Phi}$. Such inversions can be achieved efficiently for many dictionaries $\mathbf{\Phi}$, such as tight frames, or finite differences, etc.

■ Setting 6: equation (7.9) can also be put in the form that qualifies for this setting. This suggests applying the ADMM algorithm, which would entail inverting $\mathbf{I} + \mathbf{H}^T\mathbf{H}$ and $\mathbf{I} + \mathbf{\Phi}\mathbf{\Phi}^T$.

In the following, we restrict ourselves to the first identification and the corresponding algorithm in equation (7.55). The other options and corresponding algorithms are left as exercices to the interested reader. Algorithm 27 summarizes the main steps when specializing equation (7.55).

Algorithm 27 Primal-Dual algorithms to solve (7.9)

Initialization: choose some $(x^{(0)}, u^{(0)})$, $\mu, \nu > 0$ s.t. $1 - \mu\nu\|\mathbf{\Phi}\|^2 > \mu\|\mathbf{H}\|^2/2$, $\tau_t \in [\epsilon, 1], \epsilon \in]0, 1[$.

Main iteration:

for $t = 0$ **to** $N_{\text{iter}} - 1$ **do**

   1. *Descent step on the primal:*
$$p^{(t+1)} = x^{(t)} + \mu\mathbf{H}^T\left(y - \mathbf{H}x^{(t)}\right) - \mu\mathbf{\Phi}u^{(t)}.$$

   2. *Thresholded ascent step on the dual:*
$$q^{(t+1)} = \text{SoftThresh}_\lambda\left(u^{(t)} + \nu\mathbf{\Phi}^T(2p^{(t+1)} - x^{(t)})\right).$$

   3. *Relaxation step:*
$$\left(x^{(t+1)}, u^{(t+1)}\right) = \tau_t\left(p^{(t+1)}, q^{(t+1)}\right) + (1 - \tau_t)\left(x^{(t)}, u^{(t)}\right).$$

Output: $x^{(N_{\text{iter}})}$.

7.5.1.3 Computational complexity

The bulk of the computation in Algorithms 25–27 is essentially invested in applying $\mathbf{\Phi}$ and $\mathbf{H}$ and their adjoints. In most practical cases, these operators are never constructed explicitly; rather they are implemented as fast implicit operators taking a vector α (respectively x), and returning $\mathbf{\Phi}\alpha$ (respectively $\mathbf{\Phi}^T x$) and $\mathbf{H}x$ (respectively $\mathbf{H}^T y$). For example, if $\mathbf{H} \in \mathbb{R}^{m \times N}$ is the circular convolution operator ($m = N$), or the Fourier measurement operator in compressed sensing (see Chapter 13), multiplication by $\mathbf{H}$ or $\mathbf{H}^T$ costs at most $O(N \log N)$ operations. For an inpainting problem, the cost is linear in N. The complexity of multiplying by $\mathbf{\Phi}$ and $\mathbf{\Phi}^T$ depends on the transforms in the dictionary: for example, the DWT costs $O(N)$ operations, the UWT transform costs $O(N \log N)$, and so does the second-generation curvelet transform.

Refer to Chapters 2, 3, and 5 for a detailed description of these and other multiscale transforms.

7.5.2 Choice of the Regularization Parameter(s) in BPDN/Lasso

In regularized inverse problems, the choice of λ when solving (7.4) or (7.9) is crucial as it represents the desired balance between sparsity (regularization) and data fidelity. The appropriate choice of this parameter is an important topic and we here provide some guidelines. Before delving into the details, observe that λ should always be chosen in $]0, \|\mathbf{F}^T y\|_\infty[$. Indeed, $\alpha^\star$ is a global minimizer of (7.4) if and only if

$$\mathbf{F}^T(y - \mathbf{F}\alpha^\star) \in \lambda \partial \|\cdot\|_1 (\alpha^\star) \subseteq \lambda \partial \|\cdot\|_1 (0) = \mathbb{B}_\infty^\lambda, \tag{7.57}$$

where we used the well-known expression of the subdifferential of the ℓ_1-norm, and the inclusion becomes an equality for $\alpha^\star = 0$. Thus, if $\|\mathbf{F}^T y\|_\infty \leq \lambda$, then 0 is a trivial solution to (7.4).

7.5.2.1 BPDN/Lasso consistency with Gaussian noise
Assume that the noise in equation (7.1) is zero-mean Gaussian noise of variance σ_ε^2. In the statistical community, many authors have studied consistency and correct sparsity recovery properties of BPDN/Lasso with a synthesis prior; see Meinshausen and Bühlmann (2006); Bickel et al. (2009); Wainwright (2009); Candès and Plan (2009); and references therein. These works established that if the regularization parameter is set to[5]

$$\lambda = c\sigma_\varepsilon \sqrt{2 \log T}, \tag{7.58}$$

for large enough c ($c > 2\sqrt{2}$), then BPDN can recover the correct sparsity pattern or be consistent with the original sparse vector under additional conditions on $\mathbf{F}$ (e.g., incoherence, appropriate spectrum). This choice of λ was also advocated in Chen et al. (1999), as inspired by the universal threshold that we discussed in Section 6.2.2.4 in the orthogonal case.

7.5.2.2 Probing the Pareto front
In his attempt to solve the constrained form of the (discrete) total variation denoising, Chambolle (2004) devised a sequence of regularized problems each with a different value of λ. To meet a constraint size σ, an intuitive update of the λ is $\lambda_{new} = \lambda_{old}\sigma / \|residuals_{old}\|$. The theoretical analysis is rigorous for denoising. In practice, it was observed by Chambolle (2004) that this rule still works when λ is updated at each step of the algorithm solving the regularized problem, and even with inverse problems. Transposed to our setting, for a given target size of the residuals σ, the update rule reads

$$\lambda_{t+1} = \lambda_t \sigma / \|r^{(t)}\| \tag{7.59}$$

where $r^{(t)} = y - \mathbf{F}\alpha^{(t)}$ in the synthesis case and $r^{(t)} = y - \mathbf{H}x^{(t)}$ in the analysis case. Van Den Berg and Friedlander (2008) establish a precise characterization of the curve $\rho \leftrightarrow \sigma$ for problems (7.5)–(7.6), and propose a root-finding procedure to probe this curve and find the value ρ corresponding to a given σ, such that solutions of (7.5) with ρ are also solutions to (7.6).

7.5.2.3 Stein Unbiased Risk Estimation

When the noise ε in equation (7.1) is assumed zero-mean white Gaussian of variance σ_ε^2, the Stein Unbiased Risk Estimation (SURE) (Stein 1981) gives a principled framework to automatically tune the regularization parameter by minimizing an objective quality measure. We here focus on the BPDN/Lasso with a synthesis-sparsity prior. Extension to the analysis case can be found in Vaiter et al. (2013a).

Denote the mapping $\mu_\lambda^\star : y \mapsto \mathbf{F}\alpha_\lambda^\star(y)$, where $\alpha_\lambda^\star(y)$ is any global minimizer of equation (7.4) with observations y. The careful reader may recognize that $\mu_\lambda^\star(y)$ is single valued, though $\alpha_\lambda^\star(y)$ may not be unique. We similarly write $\mu_0 = \mathbf{F}\alpha_0$. Ideally, one would like to choose λ that minimizes the quadratic risk

$$\mathbb{E}_\varepsilon \left(\left\| \mathbf{A}\mu_0 - \mathbf{A}\mu_\lambda^\star(y) \right\|^2 \right), \tag{7.60}$$

for a matrix $\mathbf{A} \in \mathbb{R}^{n \times m}$, where $\mathbb{E}_\varepsilon$ is the expectation taken under the distribution of ε. Several choices are possible for $\mathbf{A}$: $\mathbf{A} = \mathbf{I}$ corresponds to the so-called prediction risk (risk on μ_0); when $\mathbf{F}$ is rank deficient, $\mathbf{A} = \mathbf{F}^\mathrm{T}(\mathbf{F}\mathbf{F}^\mathrm{T})^+$ yields the projection risk (the risk on $\ker(\mathbf{F})^\perp$); and when $\mathbf{F}$ has full rank, $\mathbf{A} = \mathbf{F}^+ = (\mathbf{F}^\mathrm{T}\mathbf{F})^{-1}\mathbf{F}^\mathrm{T}$ gives the estimation risk (risk on x_0). In inverse problems, where $\mathbf{H}$ is generally singular, the projection risk is preferable to the prediction risk. However, minimizing the quadratic risk, equation (7.60), is not possible since x_0 is unknown.

We now describe a Generalized SURE (GSURE) that unbiasedly estimates equation (7.60). The GSURE associated with $\mathbf{A}$ is defined as

$$\mathrm{GSURE}^{\mathbf{A}}(\mu_\lambda^\star(y)) = \|\mathbf{A}(y - \mu_\lambda^\star(y))\|^2 - \sigma^2 \operatorname{trace}(\mathbf{A}^\mathrm{T}\mathbf{A}) + 2\sigma^2 df^{\mathbf{A}}(y), \tag{7.61}$$

where

$$df^{\mathbf{A}}(y) = \operatorname{trace} \left(\mathbf{A} \frac{\partial \mu_\lambda^\star(y)}{\partial y} \mathbf{A}^\mathrm{T} \right)$$

and $\frac{\partial \mu_\lambda^\star(y)}{\partial y}$ is the (weak) Jacobian of the mapping $\mu_\lambda^\star$. $df^{\mathbf{A}}(y)$ is an estimator of the so-called effective number of degrees of freedom, which, roughly speaking, quantifies the intrinsic complexity of an estimator.

$\mathrm{GSURE}^{\mathbf{A}}(\mu_\lambda^\star(y))$ is indeed an unbiased estimator of the risk, equation (7.60), i.e.

$$\mathbb{E}_\varepsilon \left(\mathrm{GSURE}^{\mathbf{A}}(\mu_\lambda^\star(y)) \right) = \mathbb{E}_\varepsilon \left(\left\| \mathbf{A}\mu_0 - \mathbf{A}\mu_\lambda^\star(y) \right\|^2 \right).$$

GSURE only depends on the observation y and thus can be computed as long as $df^{\mathbf{A}}(y)$ can be computed efficiently. This is indeed true for the solutions of the BPDN/Lasso problem.

It can be shown that (see Zou et al. (2007) for the case where $\mathbf{F}$ is full column rank and Dossal et al. (2013) in the general case)

$$\frac{\partial \mu_\lambda^\star(y)}{\partial y} = \mathbf{F}_\Lambda \left(\mathbf{F}_\Lambda^\mathrm{T} \mathbf{F}_\Lambda \right)^{-1} \mathbf{F}_\Lambda^\mathrm{T},$$

where $\mathbf{F}_\Lambda$ is the restriction of $\mathbf{F}$ to the columns indexed by the support of a solution $\alpha_\lambda^\star(y)$ such that $\mathbf{F}_\Lambda$ is full column rank. For instance, for the prediction risk (i.e., $\mathbf{A} = \mathbf{I}$), we get

$$df^{\mathbf{I}}(y) = |\Lambda| \qquad \mathrm{GSURE}^{\mathbf{I}}(\mu_\lambda^\star(y)) = \left\| y - \mu_\lambda^\star(y) \right\|^2 - m\sigma^2 + 2\sigma^2 |\Lambda|.$$

For the general case of arbitrary $\mathbf{A}$, $df^{\mathbf{A}}(y)$ takes the form

$$df^{\mathbf{A}}(y) = \text{trace}\left(\mathbf{A}\mathbf{F}_{\Lambda}\mathbf{F}_{\Lambda}^{+}\mathbf{A}^{\mathsf{T}}\right) = \mathbb{E}_Z\left(\langle\mathbf{F}_{\Lambda}^{\mathsf{T}}\mathbf{A}^{\mathsf{T}}\mathbf{A}Z, \mathbf{F}_{\Lambda}^{+}Z\rangle\right), \ Z \sim \mathcal{N}(0, \mathbf{I}) ,$$

which can be estimated in practice by the sample moment

$$\frac{1}{K}\sum_{k=1}^{K}\langle\mathbf{F}_{\Lambda}^{\mathsf{T}}\mathbf{A}^{\mathsf{T}}\mathbf{A}z_k, \mathbf{F}_{\Lambda}^{+}z_k\rangle$$

for K realizations of Z (even $K = 1$ works well in practice). The computational bulk of implementing such an estimate is invested in computing $\mathbf{F}_{\Lambda}^{+}z_k$ for each z_k, which corresponds to solving a linear system using, for example, a conjugate gradient solver.

7.5.2.4 Differentiation of an iterative scheme

The GSURE-based framework we have just developed for choosing λ extends in fact to any simple convex function J_1, beyond the ℓ_1 norm. This approach however has some important bottlenecks. First, deriving the closed-form expression of the Jacobian of $\mu_{\lambda}^{\star}(y)$ is in general challenging and has to be addressed on a case-by-case basis. Second, in large-dimensional problems, evaluating numerically and storing this Jacobian are barely possible, while we are instead interested in its trace. Even if it were possible, it might be subject to serious numerical instabilities. Indeed, solutions of variational problems such as BPDN/Lasso are achieved via iterative schemes such as those described above, which eventually converge to the set of solutions as $t \to +\infty$. Yet, for ℓ_1 for instance, substituting the support of the true solution by the support of the tth iterate, obtained at a prescribed convergence accuracy, might be imprecise.

A practical way to get around these difficulties is to compute the differential quantities recursively from the sequence of iterates by relying on the chain rule. This idea was first suggested in Vonesch et al. (2008); see also Giryes et al. (2011). It has been extended to the general class of proximal splitting algorithms in Deledalle et al. (2012, 2014), including all those described in Section 7.4.

7.5.2.5 Multiple regularization parameters from noise properties

We restrict the presentation to (7.4), in which a similar reasoning can be carried out for the analysis-sparsity case (7.9). In (7.4), all the entries of α are equally penalized through λ. In real applications however, the sought-after coefficients are likely to have very different scalings, and it would be wiser to adapt the regularization parameter to each coefficient. This corresponds to solving

$$\min_{\alpha \in \mathbb{R}^T} \frac{1}{2}\|y - \mathbf{H}\Phi\alpha\|^2 + \sum_{i=1}^{T}\lambda_i|\alpha[i]| . \tag{7.62}$$

Choosing, however, as many as T parameters λ_i is highly challenging as T is very large in real applications (remember the redundancy of the different transforms from the previous chapters). The number of λ_i's can be reduced for subband transforms (such as UWT or curvelets), setting one λ_i per subband. But even in this case the methods described in the above sections are barely applicable.

Unlocking such a bottleneck is of paramount importance, especially from a practical perspective. At first sight, it seems impossible to devise a general recipe to choose properly these regularization parameters that would work for general inverse problems. But let us take a different look at ISTA or FISTA algorithms used to solve (7.62). These schemes involve at each iteration a denoising step (hence the name iterative soft-thresholding) that consists of an entry-wise soft-thresholding with threshold λ_i. Indeed, let $r^{(t)} = y - \mathbf{H}\boldsymbol{\Phi}\alpha^{(t)}$ be the residual vector at iteration t, and $\xi^{(t)} = \boldsymbol{\Phi}^{\mathrm{T}}\mathbf{H}^{\mathrm{T}}r^{(t)}$ its transform coefficients vector. Therefore, ISTA reads (see Algorithm 25 with $\tau_t \equiv 1$)

$$\alpha^{(t+1)}[i] = \mathrm{SoftThresh}_{\mu\lambda_i}\left(\alpha^{(t)}[i] + \mu\xi^{(t)}[i]\right), \quad i = 1, \ldots, T .$$

If we think of $\xi^{(t)}$ as some sort of "noise" contaminating $\alpha^{(t)}$, soft-thresholding is supposed to forbid $\xi^{(t)}$ from propagating through iterations. Thus, one should adapt the choice of λ_i to the power level of $\xi^{(t)}[i]$ similarly to what was advocated in Chapter 6. This is the idea underlying the practical, yet very effective approach proposed in Ngolè Mboula et al. (2015); Garsden et al. (2015) and Lanusse et al. (2014). We now consider two possible strategies.

Noise-driven strategy

Recall that the noise ε in (7.1) is supposed zero-mean additive with known covariance matrix $\boldsymbol{\Sigma}^6$. If α_0 ($x_0 = \boldsymbol{\Phi}\alpha_0$) were perfectly recovered by ISTA or FISTA, then the residual $r^{(\infty)}$ would be exactly ε, and its coefficients $\xi^{(\infty)} = \boldsymbol{\Phi}^{\mathrm{T}}\mathbf{H}^{\mathrm{T}}\varepsilon$, whose covariance matrix is $\boldsymbol{\Phi}^{\mathrm{T}}\mathbf{H}^{\mathrm{T}}\boldsymbol{\Sigma}\mathbf{H}\boldsymbol{\Phi}$. The crude assumption that is made now is that $\xi^{(t)} \approx \boldsymbol{\Phi}^{\mathrm{T}}\mathbf{H}^{\mathrm{T}}\varepsilon$, for any t, and to choose $\lambda_i = \tau\sigma_i$, where τ is generally chosen between 3 and 5 (see Section 6.2.1.1) and σ_i is the square root of the ith entry on the diagonal of $\boldsymbol{\Phi}^{\mathrm{T}}\mathbf{H}^{\mathrm{T}}\boldsymbol{\Sigma}\mathbf{H}\boldsymbol{\Phi}$ (i.e., standard deviation of $(\boldsymbol{\Phi}^{\mathrm{T}}\mathbf{H}^{\mathrm{T}}\varepsilon)[i]$). This can be done analytically in many cases discussed in this book. Alternatively, one can estimate σ_i using the sample moment by averaging over K realizations $\tilde{\varepsilon}_k$ drawn from the distribution of ε, for K large enough,

$$\sqrt{\frac{1}{K}\sum_{i=1}^{K}\left(\boldsymbol{\Phi}^{\mathrm{T}}\mathbf{H}^{\mathrm{T}}\tilde{\varepsilon}_k\right)[i]^2} .$$

Residual-driven strategy for subband transforms

The noise-driven strategy is versatile enough to handle many types of noise, and it minimizes exactly (7.62). However, it makes an important and crude assumption. When the noise ε is stationary and Gaussian, this assumption may be relaxed, as the residual vector $r^{(t)}$ itself may serve as a way of estimating λ_i. Suppose that $\mathbf{H}$ is a convolution operator, and $\boldsymbol{\Phi}$ corresponds to a subband band-pass transform with $J \ll T$ subbands. Wavelets and curvelets are typical transforms fulfilling this assumption. In this case, it is immediately apparent that $\boldsymbol{\Phi}_j^{\mathrm{T}}\mathbf{H}^{\mathrm{T}}\varepsilon$ is also Gaussian and stationary in each subband $j \in \{1, \ldots, J\}$. If the band-pass and convolution kernel are almost constant in subband j, then $\boldsymbol{\Phi}_j^{\mathrm{T}}\mathbf{H}^{\mathrm{T}}\varepsilon$ is even (almost) white. One can then be tempted to use the coefficients in $\xi_j^{(t)} = \boldsymbol{\Phi}_j^{\mathrm{T}}\mathbf{H}^{\mathrm{T}}r^{(t)}$ to estimate standard deviation σ_j. But this would not be a wise choice as $r^{(t)}$ contains also structure and not only noise. Recalling that the MAD estimator that we described in Section 6.2.1.2 is robust to the presence of (sparse) structure, one can apply the MAD formula (6.9) directly to $\xi_j^{(t)}$ to estimate σ_j. An important consequence of this choice, however, is that now, the regularization parameter λ_i becomes iteration dependent. Thus, convergence of either

ISTA or FISTA is not guaranteed, and even if they do converge, the corresponding accumulation point is not gauranteed to be a (global) minimizer of (7.62). Nonetheless, several experiments in the literature suggest that the procedure exhibits good convergence behavior (Ngolè Mboula et al. 2015; Garsden et al. 2015).

7.5.3 BPDN/Lasso in Constrained Form

7.5.3.1 Synthesis-sparsity prior

We now consider equation (7.6). We assume that $\sigma < \|y\|$ to avoid the unique trivial solution $\alpha^\star = 0$. Equation (7.6) only asks that the reconstruction be consistent with the data such that the residual error is bounded by σ in norm. Solving (7.6) is challenging for large-scale problems.

Recall that (7.6) is a particular case of equation (P) with $D(\cdot, y)$ being the indicator of $y + \mathbb{B}_2^\sigma$, and $J_1 = \|\cdot\|_1$. This problem has a nonempty set of solutions by coercivity of J_1. Moreover, both $D(\cdot, y)$ and J_1 are simple (the projector on $y + \mathbb{B}_2^\sigma$ is obtained by combining equation (7.24) and Property 3(i)). Thus (P) takes a form captured by several settings described earlier:

- If $\mathbf{F}$ is a tight frame, in which case $D(\mathbf{F}\cdot, y)$ is simple, then this is Setting 2 for which the DR splitting algorithm (7.41) can be applied.
- If $\mathbf{I} + \mathbf{F}^\mathsf{T}\mathbf{F}$ can be easily inverted, then this is Setting 5, for which ADMM (7.48) can be applied.
- In all cases, we are in the scope of Setting 8, for which one can apply (7.53).

The iterative scheme obtained in the general situation as an application of (7.53) is given in Algorithm 28. The algorithms corresponding to applying DR or ADMM can be written easily and are left as exercises.

Algorithm 28 Primal-Dual splitting to solve (7.6)

Initialization: choose some $(\alpha^{(0)}, u^{(0)})$, $\mu, \nu > 0$ s.t. $\mu\nu\|\mathbf{H}\|^2\|\mathbf{\Phi}\|^2 < 1$, $\tau_t \in [\epsilon, 1]$, $\epsilon \in \,]0, 1[$.
Main iteration:
for $t = 0$ **to** $N_{\text{iter}} - 1$ **do**

    1. *Thresholded descent step on the primal:*
$$p^{(t+1)} = \text{SoftThresh}_{\mu\lambda}\left(\alpha^{(t)} - \mu\mathbf{\Phi}^\mathsf{T}\mathbf{H}^\mathsf{T}u^{(t)}\right).$$

    2. *Projected ascent step on the dual:*
$$q^{(t+1)} = \left(\mathbf{I} - \mathrm{P}_{\mathbb{B}_2^{\nu\sigma}}\right)\left(u^{(t)} + \nu\mathbf{H}\mathbf{\Phi}\left(2p^{(t+1)} - \alpha^{(t)}\right) - \nu y\right).$$

    3. *Relaxation step:*
$$\left(\alpha^{(t+1)}, u^{(t+1)}\right) = \tau_t\left(p^{(t+1)}, q^{(t+1)}\right) + (1 - \tau_t)\left(\alpha^{(t)}, u^{(t)}\right).$$

Output: $\alpha^{(N_{\text{iter}})}$.

We can handle just as well any ℓ_p-constraint, $p \geq 1$. It is sufficient to replace $\mathrm{P}_{\mathbb{B}_2^\sigma}$ by $\mathrm{P}_{\mathbb{B}_p^\sigma}$, where the latter is detailed in Section 7.3.2.3 for the different values of p.

7.5.3.2 Analysis-sparsity prior

For equation (7.11), the set of minimizers is nonempty and compact if $\ker(\mathbf{\Phi}^{\mathrm{T}}) \cap \ker(\mathbf{H}) = \{0\}$. This is a particular case of equation (7.54) with $D(\cdot, y)$ being the indicator of $y + \mathbb{B}_2^\sigma$, and $J_1 = \|\cdot\|_1$. Again, problem (7.9) can be formulated according to the different settings we described in Section 7.4. Here we focus on the most general one (i.e., Setting 10) since $D(\cdot, y)$ and J_1 are simple. Algorithm 29 summarizes the specialization of equation (7.56) to this case.

Algorithm 29 Primal-Dual algorithms to solve equation (7.11)

Initialization: choose some $(x^{(0)}, u_1^{(0)}, u_2^{(0)})$, $\mu, \nu > 0$ s.t. $\mu\nu(\|\mathbf{H}\|^2 + \|\mathbf{\Phi}\|^2) < 1$, $\tau_t \in [\epsilon, 1]$, $\epsilon \in]0, 1[$.
Main iteration:
for $t = 0$ **to** $N_{\mathrm{iter}} - 1$ **do**

    1. *Descent step on the primal:*

$$p^{(t+1)} = x^{(t)} - \mu\big(\mathbf{H}^{\mathrm{T}} u_1^{(t)} + \mathbf{\Phi} u_2^{(t)}\big).$$

    2. *Thresholded ascent step on the dual:*

$$q_1^{(t+1)} = \big(\mathbf{I} - \mathrm{P}_{\mathbb{B}_2^{\nu\sigma}}\big)\big(u_1^{(t)} + \nu\mathbf{H}(2p^{(t+1)} - x^{(t)}) - \nu y\big),$$
$$q_2^{(t+1)} = (\mathbf{I} - \mathrm{SoftThresh}_1)\big(u_2^{(t)} + \nu\mathbf{\Phi}^{\mathrm{T}}(2p^{(t+1)} - x^{(t)})\big).$$

    3. *Relaxation step:*

$$\big(x^{(t+1)}, u_1^{(t+1)}, u_2^{(t+1)}\big) = \tau_t\big(p^{(t+1)}, q_1^{(t+1)}, q_2^{(t+1)}\big) + (1 - \tau_t)\big(x^{(t)}, u_1^{(t)}, u_2^{(t)}\big).$$

Output: $x^{(N_{\mathrm{iter}})}$.

It goes without saying that this algorithm can be easily extended to any ℓ_p-constraint, $p \geq 1$.

7.5.3.3 Computational complexity

Again, the computational complexity of each iteration of Algorithm 28 and equation (29) is dominated by that of applying $\mathbf{H}, \mathbf{\Phi}$, and their adjoints. See Section 7.5.1.3 for typical examples of their cost.

7.5.3.4 Choice of σ

In general, the choice of the constraint size σ is simpler than that of λ in the penalized forms, equations (7.4) and (7.9). For instance, for the solution to equation (7.6) (respectively, equation (7.11)) to be a good approximation to the true vector α_0 (resp. x_0), it is necessary that the latter be feasible; $\|\varepsilon\| \leq \sigma$. For instance, if $\varepsilon \sim \mathcal{N}(0, \sigma_\varepsilon^2)$ (i.e., $\|\varepsilon\|^2$ is χ_m^2-distributed), by standard concentration inequalities on χ_m^2 variables, the latter condition holds with probability higher than $1 - e^{-\nu\sqrt{m/8}}$ if

$$\sigma^2 = \mathbb{E}(\|\varepsilon\|^2) + c\sqrt{\mathrm{Var}\left[\|\varepsilon\|^2\right]}. \tag{7.63}$$

Taking $c = 2$, it follows easily that $\sigma = \sqrt{m}\sigma_\varepsilon \sqrt{1 + 2\sqrt{2/m}}$ ensures feasibility with probability greater than $1 - e^{-\sqrt{m/2}}$. Similar arguments can be developed for other ℓ_p constraints (Jacques et al. 2009).

7.5.4 Basis Pursuit

7.5.4.1 Synthesis-sparsity prior

Let us turn to equation (7.2). This problem can be turned into a linear program and used to solve popular solvers such as interior points. However, these may scale badly with the dimension. We prefer proximal splitting solvers. It is immediately apparent that equation (7.2) is a particular case of equation (7.6) for $\sigma = 0$, and thus can be solved efficiently using Algorithm 28 with $P_{\mathbb{B}_2^0}(u) = 0$. An alternative that we detail for the reader's convenience would also be based on DR combining equations (7.41) with (7.21) and (7.27). This gives Algorithm 30.

Algorithm 30 Douglas-Rachford splitting to solve BP

Initialization: choose some $z^{(0)}, \gamma > 0, \tau_t \in [0, 2]$ s.t. $\sum_{t \in \mathbb{N}} \tau_t(2 - \tau_t) = +\infty$.
Main iteration:
for $t = 0$ **to** $N_{\text{iter}} - 1$ **do**

1. *Compute the residual:* $r^{(t)} = y - \mathbf{F}z^{(t)}$.
2. *Projection on the equality constraint:* $\alpha^{(t+1/2)} = z^{(t)} + \mathbf{F}^+ r^{(t)}$.
3. *Reflected projector:* $\zeta^{(t)} = 2\alpha^{(t+1/2)} - z^{(t)}$.
4. *Reflected soft-thresholding:* $\xi^{(t)} = 2\,\mathrm{SoftThresh}_\gamma(\zeta^{(t)}) - \zeta^{(t)}$.
5. *Relaxation step:* $z^{(t+1)} = (1 - \tau_t/2)z^{(t)} + \tau_t/2(\xi^{(t)})$.

Output: $\alpha^{(N_{\text{iter}}-1/2)}$.

7.5.4.2 Analysis-sparsity prior

As for the synthesis case, identifying (7.8) with (7.11) for $\sigma = 0$, one can just apply Algorithm 29 with $P_{\mathbb{B}_2^0}(u) = 0$.

7.5.5 Dantzig Selector

We finally consider problems (7.7) and (7.12).

7.5.5.1 Synthesis-sparsity prior

This is problem (7.7). We assume that $\delta < \|\mathbf{F}^T y\|_\infty$ to avoid the unique trivial solution $\alpha^\star = 0$. Equation (7.7) forces the residual to contain features that have correlations with the columns of $\mathbf{F}$ of at most δ. Solving problem (7.7) is also challenging for large-scale problems.

In fact, this problem can be rewritten as

$$\min_{\alpha \in \mathbb{R}^T} \|\alpha\|_1 \quad \text{s.t.} \quad \|\mathbf{G}\alpha - z\| \le \delta$$

where $\mathbf{G} = \mathbf{F}^T \mathbf{F}$ is the Gram operator of $\mathbf{F}$ and $z = \mathbf{F}^T y$. Clearly, this problem shares essentially the same structure as problem (7.6), replacing the ℓ_2 ball with the ℓ_∞ ball,

F with **G**, and y with z. Thus, Algorithm 28 applies, mutatis mutandis, to solve equation (7.7).

7.5.5.2 Analysis-sparsity prior

Problem (7.12) is equivalent to

$$\min_{x \in \mathbb{R}^T} \|\mathbf{\Phi}^T x\|_1 \quad \text{s.t.} \quad \|\mathbf{G}x - z\| \leq \delta ,$$

where now $\mathbf{G} = \mathbf{H}^T \mathbf{H}$ and $z = \mathbf{F}^T y$. As in the synthesis case, it is now sufficient to identify equation (7.12) with (7.11), and apply Algorithm 29 with the appropriate changes.

7.5.6 Nonlinear Inverse Problems

This chapter addresses mainly inverse problems when the operator **H** is linear. However, some of the material we developed on operator splitting applies also when the degradation operator is nonlinear. Suppose, for instance, that the degradation equation is now

$$y = \mathcal{H}(x_0) + \varepsilon ,$$

where $\mathcal{H} : \mathbb{R}^N \mapsto \mathbb{R}^m$ is a nonlinear mapping. The goal is to recover x_0 known to be sparse in $\mathbf{\Phi}$ according to a synthesis-sparsity prior. Thus it is natural to solve, e.g.,

$$\min_{\alpha \in \mathbb{R}^T} D(\mathcal{H}(\mathbf{\Phi}\alpha), y) + \sum_{k=1}^{l} J_k(\alpha) , \tag{7.64}$$

where $J_k \in \Gamma_0(\mathbb{R}^T)$. If $\mathcal{H}$ is such that $D(\mathcal{H}(\mathbf{\Phi}\cdot), y) \in \Gamma_0(\mathbb{R}^T)$, then one can hope to apply the proximal splitting algorithms of Section 7.4. For instance, if $l = 1, J_1$ is simple and $D(\mathcal{H}(\mathbf{\Phi}\cdot), y)$ has a Lipschitz-continuous gradient, then the FB applies straightforwardly which gives the recursion

$$\alpha^{(t+1)} = \text{prox}_{\mu J_1} \left(\alpha^{(t)} - \mu \mathbf{\Phi}^T \mathcal{H}'^*\left(\mathbf{\Phi}\alpha^{(t)}\right) \nabla D\left(\mathcal{H}\left(\mathbf{\Phi}\alpha^{(t)}\right), y\right) \right) , \tag{7.65}$$

for a step size μ depending on the Lipschitz constant, where $\mathcal{H}'$ stands for the (Fréchet) derivative of $\mathcal{H}$. This has been used, for instance, in Dupé et al. (2009) for deconvolution with Poisson noise.

Ramlau and Teschke (2006) and Bonesky et al. (2007) tackled the case where the data fidelity in equation (7.64) is not convex. Both assume that $\mathcal{H}$ is (Fréchet) differentiable with a Lipschitz continuous derivative, and $J_1 \in \Gamma_0(\mathbb{R}^T)$. Ramlau and Teschke (2006) assumed that J_1 is positively 1-homogeneous and proved convergence of an iteration very similar to equation (7.65) ($\mathcal{H}'^*(\mathbf{\Phi}\alpha^{(t+1)})$ instead of $\mathcal{H}'^*(\mathbf{\Phi}\alpha^{(t)})$) to a stationary point using a surrogate approach. Bonesky et al. (2007) dealt with more general penalties J_1 but coercive, and proved also convergence of equation (7.65) to a stationary point. In the next section we describe an even more general framework for extending FB-like splitting to the non-convex setting.

7.6 NON-CONVEX PROBLEMS

7.6.1 Forward-Backward with Non-Convexity

Sparse regularization by the ℓ_1-norm is only a convex surrogate (tight relaxation) for the ℓ_0 sparsity penalty. Moreover, ℓ_1 regularized solutions are prone to bias (remember soft-thresholding is involved in this case). This may cause harm for applications where the amplitude of the recovered features must be preserved.

Iterative hard-thresholding (IHT) (Starck et al. 2004b, 2003c; Elad et al. 2005; Herrity et al. 2006; Blumensath and Davies 2008; Ramlau et al. 2008) consists of replacing soft-thresholding by hard-thresholding in the ISTA Algorithm 25. This then gives

$$\alpha^{(t+1)} = \text{HardThresh}_{\mu\lambda}\left(\alpha^{(t)} + \mu\mathbf{F}^{\text{T}}\left(y - \mathbf{F}\alpha^{(t)}\right)\right) , \tag{7.66}$$

for $\mu \in]0, 1/(\|\mathbf{F}\|^2]$ (no factor 2 as in ISTA). The goal pursued by this iteration is to solve the ℓ_0-regularized problem

$$\min_{\alpha \in \mathbb{R}^T} \|y - \mathbf{F}\alpha\|^2 + \lambda^2 \|\alpha\|_0 . \tag{7.67}$$

In general, the sequence $\alpha^{(t)}$ is only guaranteed to converge to a stationary point (Blumensath and Davies 2008; Attouch et al. 2013) (assuming the sequence is bounded).

The FB recursion (7.39) was also proposed to deal with other non-convex penalties. For instance, Bredies and Lorenz (2009) considered ℓ_p-regularization for $0 < p < 1$,

$$\min_{\alpha \in \mathbb{R}^T} \frac{1}{2} \|y - \mathbf{F}\alpha\|^2 + \lambda \|\alpha\|_p^p . \tag{7.68}$$

The FB iteration in this case reads

$$\alpha^{(t+1)} = \text{prox}_{\mu\lambda\|\cdot\|_p^p}\left(\alpha^{(t)} + \mu\mathbf{F}^{\text{T}}\left(y - \mathbf{F}\alpha^{(t)}\right)\right) , \tag{7.69}$$

with $\mu_t \in]0, 1/(\|\mathbf{F}\|^2]$ and the proximity operator is separable in each coordinate. Even if the ℓ_p penalty is now non-convex, it was shown that its proximity operator has a unique closed-form solution given by Antoniadis and Fan (2001); Fadili and Bullmore (2005) and Fadili et al. (2009b):

$$\tilde{\alpha}[i] = \text{prox}_{\mu\lambda|\cdot|^p}(\alpha[i]) = \begin{cases} 0 & \text{if } |\alpha[i]| \leq \mu\lambda\kappa_p , \\ \alpha[i] - \mu\lambda p \, \text{sign}(\tilde{\alpha}[i])|\tilde{\alpha}[i]|^{p-1} & \text{if } |\alpha[i]| > \mu\lambda\kappa_p . \end{cases} \tag{7.70}$$

$\kappa_p = (2 - p)(\mu\lambda p(1 - p)^{p-1})^{\frac{1}{2-p}}$. For $|\alpha[i]| > \mu\lambda\kappa_p$, equation (7.70) has a shrinkage amount sandwiched between soft- and hard-thresholding. Bredies and Lorenz (2009) have shown subsequent convergence of equation (7.69) to a stationary point. Global convergence to a stationary point was established in Attouch et al. (2013) (if the sequence is bounded).

It turns out that the FB proximal splitting scheme can be elegantly extended much beyond the ℓ_p-regularization and quadratic data fidelity. We follow here the same approach as in Attouch et al. (2013). Consider solving

$$\min_{\alpha \in \mathbb{R}^T} D(\mathbf{F}\alpha, y) + J(\alpha) , \tag{7.71}$$

where

- $D(\cdot, y)$ is differentiable with a β-Lipschitz-continuous gradient. It is not necessarily convex.
- J is not necessarily convex. It is, however, simple, meaning that its proximity operator $\text{prox}_{\mu J}$ is easily computable. Observe that $\text{prox}_{\mu J}$ may be multivalued in the non-convex case. But, luckily, this does not affect the rest of our exposition.
- $D(\cdot, y) + J$ is a proper lsc function that is bounded from below and that satisfies the so-called Kurdyka-Łojasiewicz (KL) property.

We do not elaborate on the details of the KL property, which would require substantial material from nonsmooth and variational analysis. Moreover, this elaboration is not essential to the reader interested in algorithmic details. But roughly speaking, the KL property means that the function under consideration looks sharp under a suitable reparametrization. In the context of optimization, the KL property is important because a wide range of problems involve functions satisfying it, and it is often elementary to check that such a property is satisfied. Typical functions satisfying the KL property are (possibly nonsmooth) semi-algebraic functions. These are functions whose graph can be represented as a finite union of finitely many polynomial inequalities. Semi-algebraic functions comprise a rich class that is stable under many mathematical operations, including addition, multiplication, composition by a linear operator, and derivation, to name a few. They are usually easy to recognize, even without going through their original definition. For instance, the ℓ_p-penalty, for $p \geq 0$ and rational, is semi-algebraic. Thus, since the quadratic function is algebraic, the objectives in equations (7.67) and (7.68), for p rational, are also semi-algebraic.

Many other functions that are met in the sparsity world and that are not semi-algebraic, very often satisfy the KL property. An important class is given by functions definable in an o-minimal structure; see van den Dries and Miller (1996). We do not give a precise definition of definability, which is outside the scope of this book, but the flexibility of this concept is illustrated by the ℓ_p penalty for any $p \geq 0$ (rational or not). Indeed, $t \in]0, +\infty] \to t^p$, $p \in \mathbb{R}$, is definable (van den Dries and Miller 1996), and thus so is the ℓ_p penalty.

Consider the FB splitting algorithm to solve equation (7.71)

$$\begin{cases} \mu \in]0, \frac{1}{\beta \|\mathbf{F}\|^2}], \\ \alpha^{(t+1)} \in \text{prox}_{\mu J}\left(\alpha^{(t)} - \mu \mathbf{F}^{\mathrm{T}} \nabla D\left(\mathbf{F}\alpha^{(t)}, y\right)\right), \end{cases} \tag{7.72}$$

and inclusion in $\text{prox}_{\mu J}$ implies that it might be multivalued. Clearly, equation (7.72) covers both (7.66) and (7.69) as particular cases. When the sequence provided by equation (7.72) is bounded, it converges to a stationary point of (7.71). Iteration (7.72) is also provably stable to relative errors. There are standard assumptions that automatically guarantee the boundedness of the sequence $\alpha^{(t)}$, and thus its convergence. For instance, coercivity of J would be sufficient, as is the case for ℓ_p, $p > 0$.

We close this section by briefly looking at the analysis-sparsity version of equation (7.71), i.e.,

$$\min_{x \in \mathbb{R}^N} D(\mathbf{H}x, y) + J(\mathbf{\Phi}^{\mathsf{T}} x) , \tag{7.73}$$

where $D(\cdot, y)$ and J satisfy the same assumptions as above. The FB still applies with its convergence guarantees. The main difficulty that remains, however, is to compute the proximity operator of $J \circ \mathbf{\Phi}^{\mathsf{T}}$. There is no general recipe, and this has be to be done on a case-by-case basis.

7.6.2 Iterative Reweighted Algorithms

Iterative reweighted algorithms provide a framework where one replaces the original non-convex by a sequence of subproblems, where the latter are much easier to solve (i.e. a convex or even closed-form solution). Such algorithms fall within the general class of majorization-minimization (MM) algorithms; see Lange (2004). In a nutshell, MM algorithms are a generalization of EM algorithms and work by iteratively minimizing a simple surrogate function majorizing the original objective function. A qualified surrogate majorant at a point, say $\alpha^{(t)}$, lies above the original function and is tangent to it at $\alpha^{(t)}$. In general, many majorizing or minorizing relationships may be derived from various inequalities stemming from convexity or concavity. The important ingredient is then to find a qualified majorant.

Iterative Reweighted Least-Squares (IRLS)

IRLS was proposed as an iterative MM-type algorithm in robust statistics to minimize the ℓ_1-norm (Karlovitz 1970). It was then revitalized for $\ell_p, p \leq 1$, sparse recovery as FOCUSS (FOcal Underdetermined System Solver) by Gorodnitsky and Rao (1997); see also (Daubechies et al. 2010) for a rigrous convergence analysis in a compressed sensing scenario (Chapter 13).

Consider the general version of problem (7.68):

$$\min_{\alpha \in \mathbb{R}^T} \frac{1}{2} \|y - \mathbf{F}\alpha\|^2 + \sum_{i=1}^{T} g_i \left(\sqrt{\alpha[i]^2 + \epsilon^2} \right) , \tag{7.74}$$

where $\epsilon > 0$ is sufficiently small, and for any i, g_i is differentiable, non-decreasing, and concave on $[0, +\infty[$ with $g_i(0) = 0$. Typically, ℓ_p, with $p \in]0, 1[$ satisfies these requirements. It is clear that $g_i \circ \sqrt{\cdot}$ is concave on $[0, +\infty[$. By concavity, it is below its tangent at $\alpha^{(t)}[i]$,

$$g_i \left(\sqrt{\alpha[i]^2 + \epsilon^2} \right) + g_i' \left(\sqrt{\alpha^{(t)}[i]^2 + \epsilon^2} \right) (\alpha[i]^2 - (\alpha^{(t)}[i])^2) \Big/ \left(2\sqrt{\alpha^{(t)}[i]^2 + \epsilon^2} \right) .$$

One can then improve the accuracy of the guess of the solution of equation (7.74) by inductively replacing the penalty by its affine majorant, and minimizing

$$\min_{\alpha \in \mathbb{R}^T} \frac{1}{2} \|y - \mathbf{F}\alpha\|^2 + \frac{1}{2} \sum_{i=1}^{T} w^{(t)}[i]\alpha[i]^2 , \tag{7.75}$$

where the weights

$$w^{(t)}[i] := \frac{g_i'\left(\sqrt{\alpha^{(t)}[i]^2 + \epsilon^2}\right)}{\sqrt{\alpha^{(t)}[i]^2 + \epsilon^2}} \geq 0 . \tag{7.76}$$

For ℓ_p, the weights read $w^{(t)}[i] = p(\alpha^{(t)}[i]^2 + \epsilon^2)^{p/2-1}$. The role of ϵ is now apparent, as it prevents the weights from blowing up or being degenerate when $\alpha^{(t)}[i] = 0$, and ensures that this value does not strictly prohibit a non-zero estimate at the next iterate. In practice, ϵ should be set slightly sufficiently small, typically smaller than the non-zero magnitudes of the original vectors (unknown) α_0.

The solution to equation (7.75) can be computed in closed form as

$$\alpha^{(t+1)} = \left(\mathbf{F}^{\mathsf{T}}\mathbf{F} + \mathrm{Diag}\left(w^{(t)}\right)\right)^{-1}\mathbf{F}^{\mathsf{T}}y \tag{7.77}$$

whenever the inverse exists. The IRLS algorithm then alternates between equations (7.76) and (7.77).

By construction, because IRLS is an instance of MM, the objective function in (7.75) at $\alpha^{(t)}$ decreases, but this does not say anything about the convergence of the iterates. Using additional regularity assumptions, such as smoothness of D and assuming coercivity, for instance, one can ensure convergence to a stationary point; see Lange (2004). Again, given non-convexity, convergence to a global minimizer cannot be ensured in general. It is thus important to choose a suitable starting point (e.g., BPDN/Lasso minimizer for IRLS with ℓ_p), for IRLS to be effective.

The IRLS reweighted scheme can be applied to the analysis-sparsity prior $\sum_{i=1}^{T} g_i(\sqrt{(\mathbf{\Phi}^{\mathsf{T}}x)[i]^2 + \epsilon^2})$ just as well, in which case the weights and updates become

$$\begin{cases} w^{(t)}[i] = \dfrac{g_i'\left(\sqrt{(\mathbf{\Phi}^{\mathsf{T}}x^{(t)})[i]^2 + \epsilon^2}\right)}{\sqrt{(\mathbf{\Phi}^{\mathsf{T}}x^{(t)})[i]^2 + \epsilon^2}}, \\[2ex] \alpha^{(t+1)} = \left(\mathbf{H}^{\mathsf{T}}\mathbf{H} + \mathbf{\Phi}\,\mathrm{Diag}\left(w^{(t)}\right)\mathbf{\Phi}^{\mathsf{T}}\right)^{-1}\mathbf{H}^{\mathsf{T}}y , \end{cases}$$

with the proviso that the above inverse makes sense.

Iterative Reweighted ℓ_1-minimization (IRℓ_1)

IRℓ_1 was proposed in Candès et al. (2008) as a way of approximately minimizing problems with the ℓ_0-penalty. We consider now the following problem,

$$\min_{\alpha \in \mathbb{R}^T} D(\mathbf{F}\alpha, y) + \sum_{i=1}^{T} g_i(|\alpha[i]| + \epsilon), \tag{7.78}$$

under the same assumptions on g_i, and where $D(\cdot, y) \in \Gamma_0(\mathbb{R}^m)$. This problem is equivalent to

$$\min_{\alpha, \xi \in \mathbb{R}^T} D(\mathbf{F}\alpha, y) + \sum_{i=1}^{T} g_i(\xi[i] + \epsilon) \quad \text{s.t.} \quad |\alpha[i]| \leq \xi[i] .$$

Using concavity and differentiability of g_i, its affine majorant at $\xi^{(t)}[i]$ is

$$g_i\left(\xi^{(t)}[i] + \epsilon\right) + g_i'\left(\xi^{(t)}[i] + \epsilon\right)\left(\xi[i] - \xi^{(t)}[i]\right) .$$

In Candès et al. (2008), $g_i = \log$ is proposed. Thus, a qualified majorant to equation (7.78) at $\alpha^{(t)}$ is

$$\min_{\alpha, \xi \in \mathbb{R}^T} D(\mathbf{F}\alpha, y) + \frac{1}{2} \sum_{i=1}^{T} w^{(t)}[i]\xi[i] \quad \text{s.t.} \quad |\alpha[i]| \le \xi[i]$$

$$\Longleftrightarrow \min_{\alpha \in \mathbb{R}^T} D(\mathbf{F}\alpha, y) + \frac{1}{2} \sum_{i=1}^{T} w^{(t)}[i]|\alpha[i]| \tag{7.79}$$

where the weights are

$$w^{(t)}[i] := g_i'\left(|\alpha^{(t)}[i]| + \epsilon\right) \ge 0. \tag{7.80}$$

Problem (7.79) is convex with a weighted ℓ_1 norm as a regularizer. It can then be solved by applying any proximal splitting solver that we designed above for the ℓ_1 norm and $D(\cdot, y)$ (see, e.g. Section 7.5). IRℓ_1 minimization consists then in alternating between equations (7.80) and (7.79). As for IRLS, the choice of a suitable starting point is important given non-convexity of the original problem.

In the case of an analysis-sparsity prior $\sum_{i=1}^{T} g_i(|(\mathbf{\Phi}^{\mathrm{T}}x)[i]| + \epsilon)$, IR$\ell_1$ corresponds to alternating between

$$\begin{cases} w^{(t)}[i] = g_i'\left(|(\mathbf{\Phi}^{\mathrm{T}}x^{(t)})[i]| + \epsilon\right), \\ \alpha^{(t+1)} \in \underset{\alpha \in \mathbb{R}^T}{\operatorname{argmin}} \ D(\mathbf{F}\alpha, y) + \frac{1}{2} \sum_{i=1}^{T} w^{(t)}[i]|\alpha[i]|. \end{cases}$$

7.7 GENERAL DISCUSSION: SPARSITY, INVERSE PROBLEMS, AND ITERATIVE THRESHOLDING

7.7.1 Iterative Thresholding: Simplicity and Robustness

The proximal schemes presented above involve computing the proximity operators of simple functions, such as the ℓ_1-norm, whose cost is generally linear or almost linear (up to log factors). These schemes are also very easy to implement. Furthermore, as explained in Section 7.4.9, they are robust with regard to numerical errors.

However, their local convergence behavior and speed strongly depend on the operator $\mathbf{H}$, and slow convergence may be observed for severely ill-conditioned $\mathbf{H}$. See Liang et al. (2014) for a rigorous analysis. For the case of ISTA, acceleration can be achieved in several ways, including FISTA, or by exploiting the structure of the operator such as convolution (Vonesch and Unser 2007), or by using elaborated step sizes, line search, (Elad 2006; Nesterov 2007), or the Barzilai-Borwein method (Wright et al. 2009). Other principled ways are to use variable metric proximal splitting, including the variable metric FB algorithm (Chen and Rockafellar 1997; S. Becker 2012; Combettes and Vũ 2014; Lee et al. 2014), or exploiting the fact that the regularizers that we use in sparse recovery are locally smooth when restricted to appropriate subsets (Liang et al. 2014) (e.g., the ℓ_1 norm).

7.7.2 Varying the Regularization Parameter in ISTA

The idea of iterative thresholding with a varying threshold was pioneered in Starck et al. (2004b) and Elad et al. (2005) for sparse signal decomposition and inpainting in order to accelerate the convergence. The proposal of these authors was to use a different λ_t at each iteration. The first threshold λ_0 should be set to a large value (i.e., $\|\mathbf{F}^{\mathrm{T}} y\|_\infty$) and λ_t should decrease with the iterations, following a given policy, typically linear or exponential.

The idea underlying this threshold update recipe has a flavor of homotopy continuation or path following. In Osborne et al. (2000), a homotopy method was to compute the regularization path of the Lasso (7.4) (i.e., the behavior of the solutions $\alpha_\lambda^\star$ as a mapping of $\lambda \in]0, \|\mathbf{F}^{\mathrm{T}} y\|_\infty[$). The key is that the solutions $\alpha_\lambda^\star$ of BPDN identify a polygonal path, and the homotopy method follows this solution path by jumping from vertex to vertex. Inspired by this approach, Fadili et al. (2009b) introduced a continuation method that solves a sequence of problems (7.4) for a decreasing value of λ (e.g., linearly or exponentially) and uses the previous solution as a warm start for the next problem. This approach has been used by several authors with different update schemes of λ (Figueiredo et al. 2007b; Hale et al. 2008; Wright et al. 2009). Continuation has been shown to speed up convergence, to confer robustness to initialization, and to enable the better recovery of signals with high dynamic range. Convergence and recovery guarantees of ISTA with varying threshold have been investigated recently in Xiao and Zhang (2013), under an exponential update schedule of λ, and adaptive line search for the step size. They prove that if $\mathbf{F}$ satisfies the restricted isometry property (see Chapter 13), the procedure indeed converges.

For non-convex minimization problems, starting with a high threshold level and decreasing it with iterations, we have observed in practice that it may allow local minima to be avoided.

7.7.3 Iterative Reweighting

The Iterative Reweighted ℓ_1-minimization (IRℓ_1) discussed in Section 7.6.2, is a convenient way to solve ℓ_0-regularized inverse problems that has proven to be efficient in different applications such as superresolution (Ngolè Mboula et al. 2015), non-negative blind source separation (Rapin et al. 2014), spectral estimation (Paykari et al. 2014), and sparse signal decomposition (see Chapter 8) (Peng and Hwang 2014). For blind source separation problems with correlated sources, Bobin et al. (2014) show how a specific reweighting can improve the results significantly.

7.8 GUIDED NUMERICAL EXPERIMENTS

The splitting framework described in this chapter has been applied to solve several inverse problems such as signal decomposition, sparse spike deconvolution, and recovery in compressed sensing. The Matlab `SplittingSolvers` toolbox is made available freely under the CeCILL license for download at the address www.SparseSignalRecipes.info. This toolbox is a collection of Matlab functions and scripts implementing the algorithms discussed in this chapter and reproducing the guided numerical experiments described later. It has the same structure as the MCALab toolbox discussed in Section 8.8.1.

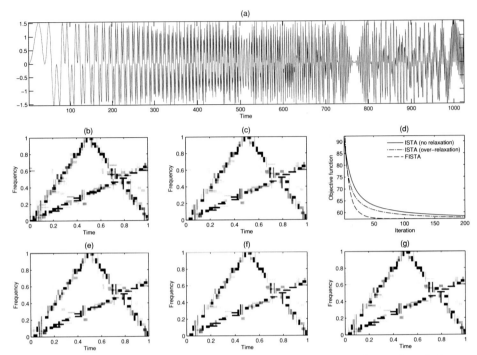

Figure 7.2. Sparse representation of two-chirps $N = 1024$ in a wavelet packet dictionary. (a) Noisy two-chirp signal (PSNR = 25 dB). (b)–(c) Wavelet packet phase-plane tiling of recovered signals by solving (7.4) using Algorithms 25 and 26. (d) Convergence profile in terms of the objective function in equation (7.4) for ISTA (over-relaxed or not) and FISTA. (e) Wavelet packet phase-plane tiling of recovered signal by solving (7.2) using Algorithm 30. (f) Wavelet packet phase-plane tiling of recovered signal by solving (7.6) using (7.41). (g) Wavelet packet phase-plane tiling of recovered signal by solving (7.7). Except for Algorithm 30, which was applied with the noiseless measurements, all other algorithms were run on the noisy ones.

7.8.1 Sparse Representation

The results of this experiment can be reproduced with the script `1D/Demos/testsSparseApproxSynthesis1D.m` of the toolbox. The proximal splitting algorithms are applied to a sparse decomposition problem of a 1D signal of $N = 1024$ samples ($\mathbf{H} = \mathbf{I}$). The signal is a superposition of two chirps (i.e., two frequency-modulated sines) and corrupted with an additive white Gaussian noise of standard deviation σ_ε (PSNR = 25 dB). The dictionary Φ is taken as the wavelet packets since chirps are compressible in such a dictionary. Five algorithms applied to solve different problems were tested with 200 iterations: ISTA in Algorithm 25 and FISTA in Algorithm 26 to solve problem (7.4), DR splitting in Algorithm 30 to solve BP (7.2), DR also to solve problem (7.6) since Φ is a tight frame, and primal-dual splitting (adapted from Algorithm 28) to solve (7.7). We also applied an over-relaxed version of ISTA. Except for (7.2), which used the noiseless measurements, all other algorithms were run on the noisy ones. To solve problem (7.6), the radius of the ℓ_2-constraint was set slightly larger than $\sqrt{N}\sigma_\varepsilon$ (i.e., $\sigma = \sqrt{N}\sigma_\varepsilon\sqrt{1 + 2\sqrt{2/N}}$ as advocated in Section 7.5.3.4). For Algorithms 25 and 26, the choice of the regularization

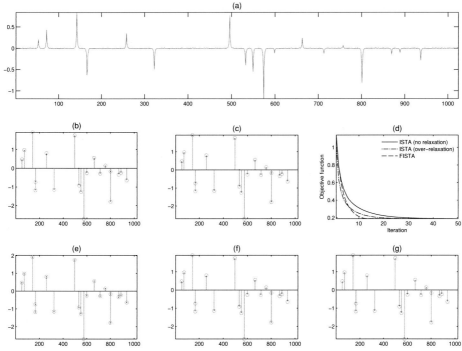

Figure 7.3. Sparse spike train deconvolution $N = 1024, k = 20$. (a) Blurred noisy, SNR = 25 dB. (b)–(c) Recovered spikes by solving problem (7.4) using Algorithms 25 and 26. (c) Convergence profile in terms of the objective function in equation (7.4) for ISTA (over-relaxed or not) and FISTA. (e)–(g) Recovered by solving respectively (7.2), (7.6), and (7.7). Except for problem (7.2), which was solved with the noiseless measurements, all other algorithms were run on the noisy ones.

parameter λ in (7.4) was done on a trial-test basis to get a residual error of σ (alternative ways are described in Section 7.5.2). For problem (7.7), the parameter δ was set to λ, since the ℓ_∞ constraint is nothing but the first-order optimality condition (7.57) of (7.4). The results are shown in Fig. 7.2. Observe that as expected, FISTA is faster than ISTA (whether it is relaxed or not), and the latter exhibits an improved convergence behavior when over-relaxed.

7.8.2 Sparse Spike Deconvolution

In this experiment, we generated a 1D 20-sparse vector α with the position selected uniformly at random among $N = 1024$ positions, where the non-zero entries are drawn iid (independently and identically distributed) from the standard Gaussian distribution. As the spikes are sparse in the standard basis, the dictionary is $\boldsymbol{\Phi} = \mathbf{I}$. The sparse spike train is then convolved with a double exponential point spread function, and thus $\mathbf{H}$ is an $N \times N$ circular convolution matrix. Additive zero-mean white Gaussian noise with standard deviation σ_ε (SNR = 25 dB) was added to $\mathbf{H}\alpha$ to get the observed blurred and noisy signal y. The same algorithms as in the previous experiment are tested, but as $\mathbf{H}\boldsymbol{\Phi}$ is no longer a tight frame, Algorithm 28 was used to solve equation (7.6) and (7.2) ($\sigma = 0$). The radius of the

ℓ_2-constraint in equation (7.6), that of the ℓ_∞-constraint in equation (7.7), and the regularization parameter in equation (7.4) were chosen as in the previous experiment. The results are depicted in Fig. 7.3. They can be reproduced with the script `1D/Demos/testsSparseSpikeDeconv1D.m` of the toolbox.

7.9 SUMMARY

In this chapter, we emphasized the role of sparsity in solving linear inverse problems. We introduced and developed a unified framework, namely proximal splitting, for solving a large class of convex sparsity-regularized linear inverse problems. Practical algorithms were provided in detail, and only a few important theoretical properties were discussed. We also discussed extension to the non-convex case. The goal was to have a clear picture of the state-of-the-art in the field. We finally provided some guided numerical experiments based on a Matlab toolbox that we make available on the web. This is a complete library that implements the algorithms described in the chapter and allows the reader to reproduce the tutorial examples shown here, as well as many others.

In the next two chapters, we see more specific linear inverse problems where non-convex sparsity penalties, such as the ℓ_0 pseudo-norm, can be used. We show that hard-thresholding is at the heart of the iterative stagewise pursuit algorithms that are proposed, leading to very good results, if appropriately combined with a varying threshold strategy.

8

Morphological Diversity

8.1 INTRODUCTION

The content of an image is often complex, and there is no single transform which is optimal to represent effectively all the contained features. For example, the Fourier transform is better at sparsifying globally oscillatory textures, while the wavelet transform does a better job with isolated singularities. Even if we limit our class of transforms to the wavelet one, decisions have to be made between e.g. the starlet transform (see Section 3.5) which yields good results for isotropic objects (such as stars and galaxies in astronomical images, or cells in biological images), and the orthogonal wavelet transform (see Section 2.5) which is good for bounded variation images (Cohen et al. 1999).

If we do not restrict ourselves to fixed dictionaries related to fast implicit transforms such as the Fourier or the wavelet dictionaries, one can even design very large dictionaries including many different shapes to represent the data effectively. Following Olshausen and Field (1996b), we can even push the idea one step forward by requiring that the dictionary is not fixed but rather learned to sparsify a set of typical images (patches). Such a dictionary design problem corresponds to finding a sparse matrix factorization and was tackled by several authors (Field 1999; Olshausen and Field 1996a; Simoncelli and Olshausen 2001; Lewicki and Sejnowski 2000; Kreutz-Delgado et al. 2003; Aharon et al. 2006; Peyré et al. 2007). In the rest of the chapter, we restrict ourselves to fixed dictionaries with fast transforms.

8.1.1 The Sparse Decomposition Problem

In the general sparse representation framework, a signal vector $x \in \mathbb{R}^N$ is modeled as the linear combination of T elementary waveforms according to (1.1). In the case of overcomplete representations, the number of waveforms or atoms $(\varphi_i)_{1 \leq i \leq T}$ that are columns of the dictionary Φ is higher than the dimension of the space in which x lies: $T > N$, or even $T \gg N$ for highly redundant dictionaries.

The decomposition problem of a signal or image in Φ amounts to recovering the coefficient vector α in (1.1) from $x = \Phi\alpha$. However, we can easily see that there is a fundamental problem; the N-sample signal or image offers us N data (the sample) values but there are as many as $T > N$ unknowns. Traditional mathematical reasoning, in fact the fundamental theorem of linear algebra, tells us not to attempt this: there are more unknowns than equations and the problem has *no unique solution*.

On the other hand, solving the underdetermined system of linear equations $x = \Phi \alpha$ can be made possible by reducing the space of candidate solutions to those satisfying some side constraints. For instance, among all solutions of $x = \Phi \alpha$, we would like the sparsest one (with the least number of non-zero entries $\alpha[i]$). Put formally, the sparse decomposition problem requires to solve the following minimization problem:

$$\min_{\alpha \in \mathbb{R}^T} \|\alpha\|_0 \quad \text{s.t.} \quad x = \Phi \alpha . \tag{8.1}$$

As stated, this may appear hopeless. Clearly equation (8.1) is a *combinatorial* optimization problem that requires enumerating all the collections of atoms in Φ looking for the smallest set that synthesizes x. This is why authors turned to approximations or relaxations of (8.1). Donoho and Huo (2001b) proposed to relax the non-convex ℓ_0 sparsity measure by substituting the problem in (8.1) with the convex problem

$$\min_{\alpha \in \mathbb{R}^T} \|\alpha\|_1 \quad \text{s.t.} \quad x = \Phi \alpha . \tag{8.2}$$

This problem is known as *Basis Pursuit* (BP) (Chen et al. 1999) (see also Chapters 7 and 13). Unlike (8.1), (8.2) is a computationally tractable convex optimization problem that can be solved very efficiently as we described in detail in Section 7.5.4.

BP however does not solve equation (8.1) in general. But, under appropriate conditions on Φ and x, BP can produce the globally optimal solution of equation (8.1). Thus, practical algorithms can solve problems that at first glance seem computationally intractable. Extensive work has focused on sufficient (and sometimes necessary) conditions under which the problem in (8.2) recovers the sparsest solution of an underdetermined system of linear equations, both in the noiseless and noisy cases. Our aim here is not to give an exhaustive overview of the literature on the subject but only to outline the main contributions.

For instance, sufficient conditions based on the mutual coherence of Φ were introduced by several authors, see, for example, Donoho and Huo (2001b); Donoho and Elad (2003); Bruckstein and Elad (2002); Gribonval and Nielsen (2003); Feuer and Nemirovsky (2003); Donoho et al. (2006); Tropp (2006b). The *mutual coherence* μ_Φ of Φ is defined as

$$\mu_\Phi = \max_{i \neq j} |\langle \varphi_i, \varphi_j \rangle| . \tag{8.3}$$

This quantity can be viewed as a worst-case measure of resemblance between all pairs of atoms. Donoho and Huo (2001b) and others showed that if a k-sparse vector α whose support $\Lambda(\alpha) = \{1 \leq i \leq N \mid \alpha[i] \neq 0\}$ satisfies

$$\text{Card}(\Lambda(\alpha)) = k < C(\mu_\Phi^{-1} + 1) , \tag{8.4}$$

for some constant $C > 0$ (typically $C = 1/2$ (Donoho and Huo 2001b)), then the solution of BP is unique and is a point of equivalence of (8.1) and (8.2), hence ensuring identifiability of the unique sparsest solution by ℓ_1 minimization. In a nutshell, this results tells us that the more incoherent the dictionary, the higher level of sparsity that can be recovered exactly by ℓ_1-minimization. Note however that despite its simplicity and stability to compressibility and noise (Donoho et al. 2006), the identifiability test of equation (8.4) leads to pessimistic sparsity bounds which are at best $O(\sqrt{N})$ (e.g. for a Sines+Diracs dictionary). The coherence-based sufficient recovery conditions can be refined using the Spark[1] of Φ (Donoho et al. 2006), or by considering not only the sparsity but also the support and the sign pattern of the non-zero entries of α (Fuchs 2004; Tropp 2006b; Wainwright 2009). Sufficient ℓ_1-identifiability condition based on the restricted isometry property will be discussed in more detail in the context of compressed sensing in Chapter 13. Based on topological properties of random projection of the unit ℓ_1-ball under Φ, Donoho (2006); Donoho and Tanner (2005) determine a very sharp sparsity upper-bound that is (almost) linear in N, which is much better than $O(\sqrt{N})$ dictated by (8.4). However, this identifiability condition does not ensure stability to noise. The interested reader may refer to Bruckstein et al. (2009) for a comprehensive review of sparse recovery conditions by ℓ_1 minimization and greedy algorithms.

8.1.2 The Concept of Morphological Diversity

The morphological diversity concept introduces a new data modeling framework which allows us to have both a sparse representation and fast algorithms that exploit the structure of the dictionary. Morphological diversity assumes that the data x can be modeled as the sum of K components x_k that look *morphologically* different:

$$x = \sum_{k=1}^{K} x_k \,, \tag{8.5}$$

where each component x_k is sparse in a given dictionary Φ_k which is associated with implicit fast analysis/synthesis operators. Each x_k is called a *morphological component*. For instance, by combining the Fourier and the wavelet dictionaries, we can well represent signals which contain both stationary and localized features.

The core idea of this chapter is then to encode a priori knowledge on the salient features of the sought-after signal or image in a large dictionary, built by combining several subdictionaries, each specialized in sparsifying a certain type of structure. Owing to advances in modern computational harmonic analysis, many transforms such as those described in Chapters 2–5, were shown to be very effective in sparsely representing certain kinds of signals and images. Each sub-dictionary can then be chosen appropriately from these transforms.

Further reasoning behind this is borrowed from an old idea in signal processing: the matched filter. The matched filter theorem asserts that to optimally detect the presence of a known template in an observed noisy signal, the latter must be correlated with the template, and the SNR will be maximal if the template is present. The lesson taught by this result is that to analyze effectively a signal or image, we just have to pick up a dictionary with atoms that are morphologically similar to the features in the signal or image.

On the basis of this morphological diversity concept, we present in the rest of this chapter how we can derive fast algorithms for applications which involve such complex dictionaries, i.e. a union of several sub-dictionaries, where each of them has fast analysis and synthesis operators. Applications tackled in this chapter are denoising, deconvolution, component separation and inpainting.

8.2 DICTIONARY AND FAST TRANSFORMATION

From a practical point of view, given a signal x, we will need to compute its forward (or analysis) transform by multiplying it by $\mathbf{\Phi}^{\mathrm{T}}$.[2] We also need to reconstruct (synthesize) any signal from its coefficients α. In fact, the matrix $\mathbf{\Phi}$ and its transpose $\mathbf{\Phi}^{\mathrm{T}}$ corresponding to each transform are never explicitly constructed in memory. Rather they are implemented as fast implicit analysis and synthesis operators taking a signal vector x, and returning $\mathbf{\Phi}^{\mathrm{T}}x = \mathbf{T}x$ (analysis side), or taking a coefficient vector α and returning $\mathbf{\Phi}\alpha$ (synthesis side). In the case of a simple orthogonal basis, the inverse of the analysis transform is trivially $\mathbf{T}^{-1} = \mathbf{\Phi}$; whereas assuming that $\mathbf{\Phi}$ is a tight frame ($\mathbf{\Phi}\mathbf{\Phi}^{\mathrm{T}} = c\mathbf{I}$) implies that $\mathbf{T}^{+} = c^{-1}\mathbf{\Phi}$ is the Moore-Penrose pseudo-inverse transform (corresponding to the minimal dual synthesis frame). In other words, computing $\mathbf{\Phi}\alpha$ is equivalent to applying $\mathbf{T}^{+}$ to α up to a constant. It turns out that $\mathbf{T}^{+}\alpha$ is the reconstruction operation implemented by most implicit synthesis algorithms including some of those discussed in Chapters 2–5.

8.3 COMBINED DENOISING

8.3.1 Several Transforms Are Better than One

Suppose that we observe

$$y = x + \varepsilon \, ,$$

where $\varepsilon \sim \mathcal{N}(0, \sigma_\varepsilon^2)$, and x is a superposition of type (8.5). Our goal is to build an estimator of x by exploiting the morphological diversity of its content.

Suppose that we are given K dictionaries $\mathbf{\Phi}_k$ each associated with a linear transform (analysis) operator $\mathbf{T}_k$. Let $\mathbf{\Phi} = [\mathbf{\Phi}_1, \ldots, \mathbf{\Phi}_K]$ be the amalgamated dictionary and $\mathbf{T} = \mathbf{\Phi}^{\mathrm{T}}$ the analysis operator of $\mathbf{\Phi}$.

According to Chapter 6, a sequence of estimates $(\tilde{x}_k)_{1 \leq k \leq K}$ of x can be built by hard thresholding each α_k

$$\tilde{x}_k = \mathbf{T}_k^{+} \, \mathrm{HardThresh}_\lambda (\mathbf{T}_k y) \, , \tag{8.6}$$

with a threshold λ typically 3–4 times the noise standard deviation. Given the K individual estimates $\tilde{x}_k$, a naive but simple aggregated estimator is given by averaging them, i.e.

$$\tilde{x} = \frac{1}{K} \sum_{k=1}^{K} \tilde{x}_k \, . \tag{8.7}$$

This is for instance the idea underlying translation-invariant wavelet denoising by cycle-spinning (Coifman and Donoho 1995), where the averaging estimator is constructed from the thresholded orthogonal wavelet coefficients of translated versions of the original signal. However, this simple solution is not always relevant as it weights equally both low- and high-quality estimates. In fact, the question is deeper than that: suppose that we are given a sequence of estimates, each from a sparse representation explaining the signal differently. Is there an effective way to merge these estimates that leads to a better estimate by taking benefit of each transform? Answering this question is difficult in general. The problem amounts to figuring out a set of weights that are constructed in such a way to optimize the performance of the resulting estimator (in equation (8.7), all estimates are equi-weighted with $1/K$). An interesting solution was proposed by Fadili et al. (2007) who deployed a data-adaptive Bayesian framework to optimally combine the individual closed-form minimum mean-squares estimators (MMSE). The idea is to weight each estimate $\tilde{x}_k$ at each sample according to the significance that the atoms in Φ_k have in synthesizing $\tilde{x}_k$ at that sample. This procedure can however be time-consuming in practice. A rigorous statistical framework that studies these weights and the properties of the resulting estimators is known as *aggregation estimators*. Aggregation estimators with exponential weights and sparse representations have been studied (Dalalyan and Tsybakov 2008; Juditsky et al. 2008; Dalalyan and Tsybakov 2009). Sparsity oracle inequalities and other optimality properties of the estimators have been established. However, practical algorithms for large-scale data are still lacking. Recently, Elad and Yavneh (2009) started working in this direction and proposed a randomized orthogonal matching pursuit (OMP) algorithm to obtain a collection of competing representations, and those are averaged to lead to better denoising performance. This approach still needs some more work to be applicable to large data and dictionaries.

In the next section, we describe a fast combined denoising algorithm that can handle real-world images and large-scale dictionaries.

8.3.2 Combined Denoising Algorithm

The starting point of this approach is the sequence of multiresolution supports $(\mathcal{M}_k)_{1 \le k \le K}$ (see Section 6.2.3.1) that are obtained from the significant coefficients in $\mathbf{T}_k y$ after hard thresholding as in equation (8.6). Now, we seek a solution $\tilde{x}$ which has the sparsest representation *simultaneously* in each sub-dictionary Φ_k, such that its coefficients $\mathbf{T}_k \tilde{x}$ approach the empirical coefficients $\mathbf{T}_k y$ but only at the locations retained in $\mathcal{M}_k$. Put formally, our goal is to solve the following optimization problem:

$$\min_{x \in \mathcal{C}} \left[\|\mathbf{T}_1 x\|_1, \dots, \|\mathbf{T}_K x\|_1 \right], \tag{8.8}$$

where $\mathcal{C}$ is the set of linear constraints

$$\mathcal{C} = [0, +\infty)^N \cap \left(\cap_{k=1}^K \mathcal{C}_k \right), \ \mathcal{C}_k = \{x \in \mathbb{R}^N \|| (\mathbf{T}_k (y - x))[i]\| \le e_k[i], \forall i \in \mathcal{M}_k \}. \tag{8.9}$$

The positivity constraint can be replaced with other linear constraints on the dynamic range of the solution. In practice, the constraint size $e_k[i]$ is typically set to $e_k[i] = \sigma_k[i]/2$ where $\sigma_k[i]$ is the standard deviation of the noise in the kth transform domain at the coefficient index i. See Section 6.2.1.1 on how to compute them from σ_ε. In brief, these constraints guarantee that the solution will preserve any pattern which is detected as significant by any of the K transforms.

Problem (8.8) is a non-smooth *multiobjective* minimization problem (the objective is vector-valued). It is nontrivial to solve. The scalar concept of minimality (see e.g. Chapter 7) does not apply directly in the multiobjective setting. A useful replacement is the notion of Pareto optimality (Miettinen 1999). The multiobjective problem is almost always solved by combining the multiple objectives into one scalar objective whose solution is a Pareto optimal point for the original multiobjective problem. Interestingly, for our denoising problem, solving equation (8.8) boils down again to finding some appropriate weights as discussed above, although the weights here play a different role.

There are various solvers for multiobjective minimization which include homotopy techniques, normal-boundary intersection, multilevel programming and evolutionary algorithms (Miettinen 1999). The most intuitive technique is to minimize a positively weighted convex sum of the objectives for various settings of the convex weights. But the computational expense forces us to restrict ourselves to performing only one minimization. More precisely, our heuristic solver starts at $k = 1$, puts a weight one on its objective in equation (8.8), solves the corresponding scalar objective minimization problem, and then uses the obtained solution as an input for $k + 1$, and the process is repeated.

The scalar objective optimization problem that we have to solve for each k is of type

$$\min_{x \in [0, +\infty)^N \cap \mathcal{C}_k} \|\mathbf{T}_k x\|_1 . \tag{8.10}$$

This a non-smooth convex optimization problem, and the Douglas-Rachford splitting described in Chapter 7 appears as a natural candidate to solve it. The bottleneck of this approach is however that the proximity operators of both the objective and the constraint will necessitate two inner iterations to be computed. Below we propose an alternative based on the hybrid steepest descent (HSD) (Yamada 2001). The HSD algorithm allows minimizing convex but Lipschitz differentiable functionals over the intersection of fixed point sets of nonexpansive mappings. Unlike the projector on the constraint in equation (8.10), the nonexpansive mappings with the desired fixed point sets in our case do have closed forms. To overcome the difficulty of differentiability, we replace the ℓ_1 objective (8.10) by a smoothed (strictly convex) version $F_\epsilon(\alpha_k) = \sum_i \sqrt{\alpha_k[i]^2 + \epsilon} \ (\epsilon \geq 0)$.

Define the HSD iteration scheme ($t \geq 0$):

$$x_\epsilon^{(t+1)} = \mathbf{T}_k^+ \circ (\mathbf{I} - \gamma_t \nabla F_\epsilon) \circ \mathbf{T}_k \circ \mathcal{Q}_k \left(x_\epsilon^{(t)} \right) \tag{8.11}$$

where ∇F_ϵ is the gradient of F_ϵ, and $\mathcal{Q}_k = (\mathbf{T}_k^+ \circ \mathrm{P}_{\mathcal{P}_{\mathcal{P}_k}} \circ \mathbf{T}_k) \circ \mathrm{P}_{\mathcal{P}_+}$, $\mathrm{P}_{\mathcal{P}_+}$ is the projector on the positive orthant $\mathcal{P}_+$ and $\mathrm{P}_{\mathcal{P}_k}(\alpha_k)$ is the componentwise orthogonal projector that leaves all entries $i \notin \mathcal{M}_k$ of α_k unchanged and otherwise:

$$\mathrm{P}_{\mathcal{P}_k}(\alpha_k)[i] = \begin{cases} \alpha_k[i] & \text{if } [\alpha_k[i] - (\mathbf{T}_k y)[i]] \leq e_k[i] \\ (\mathbf{T}_k y)[i] + \mathrm{sign}(\alpha_k[i] - (\mathbf{T}_k y)[i]) e_k[i] & \text{otherwise} . \end{cases} \tag{8.12}$$

The step-size sequence γ_t obeys:

$$\lim_{t\to\infty}\gamma_t = 0, \quad \sum_{t\ge 1}\gamma_t = +\infty \quad \text{and} \quad \sum_{t\ge 1}|\gamma_t - \gamma_{t+1}| < +\infty\,.$$

A typical choice is $\gamma_t = (N_{\text{iter}} - t)/(N_{\text{iter}} - 1)$, which satisfies the requirements as $N_{\text{iter}} \to +\infty$.

Using a proof similar to Zhang et al. (2008b, Theorem 3), it can be shown that if $\boldsymbol{\Phi}_k$ corresponds to a tight frame, then instead of directly solving equation (8.10), one can solve its smoothed strictly convex version by applying equation (8.11) with a small ϵ. Formally, as $\epsilon \to 0^+$, every limit of the solution to the smoothed problem is a solution to equation (8.10). We also point out that, in practice, the recursion (8.11) applies equally well even with $\epsilon = 0$. For $\epsilon = 0$, from the subdifferential of the ℓ_1 norm (see equation (7.16)), the operator $\mathbf{I} - \gamma_t \nabla F_\epsilon$ in equation (8.11) can be implemented in practice as a soft thresholding with a threshold γ_t.

Now we have all ingredients for the combined denoising algorithm summarized in Algorithm 31. In our experiments, we observed that step c. of the inner loop can be discarded without loss of quality, and the benefit is computational savings. Hence, the computational cost of this algorithm can be reduced to $O(2N_{\text{iter}}\sum_{k=1}^{K}V_k)$, where V_k is the computational cost of each transform.

Algorithm 31 Combined Denoising Algorithm

Task: Denoising using several transforms.
Parameters: The data y, the dictionaries $\boldsymbol{\Phi}_1, \dots, \boldsymbol{\Phi}_K$ (with atoms assumed normalized to a unit norm), the number of iterations N_{iter}.
Initialization: Initialize $\gamma_0 = 1$ and the solution $x^{(0)} = 0$. Estimate the noise standard deviation σ_ε in y (e.g. see equation (6.9)), and set $e_k = \sigma_\varepsilon/2, \forall k$.
for $k = 1$ to K **do**
$\quad$ Compute the transform coefficients $\beta_k = \mathbf{T}_k y$; deduce the multiresolution support $\mathcal{M}_k$.

for $t = 0$ to $N_{\text{iter}} - 1$ **do**

$\quad$ 1. $z = x^{(t)}$.
$\quad$ 2. **for** $k = 1$ to K **do**

$\qquad$ a. Compute the transform coefficients $\alpha_k = \mathbf{T}_k z$.
$\qquad$ b. From (8.12), compute the projection $\zeta_k[i] = \mathrm{P}_{\mathcal{P}_k}(\alpha_k)[i]$ if $i \in \mathcal{M}_k$, and $\zeta_k[i] = \alpha_k[i]$ otherwise.
$\qquad$ c. Project onto the column-span of $\mathbf{T}_k$: $\zeta_k \leftarrow \mathbf{T}_k\mathbf{T}_k^+(\zeta_k)$.
$\qquad$ d. Apply soft thresholding with threshold λ to ζ_k:
$$\tilde{\zeta}_k = \text{SoftThresh}_{\gamma_t}(\zeta_k).$$
$\qquad$ e. Reconstruct and project onto the positive orthant:
$$z = \mathrm{P}_{\mathcal{P}_+}(\mathbf{T}_k^+\tilde{\zeta}_k).$$

$\quad$ 3. Update the image: $x^{(t+1)} = z$.
$\quad$ 4. $\gamma_{t+1} = (N_{\text{iter}} - t - 1)/N_{\text{iter}}$.

Output: $x^{(N_{\text{iter}})}$ the denoised image.

Figure 8.1. (top left) Noisy image $\sigma_\varepsilon = 20$, PSNR $= 22.13$ dB, and denoised images by hard thresholding (top right) in the UWT domain (PSNR $= 31.94$ dB), (bottom left) in the curvelet domain (PSNR $= 31.95$ dB), and (bottom right) using the combined denoising algorithm with both transforms (32.72 dB).

Example

The noisy "Lena" image ($\sigma_\varepsilon = 20$, PSNR $= 22.13$ dB) was denoised by hard thresholding in the undecimated wavelet transform (UWT) domain, in the curvelet domain, and using the combined denoising Algorithm 31 with both transforms. Figure 8.1 (top left) displays the noisy image; the denoised images are shown on the top right (UWT), bottom left (curvelet transform), and bottom right (combined denoising). A zoom on Lena's hat is depicted in Fig. 8.2 (left). Figure (right) 8.2 shows the full residual image. The residual is much better when the combined denoising is applied, and no further structure is visible. This is not the case if either the wavelet or the curvelet transform is used alone.

Figure 8.3 shows the PSNR of the solution versus the iteration counter. In this example, the algorithm converges rapidly. From a practical viewpoint, only four or five iterations were needed. Note that the PSNR obtained after a single iteration is already superior to that obtained based on simple thresholding of wavelet or curvelet coefficients.

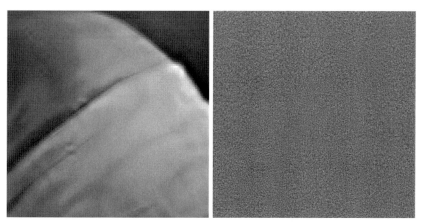

Figure 8.2. (left) A zoom on the hat of the denoised image by the combined method. (right) The full residual image.

8.4 COMBINED DECONVOLUTION

8.4.1 Problem Formulation

In the same vein as for denoising, we expect that the combination of different transforms can improve the quality of the result in a deconvolution problem, where now we observe

$$y = \mathbf{H}x + \varepsilon \,,$$

where $\mathbf{H}$ is the circular convolution operator associated with a point spread function (PSF) h (typically low pass), and ε is the noise. The combined deconvolution problem can be approached in two different ways.

If the noise is additive white Gaussian with variance σ_ε^2, and the Fourier transform $\hat{h}$ of the PSF does not vanish, then the deconvolution problem can be brought to a denoising problem by inverting the degradation $\mathbf{H}$. The resulting noise after inversion remains Gaussian, is not white, but colored, with a spectral density $\sigma_\varepsilon^2/|\hat{h}|^2$. The combined denoising algorithm, Algorithm 31, can then be applied with the wavelet

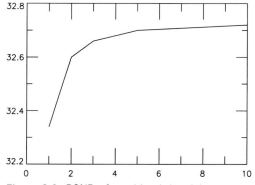

Figure 8.3. PSNR of combined denoising versus the iteration counter.

and curvelet transforms. This necessitates, first, the estimation of the standard deviations of the noise in the different subbands of both transforms; see the case of colored Gaussian noise in Section 6.2.1.1. As h is generally low pass, the traditional wavelet basis does not diagonalize the covariance of the noise after inverting $\mathbf{H}$. For this purpose, Khalifa et al. (2003) introduced mirror wavelets as particular wavelet packets that subdecompose the finest wavelet scale. It is recommended to use them as they may produce better results in practice.

An iterative deconvolution algorithm is more general and can be applied without stringent restrictions on h. For the sake of simplicity, we assume that the noise $\varepsilon \sim \mathcal{N}(0, \sigma_\varepsilon^2)$. Again, this approach begins by computing K multiresolution supports $(\mathcal{M}_k)_{1 \leq k \leq K}$ obtained from the significant coefficients in each $\mathbf{T}_k y$. For other noise models, for example, Poisson (see Section 6.4), the multiresolution supports are computed on the stabilized observations using the appropriate variance stabilizing transform (Anscombe for Poisson noise). Let $\mathbf{M}_k$ be the binary (nonsquare) matrix that extracts the coefficients indexed in $\mathcal{M}_k$ from any coefficient vector.

With the multiresolution supports to hand, the combined deconvolution approach seeks a solution to the following optimization problem (Starck et al. 2003c):

$$\min_{x \in \mathcal{C}'} \|x\|_{\mathrm{TV}_p}^p \, , \qquad (8.13)$$

where $\mathcal{C}' = [0, +\infty)^N \cap (\cap_{k=1}^K \{x \in \mathbb{R}^N \mid \|\mathbf{M}_k \mathbf{T}_k (y - \mathbf{H}x)\|_2 \leq \sigma_k\})$, $\|x\|_{\mathrm{TV}_p}$ is the pth norm of the discrete gradient of x. The discrete total variation seminorm (6.21) obviously corresponds to $p = 1$. Here we took $p = 1.1$ in order to approach the case $p = 1$ while dealing with a strictly convex and differentiable functional. The regularization in equation (8.13) promotes piecewise smooth candidate solutions. The constraint imposes fidelity to the data, or more exactly, on the significant coefficients of the data, obtained by the different transforms. Non-significant (i.e. due to noise) coefficients are excluded, hence, avoiding noise amplification in the solution.

8.4.2 Combined Deconvolution Algorithm

To solve (8.13), and if one can afford to subiterate to compute the projector on the constraint, the splitting framework of Chapter 7 can be used advantageously. Otherwise, one can think of using the HSD algorithm as for denoising. However, because of the convolution operator $\mathbf{H}$, it turns out that the computation of a nonexpansive operator associated with the constraint on the multiresolution support having the proper fixed point set is difficult without subiterating.

We then turn to another alternative by relaxing the multiresolution constraints in equation (8.13) into an augmented Lagrangian form:

$$\min_{x \in [0, +\infty)^N} \frac{1}{2} \sum_{k=1}^K \|\mathbf{M}_k \mathbf{T}_k (y - \mathbf{H}x)\|_2^2 + \lambda \|x\|_{\mathrm{TV}_p}^p \, , \qquad (8.14)$$

where λ is a regularization parameter. Let $F(x) = \|x\|_{\mathrm{TV}_p}^p$. Its gradient with respect to x is

$$\nabla F(x) = \left(-\overline{\mathrm{div}} \circ G \circ \overline{\nabla}(x) \right)_{1 \leq i \leq N} \, , \qquad (8.15)$$

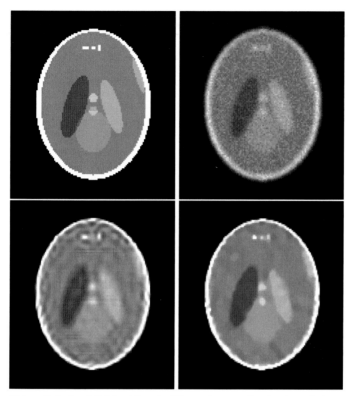

Figure 8.4. (top) Original image (Shepp-Logan phantom) and simulated degraded image (i.e. blurred and contaminated with Poisson noise). (bottom) Deconvolved image using (left) only the wavelet transform and (right) the combined approach.

where $\overline{\mathrm{div}}$ is the discrete divergence operator (Chambolle 2004), and $G : \mathbb{R}^{N \times 2} \to \mathbb{R}^{N \times 2}$ is a multivalued function whose ith entry is the vector field $p\zeta |\zeta|^{p-2}$ for $\zeta \in \mathbb{R}^2$ and $|\zeta| = \sqrt{\zeta^T \zeta}$.

A solution to (8.13) is computed via projected gradient descent

$$x^{(t+1)} = \mathrm{P}_{\mathcal{P}_+} \left(x^{(t)} + \mu \left(\sum_{k=1}^{K} \mathbf{H}^* \mathbf{\Phi}_k \mathbf{M}_k^T \mathbf{M}_k \mathbf{T}_k \left(y - \mathbf{H}x^{(t)} \right) - \lambda \nabla F \left(x^{(t)} \right) \right) \right) , \quad (8.16)$$

where $\mu > 0$ is a descent step-size parameter, chosen either by a line search or as a fixed step size of moderate value to ensure convergence[3]. In fact, with the upper-bound estimate $2/(\|\mathbf{H}\|^2 \sum_k \|\mathbf{\Phi}_k\|^2 + 8\lambda)$ as $p \to 1^+$, we observed convergence. Note that since the noise is controlled by the multiresolution supports, the regularization parameter λ does not have the same importance as in standard deconvolution methods. A much lower value is enough to remove the artifacts produced by the wavelets and the curvelets.

Example

Figure 8.4 (top) shows the Shepp-Logan phantom and the degraded image; that is, the original image is blurred with a Gaussian PSF (full width at half maximum

(FWHM) = 3.2 pixels) and then corrupted with Poisson noise. The multiresolution supports were obtained from the Anscombe stabilized image. Figure 8.4 (bottom) shows the deconvolution with (left) only the wavelet transform (no penalization term) and (right) the combined deconvolution method ($\lambda = 0.4$).

8.5 MORPHOLOGICAL COMPONENT ANALYSIS

8.5.1 Signal and Image Decomposition

Although mathematics has its million-dollar problems, in the form of Clay Math Prizes, there are several billion dollar problems in signal and image processing. Famous ones include the cocktail party problem. These signal processing problems seem to be intractable according to orthodox arguments based on rigorous mathematics, and yet they keep cropping up in problem after problem.

One such fundamental problem involves decomposing a signal or image into superposed contributions from different sources. Think of symphonic music which may involve superpositions of acoustic signals generated by many different instruments – and imagine the problem of separating these contributions. More abstractly, we can see many forms of media content that are superpositions of contributions from different content types (i.e. the morphological components), and we can imagine wanting to separate out the contributions from each. We again see that there is a fundamental obstacle to this: for an N-sample signal or image x created by superposing K different components, we have as many as $N \cdot K$ unknowns (the contribution of each content type to each pixel) but only N equations. But as we argued in Section 8.1.1, if we have information about the underlying components – using a sparsity prior – there are some rigorous results showing that such separation is possible.

We embark from equation (8.5) and suppose now that the observed linear mixture is possibly noisy (see the illustration in Fig. 8.5):

$$y = \sum_{k=1}^{K} x_k + \varepsilon = \sum_{k=1}^{K} \Phi_k \alpha_k + \varepsilon, \; \varepsilon \sim \mathcal{N}\left(0, \sigma_\varepsilon^2\right). \tag{8.17}$$

The morphological component analysis (MCA) framework (Starck et al. 2004b) aims at recovering *all* morphological components $(x_k)_{k=1,...,K}$ from y, which is an ill-posed inverse problem. MCA assumes that a dictionary can be built by amalgamating several subdictionaries $(\Phi_1, \ldots, \Phi_K)$ such that, for each k, the representation of x_k in Φ_k is sparse and not, or at least not as sparse, in other $\Phi_l, l \neq k$. In other words, the subdictionaries $(\Phi_k)_k$ must be mutually incoherent. Thus, the dictionary Φ_k plays a role of a discriminant between content types, preferring the component x_k over the other parts. This is a key observation for the success of the separation algorithm. Once such dictionaries are identified, the use of a pursuit algorithm searching for the sparsest representation leads to the desired separation. MCA is capable of creating atomic sparse representations containing as a by-product a decoupling of the signal content.

As an illustrative example, let our image contain lines and Gaussians (as in Fig. 8.5 (bottom)). Then the ridgelet transform would be very effective at sparsely

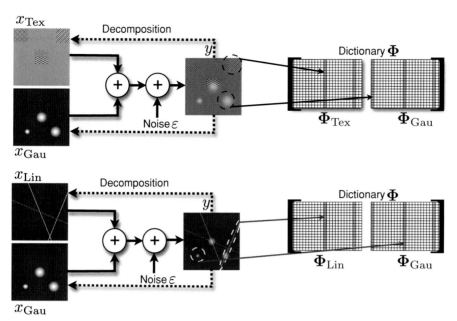

Figure 8.5. Illustration of the image decomposition problem with sparse representation.

representing the global lines and poor for Gaussians. On the other hand, wavelets would be very good at sparsifying the Gaussians and clearly worse than ridgelets for lines.

8.5.2 The Morphological Component Analysis Algorithm

Starck et al. (2004b, 2005b) proposed estimating the components $(x_k)_{1 \le k \le K}$ by solving the following constrained optimization problem:

$$\min_{\alpha_1, \dots, \alpha_K} \sum_{k=1}^{K} \|\alpha_k\|_p^p \quad \text{s.t.} \quad \left\| y - \sum_{k=1}^{K} \Phi_k \alpha_k \right\|_2 \le \sigma , \qquad (8.18)$$

where $\|\alpha\|_p^p$ is sparsity promoting (the most interesting regime is for $0 \le p \le 1$), and σ is typically chosen as a constant times $\sqrt{N}\sigma_\varepsilon$. The constraint in this optimization problem accounts for the presence of noise and model imperfection. If there is no noise and the linear superposition model is exact ($\sigma = 0$), an equality constraint is substituted for the inequality constraint.

Problem (8.18) is not easy to solve in general, especially for $p < 1$ (for $p = 0$ it is even NP-hard). Nonetheless, if all component coefficients α_l but the kth are fixed, then a solution can be achieved through hard thresholding (for $p = 0$) or soft thresholding (for $p = 1$) the coefficients of the marginal residuals $r_k = y - \sum_{l \ne k} \Phi_l \alpha_l$ in Φ_k. The other components are relieved of these marginal residuals r_k, and are likely to contain mainly the salient information of x_k. This intuition dictates a coordinate relaxation algorithm that cycles through the components at each iteration and applies a thresholding to the marginal residuals. This is what justifies the steps of the MCA algorithm summarized in Algorithm 32.

Algorithm 32 MCA Decomposition Algorithm

Task: Signal/image decomposition.
Parameters: The signal/image x, the dictionary $\boldsymbol{\Phi} = [\boldsymbol{\Phi}_1 \cdots \boldsymbol{\Phi}_K]$, number of iterations N_{iter}, stopping threshold $\lambda_{\min}$, threshold update schedule.
Initialization:

- Initial solution $x_k^{(0)} = 0, \forall k$.
- Initial residual $r^{(0)} = y$.
- Initial threshold: let $k^\star = \arg\max_k \|\mathbf{T}_k y\|_\infty$, set $\lambda_0 = \max_{k \neq k^\star} \|\mathbf{T}_k y\|_\infty$.

Main iteration:
for $t = 1$ **to** N_{iter} **do**
    for $k = 1$ **to** K **do**
        Compute marginal residuals $r_k^{(t)} = r^{(t-1)} + x_k^{(t-1)}$.
        Update kth component coefficients by hard (or soft) thresholding
        $\alpha_k^{(t)} = \text{HardThresh}_{\lambda_{t-1}}(\mathbf{T}_k r_k^{(t)})$.
        Update kth component $x_k^{(t)} = \boldsymbol{\Phi}_k \alpha_k^{(t)}$.

    Update the residuals $r^{(t)} = y - \sum_{k=1}^{K} x_k^{(t)}$.
    Update the threshold λ_t according to the given schedule.
    if $\lambda_t \leq \lambda_{\min}$ **then** stop.
Output: Morphological components $\left(x_k^{(N_{\text{iter}})}\right)_{k=1,\ldots,K}$.

Besides coordinate relaxation, another important ingredient of MCA is iterative thresholding with *varying threshold*. Thus, MCA can be viewed as a stage-wise hybridization of matching pursuit (MP) (Mallat and Zhang 1993) with block-coordinate relaxation (BCR) (Sardy et al. 2000) that attempts to solve (8.18). The adjective "stagewise" is because MCA exploits the fact that the dictionary is structured (union of transforms), and the atoms enter the solution by groups rather than individually, unlike MP. As such, MCA is a *salient-to-fine* process where at each iteration, the most salient content of each morphological component is iteratively computed. These estimates are then progressively refined as the threshold λ evolves towards $\lambda_{\min}$. It is worth noting that in practice, hard thresholding leads generally to better results than soft thresholding.

8.5.3 Thresholding Strategies

The way the threshold is decreased along the iterations of the MCA algorithm is paramount in terms of separation quality.

Prefixed decreasing threshold
In the work of Starck et al. (2004b, 2005b), linear and exponential decrease were advocated. For the linear decrease, the threshold λ_s sequence is

$$\lambda_t = \lambda_0 - t(\lambda_0 - \lambda_{\min})/N_{\text{iter}} . \tag{8.19}$$

The first threshold λ_0 can be set automatically to a large enough value (e.g. $\lambda_0 = \max_{k \neq k^\star} \|\mathbf{T}_k y\|_\infty$ where $k^\star = \arg\max_{1 \leq k \leq K} \|\mathbf{T}_k y\|_\infty$). For an exact representation of the data with the morphological components, $\lambda_{\min}$ must be set to zero. Noise can be handled (see Section 8.5.5).

Adaptive strategies

Although the simplicity of linear or exponential threshold update is an advantage, there is no general recipe to estimate the minimum number of iterations yielding a successful separation. A too small number of iterations leads to poor separation while a large number of iterations is computationally expensive. Experiments have clearly shown that the best number of iterations (typically, hundreds) depends on the data, and more precisely on contrast between the components. Therefore, a desirable thresholding strategy would provide a fast decomposition with a data-adaptive threshold update schedule.

Two data-adaptive strategies have been proposed, namely, median absolute deviation (MAD) (Donoho et al. 2012) and mean of maximum (MOM) (Bobin et al. 2007b). For simplicity, let $K = 2$; generalizing to $K \geq 2$ is straightforward.

- MAD: Let $y = x_1 + x_2 = \mathbf{\Phi}_1 \alpha_1 + \mathbf{\Phi}_2 \alpha_2$, where both $\mathbf{\Phi}_{k=1,2}$ are orthonormal bases. Decomposing y in $\mathbf{\Phi}_1$ leads to $\mathbf{T}_1 y = \alpha_1 + \mathbf{T}_1 \mathbf{\Phi}_2 \alpha_2$. Provided that the mutual coherence of $\mathbf{\Phi}_1$ and $\mathbf{\Phi}_2$ is low, x_2 has no particular structure in $\mathbf{\Phi}_1$ and hence it is tempting to model $\mathbf{\Phi}_1^T x_2$ as an additive noise possibly Gaussian. Its standard deviation can be estimated using a robust estimator such as the MAD (see equation (6.9)). It follows that estimating the significant entries $\tilde{\alpha}_1$ in α_1 is a denoising problem readily solved by thresholding $\mathbf{T}_1 y$ with a threshold 3–4× the standard deviation estimated by the MAD from $\mathbf{T}_1 y$. The following step is to transform the residuals $y - \tilde{x}_1 = y - \mathbf{\Phi}_1 \tilde{\alpha}_1$ in $\mathbf{\Phi}_2$ and so on. Clearly, the variance of the residual is likely to decrease along iterations and this provides a simple strategy to adaptively control the threshold in the MCA algorithm. In practice, this strategy remains fruitful even if each $\mathbf{\Phi}_k$ is redundant. Donoho et al. (2012) proposed a similar strategy to find sparse solutions of underdetermined linear systems with random dictionaries.
- MOM: Let $x_1^{(t)}$ and $x_2^{(t)}$ denote the current estimates of the corresponding components at iteration t of the MCA algorithm. The current residual is $r^{(t)} = y - x_1^{(t)} - x_2^{(t)}$. In the strategy coined MOM, the value of the threshold at iteration t is given by

$$\lambda_t = \frac{1}{2} \left(\left\| \mathbf{T}_1 r^{(t)} \right\|_\infty + \left\| \mathbf{T}_2 r^{(t)} \right\|_\infty \right), \qquad (8.20)$$

which is easily computed at each step of the iterative process. For $K > 2$ dictionaries, λ_t is taken as the mean of the two largest values of $\|\mathbf{T}_k r^{(t)}\|_\infty$. The intuition underlying this strategy is that the next significant coefficients to be selected should be attached to the dictionary in which the transform of the residual has coefficients of largest magnitudes.

8.5.4 Recovery Guarantees

In the noiseless case, a careful analysis of the recovery properties (uniqueness and support recovery) of the MCA algorithm and its convergence behavior when all Φ_k are orthobases was provided by Bobin et al. (2007b, 2009). These results can be summarized as follows.

Let $y = \sum_{k=1}^{K} x_k = \sum_{k=1}^{K} \sum_{i \in \Lambda_k} \alpha_k[i] \varphi_{k,i}$, where Λ_k is the support of the kth morphological component coefficients and $\Lambda = \cup_{k=1}^{K} \Lambda_k(\alpha_k)$. Assume that the residual at iteration t can be written as $r^{(t)} = \sum_{k=1}^{K} \tilde{\alpha}_k^{(t)}[i] \varphi_{k,i}$. Let us denote

$$(k^\star, i^\star) = \arg\max_{k, i \in \Lambda_k} \left| \tilde{\alpha}_k^{(t)}[i] \right|, \quad \tilde{\alpha}^\star = \left| \tilde{\alpha}_{k^\star}^{(t)}[i^\star] \right|,$$

$$(k^\dagger, i^\dagger) = \arg\max_{k \neq k^\star, i \in \Lambda_k} \left| \tilde{\alpha}_k^{(t)}[i] \right|, \quad \tilde{\alpha}^\dagger = \left| \tilde{\alpha}_{k^\dagger}^{(t)}[i^\dagger] \right|.$$

Let ρ such that $\tilde{\alpha}^\dagger = \rho \tilde{\alpha}^\star$ for $0 < \rho < 1$. The parameter ρ can be interpreted as a measure of contrast between the morphological components.

It was shown in Fadili et al. (2009a); Bobin et al. (2009) that if $\mathrm{Card}(\Lambda) < \mu_\Phi^{-1}/4$ and $\rho \leq 1/5$, then at each iteration t and for each morphological component $k^\star$, the MCA-MOM algorithm does not select any wrong atom outside the correct support $\Lambda_{k^\star}$, and selects at least one atom to enter the active set from the correct support $\Lambda_{k^\star}$. Moreover, the MCA-MOM algorithm converges linearly[4] to the correct component separation and its sparsest representation in Φ.

In a nutshell, MCA-MOM recovers the correct separation if the components are contrasted, and the solution is sufficiently sparse in an incoherent dictionary Φ.

8.5.5 Handling Additive Gaussian Noise

From a Bayesian point of view, the ℓ_2-norm constraint in equation (8.18) is equivalent to the log-likelihood assuming that the noise is additive white Gaussian. Hence MCA can handle intrinsically data perturbed by such a noise. Indeed, as MCA is a coarse-to-fine iterative procedure, bounded noise can be handled just by stopping iterating when the residual is at the noise level. Assuming that the noise variance σ_ε^2 is known, the algorithm may be stopped at iteration t when the ℓ_2-norm of the residual satisfies $\|r^{(t)}\|_2 \leq \sqrt{N}\sigma_\varepsilon$. Alternatively, one may use a strategy reminiscent of denoising methods, by taking $\lambda_{\min} = \tau \sigma_\varepsilon$ where τ is a constant, typically between 3 and 4.

For non-Gaussian noise, a similar strategy as before could also be used, but a noise modeling step in the transform domain must be accomplished in order to derive the probability density function (pdf) for each coefficient of the dictionary to be due to noise. The distribution of many noise models in different dictionaries such as wavelets or curvelets have been proposed (Starck and Murtagh 2006), see also Chapter 6.

8.5.6 Morphological Component Analysis versus Basis Pursuit for Sparse Recovery

Performance of BP and MCA-MOM for sparse recovery were compared. BP was solved with the DR splitting algorithm, Algorithm 30. We define $\mathcal{BG}(p_1, p_2)$ as the

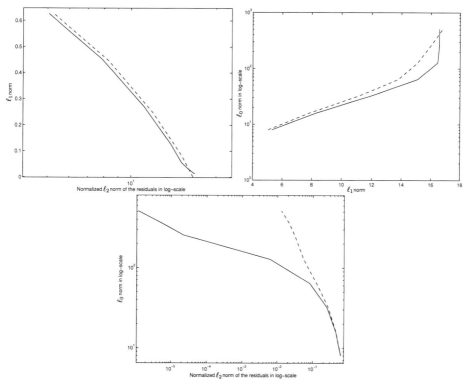

Figure 8.6. Comparison of MCA-MOM (solid line) to BP (dashed line) for sparse recovery. (top left) ℓ_1/ℓ_2-curve of both MCA-MOM and BP (dashed line); (top right) ℓ_0/ℓ_1-curve of both MCA-MOM and BP; and (bottom) nonlinear approximation error curve (ℓ_0/ℓ_2) of both MCA-MOM and BP. See text for details.

class of signals such that if y is drawn from this model, then $y = \mathbf{\Phi}_1\alpha_1 + \mathbf{\Phi}_2\alpha_2$ where α_1 and α_2 are Bernoulli-Gaussian random vectors whose entries are nonzero with probabilities p_1 and p_2 respectively. Nonzero coefficients are drawn from $\mathcal{N}(0, 1)$. Signals drawn from this class are compressible in $\mathbf{\Phi}$. The dictionary $\mathbf{\Phi}$ used in this experiment is taken as the union of the 1-D orthogonal wavelet transform and the DCT. The results are pictured in Fig. 8.6. The graphs were computed as an average over 50 decompositions of signals belonging to the model $\mathcal{BG}(p_1, p_2)$ with random p_1 and p_2.

Figure 8.6 (top right and bottom) show the ℓ_0 and the ℓ_1 norm of the decomposition coefficients recovered by MCA (solid line) and BP (dashed line) as a function of the residual ℓ_2 norm (in log scale), respectively. The top right graph depicts the ℓ_0 pseudo-norm of the coefficients as a function of their ℓ_1 norm: the MCA-MOM curve is below the BP one. Informally, while MCA and BP solutions have very close ℓ_1 norms (for the same quality of approximation), MCA-MOM provide sparser solutions. In terms of ℓ_0 sparsity, MCA-MOM achieves better nonlinear approximation as illustrated in Figure 8.6 (bottom). Thus MCA-MOM appears as a good and fast candidate for sparse decomposition of signals in union of bases.

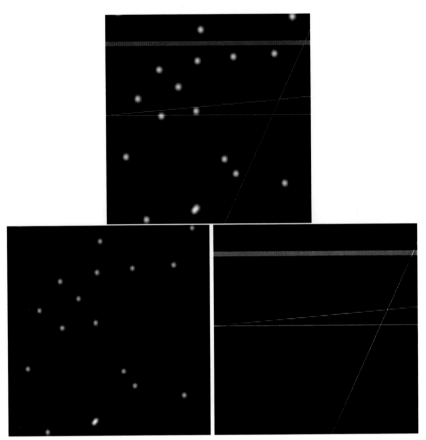

Figure 8.7. (top) Original image containing lines and Gaussians. (bottom left) Reconstructed image from the starlet coefficients. (bottom right) Reconstructed image from the ridgelet coefficients.

8.5.7 Examples

Lines-Point Separation

Figure 8.7 illustrates the separation result in the case where the input image (256×256) contains only lines and Gaussians without noise. In this experiment, we used $N_{\mathrm{iter}} = 20$. Based on the morphological content of this image, natural candidate dictionaries are the starlet (to serve the Gaussians) and the ridgelet transform (for the lines). Figure 8.7 represents the original image, the reconstructed image from the starlet coefficients, and the image reconstructed from the ridgelet coefficients.

While this dataset is synthetic it has relevance for any case involving separation of Gaussian-like features (e.g., stars in astronomy) with anisotropic features (e.g., in astronomy, dust emission, supernova remnants, filaments).

Real Astronomical Data

Figure 8.8 (top left) shows a compact blue galaxy. The data were obtained on ground with the Gemini/Observatory Spectrometer and Camera for the Infrared (OSCIR) instrument at 10 μm. The pixel field of view is 0.089″/pixel, and the source was

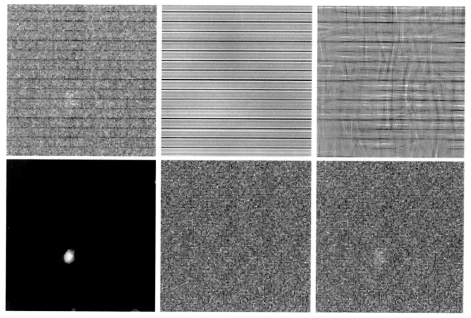

Figure 8.8. (top left) Galaxy SBS 0335-052 (10 μm). Reconstructions from the (top middle) ridgelet, (top right) curvelet, and (bottom left) wavelet coefficients. (bottom middle) Residual image. (bottom right) Artifact free image.

observed for 1500 seconds. The data are contaminated by noise and a stripping artifact due to the instrument electronics.

This image was decomposed using a dictionary containing wavelets, ridgelets, and curvelets. Figure 8.8 shows the three images reconstructed from the recovered ridgelet, curvelet, and wavelet coefficients. The image in Fig. 8.8 (bottom middle) shows the residual after removing all recovered morphological components from the observed image. Another interesting image is the artifact-free one, obtained by subtracting the ridgelet and curvelet-associated morphological components from the observed image (see Fig. 8.8 (bottom right)). The galaxy has been detected well in the wavelet domain, while all stripping artifacts have been captured by the ridgelets and curvelets.

8.6 TEXTURE-CARTOON SEPARATION

An especially interesting and complicated image content separation problem is the one targeting decomposition of an image into texture and piece-wise-smooth (cartoon) parts. The importance of such separation is for applications in image compression, image analysis, synthesis and more: see for example Bertalmío et al. (2003). A functional-space characterization of oscillating textures was proposed by Meyer (2002), and was then used within a variational framework in Vese and Osher (2003); Lieu and Vese (2008) and later followed by others (Aujol et al. 2005; Aujol and Chambolle 2005; Aujol et al. 2006) for the design of such an image separation algorithm. Since these pioneering contributions, we have witnessed a flurry of research activity in this application field. A different methodology towards the same separation task is proposed in Meyer et al. (2002) and Guo et al. (2003). The work in

Meyer et al. (2002) describes a novel image compression algorithm based on image decomposition into cartoon and texture layers using the wavelet packet transform. The work presented in Guo et al. (2003) shows a separation based on matching pursuit and a MRF (Markov random field) modeling.

In this section, we focus on the same decomposition problem, that is, texture and natural (piecewise smooth) additive layers. In the rest of this section, we will essentially deal with locally periodic/oscillating textures. The core idea here is to choose two appropriate dictionaries, one known to sparsify the textured part and the second the cartoon part. Each dictionary will play the role of a discriminant, preferring the part of the image it is serving, while yielding nonsparse representations on the other content type. Then MCA is expected to lead to the proper separation, as it seeks the overall sparsest solution, and this should align with the sparse representation for each part.

8.6.1 Choosing a Dictionary

As already discussed in Section 8.5, identifying the appropriate dictionary is a key step towards a good separation. We discuss here the dictionary for the texture and the piecewise smooth content.

8.6.1.1 Dictionaries for Textures: The (Local) Discrete Cosine Transform

The DCT is a variant of the discrete Fourier transform, replacing the complex analysis with real numbers by a symmetric signal extension. The DCT is an orthonormal transform, known to be well suited for first order Markov stationary signals. Its coefficients essentially represents frequency content, similar to the ones obtained by Fourier analysis. When dealing with locally stationary signals, DCT is typically applied in blocks. Such is the case in the JPEG image compression algorithm. Having overlapping blocks is used to prevent blocking artifacts, in this case an overcomplete transform corresponding to a tight frame with redundancy 4 for an overlap of 50%. A fast algorithm with complexity $O(N^2 \log N)$ exists for its computation. The DCT is appropriate for sparse representation of either smooth or locally periodic behaviors. Other dictionaries that could be considered are Gabor, brushlets, wavelet packets or wave atoms (Demanet and Ying 2007).

8.6.1.2 Dictionaries for Piecewise Smooth Content: the Curvelet Transform

As we have seen in Chapter 5, the curvelet transform enables the directional analysis of an image in different scales. This transform provides a near-optimal sparse representation of piecewise smooth (C^2) images away from C^2 contours. It is well suited for anisotropic structures and smooth curved edges. Other dictionaries that could be considered are wavelets, bandlets (Peyré and Mallat 2007) or shearlets (Labate et al. 2005).

8.6.2 Separation Algorithm

Assume hereafter that the local DCT is chosen for the locally periodic textured part – denoted as $\boldsymbol{\Phi}_D$ with associated transform operator $\mathbf{T}_D$. Moreover, we choose the curvelet dictionary for the natural part that we denote $\boldsymbol{\Phi}_C$. As both these transforms correspond to tight frames, then $\boldsymbol{\Phi}_D$ is the pseudo-inverse reconstruction operator $\mathbf{T}_D^+$ up to a constant and similarly for $\boldsymbol{\Phi}_C$.

Returning to the separation problem as posed earlier, we have to solve equation (8.18) for the two unknown morphological components x_D and x_C: the texture and the piecewise smooth images. This formulation is flexible enough to incorporate external forces that direct the morphological components to better suit their expected content. These forces will fine tune the separation process to achieve its task. As an example for such successful external force, a total variation (TV) penalty can be added to x_C in order to direct the cartoon component to fit the piecewise smooth model. This leads to

$$\min_{\alpha_D,\alpha_C} \|\alpha_D\|_p^p + \|\alpha_C\|_p^p + \gamma \|\Phi_C\alpha_C\|_{TV} \quad \text{s.t.} \quad \|y - \Phi_D\alpha_D - \Phi_C\alpha_C\|_2 \leq \sigma . \quad (8.21)$$

Regularizing with TV to enhance restoration quality has appeared in Starck et al. (2001); Candès and Guo (2002); Starck et al. (2003c), where TV was used to damp ringing artifacts near edges, caused by the oscillations of the curvelet atoms. Combining TV with wavelets has also been proposed for similar reasons in Malgouyres (2002b); Durand and Froment (2003), although in a different fashion.

The steps of the MCA separation are summarized in Algorithm 33. In this algorithm, hard or soft thresholding can be used. Better results are generally obtained using a hard thresholding.

Algorithm 33 MCA Texture-Cartoon Part Separation

Task: Texture-piecewise smooth component separation, solve (8.21).
Parameters: The signal/image y, the local DCT and curvelet dictionaries Φ_D and Φ_C, number of iterations N_{iter}, γ and index of the cartoon part, stopping threshold λ_{min}, threshold update schedule.
Initialization: $x_D^{(0)} = x_C^{(0)} = 0, \lambda^{(0)} = \min(\|T_D y\|_\infty, \|T_C y\|_\infty)$.
Main iteration:
for $t = 1$ to N_{iter} **do**

1. **Texture Part – Update of x_D assuming x_C is fixed:**
   - Compute the residual $r^{(t)} = y - x_D^{(t)} - x_C^{(t)}$.
   - Compute the local DCT coefficients $\alpha_D^{(t)} = T_D(x_D + r^{(t)})$.
   - Hard (or soft) with threshold λ_t: $\tilde{\alpha}_D^{(t)} = \text{HardThresh}_{\lambda_t}(\alpha_D^{(t)})$.
   - Update $x_D^{(t)} = \Phi_D\tilde{\alpha}_D^{(t)}$.

2. **Cartoon Part – Update of x_C assuming x_D is fixed:**
   - Compute the residual $r^{(t)} = y - x_C^{(t)} - x_C^{(t)}$.
   - Compute the curvelet coefficients $\alpha_C^{(t)} = T_C(x_C + r^{(t)})$.
   - Hard (or soft) with threshold λ_t: $\tilde{\alpha}_C^{(t)} = \text{HardThresh}_{\lambda_t}(\alpha_C^{(t)})$.
   - Update $x_C^{(t)} = \Phi_C\tilde{\alpha}_C^{(t)}$.

3. **TV Regularization of x_C:** see Algorithm 34.
4. Update the threshold $\lambda^{(t+1)}$ according to the given schedule (see Section 8.5.3).
5. **if** $\lambda^{(t+1)} \leq \lambda_{min}$ **then** stop.

End iteration
Output: Texture and Cartoon components $(x_D^{(N_{iter})}, x_C^{(N_{iter})})$.

TV and Undecimated Haar Transform

A link between the TV regularization and the undecimated Haar wavelet soft thresholding has been studied in Steidl et al. (2004), arguing that in the 1-D case, the TV seminorm and the ℓ_1-norm of the undecimated single resolution Haar detail coefficients are equivalent. When going to 2-D, this relation does not hold anymore, but the two approaches share some similarities. Whereas the TV seminorm is translation- and rotation-invariant, the undecimated 2-D Haar wavelet transform has translation- and scale-invariance. In light of this interpretation, the TV regularization step of Algorithm 33 can be implemented as in Algorithm 34.

Algorithm 34 Approximate TV Regularization by Soft Thresholding Undecimated Haar Wavelet Coefficients

---

Parameters: The image x_C and regularization parameter γ.

- Compute the undecimated Haar wavelet transform coefficients of x_C.
- Soft threshold the finest scale coefficients with threshold γ.
- Reconstruct by inverse undecimated Haar wavelet transform.

To keep the link between the TV penalty and the undecimated Haar wavelet transform, we have to use only one level in the Haar wavelet transform. Choosing more levels would lead to a kind of multiscale-TV penalty. It is worth remarking that what we have just presented is an approximation to the proximity operator of the TV penalty. An alternative exact way of computing it is the duality-based algorithms of Section 7.3.2.5 with the discrete gradient. The exact solution would, however, entail an iterative algorithm.

8.6.3 Examples

Boy + Texture

In this example, we generated a synthetic image composed of a natural scene and a texture, where we have the ground truth parts to compare against. We used the MCA decomposition, Algorithm 33, with the curvelet transform for the natural scene part, and a global DCT transform for the texture. We used the soft thresholding Haar as a substitute for TV, as described in Algorithm 34. The parameter γ was fixed to 0.1. In this example, as for the example of "Barbara", to be described below, we got better results if the very low frequencies were ignored in the textured part. The reason for this is the evident coherence between the two dictionary elements at low frequencies – both consider the low frequency content as theirs. Figure 8.9 shows the original image (addition of the texture and the natural parts), the reconstructed cartoon (natural) component and the texture part.

Barbara

We also applied the MCA separation, Algorithm 33, to the "Barbara" image. We used the curvelet transform for the cartoon part, and a local DCT transform with a smooth sine window of size size 32×32 for the locally oscillating texture. Again, we used Algorithm 34 to approximate the TV regularization. The parameter γ was

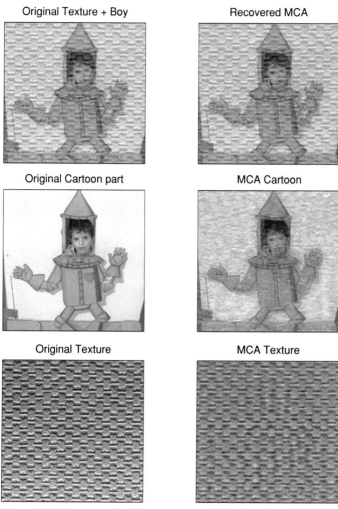

Original Texture + Boy   Recovered MCA

Original Cartoon part   MCA Cartoon

Original Texture   MCA Texture

Figure 8.9. Decomposing the "Boy+Texture" image. See Table 8.2 for the experimental details.

set to 2. Figure 8.10 displays the "Barbara" image, the recovered cartoon component and the reconstructed texture component.

8.6.4 Applications

The ability to separate the image into different contents, as we show, has many potential applications. We sketch here two simple examples to illustrate the importance of a successful separation.

8.6.4.1 Edge Detection

Edge detection is a crucial processing step in many computer vision applications. When the texture is highly contrasted, most of the detected edges are due the texture rather than the natural part. By separating first the two components we can recover

Original Barbara

MCA Barbara

Barbara Cartoon

Barbara Texture

Figure 8.10. Decomposing the "Barbara" image. See Table 8.2 for the experimental details.

the true object's edges. Figure 8.11 shows the edges revealed by the Canny edge detector on both the original image and the curvelet reconstructed component (see Fig. 8.9).

8.6.4.2 Nonlinear Approximation

The efficiency of a sparse decomposition can be assessed through the decay of its nonlinear approximation (NLA) error as a function of the sparsity level as explained in Section 1.1.2. An NLA-curve is obtained by reconstructing the image from its best m-term in the decomposition. Throughout the chapters, we discussed decay rates of the NLA achieved by different transforms for given class of functions. For instance, for smooth functions away from a discontinuity across a C^2 curve, the NLA error decays as $O(m^{-1/2})$ in squared L_2 norm in a Fourier basis, as $O(m^{-1})$ in a wavelet basis (Mallat 2008) and as $O(m^{-2}(\log m)^3)$ (see Section 5.4).

Using the separation algorithm described above, the "Barbara" image was decomposed in the redundant dictionary local DCT+orthogonal wavelet transform (OWT). Since the dictionary used is highly redundant, the exact overall

Figure 8.11. (left) Detected edges on the original image. (right) Detected edges on the curvelet reconstruct component.

representation of the original image may require a relatively small number of coefficients due to the promoted sparsity, and this essentially yields a better NLA curve.

Figure 8.12 presents the NLA curves for the image "Barbara" using the OWT (dotted line), the DCT (solid line), and of the algorithm discussed here (dashed line), based on the local DCT+OWT dictionary. We see that for low sparsity levels, typically $m < 15$ percent N, the combined representation leads to a better NLA curve than the local DCT or the OWT alone.

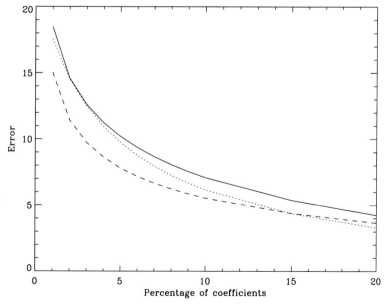

Figure 8.12. Best m-term nonlinear approximation error of reconstructed "Barbara" image versus the m largest coefficients used in the reconstruction. Local DCT transform (solid line), OWT (dotted line), and our texture-cartoon decomposition (dashed line).

8.7 INPAINTING

8.7.1 Problem Formulation

Inpainting is to restore missing image information based upon the still available (observed) cues from destroyed, occluded or deliberately masked subregions of the images. The key to successful inpainting is to infer robustly the lost information from the observed cues. The inpainting can also be viewed as an interpolation or a desocclusion problem. The classical image inpainting problem can be stated as follows. Suppose the ideal complete image is x defined on a finite domain. The observed incomplete image y is the result of applying the lossy operator $\mathbf{M}$:

$$y = \mathbf{M}[x + \varepsilon] \tag{8.22}$$

where ε is the noise (typically here $\sim \mathcal{N}(0, \sigma_\varepsilon^2)$). A typical example of $\mathbf{M}$ is the binary mask; a diagonal matrix with ones (observed pixel) or zeros (missing pixel), and y is a masked image with zeros wherever a pixel is missing. Inpainting is to recover x from y which is an inverse ill-posed problem.

Nontexture image inpainting has received considerable interest and excitement since the pioneering paper by Masnou and Morel (1998, 2002) who proposed variational principles for image desocclusion (the term inpainting was not yet used). A wave of interest in nontexture inpainting was also started from the paper of Bertalmío et al. (2000), where applications in the movie industry, video, and art restoration were unified. Basically, the major mechanisms to get information into the inpainting domain are as follows:

■ *Diffusion and transport partial diffusion equation (PDE)/variational principle*: There is an abundant literature on PDE/variational non-texture inpainting. For an extended survey of the mathematics involved in the above frameworks and some applications, see Chan and Shen (2005, Chapter 6) and Bertalmío et al. (2005). Note however that the main intrinsic limitations of these approaches is that they cannot deal with texture inpainting. They are suitable for geometrical parts of the image and perform well only for non-texture inpainting. Thus texture and large empty gaps can be a major issue.

■ *Nonlocal exemplar region fill-in*: The basic idea behind these algorithms is to fill in the missing regions with available information from some best matching candidates assuming self-similarity of the image (e.g., surrounding pixels/regions (Efros and Leung 1999; Bertalmío et al. 2003; Criminisi et al. 2004; Demanet et al. 2003)). The goal is to synthesize a complete, visually plausible and coherent image, where the visible parts of the image serve as a reference/training set to infer the unknown parts. Bertalmío et al. (2003); Rane et al. (2002) adapted Meyer's variational decomposition model to decompose the image into its natural (cartoon) and texture parts, then inpaint the natural part using a PDE-based method and a fill-in-based approach for the texture part following the work of Efros and Leung (1999). Other work in this direction includes Jia and Tang (2005); Acton et al. (2001). Criminisi et al. (2004) proposed an algorithm that allows one to fill-in an image progressively by looking for best-matching prototypes in a dictionary built from a set of patterns around the missing subregions.

■ *Sparsity regularization*: Elad et al. (2005) introduced a novel inpainting algorithm that is capable of reconstructing both texture and cartoon image contents. This algorithm is a direct extension of the MCA (see Section 8.7.2). Fadili and Starck (2005); Fadili et al. (2009b) also proposed sparse regularization over a global dictionary for inpainting (see Section 8.7.3). Because of missing measurements, the arguments supporting the success of this approach are borrowed from the theory of compressed/ive sensing that will be discussed in Chapter 13. Sparse regularization over non-local dictionaries (learned from patches of the data) have recently proved very effective for texture and cartoon inpainting (Mairal et al. 2008; Peyré et al. 2007).

In the next section, we describe two inpainting algorithms relying on sparse regularization. The first one is based on the MCA algorithm that can be extended to treat missing parts. The second one casts the inpainting as a maximum penalized estimator with missing data, and solves it with the splitting algorithms described in the previous chapter. Both approaches have desirable features, such as handling large gaps, textures, and additive noise properly.

8.7.2 Morphological Component Analysis for Inpainting

Assume that the missing pixels are indicated by a diagonal mask matrix $\mathbf{M} \in \mathbb{R}^{N \times N}$. The main diagonal of $\mathbf{M}$ encodes the pixel status, namely, 1 for an existing pixel and 0 for a missing one.

As proposed by Elad et al. (2005) for texture and cartoon inpainting, (8.21) can be extended to incorporate missing data through the mask $\mathbf{M}$ by minimizing:

$$\min_{\alpha_1,\ldots,\alpha_K} \sum_{k=1}^{K} \|\alpha_k\|_p^p + \gamma \|\boldsymbol{\Phi}_C \alpha_C\|_{\text{TV}}, \quad \text{s.t.} \quad \left\| y - \mathbf{M} \sum_{k=1}^{K} \boldsymbol{\Phi}_k x_k \right\|_2 \leq \sigma . \tag{8.23}$$

To solve this optimization problem, we only need to adapt slightly the MCA Algorithm 32 or 33, modifying the residual update rule to $r^{(t)} = y - \mathbf{M} \sum_{k=1}^{K} x_k^{(t)}$ to account for the masking matrix $\mathbf{M}$. The other steps of the algorithm remain unchanged.

8.7.3 Iterative Soft Thresholding for Inpainting

When taking $p = 1$ and the TV regularization term is dropped in equation (8.23), Fadili and Starck (2005); Fadili et al. (2009b) formulated the inpainting problem as a maximum penalized likelihood estimator with missing data and sparsity-promoting penalties:

$$\min_{\alpha_1,\ldots,\alpha_K,\sigma_\varepsilon^2} \frac{1}{2\sigma_\varepsilon^2} \left\| y - \mathbf{M} \sum_{k=1}^{K} \boldsymbol{\Phi}_k x_k \right\|_2^2 + \lambda \sum_{k=1}^{K} \|\alpha_k\|_1 . \tag{8.24}$$

Any other convex sparsity penalty can be used instead of the ℓ_1 norm. Note that now σ_ε^2 may not be known nor easily estimated (due to missing pixels) from the observed data. The above estimator can be also interpreted in the light of the expectation-maximization (EM) algorithm, a rigorous statistical framework for estimation with missing samples (Fadili et al. 2009b). To solve equation (8.24) for the coefficients

$(\alpha_k)_{1 \le k \le K}$, it is natural to resort to the forward-backward splitting developed in Chapter 7 (i.e., the measurement operator $\mathbf{H}$ corresponds to the binary mask $\mathbf{M}$). Besides rigorous convergence guarantees, a chief advantage of this algorithm is its ability to estimate the noise variance. Let the stepsize sequence $0 < \mu_t < 2/(\sum_k \|\mathbf{\Phi}_k\|^2)$, where $\|\mathbf{\Phi}_k\|^2$ corresponds to the largest frame bound of $\mathbf{\Phi}_k$. Denote Ω_o the set of observed samples and N_o its cardinality. The main inpainting algorithm to solve equation (8.24) is summarized in Algorithm 35.

Algorithm 35 EM-Inspired Inpainting Algorithm

Task: Signal/image inpainting.
Parameters: Observed masked image y, the mask $\mathbf{M}$, the dictionary $\mathbf{\Phi} = [\mathbf{\Phi}_1 \cdots \mathbf{\Phi}_K]$, regularization parameter λ, initial $\sigma_\varepsilon^{(0)}$, convergence tolerance δ.
Initialization: Initial solution $\alpha_k^{(0)} = 0, \forall k$.
Main iteration:
repeat

    1. Update the residual $r^{(t)} = y - \mathbf{M}\mathbf{\Phi}\alpha^{(t)}$.
    2. Update the coefficients $\alpha^{(t)}$

$$\alpha^{(t+1)} = \mathrm{SoftThresh}_{\lambda \mu_t}\left(\alpha^{(t)} + \mu_t \mathbf{\Phi}^{\mathrm{T}} r^{(t)}\right) .$$

    3. If desired, update $\sigma_\varepsilon^{2^{(t+1)}}$ according to

$$\sigma_\varepsilon^{2^{(t+1)}} = \frac{1}{N}\left[\sum_{i \in \Omega_o}\left(y[i] - \left(\mathbf{\Phi}\alpha^{(t)}\right)[i]\right)^2 + (N - N_o)\sigma_\varepsilon^{2^{(t)}}\right] .$$

until $\left\|\alpha^{(t+1)} - \alpha^{(t)}\right\|_2 \le \delta$;
Output: Inpainted image $\tilde{x} = \mathbf{\Phi}\alpha^{(t)} = \sum_k \mathbf{\Phi}_k \alpha_k^{(t)}$.

If the data fidelity term in equation (8.24) is in its constrained form, and if the dictionary is formed from orthobases or tight frames, the Douglas-Rachford splitting can be used and the projector on the constraint set has a closed-form (see Section 7.5.3). Other variants are described by Fadili et al. (2009b) and the interested reader may refer to that paper for further details.

Let us conclude this subsection by noting some differences and similarities between the two preceding inpainting algorithms.

■ *Target*: in the MCA-based formulation, the targets are the morphological components, and component separation is a by-product of the inpainting process; while in the second algorithm, the goal is to achieve a good inpainting of the whole image, and not necessarily a good separation and inpainting of each component.
■ *Parameters*: in the MCA-based inpainting, the user provides the algorithm with a threshold-lowering schedule and a stopping threshold λ_{min}, while in the second version, the regularization parameter λ is either fixed, or a continuation method, which solves a sequence of problems (8.24) for a decreasing value of λ, can be used. See Section 7.7.2 and (Fadili et al. 2009b).

■ *Noise*: both algorithms handle the presence of noise. The second formulation is able to estimate the noise variance along with inpainting.

■ *Optimization algorithms*: despite apparent similarities, the two formulations use different optimization frameworks. MCA is a stagewise algorithm, formed by hybridizing MP with BCR. The second formulation yields an iterative thresholding algorithm with a rigorous convergence analysis guaranteed for convex penalties, as explained in Chapter 7.

8.7.3.1 Examples
Barbara
Figure 8.13 shows the "Barbara" image (512×512) and its inpainted results for three random masks of 20, 50, and 80 percent missing pixels. The unstructured random form of the mask makes the recovery task easier which is predictable using a compressed sensing argument (see Chapter 13). Again, the dictionary contained the curvelet and local DCT transforms. The algorithm is not only able to recover the geometric part (cartoon), but it performs particularly well inside the textured areas.

Lena
We compared the two inpainting algorithms given in Algorithm 32 and Algorithm 35 on "Lena" 512×512. The masked image is depicted in Fig. 8.14 (top right), where 80 percent of the pixels were missing, with large gaps. The dictionary contained the curvelet transform. The parameters chosen for each algorithm are given in Table 8.2. Despite the challenging nature of this example (large gaps), both inpainting algorithms performed well. They managed to recover the most important details of the image that are hardly distinguishable by eye in the masked image. The visual quality is confirmed by measures of the PSNR, as reported in Fig. 8.14.

Lines + Gaussians
We repeated the same comparison with a synthetic image which is a composite of three Gaussians and three lines; see Fig. 8.15 (top left). On the basis of this morphological content, the UWT and the curvelet transforms were chosen as candidate dictionaries. The parameters chosen for each algorithm are summarized in Table 8.2. The masked and filled-in images are portrayed in Fig. 8.15. Both inpainting algorithms performed well, although the result of Algorithm 35 is somewhat smoother.

8.8 GUIDED NUMERICAL EXPERIMENTS

8.8.1 MCALab

8.8.1.1 The MCALab Distribution
MCALab is a library of Matlab routines that implements the algorithms described here for signal/image decomposition and inpainting. The MCALab library provides open source tools for sparse decomposition and inpainting, and may be used to reproduce the figures here and to redo those figures with variations in the parameters. The library is accessible via the book's software web address (http://www.SparseSignalRecipes.info). The current version of MCALab is 110 and is distributed under the CeCILL license.

Original

Masked 20% missing pixels   Inpainted MCA (Alg. 31) PSNR=35.3 dB

Masked 50% missing pixels   Inpainted MCA (Alg. 31) PSNR=31.7 dB

Masked 80% missing pixels   Inpainted MCA (Alg. 31) PSNR=26.5 dB

Figure 8.13. Inpainting the "Barbara" image. See Table 8.2 for the experimental details.

The structure of the MCALab package is depicted in Fig. 8.16. This structure is also the backbone of the other Matlab toolboxes described in this book. MCALab has two main directories, one for 1-D signals and the second for 2-D images. Each of these directories has the same architecture and contains the following subdirectories:

Original Lena

Masked PSNR=6.44 dB

Inpainted (Alg. 33) PSNR=19.9 dB

Inpainted MCA (Alg. 30) PSNR=19.9 dB

Figure 8.14. Inpainting the "Lena" image. See Table 8.2 for the experimental details.

- *Dictionaries*: A directory MCALab110/xxx-D/Dictionaries (relating to either 1-D or 2-D functionality) containing various fast implicit analysis and synthesis transforms such as DCT, wavelets, and curvelets.
- *Decomposition*: A directory MCALab110/xxx-D/Decomposition containing the implementation of Algorithms 32–35.
- *Datasets*: A directory MCALab110/xxx-D/Datasets containing signal and image datasets used to illustrate decomposition and inpainting. MCALab110/One-D/Datasets also contains a Matlab function that generates many artificial signals and reads input signals.
- *DemoGUI*: A directory MCALab110/xxx-D/Datasets containing a graphical user-friendly interface to decompose and inpaint the user's own data or data supplied with MCALab.
- *Scripts*: A directory MCALab110/xxx-D/Scripts containing pedagogical examples with synthetic and real data that illustrate the use of MCA and inpainting algorithms. They also help getting started with the package.

There are MCALab functions which call WaveLab functions. We recommend that the user downloads and installs WaveLab (Buckheit and Donoho 1995) for MCALab to be comprehensively supported.

MCALab also incorporates software for two other transforms not distributed with WaveLab. These are the wrapping version of the second generation

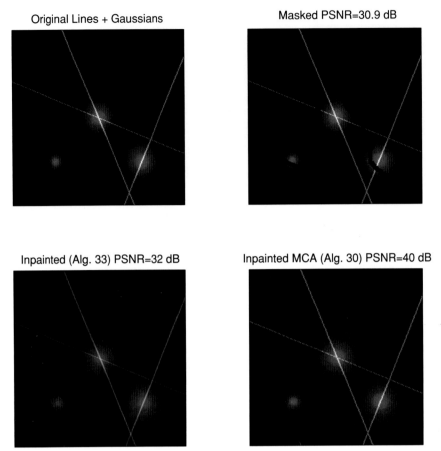

Figure 8.15. Inpainting lines + Gaussians image. See Table 8.2 for the experiment details.

discrete curvelet transform (DCTG2) implemented in CurveLab (Curvelab 2005), and the undecimated discrete wavelet transform from the DSP group of Rice (Rice Wavelet Toolbox). Note that some of the DCTG2 functions have been slightly modified to match our dictionary data structure, and to implement curvelets at the finest scale. We strongly recommend that the user downloads our modified version. Both of these transforms are available in a version of MCALab named MCAL-abWithUtilities; see the dashed rectangle in Fig. 8.16. They are in the subdirectories `MCALabWithUtilities/CurveleToolbox` and `MCALabWithUtilities/UDWT`. The user may read `Contents.m` in `MCALabWithUtilities/` for further details. The user also is invited to read carefully the license agreement details of these transforms on their respective websites prior to use.

8.8.1.2 Dictionaries and Data Structures
The functions in the `xxx-D/Dictionary` subdirectories provide fast implicit analysis and synthesis operators for all dictionaries implemented in MCALab. It is worth noting that except for the DCTG2 with the wrapping implementation, all

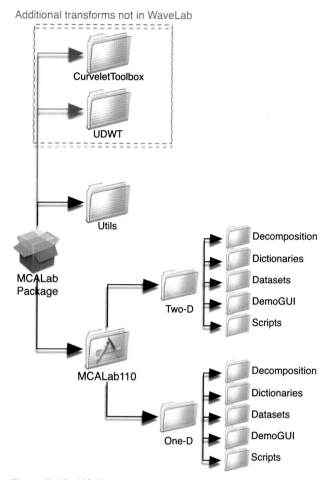

Figure 8.16. MCALab package architecture.

dictionaries provided in MCALab are normalized such that atoms have unit ℓ_2-norm. The DCTG2 implements a non-normalized Parseval tight frame. Thus, a simple rule to compute the ℓ_2-norm of the atoms is $1/\sqrt{\text{redundancy}}$ of the frame, see Section 5.4.2. Normalization has an important impact on the thresholding step involved in the decomposition/inpainting engines. The thresholding functions coded in MCALab take care of these normalization issues for the dictionaries it implements.

The dictionaries are implemented in an object-oriented way. The top level routines are FastLA and FastLS. Each transform has a fast analysis and a fast synthesis function named, respectively, FasNAMEOFTRANSFORMAnalysis and FasNAMEOFTRANSFORMSynthesis. Four arguments (NameOfDict, par1, par2, par3) are used to specify a dictionary. The meaning of each parameter is explained in the corresponding routine. Each FasNAMEOFTRANSFORMAnalysis computes the transform coefficients of an image or a signal and stores them in a structure array. We also define the List data structure, which allows us to create and easily manipulate overcomplete merged dictionaries.

Table 8.1. Experimental Setup for the 1-D Separation Examples

Signal	Dictionaries	Task	Algorithm parameters
TwinSine + Diracs $n = 1024$	**Global DCT** (fineness = 4) **Dirac**	Decomposition	$N_{\text{iter}} = 200$, $\lambda_{\min} = 0$, linearly decreasing threshold
EEG-fMRI signal $n = 8192$	**Local DCT** (square window, width = 32, overlap = 50% × width) **UWT** (Symmlet 6, coarsest scale 2)	Decomposition and denoising	$N_{\text{iter}} = 100$, σ_ε: estimated from data, $\lambda_{\min} = 4\tilde{\sigma}_\varepsilon$, exponentially decreasing threshold

8.8.1.3 Decomposition and Inpainting Engines

The routines in this directory perform either signal/image decomposition and inpainting using the MCA-based Algorithms 32–33, or signal and image inpainting using Algorithm 35 described above. This set of routines is for dictionaries with fast implicit operators.

8.8.1.4 Scripts and GUI

The subdirectory `MCALab110/xxx-D/Scripts` contains a variety of scripts, each of which contains a sequence of commands, datasets and parameters generating some figures shown in this chapter (as summarized in Tables 8.1 and 8.2), as well as other exploratory examples. The user can also run the same experiments on his or her own data, or tune the parameters by simply modifying the scripts. By studying these scripts one can quickly learn the practical aspects of sparse-representation based image decomposition and inpainting.

The routines in `MCALab110/xxx-D/DemoGUI` implement a point-and-click graphical user interface (GUI) that allows the user to select data and masks (signals or images), and then decompose or inpaint them using MCA Algorithms 32–33. Only signals and images with two morphological components, hence two dictionaries, can be processed with this GUI; see Fadili et al. (2010) for details.

8.8.2 Reproducible Experiments

Data description, dictionaries and algorithm parameters used in the experiments of this section are summarized in Table 8.1 and Table 8.2.

8.8.2.1 One-Dimensional Examples
TwinSine + Diracs

The synthetic signal of Fig. 8.17(a) (dashed line) consists of three randomly located spikes and the TwinSine signal: two cosines with frequencies separated by less than the Rayleigh distance. The TwinSine appears in Chen et al. (1999). We analyzed this signal with an overcomplete dictionary formed by merging a four-fold overcomplete DCT and a standard (Dirac) basis. The parameters chosen for this experiment are summarized in Table 8.1. The results are shown in Figs. 8.17(b)–(d). MCA managed to

Table 8.2. Experimental Setup for 2-D Separation and Inpainting Examples

Image	Dictionaries	Task	Algorithm parameters
Boy + Texture 256 × 256	**Curvelets** (cartoon) (coarsest scale 2) **Global DCT** (texture) (low-frequencies removed)	Decomposition (Alg. 33)	$N_{iter} = 50$, $\gamma = 0.1$ (TV on cartoon part), $\lambda_{min} = 0$, exponentially decreasing threshold
Barbara 512 × 512	**Curvelets** (cartoon) (coarsest scale 2)	Decomposition (Alg. 33)	$N_{iter} = 300$, $\gamma = 2$ (TV on cartoon part), $\lambda_{min} = 0$, exponentially decreasing threshold
	Local DCT (texture) (sine-bell window, width = 32, low-frequencies removed)	Inpainting (Alg. 33 – sect. 8.7.2)	$N_{iter} = 300$, $\gamma = 0$ (no TV), $\lambda_{min} = 0$, linearly decreasing threshold
Lines + Gaussians 256 × 256	**Curvelets** (lines) (coarsest scale 3)	Inpainting (Alg. 32 – sect. 8.7.2)	$N_{iter} = 50$, $\gamma = 0$ (no TV), $\lambda_{min} = 0$, linearly decreasing threshold
	UWT (Gaussians) (Symmlet 6, coarsest scale 2)	Inpainting (Alg. 35 – sect. 8.7.3)	no noise, $\delta = $ 1E-6, $\lambda = 3$
Lena 512 × 512	**Curvelets** (coarsest scale 2)	Inpainting (Alg. 32 – sect. 8.7.2)	$N_{iter} = 300$, $\gamma = 0$ (no TV), $\lambda_{min} = 0$, exponentially decreasing threshold
		Inpainting (Alg. 35 – sect. 8.7.3)	no noise, $\delta = $ 1E-6, $\lambda = 10$

resolve the frequencies of the oscillating (TwinSine (b)–(c)) component and to separate it properly from the spikes shown in (d), although some spurious frequencies are still present in the oscillating part. The locations of the true frequencies correspond to the dotted lines in Fig 8.17(c), and the original spikes are indicated by the crosses in Fig 8.17(d).

Electroencephalography-Functional Magnetic Resonance Imaging

MCA was also applied to a real signal acquired during a multi-modal neuroimaging experiment. During such an experiment, electroencephalography (EEG) and functional magnetic resonance imaging (fMRI) data are recorded synchronously for the study of the spatio-temporal dynamics of the brain activity. However, this simultaneous acquisition of EEG and fMRI data faces a major difficulty because of currents induced by the scanner magnetic fields yielding strong artifacts that generally dominate the useful EEG signal. In a continuous acquisition protocol, both modalities are

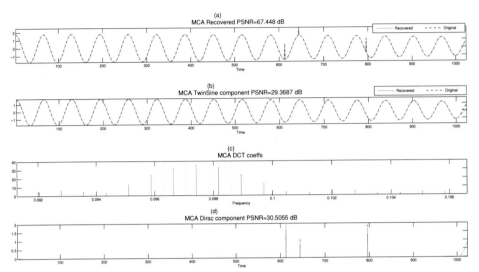

Figure 8.17. Decomposing TwinSine + Diracs signal. See Table 8.1 for the experimental details.

able to record data. But a postprocessing step for EEG artifact reduction is necessary for the EEG signal to be exploitable.

An example of such a signal[5] is depicted in Fig. 8.18(a). The periods where the scanner sequence is switched on are clearly visible, inducing strong oscillations on the EEG signal with an amplitude 10 to 20 times higher that the expected EEG amplitude. This locally oscillating behavior is expected because of the shape of the magnetic field gradients of the scanner. Therefore, to get rid of the magnetic field-induced component and clean the EEG signal from these artifacts, we decomposed it using an overcomplete dictionary of local DCT (for the magnetic field artifacts) and the UWT (for the EEG smooth and localized component). The parameters of this experiment are detailed in Table 8.1. The results are displayed in Figs. 8.18(c)–(d). As a by-product, the signal was also cleaned from measurement noise.

8.8.2.2 Two-Dimensional Examples

All figures presented in this chapter in Sections 8.6.3, 8.7.3.1 and 8.8.2 can be reproduced using the MCAlab software. We summarize in Table 8.2 the parameters needed to reproduce these figures.

8.9 SUMMARY

In this chapter, we described the morphological diversity concept and the MCA algorithm for sparse signal/image decomposition. The approach heavily relies on the ability to identify, for each part, a dictionary that will sparsify it, while leading to a non-sparse (or at least less sparse) representation on the other content type. We applied the MCA method for separating an image into its textured and piecewise smooth parts. A total variation regularization is used as a successful external force to enhance the texture-cartoon separation quality. A very nice property of this MCA

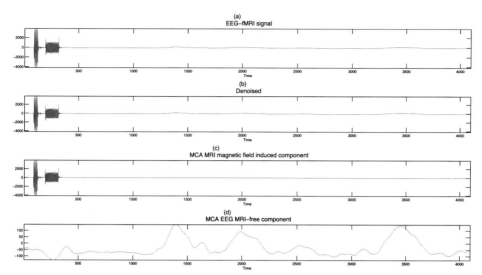

Figure 8.18. Decomposing and denoising the EEG–MRI real signal. See Table 8.1 for the experimental details.

decomposition framework is that it can be easily extended to automatically fill in missing samples.

More experiments relative to this MCA decomposition and inpainting technique can be found in the MCALab package. MCALab is a complete software environment for sparse-representation-based signal/image decomposition and inpainting. We described its architecture and discussed some results that can be reproduced by running corresponding scripts in the MCALab package. Other exploratory examples not included in this chapter may be reproduced just as well.

In this chapter, we were only concerned with scalar-valued observations, the so-called monochannel case. Building on sparsity and morphological diversity ingredients, we will describe in the next chapter extensions of the MCA to multichannel data.

9

Sparse Blind Source Separation

9.1 INTRODUCTION

Over the past few years, the development of multi-channel sensors has motivated interest in methods for the coherent processing of multivariate data. Areas of application include biomedical engineering, medical imaging, speech processing, astronomical imaging, remote sensing, communication systems, seismology, geophysics, econometrics.

Consider a situation where there is a collection of signals emitted by some physical objects or sources. These physical sources could be, for example, different brain areas emitting electrical signals; people speaking in the same room (the classical cocktail party problem), thus emitting speech signals; or radiation sources emitting their electromagnetic waves. Assume further that there are several sensors or receivers. These sensors are in different positions, so that each records a mixture of the original source signals with different weights. It is assumed that the mixing weights are unknown, since knowledge of that entails knowing all the properties of the physical mixing system, which is not accessible in general. Of course, the source signals are unknown as well, since the primary problem is that they cannot be recorded directly. The *blind source separation* (BSS) problem is to find the original signals from their observed mixtures, without prior knowledge of the mixing weights, and by knowing very little about the original sources. In the classical example of the cocktail party, the BSS problem amounts to recovering the voices of the different speakers, from the mixtures recorded at several microphones.

There has been much recent research activity on BSS. Some specific issues have already been addressed using a blend of heuristic ideas and rigorous derivations. This is testified to by the extensive literature on the subject. As clearly emphasized by previous work, it is fundamental that the sources to be retrieved present some quantitatively measurable diversity (e.g. decorrelation, independence, morphological diversity, etc.). Recently, sparsity and morphological diversity have emerged as a novel and effective source of diversity for BSS.

In the BSS setting, the instantaneous linear mixture model assumes that we are given N_c observations or channels $(y_1, \ldots, y_{N_c})$ where each y_i is a vector of length

N (an image or higher-dimensional data is treated by reordering its samples in a 1-D vector of length N); each measurement is the linear mixture of N_s vectors $(s_1, \ldots, s_{N_s})$ called sources, each one having the same length N. In the noisy case, this reads

$$y_i[l] = \sum_{j=1}^{N_s} \mathbf{A}[i, j] s_j[l] + \varepsilon_i[l], \quad \forall i \in \{1, \ldots, N_c\}, \quad \forall l \in \{1, \ldots, N\}, \quad (9.1)$$

where $\mathbf{A}$ is the $N_c \times N_s$ mixing matrix whose columns will be denoted a_i, and ε_i is the noise vector in channel i supposed to be bounded. $\mathbf{A}$ defines the contribution of each source to each measurement. As the measurements are N_c different mixtures, source separation techniques aim at recovering the original sources $(s_i)_{i=1\ldots,N_s}$ by taking advantage of some information contained in the way the signals are mixed in the observed channels. This mixing model is conveniently rewritten in matrix form:

$$\mathbf{Y} = \mathbf{AS} + \mathbf{E}, \quad (9.2)$$

where $\mathbf{Y}$ is the $N_c \times N$ measurement matrix whose rows are $y_i^{\mathrm{T}}, i = 1, \ldots, N_c$ (i.e. observed data), and $\mathbf{S}$ is the $N_s \times N$ source matrix with rows $s_i^{\mathrm{T}}, i = 1, \ldots, N_s$. The $N_c \times N$ matrix $\mathbf{E}$, with rows $\varepsilon_i^{\mathrm{T}}$, is added to account for instrumental noise and/or model imperfections. In this chapter, we will discuss the overdetermined case, which corresponds to $N_c \geq N_s$ (i.e. we have more channels than sources); the converse underdetermined case ($N_c < N_s$) is an even more difficult problem (see Jourjine et al. (2000) or Georgiev et al. (2005) for further details).

In the BSS problem, both the mixing matrix $\mathbf{A}$ and the sources $\mathbf{S}$ are unknown and must be estimated jointly. In general, without further a priori knowledge, decomposing a rectangular matrix $\mathbf{Y}$ into a linear combination of N_s rank-one matrices is clearly ill-posed. The goal of BSS is to understand the different cases in which this or that additional prior constraint allows us to reach the land of well-posed inverse problems and to devise separation methods that can handle the resulting models.

Source separation is overwhelmingly a question of contrast and diversity to disentangle the sources. Depending on the way the sources are distinguished, most BSS techniques can be categorized into two main classes:

- Statistical approaches – ICA: the well-known independent component analysis (ICA) methods assume that the sources $(s_i)_{i=1,\ldots,N_s}$ (modeled as random processes) are statistically independent and non-Gaussian. These methods (e.g., joint approximate diagonalization of eigen-matrices (JADE) Cardoso (1999); FastICA and its derivatives, Hyvärinen et al. (2001); and InfoMax Koldovsky et al. (2006)) already provided successful results in a wide range of applications. Moreover, even if the independence assumption is strong, it is in many cases physically plausible. Theoretically, Lee et al. (2000) focus on the equivalence of most ICA techniques with mutual information minimization processes. Then, in practice, ICA algorithms are about devising adequate contrast functions which are related to approximations of mutual information. In terms of discernibility, statistical independence is a "source of diversity" between the sources.
- Sparsity and morphological diversity: Zibulevsky and Pearlmutter (2001) introduced a BSS method that focuses on sparsity to distinguish the sources. They

assumed that the sources are sparse in a particular basis Φ (for instance, the wavelet orthobasis). The sources $\mathbf{S}$ and the mixing matrix $\mathbf{A}$ are estimated by minimizing a maximum a posteriori criterion with a sparsity-promoting prior on the sources in Φ. They showed that sparsity clearly enhances the diversity between the sources. The extremal sparse case assumes that the sources have mutually disjoint supports in the original or transform domain (see (Jourjine et al. 2000; Li et al. 2006)). Nonetheless this simple case requires highly sparse signals. Unfortunately, this is not the case for large classes of signals and especially in image processing.

Another approach based on the concept of morphological diversity developed in the previous chapter has been proposed by Bobin et al. (2006) which assumes that the N_s sources $(s_i)_{i=1,...,N_s}$ are sparse in different dictionaries. For instance, a piecewise smooth source s_1 (e.g., cartoon image) is well sparsified in a curvelet tight frame while a warped globally oscillating source s_2 (oscillating texture) is better represented using the local DCT or the waveatom dictionary. This model takes advantage of the fact that the sources are morphologically distinct to differentiate between them with accuracy. The method has been extended to the more general case where each source s_i is the sum of several components ($\forall i$, $s_i = \sum_{k=1}^{K} x_{i,k}$), each of which is sparse in a given dictionary Φ_k (Bobin et al. 2007a). This, in fact, generalizes the MCA framework of Section 8.5 to multichannel data. This sparsity- and morphological diversity-based model has been shown to enjoy several advantages such as enhanced separation quality and robustness to noise.

In this chapter, we give some new and essential insights into the use of sparsity in BSS and we highlight the central role played by morphological diversity as a source of contrast between the sources. We provide fast and practical algorithms, and we describe an extension to Non-negative Matrix Factorization (NMF).

9.2 INDEPENDENT COMPONENT ANALYSIS

9.2.1 Independence as a Contrast Principle

Throughout this section, we consider the noiseless instantaneous linear mixture model assuming that $\mathbf{Y} = \mathbf{AS}$. This can be written equivalently in the following form:

$$\mathbf{Y} = \sum_{i=1}^{N_s} \mathbf{Y}^{(i)} = \sum_{i=1}^{N_s} a_i s_i^{\mathrm{T}}, \tag{9.3}$$

where $\mathbf{Y}^{(i)}$ is the contribution of the source s_i to the data $\mathbf{Y}$. Thus, BSS is equivalent to decomposing the matrix $\mathbf{Y}$ of rank N_s into a sum of N_s rank-one matrices $\{\mathbf{Y}^{(i)} = a_i s_i^{\mathrm{T}}\}_{i=1,...,N_s}$. Obviously, there is no unique way to achieve such a decomposition. Further information is required to disentangle the sources.

Let us assume that the sources are random vectors (of zero mean without loss of generality). These may be known a priori to be different in the sense of being simply decorrelated. A separation scheme will then look for sources $(s_i)_{i=1,...,N_s}$ such that their covariance matrix $\Sigma_{\mathbf{S}}$ is diagonal. Unfortunately, the covariance matrix $\Sigma_{\mathbf{S}}$ is invariant to orthonormal transformations such as rotations. Therefore an effective BSS method has to go beyond decorrelation (see Cardoso (1999) for further reflections about the need for stronger a priori constraints going beyond the decorrelation assumption).

The seminal work by Comon (1994) paved the way for the outgrowth of *independent component analysis* (ICA). In the ICA framework, the sources are assumed to be independent random variables which is true if and only if the joint probability density function (pdf) $\mathrm{pdf_S}$ obeys

$$\mathrm{pdf_S}(s_1, \ldots, s_{N_s}) = \prod_{i=1}^{N_s} \mathrm{pdf}_{s_i}(s_i) . \qquad (9.4)$$

As statistical independence is a property to be verified by the PDF of the sources, devising a good measure of independence is not trivial. In this setting, ICA then boils down to finding a multichannel representation/basis on which the estimated sources $\tilde{\mathbf{S}}$ are as independent as possible. Equivalently, ICA looks for a *separating/demixing* matrix $\mathbf{B}$ such that the estimated sources $\tilde{\mathbf{S}} = \mathbf{BAS}$ are independent. Until the end of this section devoted to ICA, we will assume that the mixing matrix $\mathbf{A}$ is square and invertible.

We could ask if independence makes the sources identifiable. Under mild conditions, the Darmois theorem (Darmois 1953) shows that statistical independence means separability (Comon 1994). It states that if at most one of the sources is generated from a Gaussian distribution then, if the entries of $\tilde{\mathbf{S}} = \mathbf{BAS}$ are independent, $\mathbf{B}$ is a separating matrix and $\tilde{\mathbf{S}}$ is equal to $\mathbf{S}$ up to a scale factor (multiplication by a diagonal matrix with strictly positive diagonal entries) and permutation. As a consequence, if at most one source is Gaussian, maximizing independence between the estimated sources leads to perfect estimation of $\mathbf{S}$ and $\mathbf{A} = \mathbf{B}^{-1}$. The Darmois theorem then motivates the use of independence in BSS.

9.2.2 Independence and Gaussianity

The Kullback-Leibler (KL) divergence between two densities is defined as

$$\mathrm{KL}(\mathrm{pdf}_1 \| \mathrm{pdf}_2) = \int_{\mathbf{u}} \mathrm{pdf}_1(\mathbf{u}) \log\left(\frac{\mathrm{pdf}_1(\mathbf{u})}{\mathrm{pdf}_2(\mathbf{u})}\right) d\mathbf{u} . \qquad (9.5)$$

The mutual information (MI) in the form of the KL divergence between the joint density $\mathrm{pdf_S}(s_1, \ldots, s_{N_s})$ and the product of the marginal densities $\mathrm{pdf}_{s_i}(s_i)$ is a popular measure of statistical independence:

$$\mathrm{MI}(\mathbf{S}) = \mathrm{KL}\left(\mathrm{pdf_S} \| \prod_{i=1}^{N_s} \mathrm{pdf}_{s_i}\right) , \qquad (9.6)$$

which is nonnegative and vanishes if and only if the sources s_i are mutually independent. Using the Pythagorean identity of the KL divergence, the mutual information can be equivalently written (Cardoso 2003; Comon 1994):

$$\text{MI}(\mathbf{S}) = \text{KL}(\phi(\cdot; 0, \mathbf{\Sigma_S}) \| \phi(\cdot; 0, \text{diag}(\mathbf{\Sigma_S})))$$

$$- \sum_{i=1}^{N_s} \text{KL}\big(\text{pdf}_{s_i} \| \phi(\cdot; 0, \sigma_{s_i}^2)\big) + \text{KL}(\text{pdf}_{\mathbf{S}} \| \phi(\cdot; 0, \mathbf{\Sigma_S})) , \qquad (9.7)$$

where $\sigma_{s_i}^2 = \mathbf{\Sigma_S}[i, i]$ is the variance of s_i, and $\phi(.; 0, \mathbf{\Sigma})$ is the multivariate Gaussian PDF with zero mean and covariance $\mathbf{\Sigma}$. The first term in (9.7) vanishes when the sources are decorrelated. The second term measures the marginal non-Gaussianity of the sources. The last term measures the joint non-Gaussianity of the sources, and is invariant under affine transforms. As ICA looks for a demixing matrix $\mathbf{B}$ which minimizes $\text{MI}(\tilde{\mathbf{S}} = \mathbf{BY})$, this term is a constant independent of all $\mathbf{B}$. Consequently, maximizing independence of the estimated sources $\tilde{\mathbf{S}}$ is equivalent to minimizing the correlation between the sources and maximizing their non-Gaussianity. Note that, with a taste of the Central Limit Theorem, intuition tells us that mixing independent signals should lead to a kind of Gaussianization. It then seems natural that demixing leads to processes that deviate from Gaussian processes.

9.2.3 Independent Component Analysis Algorithms

Since the seminal paper of Comon (1994), a variety of ICA algorithms have been proposed. They all merely differ in the way they devise assessable measures of independence. Some popular approaches have given the following measures of independence:

- Information Maximization: Bell and Sejnowski (1995); Nadal and Parga (1994) proposed the InfoMax principle implemented by maximizing with respect to $\mathbf{B}$ the differential entropy of an appropriate nonlinear function of $\mathbf{BY}$. They showed that information maximization is equivalent to minimizing a measure of independence based on the KL divergence.
- Maximum Likelihood (ML): ML has also been proposed to solve the BSS problem (Cardoso 1997; Pearlmutter and Parra 1997; Pham et al. 1992). In the ICA framework, it was shown that the ML approach coincides with InfoMax provided that $\mathbf{B}$ is identified with $\mathbf{A}^{-1}$ (Cardoso 1997).
- Higher Order Statistics: As we pointed out above, maximizing the independence of the sources is equivalent to maximizing their non-Gaussianity under a strict decorrelation constraint. Because Gaussian random variables have vanishing higher order cumulants, devising a separation algorithm based on these higher order statistics should provide a way of accounting for the non-Gaussianity of the estimated sources. A wide range of ICA algorithms have been proposed along these lines, see (Hyvärinen et al. 2001; Belouchrani et al. 1997; Cardoso 1999) and references therein. Historical papers (Comon 1994) proposed ICA algorithms that use approximations of the Kullback-Leibler divergence (based on truncated Edgeworth expansions). Those approximations explicitly involve higher order cumulants.

Lee et al. (2000) showed that most ICA-based algorithms are similar in theory and in practice.

9.2.4 Limits of Independent Component Analysis

Despite its theoretical strength and elegance, ICA suffers from several limitations:

- PDF assumption: While even implicit, the ICA algorithm requires information on the source distribution. As stated in Lee et al. (2000), whatever the contrast function to optimize, most ICA algorithms can be equivalently restated in a "natural gradient" form (Amari 1999; Amari and Cardoso 1997). In such a setting, the demixing matrix **B** is estimated iteratively: $\mathbf{B}^{(t+1)} = \mathbf{B}^{(t)} + \mu \nabla_{\mathbf{B}}(\mathbf{B}^{(t)})$. The "natural gradient" $\nabla_{\mathbf{B}}$ at **B** is given by:

$$\nabla_{\mathbf{B}}(\mathbf{B}) \propto \left(\mathbf{I} - \frac{1}{N} \mathscr{H}(\tilde{\mathbf{S}})\tilde{\mathbf{S}}^{\mathrm{T}} \right) \mathbf{B} \,, \tag{9.8}$$

where $\tilde{\mathbf{S}}$ is the estimate of $\mathbf{S}$: $\tilde{\mathbf{S}} = \mathbf{BY}$. The matrix $\mathscr{H}(\tilde{\mathbf{S}})$ in (9.8) is the so-called score function which is closely related to the PDF of the sources (Cichocki and Amari 2002; Amari and Cardoso 1997). Assuming that all the sources are generated from the same joint PDF $\mathrm{pdf}_{\mathbf{S}}$, the entries of $\mathscr{H}(\tilde{\mathbf{S}})$ are the partial derivatives of the log-likelihood function

$$\mathscr{H}(\tilde{\mathbf{S}})[i, l] = -\frac{\partial \log(\mathrm{pdf}_{\mathbf{S}}(\tilde{\mathbf{S}}))}{\partial \tilde{\mathbf{S}}[i, l]}, \quad \forall (i, l) \in \{1, \ldots, N_s\} \times \{1, \ldots, N\} \,. \tag{9.9}$$

As expected, the way the demixing matrix (and thus the sources) is estimated closely depends on the way the sources are modeled (from a statistical point of view). For instance, separating platykurtic (distribution with negative kurtosis) or leptokurtic (distribution with positive kurtosis) sources will require completely different score functions. Even if ICA is shown in Amari and Cardoso (1997) to be quite robust to so-called mismodeling, the choice of the score function is crucial with respect to the convergence (and rate of convergence) of ICA algorithms. Some ICA-based techniques (Koldovsky et al. 2006) focus on adapting the popular FastICA algorithm to adjust the score function to the distribution of the sources. They particularly focus on modeling sources whose distribution belongs to specific parametric classes of distributions such as generalized Gaussian distribution (GGD).

- Noisy ICA: Only a few works have investigated the problem of noisy ICA (Davies 2004; Koldovsky and Tichavsky 2006). As pointed out by Davies (2004), noise clearly degenerates the ICA model: it is not fully identifiable. In the case of additive Gaussian noise as stated in equation (9.2), using higher order statistics yields an effective estimate of the mixing matrix $\mathbf{A} = \mathbf{B}^{-1}$ (higher order cumulants are indeed blind to additive Gaussian noise; this property does not hold for non-Gaussian noise). But in the noisy ICA setting, applying the demixing matrix to the data does not yield an effective estimate of the sources. Furthermore, most ICA algorithms assume the mixing matrix **A** to be square. When there are more observations than sources ($N_c > N_s$), a dimension reduction step is first applied. When noise perturbs the data, this subspace projection step can dramatically deteriorate the performance of the separation stage.

In the following, we will introduce a new way of modeling the data so as to avoid most of the aforementioned limitations of ICA.

9.2.5 Toward Sparsity

The seminal paper of Zibulevsky and Pearlmutter (2001) introduced sparsity as an alternative to standard contrast functions in ICA. In their work, each source s_i was assumed to be sparsely represented in a dictionary Φ:

$$s_i = \Phi \alpha_i \quad \forall i = 1, \ldots, N_s \, . \tag{9.10}$$

where the coefficients were assumed independent with a sharply peaked (i.e., leptokurtic) and heavy-tailed pdf:

$$\text{pdf}_{\boldsymbol{\alpha}}(\alpha_1, \ldots, \alpha_{N_s}) \propto \prod_{i,l} e^{-\lambda_i \psi(\alpha_i[l])} \, , \tag{9.11}$$

where $\psi(\alpha_i[l])$ is a sparsity-promoting penalty; e.g. the ℓ_p-norm corresponding to a GGD prior. Zibulevsky and Pearlmutter (2001) used a convex smooth approximation of the ℓ_1 norm (Laplacian prior) and proposed to estimate $\mathbf{A}$ and $\mathbf{S}$ via a maximum a posteriori (MAP) estimator. The resulting optimization problem was solved with a relative Newton algorithm (RNA) (Zibulevski 2003). This work paved the way for the use of sparsity in BSS. Note that several other works emphasized the use of sparsity in a parametric Bayesian approach; see Ichir and Djafari (2006) and references therein. Recently, sparsity has emerged as an effective tool for solving underdetermined source separation problems; see (Li et al. 2006; Georgiev et al. 2005; Bronstein et al. 2005; Vincent 2007; Bobin et al. 2007a, 2008; Rapin et al. 2012, 2014).

9.3 SPARSITY AND MULTICHANNEL DATA

In this section, will see how the story of monochannel sparse decomposition problem described and characterized in Section 8.1.1 can be told in the language of multichannel data. This will be a consequence of a key observation dictated by equation (9.3).

9.3.1 Morphospectral Diversity

Extending the redundant representation framework to the multichannel case requires defining what a multichannel overcomplete representation is. Let us assume in this section that $\mathbf{A} = [\varphi_{v,1}, \ldots, \varphi_{v,N_c}] \in \mathbb{R}^{N_c \times N_s}$ is a *known spectral* dictionary, and $\Phi = [\varphi_1, \ldots, \varphi_T] \in \mathbb{R}^{N \times T}$ is a *spatial* or *temporal* dictionary[1]. We assume that each source s_i can be represented as a (sparse) linear combination of atoms in Φ; $s_i = \Phi \alpha_i$. Let $\boldsymbol{\alpha}$ the $N_s \times T$ matrix whose rows are α_i^T.

From (9.3), the multichannel noiseless data $\mathbf{Y}$ can be written as

$$\mathbf{Y} = \mathbf{A} \boldsymbol{\alpha} \Phi^T = \sum_{i=1}^{N_s} \sum_{j=1}^{T} \left(\varphi_{v,i} \varphi_j^T \right) \alpha_i[j] \, . \tag{9.12}$$

Consequently, each column in of $\mathbf{Y}$ reads

$$\text{vect}(\mathbf{Y}) = (\mathbf{A} \otimes \Phi) \, \text{vect}(\boldsymbol{\alpha}) \, , \tag{9.13}$$

where $\otimes$ is the tensor (Kronecker) product and the operator vect stacks the columns of its argument in a long 1D vector. This latter equation brings a clear and simple insight: the sparsity of the sources in Φ translates into sparsity of the multichannel data $\mathbf{Y}$ in the multichannel tensor product dictionary $\mathbf{\Psi} = \mathbf{A} \otimes \mathbf{\Phi}$. This concept of multichannel dictionary has also been noted in Gribonval and Nielsen (2008).

The multichannel dictionary $\mathbf{\Psi}$ can also be seen as concatenation of multichannel atoms $\mathbf{\Psi}^{(ij)} = \varphi_{v,i} \varphi_j^\mathrm{T}$ which are rank-one matrices obtained from each atomic spectrum $\varphi_{v,i}$ and each spatial elementary atom φ_j (see equation (9.12)).

In Chapter 8, we have seen that some of the popular sparse recovery results in the monochannel setting rely on the mutual coherence of the dictionary. In the multichannel case a similar quantity can be defined. In fact, by standard properties of the tensor product, one can easily show that the Gram matrix of a tensor product is the tensor product of the Gram matrices. Thus the mutual coherence of the multichannel dictionary $\mathbf{\Psi}$ is

$$0 \leq \mu_{\mathbf{\Psi}} = \max\{\mu_{\mathbf{A}}, \mu_{\mathbf{\Phi}}\} < 1 . \tag{9.14}$$

This expression of mutual coherence is instructive as it tells us that multichannel atoms can be distinguished based on their spatial or spectral morphology. In other words, discriminating two multichannel atoms $\mathbf{\Psi}_{ij}$ and $\mathbf{\Psi}_{i'j'}$ may put on different faces:

- Spatial or temporal (respectively, spectral) diversity: in this case $i = i'$ and $j \neq j'$ (respectively, $i \neq i'$ and $j = j'$). These atoms have the same spectrum (respectively, spatial shape) but one can discriminate between them based on their spatial (respectively, spectral) diversity. From equation (9.14), their coherence is lower than $\mu_{\mathbf{\Phi}}$ (respectively, $\mu_{\mathbf{A}}$). Disentangling these multichannel atoms can equivalently be done in the monochannel case.
- Both diversities: $i \neq i'$ and $j \neq j'$, this seems to be a more favorable scenario to differentiate the atoms as they do not share either the same spectrum or the same spatial (or temporal) shape. Note that from equation (9.14), the coherence between these atoms in this case is lower than $\mu_{\mathbf{A}}\mu_{\mathbf{\Phi}} \leq \max\{\mu_{\mathbf{A}}, \mu_{\mathbf{\Phi}}\}$.

9.3.2 Multichannel Sparse Decomposition

We embark from equation (9.12), where the multichannel dictionary $\mathbf{\Psi}$ is supposed to be overcomplete, i.e. $NN_c < TN_s$. The goal is to recover the sparsest solution α from $\mathbf{Y}$ which requires solving:

$$\min_{\alpha \in \mathbb{R}^{N_s \times T}} \sum_{i=1}^{N_s} \|\alpha_i\|_0 \quad \text{s.t.} \quad \mathbf{Y} = \mathbf{A}\alpha\mathbf{\Phi}^\mathrm{T}. \tag{9.15}$$

As justified in Chapter 8, this combinatorial problem can be replaced by its convex relaxation substituting the ℓ_1 norm for the ℓ_0 pseudo-norm, hence giving

$$\min_{\alpha \in \mathbb{R}^{N_s \times T}} \sum_{i=1}^{N_s} \|\alpha_i\|_1 \quad \text{s.t.} \quad \mathbf{Y} = \mathbf{A}\alpha\mathbf{\Phi}^\mathrm{T}. \tag{9.16}$$

As equation (9.13) is a vectorized monochannel form of equation (9.12), what we are trying to do is actually to find the sparsest solution of a monochannel underdetermined system of linear equations where the solution is sparse in an overcomplete tensor product dictionary. Recovery properties of monochannel sparse decomposition by ℓ_1 minimization were overviewed in Section 8.1.1. Therefore, if one is able to translate those identifiability criteria in the language of tensor product dictionaries, then we are done.

In particular, the coherence-based sparse recovery criterion (8.4) is trivial to adapt, owing to equation (9.14). Indeed, if $\mathbf{Y}$ is k-sparse in the multichannel dictionary $\mathbf{\Psi}$ with $k < C(\mu_{\mathbf{\Psi}}^{-1} + 1)$ for some $C > 0$ (typically $C = 1/2$), and the dictionary is sufficiently incoherent (both spectrally and spatially), then the solution of (9.16) is unique, is a point of equivalence of equations (9.15) and (9.16), and the recovery is stable to bounded noise on $\mathbf{Y}$.

Earlier, we addressed the multichannel sparse decomposition problem without assuming any constraint on the sparsity pattern of the different channels. It is worth however pointing out that sparse recovery conditions from multichannel measurements can be refined if some structured sparsity is hypothesized. For instance, for structured multichannel representation (e.g., sources with disjoint supports) Gribonval and Nielsen (2008) provided coherence-based sufficient recovery conditions by solving equation (9.16). One should note that despite apparent similarities, the multichannel sparse decomposition problem discussed here is conceptually different from the one targeting *simultaneous* sparse recovery of multiple measurements vectors (MMV) considered by several authors; see, for example, Cotter et al. (2005); Malioutov et al. (2005); Tropp (2006a); Chen and Huo (2006); Argyriou et al. (2008); Bach (2008); Gribonval et al. (2008); Eldar and Mishali (2009); Lounici et al. (2009); Negahban and Wainwright (2009). The latter are not aware of any mixing process via $\mathbf{A}$, and their goal is to recover α from MMV $\mathbf{Y} = \alpha\mathbf{\Phi}^{\mathrm{T}}$ in which the vectors α_i, i.e. rows of α, have a common sparsity pattern. However the MMV model can also be written $\mathrm{vect}(\mathbf{Y}^{\mathrm{T}}) = (\mathbf{\Phi} \otimes \mathbf{I})\,\mathrm{vect}(\alpha^{\mathrm{T}})$ as in (9.13). The most widely used approach to solve the simultaneous sparse recovery problem with joint sparsity is to minimize a mixed $\ell_p - \ell_q$ norm of the form $\sum_{j=1}^{T}(\|\alpha[.,j]\|_p^q)^{1/q}$ for $p \geq 1, 0 \leq q \leq +\infty$.

9.4 MORPHOLOGICAL DIVERSITY AND BLIND SOURCE SEPARATION

9.4.1 Generalized Morphological Component Analysis

We now turn to the BSS problem and we highlight the role of sparsity and morphological diversity as a source of contrast to solve it. Towards this goal, we assume that the sources are sparse in the spatial dictionary $\mathbf{\Phi}$ that is the concatenation of K orthonormal bases $(\mathbf{\Phi}_k)_{k=1,\ldots,K}$: $\mathbf{\Phi} = [\mathbf{\Phi}_1, \ldots, \mathbf{\Phi}_K]$. The restriction to orthonormal bases is only formal and the algorithms to be presented later still work in practice even with redundant subdictionaries $\mathbf{\Phi}_k$.

The generalized morphological component analysis (GMCA) framework assumes a priori that each source is modeled as the linear combination of K morphological components, where each component is sparse in a specific basis:

$$\forall i \in \{1, \ldots, N_s\}; \qquad s_i = \sum_{k=1}^{K} x_{i,k} = \sum_{k=1}^{K} \mathbf{\Phi}_k \alpha_{i,k} \tag{9.17}$$

$$= \mathbf{\Phi}\alpha_i \qquad \text{where } \alpha_i = \left[\alpha_{i,1}^{\mathrm{T}}, \ldots, \alpha_{i,K}^{\mathrm{T}}\right]^{\mathrm{T}}.$$

GMCA seeks an unmixing scheme, through the estimation of $\mathbf{A}$, which leads to the sparsest sources $\mathbf{S}$ in the dictionary $\boldsymbol{\Phi}$. This is expressed by the following optimization problem, written in the augmented Lagrangian form:

$$\min_{\mathbf{A}, \alpha_{1,1}, \ldots, \alpha_{N_s,K}} \frac{1}{2} \|\mathbf{Y} - \mathbf{A}\alpha\boldsymbol{\Phi}^{\mathrm{T}}\|_{\mathrm{F}}^2 + \lambda \sum_{i=1}^{N_s} \sum_{k=1}^{K} \|\alpha_{i,k}\|_p^p$$

$$\text{s.t.} \quad \|a_i\|_2 = 1 \quad \forall i \in \{1, \ldots, N_s\}, \quad (9.18)$$

where, typically $p = 0$ or its relaxed convex version with $p = 1$, and $\|\mathbf{X}\|_{\mathrm{F}} = (\mathrm{trace}(\mathbf{X}^{\mathrm{T}}\mathbf{X}))^{1/2}$ is the Frobenius norm. The unit ℓ_2-norm constraint on the columns of $\mathbf{A}$ avoids the classical scale indeterminacy of the product $\mathbf{AS}$ in equation (9.2). The reader may have noticed that the MCA problem (8.18) in Chapter 8 is a special case of the GMCA problem (9.18) when there is only one source $N_s = 1$ and one channel $N_c = 1$ (no mixing). Thus GMCA is indeed a multichannel generalization of MCA.

The program (9.18) is a notoriously difficult nonconvex optimization problem even for convex penalties when $p \geq 1$. More conveniently, following equation (9.3), the product $\mathbf{AS}$ can be split into $N_s \cdot K$ multichannel morphological components: $\mathbf{AS} = \sum_{i,k} a_i x_{i,k}^{\mathrm{T}} = \sum_{i,k} (a_i \alpha_{i,k}^{\mathrm{T}}) \boldsymbol{\Phi}_k^{\mathrm{T}}$. Based on this decomposition, and inspired by the block-coordinate relaxation as for MCA, GMCA yields an alternating minimization algorithm to estimate iteratively one term at a time (Bobin et al. 2007a). We will show shortly that the estimation of each morphological component $x_{i,k} = \boldsymbol{\Phi}_k \alpha_{i,k}$ assuming $\mathbf{A}$ and $x_{\{i',k'\} \neq \{i,k\}}$ are fixed is obtained by simple hard or soft thresholding for $p = 0$ and $p = 1$.

Define the (i, k)th multichannel marginal residual by

$$\mathbf{R}_{i,k} = \mathbf{Y} - \sum_{i' \neq i} \sum_{k' \neq k} a_{i'} x_{i',k'}^{\mathrm{T}} . \quad (9.19)$$

as the part of the data $\mathbf{Y}$ unexplained by the multichannel morphological component $a_i x_{i,k}^{\mathrm{T}}$. Estimating $x_{i,k} = \boldsymbol{\Phi}_k \alpha_{i,k}$, assuming $\mathbf{A}$ and the other components $x_{(i',k') \neq (i,k)}$ are fixed, leads to the component-wise optimization problem:

$$\min_{x_{i,k} \in \mathbb{R}^N} \frac{1}{2} \left\| \mathbf{R}_{i,k} - \left(a_i \alpha_{i,k}^{\mathrm{T}} \right) \boldsymbol{\Phi}^{\mathrm{T}} \right\|_{\mathrm{F}}^2 + \lambda \|\alpha_{i,k}\|_p^p , \quad (9.20)$$

Because here, $\boldsymbol{\Phi}_k$ is an orthogonal matrix, with calculations similar to those of Sections 7.3.2.2 and 7.6.1[2], it can be shown that the unique solution of (9.20) is obtained by a hard ($p = 0$) or soft ($p = 1$) thresholding. Hence, the closed-form estimate of the morphological component $x_{i,k}$ is

$$\tilde{x}_{i,k} = \Delta_{\boldsymbol{\Phi}_k, \lambda'} \left(\frac{1}{\|a_i\|_2^2} \mathbf{R}_{i,k}^{\mathrm{T}} a_i \right) , \quad (9.21)$$

where $\lambda' = \lambda / \|a_i\|_2^2$ for soft thresholding and $\lambda' = \sqrt{2\lambda} / \|a_i\|_2$ for hard thresholding. As described in Chapter 8, the operator $\Delta_{\mathbf{D}, \lambda}(x)$ consists of (1) computing the coefficients of x in the dictionary $\mathbf{D}$, (2) thresholding (soft or hard) the obtained coefficients with the threshold λ, and (3) reconstructing from thresholded coefficients

$$\Delta_{\mathbf{D}, \lambda}(x) = \mathbf{D} \, \mathrm{Thresh}_\lambda (\mathbf{D}^{\mathrm{T}} x). \quad (9.22)$$

Thresh$_\lambda$ is either a hard or a soft thresholding. When $\boldsymbol{\Phi}_k$ is redundant, (9.21) is only the first iteration of the iterative thresholding recursion described in Chapter 7 (see Algorithm 25 and equation (7.66)), and which should be used when $\boldsymbol{\Phi}_k$ is overcomplete. However, in practice, (9.21) can still be used to save computation time.

Now, considering $\{a_{i'}\}_{i'\neq i}$ and all morphological components as fixed, and recalling that $N_c \geq N_s$, updating the column a_i is then just a least-squares estimate

$$\tilde{a}_i = \frac{1}{\|s_i\|_2^2}\left(\mathbf{Y} - \sum_{i'\neq i} a_{i'} s_{i'}^{\mathrm{T}}\right) s_i . \tag{9.23}$$

where $s_i = \sum_{k=1}^K x_{i,k}$. This estimate is then projected onto the unit sphere to meet the unit ℓ_2-norm constraint in equation (9.18). The GMCA algorithm is summarized in Algorithm 36.

Algorithm 36 GMCA Algorithm

Task: Sparse Blind Source Separation.
Parameters: The data $\mathbf{Y}$, the dictionary $\boldsymbol{\Phi} = [\boldsymbol{\Phi}_1 \cdots \boldsymbol{\Phi}_K]$, number of iterations N_{iter}, number of sources N_s and channels N_c, stopping threshold $\lambda_{\min}$, threshold update schedule.
Initialization: $x_{i,k}^{(0)} = 0$ for all (i,k), $\mathbf{A}^{(0)}$ random and threshold λ_0.
Main iteration:
for $t = 1$ **to** N_{iter} **do**
    for $i = 1, \ldots, N_s$ **do**
        for $k = 1, \ldots, K$ **do**
            Compute the marginal residuals:

$$\mathbf{R}_{i,k}^{(t)} = \mathbf{Y} - \sum_{(i',k')\neq(i,k)} a_{i'}^{(t-1)} x_{i',k'}^{(t-1)^{\mathrm{T}}} .$$

            Estimate the current component $x_{i,k}^{(t)}$ via thresholding with threshold λ_t:
            $x_{i,k}^{(t)} = \Delta_{\boldsymbol{\Phi}_k, \lambda_t}\left(\mathbf{R}_{i,k}^{(t)^{\mathrm{T}}} a_i^{(t-1)}\right).$
        Update ith source $s_i^{(t)} = \sum_{k=1}^K x_{ik}^{(t)}$.
        Update a_i assuming $a_{i'\neq i}^{(t)}$ and the morphological components $x_{i,k}^{(t)}$ are fixed :
        $a_i^{(t)} = \frac{1}{\|s_i^{(t)}\|_2^2}\left(\mathbf{Y} - \sum_{i'\neq i}^{N_s} a_{i'}^{(t-1)} s_{i'}^{(t)^{\mathrm{T}}}\right) s_i^{(t)}$ and normalize to a unit ℓ_2 norm.
    Update the threshold λ_t according to the given schedule.
    if $\lambda_t \leq \lambda_{\min}$ **then** stop.
Output: Estimated sources $\left(s_i^{(N_{\text{iter}})}\right)_{i=1,\ldots,N_s}$ and mixing matrix $\mathbf{A}^{(N_{\text{iter}})}$.

For $p = 1$ and fixed threshold λ, Algorithm 36 can be shown to converge to a stationary point, see Tseng (2001); Bobin et al. (2008). This point is not guaranteed to be even a local minimum of the energy, and this is even less clear for $p = 0$. Thus, in the same vein as MCA, GMCA relies on a salient-to-fine strategy using a varying threshold to mitigate the problem of sensitivity to initialization. More precisely,

GMCA first computes coarse versions of the morphological components for any fixed source s_i. These raw sources are estimated from their most significant coefficients in Φ. Then, the corresponding column a_i is estimated from the most significant features of s_i. Each source and its corresponding column of $\mathbf{A}$ are then alternately and progressively refined as the threshold decreases towards $\lambda_{\min}$. This particular iterative thresholding scheme provides robustness to noise and initialization by working first on the most significant features in the data and then progressively incorporating smaller details to finely tune the model parameters. GMCA can be used with either linear or exponential decrease of the threshold as for MCA in Chapter 8.

If $\mathbf{A}$ were known and fixed, the GMCA would be equivalent to performing an MCA sparse decomposition of $\mathbf{Y}$ in the tensor product multichannel dictionary $\mathbf{A} \otimes \Phi$. But as GMCA also updates the mixing matrix at each iteration, it is able to learn the spectral part of the multichannel dictionary directly from the data.

9.4.1.1 Complexity Analysis

We begin by noting that the bulk of the computation is invested in the application of Φ_k^T and Φ_k at each iteration and for each of the $N_s K$ morphological components $x_{i,k}$. Hence, fast implicit operators associated with Φ_k or its adjoint are of key importance in large-scale applications. Let V_k denote the cost of one application of the analysis and synthesis operators Φ_k^T and Φ_k. The computation of the multichannel residuals for all (i, k) costs $O(N_s K N_c N)$ operations. Each step of the double "For" loop computes the correlation of this residual with a_i costing $O(N_c N)$ operations. Next, it computes the residual correlations (application of Φ_k^T), thresholds them, and then reconstructs the morphological component $x_{i,k}$. This costs $O(2V_k + T)$ operations. The sources are then reconstructed with $O(N_s K N)$, and the update of each mixing matrix column involves $O(N_c N)$ operations. Noting that in our setting, $N_s \approx N_c \ll N$, and $V_k = O(N)$ or $O(N \log N)$ for most popular transforms (see previous chapters for details), the whole GMCA algorithm then costs $O(N_{\text{iter}} N_s^2 K N) + O(2 N_{\text{iter}} N_s \sum_{k=1}^{K} V_k + N_s K T)$. Thus in practice GMCA could be computationally demanding for large-scale high dimensional problems. In Section 9.4.3, we will see that under appropriate assumptions, GMCA can be accelerated yielding a simple and much faster algorithm that enables handling of very large scale problems.

9.4.1.2 The Thresholding Strategy

Hard or soft thresholding?

In practice, it was observed that hard thresholding leads to better results (Bobin et al. 2006, 2007a). Furthermore, if $\mathbf{A}$ is known and no noise contaminates the data, GMCA with hard thresholding will enjoy the sparse recovery guarantees given in Section 8.5.4, with the proviso that the morphological components are contrasted and sparse in a sufficiently incoherent multichannel dictionary $\mathbf{A} \otimes \Phi$. A good alternative could be to use a reweighing ℓ_1 alogrithm (Candès *et al.* 2007), as proposed by Rapin et al. (2014). This solution has the advantage of keeping the properties of robustness and convergence of ℓ_1 minimization, but without having a bias on the solution as in ℓ_0 minimization. There is unfortunately a drawback, a higher computation time.

Handling additive Gaussian noise

The GMCA algorithm is well suited to deal with data contaminated with additive Gaussian noise (see the next section for a Bayesian interpretation). For instance, assume that the noise $\mathbf{E}$ in equation (9.2) is additive white Gaussian in each channel, that is, its covariance matrix $\mathbf{\Sigma_E}$ is diagonal, and let $\sigma_\mathbf{E}$ be its standard deviation supposed equal for all channels for simplicity. Then, Algorithm 36 can be applied as described above with $\lambda_{\min} = \tau\sigma_\mathbf{E}$, where τ is chosen as in denoising methods, typically taking its value in the range [3, 4]. This attribute of GMCA makes it a suitable choice for use in noisy BSS. GMCA not only manages to separate the sources, but also succeeds in removing additive noise as a by-product.

9.4.2 The Bayesian Perspective

GMCA can be interpreted from a Bayesian standpoint. For instance, let us assume that the entries of the mixtures $(y_i)_{i=1,\ldots,N_c}$, the mixing matrix $\mathbf{A}$, the sources $(s_i)_{i=1,\ldots,N_s}$ and the noise matrix $\mathbf{E}$ are random processes. We assume that the noise $\mathbf{E}$ is zero mean Gaussian where the noise vector ε_i in each channel is white, but the noise between channels is possibly correlated with known covariance matrix $\mathbf{\Sigma_E}$. This means that the log-likelihood function takes the form

$$LL(\mathbf{Y}|\mathbf{S}, \mathbf{A}, \mathbf{\Sigma_E}) = \frac{1}{2}\|\mathbf{Y} - \mathbf{AS}\|_{\mathbf{\Sigma_E}}^2, \quad \text{where } \|\mathbf{X}\|_{\mathbf{\Sigma_E}}^2 = \text{trace}\left(\mathbf{X}^\mathsf{T}\mathbf{\Sigma_E}^{-1}\mathbf{X}\right).$$

We further assume that the uniform prior is imposed on entries of $\mathbf{A}$. Other priors on $\mathbf{A}$ could be imposed, for example, a known fixed column. As far as the sources are concerned, they are known from equation (9.17) to be sparse in the dictionary $\mathbf{\Phi}$. Thus their coefficients $\boldsymbol{\alpha} = [\alpha_1, \ldots, \alpha_{N_s}]^\mathsf{T}$ will be assumed as drawn independently from a leptokurtic pdf with heavy tails such as the generalized Gaussian distribution form

$$\text{pdf}_{\boldsymbol{\alpha}}(\alpha_{1,1}, \ldots, \alpha_{N_s,K}) \propto \prod_{i=1}^{N_s}\prod_{k=1}^{K} \exp\left(-\lambda_{i,k}\|\alpha_i\|_{p_{i,k}}^{p_{i,k}}\right),$$

$$0 \le p_{i,k} < 2 \,\forall(i, k) \in \{1, \ldots, N_s\} \times \{1, \ldots, K\}. \quad (9.24)$$

Putting together the log-likelihood function and the priors on $\mathbf{A}$ and $\boldsymbol{\alpha}$, the MAP estimator leads to the following optimization problem

$$\min_{\mathbf{A},\alpha_{1,1},\ldots,\alpha_{N_s,K}} \frac{1}{2}\|\mathbf{Y} - \mathbf{A}\boldsymbol{\alpha}\mathbf{\Phi}^\mathsf{T}\|_{\mathbf{\Sigma_E}}^2 + \sum_{i=1}^{N_s}\sum_{k=1}^{K}\lambda_{i,k}\|\alpha_{i,k}\|_{p_{i,k}}^{p_{i,k}}, \quad (9.25)$$

This problem has strong similarity with that of equation (9.18). More precisely, if the noise is homoscedastic and decorrelated between channels (i.e. $\mathbf{\Sigma_E} = \sigma_\mathbf{E}^2\mathbf{I}$), if the shape parameters $p_{i,k}$ of the generalized Gaussian distribution prior are all equal to p and the scale parameters are all taken as $\lambda_{i,k} = \lambda/\sigma_\mathbf{E}^2$, and if the columns of $\mathbf{A}$ are assumed uniform on the unit sphere, then equation (9.25) is exactly equation (9.18). Note that in the development above, the independence assumption in (9.24) does not necessarily entail independence of the sources. Rather it means that there are no a priori assumptions that indicate any dependency between the sources.

9.4.3 The Fast Generalized Mophological Component Analysis Algorithm

The goal here is to speed up the GMCA algorithm. As a warm-up, assume that the dictionary $\boldsymbol{\Phi}$ is no longer redundant and reduces to a single orthobasis (i.e., $K = 1$). Let us denote $\boldsymbol{\beta} = \mathbf{Y}\boldsymbol{\Phi}$ the matrix where each of its rows stores the coefficients of each channel y_i. The optimization problem (9.18) then becomes (we omit the ℓ_2 constraint on $\mathbf{A}$ to lighten the notation)

$$\min_{\mathbf{A},\boldsymbol{\alpha}} \frac{1}{2} \|\boldsymbol{\beta} - \mathbf{A}\boldsymbol{\alpha}\|_{\mathrm{F}}^2 + \lambda \sum_{i=1}^{N_s} \|\alpha_i\|_p^p \,. \tag{9.26}$$

where $p = 0$ or $p = 1$. The GMCA algorithm no longer needs to apply the analysis and synthesis operators at each iteration as only the channels $\mathbf{Y}$ have to be transformed once in $\boldsymbol{\Phi}$. Clearly, this case is computationally much cheaper.

However, this is rigorously valid only for an orthobasis dictionary, and no orthonormal basis is able to sparsely represent large variety of signals and yet we would like to use very sparse signal representations which motivated the use of redundancy in the first place. Arguments supporting the substitution of equation (9.26) for equation (9.18) for a redundant dictionary $\boldsymbol{\Phi}$ were given in Bobin et al. (2007a, 2008). The idea is first to compute the sparsest representation of each channel y_i in the redundant dictionary $\boldsymbol{\Phi}$ using an appropriate (nonlinear) decomposition algorithm (e.g., BP, MCA). Now, $\boldsymbol{\beta}$ denotes the matrix where each row contains the sparse decomposition of the corresponding channel. Because the channels are linear mixtures of the sources via the mixing matrix $\mathbf{A}$, the key argument developed by Bobin et al. (2007a) is that the sparse decomposition algorithm must preserve linear mixtures. Descriptively, the sparsest decomposition provided by the algorithm when applied to each channel must be equal to the linear combination of the sparsest decompositions of the sources. This statement is valid if the sources and the channels are identifiable, meaning that they verify sufficient conditions so that their unique sparsest representation can be recovered by the decomposition algorithm. For instance, if MCA is used, then following Section 8.5.4, it is sufficient that the channels and the sources be sparse enough in an incoherent dictionary $\boldsymbol{\Phi}$, and their morphological components be sufficiently contrasted. See Bobin et al. (2007a, 2008) for details.

Hence, under these circumstances, a fast GMCA algorithm can be designed to solve equation (9.26) by working in the transform domain after decomposing each observed channel y_i in $\boldsymbol{\Phi}$ using a sparse decomposition algorithm such as MCA. There is an additional important simplification when substituting problem (9.26) for (9.18). Indeed, since $N_c \geq N_s$ (i.e., overdetermined BSS), it turns out that equation (9.26) is a multichannel overdetermined least-squares fit with ℓ_0/ℓ_1-sparsity penalization. We again use an alternating minimization scheme to solve for $\mathbf{A}$ and $\boldsymbol{\alpha}$:

- *Update the coefficients*: When $\mathbf{A}$ is fixed, since the quadratic term is strictly convex ($\mathbf{A}$ has full column-rank), the marginal optimization problem can be solved by a general form of the forward-backward splitting iteration (Chen and Rockafellar 1997):

$$\boldsymbol{\alpha}^{(t+1)} = \mathrm{Thresh}_{\mu\lambda} \left(\boldsymbol{\alpha}^{(t)} + \mu \, \boldsymbol{\Xi} \mathbf{A}^{\mathrm{T}} \left(\boldsymbol{\beta} - \mathbf{A}\boldsymbol{\alpha}^{(t)} \right) \right) \,, \tag{9.27}$$

where $\boldsymbol{\Xi}$ is a relaxation matrix such that the spectral radius of $(\mathbf{I} - \mu \boldsymbol{\Xi} \mathbf{A}^{\mathrm{T}} \mathbf{A})$ is bounded above by 1, and the step-size $0 < \mu \leq 1/\|\boldsymbol{\Xi} \mathbf{A} \mathbf{A}^{\mathrm{T}}\|$. Taking $\boldsymbol{\Xi} = (\mathbf{A}^{\mathrm{T}} \mathbf{A})^{-1}$ ($\mathbf{A}^{\mathrm{T}} \mathbf{A}$ is nonsingular and a kind of Newton's method ensues) yields the closed form

$$\tilde{\boldsymbol{\alpha}} = \mathrm{Thresh}_\lambda (\mathbf{A}^+ \boldsymbol{\beta}), \tag{9.28}$$

where Thresh_λ is a thresholding operator (hard for $p = 0$ and soft for $p = 1$).

- If $\boldsymbol{\alpha}$ is fixed, and since $\boldsymbol{\alpha}$ is full row rank, the mixing matrix $\mathbf{A}$ is given by the least squares estimate:

$$\tilde{\mathbf{A}} = \boldsymbol{\beta} \boldsymbol{\alpha}^{\mathrm{T}} (\boldsymbol{\alpha} \boldsymbol{\alpha}^{\mathrm{T}})^{-1} = \boldsymbol{\beta} \boldsymbol{\alpha}^+ , \tag{9.29}$$

and the columns of $\tilde{\mathbf{A}}$ are then normalized.

Note that the latter two-step estimation scheme has a flavor of the alternating sparse coding/dictionary learning algorithm presented by Aharon et al. (2006); Peyré et al. (2007) in a different framework.

This two-stage iterative process leads to the accelerated version of GMCA summarized in Algorithm 37.

Algorithm 37 Fast GMCA Algorithm

Task: Sparse Blind Source Separation.
Parameters: The data $\mathbf{Y}$, the dictionary $\boldsymbol{\Phi} = [\boldsymbol{\Phi}_1 \cdots \boldsymbol{\Phi}_K]$, number of iterations N_{iter}, number of sources N_s and channels N_c, stopping threshold λ_{min}, threshold update schedule.
Initialization:

- $\boldsymbol{\alpha}^{(0)} = 0$, $\mathbf{A}^{(0)}$ a random matrix.
- Apply the MCA Algorithm 32 with $\boldsymbol{\Phi}$ to each data channel y_i to get $\boldsymbol{\beta}$.
- Set threshold $\lambda_0 = \max_{i,l} |\boldsymbol{\beta}[i, l]|$.

Main iteration:
for $t = 1$ **to** N_{iter} **do**

- Update the coefficients $\boldsymbol{\alpha}$: $\boldsymbol{\alpha}^{(t+1)} = \mathrm{Thresh}_{\lambda_t} (\mathbf{A}^{(t)^+} \boldsymbol{\beta})$.
- Update the mixing matrix $\mathbf{A}$: $\mathbf{A}^{(t+1)} = \boldsymbol{\beta} \boldsymbol{\alpha}^{(t+1)^+}$, normalize columns to a unit ℓ_2 norm.
- Update the threshold λ_t according to the given schedule.

if $\lambda_t \leq \lambda_{\mathrm{min}}$ **then** stop.
Reconstruct the sources: $\tilde{s}_i = \sum_{k=1}^K \boldsymbol{\Phi}_k \boldsymbol{\alpha}_{i,k}^{(N_{\mathrm{iter}})}$, $i = 1, \ldots, N_s$.
Output: Estimated sources $(\tilde{s}_i)_{i=1,\ldots,N_s}$ and mixing matrix $\mathbf{A}^{(N_{\mathrm{iter}})}$.

In the same vein as in Section 9.4.1, the coarse-to-fine process is also at the heart of this fast version of GMCA with the threshold that decreases with increasing iteration count. This again brings robustness to noise and initialization.

Complexity analysis.
When the assumptions discussed above for the redundant dictionary case are valid, the fast GMCA version requires only one application of MCA on each channel, which is faster than the first version of GMCA (see Section 9.4.1.1). Once MCA is applied to each channel, and assuming as before that $N_s \approx N_c \ll N \leq T$, it can be easily shown that the rest of the algorithm requires $O(N_{\mathrm{iter}}N_s^2 T)$ operations. In the case where only one orthogonal dictionary is used (e.g., Fourier orthogonal wavelet transform), the algorithm becomes even faster, since the MCA step is replaced by application of the fast analysis operator to each channel.

9.4.4 Estimating the Number of Sources

In BSS, the number of sources N_s is assumed to be a fixed known parameter of the problem. In practical situations, this is rather an exception than a rule, and estimating N_s from the data is a crucial and strenuous problem.

As we supposed $N_s \leq N_c$, the number of sources is the dimension of the subspace of the whole N_c-dimensional space (recall that N_c is the number of channels) in which the data lie. A misestimation of the number of sources N_s may entail two difficulties:

- Underestimation: in the GMCA algorithm, underestimating the number of sources will clearly lead to poor unmixed solutions that are made of linear combinations of "true" sources. The solution may then be suboptimal with respect to the sparsity of the estimated sources.
- Over-estimation: in such case, the GMCA algorithm may have to cope with a mixing matrix estimate that becomes ill conditioned.

Relatively little work has focused on the estimation of the number of sources N_s. One can think of using model selection criteria such as the minimum description length (MDL) devised in Balan (2007). Such criteria, including Akaike information criterion (AIC) (Akaike 1970) and the Bayesian information criterion (BIC) (Schwarz 1978), would provide a balance between the complexity of the model (here the number of sources) and its ability to faithfully represent the data. It would amount to adding a penalty term in equation (9.18). This penalty term would merely prevent a high number of sources. But a sparsity-based method to estimate N_s within the GMCA framework can be designed.

For a fixed number of sources $n_s < N_s$, the sparse BSS problem (9.18) can be written in the constrained from

$$(\mathrm{P}_{n_s,\sigma}) : \quad \min_{\mathbf{A},\boldsymbol{\alpha} \mid \mathrm{rank}(\mathbf{A})=n_s} \sum_{i=1}^{n_s} \|\alpha_i\|_p^p \quad \mathrm{s.t.} \quad \|\mathbf{Y} - \mathbf{A}\boldsymbol{\alpha}\boldsymbol{\Phi}^{\mathrm{T}}\|_{\mathrm{F}} \leq \sigma . \quad (9.30)$$

To jointly estimate the $\mathbf{S} = \boldsymbol{\alpha}\boldsymbol{\Phi}^{\mathrm{T}}$, $\mathbf{A}$ and the number of sources, the problem we would like to tackle is then

$$\min_{n_s \in \{1,\dots,N_c\}} \left\{ \min_{\mathbf{A},\boldsymbol{\alpha} \mid \mathrm{rank}(\mathbf{A})=n_s} \sum_{i=1}^{n_s} \|\alpha_i\|_p^p \quad \mathrm{s.t.} \quad \|\mathbf{Y} - \mathbf{A}\boldsymbol{\alpha}\boldsymbol{\Phi}^{\mathrm{T}}\|_{\mathrm{F}} \leq \sigma \right\} .$$

If $n_s < N_s$, there exists a minimal value $\sigma^\star(n_s)$ such that if $\sigma < \sigma^\star(n_s)$, $(\mathrm{P}_{n_s,\sigma})$ has no feasible solution in $\mathbf{A}$ that satisfies the rank condition. For a fixed $n_s < N_s$, this minimal value $\sigma^\star(n_s)$ is the approximation error between $\mathbf{Y}$ and its projection in the subspace spanned by its singular vectors corresponding to the n_s largest singular values. Furthermore, in the noiseless case, for $n_s < N_s, \sigma^\star(n_s)$ is always strictly positive as the data lies in a subspace whose dimension is exactly N_s. When $n_s = N_s$, the problem $(\mathrm{P}_{N_s,\sigma})$ has at least one solution for $\sigma = \sigma^\star(N_s) = 0$.

This discussion suggests a constructive approach to jointly estimate the number of sources $N_s, \mathbf{S} = \alpha\mathbf{\Phi}^\mathrm{T}$ and $\mathbf{A}$. This selection procedure uses GMCA to solve a sequence of problems $(\mathrm{P}_{n_s,\sigma(n_s)})$ for each constraint radius $\sigma(n_s)$ with increasing $n_s, 1 \leq n_s \leq N_c$. This is summarized in Algorithm 38 (Bobin et al. 2008).

Algorithm 38 GMCA-Based Selection of the Number of Sources

Task: Jointly estimate the number of sources, source coefficients α and mixing matrix $\mathbf{A}$.

Parameters: The data $\mathbf{Y}$, the dictionary $\mathbf{\Phi} = [\mathbf{\Phi}_1 \cdots \mathbf{\Phi}_K]$, number of iterations N_{iter}, stopping threshold $\lambda_{\min}$, threshold update schedule.

Main iteration:

for $n_s = 1$ to N_c **do**

> 1. Add a new column to $\mathbf{A}$.
> 2. Solve $(\mathrm{P}_{n_s,\sigma^\star(n_s)})$ with the GMCA algorithm using $(\mathbf{\Phi}, N_{\mathrm{iter}}, n_s, N_c, \lambda_{\min})$ as its parameters.
>
> **if** $\|\mathbf{Y} - \mathbf{A}\alpha\mathbf{\Phi}^\mathrm{T}\|_\mathrm{F} \leq \sigma^\star(N_s)$ **then** stop.

Output: Estimated number of sources n_s.

Choice of the new columns of A

In the aforementioned algorithm, step 1 amounts to adding a column vector to the current mixing matrix $\mathbf{A}$. The most simple choice would amount to choosing this vector at random. Wiser choices can also be made based on additional prior information:

■ *Decorrelation:* If the mixing matrix is assumed to be orthogonal, the new column vector can be chosen as being orthogonal to the subspace spanned by the columns of $\mathbf{A}$ with rank $(\mathbf{A}) = n_s - 1$.

■ *Known spectra:* If a library of spectra is known a priori, the new column can be chosen amongst the set of unused ones. The new spectrum can be chosen based on its correlation with the residual. Let $\mathcal{A}$ denote a library of spectra $\{\mathsf{a}_i\}_{i=1,\dots,\mathrm{Card}(\mathcal{A})}$ and let $\mathcal{A}^c_{n_s}$ denote the set of spectra that have not been chosen yet, then the n_sth new column of $\mathbf{A}$ is chosen such that:

$$\mathsf{a}_{i^\star} = \underset{\mathsf{a}_i \in \mathcal{A}^c_{n_s}}{\mathrm{argmax}} \left| \sum_{l=1}^{N} \frac{1}{\|\mathsf{a}_i\|_2^2} \mathsf{a}_i^\mathrm{T} (\mathbf{Y} - \mathbf{A}\mathbf{S})[.,l] \right| . \tag{9.31}$$

Any other prior information can be taken into account which will guide the choice of a new column vector of $\mathbf{A}$.

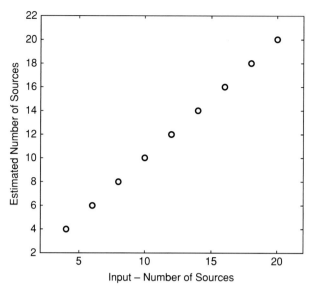

Figure 9.1. Estimating the number of sources with GMCA. Each point is the average number of sources computed from 25 trials. For each point, the estimation variance was zero.

The noisy case

In the noiseless case, step 2 of Algorithm 38 amounts to running the GMCA algorithm to estimate $\mathbf{A}$ and $\mathbf{S} = \alpha\mathbf{\Phi}^{\mathrm{T}}$ for a fixed n_s with a final threshold $\lambda_{\min} = 0$. In the noisy case, σ in $(\mathrm{P}_{n_s,\sigma})$ can be closely related to the noise level For instance, if the noise $\mathbf{E}$ is additive Gaussian with $\mathbf{\Sigma_E} = \sigma_{\mathbf{E}}^2$, $\lambda_{\min} = \tau\sigma_{\mathbf{E}}$ with $\tau = 3$–4 as suggested throughout the chapter. If the GMCA algorithm recovers the correct sources and mixing matrix, this ensures that the residual mean-squares is bounded by $\tau^2\sigma_{\mathbf{E}}^2$ with probability higher than $1 - \exp(-\tau^2/2)$.

Illustrative example

In this experiment, 1-D channels are generated following the instantaneous linear mixture model (9.2) with N_s sources, where N_s varies from 2 to 20. The number of channels is $N_c = 64$, each having $N = 256$ samples. The dictionary $\mathbf{\Phi}$ is chosen as the Dirac basis, and the entries of $\mathbf{S}$ have been independently drawn from a Laplacian PDF with unit scale parameter (i.e. $p = 1$ and $\lambda = 1$ in equation (9.24)). The entries of the mixing matrix are independent and identically distributed $\sim \mathcal{N}(0, 1)$. The observations are not contaminated by noise.

This experiment will focus on comparing the classical principal components analysis (PCA), the popular subspace selection method, and the GMCA algorithm assuming N_s is unknown. In the absence of noise, only the N_s highest eigenvalues provided by the PCA, which coincide with the Frobenius norm of the rank 1 matrices $(a_i s_i^{\mathrm{T}})_{i=1...,N_s}$, are nonzero. PCA therefore provides the true number of sources. The GMCA-based selection procedure in Algorithm 38 has been applied to the same data in order to estimate the number of sources N_s. Figure 9.1 depicts the mean number of sources estimated by GMCA. Each point has been averaged over 25

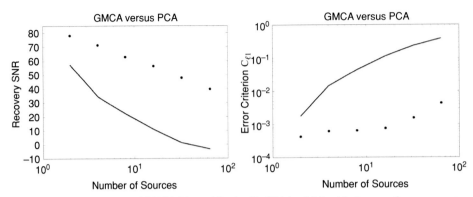

Figure 9.2. Comparison of GMCA (dotted line) with PCA (solid line) in terms of source recovery. (left) Recovery SNR in dB as N_s increases. (right) Source recovery criterion C_{ℓ_1}. Each point is an average over 25 realizations.

random realizations of $\mathbf{S}$ and $\mathbf{A}$. The estimation variance was zero indicating that for each of the 25 trials, GMCA provides exactly the true number of sources.

Figure 9.2 reports the comparative performances of PCA and GMCA in recovering the true input sources. In this experiment, the number of channels is $N_c = 128$, and each channel has $N = 2048$ samples. Figure 9.2 (left) shows the mean (over 25 realizations) recovery SNR of the estimated sources. The SNR for both methods decreases as N_s increases which is expected, but clearly the GMCA provides sources that are far closer to the true sources than PCA. We define the following ℓ_1 norm-based error criterion between the original sources and mixing matrix and their estimates:

$$
C_{\ell_1} = \frac{\sum_{i=1}^{N_s} \sum_{j=1}^{N_c} \sum_{l=1}^{N} \left| (a_i s_i^{\mathsf{T}})[j,l] - (\tilde{a}_i \tilde{s}_i^{\mathsf{T}})[j,l] \right|}{\sum_{i=1}^{N_s} \sum_{j=1}^{N_c} \sum_{l=1}^{N} \left| (a_i s_i^{\mathsf{T}})[j,l] \right|}, \tag{9.32}
$$

C_{ℓ_1} provides a sparsity-based criterion that quantifies the deviation between the estimated sources and the true sparsest sources. Figure 9.2 (right) shows the evolution of C_{ℓ_1} as N_s varies. As expected, the GMCA-based algorithm also provides much sparser sources.

9.4.5 Illustrative Experiments

9.4.5.1 The Sparser, the Better

So far in this chapter, sparsity and morphological diversity were claimed as the clue for good separation results. The role of morphological diversity is twofold:

- *Separability*: The sparser and the more morphologically diverse the sources in the dictionary $\mathbf{\Phi}$, the more "separable" they are.
- *Robustness to noise/model imperfections*: The sparser the sources, the less dramatic the noise. This is the essence of sparsity-based denoising methods as discussed in Chapter 6.

To illustrate these points, let us consider $N_s = 2$ 1-D sources with $N = 1024$ samples. These sources are the Bump and HeaviSine signals available in Wavelab 802

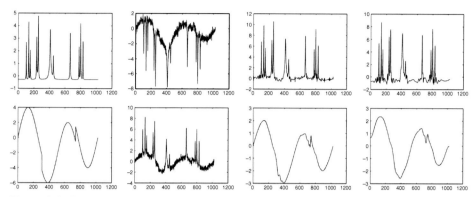

Figure 9.3. The sparser the better. The first column shows the original sources. The second column shows the mixtures with additive white Gaussian noise (SNR = 19 dB). The third column shows sources estimated with GMCA using only the OWT dictionary. The fourth column shows sources estimated with GMCA using a redundant dictionary made of the union of the DCT and the OWT.

(2001). The first column of Fig. 9.3 shows the two synthetic sources. The sources are randomly mixed, and a white Gaussian noise with variance corresponding to SNR = 19 dB is added so as to provide $N_c = 2$ observations portrayed in the second column of Fig. 9.3. To apply the fast GMCA Algorithm 37, MCA was assumed to preserve linearity with such sources and mixtures (see our choice of the dictionary later on). The mixing matrix is assumed to be unknown. The third and fourth columns of Fig. 9.3 depict the GMCA estimated sources computed with a dictionary containing respectively the OWT, and the DCT+OWT. Visually, GMCA performs quite well in both cases.

We define the mixing matrix criterion

$$C_\mathbf{A} = \sum_{i,j} |\mathbf{I}[i, j] - (\mathbf{P}\tilde{\mathbf{A}}^+\mathbf{A})[i, j]| ,$$

where $\mathbf{I}$ is the identity matrix as usual, $\mathbf{P}$ is a matrix that reduces the scale/permutation indeterminacy of the mixing model and $\tilde{\mathbf{A}}^+$ is the pseudo-inverse of the estimated mixing matrix. In the simulation experiments, the true sources and mixing matrix are obviously known and thus $\mathbf{P}$ can be computed easily. The mixing matrix criterion is thus strictly positive unless the mixing matrix is perfectly estimated up to scale and permutation. This mixing matrix criterion is experimentally much more sensitive to separation errors.

Figure 9.4 portrays the evolution of the criterion $C_\mathbf{A}$ as the SNR increases. The dashed line corresponds to the behavior of GMCA with the OWT dictionary, and the solid line to that when Φ is the union of the DWT and the DCT. On the one hand, GMCA gives satisfactory results as $C_\mathbf{A}$ is rather low for both experiments. On the other hand, the values of $C_\mathbf{A}$ provided by the fast GMCA with the redundant dictionary are approximately 5 times better than those achieved using solely the orthogonal dictionary OWT. In summary, this simple toy experiment clearly underlines the role of sparsity and overcompleteness for successful BSS.

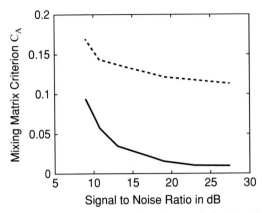

Figure 9.4. The sparser the better; behavior of the mixing matrix criterion C_A with varying SNR. OWT–fast GMCA (dashed line) and (DCT+OWT)–fast GMCA (solid line).

9.4.5.2 Generalized Morphological Component Analysis and Noisy Data

The goal here is to compare several BSS techniques with GMCA for image separation in a noisy environment. Three different reference BSS methods are chosen:

- *JADE* (Cardoso 1999): The well-known ICA based on fourth-order statistics, see Section 9.2.3.
- *Relative Newton Algorithm (RNA)* (Zibulevski 2003): The seminal sparsity-based BSS technique described in Section 9.2.5. In the experiments reported hereafter, we used the RNA on the channels transformed in the 2-D OWT domain.
- *EFICA*: This separation method improves the FastICA algorithm for sources following a GGD prior. We thus applied EFICA on the channels transformed by a 2-D OWT to sparsify them and hence the leptokurticity assumption on the source marginal statistics becomes valid.

Figure 9.5 shows the original $N_s = 2$ sources (top) and $N_c = 2$ mixtures (bottom). The sources s_1 and s_2 are normalized to a unit variance. The mixing matrix $\mathbf{A}$ is such that $y_1 = 0.25s_1 + 0.5s_2 + \varepsilon_1$ and $y_2 = -0.75s_1 + 0.5s_2 + \varepsilon_2$, where ε_1 and ε_2 are zero mean white Gaussian noise vectors that are mutually independent.

The comparisons we carry out here are twofold: (1) we assess the separation quality in terms of the correlation between the original and estimated sources as the SNR varies; (2) as the estimated sources are also perturbed by noise, we also quantify the performance of each method by computing the mixing matrix criterion C_A. The GMCA algorithm was applied using a dictionary containing the DCTG2 and the Local DCT.

Figure 9.6 portrays the evolution of the correlation coefficient of source 1 and source 2 as a function of the SNR. At first glance, GMCA, RNA and EFICA are very robust to noise as they give correlation coefficients close to the optimal value 1. On these images, JADE behaves rather poorly. It might be due to the correlation between these two sources. For higher noise levels (SNR lower than 10 dB), EFICA tends to perform slightly worse than GMCA and RNA.

Figure 9.5. (top) The 256×256 source images. (bottom) Two noisy mixtures SNR $= 10$ dB.

The mixing matrix-based criterion C_A turns out to be more sensitive to separation errors and then better discriminates between the methods. Figure 9.7 depicts the behavior of C_A with increasing SNR. While the correlation coefficient was unable to discriminate between GMCA and RNA, C_A clearly reveals their differences. First, it

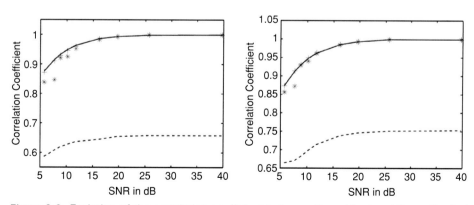

Figure 9.6. Evolution of the correlation coefficient between the original and the estimated sources as a function of the SNR: (left) source 1; (right) source 2. Solid line is GMCA; dashed line is JADE; stars are EFICA; and plusses are RNA.

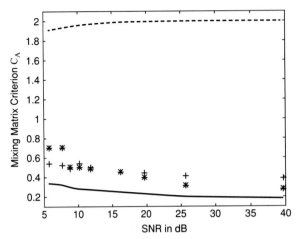

Figure 9.7. Evolution of the mixing matrix criterion C_A as a function of the SNR. Solid line is GMCA; dashed line is JADE; stars are EFICA; and plusses are RNA.

confirms the dramatic behavior of JADE on that set of mixtures. Secondly, RNA and EFICA behave rather similarly. Thirdly, GMCA seems to provide far better results with C_A values that are up to 10 times better than JADE and approximately 2 times better than with RNA or EFICA.

In summary, the findings of this experiment allow us to conclude the following safely:

■ Sparsity brings better results. Amongst the methods we used, only JADE is not a sparsity-based separation algorithm. Whatever the method, separating in a sparse representation-domain enhances the separation quality: RNA, EFICA and GMCA clearly outperform JADE.
■ GMCA takes better advantage of overcompleteness and morphological diversity. GMCA takes better advantage of overcomplete sparse representations than RNA and EFICA.

9.4.5.3 Multichannel Image Inpainting

Similarly to the MCA (see Section (8.7.2)), GMCA can be readily extended to handle multichannel missing data. Although the rest of the section holds for any overdetermined multichannel data, without loss of generality, we consider color images where the observed data $\mathbf{Y}$ consist of $N_c = 3$ observed channels corresponding to each color layer (for instance red, green and blue), and the number of sources is also $N_s = 3$.

GMCA-inpainting seeks an unmixing scheme, through the estimation of $\mathbf{A}$, which leads to the sparsest sources $\mathbf{S}$ in the dictionary $\mathbf{\Phi}$, taking into account the missing data mask $\mathbf{M}_j$ (the main diagonal of $\mathbf{M}_j$ encodes the pixel status in channel j; see Section 8.7.2 for more details). The resulting optimization problem to be solved is

Figure 9.8. Inpainting color images. (top left) Original "Barbara" color image (left) and (top right) a zoom on the scarf. (middle) Masked image – 90 percent of the color pixels are missing. (bottom) Inpainted image using the adaptive GMCA algorithm. (See *color plates*.)

then

$$\min_{\mathbf{A}, \alpha_{1,1},\dots,\alpha_{N_s,K}} \sum_{j=1}^{N_c} \frac{1}{2} \left\| y_j - \mathbf{M}_j \left(\sum_{i=1}^{N_s} \mathbf{A}[j,i]\mathbf{\Phi}\alpha_i \right) \right\|_2^2 + \lambda \sum_{i=1}^{N_s} \sum_{k=1}^{K} \|\alpha_{i,k}\|_p^p$$

$$\text{s.t.} \quad \|a_i\|_2 = 1 \quad \forall i \in \{1,\dots,N_s\} . \quad (9.33)$$

If $\mathbf{M}_j = \mathbf{M}$ for all channels, (9.33) becomes

$$\min_{\mathbf{A}, \alpha_{1,1}, \ldots, \alpha_{N_s, K}} \frac{1}{2} \|\mathbf{Y} - \mathbf{A}\alpha\mathbf{\Phi}^{\mathrm{T}}\mathbf{M}\|_{\mathrm{F}}^2 + \lambda \sum_{i=1}^{N_s} \sum_{k=1}^{K} \|\alpha_{i,k}\|_p^p$$

$$\text{s.t.} \quad \|a_i\|_2 = 1 \quad \forall i \in \{1, \ldots, N_s\}. \quad (9.34)$$

The GMCA-inpainting algorithm is similar to Algorithm 36, except that the update of the residual $\mathbf{R}_{i,k}^{(t)}$ is modified to

$$\mathbf{R}_{i,k}^{(t)} = \left(\mathbf{Y} - \sum_{(i',k') \neq (i,k)} a_{i'}^{(t-1)} x_{i',k'}^{(t-1)^{\mathrm{T}}} \right) \mathbf{M}.$$

Figure 9.8 (top) shows the original "Barbara" color image (in RGB space) and a zoom. (middle) Masked color images where 90 percent of the color pixels were missing. (bottom) Recovered images with the color space-adaptive GMCA algorithm, where $\mathbf{A}$ was estimated along with the inpainted sources. It was shown by Bobin et al. (2009) that the adaptive color space GMCA inpainting performs much better than inpainting each color channel separately using the algorithms of Section 8.7.

9.5 NON-NEGATIVE MATRIX FACTORIZATION

GMCA has recently been extended to the case of non-negative sources mixed through non-negative coefficients (Rapin et al. 2013a) (i.e., nonnegative matrix factorization (NMF)). Under these conditions, it was shown that improperly constraining the problem could lead to instabilities. We should therefore consider solving the ℓ_1-constrained problem:

$$\underset{\mathbf{A} \geq 0, \, \mathbf{S} \geq 0}{\operatorname{argmin}} \|\mathbf{Y} - \mathbf{A}\mathbf{S}\|_2^2 + \|\mathbf{\Lambda} \odot \mathbf{S}\|_1, \quad (9.35)$$

by alternately and optimally solving both the following convex subproblems:

$$\underset{\mathbf{S} \geq 0}{\operatorname{argmin}} \|\mathbf{Y} - \mathbf{A}\mathbf{S}\|_2^2 + \|\mathbf{\Lambda} \odot \mathbf{S}\|_1, \quad (9.36)$$

$$\underset{\mathbf{A} \geq 0}{\operatorname{argmin}} \|\mathbf{Y} - \mathbf{A}\mathbf{S}\|_2^2, \quad (9.37)$$

using the forward-backward algorithm (Combettes and Wajs 2005), fully described in 7.4.2. Here, $\odot$ is the term-by-term multiplication operator.

In the same way as in the standard version of GMCA, the sparsity parameter $\mathbf{\Lambda}$ is automatically controlled so as to deal with a Gaussian noise contamination. A full implementation is available online on the GMCALab webpage www.cosmostat .org/GMCALab.html. This framework was later updated (Rapin et al. 2014, 2013b,c) so as to encompass sparse priors in a possibly redundant transform domain, using either the synthesis formulation with the Generalized Forward-Backward algorithm (Raguet et al. 2013) (see Section 7.4.6):

$$\underset{\mathbf{A} \geq 0, \, \mathbf{S}_w \mathbf{W} \geq 0}{\operatorname{argmin}} \|\mathbf{Y} - \mathbf{A}\mathbf{S}_w\mathbf{W}\|_2^2 + \lambda\|\mathbf{\Lambda} \odot \mathbf{S}_w\|_1, \quad (9.38)$$

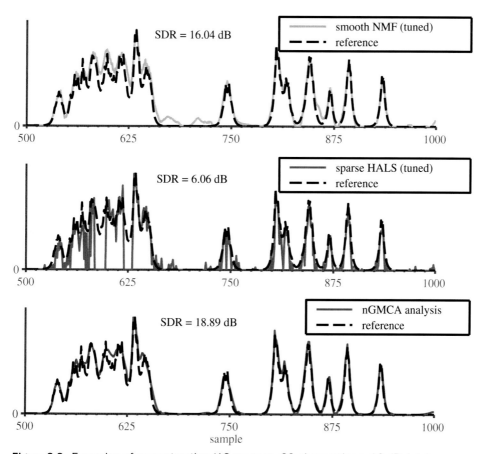

Figure 9.9. Examples of reconstruction (12 sources, 32 observations, 10 dB data).

or the analysis formulation with the Chambolle-Pock algorithm Chambolle and Pock (2010):

$$\operatorname*{argmin}_{\mathbf{A}\geq 0,\ \mathbf{S}\geq 0} \|\mathbf{Y} - \mathbf{AS}\|_2^2 + \lambda \|\mathbf{\Lambda} \odot (\mathbf{SW}^T)\|_1 . \tag{9.39}$$

The analysis formulation gives a better result (Rapin et al. 2013a), and the new algorithm, nGMCA, has been tested on simulated nuclear magnetic resonance (NMR) data together with sparse hierarchical alternating least squares (HALS) (Cichocki et al. 2007, 2009), which uses sparsity in the direct domain, and smooth NMF (Zdunek and Cichocki 2007), which uses a smooth regularization. Figure 9.9 shows the estimation of one of the mixed sources (dashed black line) using smooth NMF, sparse HALS, and nGMCA. While the smooth regularization of smooth NMF smooths out the peaks and the sparse prior of sparse HALS does not capture the continuity of the source, nGMCA is able to properly capture the structure of the source.

The source-to-distortion ratio (SDR) displayed on the plots was developed in Vincent et al. (2006). It increases when the quality of the estimation increases, with less interference, less noise, and fewer artifacts. Their values confirm that using sparsity in the wavelet domain yields higher quality reconstructions.

Figure 9.10 provides more quantitative results. This benchmark shows the behavior of the algorithms for various levels of noise, still on simulated NMR data. It

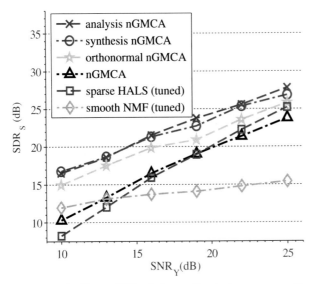

Figure 9.10. Mean SDR of the estimated sources with respect to the noise level in dB (simulated NMR spectra, 12 sources, 32 observations, average of 36 simulations).

includes the synthesis and the analysis formulations using redundant wavelet transforms, as well as a version using orthonormal wavelets — for which both formulations are equivalent. The algorithms using sparsity in the wavelet domain outperform the other ones. The redundancy of the transform in the algorithms using the analysis and the synthesis formulations provides an additional 3 dB compared to the one using orthonormal wavelets. All these versions are also available on the GMCALab webpage, and more details are provided in Rapin et al. (2014).

9.6 GUIDED NUMERICAL EXPERIMENTS

9.6.1 GMCAlab

GMCALab is a library of Matlab routines that implements the algorithms described here for multichannel signal/image bind source separation. The GMCALab library provides open source tools for BSS, and may be used to reproduce the BSS experiment below and to redo the figures with variations in the parameters. The library is available at the book's web site (http://www.SparseSignalRecipes.info). It requires at least WaveLab (see Section 2.9.1) to avail of full functionality. It has been successfully tested for all major operating systems, under Matlab 6.x and Matlab 7.x. GMCALab is distributed for noncommercial use.

9.6.2 Reproducible Experiment

Figure 9.11 illustrates the results provided by the script `sparse_noisy_examples.m` which applies the fast GMCA Algorithm 37 to a BSS problem with $N_s = 4$ sources, $N_c = 10$ noisy channels, and SNR = 10 dB. The mixing matrix is randomly generated

Figure 9.11. Results of the BSS guided experiment: $N_s = 4$ sources, $N_c = 10$ noisy channels, with SNR $= 10$ dB. The mixing matrix is randomly generated with entries independent and identically distributed $\sim \mathcal{N}(0, 1)$. The dictionary used in GMCA contained the OWT. (left) Original sources. (middle) Four out of ten noisy mixtures. (right) Sources estimated using the fast GMCA Algorithm 37.

with entries independent and identically distributed $\sim \mathcal{N}(0, 1)$. The fast GMCA was applied using the OWT dictionary.

9.7 SUMMARY

In this chapter, the role of sparsity and morphological diversity was highlighted to solve the blind source separation problem. Based on these key ingredients, a fast algorithmic approach coined GMCA was described together with variations to solve several problems including BSS. The conclusions that one has to keep in mind are essentially twofold: first, sparsity and morphological diversity lead to enhanced separation quality, and second, the GMCA algorithm takes better advantage of sparsity yielding better and robust-to-noise separation. When the number of sources is unknown, a GMCA-based method was described to objectively estimate the correct number of sources. This chapter also extends the GMCA framework to cope with the nonnegative matrix factorization. The results are given that illustrate the reliability of morpho-spectral sparsity regularization. In a wider framework, GMCA is shown to provide an effective basis for solving classical multichannel restoration problems such as color image inpainting.

Nonetheless, this exciting field of sparse BSS still has many interesting open problems. Among them, one may cite, for instance, the extension to the underdetermined case with more sources than channels, and the theoretical guarantees of the sparsity-regularized BSS problem.

10

Dictionary Learning

10.1 INTRODUCTION

A data set can be decomposed in many dictionaries, and we argue in this book that the "best" dictionary is the one providing the sparsest (most economical) representation. In practice, it is convenient to use dictionaries with a fast implicit transform (such as those described in detail in the previous chapters), which allows us to directly obtain the coefficients and reconstruct the signal from these coefficients using fast algorithms running in linear or almost linear time (unlike matrix-vector multiplications). We have also seen in Chapter 8 that fixed dictionaries can be gathered together in order to build a larger dictionary that can describe the data in a more versatile way. All these dictionaries are designed to handle specific contents and are restricted to signals and images that are of a certain type. For instance, Fourier represents stationary and periodic signals well, wavelets are good for analyzing isotropic objects of different scales, curvelets are designed for anisotropic and curvilinear features. Hence, the representation space that we use in our analysis can be seen as a prior we have on our data. Fixed dictionaries, though they have very fast implicit analysis and synthesis operators, which makes them attractive from a practical point of view, cannot guarantee sparse representations of new classes of signals of interest that present more complex patterns and features. What can one do if the data cannot be sufficiently sparsely represented by any of these fixed (or combined) existing dictionaries or if is not known the morphology of features contained in our data? Is there a way to make our data analysis more adaptive by optimizing for a dedicated dictionary? To answer these questions, a new field has emerged called **Dictionary Learning** (DL). Dictionary learning offers the possibility of learning an adaptive dictionary Φ directly from the data (or from a set of exemplars that we believe represent the data well). DL is at the interface of machine learning and signal processing.

The problem of dictionary learning in its overdetermined form (that is, when the number of atoms in the dictionary is smaller than or equal to the ambient dimension of the signal) has been studied in depth and can be approached using many viable techniques such as principal component analysis (PCA) and its variants. These approaches are based on algorithms minimizing the reconstruction errors on a training set of samples while representing them as a linear combination of the dictionary elements (Bishop 2006). Inspired by an analogy to the learning mechanism used by the simple cells in the visual cortex, Olshausen and Field (1996b) were the first to propose a way of learning the dictionary from the data and to insist on the dictionary redundancy. They have applied this learning scheme to small blocks, termed patches, extracted from natural images. The major conclusion of this line of research is that learning over a large set of disparate natural images leads to localized atoms that look like oriented edge filters. Since then, other approaches to dictionary learning have been proposed; see, e.g., Bell and Sejnowski (1997); Lewicki and Sejnowski (2000); Kreutz-Delgado et al. (2003); Engan et al. (1999) and Aharon et al. (2006).

Recent works have shown that designing adaptive dictionaries and learning them on the data themselves, instead of using predesigned selections of analytically driven atoms, leads to state-of-the-art performance in various tasks of image and signal processing, including denoising (Elad and Aharon 2006), inpainting (Mairal et al. 2010), or more generally inverse problems (Peyré et al. 2010).

In this chapter, we will only tackle DL in its sparsity-synthesis version. Its analysis counterpart is more intricate and has started to be developed in the literature only recently (Peyré et al. 2010; Rubinstein et al. 2013; Yaghoobi Vaighan et al. 2013).

10.2 DICTIONARY LEARNING STRATEGY

10.2.1 A Matrix Factorization Problem

Let $x_i \in \mathbb{R}^N, i = 1, \ldots, P$, be a set of exemplar signals. Denote the matrix $\mathbf{X} \in \mathbb{R}^{N \times P}$, storing the x_i vectors as its columns. The aim of DL is to solve the (possibly approximate) factorization problem of $\mathbf{X}$:

$$\text{find } \mathbf{\Phi} \text{ and } \alpha \text{ such that } \quad \mathbf{X} \approx \mathbf{\Phi}\alpha \tag{10.1}$$

where $\mathbf{\Phi} \in \mathbb{R}^{N \times T}$ is the dictionary of T atoms, and $\alpha \in \mathbb{R}^{T \times P}$ is the matrix whose i-th column is the synthesis coefficients vector α_i of the exemplar x_i in $\mathbf{\Phi}$, i.e. $x_i \approx \mathbf{\Phi}\alpha_i$. The goal of DL is to jointly infer $\mathbf{\Phi}$ and α from the sole knowledge of $\mathbf{X}$. Observe in passing that this problem bears close similarities with the blind source separation (BSS) problem considered in Chapter 9, where the role of the dictionary in DL parallels that of the mixing matrix in BSS, and the coefficients α that of the sources.

In general, (10.1) is clearly ill posed because the number of uknowns, $\mathbf{\Phi}$ and α, is much higher than the number of observations. Even in the overdetermined case, the components in (10.1) can only be identified up to a scale change and permutation. Thus, additional a priori knowledge is required to bring back this problem to the land of well posedness.

Our main prior here is that α is sparse. Therefore, DL can be cast as the following optimization problem:

$$\min_{\mathbf{\Phi},\alpha} \frac{1}{2} \|\mathbf{X} - \mathbf{\Phi}\alpha\|_{\mathrm{F}}^2 + \sum_{i=1}^{T} \lambda_i \|\alpha_i\|_p^p \quad \text{s.t.} \quad \mathbf{\Phi} \in \mathcal{D}, \tag{10.2}$$

where $p \in [0, 1]$, $\lambda_i > 0$ is the regularization parameter for vector α_i. Usually, $\lambda_i \equiv \lambda > 0$, for all i. The quadratic data fidelity accounts for the approximation error, and

$\mathcal{D}$ is a nonempty closed constraint set. An important constraint that $\mathcal{D}$ must deal with is to remove the scale ambiguity. Indeed, if $(\Phi^\star, \alpha^\star)$ is a minimizer of (10.2), then by bilinearity, for any $s \in \mathbb{R}$, $(s\Phi^\star, \alpha^\star/s)$ is also a minimizer with regularization parameter $|s|^p \lambda_i$. A standard constraint to remove this ambiguity is to enforce the atoms (columns of Φ) to be scaled to a norm equal to (resp. less than) 1, in which case $\mathcal{D}$ is the Cartesian product of unit Euclidean spheres (resp. balls). Additional constraints might be considered; for example, zero-mean atoms, orthogonality, or even physical constraints to accommodate for the specific sought-after applications.

10.2.2 Patch-Based Learning

It is in general numerically intractable to deploy the above DL strategy on large-scale exemplars. However, in many applications, this can be avoided. For instance, natural images are known to exhibit nonlocal self-similarities, meaning that non-necessarily nearby fragments (blocks/patches) carry very close information content. Based on this simple observation, several authors have proposed applying DL directly on the image patches, which would serve as the exemplars (Elad and Aharon 2006; Mairal et al. 2010; Peyré et al. 2010). This leads to patch-sized atoms, which entail a locality of the resulting algorithms. This locality can be turned back into a global treatment of larger images by appropriate tiling of the patches as we describe concretely now.

Consider an image x of $N = n^2$ pixels, arranged as a vector in $\mathbb{R}^N$. We consider square patches of size $Q = q \times q$, and the number of patches is $P = n/\Delta \times n/\Delta = N/\Delta^2$, where $1 \leq \Delta \leq q$ controls the subsampling of the patch extraction process. We denote by $R_k(x) \in \mathbb{R}^Q$ the patch extracted from x, where $k = (k_1, k_2)$ indexes the central location of the patch ($0 \leq k_{1,2} < n/\Delta$) in the image. Although k is a pair of integers to index two-dimensional patches, it is conveniently converted into a single integer in $\{1, \ldots, P\}$ after rearranging the patches in a vectorized form to store them as column vectors in a matrix.

Let $\alpha_k \in \mathbb{R}^T$ be the synthesis coefficients vector representing the patch $R_k(x)$ in Φ. Collect now the patches $R_k(x)$ as the P columns in the matrix $\mathbf{X} \in \mathbb{R}^{Q \times P}$, and the vectors α_k as the columns of $\alpha \in \mathbb{R}^{T \times P}$. The DL problem from these patches amounts to solving (10.2) for $\Phi \in \mathbb{R}^{Q \times T}$ and α.

10.2.3 Learning from Large Exemplars or Patches?

As just seen, the dictionary can be learned either from a database of exemplars or from patches extracted from the observed data. Each method has its pros and cons. For instance, it may happen that one has a sufficiently rich databases of exemplars. In some applications, such as astronomy, one may even be able to simulate replications from the class to which the observed data belong. In this case, the dictionary is learned once and for all on the whole data and can be used for subsequent treatments. However, this can become computationally expensive even at moderate sizes, not to mention the storage and the cost of applying the dictionary and its tranpose. Moreover, good exemplar databases with sufficiently rich and diverse content are not always available. In such a case, patch-based learning may be a good option, with the proviso that the self-similarity assumption holds. The resulting dictionary is of small size, which makes the overall treatment computationally simpler and tractable.

However, if the observed data are degraded, typically with noise or even a forward operator, then DL cannot be applied directly to the patches of the observations, instead a proxy has to be created in a wise way as we see in Section 10.3.

10.2.4 Alternating Minimization

Problem (10.2) is non-convex even if $\mathcal{D}$ is convex and $p = 1$. It is therefore very challenging to optimize. In the same vein as what has been done for BSS, we can adopt the following alternating (à la Gauss-Seidl) minimization strategy:

$$\alpha^{(t+1)} \in \underset{\alpha}{\operatorname{argmin}} \frac{1}{2} \left\| \mathbf{X} - \mathbf{\Phi}^{(t)} \alpha \right\|_{\mathrm{F}}^2 + \lambda \|\alpha_i\|_p^p, \tag{10.3}$$

$$\mathbf{\Phi}^{(t+1)} \in \underset{\mathbf{\Phi} \in \mathcal{D}}{\operatorname{argmin}} \left\| \mathbf{X} - \mathbf{\Phi} \alpha^{(t+1)} \right\|. \tag{10.4}$$

When $p = 1$ and $\mathcal{D}$ is convex (e.g., Euclidean ball), it was shown in Peyré et al. (2010), using tools from Tseng (2001), that this alternating scheme converges to a stationary point. For $p \in [0, 1]$ and $\mathcal{D}$ semi-algebraic (e.g., Cartesian product of Euclidean balls or spheres; see Section 7.6.1 for discussion of semi-algebraicity), it can be shown that again the alternating strategy converges to a stationary point, based on the arguments in (Bolte et al. 2014).

Most DL methods are based on a similar alternating strategy, and they differ essentially in the specific schemes used to solve the sparse coding and/or the dictionary update problem. Algorithm 39 summarizes the two main steps of a typical DL algorithm with the different schemes used in each step, and that which we describe in the next section.

Algorithm 39 Dictionary Learning via Alternating Minimization

---

Input: exemplars or patches $\mathbf{X}$, regularization parameter or target sparsity level.
Initialization: initial dictionary $\mathbf{\Phi}^{(0)}$.
Main iteration:
for $t = 0$ **to** $N_{\mathrm{iter}} - 1$ **do**

- Sparse coding: Update $\alpha^{(t+1)}$ for fixed $\mathbf{\Phi}^{(t)}$ (Section 10.2.4.1).
- Dictionary update: Update $\mathbf{\Phi}^{(t+1)}$ for fixed $\alpha^{(t+1)}$ (Section 10.2.4.2).

Output: Sparse codes $\alpha^{(N_{\mathrm{iter}})}$ and dictionary $\mathbf{\Phi}^{(N_{\mathrm{iter}})}$.

10.2.4.1 Sparse Coding

In (10.3), the dictionary is fixed, and the problem is marginally minimized with respect to the cofficients. This corresponds to a standard sparse coding problem as we extensively described in Chapter 7. Indeed, for $p = 1$, (10.3) is in fact the Lasso problem (7.4). It can then be solved using the Forward-Backward Algorithm 25 or its accelerated version FISTA, Algorithm 26. For the non-convex case $p \in [0, 1[$, problem (10.3) has the structure of (7.68). It can then be solved efficiently with the provably convergent forward-backward algorithm (7.69).

Greedy-type algorithms (such as matching pursuit) are also widely used in the sparse coding step, though there is no guarantee in general that they solve any optimization problem, and even less so the alternating minimization (10.3). An alternative choice is to use iteratively reweighted algorithms (see Section 7.6.2), such as advocated in Engan et al. (1999) who used IRLS. Convergence to a stationary point of (10.3) can be ensured in this case.

10.2.4.2 Dictionary update
For (10.4), the coefficients are held fixed and the dictionary is updated. There are several strategies for this step.

Projected Gradient Descent
If $\mathcal{D}$ were simple, meaning that the projector on $\mathcal{D}$ is easy to compute (typically for $\mathcal{D}$ the Cartesian product of Euclidean balls or spheres), then step (10.4) can be achieved via a projected gradient descent, which is a special instance of the forward-backward algorithm (7.39) (with some care taken on the choice of the descent stepsize in the non-convex case). When $\mathcal{D}$ is also convex, then the accelerated version FISTA (7.40) can be a good choice.

To be concrete, consider the case where the atoms are constrained to a zero-mean and unit norm, i.e., $\mathcal{D} = \mathcal{D}_1 \times \mathcal{D}_2 \times \cdots \times \mathcal{D}_T$ where, for $k = 1, \ldots, T$,

$$\mathcal{D}_k = \left\{ \varphi \in \mathbb{R}^Q | \sum_{i=1}^{Q} \varphi[i] = 0 \right\} \cap \{ \varphi \in \mathbb{R}^Q | \|\varphi\| = 1 \} .$$

Then, the projected gradient descent algorithm for problem (10.4) starts at $\mathbf{\Phi}^{(t)}$ and iterates as

$$\mathbf{\Phi}^{(l+1)} = \mathrm{P}_{\mathcal{D}} \left(\mathbf{\Phi}^{(l)} + \mu \left(\mathbf{X} - \mathbf{\Phi}^{(l)} \boldsymbol{\alpha}^{(t+1)} \right) \boldsymbol{\alpha}^{(t+1)\mathrm{T}} \right) , \qquad (10.5)$$

where $\mu \in]0, 1/\|\boldsymbol{\alpha}^{(t+1)}\|^2[$,

$$\mathrm{P}_{\mathcal{D}}(\mathbf{\Phi}) = \left(\mathrm{P}_{\mathcal{D}_1}(\varphi_1) \cdots \mathrm{P}_{\mathcal{D}_k}(\varphi_k) \cdots \cdots \mathrm{P}_{\mathcal{D}_T}(\varphi_T) \right) ,$$

and $\mathrm{P}_{\mathcal{D}_k}(\varphi_k)$ has the explicit expression

$$\mathrm{P}_{\mathcal{D}_k}(\varphi_k) = \begin{cases} \frac{\varphi_k - c}{\|\varphi_k - c\|} & \text{if } \varphi_k - c \neq 0 \\ \text{any vector on } \mathcal{D}_k & \text{otherwise} , \end{cases} \qquad (10.6)$$

where $c = \frac{1}{Q} \sum_{i=1}^{Q} \varphi_k[i]$.

The projected gradient descent can be quite slow, especially depending on the estimate of the Lipschitz constant in the choice of the descent stepsize μ. When the constraint set $\mathcal{D}$ is convex and simple, one can appeal to the accelerated version, FISTA (7.40).

Method of Optimal Directions (MOD)

Suppose that the constraint in (10.4) is ignored. Then, we recover a least-squares problem. If $P \geq T$ (i.e., more patches/exemplars than atoms), this problem has a unique solution given by

$$\boldsymbol{\Phi}^{(t+1)} = \mathbf{X}\boldsymbol{\alpha}^{(t+1)+} = \mathbf{X}\boldsymbol{\alpha}^{(t+1)\mathrm{T}}\big(\boldsymbol{\alpha}^{(t+1)}\boldsymbol{\alpha}^{(t+1)\mathrm{T}}\big)^{-1}. \tag{10.7}$$

For small to moderate values of T, computing the least-squares solution (10.7) is affordable, while for large T, a conjugate gradient solver would be preferred. This is the MOD update proposed by (Engan et al. 1999).

Now, if the constraint on $\mathcal{D}$ is considered, the update (10.7) is no longer valid. It is then tempting, and is actually done in Engan et al. (1999) and other works, to just project $\boldsymbol{\Phi}^{(t+1)}$ in (10.7) on $\mathcal{D}$. However, despite its simplicity, one must be aware that the MOD update does not solve (10.4).

K-SVD

The K-SVD dictionary update proposed by (Aharon et al. 2006) consists of sweeping through the atoms and updating each atom one at a time. More precisely, assume that $\mathcal{D}$ is ignored for the moment in (10.4). To lighten the notation, we remove superscript $(t+1)$. Then the objective in equation (10.4) equivalently reads (remember also (9.3)),

$$\|\mathbf{X} - \boldsymbol{\Phi}\boldsymbol{\alpha}\|_{\mathrm{F}} = \|\mathbf{R}_k - \varphi_k\alpha^k\|, \tag{10.8}$$

where $\mathbf{R}_k = \mathbf{X} - \sum_{j \neq k} \varphi_j\alpha^j$, and α^j is the i-th row of $\boldsymbol{\alpha}$. Minimizing the objective (10.8) with respect to φ_k and α^k amounts to finding the best rank-1 approximation to $\mathbf{R}_k$, which has a closed-form solution given by the singular value decomposition (SVD) of $\mathbf{R}_k$. However, this is not a wise choice because it is likely to produce dense vectors α^k, and in turn, dense matrices $\boldsymbol{\alpha}$ after sweeping and updating all the atoms, while we are seeking sparse $\boldsymbol{\alpha}$.

The nice proposal of K-SVD is rather to apply SVD, but only to $\mathbf{R}_k$ restricted to the exemplars/patches that are actually using atom φ_k. Let $\Lambda(\alpha^k) = \{i|\alpha^k[i] \neq 0\}$ be the support of α^k. Denote, $\widetilde{\mathbf{R}}_k \in \mathbb{R}^{N \times |\Lambda(\alpha^k)|}$ as the restriction of $\mathbf{R}$ to its columns indexed by $\Lambda(\alpha^k)$, and similarly $\widetilde{\alpha}^k$ as the restriction of α^k to its entries indexed by $\Lambda(\alpha^k)$. Then (10.8) becomes

$$\left\|\widetilde{\mathbf{R}}_k - \varphi_k\widetilde{\alpha}^k\right\|_{\mathrm{F}}. \tag{10.9}$$

Let the SVD of $\widetilde{\mathbf{R}}_k = \mathbf{U}\boldsymbol{\Sigma}\mathbf{V}^*$. Take the solution of (10.9) $\varphi_k^{(t+1)}$ as the first column of $\mathbf{U}$, and the update of the coefficients vector $(\widetilde{\alpha}^k)^{(t+1)}$ as the first colmun of $\mathbf{V}$ multiplied by the leading singular value $\boldsymbol{\Sigma}[1, 1]$. An important consequence of this update is that the unit norm constraint is automatically ensured and the supports of the updated coefficients vectors are never enlarged. The name K-SVD is a tribute to K-Means, since the K-SVD obtains the updated dictionary by K (rather than T in our case) SVD computations, each determining one atom.

10.3 DICTIONARY LEARNING AND LINEAR INVERSE PROBLEMS

10.3.1 Problem Formulation

Suppose we observe (recall (7.1) in Chapter 7)

$$y = \mathbf{H}x_0 + \varepsilon \, ,$$

where the noise ε is bounded and $\mathbf{H} : \mathbb{R}^N \to \mathbb{R}^m$. The goal here is to solve this inverse problem and stably recover x_0 from the observations y. In Chapter 7, we tackled this in a very general framework where the dictionary was known and fixed. The goal in this section is also to adapt to the content of signals/images by simultaneously solving the inverse problem and learning the dictionary $\mathbf{\Phi}$. This can be cast as solving the following optimization problem (we focus on the ℓ_1 sparsity penalty):

$$\min_{x, \mathbf{\Phi} \in \mathcal{D}, (\alpha_k)_{1 \le k \le P}} \frac{1}{2} \|y - \mathbf{H}x\|^2 + \frac{\mu}{P} \left(\sum_{k=1}^{P} \frac{1}{2} \|R_k(x) - \mathbf{\Phi}\alpha_k\|^2 + \lambda \|\alpha_k\|_1 \right) \qquad (10.10)$$

where we recall from Section 10.2.2 that $R_k(x)$ stands for the patch extraction operator at location k, P is the number of patches (possibly overlapping), and μ and $\lambda > 0$ are parameters (whose choice is to be discussed later on). Clearly, if x were known and fixed to x_0, this problem is nothing but DL in (10.2). Thus, problem (10.10) attempts to use x as a proxy of x_0 to learn the corresponding dictionary. The weight $1/P$ compensates for the redundancy factor introduced by the overlap between the patches. This normalization allows one to rescale the learned dictionary energy, but obviously it could be also absorbed in the parameter μ.

10.3.2 Alternating Minimization

We again appeal to alternating minimization to solve (10.10). At iteration t, for fixed $x^{(t)}$, we recover a standard DL problem that can be solved using Algorithm 39. Updating x for fixed dictionary $\mathbf{\Phi}^{(t+1)}$ and sparse codes $\alpha_k^{(t+1)}$ involves solving

$$\min_{x \in \mathbb{R}^N} \|y - \mathbf{H}x\|^2 + \frac{\mu}{P} \sum_{k=1}^{P} \left\| R_k(x) - \mathbf{\Phi}^{(t+1)} \alpha_k^{(t+1)} \right\|^2$$

whose minimizer is unique and has the closed form

$$x^{(t+1)} = \left(\mathbf{H}^{\mathrm{T}} \mathbf{H} + \mu \mathbf{I} \right)^{-1} \left(\mathbf{H}^{\mathrm{T}} y + \frac{\mu}{P} \sum_{k=1}^{P} R_k^* \left(\mathbf{\Phi}^{(t+1)} \alpha_k^{(t+1)} \right) \right) , \qquad (10.11)$$

where R_k^* is the adjoint of the patch extraction operator. To derive this expression, we used the fact that $\frac{1}{P} \sum_{k=1}^{P} R_k^* R_k = \mathbf{I}$ (with special care at the boundaries). For a general operator $\mathbf{H}$, the update (10.11) requires solving a well-conditioned linear system, which can be computed by conjugate gradient. If $\mathbf{H}$ is known to be diagonalized in some domain (e.g., Fourier for convolution or space domain for inpainting), then (10.11) can be implemented very efficiently. For image denoising, where $\mathbf{H} = \mathbf{I}$, the update of $x^{(t+1)}$ reduces to the convex combination

$$x^{(t+1)} = (1+\mu)^{-1} \left(y + \frac{\mu}{P} \sum_{k=1}^{P} R_k^* (\boldsymbol{\Phi}^{(t+1)} \alpha_k^{(t+1)}) \right).$$

In plain words, this formula states that the updated image is computed by putting the patches reconstructed from their sparse codes back to their locations, averaging them (effector overlapping), and then averaging the result with y with weights, respectively, μ and 1.

Algorithm 40 recaps the main steps followed when solving (10.10). This algorithm is again guaranteed to converge; see Peyré et al. (2010).

Algorithm 40 Joint Dictionary Learning and Inverse Problem Solving

---

Input: observation y, operator $\mathbf{H}$, parameters μ and λ (or target sparsity level).
Initialization: $x^{(0)} = 0$, initial dictionary $\boldsymbol{\Phi}^{(0)}$.
for $t = 0$ **to** $N_{\text{iter}} - 1$ **do**

- Update $x^{(t+1)}$ using (10.11).
- Update $\alpha^{(t+1)}$ and $\boldsymbol{\Phi}^{(t+1)}$ with Algorithm 39 using $\boldsymbol{\Phi}^{(t)}$ as an initialization.

Output: Recovered $x^{(N_{\text{iter}})}$, sparse codes $\alpha^{(N_{\text{iter}})}$, and dictionary $\boldsymbol{\Phi}^{(N_{\text{iter}})}$.

10.3.3 Parameter Choice

The choice of the size of the learned dictionaries (size of the patch size $Q = q^2$, overlap Δ, and redundancy T/Q) is still an open problem in dictionary learning. For inpainting, for example, the size of the patches should be larger than that of the missing regions. Increasing the redundancy of the dictionary enables us to capture more complicated structures in the data, and a high overlap parameter allows us to reduce block artifacts. But this makes the learning more difficult (complexity increases with redundancy and overlap, and conditioning of the dictionary deteriorates with overcompleteness).

Selecting good values for μ and λ (or the target sparsity level) is also a delicate and difficult issue. The parameter μ should be adapted to the noise level. In the case where ε is a Gaussian white noise of variance σ_ε^2, μ is set so that the norm of the residuals is $\approx \sqrt{N}\sigma_\varepsilon$. As far as λ is concerned, the value $\lambda = \sigma^2/30$ has been advocated in Elad and Aharon (2006) and leads to good performance for denoising.

10.3.4 Centering-Invariant Dictionary Learning

In the previous sections, we considered only zero-mean and unit-norm constraints on the learned atoms. In many applications, many patches can be translated versions of each other. It is then wise to take such translation invariance[1] in the structure of the learned dictionary from the very beginning. This can, for instance, be achieved by taking the dictionary $\boldsymbol{\Phi}$ as a concatenation of convolution operators, whose respective kernels are prototypical atoms (to be learned). Another way is to observe that a translation-invariant dictionary should be insensitive to a shift of the patches. This is the proposal in Beckouche et al. (2013), who used a simple centering operator to capture such an invariance.

Given a patch $R_k(x)$, we define the centering operator C_k as

$$C_k\left(R_k(x)\right)[l] = \begin{cases} R_k(x)[l+i_k] & \text{if } 1 \leq l \leq q - i_k \\ R_k(x)[l+i_k-q] & \text{if } q - i_k < l \leq q \end{cases} \qquad (10.12)$$

and i_k is the smallest integer verifying

$$\begin{cases} C_k\left(R_k(x)\right)[q/2] = \max_l(|R_k(x)[l]|) & \text{if } q \text{ is even} \\ C_k\left(R_k(x)\right)[(q-1)/2] = \max_l(|R_k(x)[l]|) & \text{if } q \text{ is odd.} \end{cases}$$

The centering operator translates the original vector values in order to place the maximum value in magnitude in the central index position with periodic boundary conditions. When the original vector has more than one entry that reaches its maximum value in magnitude, the smallest index i_k is chosen. Observe that centering transfers translation to the patches, which has to be done once and for all.

The centering-invariant version of (10.10) is

$$\min_{x,\Phi\in\mathcal{D},(\alpha_k)_{1\leq k\leq P}} \frac{1}{2}\|y-\mathbf{H}x\|^2 + \frac{\mu}{P}\left(\sum_{k=1}^{P}\frac{1}{2}\|C_k(R_k(x)) - \Phi\alpha_k\|^2 + \lambda\|\alpha_k\|_1\right). \qquad (10.13)$$

The new problem does not change the update of the dictionary and sparse codes, except that they are learned from the centered patches $C_k\left(R_k(x)\right)$ rather than from the patches $R_k(x)$, as was done in (10.10). However, the update of $x^{(t+1)}$ changes slightly to become

$$x^{(t+1)} = \left(\mathbf{H}^\mathsf{T}\mathbf{H} + \mu\mathbf{I}\right)^{-1}\left(\mathbf{H}^\mathsf{T}y + \frac{\mu}{P}\sum_{k=1}^{P}C_k^*\left(R_k^*\left(\Phi^{(t+1)}\alpha_k^{(t+1)}\right)\right)\right). \qquad (10.14)$$

For $\mathbf{H} = \mathbf{I}$ (i.e., denoising), the update reads

$$x^{(t+1)} = (1+\mu)^{-1}\left(y + \frac{\mu}{P}\sum_{k=1}^{P}C_k^*\left(R_k^*\left(\Phi^{(t+1)}\alpha_k^{(t+1)}\right)\right)\right).$$

Compared to the previous non-centering aware version, the new update consists of applying the opposite translation to the patches reconstructed from their sparse codes, then putting them back in their locations, and finally averaging them. We leave as a simple exercise to the reader the adaptation of Algorithm 40 to incorporate the centering operator.

10.4 GUIDED NUMERICAL EXPERIMENTS

Dictionary learning with the different updating schemes presented in this chapter are implemented in the DictLearn toolbox made available freely under the CeCILL license for download at www.SparseSignal-Recipes.info. This toolbox is a collection of Matlab functions and scripts and uses some of the proximal splitting algorithms described in Chapter 7.

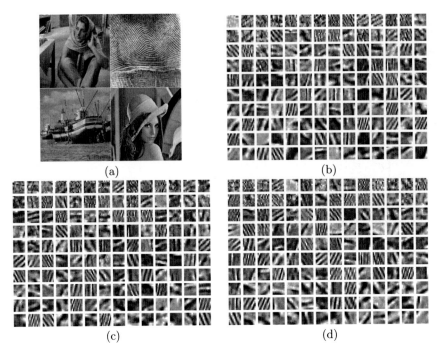

Figure 10.1. (a) Exemplars from which random patches were extracted. (b)-(d) Atoms learned using Algorithm 39 where the sparse codes are updated using ISTA ($\lambda = 0.02$), and the dictionary is updated using (b) projected gradient descent, (c) MOD, and (d) K-SVD. The number of extracted patches for learning is 3000, each patch is 10×10 ($Q = 10^2$), and the dictionary redundancy is $T/Q = 2$. Only 140 atoms out of 200 (selected at random) are shown.

10.4.1 Dictionary Learning

The results of this experiment can be reproduced with the script `Demos/testsDictionaryLearning.m` of the toolbox. Figure 10.1 shows two examples of dictionaries learned using Algorithm 39 from patches randomly extracted from some exemplar images shown in panel (a). The sparse codes are updated using ISTA (see Chapter 7) with $\lambda = 0.02$, and the dictionary updated using (b) projected is gradient descent, (c) MOD, and (d) K-SVD. The number of extracted patches is 3000, each patch is 10×10 ($Q = 10^2$), and the dictionary redundancy is $T/Q = 2$. One can see that the learned atoms exhibit both locally oscillatory patterns (textured areas) and piecewise smooth ones with oriented edges.

10.4.2 Centering-Invariant Learning and Denoising

In this experiment, we use a Hubble Space Telescope image of a nebula ($N = 512^2$ pixels) that we contaminate with an additive white Gaussian noise. We then apply Algorithm 40 in its centering version. Patches are of size 9×9 ($Q = 81$) with an overlap of eight pixels between patches. The dictionary redundancy is chosen to be

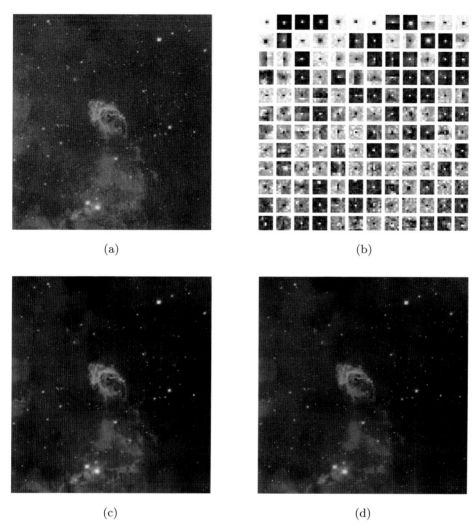

Figure 10.2. Results on a noisy nebula image. (a) Noisy image with input PSNR = 26.67 dB.
(b) Centering-invariant learned dictionary. (c) Wavelet-based denoising (PSNR = 33.61 dB).
(d) Joint centering-invariant dictionary learning and denoising (PSNR = 35.24 dB).

$T/Q = 2$. The number of extracted patches for learning is 6480. Figure 10.2 displays
the obtained results. Compared to wavelet-based denoising (see Chapter 6), which
achieves a PSNR = 33.61 dB, centering-invariant dictionary learning and denoising
shows a PSNR = 35.24 dB.

10.5 SUMMARY

Dictionary learning is a promising paradigm that allows us to capture complex geometrical content in images and can thus be exploited for many tasks. We described
how it can be combined wisely to solve linear inverse problems. On the practical side,

we showed its efficiency in image denoising and how it overcomes the performances of state-of-the-art denoising algorithms that use nonlearned dictionaries. The use of dictionary learning requires us to choose several parameters such as the patch size, the number of atoms in the dictionary, or the sparsity imposed during the learning process. Those parameters can have a significant impact on the quality of the recovered image or the computational cost of the processing.

11

Three-Dimensional Sparse Representations

11.1 INTRODUCTION

With the increasing computing power and memory storage capabilities of computers, it has become feasible to analyze 3-D data as a volume. Among the most simple transforms extended to 3-D are the separable wavelet transform (decimated, undecimated, or any other kind) and the discrete cosine transform (DCT), because these are separable transforms and thus the extension is straightforward. The DCT is mainly used in video compression, but has also been used in denoising (Rusanovskyy and Egiazarian 2005). As for the 3-D wavelets, they have already been used in denoising applications in many domains (Selesnick and Li 2003; Dima et al. 1999; Chen and Ning 2004).

However these separable transforms lack the directional nature that has facilitated the success of 2-D transforms such as curvelets. Consequently, a lot of effort has been made in recent years to build sparse 3-D data representations that better represent geometrical features contained in the data. The 3-D beamlet transform (Donoho and Levi 2002) and the 3-D ridgelet transform (Starck et al. 2005a) were, respectively, designed for 1-D and 2-D feature detection. Video denoising using the ridgelet transform was proposed in Carre et al. (2003). These transforms were combined with 3-D wavelets to build BeamCurvelets and RidCurvelets (Woiselle et al. 2010), which are extensions of the first-generation curvelets (Starck et al. 2002). Whereas most 3-D transforms are adapted to plate-like features, the BeamCurvelet transform is adapted to filaments of different scales and different orientations. Another extension of the curvelets to 3-D is the 3-D fast curvelet transform (Ying et al. 2005), which consists in of paving the Fourier domain with angular wedges in dyadic concentric squares, using the parabolic scaling law to fix the number of angles depending on the scale; it has atoms designed for representing surfaces in 3-D. The Surflet transform (Chandrasekaran et al. 2004) – a d-dimensional extension of the 2-D wedgelets (Donoho 1999; Romberg et al. 2002) – has been studied for compression purposes (Chandrasekaran et al. 2009). Surflets are an adaptive transform estimating each cube of a quad-tree decomposition of the data by two regions of constant value separated by a polynomial surface. Another possible representation uses the Surfacelets developed by Lu and Do (2005). It relies on the combination of a Laplacian pyramid and a d-dimensional directional filter bank. Surfacelets produce a tiling of the Fourier space in angular wedges in a way close to the curvelet transform, and can be interpreted as a 3-D adaptation of the 2-D contourlet transform. This transformation has also been applied to video denoising (Lu and Do 2007). More recently, Shearlets (Labate et al. 2005) have also been extended to 3-D (Negi and Labate 2012) and subsequently applied to video denoising and enhancement.

All these 3-D transforms are developed on Cartesian grids and are therefore appropriate to process 3-D cubes. However, in fields like geophysics and astrophysics, data are often naturally accessible on the sphere. This fact has led to the development of sparse representations on the sphere. Many wavelet transforms on the sphere have been proposed in recent years. (Starck et al. 2006) proposed an invertible isotropic undecimated wavelet transform (UWT) on the sphere, based on spherical harmonics. A similar wavelet construction (Marinucci et al. 2008; Faÿ and Guilloux 2011; Faÿ et al. 2008) used the so-called needlet filters. (Wiaux et al. 2008) also proposed an algorithm that permits reconstruction of an image from its steerable wavelet transform. Since reconstruction algorithms are available, these tools have been used for many applications such as denoising, deconvolution, component separation (Moudden et al. 2005; Bobin et al. 2008; Delabrouille et al. 2009), and inpainting (Abrial et al. 2007; Abrial et al. 2008). However, they are limited to 2-D spherical data.

The aim of this chapter is to review different kinds of 3-D sparse representations among those mentioned earlier, providing descriptions of the different transforms and examples of practical applications. In Section 11.2, we present several constructions of separable 3-D and 2-D-1-D wavelets. Section 11.3 describes the 3-D Ridgelet and Beamlet transforms that are, respectively, adapted to surfaces and lines spanning the entire data cube. These transforms are used as building blocks of the first-generation 3-D curvelets presented in Section 11.4. which can sparsely represent either plates or lines of different sizes, scales, and orientations. In Section 11.5, the 3-D Fast Curvelet is presented along with a modified Low Redundancy implementation to address the issue of the prohibitively redundant original implementation.

11.2 3-D WAVELETS

In this section we present two 3-D discrete wavelet constructions based on filter banks to enable fast transforms (in $O(N^3)$ where N^3 is the size of the data cube). These transforms, namely the 3-D biorthogonal wavelet and the 3-D Isotropic Undecimated Wavelet Transform, are built by separable tensor products of 1-D wavelets and are thus simple extensions of the 2-D transforms. They are complementary in the sense that the biorthogonal wavelet has no redundancy, which is especially appreciable in 3D at the cost of low performance for data restoration purposes, while the IUWT is redundant but performs very well in restoration applications. We also present a 2-D–1-D wavelet transform in Cartesian coordinates. In the final part of this section, this 2-D–1-D transform is demonstrated in an application to time-varying source detection in the presence of Poisson noise.

11.2.1 3-D Biorthogonal Wavelets

The DWT algorithm can be extended to any dimension by *separable* (tensor) products of a scaling function ϕ and a wavelet ψ.

In the three-dimensional algorithm, the scaling function is defined by $\phi(x, y, z) = \phi(x)\phi(y)\phi(z)$, and the passage from one resolution to the next is achieved by

$$c_{j+1}[k, l, m] = \sum_{p,q,r} h[p - 2k]h[q - 2l]h[r - 2m]c_j[p, q, r]$$

$$= [\bar{h}\bar{h}\bar{h} \star c_j]_{\downarrow 2,2,2}[k, l, m] \,, \tag{11.1}$$

where $[.]_{\downarrow 2,2,2}$ stands for the decimation by factor 2 along all x-, y-, and z-axes (i.e., only even pixels are kept) and $h_1 h_2 h_3 \star c_j$ is the 3-D discrete convolution of c_j by the separable filter $h_1 h_2 h_3$ (i.e., convolution first along the x-axis by h_1, then convolution along the y-axis by h_2, and finally convolution allong the z-axis by h_3).

The detail coefficients are obtained from seven wavelets:

- x wavelet: $\psi^1(x, y, z) = \psi(x)\phi(y)\phi(z)$,
- x-y wavelet: $\psi^2(x, y, z) = \psi(x)\psi(y)\phi(z)$,
- y wavelet: $\psi^3(x, y, z) = \phi(x)\psi(y)\phi(z)$,
- y-z wavelet: $\psi^4(x, y, z) = \phi(x)\psi(y)\psi(z)$,
- x-y-z wavelet: $\psi^5(x, y, z) = \psi(x)\psi(y)\psi(z)$,
- x-z wavelet: $\psi^6(x, y, z) = \psi(x)\phi(y)\psi(z)$,
- z wavelet: $\psi^7(x, y, z) = \phi(x)\phi(y)\psi(z)$,

which leads to seven wavelet subcubes (subbands) at each resolution level (see Fig. 11.1):

$$w^1_{j+1}[k, l, m] = \sum_{p,q,r} g[p - 2k]h[q - 2l]h[r - 2m]c_j[p, q, r] = [\bar{g}\bar{h}\bar{h} \star c_j]_{\downarrow 2,2,2}[k, l, m]$$

$$w^2_{j+1}[k, l, m] = \sum_{p,q,r} g[p - 2k]g[q - 2l]h[r - 2m]c_j[p, q, r] = [\bar{g}\bar{g}\bar{h} \star c_j]_{\downarrow 2,2,2}[k, l, m]$$

$$w^3_{j+1}[k, l, m] = \sum_{p,q,r} h[p - 2k]g[q - 2l]h[r - 2m]c_j[p, q, r] = [\bar{h}\bar{g}\bar{h} \star c_j]_{\downarrow 2,2,2}[k, l, m]$$

$$w^4_{j+1}[k, l, m] = \sum_{p,q,r} h[p - 2k]g[q - 2l]g[r - 2m]c_j[p, q, r] = [\bar{h}\bar{g}\bar{g} \star c_j]_{\downarrow 2,2,2}[k, l, m]$$

$$w^5_{j+1}[k, l, m] = \sum_{p,q,r} g[p - 2k]g[q - 2l]g[r - 2m]c_j[p, q, r] = [\bar{g}\bar{g}\bar{g} \star c_j]_{\downarrow 2,2,2}[k, l, m]$$

$$w^6_{j+1}[k, l, m] = \sum_{p,q,r} g[p - 2k]h[q - 2l]g[r - 2m]c_j[p, q, r] = [\bar{g}\bar{h}\bar{g} \star c_j]_{\downarrow 2,2,2}[k, l, m]$$

$$w^7_{j+1}[k, l, m] = \sum_{p,q,r} h[p - 2k]h[q - 2l]g[r - 2m]c_j[p, q, r] = [\bar{h}\bar{h}\bar{g} \star c_j]_{\downarrow 2,2,2}[k, l, m] \,.$$

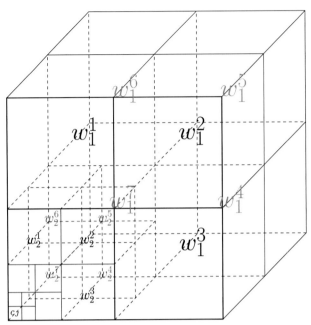

Figure 11.1. Decomposition of initial data cube into pyramidal wavelet bands. The bottom left cube c_J is the smoothed approximation, and the w_j^i are the different wavelet subbands at each scale j.

For a discrete $N \times N \times N$ data cube X, the transform is summarized in Algorithm 41.

Algorithm 41 The 3-D Biorthogonal Wavelet Transform

Data: $N \times N \times N$ data cube X
Result: $\mathcal{W} = \{w_1^1, w_1^2, \dots, w_1^7, w_2^1, \dots, w_J^1, \dots, w_J^7, c_J\}$ the 3-D DWT of X.
begin
    $c_0 = X, J = \log_2 N$
    for $j = 0$ to $J - 1$ **do**
        Compute $c_{j+1} = \bar{h}\bar{h}\bar{h} \star c_j$, down-sample by a factor 2 in each dimension.
        Compute $w_{j+1}^1 = \bar{g}\bar{h}\bar{h} \star c_j$, down-sample by a factor 2 in each dimension.
        Compute $w_{j+1}^2 = \bar{g}\bar{g}\bar{h} \star c_j$, down-sample by a factor 2 in each dimension.
        Compute $w_{j+1}^3 = \bar{h}\bar{g}\bar{h} \star c_j$, down-sample by a factor 2 in each dimension.
        Compute $w_{j+1}^4 = \bar{h}\bar{g}\bar{g} \star c_j$, down-sample by a factor 2 in each dimension.
        Compute $w_{j+1}^5 = \bar{h}\bar{g}\bar{g} \star c_j$, down-sample by a factor 2 in each dimension.
        Compute $w_{j+1}^6 = \bar{g}\bar{h}\bar{g} \star c_j$, down-sample by a factor 2 in each dimension.
        Compute $w_{j+1}^7 = \bar{h}\bar{h}\bar{g} \star c_j$, down-sample by a factor 2 in each dimension.
end

In a similar way to the 1-D case in (2.19) and with the proper generalization to 3-D, the reconstruction is obtained by

$$
\begin{aligned}
c_j = 8\big(&\tilde{h}\tilde{h}\tilde{h} \star [c_{j+1}]_{\uparrow 2,2,2} + \tilde{g}\tilde{h}\tilde{h} \star [w^1_{j+1}]_{\uparrow 2,2,2} + \tilde{g}\tilde{g}\tilde{h} \star [w^2_{j+1}]_{\uparrow 2,2,2} \\
&+ \tilde{h}\tilde{g}\tilde{h} \star [w^3_{j+1}]_{\uparrow 2,2,2} + \tilde{h}\tilde{g}\tilde{g} \star [w^4_{j+1}]_{\uparrow 2,2,2} + \tilde{g}\tilde{g}\tilde{g} \star [w^5_{j+1}]_{\uparrow 2,2,2} \\
&+ \tilde{g}\tilde{h}\tilde{g} \star [w^6_{j+1}]_{\uparrow 2,2,2} + \tilde{h}\tilde{h}\tilde{g} \star [w^7_{j+1}]_{\uparrow 2,2,2}\big) \ .
\end{aligned}
\tag{11.2}
$$

11.2.2 3-D Isotropic Undecimated Wavelet Transform

The main advantage of the biorthogonal wavelet transform introduced in the previous section is its nonredundancy: the transform of an $N \times N \times N$ cube is a cube of the same size. This property is particularly appreciable in three dimensions as the resources needed to process a 3-D signal scale faster than in lower dimensions. However, this discrete wavelet transform (DWT) is far from optimal for applications such as restoration (e.g., denoising or deconvolution), detection, or, more generally, analysis of data. Indeed, modifications of DWT coefficients introduce a large number of artifacts in the signal after reconstruction, mainly due to the loss of the translation-invariance in the DWT.

For this reason, for restoration and detection purposes, redundant transforms are generally preferred. Here, we present the 3-D version of the Isotropic Undecimated Wavelet Transform (IUWT) also known as the *starlet wavelet transform* because its 2-D version is well adapted to the more or less isotropic features found in astronomical data (Starck and Murtagh 1994; Starck and Murtagh 2006).

The starlet transform is based on a separable isotropic scaling function

$$
\phi(x, y, z) = \phi_{1D}(x)\phi_{1D}(y)\phi_{1D}(z) \ ,
\tag{11.3}
$$

where ϕ_{1D} is a 1-D B-spline of order 3:

$$
\phi_{1D}(x) = \frac{1}{12}\left(|x - 2|^3 - 4|x - 1|^3 + 6|x|^3 - 4|x + 1|^3 + |x + 2|^3\right).
\tag{11.4}
$$

The separability of ϕ is not a required condition but it allows fast computation, which is especially important for large-scale data sets in three dimensions.

The wavelet function is defined as the difference between the scaling functions of two successive scales:

$$
\frac{1}{8}\psi\left(\frac{x}{2}, \frac{y}{2}, \frac{z}{2}\right) = \phi(x, y, z) - \frac{1}{8}\phi\left(\frac{x}{2}, \frac{y}{2}, \frac{z}{2}\right).
\tag{11.5}
$$

This choice of wavelet function allows for a very simple reconstruction formula where the original data cube can be recovered by simple co-addition of the wavelet coefficients and the last smoothed approximation. Furthermore, since the scaling function is chosen to be isotropic, the wavelet function is therefore also isotropic. Figure 11.2 shows an example of such 3-D isotropic wavelet function.

The implementation of the starlet transform relies on the very efficient *à trous* algorithm; this French term means "with holes" (Holschneider et al. 1989; Shensa

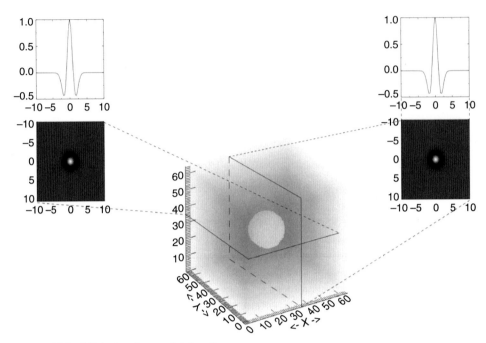

Figure 11.2. 3-D isotropic wavelet function.

1992). Let h be the filter associated with ϕ:

$$h[k, l, m] = h_{1D}[k]h_{1D}[l]h_{1D}[m] ,$$
$$h_{1D}[k] = [1, 4, 6, 4, 1]/16, \qquad k \in [-2, 2] , \tag{11.6}$$

and g the filter associated with the wavelet ψ:

$$g[k, l, m] = \delta[k, l, m] - h[k, l, m] . \tag{11.7}$$

The à trous algorithm defines for each j a scaled versions $h_{1D}^{(j)}$ of the 1-D filter h_{1D} such that

$$h_{1D}^{(j)}[k] = \begin{cases} h_{1D}[k] & \text{if } k \in 2^j\mathbb{Z} \\ 0 & \text{otherwise} . \end{cases} \tag{11.8}$$

For example, we have

$$h_{1D}^{(1)} = [\dots, h_{1D}[-2], 0, h_{1D}[-1], 0, h_{1D}[0], 0, h_{1D}[1], 0, h_{1D}[2], \dots] . \tag{11.9}$$

Due to the separability of h, for each j we can also define

$$h^{(j)}[k, l, m] = h_{1D}^{(j)}[k]h_{1D}^{(j)}[l]h_{1D}^{(j)}[m] \tag{11.10}$$
$$g^{(j)}[k, l, m] = \delta[k, l, m] - h_{1D}^{(j)}[k]h_{1D}^{(j)}[l]h_{1D}^{(j)}[m] . \tag{11.11}$$

From the original data cube c_0, the wavelet and approximation coefficients can now be recursively extracted using the filters $h^{(j)}$ and $g^{(j)}$:

$$c_{j+1}[k, l, m] = (\bar{h}^{(j)} \star c_j)[k, l, m] \tag{11.12}$$

$$= \sum_{p,q,r} h_{1D}[p]h_{1D}[q]h_{1D}[r]c_j[k + 2^j p, l + 2^j q, m + 2^j r]$$

$$w_{j+1}[k, l, m] = (\bar{g}^{(j)} \star c_j)[k, l, m] \tag{11.13}$$

$$= c_j[k, l, m] - \sum_{p,q,r} h_{1D}[p]h_{1D}[q]h_{1D}[r]c_j[k + 2^j p, l + 2^j q, m + 2^j r] .$$

Finally, due to the choice of wavelet function, the reconstruction is obtained by a simple co-addition of all the wavelet scales and the final smooth subband:

$$c_0[k, l, m] = c_J[k, l, m] + \sum_{j=1}^{J} w_j[k, l, m] . \tag{11.14}$$

The algorithm for the 3-D starlet transform is provided in Algorithm 42.

Algorithm 42 3-D Starlet Transform Algorithm

Data: $N \times N \times N$ data cube X
Result: $\mathcal{W} = \{w_1, w_2, \ldots, w_J, c_J\}$ the 3-D starlet transform of X.
begin

> $c_0 = X, J = \log_2 N, h_{1D}[k] = [1, 4, 6, 4, 1]/16, \ k = -2, \ldots, 2.$
> **for** $j = 0$ to $J - 1$ **do**
>> **for** each $k, l = 0$ to $N - 1$ **do**
>>> Carry out a 1-D discrete convolution of the cube c_j with periodic or reflexive boundary conditions, using the 1-D filter h_{1D}. The convolution is an interlaced one, where the $h_{1D}^{(j)}$ filter's sample values have a gap (growing with level, j) between them of 2^j samples, giving rise to the name à trous ("with holes").
>>>
>>> $$\alpha[k, l, \cdot] = h_{1D}^{(j)} \star c_j[k, l, \cdot] .$$
>>
>> **for** each $k, m = 0$ to $N - 1$ **do**
>>> Carry out a 1-D discrete convolution of α, using 1-D filter h_{1D}:
>>>
>>> $$\beta[k, \cdot, m] = h_{1D}^{(j)} \star \alpha[k, \cdot, m].$$
>>
>> **for** each $l, m = 0$ to $N - 1$ **do**
>>> Carry out a 1-D discrete convolution of β, using 1-D filter h_{1D}:
>>>
>>> $$c_{j+1}[\cdot, l, m] = h_{1D}^{(j)} \star \beta[\cdot, l, m].$$
>>
>> From the smooth subband c_j, compute the IUWT detail coefficients,
>>
>> $$w_{j+1} = c_j - c_{j+1}.$$

end

At each scale j, the starlet transform provides only one subband w_j, instead of the seven subbands produced by the biorthgonal transform. However, since the subbands are not decimated in this transform, each w_j has exactly the same number of voxels as the input data cube. The redundancy factor of the 3-D starlet transform is therefore $J + 1$ where J is the number of scales. Although it has a higher redundancy factor than the biorthogonal transform (equal to 1), the starlet transform offers a far reduced redundancy compared to a standard undecimated wavelet transform (the undecimated version of the DWT introduced in the previous section; see (Starck et al. 2010)), which has a redundancy factor of $7J + 1$.

11.2.3 2-D–1-D Wavelet Transform

So far, the 3-D wavelet transforms we have presented are constructed to handle full 3-D signals. However, in some situations the signals of interest are not intrinsically 3-D, but are constructed from a set of 2-D images where the third dimension is not spatial but can be temporal or in energy. In this case, analyzing the data with the previous 3-D wavelets makes no sense, and a separate treatment of the third dimension, not connected to the spatial domain, is required. One can define an appropriate wavelet for this kind of data by the tensor product of a 2-D spatial wavelet and a 1-D temporal (or energy) wavelet:

$$\psi(x, y, z) = \psi^{(xy)}(x, y)\psi^{(z)}(z) , \tag{11.15}$$

where $\psi^{(xy)}$ is the spatial wavelet and $\psi^{(z)}$ the temporal wavelet (respectively, energy). In the following, we consider only the isotropic spatial scale and dyadic scale, and we denote as j_1 the spatial scale index (i.e., scale $= 2^{j_1}$) and j_2 as the time (respectively, energy) scale index.

$$\psi^{(xy)}_{j_1, k_x, k_y}(x, y) = \frac{1}{2^{j_1}} \psi^{(xy)}\left(\frac{x - k_x}{2^{j_1}}, \frac{y - k_y}{2^{j_1}}\right) \tag{11.16}$$

$$\psi^{(z)}_{j_2, k_z}(z) = \frac{1}{\sqrt{2^{j_2}}} \psi^{(z)}\left(\frac{z - k_z}{2^{j_2}}\right) . \tag{11.17}$$

Hence, given a continuous data set D, we derive its 2-D–1-D wavelet coefficients $w_{j_1, j_2}(k_x, k_y, k_z) - k_x$ and k_y are spatial indices and k_z is a time (respectively, energy) index – according to

$$w_{j_1, j_2}(k_x, k_y, k_z) = \frac{1}{2^{j_1}} \frac{1}{\sqrt{2^{j_2}}} \int\!\!\!\int\!\!\!\int_{-\infty}^{+\infty} D(x, y, z) \quad \psi^{(z)*}\left(\frac{z - k_z}{2^{j_2}}\right)$$

$$\times \psi^{(xy)*}\left(\frac{x - k_x}{2^{j_1}}, \frac{y - k_y}{2^{j_1}}\right) dx dy dz$$

$$= \left\langle D, \psi^{(xy)}_{j_1, k_x, k_y} \psi^{(z)}_{j_2, k_z} \right\rangle . \tag{11.18}$$

11.2.3.1 Fast Undecimated 2-D–1-D Decomposition/Reconstruction

In order to have a fast algorithm, wavelet functions associated with a filter bank are preferred. Given a discrete data cube $D[k, l, m]$ this wavelet decomposition first applies a 2-D isotropic wavelet transform for each frame m. Using the 2-D version of the isotropic undecimated wavelet transform described in the previous section, we have

$$\forall m, \quad D[\cdot, \cdot, m] = c_{J_1}[\cdot, \cdot, m] + \sum_{j_1=1}^{J_1-1} w_{j_1}[\cdot, \cdot, m], \tag{11.19}$$

where J_1 is the number of spatial scales. Then, for each spatial location $[k, l]$ and for each 2-D wavelet scale scale j_1, an undecimated 1-D wavelet transform along the third dimension is applied on the spatial wavelet coefficients $w_{j_1}[k, l, \cdot]$

$$\forall k, l, \quad w_j[k, l, \cdot] = w_{j_1, J_2}[k, l, \cdot] + \sum_{j_2=1}^{J_2-1} w_{j_1, j_2}[k, l, \cdot], \tag{11.20}$$

where J_2 is the number of scales along the third dimension. The same processing is also applied on the coarse spatial scale $c_{J_1}[k, l, \cdot]$, and we have

$$\forall k, l, \quad c_{J_1}[k, l, \cdot] = c_{J_1, J_2}[k, l, \cdot] + \sum_{j_2=1}^{J_2-1} w_{J_1, j_2}[k, l, \cdot]. \tag{11.21}$$

Hence, we have a 2-D–1-D undecimated wavelet representation of the input data D:

$$D[k, l, m] = c_{J_1, J_2}[k, l, m] + \sum_{j_2=1}^{J_2-1} w_{J_1, j_2}[k, l, m]$$

$$+ \sum_{j_1=1}^{J_1-1} w_{j_1, J_2}[k, l, m] + \sum_{j_1=1}^{J_1-1} \sum_{j_2=1}^{J_2-1} w_{j_1, j_2}[k, l, m]. \tag{11.22}$$

In this decomposition, four kinds of coefficients can be distinguished:

- Detail-Detail coefficient ($j_1 < J_1$ and $j_2 < J_2$).

  $$w_{j_1, j_2}[k, l, \cdot] = (\delta - \bar{h}_{1D}) \star \left(h_{1D}^{(j_2-1)} \star c_{j_1-1}[k, l, \cdot] - h_{1D}^{(j_2-1)} \star c_{j_1}[k, l, \cdot] \right).$$

- Approximation-Detail coefficient ($j_1 = J_1$ and $j_2 < J_2$).

  $$w_{J_1, j_2}[k, l, \cdot] = h_{1D}^{(j_2-1)} \star c_{J_1}[k, l, \cdot] - h_{1D}^{(j_2)} \star c_{J_1}[k, l, \cdot].$$

- Detail-Approximation coefficient ($j_1 < J_1$ and $j_2 = J_2$).

  $$w_{j_1, J_2}[k, l, \cdot] = h_{1D}^{(J_2)} \star c_{j_1-1}[k, l, \cdot] - h_{1D}^{(J_2)} \star c_{j_1-1}[k, l, \cdot].$$

- Approximation-Appoximation coefficient ($j_1 = J_1$ and $j_2 = J_2$).

  $$c_{J_1, J_2}[k, l, \cdot] = h_{1D}^{(J_2)} \star c_{J_1}[k, l, \cdot].$$

As this 2-D–1-D transform is fully linear, a Gaussian noise remains Gaussian after transformation. Therefore, all thresholding strategies that have been developed for wavelet Gaussian denoising are still valid with the 2-D–1-D wavelet transform. Denoting δ, the thresholding operator, the denoised cube is obtained by

$$\tilde{D}[k, l, m] = c_{J_1, J_2}[k, l, m] + \sum_{j_1=1}^{J_1-1} \delta\big(w_{j_1, J_2}[k, l, m]\big)$$

$$+ \sum_{j_2=1}^{J_2-1} \delta\big(w_{J_1, j_2}[k, l, m]\big) + \sum_{j_1=1}^{J_1-1}\sum_{j_2=1}^{J_2-1} \delta\big(w_{j_1, j_2}[k, l, m]\big) . \quad (11.23)$$

A typical operator is the hard-threshold (i.e., $\delta_T(x) = 0$ is $|x|$ is below a given threshold T, and $\delta_T(x) = x$ is $|x| \geq T$). The threshold T is generally chosen between three and five times the noise standard deviation (Starck and Murtagh 2006).

11.2.4 Application: Time-Varying Source Detection

An application of the 2-D–1-D wavelets presented in the previous section has been developed in (Starck et al. 2009) in the context of source detection for the Large Area Telescope (LAT) instrument aboard the Fermi Gamma-Ray Space Telescope. Source detection in the high-energy gamma-ray band observed by the LAT is complicated by three factors: the low fluxes of point sources relative to the celestial foreground, the limited angular resolution, and the intrinsic variability of the sources.

The fluxes of celestial gamma rays are low, especially relative to the $\sim$1 m^2 effective area of the LAT (by far, the largest effective collecting area ever in the GeV range). An additional complicating factor is that diffuse emission from the Milky Way itself (which originates in cosmic-ray interactions with interstellar gas and radiation) makes a relatively intense, structured foreground emission. The few very brightest gamma-ray sources provide approximately 1 detected gamma ray per minute when they are in the field of view of the LAT, while the diffuse emission of the Milky Way typically provides about 2 gamma rays per second. Furthermore, in this energy band, the gamma-ray sky is quite dynamic, with a large population of sources such as gamma-ray blazars (distant galaxies whose gamma-ray emission is powered by accretion onto supermassive black holes) that flare episodically. The time scales of flares, which can increase the flux by a factor of 10 or more, can be minutes to weeks; the duty cycle of flaring in gamma rays is not well determined yet, but individual blazars can go months or years between flares. In general we do not know in advance where in the sky the sources will be found.

For previous high-energy gamma-ray missions, the standard method of source detection has been model fitting – maximizing the likelihood function while moving around trial point sources in the region of the sky being analyzed. This approach has been driven by the limited photon counts and the relatively limited resolution of gamma-ray telescopes.

Here, we present the different approach adopted by (Starck et al. 2009), which is based on a non-parametric method combining a MutliScale Variance Stabilization Transform (MS-VST) proposed for Poisson data denoising by (Zhang et al. 2008b) and a 2-D–1-D representation of the data. Using the time as the 1-D component of the 2-D–1-D transform, the resulting filtering method is particularly adapted to the rapidly time-varying low-flux sources in the Fermi LAT data.

Extending the MS-VST developed for the isotropic undecimated wavelet transform in (Zhang et al. 2008b), the 2-D–1-D MS-VST is implemented by applying a square root variance stabilization transform (VST) $\mathcal{A}_{j_1, j_2}$ to the approximation coefficients c_{j_1, j_2} before computing the wavelet coefficients as the difference of the stabilized approximation coefficients. The VST operator $\mathcal{A}_{j_1, j_2}$ is entirely determined by the filter h used in the wavelet decomposition and by the scales j_1, j_2; see (Zhang et al. 2008b) for the complete expression.

Plugging the MS-VST into the 2-D–1-D transform yields four kinds of coefficients:

■ Detail-Detail coefficient ($j_1 < J_1$ and $j_2 < J_2$).

$$w_{j_1, j_2}[k, l, \cdot] = (\delta - \overline{h}_{1D})$$
$$\star \left(\mathcal{A}_{j_1-1, j_2-1}\left[h_{1D}^{(j_2-1)} \star c_{j_1-1}[k, l, \cdot] \right] - \mathcal{A}_{j_1, j_2-1}\left[h_{1D}^{(j_2-1)} \star c_{j_1}[k, l, \cdot] \right] \right) .$$

■ Approximation-Detail coefficient ($j_1 = J_1$ and $j_2 < J_2$).

$$w_{J_1, j_2}[k, l, \cdot] = \mathcal{A}_{J_1, j_2-1}\left[h_{1D}^{(j_2-1)} \star c_{J_1}[k, l, \cdot] \right] - \mathcal{A}_{J_1, j_2}\left[h_{1D}^{(j_2)} \star c_{J_1}[k, l, \cdot] \right] .$$

■ Detail-Approximation coefficient ($j_1 < J_1$ and $j_2 = J_2$).

$$w_{j_1, J_2}[k, l, \cdot] = \mathcal{A}_{j_1-1, J_2}\left[h_{1D}^{(J_2)} \star c_{j_1-1}[k, l, \cdot] \right] - \mathcal{A}_{j_1-1, J_2}\left[h_{1D}^{(J_2)} \star c_{j_1-1}[k, l, \cdot] \right] .$$

■ Approximation-Appoximation coefficient ($j_1 = J_1$ and $j_2 = J_2$).

$$c_{J_1, J_2}[k, l, \cdot] = h_{1D}^{(J_2)} \star c_{J_1}[k, l, \cdot] .$$

All wavelet coefficients are now stabilized, and the noise on all wavelet coefficients w is Gaussian. Denoising is, however, not straightforward because there is no reconstruction formulas because the stabilizing operators $\mathcal{A}_{j_1, j_2}$ and the convolution operators along (x, y) and z do not commute. To circumvent this difficulty, this reconstruction problem can be solved by defining the multiresolution support (Murtagh et al. 1995) from the stabilized coefficients and by using an iterative reconstruction scheme.

As the noise on the stabilized coefficients is Gaussian, and without loss of generality we let its standard deviation equal 1, we consider that a wavelet coefficient $w_{j_1, J_2}[k, l, m]$ is significant (i.e., not due to noise) if its absolute value is larger than or equal to k, where k is typically between 3 and 5. The multiresolution support is obtained by detecting at each scale the significant coefficients. The multiresolution support for $j_1 \leq J_1$ and $j_2 \leq J_2$ is defined by

$$M_{j_1, j_2}[k, l, m] = \begin{cases} 1 & \text{if } w_{j_1, j_2}[k, l, m] \text{ is significant} \\ 0 & \text{if } w_{j_1, j_2}[k, l, m] \text{ is not significant} . \end{cases} \tag{11.24}$$

We denote $\mathcal{W}$ as the 2-D–1-D isotropic wavelet transform, $\mathcal{R}$ the inverse wavelet transform, and Y the input data. We want our solution X to reproduce exactly the

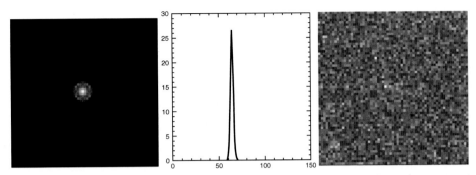

Figure 11.3. Simulated time-varying source. From left to right, simulated source, temporal flux, and co-added image along the time axis of noisy data. (See *color plates*.)

same coefficients as the wavelet coefficients of the input data Y, but only at scales and positions where significant signal has been detected in the 2-D–1-D MS-VST (i.e., $M\mathcal{W}X = M\mathcal{W}Y$). At other scales and positions, we want the smoothest solution with the lowest budget in terms of wavelet coefficients. Furthermore, since Poisson intensity functions are positive by nature, a positivity constraint is imposed on the solution. Therefore the reconstruction can be formulated as a constrained sparsity-promoting minimization problem that can be written as follows:

$$\min_{X} \| \mathcal{W}X \|_1 \quad \text{subject to} \quad \begin{cases} M\mathcal{W}X = M\mathcal{W}Y \\ X \ge 0, \end{cases} \qquad (11.25)$$

where $\| . \|_1$ is the ℓ_1-norm playing the role of regularization and is well known to promote sparsity (Donoho 2006b). This problem can be efficiently solved using the hybrid steepest descent algorithm (Yamada 2001; Zhang et al. 2008b), and requires around 10 iterations.

This filtering method is tested on a simulated time-varying source in a cube of size $64 \times 64 \times 128$, as a Gaussian centered at $(32, 32, 64)$ with a spatial standard deviation equal to 1.8 (pixel unit) and a temporal standard deviation equal to 1.2. The total flux

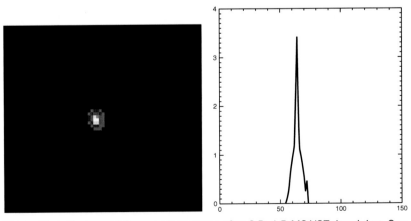

Figure 11.4. Recovered time-varying source after 2-D–1-D MS-VST denoising. One frame of the denoised cube (left) and flux per frame (right). (See *color plates*.)

of the source (i.e., spatial and temporal integration) is 100. A background level of 0.1 is added to the data cube and Poisson noise is generated. Figure 11.3 shows from left to right an image of the source, the flux per frame, and the integration of all frames along the time axis. As can be seen, the source is hardly detectable in the co-added image.

By running the 2-D MS-VST denoising method on the co-added frame, the source cannot be recovered, whereas the 2-D–1-D MS-VST denoising method is able to recover the source at 6σ from the noisy 3-D data set. Figure 11.4 (left) shows one frame (frame 64) of the denoised cube, and Figure 11.4 (right) shows the flux of the recovered source per frame.

11.3 3-D RIDGELETS AND BEAMLETS

Wavelets rely on a dictionary of roughly isotropic elements occurring at all scales and locations. They do not describe well highly anisotropic elements and contain only a fixed number of directional elements, independent of scale. Despite the fact that they have had a significant impact on image processing, they fail to efficiently represent objects with highly anisotropic elements such as lines or curvilinear structures (e.g., edges). The reason is that wavelets are non-geometrical and do not exploit the regularity of the edge curve. Following this reasoning, new constructions in 2-D have been proposed such as ridgelets (Candès and Donoho 1999) and beamlets (Donoho and Huo 2001a). Both transforms were developed as an answer to the weakness of the separable wavelet transform in sparsely representing what appear to be simple building-block atoms in an image, that is, lines and edges.

In this section, we present the 3-D extension of these transforms. In 3-D, the ridgelet atoms are sheets, while the beamlet atoms are lines. Both transforms share a similar fast implementation using the projection-slice theorem (Zhi-Oei Liang 2000) and constitute the building blocks of the first-generation 3-D curvelets presented in Section 11.4. An application of ridgelets and beamlets to the statistical study of the spatial distribution of galaxies is presented in the last part of this section.

11.3.1 The 3-D Ridgelet Transform

11.3.1.1 Continuous 3-D Ridgelet Transform

The continuous ridgelet transform can be defined in 3-D as a direct extension of the 2-D transform following (Candès and Donoho 1999). Pick a smooth univariate function $\psi : \mathbf{R} \to \mathbf{R}$ with vanishing mean $\int \psi(t)dt = 0$ and sufficient decay so that it verifies the *3D admissibility* condition:

$$\int |\hat{\psi}(v)|^2 |v|^{-3} dv < \infty . \tag{11.26}$$

Under this condition, one can further assume that ψ is normalized so that $\int |\hat{\psi}(v)|^2 |v|^{-3} dv = 1$. For each scale $a > 0$, each position $b \in \mathbf{R}$, and each orientation $(\theta_1, \theta_2) \in [0, 2\pi[\times [0, \pi[$, we can define a trivariate ridgelet function $\psi_{a,b,\theta_1,\theta_2} : \mathbf{R}^3 \to \mathbf{R}$ by

$$\psi_{a,b,\theta_1,\theta_2}(\mathbf{x}) = a^{-1/2} \psi\left(\frac{x_1 \cos\theta_1 \sin\theta_2 + x_2 \sin\theta_1 \sin\theta_2 + x_3 \cos\theta_2 - b}{a}\right), \tag{11.27}$$

where $\mathbf{x} = (x_1, x_2, x_3) \in \mathbf{R}^3$. This 3-D ridgelet function is now constant along the planes defined by $x_1 \cos \theta_1 \sin \theta_2 + x_2 \sin \theta_1 \sin \theta_2 + x_3 \cos \theta_2 = $ const. However, transverse to these ridges, it is a wavelet.

While the 2-D ridgelet transform was adapted to detect lines in an image, the 3-D ridgelet transform allows us to detect sheets in a cube.

Given an integrable trivariate function $f \in L_2(\mathbf{R}^3)$, its 3-D ridgelet coefficients are defined by:

$$\mathcal{R}_f(a, b, \theta_1, \theta_2) := \langle f, \psi_{a,b,\theta_1,\theta_2} \rangle = \int_{\mathbf{R}^3} f(\mathbf{x}) \psi^*_{a,b,\theta_1,\theta_2}(\mathbf{x}) d\mathbf{x}. \tag{11.28}$$

From these coefficients we have the following reconstruction formula:

$$f(\mathbf{x}) = \int_0^\pi \int_0^{2\pi} \int_{-\infty}^\infty \int_0^\infty \mathcal{R}_f(a, b, \theta_1, \theta_2) \psi_{a,b,\theta_1,\theta_2}(\mathbf{x}) \frac{da}{a^4} db \frac{d\theta_1 d\theta_2}{8\pi^2}, \tag{11.29}$$

which is valid almost everywhere for functions that are both integrable and square integrable. This representation of "any" function as a superposition of ridge functions is furthermore stable because it obeys the following Parseval relation:

$$\|f\|_2^2 = \int_0^\pi \int_0^{2\pi} \int_{-\infty}^\infty \int_0^\infty |\mathcal{R}_f(a, b, \theta_1, \theta_2)|^2 \frac{da}{a^4} db \frac{d\theta_1 d\theta_2}{8\pi^2}. \tag{11.30}$$

Just as can the 2-D ridgelets, the 3-D ridgelet analysis can be constructed as a wavelet analysis in the Radon domain. In 3-D, the Radon transform $\mathbf{R}(f)$ of f is the collection of hyperplane integrals indexed by $(\theta_1, \theta_2, t) \in [0, 2\pi[\times [0, \pi[\times \mathbf{R}$ given by

$$\mathbf{R}(f)(\theta_1, \theta_2, t) = \int_{\mathbf{R}^3} f(\mathbf{x}) \delta(x_1 \cos \theta_1 \sin \theta_2 + x_2 \sin \theta_1 \sin \theta_2 + x_3 \cos \theta_2 - t) d\mathbf{x}, \tag{11.31}$$

where $\mathbf{x} = (x_1, x_2, x_3) \in \mathbf{R}^3$ and δ is the Dirac distribution. Then the 3-D ridgelet transform is exactly the application of a 1-D wavelet transform along the slices of the Radon transform where the plane angle (θ_1, θ_2) is kept constant but t is varying:

$$\mathcal{R}_f(a, b, \theta_1, \theta_2) = \int \psi^*_{a,b}(t) \mathbf{R}(f)(\theta_1, \theta_2, t) dt, \tag{11.32}$$

where $\psi_{a,b}(t) = \psi((t - b)/a)/\sqrt{a}$ is a 1-dimensional wavelet.

Therefore, the basic strategy for calculating the continuous ridgelet transform in 3-D is again to compute first the Radon transform $\mathbf{R}(f)(\theta_1, \theta_2, t)$ and second to apply a 1-dimensional wavelet to the slices $\mathbf{R}(f)(\theta_1, \theta_2, \cdot)$.

11.3.1.2 Discrete 3-D Ridgelet Transform

A fast implementation of the Radon transform can be proposed in the Fourier domain thanks to the projection-slice theorem. In 3-D, this theorem states that the 1-D Fourier transform of the projection of a 3-D function onto a line is equal to the

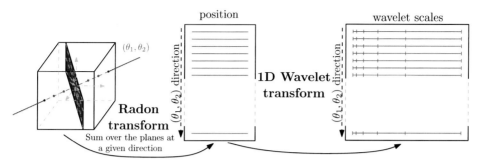

Figure 11.5. Overview of the 3-D ridgelet transform. At a given direction, sum over the normal plane to get a · point. Repeat over all its parallels to get the (θ_1, θ_2) line and apply a 1D wavelet transform on it. Repeat for all the directions to get the 3-D ridgelet transform.

slice in the 3-D Fourier transform of this function passing by the origin and parallel to the projection line.

$$\mathbf{R}(f)(\theta_1, \theta_2, t) = \mathbf{F}_{1D}^{-1}\big(u \in \mathbf{R} \mapsto \mathbf{F}_{3D}(f)(\theta_1, \theta_2, u)\big) . \tag{11.33}$$

The 3-D discrete ridgelet transform can be built in a similar way to the rectopolar 2-D transform (see Starck et al. (2010)) by applying a fast Fourier transform to the data in order to extract lines in the discrete Fourier domain. Once the lines are extracted, the ridgelet coefficients are obtained by applying a 1-D wavelet transform along these lines. However, extracting lines defined in spherical coordinates on the Cartesian grid provided by the fast Fourier transform is not trivial and requires some kind of interpolation scheme. The 3-D ridgelet is summarized in Algorithm 43 and in the flowgraph in Figure 11.5.

Algorithm 43 The 3-D Ridgelet Transform

Data: $N \times N \times N$ data cube X.
Result: 3-D Ridgelet Transform of X
begin
  – Apply a 3-D FFT to X to yield $\hat{X}[k_x, k_y, k_z]$.
  – Perform Cartesian-to-Spherical Conversion using an interpolation scheme to sample $\hat{X}$ in spherical coordinates $\hat{X}[\rho, \theta_1, \theta_2]$.
  – Extract $3N^2$ lines (of size N) passing through the origin and the boundary of $\hat{X}$.
  for each line $[\theta_1, \theta_2]$ **do**
    – apply an inverse 1D FFT
    – apply a 1-D wavelet transform to get the ridgelet coefficients
end

11.3.1.3 Local 3-D Ridgelet Transform

The ridgelet transform is optimal for finding sheets of the size of the cube. To detect smaller sheets, a partitioning must be introduced (Candès 1999). The cube c is decomposed into blocks of lower side length b so that for a $N \times N \times N$ cube, we count N/b blocks in each direction. After the block partitioning, the tranform is tuned for sheets of size $b \times b$ and of thickness a_j, a_j corresponding to the different dyadic scales used in the transformation.

11.3.2 The 3-D Beamlet Transform

The X-ray transform $\mathbf{X}f$ of a continuous function $f(x, y, z)$ with $(x, y, z) \in \mathbf{R}^3$ is defined by

$$(\mathbf{X}f)(L) = \int_L f(p)dp \, , \qquad (11.34)$$

where L is a line in $\mathbf{R}^3$, and p is a variable indexing points in the line. The transformation contains all line integrals of f. The beamlet transform (BT) can be seen as a multiscale digital X-ray transform. It is a multiscale transform because, in addition to the multiorientation and multilocation line integral calculation, it integrated also over line segments at different length. The 3-D BT is an extension to the 2-D BT proposed by Donoho and Huo (2001a).

The transform requires an expressive set of line segments, including line segments with various lengths, locations, and orientations lying inside a 3-D volume.

A seemingly natural candidate for the set of line segments is the family of *all* line segments between each voxel corner and every other voxel corner: the set of *3-D beams*. For a 3-D data set with n^3 voxels, there are $O(n^6)$ 3-D beams. It is not feasible to use the collection of 3-D beams as a basic data structure since any algorithm based on this set has a complexity with a lower bound of n^6 and hence is unworkable for the typical 3-D data size.

11.3.2.1 The Beamlet System
A dyadic cube $C(k_1, k_2, k_3, j) \subset [0, 1]^3$ is the collection of 3-D points

$$\{(x_1, x_2, x_3) : [k_1/2^j, (k_1 + 1)/2^j] \times [k_2/2^j, (k_2 + 1)/2^j] \times [k_3/2^j, (k_3 + 1)/2^j]\} \, ,$$

where $0 \le k_1, k_2, k_3 < 2^j$ for an integer $j \ge 0$, called the scale (see Fig. 11.6).

Such cubes can be viewed as descended from the unit cube $C(0, 0, 0, 0) = [0, 1]^3$ by recursive partitioning. Hence, splitting $C(0, 0, 0, 0)$ in half along each axis results

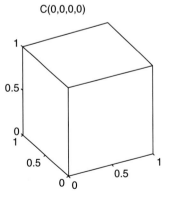
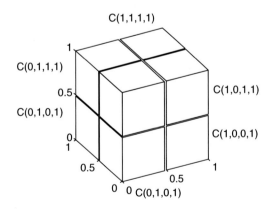

Figure 11.6. Dyadic cubes.

in eight cubes $C(k_1, k_2, k_3, 1)$ where $k_i \in \{0, 1\}$ splitting those in half along each axis results in 64 subcubes $C(k_1, k_2, k_3, 2)$ where $k_i \in \{0, 1, 2, 3\}$; and if we decompose the unit cube into n^3 voxels using a uniform n-by-n-by-n grid with $n = 2^J$ dyadic, then the individual voxels are the n^3 cells $C(k_1, k_2, k_3, J), 0 \leq k_1, k_2, k_3 < n$.

Associated with each dyadic cube, we can build a system of line segments that have both of their end-points lying on the cube boundary. We call each such segment a *beamlet*. If we consider all pairs of boundary voxel corners, we get $O(n^4)$ beamlets for a dyadic cube with a side length of n voxels (we actually work with a slightly different system in which each line is parametrized by a slope and an intercept instead of its end-points as explained later). However, we still have $O(n^4)$ cardinality. Assuming a voxel size of $1/n$ we get $J + 1$ scales of dyadic cubes where $n = 2^J$; for any scale $0 \leq j \leq J$ there are 2^{3j} dyadic cubes of scale j, and since each dyadic cube at scale j has a side length of 2^{J-j} voxels we get $O(2^{4(J-j)})$ beamlets associated with the dyadic cube and a total of $O(2^{4J-j}) = O(n^4/2^j)$ beamlets at scale j. If we sum the number of beamlets at all scales we get $O(n^4)$ beamlets.

This gives a multiscale arrangement of line segments in 3-D with controlled cardinality of $O(n^4)$. The scale of a beamlet is defined as the scale of the dyadic cube it belongs to, so lower scales correspond to longer line segments and finer scales correspond to shorter line segments. Figure 11.7 shows two beamlets at different scales.

To index the beamlets in a given dyadic cube we use slope-intercept coordinates. For a data cube of $n \times n \times n$ voxels consider a coordinate system with the cube center of mass at the origin and a unit length for a voxel. Hence, for (x, y, z) in the data cube we have $|x|, |y|, |z| \leq n/2$. We can consider three kinds of lines – *x-driven, y-driven, and z-driven* – depending on which axis provides the shallowest slopes. An *x*-driven line takes the form

$$\begin{cases} z &= s_z x + t_z \\ y &= s_y x + t_y \, , \end{cases} \tag{11.35}$$

with slopes s_z, s_y, and intercepts t_z and t_y. Here the slopes $|s_z|, |s_y| \leq 1$. The *y*- and *z*-driven lines are defined with an interchange of roles between x and y or z, as the

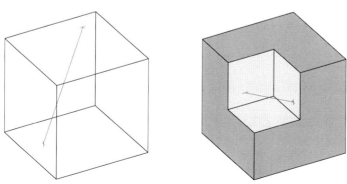

Figure 11.7. Examples of beamlets at two different scales. (a) Scale 0 (coarsest scale). (b) Scale 1 (next finer scale).

case may be. The slopes and intercepts run through equispaced sets:

$$s_x, s_y, s_z \in \{2\ell/n : \ell = -n/2, \dots, n/2 - 1\},$$

$$t_x, t_y, t_z \in \{\ell : -n/2, \dots, n/2 - 1\}.$$

Beamlets in a data cube of side n have lengths between $n/2$ and $\sqrt{3}n$ (the main diagonal).

Computational Aspects

Beamlet *coefficients* are line integrals over the set of beamlets. A digital 3-D image can be regarded as a 3-D piecewise constant function, and each line integral is just a weighted sum of the voxel intensities along the corresponding line segment. Donoho and Levi (2002) discuss in detail different approaches for computing line integrals in a 3-D digital image. Computing the beamlet coefficients for real application data sets can be a challenging computational task since, for a data cube with $n \times n \times n$ voxels, we have to compute $O(n^4)$ coefficients. By developing efficient cache-aware algorithms we are able to handle 3-D data sets of size up to $n = 256$ on a typical desktop computer in less than a day's running time. In many cases there is no interest in the coarsest scale coefficient that consumes most of the computation time, and then the overall running time can be significantly faster. The algorithms can also be easily implemented on a parallel machine of a computer cluster using a system such as message passing interface (MPI) in order to solve bigger problems.

11.3.2.2 The Fast Fourier Transform-Based Transformation

Let $\psi \in L_2(\mathbf{R}^2)$ be a smooth function satisfying the *admissibility* condition:

$$\int |\hat{\psi}(\boldsymbol{v})|^2 |\boldsymbol{v}|^{-3} d\boldsymbol{v} < \infty. \tag{11.36}$$

In this case, one can further assume that ψ is normalized so that $\int |\hat{\psi}(\boldsymbol{v})|^2 |\boldsymbol{v}|^{-3} d\boldsymbol{v} = 1$. For each scale a, each position $\mathbf{b} = (b_1, b_2) \in \mathbf{R}^2$, and each orientation $(\theta_1, \theta_2) \in [0, 2\pi[\times [0, \pi[$, we can define a trivariate *beamlet* function $\psi_{a,b_1,b_2,\theta_1,\theta_2} : \mathbf{R}^3 \to \mathbf{R}$ by

$$\psi_{a,\mathbf{b},\theta_1,\theta_2}(x_1, x_2, x_3) = a^{-1/2} \cdot \psi((-x_1 \sin\theta_1 + x_2 \cos\theta_1 + b_1)/a,$$

$$(x_1 \cos\theta_1 \cos\theta_2 + x_2 \sin\theta_1 \cos\theta_2 - x_3 \sin\theta_2 + b_2)/a). \tag{11.37}$$

The three-dimensional continuous beamlet transform of a function $f \in L_2(\mathbf{R}^3)$ is given by

$$\mathcal{B}_f : \mathbf{R}_+^* \times \mathbf{R}^2 \times [0, 2\pi[\times [0, \pi[\to \mathbf{R}$$

$$\mathcal{B}_f(a, \mathbf{b}, \theta_1, \theta_2) = \int_{\mathbf{R}^3} \psi_{a,\mathbf{b},\theta_1,\theta_2}^*(\mathbf{x}) f(\mathbf{x}) d\mathbf{x}. \tag{11.38}$$

Figure 11.8 shows an example of a beamlet function. It is constant along lines of direction (θ_1, θ_2) and a 2-D wavelet function along a plane orthogonal to this direction.

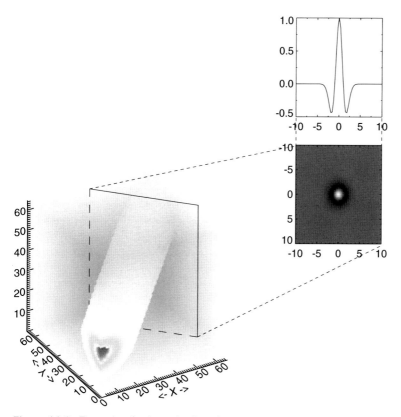

Figure 11.8. Example of a beamlet function.

The 3-D beamlet transform can be built using the "generalized projection-slice theorem" (Zhi-Oei Liang 2000). Let $f(\mathbf{x})$ be a function on $\mathbf{R}^n$, and let $\mathbf{R}_m f$ denote the m-dimensional partial Radon transform along the first m direction, $m < n$. $\mathbf{R}_m f$ is a function of $(p, \boldsymbol{\mu}_m; x_{m+1}, \ldots, x_n)$, and $\boldsymbol{\mu}_m$ is a unit directional vector in $\mathbf{R}^n$ note that for a given projection angle, the m-dimensional partial Radon transform of $f(\mathbf{x})$ has $(n - m)$ untransformed spatial dimensions and a (n-m+1) dimensional projection profile. The Fourier transform of the m-dimensional partial Radon transform, $\mathbf{R}_m f$, is related to $\mathbf{F}f$, the Fourier transform of f, by the projection-slice relation

$$\{\mathbf{F}_{n-m+1} \mathbf{R}_m f\}(k, k_{m+1}, \ldots, k_n) = \{\mathbf{F}f\}(k\boldsymbol{\mu}_m, k_{m+1}, \ldots, k_n) . \qquad (11.39)$$

Since the 3-D beamlet transform corresponds to wavelets applied along planes orthogonal to given directions (θ_1, θ_2), one can use the 2-D partial Radon transform to extract planes on which to apply a 2-D wavelet transform. Using the projection-slice theorem this partial Radon transform in this case can be efficiently performed by taking the inverse 2-D fast Fourier transforms on planes orthogonal to the direction of the beamlet extracted from the 3-D Fourier space. The FFT based 3-D beamlet transform is summarized in Algorithm 44.

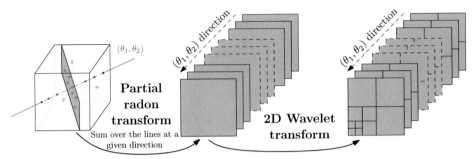

Figure 11.9. Schematic view of a 3-D beamlet transform. At a given direction, sum over the (θ_1, θ_2) line to get a ∘ point. Repeat over all its parallels to get the dark plane and apply a 2-D wavelet transform within that plane. Repeat for all the directions to get the 3-D beamlet transform. See the text (Section 11.4.2) for 1a detailed explanation and implementation clues.

Algorithm 44 The 3-D Beamlet Transform

Data: $N \times N \times N$ data cube X.
Result: 3-D Beamlet Transform of X
begin
  – Apply a 3-D FFT to X to yield $\hat{X}[k_x, k_y, k_z]$.
  – Perform Cartesian-to-Spherical Conversion using an interpolation scheme to sample $\hat{X}$ in spherical coordinates $\hat{X}[\rho, \theta_1, \theta_2]$.
  – Extract $3N^2$ planes (of size $N \times N$) passing through the origin, orthogonal to the lines used in the 3-D ridgelet transform.
  for each plane defined by $[\theta_1, \theta_2]$ **do**
  | – apply an inverse 2-D FFT
  | – apply a 2-D wavelet transform to get the Beamlet coefficients
end

Figure 11.9 gives the 3-D beamlet transform flowgraph. The 3-D beamlet transform allows us to detect filaments in a cube. The beamlet transform algorithm presented in this section differs from the one presented in Donoho et al. (2002); see the discussion in Donoho and Levi (2002).

11.3.3 Application to the Detection of Different Features

To illustrate the two transforms introduced in this section, we present an application of 3-D ridgelets and beamlets to the detection of features with different morphologies.

Three data sets are generated containing, respectively, a cluster, a plane and a line. To each data set, Poisson noise is added with eight different background levels. After applying wavelets, beamlets, and ridgelets to the 24 resulting data sets, the coefficient distribution from each transformation is normalized using 20 realizations of a Poisson noise having the same number of counts as in the data.

Figure 11.10 shows, from top to bottom, the maximum value of the normalized distribution versus the noise level for our three simulated data sets. As expected,

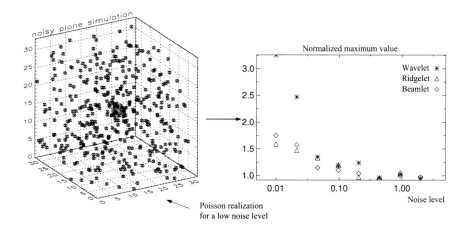

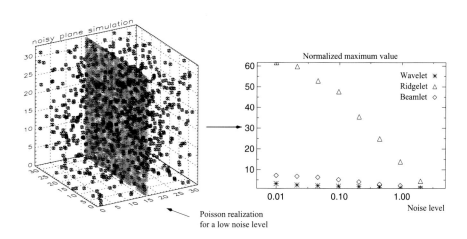

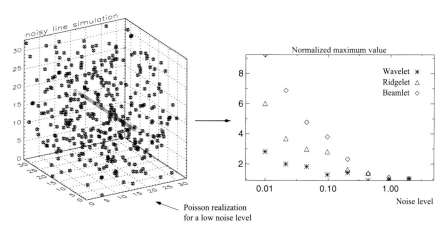

Figure 11.10. Simulation of cubes containing a cluster (top), a plane (middle), and a line (bottom).

wavelets, ridgelets, and beamlets are, respectively, the best for detecting clusters, sheets, and lines. A feature can typically be detected with a very high signal-to-noise ratio in a matched transform, while remaining indetectable in some other transforms. For example, the wall is detected at more than 60σ by the ridgelet transform, but at less than 5σ by the wavelet transform. The line is detected almost at 10σ by the beamlet transform, and with worse than a 3σ detection level by wavelets. These results show the importance of using several transforms for the optimal detection of all features contained in a data set.

11.4 FIRST-GENERATION 3-D CURVELETS

In 3-D, the 2-D ridgelet transform can either be extended using the 3-D ridgelets or 3-D beamlets introduced in the previous section. Combined with a 3-D wavelet transform, the 3-D ridgelet gives rise to the RidCurvelet, while the 3-D beamlet gives rise to BeamCurvelets.

We begin by presenting the frequency-space tiling used by both transforms before describing each one. In the last part of this section, we present denoising applications of these transforms.

11.4.1 Frequency-Space Tiling

Following the strategy of the first-generation 2-D curvelet transform, both 3-D curvelets presented in this section are based on a tiling of both frequency space and the unit cube $[0, 1]^3$.

Partitioning of the frequency space can be achieved using a filter-bank to separate the signal into spectral bands. From an adequate smooth function $\psi \in L_2(\mathbb{R}^3)$ we define for all s in $\mathbb{N}^*$, $\psi_{2s} = 2^{6s}\psi(2^{2s}\cdot)$ that extracts the frequencies around $|\nu| \in [2^{2s}, 2^{2s+2}]$, and a low-pass filter ψ_0 for $|\nu| \leq 1$. We get a partition of unity in the frequency domain:

$$\forall \nu \in \mathbf{R}^3, \quad |\hat{\psi}_0(\nu)|^2 + \sum_{s>0} |\hat{\psi}_{2s}(\nu)|^2 = 1. \tag{11.40}$$

Let $P_0 f = \psi_0 * f$ and $\Delta_s f = \psi_{2s} * f$, where $*$ is the convolution product. We can represent any signal f as $(P_0 f, \Delta_1 f, \Delta_2 f, \ldots)$.

In the spatial domain, the unit cube $[0, 1]^3$ is tiled at each scale s with a finite set $\mathcal{Q}_s$ of $n_s \geq 2^s$ regions Q of size 2^{-s}:

$$Q = Q(s, k_1, k_2, k_3) = \left[\frac{k_1}{2^s}, \frac{k_1 + 1}{2^s}\right] \times \left[\frac{k_2}{2^s}, \frac{k_2 + 1}{2^s}\right] \times \left[\frac{k_3}{2^s}, \frac{k_3 + 1}{2^s}\right] \subset [0, 1]^3. \tag{11.41}$$

Regions are allowed to overlap (for $n_s > 2^s$) to reduce the impact of block effects in the resulting 3-D transform. However, the higher the level of overlapping, the higher the redundancy of the final transform. With each region Q is associated a smooth window w_Q, so that at any point $x \in [0, 1]^3$, $\sum_{Q \in \mathcal{Q}_s} w_Q^2(x) = 1$, with

$$\mathcal{Q}_s = \left\{Q\left(s, k_1^i, k_2^i, k_3^i\right) \mid \forall i \in [\![0, n_s]\!], \left(k_1^i, k_2^i, k_3^i\right) \in [0, 2^s[^3\right\}. \tag{11.42}$$

Each element of the frequency-space $w_Q \Delta_s$ is transported to $[0, 1]^3$ by the transport operator $T_Q : L_2(Q) \rightarrow L_2([0, 1]^3)$ applied to $f' = w_Q \Delta_s f$

$$T_Q : L_2(Q) \rightarrow L_2([0, 1]^3)$$

$$(T_Q f')(x_1, x_2, x_3) = 2^{-s} f' \left(\frac{k_1 + x_1}{2^s}, \frac{k_2 + x_2}{2^s}, \frac{k_3 + x_3}{2^s} \right). \tag{11.43}$$

For each scale s, we have a space-frequency tiling operator g_Q, the output of which lives on $[0, 1]^3$

$$g_Q = T_Q w_Q \Delta_s . \tag{11.44}$$

Using this tiling operator, we can now build the 3-D BeamCurvelet and 3-D Rid-Curvelet transforms by, respectively, applying a 3-D beamlet and 3-D ridgelet transform on each space-frequency block.

11.4.2 The 3-D BeamCurvelet Transform

Given the frequency-space tiling defined in the previous section, a 3-D beamlet transform (Donoho and Levi 2002; Donoho and Huo 2001c) can now be applied on each block of each scale. Let $\phi \in L_2(\mathbf{R}^2)$ be a smooth function satisfying the following admissibility condition:

$$\sum_{s \in \mathbb{Z}} \phi^2(2^s \mathbf{u}) = 1, \quad \forall \mathbf{u} \in \mathbf{R}^2 . \tag{11.45}$$

For a scale parameter $a \in \mathbf{R}$, location parameter $\mathbf{b} = (b_1, b_2) \in \mathbf{R}^2$, and orientation parameters $\theta_1 \in [0, 2\pi[, \theta_2 \in [0, \pi[$, we define $\beta_{a,\mathbf{b},\theta_1,\theta_2}$ as the beamlet function (see Section 11.3.2) based on ϕ:

$$\beta_{a,\mathbf{b},\theta_1,\theta_2}(x_1, x_2, x_3) = a^{-1/2} \phi((-x_1 \sin \theta_1 + x_2 \cos \theta_1 + b_1)/a ,$$

$$(x_1 \cos \theta_1 \cos \theta_2 + x_2 \sin \theta_1 \cos \theta_2 - x_3 \sin \theta_2 + b_2)/a) . \tag{11.46}$$

The BeamCurvelet transform of a 3-D function $f \in L_2([0, 1]^3)$ is

$$\mathcal{BC} f = \left\{ \langle (T_Q w_Q \Delta_s) f, \beta_{a,\mathbf{b},\theta_1,\theta_2} \rangle : s \in \mathbb{N}^*, Q \in \mathcal{Q}_s \right\} . \tag{11.47}$$

As we can see, a BeamCurvelet function is parametrized in scale (s, a), position $(Q, \mathbf{b})$, and orientation (θ_1, θ_2). The following sections describe the discretization and the effective implementation of such a transform.

11.4.2.1 Discretization

For convenience, and as opposed to the continuous notation, the scales are now numbered from 0 to J, from the finest to the coarsest. As seen in the continuous formulation, the transform operates in four main steps.

(i) First the frequency decomposition is obtained by applying a 3-D wavelet transform on the data with a wavelet compactly supported in Fourier space, such as the pyramidal Meyer wavelets with low redundancy (Starck et al. 1994), or by using the 3-D isotropic à trous wavelets (see Section 11.2.2).

(ii) Each wavelet scale is then decomposed into small cubes of a size following the parabolic scaling law, forcing the block size B_s with the scale size N_s according to the formula

$$\frac{B_s}{N_s} = 2^{s/2}\frac{B_0}{N_0} , \qquad (11.48)$$

where N_0 and B_0 are the finest scale's dimension and block size.

(iii) Then we apply a partial 3-D Radon transform on each block of each scale. This is accomplished by integrating the blocks along lines at every direction and position. For a fixed direction (θ_1, θ_2), the summation gives us a plane. Each point on this plane represents a line in the original cube. We obtain projections of the blocks on planes passing through the origin at every possible angle.

(iv) Finally, we apply a two-dimensional wavelet transform on each partial Radon plane.

Steps 3 and 4 represent the beamlet transform of the blocks. The 3-D beamlet atoms aim at representing filaments crossing the whole 3-D space. They are constant along a line and oscillate like ϕ in the radial direction. Arranged blockwise on a 3-D isotropic wavelet transform, and following the parabolic scaling, we obtain the BeamCurvelet transform. Figure 11.8 summarized the beamlet transform, and Figure 11.11 the global BeamCurvelet transform.

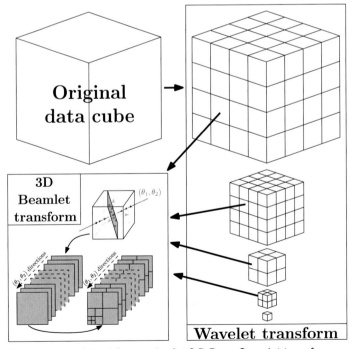

Figure 11.11. Global flowgraph of a 3-D BeamCurvelet transform.

11.4.2.2 Algorithm Summary

As with the 2-D curvelets, the 3-D BeamCurvelet transform is implemented effectively in the Fourier domain. Indeed, the integration along the lines (3-D partial Radon transform) becomes a simple plane extraction in Fourier space, using the d-dimensional projection-slice theorem, which states that the Fourier transform of the projection of a d-dimensional function onto an m-dimensional linear submanifold is equal to an m-dimensional slice of the d-dimensional Fourier transform of that function through the origin in the Fourier space, which is parallel to the projection submanifold. In our case, $d = 3$ and $m = 2$. Algorithm 45 summarizes the whole process.

Algorithm 45 The BeamCurvelet Transform

Data: A data cube X and an initial block size B
Result: BeamCurvelet transform of X
begin

    Apply a 3-D isotropic wavelet transform   **for** all scales from the finest to the second coarsest **do**

        Partition the scale into small cubes of size B **for** each block **do**

            Apply a 3-D FFT Extract planes passing through the origin at every angle (θ_1, θ_2) **for** each plane (θ_1, θ_2) **do**

                apply an inverse 2-D FFT apply a 2-D wavelet transform to get the BeamCurvelet coefficients

        if the scale number is even **then**

            according to the parabolic scaling: $B = 2B$ (in the undecimated wavelet case) $B = B/2$ (in the pyramidal wavelet case)

end

11.4.2.3 Properties

As a composition of invertible operators, the BeamCurvelet transform is invertible. Because the wavelet and Radon transform are both tight frames, so is the Beam-Curvelet transform.

Given a cube of size $N \times N \times N$, a cubic block of length B_s at scale s, and $J + 1$ scales, the redundancy can be calculated as follows.

According to the parabolic scaling, $\forall s > 0 : B_s/N_s = 2^{s/2}B_0/N_0$. The redundancy induced by the 3-D wavelet transform is

$$R_w = \frac{1}{N^3} \sum_{s=0}^{J} N_s^3 , \qquad (11.49)$$

with $N_s = 2^{-s}N$ for pyramidal Meyer wavelets, and thus $B_s = 2^{-s/2}B_0$ according to the parabolic scaling (see equation 11.48).

The partial Radon transform of a cube of size B_s^3 has a size $3B_s^2 \times B_s^2$ to which we apply 2-D decimated orthogonal wavelets with no redundancy. There are $(\rho N_s/B_s)^3$ blocks in each scale because of the overlap factor ($\rho \in [1, 2]$) in each direction. So the complete redundancy of the transform using the Meyer wavelets is

$$R = \frac{1}{N^3} \sum_{s=0}^{J-1} \left(\rho \frac{N_s}{B_s} \right)^3 3B_s^4 + \frac{N_J^3}{N^3} = 3\rho^3 \sum_{i=0}^{J-1} B_s 2^{-3s} + 2^{-3J} \quad (11.50)$$

$$= 3\rho^3 B_0 \sum_{s=0}^{J-1} 2^{-7s/2} + 2^{-3J} \quad (11.51)$$

$$= O\left(3\rho^3 B_0 \right) \quad \text{when } J \to \infty \quad (11.52)$$

$$R(J = 1) = 3\rho^3 B_0 + \frac{1}{8} \quad (11.53)$$

$$R(J = \infty) \approx 3.4\rho^3 B_0 \quad (11.54)$$

For a typical block size $B_0 = 17$, we get for $J \in [1, \infty[$:

$$R \in [51.125, 57.8[\quad \text{without overlapping} \quad (11.55)$$

$$R \in [408.125, 462.4[\quad \text{with 50\% overlapping } (\rho = 2). \quad (11.56)$$

11.4.2.4 Inverse BeamCurvelet Transform

Because all its components are invertible, the BeamCurvelet transform is invertible and the reconstruction error is comparable to machine precision. Algorithm 46 details the reconstruction steps.

Algorithm 46 The Inverse BeamCurvelet Transform

Data: An initial block size B, and the BeamCurvelet coefficients: series of wavelet-space planes indexed by a scale, angles (θ_1, θ_2), and a 3-D position $(\mathcal{B}_x, \mathcal{B}_y, \mathcal{B}_z)$

Result: The reconstructed data cube X

begin

   for all scales from the finest to the second coarsest **do**

      Create a 3-D cube the size of the current scale (according to the 3-D wavelets used in the forward transform) **for** each block position $(\mathcal{B}_x, \mathcal{B}_y, \mathcal{B}_z)$ **do**

         Create a block $\mathcal{B}$ of size $B \times B \times B$ **for** each plane (θ_1, θ_2) indexed with this position **do**

            – Apply an inverse 2-D wavelet transform   – Apply a 2-D FFT

            – Put the obtained Fourier plane to the block, such that the plane passes through the origin of the block with normal angle (θ_1, θ_2)

         – Apply a 3-D IFFT   – Add the block to the wavelet scale at the position $(\mathcal{B}_x, \mathcal{B}_y, \mathcal{B}_z)$, using a weighted function if overlapping is involved

      if the scale number is even **then**

         according to the parabolic scaling : $B = 2B$ (in the undecimated wavelet case) $B = B/2$ (in the pyramidal wavelet case)

   Apply a 3-D inverse isotropic wavelet transform

end

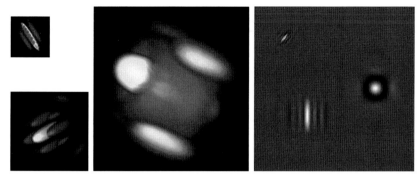

Figure 11.12. Examples of BeamCurvelet atoms at different scales and orientations. These are 3-D density plots: the values near zero are transparent, and the opacity grows with the absolute value of the voxels. Positive values are red/yellow, and negative values are blue/purple. The right map is a slice of a cube containing these three atoms in the same position as on the left. The top left atom has an arbitrary direction, the bottom left is in the slice, and the right one is normal to the slice. (See *color plates*.)

An example of a 3-D BeamCurvelet atom is represented in Figure 11.12. The BeamCurvelet atom is a collection of straight smooth segments well localized in space. Across the transverse plane, the BeamCurvelets exhibit a wavelet-like oscillating behavior.

11.4.3 The 3-D RidCurvelet Transform

As referred to in Section 11.4.2, the second extension of the curvelet transform in 3-D is obtained by using the 3-D ridgelet transform (Candès and Donoho 1999) defined in Section 11.3 instead of the beamlets.

The continuous RidCurvelet is thus defined in much the same way as the Beam-Curvelet. Given a smooth function $\phi \in L_2(\mathbf{R})$ verifying the following admissibility condition:

$$\sum_{s\in\mathbb{Z}} \phi^2(2^s u) = 1, \quad \forall u \in \mathbf{R}, \tag{11.57}$$

a three-dimensional ridge function (see Section 11.3) is given by

$$\rho_{\sigma,\kappa,\theta_1,\theta_2}(x_1, x_2, x_3) = \sigma^{-1/2}\phi\left(\frac{1}{\sigma}(x_1\cos\theta_1\cos\theta_2 + x_2\sin\theta_1\cos\theta_2 + x_3\sin\theta_2 - \kappa)\right),$$

$$\tag{11.58}$$

where σ and κ are, respectively, the scale and position parameters.

Then the RidCurvelet transform of a 3-D function $f \in L_2([0, 1]^3)$ is

$$\mathcal{R}f = \{\langle (T_Q w_Q \Delta_s)f, \rho_{\sigma,\kappa,\theta_1,\theta_2}\rangle : s \in \mathbb{N}^*, Q \in \mathcal{Q}_s\}. \tag{11.59}$$

11.4.3.1 Discretization

The discretization is made the same way, the sums over lines becoming sums over the planes of normal direction $(\theta_1; \theta_2)$, which gives us a line for each direction. The 3-D Ridge function is useful for representing planes in a 3-D space. It is constant along

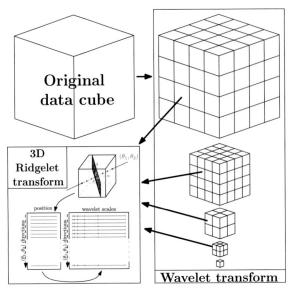

Figure 11.13. Global flowgraph of a 3-D RidCurvelet transform.

a plane and oscillates like ϕ in the normal direction. The main steps of the ridgelet transform are depicted in Figure 11.5.

11.4.3.2 Algorithm Summary
The RidCurvelet transform is also implemented in the Fourier domain, the integration along the planes becoming a line extraction in the Fourier domain. The overall process is shown in Figure 11.13, and Algorithm 47 summarizes the implementation.

Algorithm 47 The RidCurvelet Transform

Data: A data cube x and an initial block size B
Result: RidCurvelet transform of X
begin

  Apply a 3-D isotropic wavelet transform   **for** all scales from the finest to the second coarsest **do**

    Cut the scale into small cubes of size B **for** each block **do**

      Apply a 3-D FFT   Extract lines passing through the origin at every angle (θ_1, θ_2) **for** each line (θ_1, θ_2) **do**

        apply an inverse 1-D FFT   apply a 1-D wavelet transform to get the Rid-Curvelet coefficients

    if the scale number is even **then**

      according to the parabolic scaling : $B = 2B$ (in the undecimated wavelet case) $B = B/2$ (in the pyramidal wavelet case)

end

11.4.3.3 Properties

The RidCurvelet transform forms a tight frame. Additionally, given a 3-D cube of size $N \times N \times N$, a block of size length B_s at scale s, and $J + 1$ scales, the redundancy is calculated as follows. The Radon transform of a cube of size B_s^3 has a size $3B_s^2 \times B_s$, to which we apply a pyramidal 1-D wavelet of redundancy 2, for a total size of $3B_s^2 \times 2B_s = 6B_s^3$. There are $(\rho N_s / B_s)^3$ blocks in each scale because of the overlap factor ($\rho \in [1, 2]$) in each direction. Therefore, the complete redundancy of the transform using many scales of 3-D Meyer wavelets is

$$R = \sum_{s=0}^{J-1} 6B_s^3 \left(\rho \frac{N_s}{B_s} \right)^3 + 2^{-3J} = 6\rho^3 \sum_{s=0}^{J-1} 2^{-3s} + 2^{-3J} \tag{11.60}$$

$$R = O(6\rho^3) \text{ when } J \to \infty . \tag{11.61}$$

$$R(J = 1) = \qquad\qquad 6\rho^3 + 1/8 \tag{11.62}$$

$$R(J = \infty) \approx \qquad\qquad 6.86\rho^3 . \tag{11.63}$$

11.4.3.4 Inverse RidCurvelet Transform

The RidCurvelet transform is invertible, and the reconstruction error is comparable to machine precision. Algorithm 48 details the reconstruction steps.

Algorithm 48 The Inverse RidCurvelet Transform

Data: An initial block size B and the RidCurvelet coefficients: series of wavelet-space lines indexed by a scale, angles (θ_1, θ_2), and a 3-D position $(\mathcal{B}_x, \mathcal{B}_y, \mathcal{B}_z)$
Result: The reconstructed data cube X
begin
  for all scales from the finest to the second coarsest **do**
    Create a 3-D cube the size of the current scale (according to the 3-D wavelets used in the forward transform) **for** each block position $(\mathcal{B}_x, \mathcal{B}_y, \mathcal{B}_z)$ **do**
      Create a block $\mathcal{B}$ of size $B \times B \times B$ **for** each line (θ_1, θ_2) indexed with this position **do**
        − Apply an inverse 1-D wavelet transform − Apply a 1-D FFT − Put the obtained Fourier line to the block, such that the line passes through the origin of the block with the angle (θ_1, θ_2)
      − Apply a 3-D IFFT − Add the block to the wavelet scale at the position $(\mathcal{B}_x, \mathcal{B}_y, \mathcal{B}_z)$, using a weighted function if overlapping is involved
    if the scale number is even **then**
      according to the parabolic scaling : $B = 2B$ (in the undecimated wavelet case) $B = B/2$ (in the pyramidal wavelet case)
  Apply a 3-D inverse isotropic wavelet transform
end

An example of a 3-D RidCurvelet atom is represented in Figure 11.14. The Rid-Curvelet atom is composed of planes with values oscillating like a wavelet in the

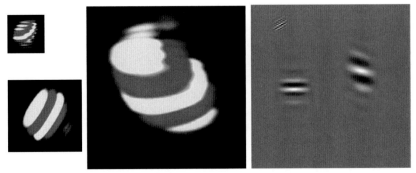

Figure 11.14. Examples of RidCurvelet atoms at different scales and orientation. The rendering is similar to that of Figure 11.12. The right plot is a slice from a cube containing the three atoms shown here. (See *color plates*.)

normal direction, and they are well localized due to the smooth function used to extract blocks on each wavelet scale.

11.4.4 Application: Structure Denoising

In sparse representations, the simplest denoising methods are performed by a simple thresholding of the discrete curvelet coefficients. The threshold level is usually taken as three times the noise standard deviation, such that for an additive Gaussian noise, the thresholding operator kills all noise coefficients except a small percentage, while keeping the big coefficients containing information. The threshold we use is often a simple $\kappa\sigma$, with $\kappa \in [3, 4]$, which corresponds, respectively, to 0.27% and $6.3 \cdot 10^{-5}$ false detections. Sometimes we use a higher κ for the finest scale (Starck et al. 2002). Other methods exist, such as the false discovery rate (FDR), that estimate automatically the threshold to use in each band (see Benjamini and Hochberg (1995); Miller et al. (2001)). The correlation between neighbor coefficients that are intra-band and/or inter-band may also be taken into account (see Sendur and Selesnik (2002); Sendur and Selesnik (2002)). In order to evaluate the different transforms, a $\kappa\sigma$ hard thresholding is used in the following experiments.

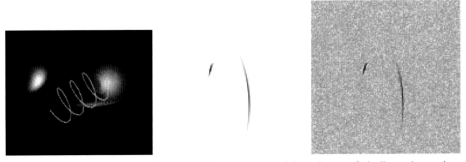

Figure 11.15. (left to right) A 3-D view of the cube containing pieces of shells and a spring-shaped filament, a slice of the previous cube, and finally a slice from the noisy cube. (See *color plates*.)

Table 11.1. PSNR of the denoised synthetic cube using wavelets, RidCurvelets, or BeamCurvelets			
	Wavelets	**RidCurvelets**	**BeamCurvelets**
Shells & spring	40.4 dB	40.3 dB	43.7 dB

Figure 11.16. (left to right) A slice from the filtered test-cube (original in Figure 11.15) by the wavelet transform (isotropic undecimated), the RidCurvelets, and the BeamCurvelets.

A way to assess the power of each transform when associated with the right structures is to denoise a synthetic cube containing plane- and filament-like structures. Figure 11.15 shows a cut and a projection of the test cube containing parts of spherical shells and a spring-shaped filament. Then this cube is denoised using wavelets, RidCurvelets, and BeamCurvelets.

As shown in Figure 11.16, the RidCurvelets denoise correctly the shells but poorly the filament, the BeamCurvelets restore the helix more properly while slightly underperforming for the shells, and wavelets are poor on the shell, give a dotted result, and miss the faint parts of both structures. The peak signal-to-noise ratios (PSNRs) obtained with each transform are reported in Table 11.1. Here, the curvelet transforms did very well for the curved image features, and the wavelets were better on the signal power. In the framework of 3-D image denoising, it was advocated in Starck et al. (2001) advocated combining several transforms in order to benefit from the advantages of each of them.

11.5 FAST CURVELETS

Despite their interesting properties, the first-generation curvelet constructions present some drawbacks. In particular, the spatial partitioning uses overlapping windows to avoid blocking effects. This leads to an increased redundancy of the transforms, which is a crucial factor in 3-D. In contrast, the second-generation curvelets (Candès and Donoho 2004; Candès et al. 2006a) exhibit a much simpler and natural indexing structure with three parameters: scale, orientation (angle), and location; hence they simplify mathematical analysis. The second-generation curvelet transform also implements a tight frame expansion (Candès and Donoho 2004) and has a much lower redundancy. Unlike the first generation transforms, the discrete second-generation implementation will not use ridgelets, therefore yielding a faster algorithm (Candès and Donoho 2004; Candès et al. 2006a).

The 3-D implementation of the fast curvelets was proposed in Ying et al. (2005) and Candès et al. (2006a) with a public code distributed (including the 2-D version) in Curvelab, a C++/Matlab toolbox available at www.curvelet.org. This 3-D fast curvelet transform has found applications mainly in seismic imaging; for instance, for denoising (Ma and Hussaini 2007) and inpainting (Herrmann and Hennenfent 2008). However, a major drawback of this transform is its high redundancy factor, of approximately 25. As a straightforward and somewhat naive remedy to this problem, Ying et al. (2005) and Candès et al. (2006a) suggest using wavelets at the finest scale instead of curvelets; doing so indeed reduces the redundancy dramatically to about 5.4 (see Section 11.5.3 for details). However, this comes at the expense of directional selectivity of fine details. On the practical side, this results in poorer performance in restoration problems compared to the full curvelet version. Note that directional selectivity was one of the main reasons curvelets were built in the first place.

In this section, we begin by describing the original 3-D fast curvelet transform (FCT) (Ying et al. 2005; Candès et al. 2006a). The FCT of a 3-D object consists of a low-pass approximation subband and a family of curvelet subbands carrying the curvelet coefficients indexed by their scale, position, and orientation in 3-D. These 3-D FCT coefficients are formed by a proper tiling of the frequency domain following two steps (see Fig. 11.17).

- ■ *Cartesian coronization or multiscale separation*: First decompose the object into (Cartesian) dyadic coronas in the Fourier domain based on concentric cubes;

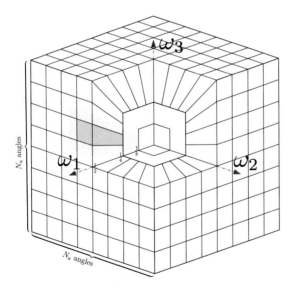

Figure 11.17. Example in 3-D of how the number of directions N_a is defined along an edge (eight in this example), and showing the overlapping region around one wedge. The dark gray area is the main part of the wedge, and the light one represents the overlapping region.

- *Angular separation*: Each corona is separated into anisotropic wedges of a trapezoidal shape obeying the so-called parabolic scaling law (to be defined shortly). The 3-D FCT coefficients are obtained by an inverse Fourier transform, applied to each wedge that has been appropriately wrapped to fit into a 3-D rectangular parallelepiped.

After detailing these two steps, we express the redundancy factor of the original 3-D FCT, which motivates the Low-Redundancy implementation (Woiselle et al. 2011) presented later. In the final part of this section, we present a few applications of the 3-D Fast Curvelet transform.

11.5.1 Cartesian Coronization

The multiscale separation is achieved using a 3-D Meyer wavelet transform (Starck et al. 1994; Mallat 2008), where the Meyer wavelet and scaling functions are defined in the Fourier domain with compactly supported Fourier transforms.

Let us denote ψ_j as the Meyer wavelet at scale $j \in \{0, \ldots, J-1\}$, and ϕ_{J-1} as the scaling function at the coarsest scale. The Meyer wavelets $\hat{\psi}(\xi)$ are defined in the Fourier domain as follows:

$$\hat{\psi}(\xi) = \begin{cases} \exp^{-i2\pi\xi} \sin\left(\frac{\pi}{2}\nu(6|\xi|-1)\right), & \text{if } 1/6 < |\xi| \le 1/3 \\ \exp^{-i2\pi\xi} \cos\left(\frac{\pi}{2}\nu(3|\xi|-1)\right), & \text{if } 1/3 < |\xi| \le 2/3 \\ 0 & \text{elsewhere} \end{cases}$$

where ν is a smooth function that goes from 0 to 1 on $[0, 1]$ and satisfies $\nu(x) + \nu(1-x) = 1$. Associated with this wavelet are the Meyer scaling functions defined by

$$\hat{\phi}(\xi) = \begin{cases} 1, & \text{if } |\xi| \le 1/6 \\ \cos\left(\frac{\pi}{2}\nu(6|\xi|-1)\right), & \text{if } 1/6 < |\xi| \le 1/3 \\ 0 & \text{if } |\xi| > 1/3 \end{cases}$$

Figure 11.18 displays (solid lines) the graphs of the Fourier transforms of the Meyer scaling and wavelet functions at three scales.

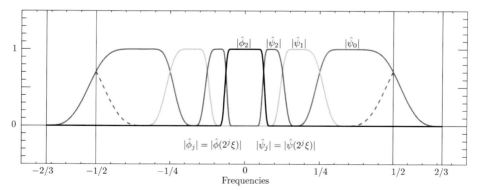

Figure 11.18. Meyer scaling and wavelet functions in the Fourier domain. In the discrete case, we only have access to the Fourier samples inside the Shannon band $[-1/2, 1/2]$, while the wavelet corresponding to the finest scale (solid red line) exceeds the Shannon frequency band to 2/3. In the original fast curvelet implementation, the Meyer wavelet basis is periodized in Fourier space, so that the exceeding end of the finest scale wavelet is replaced with the mirrored dashed line on the plot.

There is a pair of conjugate mirror filters (h, g) associated with (ϕ, ψ) whose Fourier transforms $(\hat{h}, \hat{g})$ can be easily deduced from $(\hat{\phi}, \hat{\psi})$. $\hat{h}$ and $\hat{g}$ are thus compactly supported. As a consequence, the Meyer wavelet transform is usually implemented in the Fourier domain by a classical cascade of multiplications by $\hat{h}$ and $\hat{g}$. However, the wavelet at the finest scale is supported on $[-2/3, -1/6[\cup]1/6, 2/3]$, hence exceeding the Shannon band. This necessitates knowing signal frequencies to which we do not have access.

Because the FCT makes central use of the FFT, it implicitly assumes periodic boundary conditions. Moreover, it is known that computing the wavelet transform of a periodized signal is equivalent to decomposing the signal in a periodic wavelet basis. With this in mind, the exceeding end of the finest scale wavelet is replaced with its mirrored version around the vertical axis at $|\xi| = 1/2$, as shown in the dashed line in Figure 11.18. Consequently, the support of the data to treat is $4/3$ larger than the original one, hence boosting the redundancy by a factor $(4/3)^d$ in d-D.

Denote $M_j = \hat{\psi}_j = 2^{-3j/2}\hat{\psi}(2^{-j}\cdot)$ and $M_J = \hat{\phi}_{J-1} = 2^{-3(J-1)/2}\hat{\phi}(2^{-(J-1)}\cdot)$ their Fourier transforms. M_J is a low-pass filter and the wavelet functions, $\{M_j\}_{0 \le j < J}$, are a family of bandpass frequency-localized windows that form a uniform partition of unity. Applied to a 3-D object, the family $\{M_j\}_{0 \le j < J}$ separates it into Cartesian coronas (annuli), and M_J selects its low-frequency content (see Figure 11.19). This coarsest subband is kept unaltered and, after an inverse Fourier transform, provides us with the first curvelet coefficients, which correspond to coarse-scale isotropic atoms. Only the next detail scales (i.e., those corresponding to $\{M_j\}_{0 \le j < J}$) have to be processed further.

11.5.2 Angular Separation

The FCT isolates, in the frequency domain, oriented and localized 3-D wedges. There is symmetry on a 3-D Cartesian grid: the cube has six faces that can be

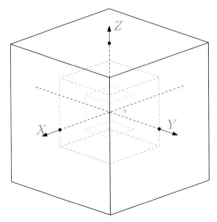

Figure 11.19. Cartesian coronization in Fourier space using compactly supported Meyer wavelets for $J = 2$. The central cube corresponds to the isotropic coarsest subband M_J.

processed in a similar way. Let $\boldsymbol{\omega} = (\omega_1, \omega_2, \omega_3) \in [-1/2, 1/2]^3$ be a frequency in the 3-D Shannon band. Exploiting the above symmetry, we only focus on the subspace $\{\omega_1 > 0, |\omega_2/\omega_1| < 1, |\omega_3/\omega_1| < 1\}$, which is a squared-based pyramid. The five other parts can be dealt with exactly in the same way by symmetry around the origin and exchange of axes.

Let N_a be the number of angles on one edge of one face of the finest scale, for a total of N_a^2 angles on each face, and thus six times more bands for the entire considered scale (see Figure 11.19). This number varies with the scale because the number of angles decreases as the scales become coarser, thereby obeying the parabolic scaling law of curvelets (Candès et al. 2006a), with a parabolic scaling matrix $\mathrm{diag}(2^{-j}, 2^{-j/2}, 2^{-j/2})$ (one short direction and two long ones). This property is essential to ensure that the 3-D curvelets are a basis for sparsely representing smooth trivariate functions with 2-D smooth surface-like singularities.

The vector indexing the angular locations on a face at the jth scale may be expressed with $\mathbf{l} = (l, l') \in \{0, \ldots, 2^{\lfloor -j/2 \rfloor} N_a - 1\}^2$, where $\lfloor \cdot \rfloor$ is the integer part of its argument.[1] Recall that a wedge is the trapezoidal region sharply localized along a given angle at a given scale; see the dark gray area in Figure 11.19. The center of the wedge is on the line going from the origin to the point $(1, \theta_l, \theta'_{l'})$, with

$$\theta_l = \left(-1 + \frac{2l+1}{2^{\lfloor -j/2 \rfloor} N_a}\right), \; \theta'_{l'} = \left(-1 + \frac{2l'+1}{2^{\lfloor -j/2 \rfloor} N_a}\right). \tag{11.64}$$

We can now define the angular separation by multiplying the dyadic annuli corresponding to the wavelet detail subbands by the smooth angular windows $V_{j,\mathbf{l}}$ in the Fourier domain. The angular windows are built from a smooth real-valued function V supported on $[-1, 1]$ and satisfying the partition property

$$\sum_{l=-\infty}^{\infty} V^2(t - 2l) = 1 \quad \forall t \in \mathbf{R} . \tag{11.65}$$

The angular window at scale j and orientation $\mathbf{l} = (l, l')$ are then constructed as

$$V_{j,\mathbf{l}}(\boldsymbol{\omega}) = V\left(2^{\lfloor -j/2 \rfloor} N_a \frac{\omega_2 - \theta_l \omega_1}{\omega_1}\right) \cdot V\left(2^{\lfloor -j/2 \rfloor} N_a \frac{\omega_3 - \theta'_{l'} \omega_1}{\omega_1}\right), \tag{11.66}$$

where θ_l and $\theta'_{l'}$ are defined in (11.64). Note the scaling factor $2^{-j/2}$ as dictated by the parabolic scaling. Owing to (11.65), the family of angular windows $\{V_{j,\mathbf{l}}\}_{\mathbf{l}}$ makes a uniform partition of the dyadic annulus at scale j, i.e.,

$$\sum_{\mathbf{l}} V_{j,\mathbf{l}}^2(\boldsymbol{\omega}) = 1 . \tag{11.67}$$

However, because of the support constraint on V, this relation does not hold for all $\boldsymbol{\omega}$, and special care should be taken at the corners where only three out of usually four windows overlap. We thus need to redefine them for (11.67) to hold for any $\boldsymbol{\omega}$. Here is a simple remedy to this problem. Let $\mathbf{l}_a, \mathbf{l}_b, \mathbf{l}_c$ be the indices of the three corner windows and redefine them on their overlapping domain Ω as

$$\forall \omega \in \Omega, \forall \mathbf{l} \in \{\mathbf{l}_a, \mathbf{l}_b, \mathbf{l}_c\}, \quad V_{j,\mathbf{l}}(\boldsymbol{\omega}) \leftarrow \frac{V_{j,\mathbf{l}}(\boldsymbol{\omega})}{\sqrt{V_{j,\mathbf{l}_a}^2(\boldsymbol{\omega}) + V_{j,\mathbf{l}_b}^2(\boldsymbol{\omega}) + V_{j,\mathbf{l}_c}^2(\boldsymbol{\omega})}}. \quad (11.68)$$

Piecing all ingredients together, the *scale-angular* wedge at scale-orientation $(j, \mathbf{l})$ is extracted by the frequency window

$$W_{j,\mathbf{l}}(\boldsymbol{\omega}) = M_j(\boldsymbol{\omega}) \cdot V_{j,\mathbf{l}}(\boldsymbol{\omega}), \quad (11.69)$$

which is sharply localized near the trapezoid

$$\left\{ (\omega_1, \omega_2, \omega_3) : 2^{j+1} < \omega_1 < 2^j, \left| \frac{\omega_2}{\omega_1} - \theta_l \right| < 2^{\lfloor j/2 \rfloor}/N_a, \left| \frac{\omega_3}{\omega_1} - \theta_{l'} \right| < 2^{\lfloor j/2 \rfloor}/N_a \right\}.$$

Once a wedge is extracted, an inverse Fourier transform must be applied to get the curvelet coefficients at the corresponding scale and orientation. Prior to this, the trapezoidal wedge has to be transformed to a convenient form for which the 3-D FFT algorithm applies. As can be seen from Figure 11.19, the wedge can be inscribed inside a 3-D parallelepiped that is $\sim 2^{j/2}$ long on the (ω_2, ω_3) coordinates (i.e., tangentially), and 2^j on ω_1 (i.e., radially). Although this expands the area including the wedge, we can still wrap it inside a rectangular parallelepiped of dimensions $\sim (2^j, 2^{j/2}, 2^{j/2})$ centered at the origin aligned with the axes of the grid (see Section 11.5.4.2 for further details about wrapping). With an appropriate choice of the size of the rectangular parallelepiped, the data do not overlap with itself after wrapping. With the wrapping trick, an inverse 3-D FFT can be readily applied to the rectangular parallelepiped to obtain the curvelet coefficients at the selected scale and orientation.

Algorithm 49 summarizes the implementation of the 3-D FCT and outlines its main steps. In order to show an atom of the 3-D FCT, we set to zero all the FastCurvelet coefficients except one, and then perform the inverse transform. We obtain a single FastCurvelet atom, which can be observed in the Fourier domain as well. Figure 11.20 displays a 3-D curvelet atom in the spatial and Fourier domain.

Algorithm 49 The 3-D Fast Curvelet Transform

Data: A 3-D data object X of size $\mathbf{N} = (N_x, N_y, N_z)$.
Input: Number of scales J, number of angles N_a on each face at the finest scale.
begin
    (i) **Multiscale separation:** apply the 3-D Meyer wavelet transform in Fourier domain, get cubes of sizes $\mathbf{N}, \mathbf{N}/2, \ldots, \mathbf{N}/2^J$.
    (ii) **Angular separation: foreach** scale $j = 0$ to J **do**
      foreach orientation $\mathbf{l} = (l, l')$ **do**
        Multiply the wavelet cube at scale j with the angular window $V_{j,\mathbf{l}}$ in Fourier; Wrapping: wrap the result in a rectangular parallelepiped centered at the origin of minimal size $(2^j 3/8 \times 2^{j/2+1}/N_a \times 2^{j/2+1}/N_a)$; Apply a 3-D inverse FFT to the rectangular parallelepiped to collect the curvelet coefficients
end
Result: 3-D FCT of X.

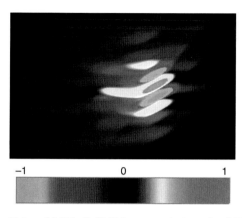 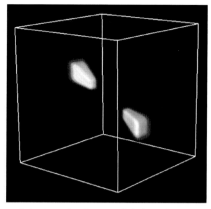

−1   0   1

Figure 11.20. (left) Volume rendering of a 3-D curvelet atom in the spatial domain corresponding to our implementation, cut by a vertical plane to see its inner structure. (right) The magnitude of its Fourier transform. The colorbar scale is valid only for the left image. (See *color plates*.)

11.5.3 Redundancy

Here, we quantify analytically the redundancy of the FCT in any dimension d. Without loss of generality, we assume that the data object is a d-D hypercube of unit side. Let N_a be the number of angles along an edge on one face at the finest scale, for a total of N_a^{d-1} orientations on each face. Let $N_f = 2d$ be the number of faces of the d-D data hypercube.

The redundancy of the Cartesian coronization, or multiscale separation assuming a dyadic frequency tiling, is given by

$$\sum_{j=0}^{J} \left(\frac{1}{2^d}\right)^j, \tag{11.70}$$

which is upper bounded by $R_w = \frac{2^d}{2^d-1}$. As explained in Section 11.5.1, an extra-redundancy R_{add} comes into play in the Meyer wavelet transform with the original FCT implementation:

$$R_{add} = \left(\frac{4}{3}\right)^d. \tag{11.71}$$

At the finest scale and on each face, there are N_a^{d-1} wedges; the size of each of them is

$$\frac{3}{8} \times \underbrace{\frac{2}{N_a} \times \cdots \times \frac{2}{N_a}}_{d-1 \text{ times}}. \tag{11.72}$$

The factor 3/8 corresponds to the radial depth of the scale; see Section 11.5.1 and Figure 11.17. In the other orthogonal directions, a wedge has a size of $\frac{1}{N_a}$ that we double because of overlapping. The redundancy of a face at the finest scale is then

$$R_f = N_a^{d-1} \cdot \frac{3}{8} \left(\frac{2}{N_a}\right)^{d-1} = 3 \cdot 2^{d-4}. \tag{11.73}$$

Table 11.2. Redundancy of the original FCT and the Low Redundancy one in 2-D and 3-D, when wavelets (W) or curvelets (C) are used at the finest scale

	Original FCT		LR-FCT	
	C	W	C	W
2-D	7.11	3.56	4.00	2.00
3-D	24.38	5.42	10.29	2.29

As can be seen, the R_f redundancy is independent of N_a, and is therefore valid at all scales. For a large enough number of scales, it can be reasonably assumed that the coarsest (wavelet) scale has the same redundancy as a curvelet subband at the same scale. Consequently, the overall redundancy of the FCT is upper bounded by (see (11.70))

$$R = N_f \cdot R_f \cdot R_w \cdot R_{add}$$
$$= 3d \frac{2^{2d-3}}{2^d - 1} \cdot R_{add} .$$

(11.74)

In the case where wavelets are used instead of curvelets at the finest scale, the redundancy upper bound is changed to

$$R' = (N_f \cdot R_f \cdot (R_w - 1) + 1) \cdot R_{add}$$
$$= \left(3d \frac{2^{d-3}}{2^d - 1} + 1 \right) \cdot R_{add} .$$

(11.75)

Table 11.2 compares numerically the redundancy of the original and the Low Redundancy FCT introduced in the next section in 2-D and 3-D, when wavelets (W) or curvelets (C) are implemented at the finest scale. It may be worth mentioning that for the practitioner, the memory storage requirement of the original FCT (as implemented in Curvelab) is twice as large as the one predicted by the redundancy formula. Indeed, the original curvelets are complex, and real curvelets are obtained by Hermitian symmetry. This explains the redundancy 40^2 claimed by Lu and Do (2007), emphasizing the need for lower redundancy curvelets.

11.5.4 Low Redundancy Implementation

In this section, we detail the Low Redundancy FCT (hereafter LR-FCT) introduced in (Woiselle et al. 2011). The overall implementation of this FCT differs from the original one in several points. The main difference lies in the way used to apply the Meyer wavelet transform to the data. Other changes are introduced as described later.

11.5.4.1 The Multiscale Separation

The extra redundancy of the curvelets as implemented in Curvelab originates mainly from the way the radial window is implemented, especially at the finest scale. As explained in Section 11.5.1, the Meyer wavelet at the finest scale is supported on

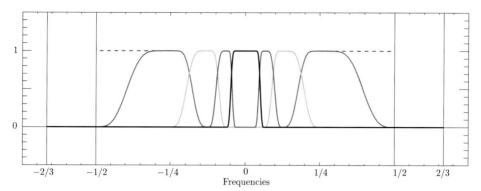

Figure 11.21. Modified Meyer filters in the Fourier domain. A scaling function is plotted in black, and in plain lines are shown the amplitude of the three following wavelet functions. In the Low Redundancy implementation, all the filters are shrunk to fit in the $[-1/2, 1/2]$ box, and the decreasing ends of the finest scale filters are replaced by a constant (dashed red line) to retain all the information.

$[-2/3, -1/6[\cup]1/6, 2/3[$, hence exceeding the Shannon band. In the original FCT, the exceeding end of the finest scale wavelet is replaced with its mirrored version around the vertical axis at $|\xi| = 1/2$.

In the LR-FCT implementation, a different approach is adopted. First, the supports of the scaling and wavelet functions (hence filters) are shrunken by a factor of $4/3$. Furthermore, to maintain the uniform partition of unity, which plays an important role for isometry of the transform, following Starck et al. (1994), the finest scale wavelet is modified by suppressing its decreasing tail so that the wavelet becomes a constant over $]-1/2, -1/4]\cup]1/4, 1/2]$ (see the dashed line in Figure 11.21). The right part of Figure 11.22 shows the impact of the proposed modifications on the 2-D curvelets in the frequency domain. This strategy and the conclusions carry over to the 3-D case.

This modification to the Meyer wavelets reduces the redundancy of the transform. Indeed, as was shown in Section 11.5.3, the redundancy of the transform is proportional to a factor R_{add} due to the Meyer wavelet transform. With this modified version of the transform, however, the wavelets do not add any redundancy, and $R_{add} = 1$ instead of $(4/3)^d$ for the original transform.

However, this comes at the cost of some changes undergone by the curvelet atoms at the finest scale. First, they are less sharply supported in the spatial domain than in the original curvelets because of the discontinuity of their Fourier transform, while the decay of the other curvelets remain unchanged. Second, they obey a parabolic scaling but with a different constant compared to the curvelets at the other scales.

11.5.4.2 Ensuring Zero-Mean Subbands

In the original wrapping-based FCT (Candès et al. 2006a; Demanet 2006), the wedges are wrapped around the origin using a simple modulo operator, which makes every point fit into a well-sized rectangular parallelepiped centered at the origin whose size is designed so that the data do not overlap with itself after wrapping. However, nothing prevents the center of the parallelepiped from receiving a significant non-zero wrapped Fourier coefficient. After an inverse FFT of the wrapped wedge, it is

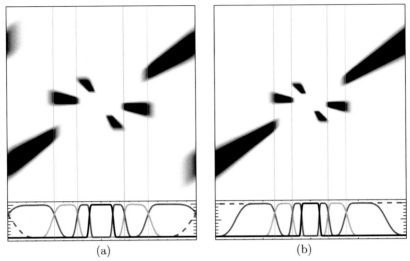

(a)   (b)

Figure 11.22. (top) Examples of 2-D (real) curvelets in the Fourier domain at three consecutive scales and different orientations, with the zero frequency at the center. From the outermost edge to the inside, a finest scale curvelet and two lower scale curvelets (a) according to the Curvelab implementation, and (b) with our modified low-redundancy implementation. (bottom) The corresponding Fourier transforms of 1-D Meyer scaling and wavelet functions.

likely to obtain curvelet coefficient subbands with non-zero means. This is obviously unsuitable since curvelet coefficients are expected to represent high-frequency content, and typical thresholding-based processing (e.g., denoising) is hampered in such a situation. One hopes that the size and position of the wedges are structured so that this misleading phenomenon is generally prevented in practice. Nevertheless, this is not guaranteed.

Therefore, to ensure zero-mean curvelet subbands, a straightforward solution is to translate each rectangular parallelepiped where a wedge has to be wrapped in such a way that the center (zero frequency) gets a true zero coefficient (i.e., a point out of the wedge support) and then to wrap the data around the translated box. Doing so, the curvelet subbands are ensured to be zero-mean valued after wrapping. Figure 11.23 illustrates the difference between the two wrapping strategies in 2-D for the sake of legibility. The technique extends readily to the 3-D case.

11.5.4.3 Properties
This section enumerates the main properties of the LR-FCT implementation.

■ *Reduced redundancy*: It has a reduction factor of $(4/3)^d$ compared to the original version. This is one of the distinctive properties of the LR-FCT and was the main goal motivating these modifications in the first place. For example, the LR-FCT with full curvelets at all scales is (almost) as redundant as the original one with wavelets at the finest scale. In 3-D, redundancy implied by this implementation is 2.5 times lower that the original FCT with curvelets at all scales. In brief, this implementation achieves a low redundancy while maintaining the directional selectivity property at the finest scale, in contrast to the original FCT where

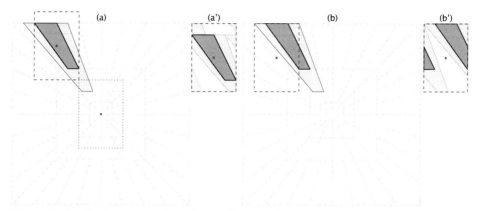

Figure 11.23. (a) Representation of the influence of a wedge and its overlapping region. The centered dotted rectangle corresponds to the minimal size in which the wedge will be wrapped. (a') The result of the wrapping. (b) The wrapping in a rectangle of the same size, but whose center is chosen such that the zero frequency (big dot) falls outside the support of the wedge. (b') The corresponding wedge after translation and wrapping.

wavelets are advocated at the finest scale to lower the redundancy (Ying et al. 2005; Candès et al. 2006a).

- *Isometry and fast exact reconstruction*: Owing to the uniform partition property of the Meyer wavelets and the coverage property (11.65) of the angular window, the collection of curvelets in Fourier space obtained by multiplication of the scale and angular windows also ensures a uniform partition of unity. Therefore, with a proper normalization of the FFT (wrapping is a simple reindexing), the proposed FCT corresponds to a Parseval tight frame (PTF) (i.e., the frame operator $CC^* = I$, where C^* is the FCT analysis operator and C its adjoint). With the PTF property, C turns out to be also the inverse transform operator associated with a fast reconstruction algorithm (each step of the forward transform is easily invertible).

- *Parabolic scaling*: By construction, the curvelets obey the parabolic scaling law with one short and two long sides $\sim (2^{-j}, 2^{-j/2}, 2^{-j/2})$. However, at the finest scale, this property is less faithful to the continuous construction compared to the original FCT (see also the discussion at the end of Section 11.5.4.1).

- *Non-equal ℓ_2-norm atoms*: Although the LR-FCT implements a PTF, the modified curvelets at the finest scale do not have the same ℓ_2 norm as the curvelets in the other (coarsest) scales. These ℓ_2 norms can nonetheless be calculated analytically so as to normalize the associated curvelets coefficients, which is important for instance in every processing that involves thresholding.

- *Guaranteed zero-mean subbands*: This is a consequence of the wise translation trick used prior to wrapping explained in Section 11.5.4.2. Of course, this operation preserves isometry and ℓ_2 norms.

11.5.4.4 Low Resolution – Fast Curvelet Transform Denoising: A Good Tradeoff Between Efficiency and Memory Storage

In this experiment, the denoising performance using the LR-FCT is compared with several other 3-D multiscale transforms on various types of data sets (3-D spatial data, hyperspectral images and videos). The noise is additive white Gaussian,

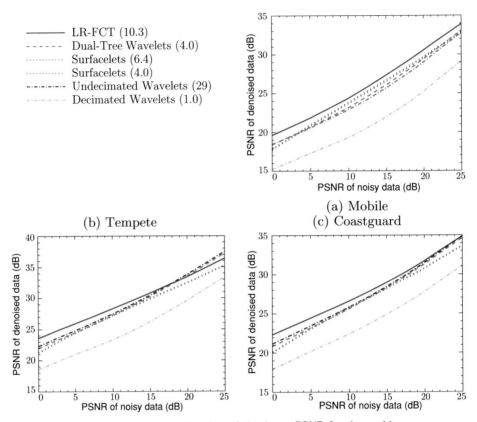

Figure 11.24. Output PSNR as a function of the input PSNR for three video sequences: (a) *mobile*, (b) *tempete*, and (c) *coastguard* CIF sequence. The redundancy of each transform is indicated in parentheses on the legend.

and simple hard-thresholding is used. The video data sets included in this experiment are the standard videos *mobile*, *tempete*, and *coastguard* Common Intermediate Format (CIF) sequences available at www.cipr.rpi.edu. For hyperspectral data, a data set from the OMEGA (Visible and Infrared Mineralogical Mapping Spectrometer) spectrometer on Mars Express was used (www.esa.int/marsexpress) with 128 wavelengths from $0.93\mu m$ to $2.73\mu m$. In addition to LR-FCT, the other transforms involved in this comparative study are the dual-tree complex wavelet transform (Kingsbury 2001; Selesnick 2004), the surfacelet transform (Lu and Do 2007), and the orthogonal (decimated) and translation-invariant (undecimated) wavelet transforms.

Figures 11.24 and 11.25 show the output peak signal-to-noise ratio (PSNR) after denoising as a function of the input PSNR for each transform. Each point on each curve is the average output PSNR on 10 noise realizations. The reader may have noticed that the wavelet results are much better here than those tabulated in Lu and Do (2007). The reason is that, unlike those authors, we used the Cohen-Daubechies-Fauveau 7/9 filterbank, which is much better for denoising. Figure 11.25 displays the results for the hyperspectral data from Mars Express (see caption for details).

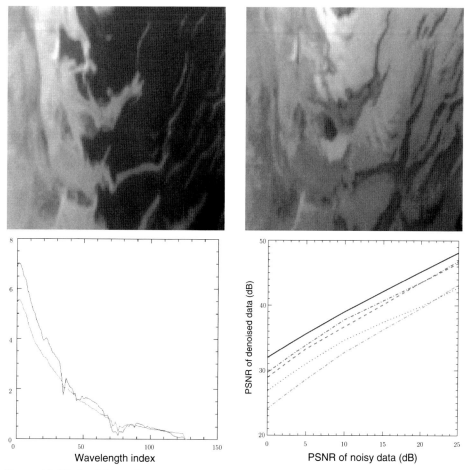

Figure 11.25. (top) Mars Express observations at two different wavelengths. (bottom) Two spectra at two distinct pixels (left) and (right) output PSNR as a function of the input PSNR for different transforms. See Figure 11.24 for details on the curves.

From these experiments, it can be clearly seen that the LR-FCT compares very favorably to the other multiscale geometrical 3-D transforms and is particularly better at the low PSNR regime. In a nutshell, it can be safely concluded that LR-FCT provides a very good compromise between denoising performance and memory/CPU requirements.

11.5.5 Application: Inpainting of Magnetic Resonance Imaging Data

Inpainting aims to restore missing data information based on still available (observed) cues from destroyed, occluded, or deliberately masked subregions of the data. Inpainting has received considerable interest and excitement and has been approached using diffusion and transport PDE/Variational principles, nonlocal exemplar region fill-in, and sparsity-based regularization; see, e.g., Elad et al. (2005); Fadili et al. (2009b); and references therein.

Let $f \in \mathbb{R}^N$ be a vectorized form of the 3-D data cube that is sought, which is $\sqrt{N} \times \sqrt{N} \times \sqrt{N}$, and let $M \in \{0, 1\}^{P \times N}, P < N$ be a binary rectangular matrix where each of its rows is zero except at the entry where a voxel is not missing. The observed (incomplete) data g is then the result of applying the lossy operator M to f:

$$g = Mf + \varepsilon .$$

where ε is some noise of finite variance σ^2 that may contaminate the observed values. Restoring f from g is an ill-posed problem, which necessitates some form of regularization to reduce the space of candidate solutions. Here, we promote solutions that are sparse in some prescribed overcomplete dictionary of atoms $\Phi \in R^{N \times L}, L \geq N$, meaning that $x := \Phi \alpha$ (a synthesis prior) can be sparsely represented to a high accuracy by a small number of atoms in Φ. Expressed formally, we are seeking to solve the following optimization problem:

$$\min_{\alpha \in \mathbb{R}^L} \|\alpha\|_0 \text{ s.t. } \|g - M\Phi\alpha\|_2 \leq \epsilon(\sigma) , \tag{11.76}$$

where $\| \cdot \|_0$ is the ℓ_0 pseudo-norm that counts the number of non-zero entries of its argument, and $\epsilon(\sigma)$ is the constraint radius that depends on the noise variance. This is a very challenging NP-hard optimization problem, and one has to resort to alternative formulations or greedy algorithms to attempt to solve it. For instance, convex ℓ_1 relaxation could be used instead of the ℓ_0 penalty.

This application makes use of the algorithm devised in Elad et al. (2005), which can be viewed as a stagewise hybridization of matching pursuit with block-coordinate relaxation. The term "stagewise" is used because the algorithm exploits the fact that the dictionary is structured (union of transforms $\Phi = [\Phi_1, \ldots, \Phi_K]$) with associated fast analysis and synthesis operators Φ_k^T and Φ_k; see Elad et al. (2005) and Starck et al. (2010) for details. For the reader's convenience, Algorithm 50 recalls the main steps of this inpainting algorithm.

Algorithm 50 Inpainting Algorithm

Data: Observed data g and mask M.
Input: Dictionary $\Phi = [\Phi_1 \cdots \Phi_K]$, number of iterations T_{iter}, final threshold τ
    (e.g. 3).
begin
| Initial components $f_k^{(0)} = 0, k = 1, \ldots, K$.   Initial residual $r^{(0)} = g$.   Initial threshold: let $k^\star = \arg \max_k \|\Phi_k^T g\|_\infty$, set $\lambda_0 = \max_{k \neq k^\star} \|\Phi_k^T g\|_\infty$. **for** $\underline{t = 1}$
| **to** T_{iter} **do**
| | **for** $k = 1$ **to** K **do**
| | | Compute marginal residuals $r_k^{(t)} = r^{(t-1)} + f_k^{(t-1)}$. Update kth component
| | | coefficients by thresholding $\alpha_k^{(t)} = \text{Thresh}_{\lambda_{t-1}}(\Phi_k^T r_k^{(t)})$. Update kth compo-
| | | nent $f_k^{(t)} = \Phi_k \alpha_k^{(t)}$.
| | Update the inpainted data $f^{(t)} = \sum_{k=1}^K f_k^{(t)}$. Update the residuals $r^{(t)} = g -$
| | $Mf^{(t)}$. Update the threshold $\lambda_t = \lambda_0 - t(\lambda_0 - \tau\sigma)/T_{\text{iter}}$.
| **end**
Result: The estimate $f^{(T_{\text{iter}})}$ of f.

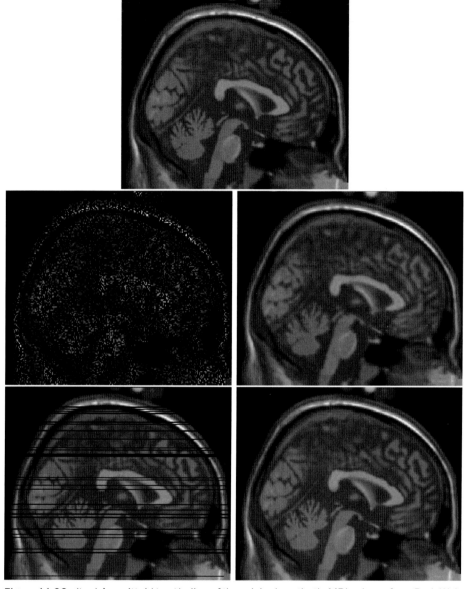

Figure 11.26. (top) A sagittal ((y, z)) slice of the original synthetic MRI volume from BrainWeb (Remi et al. 1999). Left column: the data with missing areas, 80% randomly missing voxels, and 10% missing z slices. Right: inpainting results with a LF-FCT+UDWT dictionary.

For the following experiment, this algorithm was used with a dictionary containing two transforms, the LR-FCT and the undecimated discrete wavelet transform (UDWT), to better take into account the morphological diversity of the features contained in the data. Figure 11.26 shows the inpainting result on a synthetic cerebral MRI volume available on BrainWeb (Remi et al. 1999) at www.bic.mni.mcgill.ca/brainweb/ with two masks: 80% random missing voxels and 10% missing z slices. We can see that even with 80% missing voxels, we can still see incredibly faint details in the restored anatomical structures such as in the gyri and the cerebellum.

SOFTWARE

A number of free software codes are available for different transforms described in this chapter at www.cosmostat.org/software.html. This link is on the book's software page (www.SparseSignalRecipes.info).

- MSVST-lab: Matlab code for Sparse representation-based image deconvolution with Poisson noise.
- Fast 3-D Curvelets: Matlab code for 3-D Fast curvelets.

12

Multiscale Geometric Analysis on the Sphere

12.1 INTRODUCTION

Many wavelet transforms on the sphere have been proposed in past years. Using the lifting scheme, Schröder and Sweldens (1995) developed an orthogonal Haar wavelet transform on any surface, which can be directly applied on the sphere. Its interest is, however, relatively limited because of the poor properties of the Haar function and the problems inherent to orthogonal transforms.

More interestingly, many papers have presented new continuous wavelet transforms (Antoine 1999; Tenorio et al. 1999; Cayón et al. 2001; Holschneider 1996). These works have been extended to directional wavelet transforms (Antoine et al. 2002; McEwen et al. 2007). All these continuous wavelet decompositions are useful for data analysis, but cannot be used for restoration purposes because of the lack of an inverse transform. Freeden and Windheuser (1997) and Freeden and Schneider (1998) proposed the first redundant wavelet transform, based on the spherical harmonics transform, which presents an inverse transform. Starck et al. (2006) proposed an invertible isotropic undecimated wavelet transform (IUWT) on the sphere, also based on spherical harmonics, which has the same property as the starlet transform, that is, the sum of the wavelet scales reproduces the original image. A similar wavelet construction (Marinucci et al. 2008; Faÿ and Guilloux 2011; Faÿ et al. 2008) used the so-called needlet filters. Wiaux et al. (2008) also proposed an algorithm which permits the reconstruction of an image from its steerable wavelet transform. Since reconstruction algorithms are available, these new tools can be used for many applications such as denoising, deconvolution, component separation (Moudden et al. 2005; Bobin et al. 2008; Delabrouille et al. 2009), and inpainting (Abrial et al. 2007; Abrial et al. 2008).

Extensions to the sphere of 2-D geometric multiscale decompositions, such as the ridgelet transform and the curvelet transform, were presented in Starck et al. (2006).

The goal of this chapter is to overview these multiscale transforms on the sphere. Section 12.2 overviews the hierarchical equal area isolatitude pixelization (HEALPix) of a sphere pixelization scheme and the spherical harmonics transform. Section 12.3 shows how a fast orthogonal Haar wavelet transform on the sphere can be built using HEALPix. In Section 12.5, we present an isotropic wavelet transform on the sphere which has similar properties as the starlet transform and therefore should be very useful for data denoising and deconvolution. This algorithm is directly derived from the fast Fourier transform (FFT)-based wavelet transform proposed by Starck et al. (1994) for aperture synthesis image restoration (see Section 3.7.2) and is relatively close to the Freeden and Schneider (1998) method, except that it features the same straightforward reconstruction as does the starlet transform algorithm (i.e., the sum of the scales reproduces the original data). This wavelet transform can also be easily extended to a pyramidal wavelet transform on the sphere (PWTS), allowing us to reduce the redundancy, a possibility which may be very important for larger data sets. In Section 12.6, we show how this new pyramidal transform can be used to derive a curvelet transform on the sphere. Section 12.7 describes how these new transforms can be used for denoising, component separation and inpainting. Some signals on the sphere have an additional time or energy dependency independent of the angular dimension. They are not truly 3-D but rather 2-D-1-D as the additional dimension is not linked to the spatial dimension. An extension of the wavelets on the sphere to this 2-D-1-D class of signals has been proposed in (Schmitt et al. 2010) with an application to Poisson denoising of multichannel data on the sphere. More recently, fully 3-D invertible wavelet transforms have been formulated in spherical coordinates (Lanusse et al. 2012; Leistedt and McEwen 2012). These transforms are suited to signals on the 3-D ball (i.e., on the solid sphere) which arise, for instance, in astrophysics in the study of large scale distribution of galaxies when both angular and radial positions are available.

Sections 12.10.1 and 12.10.2 present how these new tools can help us to analyze data in two real applications, in physics and in cosmology. Finally, guided numerical experiments together with a toolbox dedicated to multiscale transforms on the sphere (MR/S) are described.

12.2 DATA ON THE SPHERE

Various pixelization schemes for data on the sphere exist in the literature. These include the equidistant coordinate partition (ECP), the icosahedron method (Tegmark 1996), the quad cube (White and Stemwedel 1992), IGLOO (Crittenden 2000), HEALPix (Górski et al. 2005), hierarchical triangular mesh (HTM) (Kunszt et al. 2001) or Gauss-Legendre sky pixelization (GLESP) (Doroshkevich et al. 2005). Important properties to decide which one is the best for a given application include the number of pixels and their size; fast computation of the spherical harmonics transform; equal surface area for all pixels; pixel shape regularity; separability of variables with respect to latitude and longitude; availability of efficient software libraries including parallel implementation; and so on. Each of these properties has advantages and drawbacks. In this chapter, we use the HEALPix representation which has several useful properties.

12.2.1 HEALPix

The HEALPix representation (Górski et al. 2005)[1] is a curvilinear hierarchical partition of the sphere into quadrilateral pixels of exactly equal area but with varying

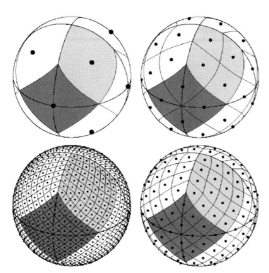

Figure 12.1. The HEALPix sampling grid for four different resolutions.

shape. The base resolution divides the sphere into 12 quadrilateral faces of equal area placed on three rings around the poles and equator. Each face is subsequently divided into N_{side}^2 pixels following a quadrilateral multiscale tree structure (see Fig. 12.1). The pixel centers are located on iso-latitude rings, and pixels from the same ring are equi-spaced in azimuth. This is critical for computational speed of all operations involving the evaluation of the spherical harmonics coefficients, including standard operations such as convolution, power spectrum estimation, and so on. HEALPix is a standard pixelization scheme in astronomy.

12.2.2 Spherical Harmonics

The equivalent of the Fourier transform on the sphere is the spherical harmonics transform. From this analogy, in the sequel, the ˆ notation that was used for Fourier transform in previous chapters will be used to denote the spherical harmonics coefficients of a function. Any function $f(\theta, \vartheta) \in L_2(S^2)$ on the sphere S^2 in $\mathbb{R}^3$ can be decomposed into spherical harmonics:

$$f(\theta, \vartheta) = \sum_{l=0}^{+\infty} \sum_{m=-l}^{l} \hat{f}_{lm} Y_{lm}(\theta, \vartheta), \tag{12.1}$$

where Y_{lm} are the spherical harmonics defined by:

$$Y_{lm}(\theta, \vartheta) = \sqrt{\frac{2l+1}{4\pi} \frac{(l-|m|)!}{(l+|m|)!}} P_{lm}(\cos \vartheta) e^{im\theta}, \tag{12.2}$$

P_{lm} are the associated Legendre functions (or polynomials) defined by the following differential equation:

$$\frac{d}{dt}\left[(1-t^2)\frac{d}{dt}P_{lm}\right] + \left(l(l+1) - \frac{m^2}{1-t^2}\right)P_{lm} = 0. \tag{12.3}$$

These functions are related to the Legendre polynomials P_l by

$$P_{lm}(t) = (-1)^m (1 - t^2)^{m/2} \frac{d^m}{dt^m} P_l(t), \tag{12.4}$$

where P_l is:

$$P_l(t) = \frac{1}{2^l l!} \frac{d^l}{dt^l} (t^2 - 1)^l. \tag{12.5}$$

Furthermore, an important property of the Legendre polynomials is that they are orthogonal:

$$\sum_{l \in \mathbb{N}} \sum_{|m| \leqslant l} Y_{lm}^*(\omega') \, Y_{lm}(\omega) = \delta(\omega' - \omega). \tag{12.6}$$

with $\omega = (\theta, \vartheta)$ et $\omega' = (\theta', \vartheta')$.

In this chapter, many multiscale decompositions will be built based on the spherical harmonics and/or the HEALPix representation.

12.3 ORTHOGONAL HAAR WAVELETS ON THE SPHERE

The Haar wavelet transform on the sphere (Schröder and Sweldens 1995) at each resolution j and pixel $\mathbf{k} = (k_x, k_y)$ on the sphere is based on a scaling function $\phi_{j,\mathbf{k}}$ ($\phi_{j,\mathbf{k}}(\mathbf{x}) = \phi(2^{-j}(\mathbf{x} - \mathbf{k}))$), where $\mathbf{x}$ is the vector of Cartesian coordinates on the sphere, and ϕ is the Haar scaling function) and three Haar wavelet functions $\psi_{j,\mathbf{k}}^d$ (see Section 2.3.3) with $d \in \{1, 2, 3\}$. It uses the idea that a given pixel on the sphere at a given resolution j in the HEALPix representation is directly related to four pixels at the next resolution $j - 1$.

Denoting $\mathbf{k}_0, \mathbf{k}_1, \mathbf{k}_2, \mathbf{k}_3$ the four pixels at scale j, hierarchically related to the pixel $\mathbf{k}$ at scale $j + 1$, scaling coefficients $c_{j+1,\mathbf{k}}$ at scale $j + 1$ are derived from those at scale j by

$$c_{j+1}[\mathbf{k}] = \frac{1}{4} \sum_{d=0}^{3} c_j[\mathbf{k}_d], \tag{12.7}$$

and wavelet coefficients at scale $j + 1$ from coefficients at scale j by

$$w_{j+1}^1[\mathbf{k}] = \frac{1}{4}(c_j[\mathbf{k}_0] + c_j[\mathbf{k}_2] - c_j[\mathbf{k}_1] - c_j[\mathbf{k}_3])$$

$$w_{j+1}^2[\mathbf{k}] = \frac{1}{4}(c_j[\mathbf{k}_0] + c_j[\mathbf{k}_1] - c_j[\mathbf{k}_2] - c_j[\mathbf{k}_3])$$

$$w_{j+1}^3[\mathbf{k}] = \frac{1}{4}(c_j[\mathbf{k}_0] + c_j[\mathbf{k}_3] - c_j[\mathbf{k}_1] - c_j[\mathbf{k}_2]). \tag{12.8}$$

The Haar wavelet transform on the sphere is orthogonal and its reconstruction is exact. The inverse transformation is obtained by

$$c_0[\mathbf{x}] = \sum_{\mathbf{k}} c_J[\mathbf{k}]\phi_{J,\mathbf{k}}(\mathbf{x}) + \sum_{j=1}^{J} \sum_{d=1}^{3} \sum_{\mathbf{k}} w_j^d[\mathbf{k}]\psi_j^d(\mathbf{x}). \tag{12.9}$$

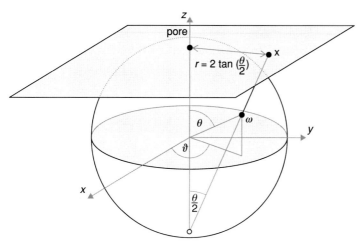

Figure 12.2. Inverse stereographic projections of a radial function from plane to the sphere.

This transform is very fast but its interest is relatively limited. Indeed, it is not rotation invariant, and more importantly the Haar wavelet shape is not well adapted for most applications, because of the nonregular shape of the wavelet function.

12.4 CONTINUOUS WAVELETS ON THE SPHERE

12.4.1 Stereoscopic Projection

To have more choice to design the wavelet function, we may want to use wavelets defined for regular 2-D images to the sphere. This is possible by using inverse stereographic projections of radial wavelet functions such the Mexican hat (Cayón et al. 2001). Defining the stereographic projection operator, $\mathbf{R} : \mathbf{t} \mapsto \omega$, with $\omega = (\theta(r), \vartheta)$, $\theta(r) = 2\arctan(r/2)$, the radial wavelets ψ_{plane} can be projected on the sphere by a unique rotation, $\omega_0 = (\theta_0, \vartheta_0)$, respectively, around the two axes O_y and O_z. Figure 12.2 shows the projection of radial functions from the plane to the sphere.

The convolution on the sphere between a radial wavelet function $\psi(\theta)$ and a function $f(\omega)$ is

$$(\psi * f)(\theta, \vartheta) = \int_{S^2} \psi^*_{\text{plane}}(\mathbf{R}^{-1}\omega) f(\omega)d\omega . \tag{12.10}$$

Such wavelets are axisymmetric by construction. This property can be used to derive fast transformation algorithms using spherical harmonics. Indeed, spherical harmonics coefficients $\hat{\psi}[l, m]$ of the wavelet function ψ on the sphere are equal to zero when $m \neq 0$, and by the Funk-Hecke theorem, the convolution can be written using spherical harmonics by

$$(\psi * f)(\theta, \vartheta) = \sum_{l=0}^{\infty} \sum_{m=-l}^{l} \sqrt{\frac{2l+1}{4\pi}} \hat{f}[l, m]\hat{\psi}[l, 0]Y_{lm}(\theta, \vartheta) . \tag{12.11}$$

where $\hat{f}[l, m]$ are the spherical harmonics coefficients of the function f, i.e. $f = \sum_{l=0}^{\infty} \sum_{m=-l}^{l} \hat{f}[l, m] Y_{lm}$ and similary for $\hat{\psi}$.

Classical wavelet dilations can also be derived on the sphere using the dilation operator $\mathcal{D}_a$ by a factor $a > 0$ (Wiaux et al. 2007):

$$\mathcal{D}_a(f)(\boldsymbol{\omega}) = \chi_a^{1/2}(a, \theta) f(D_a^{-1} \boldsymbol{\omega}), \tag{12.12}$$

where $D_a(\theta, \vartheta) = (\theta_a(\theta), \vartheta)$ with the linear relation $\tan \theta_a(\theta)/2 = a \tan \theta/2$, and D_a is the dilation operator that maps a sphere without its south pole on itself; $\chi_a^{1/2}(a, \theta)$ is a norm preservation term (i.e., $\mathcal{D}_a$ is unitary):

$$\chi_a^{1/2}(a, \theta) = a^{-1}[1 + \tan^2(\theta/2)]/[1 + a^{-2} \tan^2(\theta/2)]. \tag{12.13}$$

12.4.2 Mexican Hat Wavelet

The 2-D Mexican hat wavelet transform is the second derivative of a Gaussian:

$$\psi(r) = \frac{1}{\sqrt{2\pi}} \frac{1}{a} \left(2 - \left(\frac{r}{a}\right)^2\right) e^{-\frac{r^2}{2a^2}} \tag{12.14}$$

where a is a scale factor parameter and r the distance to the wavelet center. Using the inverse stereographic projection, it is possible to extend the Mexican hat wavelet on the sphere (Antoine 1999; Tenorio et al. 1999; Cayón et al. 2001; Holschneider 1996; Vielva et al. 2004):

$$\psi_a(r) = \frac{1}{\sqrt{2\pi} C_a} \left(1 + \left(\frac{r}{2}\right)^2\right)^2 \left(2 - \left(\frac{r}{a}\right)^2\right) e^{-\frac{r^2}{2a^2}}, \tag{12.15}$$

where a is a scale factor, C_a is a normalization term $C_a = a(1 + \frac{a^2}{2} + \frac{a^4}{4})^{\frac{1}{2}}$, and r is the distance on the tangent plane, which is related to the polar angle θ through $r = 2 \tan \frac{\theta}{2}$. This transform may be useful to analyze the data, but it does not have a reconstruction operator, and can therefore not be used for restoration applications. Figure 12.3 shows the Mexican hat wavelet on the sphere for four different scales.

12.4.3 Directional Wavelets

To study anisotropic structures, the previously described continuous wavelet transform can be extended to directional wavelets (Antoine et al. 2002; Vielva et al. 2006; McEwen et al. 2007). Figure 12.4 shows the projection of an elliptic function from the plane to the sphere.

12.4.3.1 Elongated Mexican Hat Wavelet
The elongated Mexican hat wavelet can be written as:

$$\psi_{a_x, a_y}(\theta, \vartheta) = \sqrt{\frac{2}{\pi}} C(a_x, a_y) \left(1 + \tan^2 \frac{\theta}{2}\right) \left(1 - \frac{4 \tan^2 \theta/2}{a_x^2 + a_y^2} \left(\frac{a_y^2}{a_x^2} \cos^2 \vartheta + \frac{a_x^2}{a_y^2} \sin^2 \vartheta\right)\right)$$

$$\times e^{-2 \tan \frac{\theta}{2} (\cos^2 \vartheta / a_x^2 + \sin^2 \vartheta / a_y^2)}, \tag{12.16}$$

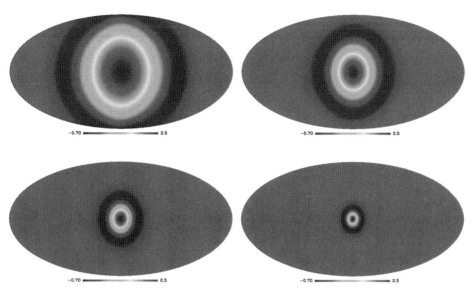

Figure 12.3. Mexican hat on the sphere for the dilation parameter equal to $a = \{1, 2, 4, 8\}$. (See *color plates*.)

where a_x and a_y are the dilation factors along the two axes O_x and O_y, $C(a_x, a_y)$ is a normalization constant defined as

$$C(a_x, a_y) = \left(a_x^2 + a_y^2\right)\left(a_x a_y\left(3a_x^4 + 3a_y^4 + 2a_x a_y\right)\right)^{-1/2}. \tag{12.17}$$

Figure 12.5 shows the wavelet functions for different dilation parameters a_x and a_y.

12.4.3.2 Morlet Wavelet
The Morlet wavelet on the sphere, derived from the stereographic projection of the 2-D function on the plane, is:

$$\psi_{a_x, a_y, \mathbf{k}}(\theta, \vartheta) = \sqrt{\frac{2}{\pi}} C(\mathbf{k}) \left(1 + \tan^2\frac{\theta}{2}\right)\left(\cos\frac{\mathbf{k}\cdot R^{-1}\mathbf{x}}{\sqrt{2}} - e^{-|\mathbf{k}|^2/4}\right)e^{-2\tan^2(\theta/2)} \tag{12.18}$$

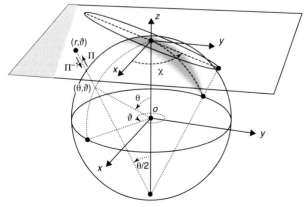

Figure 12.4. Inverse stereographic projections of a directional wavelet on the sphere. (See *color plates*.)

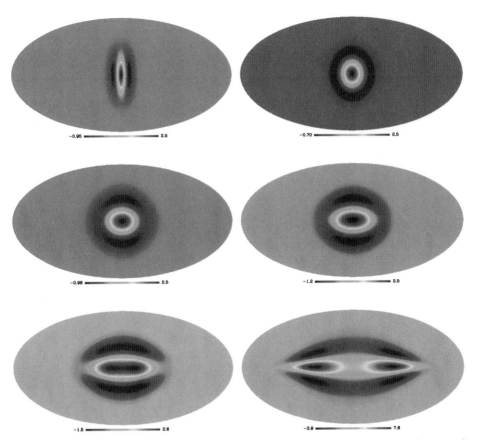

Figure 12.5. Elongated Mexican hat on the sphere for the dilation parameter equal to $a_x = 1$ and $a_y = \{0.5, 1., 1.25, 1.5, 2, 4\}$.

with $R^{-1}\mathbf{x} = (2\tan(\theta/2)\cos\vartheta, 2\tan(\theta/2)\sin\vartheta)$, $\mathbf{k} = (k_x, k_y)$, $|\mathbf{k}|^2 = k_x^2 + k_y^2$, and $C(\mathbf{k}) = (1 + 3e^{-|\mathbf{k}|^2/2} - 4e^{-3|\mathbf{k}|^2/8})^{-1/2}$. $\mathbf{k}$ allows us to control the oscillations of the wavelet functions. Figure 12.6 shows the Morlet wavelet for $\mathbf{k}$ equal respectively to $(2, 0), (4, 0), (6, 6)$ and $(9, 1)$.

Continuous wavelet transforms have been intensively used in astrophysics, mainly to analyze the cosmic microwave background (Vielva et al. 2004). Directional wavelets based on steerable filters were also proposed in Wiaux et al. (2006); McEwen et al. (2007). We present in the following a set of multiscale decompositions on the sphere which have a fast exact inverse transform, and are therefore suitable for many applications such as restoration.

12.5 REDUNDANT WAVELET TRANSFORM ON THE SPHERE WITH EXACT RECONSTRUCTION

12.5.1 Isotropic Undecimated Wavelet Transform on the Sphere

Here an undecimated isotropic transform (UWTS) is described which is similar in many respects to the starlet transform (see Chapter 3) and will therefore be a good

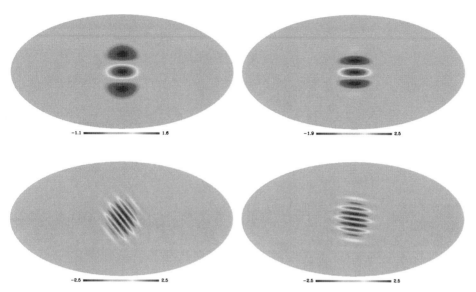

Figure 12.6. Morlet wavelets on the sphere for the parameter **k** equal to (2,0), (4,0), (6,6) et (9,1). (See *color plates*.)

candidate for restoration applications. Its isotropy is a favorable property when analyzing isotropic features. This isotropic transform is obtained using a scaling function $\phi_{l_c}(\theta, \vartheta)$ with cutoff frequency l_c and azimuthal symmetry, meaning that ϕ_{l_c} does not depend on the azimuth ϑ. Hence the spherical harmonics coefficients $\hat{\phi}_{l_c}[l, m]$ of ϕ_{l_c} vanish when $m \neq 0$ so that

$$\phi_{l_c}(\theta, \vartheta) = \phi_{l_c}(\theta) = \sum_{l=0}^{l=l_c} \hat{\phi}_{l_c}[l, 0] Y_{l0}(\theta, \vartheta). \tag{12.19}$$

Then, convolving a function $f(\theta, \vartheta) \in L_2(S^2)$ with ϕ_{l_c} is greatly simplified, and the spherical harmonics coefficients of the resulting map c_0 are readily given by

$$\hat{c}_0[l, m] = \widehat{\phi_{l_c} * f}[l, m] = \sqrt{\frac{2l+1}{4\pi}} \hat{\phi}_{l_c}[l, 0] \hat{f}[l, m]. \tag{12.20}$$

12.5.1.1 From One Resolution to the Next

A sequence of smoother approximations of f on a dyadic resolution scale can be obtained using the scaling function ϕ_{l_c} as follows:

$$\begin{aligned}
c_0 &= & \phi_{l_c} * f \\
c_1 &= & \phi_{2^{-1}l_c} * f \\
& \cdots & \\
c_j &= & \phi_{2^{-j}l_c} * f,
\end{aligned} \tag{12.21}$$

where $\phi_{2^{-j}l_c}$ is a rescaled version of ϕ_{l_c}. The above multiresolution sequence can actually be obtained recursively.

Define a low-pass filter h_j for each scale j by

$$\widehat{H}_j[l, m] = \sqrt{\frac{4\pi}{2l+1}} \hat{h}_j[l, m]$$

$$= \begin{cases} \dfrac{\hat{\phi}_{\frac{l_c}{2^{j+1}}}[l,m]}{\hat{\phi}_{\frac{l_c}{2^{j}}}[l,m]} & \text{if } l < \frac{l_c}{2^{j+1}} \quad \text{and} \quad m = 0, \\ 0 & \text{otherwise} . \end{cases} \quad (12.22)$$

It is then easily shown that c_{j+1} derives from c_j by convolution on the sphere with h_j: $c_{j+1} = c_j * h_j$.

12.5.1.2 The Wavelet Coefficients

Given an axisymmetric wavelet function ψ_{l_c}, we can derive in the same way a high-pass filter g_j on each scale j:

$$\widehat{G}_j[l, m] = \sqrt{\frac{4\pi}{2l+1}} \hat{g}_j[l, m]$$

$$= \begin{cases} \dfrac{\hat{\psi}_{\frac{l_c}{2^{j+1}}}[l,m]}{\hat{\phi}_{\frac{l_c}{2^{j}}}[l,m]} & \text{if } l < \frac{l_c}{2^{j+1}} \quad \text{and} \quad m = 0, \\ 1 & \text{if } l \geq \frac{l_c}{2^{j+1}} \quad \text{and} \quad m = 0, \\ 0 & \text{otherwise} . \end{cases} \quad (12.23)$$

From this definition, the wavelet coefficients w_{j+1} at scale $j+1$ are obtained from the previous scaling coefficients c_j by a simple convolution on the sphere with g_j: $w_{j+1} = c_j * g_j$.

As in the starlet transform algorithm, the wavelet coefficients can be defined as the difference between two consecutive resolutions, $w_{j+1}(\theta, \vartheta) = c_j(\theta, \vartheta) - c_{j+1}(\theta, \vartheta)$. This defines a zonal wavelet function ψ_{l_c} as:

$$\hat{\psi}_{\frac{l_c}{2^{j}}}[l, m] = \hat{\phi}_{\frac{l_c}{2^{j-1}}}[l, m] - \hat{\phi}_{\frac{l_c}{2^{j}}}[l, m] . \quad (12.24)$$

The high-pass filters g_j associated with this wavelet are expressed as

$$\widehat{G}_j[l, m] = \sqrt{\frac{4\pi}{2l+1}} \hat{g}_j[l, m]$$

$$= 1 - \sqrt{\frac{4\pi}{2l+1}} \hat{h}_j[l, m] = 1 - \widehat{H}_j[l, m] . \quad (12.25)$$

Obviously, other wavelet functions could be used just as well.

12.5.1.3 Choice of the Scaling Function

Any function with a cutoff frequency is a possible candidate. We retained here a B-spline function of order 3 (see Chapter 3):

$$\hat{\phi}_{l_c}[l, m] = \frac{3}{2} B_3 \left(\frac{2l}{l_c} \right) \quad (12.26)$$

where $B_3(t)$ is the scaling function defined in Section 3.5.

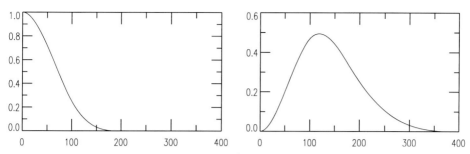

Figure 12.7. Spherical harmonic coefficients $\hat{\phi}[l, 0]$ of (left) the scaling function ϕ and (right) the wavelet function ψ.

In Figure 12.7, the spherical harmonics coefficients of the scaling function derived from a B_3-spline, and those of the associated wavelet function (12.24), are plotted as a function of l. Other functions such as the needlet function (Marinucci et al. 2008) can be used as well.

The steps of the UWT on the sphere of a discrete image X sampled from f are summarized in Algorithm 51. If the wavelet function corresponds to the choice (12.24), Step 3 in this UWTS algorithm reduces to $w_{j+1} = c_j - c_{j+1}$.

Algorithm 51 The Undecimated Wavelet Transform on the Sphere

Task: Compute the UWTS of a discrete X.
Parameters: Data samples X and number of of wavelet scales J.
Initialization:

■ $c_0 = X$.
■ Compute the B_3-spline scaling function and derive $\hat{\psi}$, $\widehat{H}$ and $\widehat{G}$ numerically.
■ Compute the corresponding spherical harmonics transform of c_0.

for $j = 0$ to $J - 1$ **do**

    1. Compute the spherical harmonics transform of the scaling coefficients: $\hat{c}_{j+1} = \hat{c}_j \widehat{H}_j$.
    2. Compute the inverse spherical harmonics transform of $\hat{c}_{j+1}$ to get c_{j+1}.
    3. Compute the spherical harmonics transform of the wavelet coefficients: $\hat{w}_{j+1} = \hat{c}_j \widehat{G}_j$.
    4. Compute the inverse spherical harmonics transform of $\hat{w}_{j+1}$ to get w_{j+1}.

Output: $\mathcal{W} = \{w_1, w_2, \ldots, w_J, c_J\}$ the UWTS of X.

Figure 12.8 shows the Mars topographic map[2] and its wavelet transform, using five scales (four wavelet scales + coarse scale). The sum of the five scales reproduces exactly the original image.

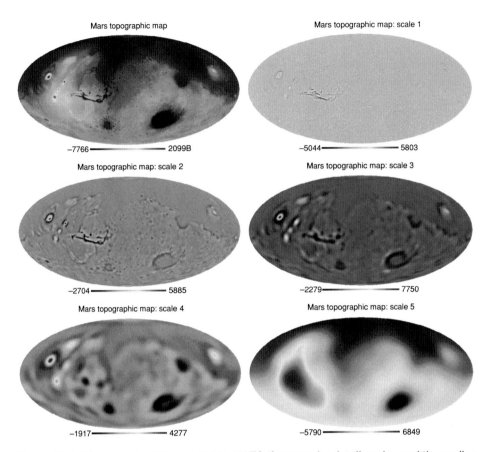

Figure 12.8. Mars topographic map and its UWTS (four wavelet detail scales and the scaling (smooth) band). (See *color plates*.)

12.5.1.4 Inverse Transform

If the wavelet is the difference between two resolutions, a straightforward reconstruction of an image from its wavelet coefficients $\mathcal{W} = \{w_1, \ldots, w_J, c_J\}$ is

$$c_0(\theta, \vartheta) = c_J(\theta, \vartheta) + \sum_{j=1}^{J} w_j(\theta, \vartheta) \,. \tag{12.27}$$

This reconstruction formula is the same as with the starlet algorithm.

But since the transform is redundant there is actually no unique way to reconstruct an image from its coefficients (the filterbank design framework of Section 3.6). Indeed, using the relations

$$\hat{c}_{j+1}[l, m] = \widehat{H}_j[l, m]\hat{c}_j[l, m]$$
$$\hat{w}_{j+1}[l, m] = \widehat{G}_j[l, m]\hat{c}_j[l, m] \tag{12.28}$$

a least-squares estimate of c_j from c_{j+1} and w_{j+1} gives

$$\hat{c}_j = \hat{c}_{j+1}\widehat{\tilde{H}}_j + \hat{w}_{j+1}\widehat{\tilde{G}}_j \,, \tag{12.29}$$

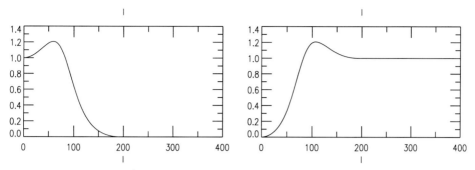

Figure 12.9. (left) Filter $\widehat{h}$, and (right) filter $\widehat{g}$.

where the dual filters $\tilde{h}$ and $\tilde{g}$ satisfy

$$\widehat{\tilde{H}}_j = \sqrt{\frac{4\pi}{2l+1}}\widehat{\tilde{h}}_j = \widehat{H}_j^*/(|\widehat{H}_j|^2 + |\widehat{G}_j|^2)$$

$$\widehat{\tilde{G}}_j = \sqrt{\frac{4\pi}{2l+1}}\widehat{\tilde{g}}_j = \widehat{G}_j^*/(|\widehat{H}_j|^2 + |\widehat{G}_j|^2).$$

(12.30)

For the scaling function, which is a B_3-spline function and a wavelet taken as the difference between two resolutions, the corresponding conjugate low-pass and high-pass filters $\widehat{\tilde{H}}$ and $\widehat{\tilde{G}}$ are plotted in Fig. 12.9. The reconstruction algorithm is given in Algorithm 52.

Algorithm 52 Inverse UWT on the Sphere

Task: Reconstruct an image from its UWTS coefficients.
Parameters: UWTS coefficients $\mathcal{W} = \{w_1, w_2, \ldots, w_J, c_J\}$.
Initialization:

■ Compute the B_3-spline scaling function and derive $\hat{\psi}, \widehat{H}, \widehat{G}, \widehat{\tilde{H}}$ and $\widehat{\tilde{G}}$ numerically.
■ Compute the spherical harmonics transform of c_J to get $\hat{c}_J$.

for $j = J - 1$ to 0, with step $= -1$ **do**

1. Compute the spherical harmonics transform of the wavelet coefficients w_{j+1} to get $\hat{w}_{j+1}$.
2. Multiply $\hat{c}_{j+1}$ by $\widehat{\tilde{H}}_j$.
3. Multiply $\hat{w}_{j+1}$ by $\widehat{\tilde{G}}_j$.
4. Get the spherical harmonics of $\hat{c}_j = \hat{c}_{j+1} + \hat{w}_{j+1}$.

Compute the inverse spherical harmonics transform of $\hat{c}_0$.
Output: c_0 is the inverse UWT on the sphere.

Figure 12.10 shows the reconstruction by setting all wavelet coefficients but one at different scales and positions. Depending on the position and scale of the nonzero

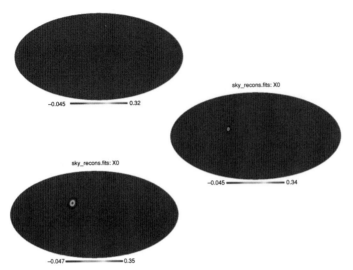

Figure 12.10. Reconstruction from a single wavelet coefficient at different scales. Each map is obtained by setting all wavelet coefficients to zero but one, and by applying an inverse UWTS. Depending on the position and scale of the nonzero coefficient, the reconstructed map shows an isotropic feature at different scales and positions. (See *color plates*.)

coefficient, the reconstructed map shows an isotropic feature at different scales and positions.

12.5.2 Isotropic Pyramidal Wavelet Transform on the Sphere

12.5.2.1 Forward Transform

In the previous algorithm, no down-sampling is performed and each scale of the wavelet decomposition has the same number of pixels as the original data set. Therefore the number of pixels in the decomposition is equal to the number of pixels in the data multiplied by the number of scales. For some applications, we may prefer to introduce a decimation in the decomposition so as to reduce the required memory size and the computation time. This can be done easily by using a specific property of the chosen scaling function. Indeed, since we are considering here a scaling function with an initial cutoff l_c in spherical harmonic multipole number l, and since the actual cutoff is reduced by a factor of two at each step, the number of significant spherical harmonics coefficients is then reduced by a factor of four after each convolution with the low pass filter h. Therefore, we need less pixels in the direct space when we compute the inverse spherical harmonics transform. Using the HEALPix pixelization scheme (Górski et al. 2005), this can be done easily by dividing by 2 the N_{side} parameter when calling the inverse spherical harmonics transform routine. The PWTS algorithm is given in Algorithm 53.

Figure 12.11 shows an Earth image and its PWTS using five scales. As the scale number increases (i.e., the resolution decreases), the pixel size becomes larger. The data are land and sea-floor elevations obtained from the ETOPO5 5-minute gridded elevation data set. A thorough explanation of the data set is provided online (www.ngdc.noaa.gov)[3].

Algorithm 53 Pyramidal wavelet transform on the sphere

Task: Compute the pyramidal WT on the sphere of a discrete image X.
Parameters: Data X and number of of wavelet scales J.
Initialization:

- $c_0 = X$.
- Compute the B_3-spline scaling function and derive $\hat{\psi}$, $\widehat{H}$ and $\widehat{G}$ numerically.
- Compute the corresponding spherical harmonics transform of c_0.

for $j = 0$ to $J - 1$ **do**

1. Compute the spherical harmonics transform of the scaling coefficients: $\hat{c}_{j+1} = \hat{c}_j \widehat{H}_j$.
2. Compute the inverse spherical harmonics transform of $\hat{c}_{j+1}$ to get c_{j+1}.
3. Down-sample c_{j+1}, since its support in the spherical harmonic domain has been divided by two.
4. Compute the spherical harmonics transform of the wavelet coefficients: $\hat{w}_{j+1} = \hat{c}_j \widehat{G}_j$.
5. Compute the inverse spherical harmonics transform of $\hat{w}_{j+1}$ to get w_{j+1}.

Output: $\mathcal{W} = \{w_1, w_2, \ldots, w_J, c_J\}$ the PWTS of X.

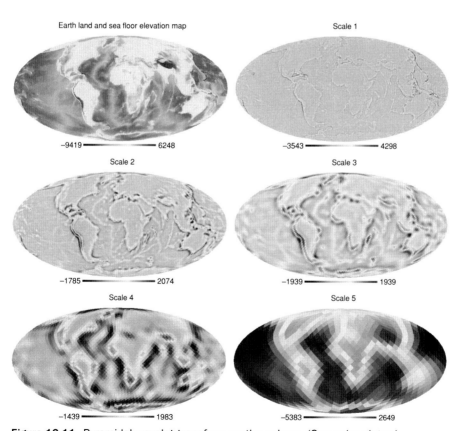

Figure 12.11. Pyramidal wavelet transform on the sphere. (See *color plates*.)

12.5.2.2 Inverse Transform

This reconstruction is not as straightforward as in the undecimated case because the different scales do not have the same resolution. For each resolution level, we have to up-sample the scaling band before coadding it to the wavelet coefficients. Algorithm 54 describes this.

Algorithm 54 Inverse Pyramidal Wavelet Transform on the Sphere

---

Task: Reconstruct an image from its PWTS.
Parameters: Pyramidal wavelet transform coefficients $W = \{w_1, w_2, \ldots, w_J, c_J\}$.
Initialization:

■ Compute the B_3-spline scaling function and derive $\hat{\psi}, \hat{H}, \hat{G}, \widehat{\tilde{H}}$ and $\widehat{\tilde{G}}$ numerically.
■ Compute the spherical harmonics transform of c_J to get $\hat{c}_J$.

for $j = J - 1$ **to** 0 **do**

    1. Upsample c_{j+1} to the resolution of c_j.
    2. Compute the spherical harmonics transform of the wavelet coefficients w_{j+1} to get $\hat{w}_{j+1}$.
    3. Multiply $\hat{c}_{j+1}$ by $\widehat{\tilde{H}}_j$.
    4. Multiply $\hat{w}_{j+1}$ by $\widehat{\tilde{G}}_j$.
    5. Get the spherical harmonics of $\hat{c}_j = \hat{c}_{j+1} + \hat{w}_{j+1}$.

Compute The inverse spherical harmonics transform of $\hat{c}_0$.
Output: c_0, the PWTS.

The wavelet transform on the sphere and its pyramidal version have both a reconstruction operator, so they are very well designed for any restoration application when the data contains isotropic features. In the following, we present other transforms on the sphere more adapted to the analysis of anisotropic features.

12.6 CURVELET TRANSFORM ON THE SPHERE

The 2-D curvelet transform enables the directional analysis of an image in different scales (see Chapter 5). The fundamental property of the curvelet transform is to analyze the data with functions of length about $2^{-j/2}$ for the jth subband $[2^j, 2^{j+1}]$ of the 2-D wavelet transform. Following the implementation of the first generation curvelet transform described in Section 5.4.1.1, the data first undergo an IUWT(i.e., starlet transform). Each scale j is then decomposed into smoothly overlapping blocks of side-length B_j pixels in such a way that the overlap between two vertically adjacent blocks is a rectangular array of size $B_j \times B_j/2$. Finally, the ridgelet transform is applied on each individual block. Recall from Chapter 5 that the ridgelet transform precisely amounts to applying a 1-D wavelet transform to the slices of the Radon transform. The first generation curvelet transform is also redundant, with a redundancy factor of $16J + 1$ whenever J scales are employed. The curvelet transform was shown to sparsely represent anisotropic structures and smooth curves and edges of different lengths.

12.6.1 Curvelets on the Sphere

The curvelet transform on the sphere (CTS) can be similar to the 2-D first generation digital curvelet transform, but replacing the starlet transform by the isotropic UWTS previously described. The CTS algorithm is the following:

- Isotropic UWTS.
- *Partitioning*: Each scale is decomposed into blocks of an appropriate scale (of side-length $\sim 2^{-s}$), using the HEALPix pixelization.
- *Ridgelet transform:* Each block is analyzed with the discrete ridgelet transform.

We now describe these three steps.

12.6.1.1 Partitioning Using the HEALPix Representation

The HEALPix representation is a curvilinear hierarchical partition of the sphere into quadrilateral pixels of exactly equal area but with varying shape. The base resolution divides the sphere into 12 quadrilateral faces of equal area placed on three rings around the poles and equator. Each face is subsequently divided into N_{side}^2 pixels following a quadrilateral multiscale tree structure (see Fig. 12.1). The pixel centers are located on isolatitude rings, and pixels from the same ring are equispaced in azimuth. This is critical for computational speed of all operations involving the evaluation of spherical harmonics transforms, including standard numerical analysis operations such as convolution, and power spectrum estimation.

An important geometrical feature of the HEALPix sampling grid is the hierarchical quadrilateral tree structure. This defines a natural one-to-one mapping of the sphere sampled according to the HEALPix grid, into twelve flat images, on all scales. It is then easy to partition a spherical map using HEALPix into quadrilateral blocks of a specified size. One first extracts the twelve base-resolution faces, and each face is then decomposed into overlapping blocks of the specified size. This decomposition into blocks is an essential step of the traditional flat 2-D curvelet transform. Based on the reversible warping of the sphere into a set of flat images made possible by the HEALPix sampling grid, the ridgelet and curvelet transforms can be extended to the sphere.

With the decomposition into blocks described above, there is no overlap between neighboring blocks belonging to different base-resolution faces. This may result for instance in blocking effects in denoising experiments via nonlinear filtering. It is possible to overcome this difficulty in some sense by working simultaneously with various rotations of the data with respect to the sampling grid. This will average out undesirable effects at edges between base resolution faces.

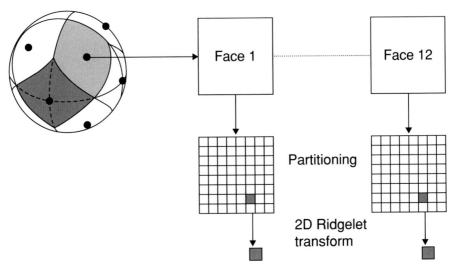

Figure 12.12. Flow graph of the ridgelet transform on the sphere.

12.6.1.2 Ridgelet Transform

Once the partitioning is performed, the standard 2-D ridgelet transform described in Chapter 5 is applied in each individual block. The ridgelet transform can be based on different implementations of the Radon transform (e.g., linogram, fast slant stack); see Chapter 5 for details.

Figure 12.12 shows the flow graph of the ridgelet transform on the sphere, and Fig. 12.13 shows the reconstruction from a single ridgelet coefficient at different scales and orientations.

12.6.2 Curvelet Transform Algorithm

The curvelet transform algorithm on the sphere is described in Algorithm 55.

Figure 12.13. Ridgelet atoms on the sphere obtained by reconstruction from a few ridgelet coefficient at different scales and orientations. (See *color plates*.)

Algorithm 55 Curvelet Transform on the sphere

Task: Compute the curvelet transform on the sphere of a discrete image X.
Parameters: Image X and number of scales J.
Initialization:

- $B_1 = B_{\min}$.
- Compute the isotropic UWTS of X with J scales, get $\{w_1, \ldots, w_J, c_J\}$.

for $j = 0$ to $J - 2$ **do**

1. Partition the wavelet subband w_j with a block size B_j.
2. Apply the digital ridgelet transform to each block; get the curvelet coefficients at scale j.

    if j modulo $2 = 1$ **then** $B_{j+1} = 2B_j$, else $B_{j+1} = B_j$.

Output: The curvelet transform on the sphere of X.

The side length of the localizing windows is doubled *at every other* dyadic subband, hence maintaining the fundamental property of the curvelet transform which says that elements of length about $2^{-j/2}$ serve for the analysis and synthesis of the jth subband $[2^j, 2^{j+1}]$. We used the default value $B_{\min} = 16$ pixels in our implementation. Figure 12.14 gives an overview of the organization of the algorithm.

Figure 12.15 shows the backprojection of curvelet coefficients at different scales and orientations.

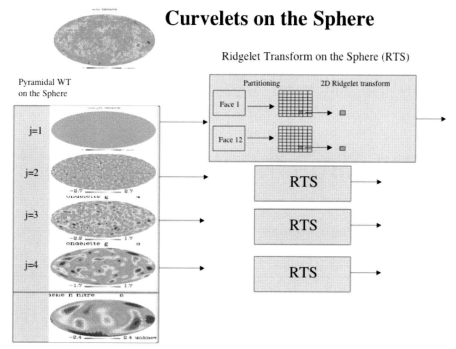

Figure 12.14. Flow graph of the curvelet transform on the sphere. (See *color plates*.)

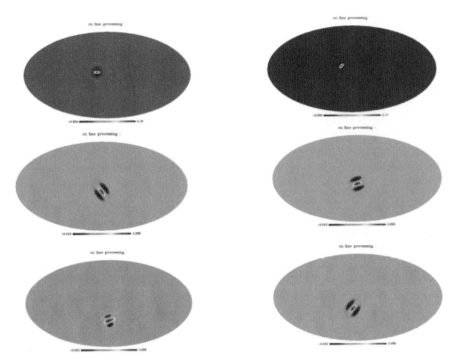

Figure 12.15. Reconstruction from a single curvelet coefficient at different scales and orientations. (See *color plates*.)

12.6.3 Pyramidal Curvelet Transform on the Sphere

The CTS is very redundant, which may be a problem for handling huge data sets such as Planck data (see Section 12.10.2 below). The redundancy can be reduced by substituting, in the curvelet transform algorithm, the pyramidal wavelet transform with the undecimated wavelet transform. The second step, which consists of applying the ridgelet transform on the wavelet scale is unchanged. The pyramidal curvelet transform (PCTS) algorithm is summarized in Algorithm 56.

Algorithm 56 Pyramidal Curvelet Transform on the Sphere

Task: Compute the PCTS of a discrete image X.
Parameters: Image X and number of scales J.
Initialization:

- $B_1 = B_{\min}$.
- Compute the pyramidal wavelet transform of X with J scales, get $\{w_1, \ldots, w_J, c_J\}$.

for $j = 0$ to $J - 2$ **do**

  1. Partition the wavelet subband w_j with a block size B_j.
  2. Apply the digital ridgelet transform to each block; get the curvelet coefficients at scale j.

  if j modulo $2 = 1$ **then** $B_{j+1} = 2B_j$, else $B_{j+1} = B_j$.
Output: The PCTS of X.

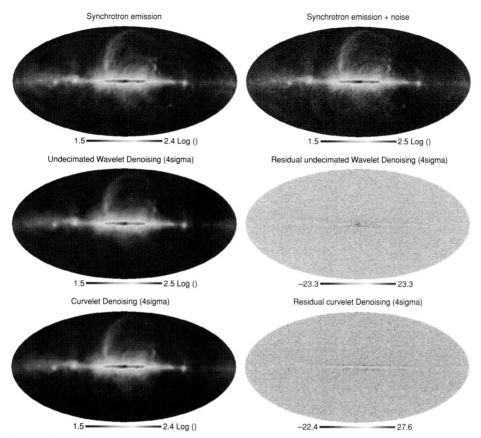

Figure 12.16. Denoising. (top) Simulated synchrotron image and same image with additive Gaussian noise (i.e., simulated data). (middle) Undecimated wavelet filtering and residual. (bottom) Pyramidal curvelet filtering and residual. (See *color plates*.)

In the next section, it is shown how the pyramidal curvelet transform can be used for image filtering.

12.7 RESTORATION AND DECOMPOSITION ON THE SPHERE

12.7.1 Denoising

Wavelets and curvelets have been used successfully for image denoising via nonlinear filtering or thresholding methods as extensively studied in Chapter 6. In the results of Fig. 12.16, denoising by hard thresholding the wavelet and curvelet coefficients on the sphere was used. The threshold was set to $4\times$ the standard deviation of the noise at each subband.

Figure 12.16 describes the setting and the results of a simulated denoising experiment: upper left, the original simulated map of the astrophysical synchrotron emission; upper right, the same image plus additive Gaussian noise ($\sigma = 5$). Since the synchrotron image has a standard deviation (after renormalization) equal to 16.26, the SNR is around 3.25. The middle panels in this figure show the UWTS denoised image and the residuals. The bottom panels show the pyramidal curvelet transform

Table 12.1. Error standard deviations after denoising the synchrotron noisy map (additive white Gaussian noise, $\sigma = 5$) by the wavelet, the curvelet and the combined denoising algorithm. See Section 8.3 for a description of the latter

Method	Error standard deviation
Noisy map	5 8
Wavelet	1.25
Curvelet	1.07
CFA	0.86

filtered image and the residuals. On such data, exhibiting very anisotropic features, the curvelets produce better results than wavelets.

The residuals after wavelet- and curvelet-based denoising presented in Fig. 12.16 show different structures. As expected, elongated features are better restored using the curvelet transform, while isotropic structures are better denoised using the wavelet transform. The combined denoising algorithm introduced in Section 8.3 can obviously also be applied on the sphere, in order to benefit from the advantages of both transforms. This iterative method detects the significant coefficients in both the wavelet domain and the curvelet domain and guarantees that the reconstructed map will take into account any pattern which is detected as significant by either of the transforms.

The results are reported in Table 12.1. The residual is much better when the combined denoising is applied, and no feature can be detected any more by eye in the residual (see Fig. 12.17). This was not the case for either the wavelet or the curvelet based denoising alone.

12.7.2 Morphological Component Analysis

The morphological component analysis (MCA) Algorithm 32 (see Section 8.5) was applied to a decomposition problem of an image on the sphere, using the transforms developed above.

The spherical maps shown in Fig. 12.18 illustrate a simple numerical experiment. We applied the MCA decomposition algorithm on the sphere, to synthetic data resulting from the linear mixture of components that were respectively sparse in the spherical harmonics and the isotropic wavelet representations. The method was able to separate the data back into its original constituents.

12.7.3 Inpainting

The inpainting algorithms described in Section 8.7 can also be applied on the sphere. In Section 8.7, a total variation penalty is shown to enhance the recovery of piecewise smooth components. Asking for regularity across the gaps of some localized statistics (e.g. enforcing the empirical variance of a given inpainted sparse component to be nearly equal outside and inside the masked areas) yields other possible constraints.

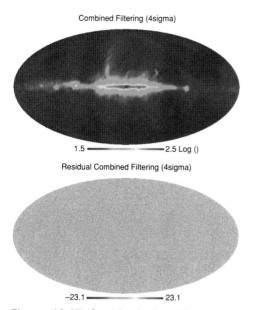

Combined Filtering (4sigma)

1.5 ——————— 2.5 Log ()

Residual Combined Filtering (4sigma)

−23.1 ——————— 23.1

Figure 12.17. Combined denoising (using both wavelets and curvelets) and residuals. (See *color plates*.)

In practice, because of the lack of accuracy of some digital transformations, additional constraints in the spherical topology can be used which may be relaxed close to convergence. These constraints were also found useful in some cases to stabilize the described iterative algorithms.

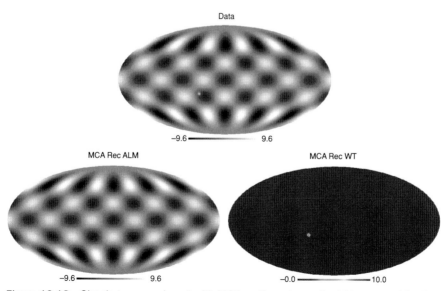

Data

−9.6 ——————— 9.6

MCA Rec ALM

−9.6 ——————— 9.6

MCA Rec WT

−0.0 ——————— 10.0

Figure 12.18. Simple toy experiment with MCA on the sphere. (top) Linear combination of a spherical harmonic function and a localized Gaussian-like function on the sphere. (bottom) Resulting separated components obtained using the proposed MCA on the sphere. (See *color plates*.)

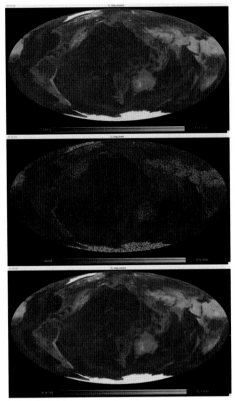

Figure 12.19. Application of the proposed MCA-inpainting algorithm on the sphere. (top) Original satellite view of the Earth. (middle) Incomplete map retaining 40 percent of the original pixels. (bottom) Inpainted map. (See *color plates.*)

A simple numerical experiment is shown in Fig. 12.19. Starting with a full satellite view of the Earth[4], an incomplete spherical map was obtained by randomly masking some of the pixels. In fact, as much as sixty percent of the pixels were masked. Using both the spherical harmonics transform and the curvelet transform on the sphere within the proposed MCA inpainting algorithm, it is possible to fill in the missing pixels in a visually undetectable way.

12.8 2-D–1-D WAVELET ON THE SPHERE

Using the isotropic undecimated wavelet transform on the sphere (IUWTS), one can extend the 2-D–1-D formalism (Starck et al. 2009) presented in Section 11.2.3 to spherical data with an additional dependency in either time or energy (Schmitt et al. 2010). As before, since the 2-D spatial dimension and the 1-D time or energy dimension do not have the same physical meaning, it appears natural that the wavelet scale along the third dimension should not be connected to the spatial scale. Hence, the 2-D–1-D wavelet function is defined by the tensor product of a 2-D wavelet and a 1-D wavelet:

$$\psi(k_\theta, k_\varphi, k_t) = \psi^{(\theta\phi)}(k_\theta, k_\varphi)\psi^{(t)}(k_t), \tag{12.31}$$

where $\psi^{(\theta\phi)}$ is the spherical spatial wavelet and $\psi^{(t)}$ the 1-D wavelet along the third dimension. Considering only isotropic and dyadic spatial scales, the discrete 2-D–1-D wavelet decomposition can be built by first taking an IUWTS for each k_t, followed by a 1-D wavelet transform (e.g., 1-D starlet) for each resulting spatial wavelet coefficient along the third dimension.

Hence for a given multichannel data set on the sphere $D[k_\theta, k_\varphi, k_t]$, applying first the IUWTS yields

$$\forall k_t, \quad D[\cdot, \cdot, k_t] = c_{J_1}[\cdot, \cdot, k_t] + \sum_{j_1=1}^{J1} w_{j_1}[\cdot, \cdot, k_t], \tag{12.32}$$

where J_1 is the number of spatial scales, a_{J_1} is the (spatial) approximation subband, and $\{w_{j_1}\}_{j_1=1}^{J_1}$ are the (spatial) detail subbands. To lighten the notation in the sequel, we replace the two spatial indices by a single index k_r which corresponds to the pixel index. Expression (12.32) reads now

$$\forall k_t, \quad D[\cdot, k_t] = a_{J_1}[\cdot, k_t] + \sum_{j_1=1}^{J1} w_{j_1}[\cdot, k_t]. \tag{12.33}$$

Then, for each spatial location k_r and for each 2-D wavelet scale j_1, a 1-D wavelet transform can be applied along t on the spatial wavelet coefficients $w_{j_1}[k_r, \cdot]$ such that

$$\forall k_t, \quad w_{j_1}[\cdot, k_t] = w_{j_1, J_2}[\cdot, k_t] + \sum_{j_2=1}^{J_2} w_{j_1, j_2}[\cdot, k_t], \tag{12.34}$$

where J_2 is the number of scales along t. The approximation spatial subband c_{J_1} is processed in a similar way, hence yielding

$$\forall k_t, \quad c_{J_1}[\cdot, k_t] = c_{J_1, J_2}[\cdot, k_t] + \sum_{j_2=1}^{J_2} w_{J_1, j_2}[\cdot, k_t]. \tag{12.35}$$

Inserting (12.34) and (12.35) into (12.33), we obtain the 2-D–1-D spherical undecimated wavelet representation of D:

$$D[k_r, k_t] = c_{J_1, J_2}[k_r, k_t] + \sum_{j_1=1}^{J_1} w_{j_1, J_2}[k_r, k_t] + \sum_{j_2=1}^{J_2} w_{J_1, j_2}[k_r, k_t] + \sum_{j_1=1}^{J_1}\sum_{j_2=1}^{J_2} w_{j_1, j_2}[k_r, k_t]. \tag{12.36}$$

Just as in Section 11.2.3, four kinds of coefficients can be distinguished in this expression:

■ Detail-Detail coefficients ($j_1 \leqslant J_1$ and $j_2 \leqslant J_2$):

$$w_{j_1, j_2}[k_r, \cdot] = (\delta - \bar{h}_{1D}) \star \left(h_{1D}^{(j_2-1)} \star a_{j_1-1}[k_r, \cdot] - h_{1D}^{(j_2-1)} \star a_{j_1}[k_r, \cdot]\right).$$

■ Approximation-Detail coefficients ($j_1 = J_1$ and $j_2 \leqslant J_2$):

$$w_{J_1, j_2}[k_r, \cdot] = h_{1\mathrm{D}}^{(j_2-1)} \star c_{J_1}[k_r, \cdot] - h_{1\mathrm{D}}^{(j_2)} \star c_{J_1}[k_r, \cdot].$$

■ Detail-Approximation coefficients ($j_1 \leqslant J_1$ and $j_2 = J_2$):

$$w_{j_1, J_2}[k_r, \cdot] = h_{1\mathrm{D}}^{(J_2)} \star c_{j_1-1}[k_r, \cdot] - h_{1\mathrm{D}}^{(J_2)} \star c_{j_1}[k_r, \cdot].$$

■ Approximation-Approximation coefficients ($j_1 = J_1$ and $j_2 = J_2$):

$$c_{J_1, J_2}[k_r, \cdot] = h_{1\mathrm{D}}^{(J_2)} \star c_{J_1}[k_r, \cdot].$$

As this 2-D–1-D transform is fully linear, a Gaussian noise remains Gaussian after transformation. Therefore, all thresholding strategies that have been developed for wavelet Gaussian denoising are still valid with the 2-D–1-D wavelet transform.

12.8.1 Application: Multichannel Poisson Deconvolution on the Sphere

In this section, we present an application of this 2-D–1-D spherical wavelet to the deconvolution of multichannel data on the sphere in the presence of Poisson noise. This application (Schmitt et al. 2012) was developed in the context of the Fermi Gamma-Ray Space Telescope, which studies the high-energy gamma-ray sky through its main instrument, the Large Area Telescope (LAT).

As mentioned in the application of the Cartesian 2-D–1-D transform in Section 11.2.4 to the same LAT data, the detection of point sources is complicated by the Poisson noise inherent in the weakness of the fluxes of celestial gamma rays and by the instrument's point spread function (PSF). In particular, the PSF is strongly energy dependent, varying from about 3.5° at 100 MeV to less than 0.1° (68% containment) at 10 GeV. Owing to large-angle multiple scattering in the tracker, the PSF has broad tails, and the 95%/68% containment ratio may be as large as 3.

Using a direct extension of the Cartesian 2-D–1-D MS-VST presented in Section 11.2.4 to spherical data with an energy dependence, it is possible to address the multichannel PSF deconvolution problem on the sphere in the presence of Poisson noise in a single general framework.

12.8.1.1 2-D–1-D Multiscale Variance Stabilization Transform on the Sphere

The extension of the 2-D–1-D MS-VST to spherical data simply amounts to replacing the Cartesian 2-D–1-D transform by the spherical transform defined in the previous section. Again, four kinds of coefficients can be identified:

■ Detail-Detail coefficients ($j_1 \leqslant J_1$ and $j_2 \leqslant J_2$):

$$w_{j_1, j_2}[k_r, \cdot] = (\delta - \bar{h}_{1\mathrm{D}})$$
$$\star \left(\mathcal{A}_{j_1-1, j_2-1}\big(h_{1\mathrm{D}}^{(j_2-1)} \star c_{j_1-1}[k_r, \cdot]\big) - \mathcal{A}_{j_1, j_2-1}\big(h_{1\mathrm{D}}^{(j_2-1)} \star c_{j_1}[k_r, \cdot]\big) \right).$$

■ Approximation-Detail coefficients ($j_1 = J_1$ and $j_2 \leqslant J_2$):

$$w_{J_1, j_2}[k_r, \cdot] = \mathcal{A}_{J_1, j_2-1}\big(h_{1\mathrm{D}}^{(j_2-1)} \star c_{J_1}[k_r, \cdot]\big) - \mathcal{A}_{J_1, j_2}\big(h_{1\mathrm{D}}^{(j_2)} \star c_{J_1}[k_r, \cdot]\big).$$

■ Detail-Approximation coefficients ($j_1 \leqslant J_1$ and $j_2 = J_2$):

$$w_{j_1,J_2}[k_r, \cdot] = \mathcal{A}_{j_1-1,J_2}\left(h_{1D}^{(J_2)} \star c_{j_1-1}[k_r, \cdot]\right) - \mathcal{A}_{j_1,J_2}\left(h_{1D}^{(J_2)} \star c_{j_1}[k_r, \cdot]\right).$$

■ Approximation-Approximation coefficients ($j_1 = J_1$ and $j_2 = J_2$):

$$c_{J_1,J_2}[k_r, \cdot] = h_{1D}^{(J_2)} \star c_{J_1}[k_r, \cdot].$$

$\mathcal{A}_{j_1,j_2}$ is the nonlinear square root VST introduced in Zhang et al. (2008a) (see Section 11.2.4). In summary, all 2-D–1-D wavelet coefficients $\{w_{j_1,j_2}\}_{j_1 \leqslant J_1, j_2 \leqslant J_2}$ are now stabilized, and the noise on all these wavelet coefficients is zero-mean Gaussian with a known variance that depends solely on h on the resolution levels (j_1, j_2). As before, these variances can be easily tabulated.

12.8.1.2 The Multichannel Deconvolution Problem
Many problems in signal and image processing can be cast as inverting the linear system:

$$Y = \mathbf{H}X + \varepsilon, \tag{12.37}$$

where $X \in \mathcal{X}$ is the data to recover, $Y \in \mathcal{Y}$ is the degraded noisy observation, ε is an additive noise, and $\mathbf{H} : \mathcal{X} \to \mathcal{Y}$ is a bounded linear operator that is typically ill behaved since it models an acquisition process that encounters a loss of information. When $\mathbf{H}$ is the identity, it is just a denoising problem that can be treated with the previously described methods. Inverting equation(12.37) is usually an ill-posed problem. This means that there is no unique and stable solution.

In the present case, the objective is to remove the effect of the instrument's PSF. $\mathbf{H}$ is the convolution operator by a blurring kernel (i.e., PSF) whose consequence is that Y lacks the high-frequency content of X. Furthermore, since the noise is Poisson, ε has a variance profile $\mathbf{H}X$. The problem at hand is then a deconvolution problem in the presence of Poisson noise. Because the PSF is channel dependent, the convolution observation model is

$$Y[\cdot, k_t] = \mathbf{H}_{k_t}X[\cdot, k_t] + \varepsilon[\cdot, k_t],$$

in each channel k_t, where $\mathbf{H}_{k_t}$ is the (spatial) convolution operator in channel k_t with known PSF. In the case of the LAT, the PSF width depends strongly on the energy, from 6.9° at 50 MeV to better than 0.1° at 10 GeV and above. Figure 12.20 shows the normalized profiles of the PSF for different energy bands.

This inversion can be performed using the well-known Richardson-Lucy algorithm with an additional regularization constraint from a multiresolution support (Murtagh et al. 1995). Let $\mathbf{H}$ be the multichannel convolution operator, which acts on a 2-D–1-D multichannel spherical data set X by applying $\mathbf{H}_{k_t}$ on each channel $X[\cdot, k_t]$ independently[5]. The regularized multichannel Richardson-Lucy scheme proposed in Schmitt et al. (2012) is

$$X^{(n+1)} = \mathrm{P}_{\mathcal{P}_+}\left(X^{(n)} \otimes \left(\mathbf{H}^T\left((\mathbf{H}X^{(n)} + \overline{R}^{(n)}) \oslash \mathbf{H}X^{(n)}\right)\right)\right), \tag{12.38}$$

where $\otimes$ (resp. $\oslash$) stands for the element-wise multiplication (resp. division) between two vectors, $\mathrm{P}_{\mathcal{P}_+}$ is the orthogonal projector onto the positive orthant $\mathcal{P}_+$, and $\overline{R}^{(n)}$ is

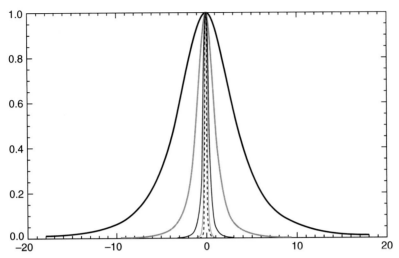

Figure 12.20. Normalized profile of the PSF for different energy bands as a function of the angle in degree. Black: 50 MeV – 82 MeV. Cyan: 220 MeV – 360 MeV. Orange: 960 MeV – 1.6 GeV. Blue: 4.2 GeV – 6.9 GeV. Green: 19 GeV – 31 GeV. (See *color plates*.)

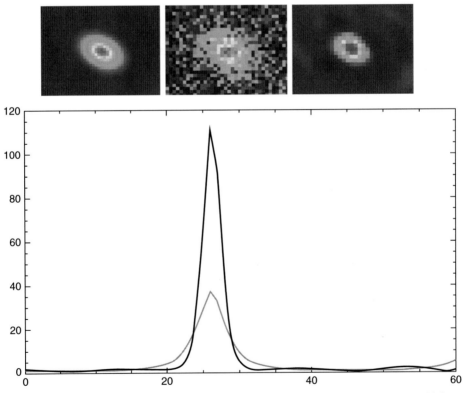

Figure 12.21. Spectrum of a single gamma-ray point source recovered using the multichannel MS-VSTS deconvolution algorithm. Top: Single gamma-ray point source on simulated (blurred) Fermi data (energy band: 360 MeV – 589 MeV) (left: simulated blurred source; middle: blurred noisy source; right: deconvolved source). Bottom: Spectrum profile of the center of the point source (cyan: simulated spectrum; black: restored spectrum from the deconvolved source). (See *color plates*.)

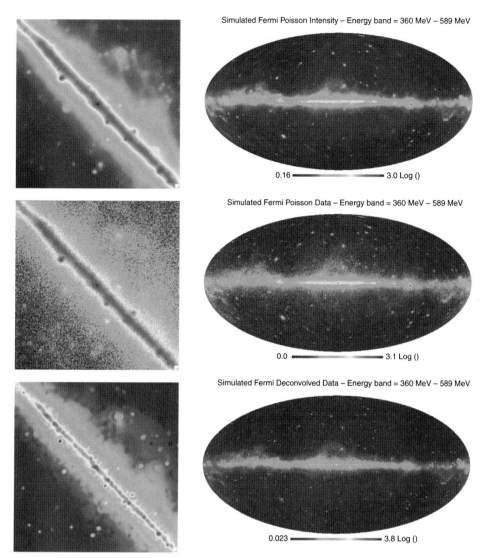

Simulated Fermi Poisson Intensity – Energy band = 360 MeV – 589 MeV

0.16 ■■■■■■ 3.0 Log ()

Simulated Fermi Poisson Data – Energy band = 360 MeV – 589 MeV

0.0 ■■■■■■ 3.1 Log ()

Simulated Fermi Deconvolved Data – Energy band = 360 MeV – 589 MeV

0.023 ■■■■■■ 3.8 Log ()

Figure 12.22. Result of the deconvolution algorithm in the 360 MeV – 589 MeV energy band. The left images are single HEALPix faces covering the galactic plane. Top Left: Simulated Fermi Poisson intensity. Top Right: Simulated Fermi noisy data. Bottom: Fermi data deconvolved with multichannel MS-VSTS. (See *color plates*.)

the regularized (significant) residual

$$\overline{R}^{(n)} = \mathcal{W}^{-1} M \mathcal{W} \left(Y - \mathbf{H} X^{(n)} \right), \tag{12.39}$$

with $\mathcal{W}$ being the IUWTS and M being the multiresolution support defined similarly to equation (11.24) by selecting significant coefficients in the MS-VSTS of the data.

Figure 12.21 shows the performance of the multichannel MS-VSTS deconvolution algorithm on a single point source. The deconvolution not only removes effectively the blur and recovers sharply localized point sorces, but it also allows restoration of all the spectral information.

Figure 12.22 depicts the result of the multichannel MS-VSTS deconvolution algorithm in one energy band on the entire sky and on a single HEALPix face covering the galactic plane. The effect of the deconvolution is strikingly good. The MS-VSTS multichannel deconvolution algorithm manages to remove a large part of the blur introduced by the PSF.

12.9 THREE-DIMENSIONAL WAVELETS ON THE BALL

In the previous sections, we have described multiresolution transforms for data provided in 3-D Cartesian coordinates or on the 2-D sphere. However, these transforms are not adapted to three-dimensional signals that are naturally expressed in spherical coordinates. Such signals arise for instance in astrophysics in the study of the 3-D distribution of galaxies (Heavens and Taylor 1995); (Rassat and Refregier 2012) for which we can have access to both angular position on the sky and distance along the line of sight. Recently two different wavelet transforms for data in spherical coordinates (i.e., on the 3-D ball) have been developed in Lanusse et al. (2012) and Leistedt and McEwen (2012). These two transforms differ mainly in the harmonic expansion used to develop data on the ball.

The expansion introduced in Leistedt and McEwen (2012) is based on exact sampling theorems in the angular domain based on McEwen and Wiaux (2011) and in the radial domain based the orthogonality of Laguerre polynomials. The resulting Fourier-Laguerre transform allows for exact decomposition and reconstruction of band-limited signals on the 3-D ball and is used to implement a wavelet transform (named flaglets) with exact decomposition and reconstruction formulas. Due to the choice of an independent basis for the radial and angular domains, flaglets probe independently angular and radial scales. However, separating angular and radial domains breaks the 3-D translational invariance of the harmonic expansion. Indeed, the apparent angular size varies depending on the radial position of an object of a given physical size. Therefore, in the flaglet transform, the same object at different radial positions will be is represented by wavelet coefficients of different angular scales.

In this section, we present the approach of Lanusse et al. (2012), which is based on the natural harmonic expansion of data in spherical coordinate using the spherical Fourier-Bessel transform. Using this transform, which is equivalent to a Fourier transform in spherical coordinates, the link between angular and radial scales is preserved. The drawback of this transform, however, is that no exact sampling theorem exists in the radial domain (Lemoine 1994). Contrary to the Fourier-Laguerre transform, the spherical Fourier-Bessel transform cannot be computed exactly for a discretely sampled band-limited signal on the ball. To circumvent this issue, a discrete spherical Fourier-Bessel transform was introduced in Lanusse et al. (2012) which allows the evaluation of this transform to any desired accuracy. Using the spherical Fourier-Bessel transform presented in the following section, an isotropic undecimated spherical 3-D wavelet transform similar to the IUWT on the sphere (see section 12.5.1) is derived in Section 12.9.3. This wavelet transform is exact in the spherical Fourier-Bessel domain, and wavelet coefficients can be recovered in the direct domain using the discrete spherical Fourier-Bessel transform described in Section 12.9.2.2.

12.9.1 Spherical Fourier-Bessel Expansion on the Ball

12.9.1.1 The Spherical Fourier-Bessel Transform

In the same way that the natural expansion of a function on the sphere is the spherical harmonics, the natural expansion of a function on the ball is the spherical Fourier-Bessel transform. This transform consists of the projection of a function $f \in L_2(\mathbf{R}^3)$ onto a set of orthogonal functions $\Psi_{lmk}(r, \theta, \varphi)$, composed of spherical harmonics and spherical Bessel functions:

$$\forall l \in \mathbb{N}, \forall m \in [\![-l, l]\!], \forall k \in \mathbb{R}^+, \quad \Psi_{lmk}(r, \theta, \varphi) = \sqrt{\frac{2}{\pi}} j_l(kr) Y_{lm}(\theta, \varphi), \quad (12.40)$$

where Y_{lm} are the spherical harmonics introduced in Section 12.2.2 and j_l are spherical Bessel functions of the first kind. These functions can be expressed in terms of the ordinary Bessel functions of the first kind J_ν for all $l \in \mathbb{N}$ and all $r \in \mathbf{R}^+$:

$$j_l(r) = \sqrt{\frac{\pi}{2r}} J_{l+1/2}(r), \quad (12.41)$$

where J_ν is defined for $z \in \mathbb{C}$ and $\nu \in \mathbb{R}$ as

$$J_\nu(z) = \sum_{k=0}^{\infty} \frac{(-1)^k z^{\nu+2k}}{2^{\nu+2k} k! \Gamma(\nu + k + 1)}. \quad (12.42)$$

Just as the spherical harmonics verify the orthonormality relation (12.6), the spherical Bessel functions are orthogonal:

$$\forall k, k' \in \mathbb{R}^+, \quad \int_0^{\infty} j_l(kr) j_l(k'r) r^2 dr = \frac{\pi}{2k^2} \delta(k - k'). \quad (12.43)$$

Using the orthogonality relations of both spherical harmonics and spherical Bessel functions, the orthogonality of the Ψ_{lmk} is easily derived:

$$\int \Psi_{lmk}^*(\mathbf{r}) \Psi_{l'm'k'}(\mathbf{r}) d\mathbf{r} = \frac{2}{\pi} \int j_l(k'r) j_l(kr) r^2 dr \int_\Omega Y_{lm}^*(\theta, \varphi) Y_{l'm'}(\theta, \varphi) d\Omega$$

$$= \frac{1}{k^2} \delta(k - k') \delta_{ll'} \delta_{mm'}. \quad (12.44)$$

From this relation, the spherical Fourier-Bessel transform of $f \in L_2(\mathbf{R}^3)$ is uniquely defined by the projection of f on the $\{\Psi_{lmk}\}$:

$$\tilde{f}_{lm}(k) = \langle f, \Psi_{lmk} \rangle = \int \Psi_{lmk}^*(r, \theta, \varphi) f(r, \theta, \varphi) r^2 \sin(\theta) d\theta d\varphi dr$$

$$= \int_0^{2\pi} \int_0^\pi \left[\sqrt{\frac{2}{\pi}} \int_0^\infty f(r, \theta, \varphi) j_l(kr) r^2 dr \right] Y_{lm}^*(\theta, \varphi) \sin(\theta) d\theta d\varphi \quad (12.45)$$

$$= \sqrt{\frac{2}{\pi}} \int_0^\infty \left[\int_0^{2\pi} \int_0^\pi f(r, \theta, \varphi) Y_{lm}^*(\theta, \varphi) \sin(\theta) d\theta d\varphi \right] j_l(kr) r^2 dr. \quad (12.46)$$

In this expression, one can recognize the commutative composition of two transforms: a spherical harmonics transform in the angular domain and a spherical Bessel transform (SBT) in the radial domain. We define the SBT and its inverse as

$$\tilde{f}_l(k) = \sqrt{\frac{2}{\pi}} \int f(r) j_l(kr) r^2 dr \tag{12.47a}$$

$$f(r) = \sqrt{\frac{2}{\pi}} \int \tilde{f}_l(k) j_l(kr) k^2 dk . \tag{12.47b}$$

In the following, the notation $\tilde{f}_l$ denotes the SBT of order l of a 1-D function f. The inversion formula for the spherical Fourier-Bessel transform is as follows:

$$f(r, \theta, \varphi) = \sqrt{\frac{2}{\pi}} \sum_{l=0}^{\infty} \sum_{m=-l}^{l} \int \tilde{f}_{lm}(k) k^2 j_l(kr) dk Y_{lm}(\theta, \varphi) . \tag{12.48}$$

12.9.1.2 Convolution in the Spherical Fourier-Bessel Domain

A key point relating to the spherical Fourier-Bessel transform is the existence of an expression for the real space convolution $h = f * g$ of two functions $f, g \in L_2(\mathbf{R}^3)$, which reduces to a very simple formula in the case of an isotropic function g. The convolution in the spherical Fourier-Bessel domain can be expressed from the well-known expression in the Fourier domain:

$$\hat{h}(k, \theta_k, \varphi_k) = \mathbf{F}\{f * g\}(k, \theta_k, \varphi_k)$$
$$= \sqrt{(2\pi)^3} \hat{f}(k, \theta_k, \varphi_k) \hat{g}(k, \theta_k, \varphi_k) , \tag{12.49}$$

using the following unitary convention for the Fourier transform:

$$\hat{f}(\mathbf{k}) = \frac{1}{\sqrt{(2\pi)^3}} \int f(\mathbf{r}) e^{-i\mathbf{k}.\mathbf{r}} d\mathbf{r} , \qquad f(\mathbf{r}) = \frac{1}{\sqrt{(2\pi)^3}} \int \hat{f}(\mathbf{k}) e^{i\mathbf{k}.\mathbf{r}} d\mathbf{k} . \tag{12.50}$$

To relate Fourier and spherical Fourier-Bessel coefficients, one can use the expansion of the Fourier kernel in spherical coordinates:

$$e^{-i\mathbf{k}.\mathbf{r}} = 4\pi \sum_{l=0}^{\infty} \sum_{m=-l}^{l} (-i)^l j_l(kr) Y_{lm}^*(\theta_r, \varphi_r) Y_{lm}(\theta_k, \varphi_k) . \tag{12.51}$$

When injected in the definition of the Fourier transform, this expression directly leads to the following relation between Fourier and spherical Fourier-Bessel transforms:

$$\hat{f}(k, \theta_k, \varphi_k) = \sum_{l=0}^{\infty} \sum_{m=-l}^{l} [(-i)^l \tilde{f}_{lm}(k)] Y_l^m(\theta_k, \varphi_k) . \tag{12.52}$$

It is worth noticing that the spherical Fourier-Bessel transform $\tilde{f}_{lm}(k)$ is merely a spherical harmonics transform applied on shells of radii k in Fourier space (up to a factor $(-i)^l$): $\hat{f}_{lm}(k) = (-i)^l \tilde{f}_{lm}(k)$.

This expression for the Fourier transform combined with the convolution equation (12.49) yields the convolution formula in the spherical Fourier-Bessel domain (see Appendix A.2 (Lanusse et al. 2012) for the full derivation):

$$
\tilde{h}_{lm}(k) = (i)^l \sqrt{(2\pi)^3} \sum_{l'=0}^{\infty} \sum_{m'=-l'}^{l'} (-i)^{l'} \tilde{f}_{l'm'}(k)
$$

$$
\times \sum_{l''=|l-l'|}^{l+l'} c^{l''}(l, m, l', m')(-i)^{l''} \tilde{g}_{l''m-m'}(k) , \tag{12.53}
$$

where $c^{l''}(l, m, l', m')$ are Slater integrals:

$$
c^{l''}(l, m, l', m') = \iint Y_{lm}^*(\theta, \varphi) Y_{l'm'}(\theta, \varphi) Y_{l''}^{m-m'}(\theta, \varphi) d\Omega . \tag{12.54}
$$

These integrals are only non-zero for $|l - l'| \le l'' \le l + l'$.

As already mentioned, this expression reduces to a simple form when g is isotropic. In this case, g has no angular dependence in the Fourier domain, and therefore $\hat{g}$ is constant on spherical shells and $\hat{g}_{lm}(k) = 0 = \tilde{g}_{lm}(k)$ for all $(l, m) \ne (0, 0)$. Then, knowing that $c^0(l, m, l, m) = 1/\sqrt{4\pi}$, equation (12.53) becomes

$$
\tilde{h}_{lm}(k) = \sqrt{2\pi} \tilde{g}_{00}(k) \tilde{f}_{lm}(k) . \tag{12.55}
$$

This expression can therefore be used to express in the spherical Fourier-Bessel domain a convolution by any isotropic filter g.

12.9.2 Discrete Spherical Fourier-Bessel Transform

The transform introduced so far yields a natural discretization in the angular domain thanks to the spherical harmonics; however, in the radial domain, the spherical Bessel transform is purely continuous. In order to implement wavelets in the harmonic domain and to be able to compute wavelet coefficients in the direct domain, a discretization scheme for the spherical Bessel transform is required. The main difficulty comes from the lack of an exact quadrature formula for this radial transform and therefore the lack of an exact sampling theorem. To circumvent this issue, we propose an approximated discrete spherical Bessel transform for a radially limited signal, which is an extension of the discrete Bessel transform introduced in Lemoine (1994). Although this discrete transform is not exact, it can be evaluated to any desired accuracy by increasing the number of sampling points. Combined with the HEALPix (Górski et al. 2005) sampling in the angular domain (see Section 12.2) we build a sampling grid in spherical coordinates that allows for back- and-forth computation of the spherical Fourier-Bessel transform.

12.9.2.1 The 1-D Discrete Spherical Bessel Transform

The transform described here is an extension to the spherical Bessel transform of the discrete Bessel transform from Lemoine (1994). The discretization of the spherical Bessel transform uses the well-known orthogonality property of the spherical Bessel functions on the interval $[0, R]$. If f is a continuous function defined on $[0, R]$ that verifies the boundary condition $f(R) = 0$, then the spherical Bessel transform defined in equation (12.47) can be expressed using a spherical Fourier-Bessel series:

$$\tilde{f}_l(k_{ln}) = \sqrt{\frac{2}{\pi}} \int_0^R f(r) j_l(k_{ln}r) r^2 dr \tag{12.56a}$$

$$f(r) = \sum_{n=1}^{\infty} \tilde{f}_l(k_{ln}) \rho_{ln} j_l(k_{ln}r) . \tag{12.56b}$$

In this expression, $k_{ln} = \frac{q_{ln}}{R}$ where q_{ln} is the nth zero of the Bessel function of the first kind of order l and the weights ρ_{ln} are defined as

$$\rho_{ln} = \frac{\sqrt{2\pi} R^{-3}}{j_{l+1}^2(q_{ln})} . \tag{12.57}$$

Although this formulation provides a discretization of the inverse spherical Bessel transform and of the k spectrum, the direct transform is still continuous, and another discretization step is necessary. Assuming that a boundary condition of the same kind can be applied to $\tilde{f}_l(k)$ so that $\tilde{f}_l(K_l) = 0$, then by using the same result, the spherical Fourier-Bessel expansion of $\tilde{f}_l(k)$ is obtained by

$$\tilde{\tilde{f}}_l(r_{ln}) = \sqrt{\frac{2}{\pi}} \int_0^K \tilde{f}_l(k) j_l(r_{ln}k) k^2 dk \tag{12.58a}$$

$$\tilde{f}_l(k) = \sum_{n=1}^{\infty} \tilde{\tilde{f}}_l(r_{ln}) \kappa_{ln} j_l(r_{ln}k) , \tag{12.58b}$$

where $r_{ln} = \frac{q_{ln}}{K_l}$ and where the weights ρ_{ln} are defined as

$$\kappa_{ln} = \frac{\sqrt{2\pi} K_l^{-3}}{j_{l+1}^2(q_{ln})} . \tag{12.59}$$

The spherical Bessel transform being an involution, $\tilde{\tilde{f}} = f$ so that $\tilde{\tilde{f}}_l(r_{ln}) = f(r_{ln})$. Much like the previous set of equations that had introduced a discrete k_{ln} grid, a discrete r_{ln} grid is obtained for the radial component. Since equations (12.56b) and (12.58b) can be used to compute f and $\tilde{f}_l$ for any value of r and k, they can in particular be used to compute $f(r_{ln})$ and $\tilde{f}_l(r_{l'n})$ where l' does not have to match l. The spherical Bessel transform and its inverse can then be expressed only in terms of series:

$$\tilde{f}_l(k_{l'n}) = \sum_{p=1}^{\infty} f(r_{lp}) \kappa_{lp} j_l(r_{lp} k_{l'n}) \tag{12.60a}$$

$$f(r_{l'n}) = \sum_{p=1}^{\infty} \tilde{f}_l(k_{lp}) \rho_{lp} j_l(r_{l'n} k_{lp}) . \tag{12.60b}$$

Thanks to this last set of equations one can compute the spherical Bessel transform and its inverse without the need to evaluate any integral. Furthermore only discrete values of f and $\hat{f}$, respectively sampled on r_{ln} and k_{ln}, are required.

However, this expression of the direct and inverse spherical Bessel transform is only valid if f is band limited ($\tilde{f}_l(K_l) = 0$) and radially limited ($f(R) = 0$) at the same time. It is well known that these two conditions can never be verified at the same time. The same problem arises for the Fourier transform: a band-limited signal necessarily has an infinite time support. In practice, by increasing the band limit K_l to any arbitrary value, one can recover an approximation of the exact transform to any required accuracy.

The second difficulty comes from the infinite sums over p in equations (12.60a) and (12.60b). In practical applications, for a given value of l only a limited number N of $\tilde{f}_l(k_{ln})$ and $f(r_{ln})$ coefficients can be stored so that $r_{lN} = R$ and $k_{lN} = K_l$. Since r_{ln} is defined by $r_{ln} = \frac{q_{ln}}{K_l}$, for $n = N$, R and K_l are bound by the following relation:

$$q_{lN} = K_l R . \qquad (12.61)$$

Therefore, the value of K_l is fixed for a choice of N and R.

The main point is that any desired accuracy in the evaluation of the direct and inverse transform can be reached by increasing the number of points N and artificially increasing R above the actual radial limit of the signal.

The truncation of the direct and inverse series to N coefficients yields a convenient matrix formulation for the discrete spherical Bessel transform and its inverse. Define a transform matrix $T^{ll'}$ as

$$T_{pq}^{ll'} = \left(\frac{\sqrt{2\pi}}{j_{l+1}^2(q_{lq})} j_l(\frac{q_{l'p} q_{lq}}{q_{lN}}) \right)_{pq} . \qquad (12.62)$$

The direct transform can be expressed as

$$\begin{bmatrix} \tilde{f}_l(k_{l'1}) \\ \tilde{f}_l(k_{l'2}) \\ \vdots \\ \tilde{f}_l(k_{l'N}) \end{bmatrix} = \frac{1}{K_l^3} T^{ll'} \begin{bmatrix} f(r_{l1}) \\ f(r_{l2}) \\ \vdots \\ f(r_{lN}) \end{bmatrix} . \qquad (12.63)$$

Reciprocally, the inverse of the values of f can be computed on any $r_{l'n}$ grid from $\tilde{f}_l$ sampled on $k_{l'n}$ using the exact same matrix:

$$\begin{bmatrix} f(r_{l'1}) \\ f(r_{l'2}) \\ \vdots \\ f(r_{l'N}) \end{bmatrix} = \frac{1}{R^3} T^{ll'} \begin{bmatrix} \tilde{f}_l(k_{l1}) \\ \tilde{f}_l(k_{l2}) \\ \vdots \\ \tilde{f}_l(k_{lN}) \end{bmatrix} . \qquad (12.64)$$

The discrete spherical Bessel transform is defined by the set of equations (12.63) and (12.64).

Finally, it can be shown (Lanusse et al. 2012) that spherical Bessel transforms of different orders can be related through the following equation:

$$\tilde{f}_l(k_{ln}) = \sum_{m=1}^{\infty} \tilde{f}_{l_0}(k_{l_0 m}) \frac{2}{j_{l_0+1}^2(q_{l_0 m})} W_{nm}^{l_0 l} . \tag{12.65}$$

where the weights $W_{nm}^{ll'}$ are defined as

$$W_{nm}^{l_0 l} = \int_0^1 j_{l_0}(q_{l_0 m}x) j_l(q_{ln}x) x^2 dx . \tag{12.66}$$

Therefore, the spherical Bessel transform of a given order can be expressed as the sum of the coefficients obtained for a different order of the transform, with the appropriate weighting. It is also worth noticing that the weights $W_{nm}^{ll'}$ are independent of the problem and can be tabulated. Using this relationship between orders, it is possible to convert the spherical Bessel coefficients of order l_0 into coefficients of any other order l, which will prove useful for the implementation of the full discrete spherical Fourier-Bessel transform.

12.9.2.2 The 3-D Discrete Spherical Fourier-Bessel Transform

As presented in Section 12.9.1, the spherical Fourier-Bessel transform is the composition of a spherical harmonics transform for the angular component and a spherical Bessel transform for the radial component. Since these two transforms can commute, they can be treated independently, and by combining discrete algorithms for both transforms, one can build a discrete spherical Fourier-Bessel transform. A convenient choice for the angular part of the transform is the HEALPix (Górski et al. 2005) pixelization scheme. The radial component can be discretized using the discrete spherical Bessel transform algorithm presented in the previous section. The choice of these two algorithms introduces a discretization of the Fourier-Bessel coefficients as well as a pixelization of the 3-D space in spherical coordinates.

The spherical Fourier-Bessel coefficients $\tilde{f}_{lm}(k)$ are defined by equation (12.45) for continuous values of k. Assuming a boundary condition on the density field f, the discrete spherical Bessel transform can be used to discretize the values of k. The discrete spherical Fourier-Bessel coefficients are therefore defined as

$$a_{lmn} = \tilde{f}_{lm}(k_{ln}) , \tag{12.67}$$

for $0 \le l \le L_{max}$, $-l \le m \le l$, and $1 \le n \le N_{max}$. These discrete coefficients are simply obtained by sampling the continuous coefficients on the k_{ln} grid introduced in the previous section.

To this discretized Fourier-Bessel spectrum corresponds a dual grid of the 3-D space defined by combining the HEALPix pixelization scheme and the discrete spherical Bessel transform.

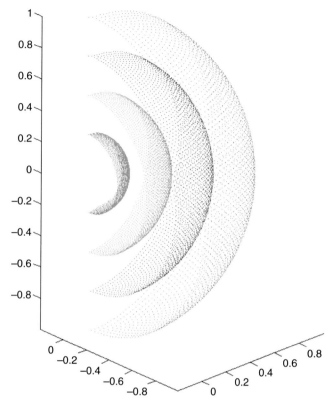

Figure 12.23. Representation of the spherical 3-D grid for the discrete spherical Fourier-Bessel transform ($R = 1$ and $N_{max} = 4$). (See *color plates*.)

In the angular domain, for a given value of r, the field $f(r, \theta, \varphi)$ can be sampled on a finite number of points using HEALPix. The radial component of the transform is conveniently performed using the discrete spherical Bessel transform. Indeed, this algorithm introduces a radial grid compatible with the discretized k_{ln} spectrum. Although this radial grid r_{ln} depends on the order l of the spherical Bessel transform, it is justified in the next section that only one grid r_{l_0n} is required to sample the field along the radial dimension. The value of l_0 is set to 0 because in this case the properties of the zeros of the Bessel function ensure that r_{0n} is regularly spaced between 0 and R:

$$r_{0n} = \frac{n}{N_{max}} R \ . \tag{12.68}$$

For given values of θ_i and φ_j, the field $f(r, \theta_i, \varphi_j)$ can now be sampled on discrete values of $r = r_{0n}$.

Combining angular and radial grids, the 3-D spherical grid is defined as a set of N_{max} HEALPix maps equally spaced between 0 and R. An illustration of this grid is provided in Figure 12.23 where only one-quarter of the space is represented for clarity.

Using this 3-D grid it becomes possible to compute back and forth the spherical Fourier-Bessel transform between a density field and its spherical Fourier-Bessel coefficients. A detailed description of the algorithm for both the direct and inverse discrete spherical Fourier-Bessel transform is provided as follows.

Inverse Transform

Let a_{lmn} be the coefficients of the spherical Fourier transform of the density field f. The reconstruction of f on the spherical 3-D grid requires two steps:

1) First, from the a_{lmn}, the inverse discrete spherical Bessel transform is computed for all l and m. This transform can be easily evaluated thanks to a matrix product:

$$
\begin{cases} \forall & 0 & \leq & l & \leq & L_{max} \\ \forall & -l & \leq & m & \leq & l \end{cases},
\begin{bmatrix} f_{lm}(r_{l_0 1}) \\ f_{lm}(r_{l_0 2}) \\ \vdots \\ f_{lm}(r_{l_0 N_{max}}) \end{bmatrix} = \frac{T^{ll_0}}{R^3}
\begin{bmatrix} a_{lm1} \\ a_{lm2} \\ \vdots \\ a_{lmN_{max}} \end{bmatrix}. \quad (12.69)
$$

Here, it is worth noting that the matrix T^{ll_0} allows the evaluation of the spherical Bessel transform of order l and provides the results on the grid of order l_0.

2) From the spherical harmonics coefficients $f_{lm}(r_{l_0 n})$ given at specific radial distances $r_{l_0 n}$ it is possible to compute the inverse spherical harmonics transform. For each n between 1 and N_{max} the HEALPix inverse spherical harmonics transform is performed on the set of coefficients $\{f_{lm}(r_{l_0 n})\}_{l,m}$. This yields N_{max} HEALPix maps, which constitute the sampling of the reconstructed density field on the 3-D spherical grid.

Direct Transform

Given a density field f sampled on the spherical 3-D grid, the spherical Fourier-Bessel coefficients a_{lmn} are computed in three steps:

1) For each n between 1 and N_{max} the spherical harmonics transform of the HEALPix map of radius $r_{l_0 n}$ is computed. This yields $f_{lm}(r_{l_0 n})$ coefficients.
2) The next step is to compute the spherical Bessel transform of order l_0 from the $f_{lm}(r_{l_0 n})$ coefficients for every (l, m). Again, this operation is a simple matrix product:

$$
\begin{cases} \forall & 0 & \leq & l & \leq & L_{max} \\ \forall & -l & \leq & m & \leq & l \end{cases},
\begin{bmatrix} \tilde{f}^{l_0}_{lm}(k_{l_0 1}) \\ \tilde{f}^{l_0}_{lm}(k_{l_0 2}) \\ \vdots \\ \tilde{f}^{l_0}_{lm}(k_{l_0 N_{max}}) \end{bmatrix} = \frac{T^{l_0 l_0}}{K^3}
\begin{bmatrix} f_{lm}(r_{l_0 1}) \\ f_{lm}(r_{l_0 2}) \\ \vdots \\ f_{lm}(r_{l_0 N_{max}}) \end{bmatrix}.
$$

$$(12.70)$$

This operation yields $\hat{f}_{lm}^{l_0}(k_{l_0 n})$ coefficients that are not yet spherical Fourier-Bessel coefficients because the order of the spherical Bessel transform l_0 does not match the order of the spherical harmonics coefficients l. An additional step is necessary.

3) The last step required to gain access to the spherical Fourier-Bessel coefficients a_{lmn} is to convert the spherical Bessel coefficients for order l_0 to the correct order l that matches the spherical harmonics order. This is done by using relation (12.65):

$$
\begin{cases}
\forall & 0 & \leq & l & \leq & L_{max} \\
\forall & -l & \leq & m & \leq & l \\
\forall & 1 & \leq & n & \leq & N_{max}
\end{cases} , \quad
\tilde{f}_{lm}(k_{ln}) = \sum_{p=1}^{N_{max}} \tilde{f}_{lm}^{l_0}(k_{l_0 p}) \frac{2W_{np}^{l_0 l}}{j_{l_0+1}^2(q_{lp})} ,
$$

(12.71)

where $W_{np}^{l_0 l}$ are defined by equation (12.66). This operation finally yields the $a_{lmn} = \tilde{f}_{lm}(k_{ln})$ coefficients.

12.9.3 Isotropic Undecimated Spherical 3-D Wavelet Transform

The aim of this section is to transpose the ideas behind the isotropic undecimated wavelet transform on the sphere introduced in Section 12.5.1 to the case of data in 3-D spherical coordinates. Indeed, the isotropic wavelet transform can be fully defined using isotropic filters that are simple to express in the spherical Fourier-Bessel domain as seen in Section 12.9.1.2. Furthermore, the practical evaluation of the direct and inverse spherical Fourier-Bessel transform was addressed in the previous section.

12.9.3.1 Wavelet Decomposition

The isotropic undecimated spherical 3-D wavelet transform is based on a scaling function $\varphi^{k_c}(r, \theta_r, \varphi_r)$ with cutoff frequency k_c and spherical symmetry. The symmetry of this function is preserved in the Fourier space, and therefore, its spherical Fourier-Bessel transform verifies $\tilde{\varphi}_{lm}^{k_c}(k) = 0$ as soon as $(l, m) \neq (0, 0)$. Furthermore, due to its cutoff frequency, the scaling function verifies $\tilde{\varphi}_{00}^{k_c}(k) = 0$ for all $k \geq k_c$. In other terms, the scaling function verifies

$$
\phi^{k_c}(r, \theta_r, \varphi_r) = \phi^{k_c}(r) = \sqrt{\frac{2}{\pi}} \int_0^{k_c} \tilde{\phi}_{00}^{k_c}(k) k^2 j_0(kr) dk Y_0^0(\theta_r, \varphi_r) .
$$

(12.72)

Using relation (12.55) the convolution of the original data $f(r, \theta, \varphi)$ with ϕ^{k_c} becomes very simple:

$$
\tilde{c}_{lm}^0(k) = [\widetilde{\phi_{k_c} * f}]_{lm}(k) = \sqrt{2\pi} \tilde{\phi}_{00}^{k_c}(k) \tilde{f}_{lm}(k) .
$$

(12.73)

Thanks to this scaling function, it is possible to define a sequence of smoother approximations $c^j(r, \theta_r, \varphi_r)$ of a function $f(r, \theta_r, \varphi_r)$ on a dyadic resolution scale. Let $\phi^{2^{-j}k_c}$ be a rescaled version of ϕ^{k_c} with cutoff frequency $2^{-j}k_c$. Then $c^j(r, \theta_r, \varphi_r)$ is obtained by convolving $f(r, \theta_r, \varphi_r)$ with $\phi^{2^{-j}k_c}$:

$$c^0 = \phi^{k_c} * f$$

$$c^1 = \phi^{2^{-1}k_c} * f$$

$$\cdots$$

$$c^j = \phi^{2^{-j}k_c} * f .$$

Applying the spherical Fourier-Bessel transform to the last relation yields

$$\tilde{c}^j_{lm}(k) = \sqrt{2\pi}\, \tilde{\phi}^{2^{-j}k_c}_{00}(k)\, \tilde{f}_{lm}(k) . \tag{12.74}$$

This leads to the following recurrence formula:

$$\forall k < \frac{k_c}{2^j}, \quad \tilde{c}^{j+1}_{lm}(k) = \frac{\tilde{\phi}^{2^{-(j+1)}k_c}_{00}(k)}{\tilde{\phi}^{2^{-j}k_c}_{00}(k)}\, \tilde{c}^j_{lm}(k) . \tag{12.75}$$

Just as for the starlet algorithm (see Section 11.2.2), the wavelet coefficients $\{w^j\}$ can be defined as the difference between two consecutive resolutions:

$$w^{j+1}(r, \theta_r, \varphi_r) = c^j(r, \theta, \varphi) - c^{j+1}(r, \theta, \varphi) . \tag{12.76}$$

This choice for the wavelet coefficients is equivalent to the following definition for the wavelet function ψ^{k_c}:

$$\tilde{\psi}^{2^{-j}k_c}_{lm}(k) = \tilde{\phi}^{2^{-(j-1)}k_c}_{lm}(k) - \tilde{\phi}^{2^{-j}k_c}_{lm}(k) , \tag{12.77}$$

so that

$$w^0 = \psi^{k_c} * f$$

$$w^1 = \psi^{2^{-1}k_c} * f$$

$$\cdots$$

$$w^j = \psi^{2^{-j}k_c} * f .$$

Applying the spherical Fourier-Bessel transform to the definition of the wavelet coefficients and using the recurrence formula verified by the c^js yields

$$\forall k < \frac{k_c}{2^j}, \quad \tilde{w}^{j+1}_{lm}(k) = \left(1 - \frac{\tilde{\phi}^{2^{-(j+1)}k_c}_{00}(k)}{\tilde{\phi}^{2^{-j}k_c}_{00}(k)}\right) \tilde{c}^j_{lm}(k) . \tag{12.78}$$

Equations (12.78) and (12.75), which define the wavelet decomposition, are in fact equivalent to convolving the resolution at a given scale j with a low-pass and a high-pass filter in order to obtain, respectively, the resolution and the wavelet coefficients at scale $j + 1$.

The low-pass filter h^j can be defined for each scale j by

$$\tilde{h}^j_{lm}(k) = \begin{cases} \dfrac{\tilde{\phi}^{2^{-(j+1)}k_c}_{00}(k)}{\tilde{\phi}^{2^{-j}k_c}_{00}(k)} & \text{if } k < \frac{k_c}{2^{j+1}} \text{ and } l = m = 0 \\ 0 & \text{otherwise .} \end{cases} \tag{12.79}$$

Then the approximation at scale $j + 1$ is given by the convolution of scale j with h^j:

$$c^{j+1} = c^j * \frac{1}{\sqrt{2\pi}} h^j .$$ (12.80)

In the same way, a high pass filter g^j can be defined on each scale j by:

$$\tilde{g}^j_{lm}(k) = \begin{cases} \frac{\tilde{\psi}^{2^{-(j+1)}k_c}_{00}(k)}{\tilde{\phi}^{2^{-j}k_c}_{00}(k)} & \text{if } k < \frac{k_c}{2^{j+1}} \text{ and } l = m = 0 \\ 1 & \text{if } k \geq \frac{k_c}{2^{j+1}} \text{ and } l = m = 0 \\ 0 & \text{otherwise .} \end{cases}$$ (12.81)

Given the definition of ψ, g^j can also be expressed in the simple form:

$$\tilde{g}^j_{lm}(k) = 1 - \tilde{h}^j_{lm}(k) .$$ (12.82)

The wavelet coefficients at scale $j + 1$ are obtained by convolving the resolution at scale j with g^j:

$$w^{j+1} = c^j * \frac{1}{\sqrt{2\pi}} g^j .$$ (12.83)

To sum up, the two relations necessary to recursively define the wavelet transform are

$$\tilde{c}^{j+1}_{lm}(k) = \tilde{h}^j_{00}(k)\tilde{c}^j_{lm}(k)$$
$$\tilde{w}^{j+1}_{lm}(k) = \tilde{g}^j_{00}(k)\tilde{c}^j_{lm}(k) .$$ (12.84)

12.9.3.2 Choice of a Scaling Function

Any function with spherical symmetry and a cutoff frequency k_c would do as a scaling function, but in this work we choose to use a B-spline function of order 3 to define our scaling function:

$$\tilde{\phi}^{k_c}_{lm}(k) = \frac{3}{2} B_3 \left(\frac{2k}{k_c} \right) \delta_{l0}\delta_{m0} .$$ (12.85)

where

$$B_3(x) = \frac{1}{12} (|x - 2|^3 - 4|x - 1|^3 + 6|x|^3 - 4|x + 1|^3 + |x + 2|^3) .$$ (12.86)

The scaling function and its corresponding wavelet function are plotted in spherical Fourier-Bessel space for different values of j in Figure 12.24.

Other functions such as Meyer wavelets or the needlet function (Marinucci et al. 2008) can be used as well. Needlet wavelet functions have a much better frequency localization than the wavelet function derived from the B_3-spline, and because nothing is perfect, the price to pay is more oscillations in the direct space. To illustrate this, we show in Figure 12.25 two different wavelet functions. Figure 12.25 (left) shows the 1-D profile of the spline (continuous line) and the needlet wavelet function (dotted line) at a given scale. Figure 12.25 (right) shows the same function, but we have plotted the absolute value to better visualize their respective ringing. As can be seen, for wavelet functions with the same main lobe, the needlet wavelet oscillates much

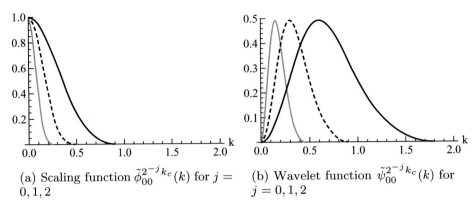

(a) Scaling function $\tilde{\phi}_{00}^{2^{-j}k_c}(k)$ for $j = 0, 1, 2$

(b) Wavelet function $\tilde{\psi}_{00}^{2^{-j}k_c}(k)$ for $j = 0, 1, 2$

Figure 12.24. Scaling function and wavelet function for $k_c = 1$.

more than the spline wavelet. Hence, the best wavelet choice certainly depends on the final applications. For statistical analysis, detection, or restoration applications, we may prefer to use a wavelet that does not oscillate too much and has a smaller support: the spline wavelet is clearly the correct choice. For spectral or bispectral analysis, where the frequency localization is fundamental, then the needlet shoud be preferred to the spline wavelet.

The complete algorithm for the isotropic undecimated spherical 3-D wavelet transform is provided in Algorithm 57. This algorithm makes use of the discrete spherical Fourier-Bessel transform described in Section 12.9.2.2. Using this transform, the spherical Fourier-Bessel coefficients are now sampled at discrete k_{ln} values, and we noted $\tilde{f}_{lm}(k_{ln}) = \tilde{f}_{lmn}$.

To illustrate this wavelet transform, a set of spherical Fourier-Bessel coefficients was extracted from a 3-D density field using the discrete spherical Fourier-Bessel transform described in the next section. The test density field was provided by a cosmological N-body simulation that was carried out by the Virgo Supercomputing Consortium using computers based at the Computing Centre of the Max Planck Society in Garching and at the Edinburgh Parallel Computing Centre. The data are publicly available at www.mpa-garching.mpg.de/Virgo/VLS.html.

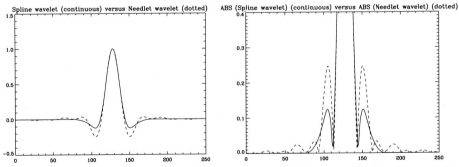

Figure 12.25. Comparison between spline, needlet, and Meyer wavelet functions on the sphere.

Algorithm 57 The Isotropic Undecimated Spherical 3-D Wavelet Transform

---

Task: Compute the isotropic undecimated spherical 3-D wavelet transform of a discrete X sampled on the spherical grid from Section 12.9.2.2.
Parameters: Data samples X and number of wavelet scales J.
Initialization:

- $c^0 = X$.
- Compute the B_3-spline scaling function and derive $\tilde{\psi}_{00n}, \tilde{h}_{00n}$, and $\tilde{g}_{00n}$ numerically.
- Compute $\tilde{c}^0_{lmn}$ the discrete spherical Fourier-Bessel transform of c^0.

for $j = 0$ to $J - 1$ **do**

    (i) Compute the discrete spherical Fourier-Bessel transform of the scaling coefficients: $\tilde{c}^{j+1}_{lmn} = \tilde{c}^j_{lmn} \tilde{h}^j_{00n}$.

    (ii) Compute the discrete spherical Fourier-Bessel transform of the wavelet coefficients: $w^{j+1}_{lmn} = c^j_{lmn} g^j_{00n}$.

    (iii) Compute the inverse spherical harmonics transform of w^{j+1}_{lmn} to get w^{j+1}.

- Compute the inverse spherical harmonics transform of c^J_{lmn} to get c^J.

Output: $\mathcal{W} = \{w^1, w^2, \ldots, w^J, c^J\}$ the isotropic undecimated spherical 3-D wavelet transform of X.

The wavelet decomposition presented earlier can then be computed from the spherical Fourier-Bessel coefficients of the test density field and yields the spherical Fourier-Bessel coefficients of the various wavelet scales and smoothed-away density. Using the inverse discrete spherical Fourier-Bessel transform, the actual wavelet coefficients can be retrieved in the form of 3-D density fields. These density fields are shown in Figure 12.26.

12.9.3.3 Inverse Transform
Since the wavelet coefficients are defined as the difference between two resolutions, the reconstruction from the wavelet decomposition $\mathcal{W} = \{w^1, \ldots, w^J, c^J\}$ is straightforward and corresponds to the reconstruction formula of the *à trous* algorithm:

$$c^0(r, \theta_r, \varphi_r) = c^J(r, \theta_r, \varphi_r) + \sum_{j=1}^{J} w^j(r, \theta_r, \varphi_r) . \tag{12.87}$$

However, given the redundancy of the transform, the reconstruction is not unique. It is possible to take advantage of this redundancy to reconstruct c^j from c^{j+1} and w^{j+1} by using a least-squares estimate.

From the recursive wavelet decomposition defined in (12.84), by respectively multiplying these equations by $\tilde{h}^{*j}_{lm}(k)$ and $\tilde{g}^{*j}_{lm}(k)$ and then adding them together, the following expression is obtained for the least-squares estimate of c^j from c^{j+1} and w^{j+1}:

$$\tilde{c}^j_{lm}(k) = \tilde{c}^{j+1}_{lm}(k)\tilde{H}^j_{lm}(k) + \tilde{w}^{j+1}_{lm}\tilde{G}^j_{lm}(k) , \tag{12.88}$$

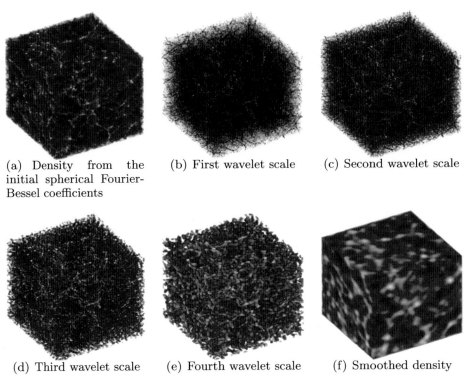

(a) Density from the initial spherical Fourier-Bessel coefficients

(b) First wavelet scale

(c) Second wavelet scale

(d) Third wavelet scale

(e) Fourth wavelet scale

(f) Smoothed density

Figure 12.26. Isotropic undecimated spherical 3-D wavelet decomposition of a density field. Only a cube at the center of the spherical field is displayed. (See *color plates*.)

where $\tilde{H}^j$ and $\tilde{G}^j$ are defined as follows:

$$\tilde{H}^j_{lm}(k) = \frac{\tilde{h}^{*j}_{lm}(k)}{\left|\tilde{h}^j_{lm}(k)\right|^2 + \left|\tilde{g}^j_{lm}(k)\right|^2} \tag{12.89}$$

$$\tilde{G}^j_{lm}(k) = \frac{\tilde{g}^{*j}_{lm}(k)}{\left|\tilde{h}^j_{lm}(k)\right|^2 + \left|\tilde{g}^j_{lm}(k)\right|^2}. \tag{12.90}$$

Among the advantages of using this reconstruction formula instead of the raw sum over the wavelet coefficients is that there is no need to perform an inverse and then direct spherical Fourier-Bessel transform to reconstruct the coefficients of the original data. Indeed, both the wavelet decomposition and reconstruction procedures only require access to spherical Fourier-Bessel coefficients, and there is no need to revert back to the direct space.

12.9.4 Application: Denoising of a Λ Cold Dark Matter Simulation

In this section, we present a simple wavelet denoising application on a density field in spherical coordinates using the isotropic undecimated spherical 3-D wavelet transform of the previous section.

Denoising using sparse transforms can be performed very easily by applying a simple thresholding on the coefficients. One can use a *soft* or *hard* thresholding according to whether we want more accuracy or less artifacts. The threshold level is usually taken as three times the noise standard deviation, such that for an additive Gaussian noise, the thresholding operator kills all noise coefficients except a small percentage, keeping the big coefficients that contain information. The threshold we use is often a simple $\kappa\sigma$, with $\kappa \in [3, 4]$, which corresponds, respectively, to 0.27% and $6.3 \cdot 10^{-5}$ false detections. Sometimes we use a higher κ for the finest scale (Starck et al. 2002). Other methods exist that estimate automatically the threshold to use in each band, such as the false discovery rate see Benjamini and Hochberg (1995) and Miller et al. (2001). The correlation between neighbor coefficients intra-band and/or inter-band may also be taken into account see Sendur and Selesnik (2002) and Sendur and Selesnick (2002).

This experiment is performed on the same N-body simulation from the Virgo Consortium as the one presented in the previous section in Figure 12.26. The Virgo large box simulation[6] provides us with a Cartesian density cube. The spherical Fourier-Bessel (SFB) coefficients of the test density field are first computed by sampling the Virgo density field on the spherical 3-D grid illustrated in Figure 12.23, for $n_{side} = 2048$, $l_{max} = 1023$ and $n_{max} = 512$. In order to perform the SFB decomposition, the observer is placed at the center of the box, and the SFB coefficients are calculated out to $R = 479/2$ h^{-1}Mpc, setting the density field to zero outside of this spherical volume.

A Gaussian noise was then added to the SFB coefficients to produce a noisy density field. Figures 12.27(a) and 12.27(b) show the central portion of slices taken in the middle of, respectively, the original and noisy spherical density fields. The level of the noise is comparable to the amplitude of the faint filamentary structures that can be seen in the original density field in Figure 12.27(a). Using hard-thresholding of the wavelet coefficients, the noisy field is filtered to yield the restored density displayed in Figure 12.27(c). The residuals after denoising are shown in Figure 12.27(d). The artificially added noise is successfully removed, without much loss to the large-scale structure, though some of the smaller filamentary structures are removed. This, however, is to be expected given the isotropic nature of the wavelet transform used here, which is better suited to restore more isotropic features such as clusters.

12.10 APPLICATIONS

12.10.1 Application in Fusion Physics

In Inertial Confinement Fusion (ICF) a spherical shell is irradiated by laser energy directly or after the laser energy has been converted to soft X-rays (Atzeni and ter Vehn 2004). Either way, the aim is to implode the capsule, which contains a shell of nuclear fusion fuel (deuterium and tritium) ready to ignite if, after it has been imploded, its density is high enough and a hot spot in its center becomes hot enough to cause a propagating nuclear burn wave to travel through the rest of the fuel. This ultimate energy process will not work if, during the implosion, hydrodynamic instabilities develop, which can break apart the shell before it assembles at the center and a hot spot forms (Lindl 1997). Hydrodynamic instabilities such as Rayleigh-Taylor occur due to nonuniformities in the laser spatial profile or imperfections in the composition of the multiple surfaces that make up the layers of thin material that

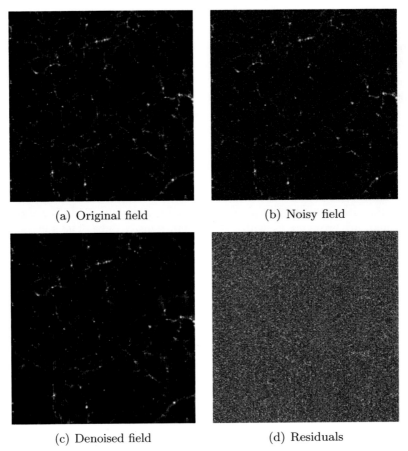

(a) Original field   (b) Noisy field

(c) Denoised field   (d) Residuals

Figure 12.27. Isotropic undecimated spherical 3-D wavelet hard-thresholding applied to a test density field. (See *color plates*.)

surround the nuclear fuel. Very small amplitude imperfections initially can result in the ultimate failure of the target due to the large compression ratios involved in ICF.

It is therefore extremely important to characterize the inner and outer surfaces of ICF shell targets so as to know whether they are worthy of consideration for ICF implosions. One day in a reactor setting tens of thousands of targets will have to be imploded daily so that checking each one will be totally out of the question. Instead, very good target fabrication quality control processes have to be adopted so that confidence levels in proper performance will be high. A major step along this path to fusion energy then is to understand why imperfections occur and to correct the systematic elements and control the harm done by random sources.

Fine structures on the surfaces of spherical shells can be measured on the nanometer scale, among methods, by atomic force microscopy or phase-shifting spherical diffractive optical interferometry. An example of such measurements is shown in Figure 12.28. As can be seen from the figure, there appears to be a super-position of global-scale variations, isolated bumps and scratches as well as artifacts that look like interference patterns on intermediate scales of localization. What looks like interference patterns must be isolated and eliminated from consideration when deciding the readiness of the target for implosion.

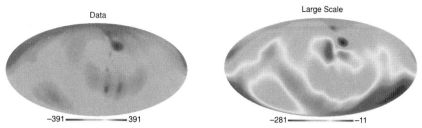

Figure 12.28. (left) Surface structures of ICF spherical shells measured on the nanometer scale are a superposition of global-scale variations, isolated bumps and scratches, as well as artifacts that look like interference patterns on intermediate scales. (right) Coarsest scale of the undecimated isotropic wavelet transform of the surface measurements of an ICF target. (See *color plates*.)

We achieved morphological feature separation by first doing an isotropic wavelet transform on the spherical data and subtracting the coarsest scale information. MCA on the sphere was used on the rest of the image using the undecimated wavelet and the local cosine transforms on the sphere. The isolated bumps were thus identified, and the artifacts caused by the measurement technique were removed easily. The resulting bumps, added to the coarsest scale, comprise the clean data with the interference patterns and artifacts removed as shown in Figure 12.29. The spherical harmonics decomposition of the cleaned image gives rise to coefficients of various ℓ modes that will be amplified by the implosion process.

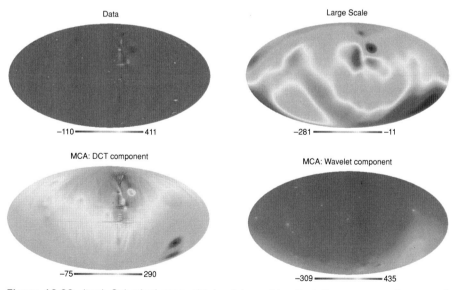

Figure 12.29. (top) Spherical map obtained by subtracting the coarse-scale map of Fig. 12.28 (right) from the initial map of Fig. 12.28 (left). (bottom) Component maps separated by the MCA method on the sphere: (left) interference patterns and measurement artifacts were caught by the local cosine functions on the sphere. whereas (right) the isolated bumps were caught using the undecimated wavelet on the sphere. Adding back the coarse scale of Fig. 12.28 (right) to the latter map results in a clean map of the surface structures of an ICF spherical shell with the interference patterns and artifacts removed. (See *color plates*.)

The implosion process can now be assessed correctly using numerical hydro-dynamic simulation generated growth factors. If the bumps are clustered and not randomly distributed, then systematic errors in the manufacturing process can be tracked down. For more details, see Afeyan et al. (2006).

12.10.2 Application in Cosmology

A major issue in modern cosmology is the measurement and the statistical charac-terization (spatial power spectrum, Gaussianity) of the slight fluctuations in the cos-mic microwave background (CMB) radiation field. These fluctuations are strongly related to the cosmological scenarios describing the properties and evolution of our universe. Some 370,000 years after the Big Bang, when the temperature of the uni-verse was around 3000 K, thermal energy was no longer sufficient to keep electrons and positively charged particles apart so they combined. Photons were then set free in a nearly transparent universe. Since the universe further expanded, these photons are now in the microwave range, but they should still be distributed according to a black body emission law. Indeed, before recombination, the universe was a highly homo-geneous opaque plasma in near-thermal equilibrium in which photons and charged particles were highly interactive. Hence the slight fluctuations in matter density, from which such large-scale structures as galaxies or clusters of galaxies have evolved, are also imprinted on the distribution of photons.

The CMB was first observed in 1965 by Penzias and Wilson, confirming a pre-diction made by Gamow in the late 1940s. But it was not until the early 1990s that evidence for small fluctuations in the CMB sky could finally be found, thanks to the observations made by the Cosmic Background Explorer (Smoot et al. 1992). They were confirmed by several subsequent observations and recently by NASA's WMAP[7]. Full-sky multi-spectral observations with unprecedented sensitivity and angular resolution are expected from ESA's Planck[8] mission, which was launched in 2009. The statistical analysis of this data set will help set tighter bounds on major cosmological parameters.

A simple numerical experiment is shown in Figure 12.30, starting with the full-sky CMB map provided by the WMAP team. This CMB map was partially masked to discard pixels where the level of contamination by residual foregrounds is expected

-0.41 ———— 0.37   -0.39 ———— 0.39

Figure 12.30. (left) CMB data map provided by the Wilkinson microwave anisotropy probe (WMAP) team. Areas of significant foreground contamination in the galactic region and at the locations of strong radio point sources have been masked out. (right) Map obtained by applying the MCA-inpainting algorithm on the sphere to the former incomplete WMAP CMB data map. (See *color plates.*)

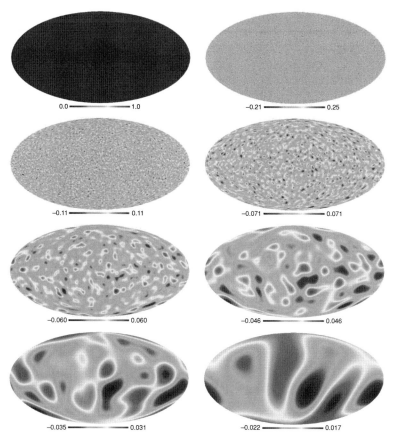

Figure 12.31. (top left) Masked area. From top to bottom and left to right, the seven wavelet scales of the inpainted map. From the visual point of view, the initially masked area cannot be distinguished any more in the wavelet scales of the inpainted map. (See *color plates*.)

to be the highest. Applying the described inpainting algorithm, which makes use of the sparsity of the representation of CMB in the spherical harmonics domain, leads to the map shown in Figure 12.30 (right): the stationarity of the CMB field appears to have been restored, and the masked region is completely undetectable to the eye. Figure 12.31 shows the wavelet decomposition of the inpainted map, allowing for further visual positive assessment of the quality of the proposed method, as again the masked regions are undetectable at all scales. It was shown by Abrial et al. (2007) and Abrial et al. (2008) that inpainting the CMB map is an interesting approach for analyzing it, especially for non-Gaussianity studies and power spectrum estimation.

12.11 GUIDED NUMERICAL EXPERIMENTS

12.11.1 MR/S Toolbox

The guided numerical experiments of this chapter are conducted using IDL with HEALPix and MR/S toolboxes.

The IDL software (http://www.idl-envi.com) is analogous to Matlab and is very widely used in astrophysics and in medical imaging. HEALPix is available online (http://sourceforge.net/projects/healpix). MR/S is a collection of IDL files that implements all the multiscale transforms described in this chapter, using HEALPix pixelization. The library is available via the book's web site (http://www.SparseSignalRecipes.info).

12.11.2 Undecimated Wavelet Transform on the Sphere

The code to generate the undecimated wavelet transform of the Mars image of Fig. 12.8 is as follows.

```
; read the data
m = mrs_read('mars_topo_mola_hpx_128.fits')

; compute the undecimated wavelet transform with 5 scales
mrs_wttrans, m, w,nbrscale=5

; Display and write the figures to the disk
tvs, m, tit='Mars topographic map', png='fig_mars.png'
tvs, w.coef[*,0], tit='Mars topographic map: scale 1', $
                  png='fig_mars_scale1.png'
tvs, w.coef[*,1], tit='Mars topographic map: scale 2', $
                  png='fig_mars_scale2.png'
tvs, w.coef[*,2], tit='Mars topographic map: scale 3', $
                  png='fig_mars_scale3.png'
tvs, w.coef[*,3], tit='Mars topographic map: scale 4', $
                  png='fig_mars_scale4.png'
tvs, w.coef[*,4], tit='Mars topographic map: scale 5', $
                  png='fig_mars_scale5.png'
```

12.11.3 Pyramidal Wavelet Transform on the Sphere

The code to generate the pyramidal wavelet transform of the Mars image of Fig. 12.11 is as follows.

```
; read the data
e = mrs_read('earth_healpix_128.fits')

; compute the pyramidal wavelet transform with 5 scales
mrs_pwttrans, e, we, nbrscale=5

; Display and write the figures to the disk
mrs_wttv, we, write='fig_earth'
```

12.11.3.1 Denoising

In the denoising experiment of Fig. 12.16 and Fig. 12.17, we have added Gaussian noise to the astronomical simulated synchrotron emission map. The code to generate the figures is as follows.

```
; read the image
s = rims('sync_res128.fits')

; add Gaussian noise
n = randomn(seed, N_ELEMENTS(s))
SigmaNoise = 5.
s1 = s + n* SigmaNoise

; Denoising using the undecimated WT on the sphere at 4sigma
Nsig = 4.
 mrs_wtfilter, s1, fwt4, nsigma= Nsig, nbrscale=5, SigmaNoise=SigmaNoise

; Denoising using the curvelet transform
mrs_curfilter, s1, fct4, nsigma= Nsig, nbrscale=5, SigmaNoise=SigmaNoise

; Denoising using the combined denoising
mrs_cbfilter, s1, fcb4, nsigma= Nsig, nbrscale=5, SigmaNoise=SigmaNoise

; Display and write the figure to the disk
tvs, s, /log, tit='Synchrotron emission', png='fig_sync.png'
tvs, s1 > 30, /log, tit='Synchrotron emission + noise', $
                png='fig_sync_noise5.png'

tvs , fwt4 > 30, /log, title='Undecimated Wavelet Denoising (4sigma)', $
                png='fig_sync_wtfilter5.png'
tvs , fct4 > 30, /log, title='Curvelet Denoising (4sigma)',  $
                png='fig_sync_curfilter5.png'
tvs , fcb4 > 30, /log, title='Combined Filtering (4sigma)',
                png='fig_sync_cbfilter5.png'

tvs , s1- fwt4,   title='Residual undecimated Wavelet Denoising (4sigma)',$
                png='fig_sync_resi_wtfilter5.png'
tvs , s1 - fct4,  title='Residual  curvelet Denoising (4sigma)',  $
                png='fig_sync_resi_curfilter5.png'
tvs , s1  - fcb4,  title='Residual  combined Filtering (4sigma)',  $
                png='fig_sync_resi_cbfilter5.png'

; Print the standard deviation (error) between the true image
; and the denoised images
print, 'Err WT = ', sigma(s-fwt4) , ', Err Cur  = ', sigma(s-fct4), ', $
                Err Comb = ', sigma(s-fcb4)
```

We find the outcome here to be:

```
==>  Err WT = 1.25,  Err Cur  = 1.07,  Err Combined = 0.86
```

SOFTWARE

A number of free software codes are available for different transforms described in this chapter at http://www.cosmostat.org/software.html:

- Fast 3-D-Curvelets: Matlab code for 3-D Fast curvelets.
- 3DEX: a code for Fast Fourier-Bessel Decomposition of Spherical 3-D Survey.
- MRS3D: 3-D Spherical Wavelet Transform on the Sphere.
- MS-VSTS: Multi-Scale Variance Stabilizing Transform on the Sphere.

  Other resources include:

- http://www.flaglets.org: For the flaglet wavelet transform on the ball.
- http://www.curvelet.org: For the Curvelab Matlab/C++ toolbox implementing the Fast Discrete Curvelet Transform.

12.12 SUMMARY

In this chapter, multiscale transforms on the sphere were presented: the wavelet transform, the ridgelet transform and the curvelet transform. The described transforms have many desirable properties such as invertibility. With the wealth of these multiscale analysis tools and the associated discrete analysis and synthesis transforms on the sphere at hand, several problems with spherical data can be attacked effectively. Applications to denoising, image decomposition and inpainting on the sphere were given. Few applications to challenging data analysis problems in physics and astrophysics were reported. These tools are expected to be valuable in many other applications. To disseminate them, a toolbox implementing both the transforms and the denoising, separation and inpainting algorithms is freely available to interested users.

13

Compressed Sensing

13.1 INTRODUCTION

In this chapter, we provide essential insights on the theory of compressed sensing (CS) that emerged in Candès et al. (2006b); Candès and Tao (2006); Donoho (2006a). Compressed sensing is also known under the names of *compressive sensing, compressed* or *compressive sampling*.

The conventional wisdom in digital signal processing is that for a band-limited continuous-time signal to be reconstructed exactly from its samples, the signal needs to be sampled at least at twice its bandwidth (the so-called Nyquist rate). This is the celebrated Shannon sampling theorem. In fact, this principle underlies nearly all signal acquisition protocols used. However, such a sampling scheme excludes many signals of interest that are not necessarily band-limited but can still be explained by a small number of degrees of freedom.

CS is paradigm that allows to sample a signal at a rate proportional to its information content rather than its bandwidth (think of sparsity as a measure of the information content). In a discrete setting, this tells us that a signal can be recovered from a small number of samples provided that it is sufficiently sparse or compressible. The sampling step is very fast since it employs nonadaptive linear projections that capture the structure of the signal. The signal is reconstructed from these projections by viewing the decoding step as a linear inverse problem that is cast as a sparsity-regularized convex optimization problem.

In this chapter, we will focus on convex ℓ_1-based recovery from CS measurements, for which the algorithms described in Chapter 7 are efficient solvers. ℓ_1-minimization is however not the only way to proceed. Other algorithms with theoretical recovery guarantees exist, for example, greedy algorithms or variants (Tropp and Gilbert 2007; Donoho et al. 2012; Needell and Tropp 2008; Needell and Vershynin 2009), or non-convex ℓ_p-regularization with $0 \le p \le 1$ (Chartrand 2007; Chartrand and Staneva 2008; Foucart and Lai 2009; Blanchard et al. 2009). We will not discuss these here.

One of the charms of the CS theory is its interdisciplinary approach, as it draws from various applied mathematical disciplines including linear algebra, probability theory, high dimensional geometry, functional analysis, computational harmonic analysis, and optimization. It also has implications in statistics, signal processing, information theory and learning theory. Nonetheless, although sparsity is an essential ingredient of the CS theory, in this chapter we emphasize the role of CS as a sampling paradigm (as testified by its name), and avoid confusion with the more general field of sparsity-regularized inverse problems.

13.2 THE SENSING PROTOCOL

Consider a general linear measurement process that records $m < N$ inner products between x_0 and a collection of vectors $(h_i)_{1 \leq i \leq m}$

$$y[i] = \langle h_i, x_0 \rangle ,\qquad(13.1)$$

or, in matrix form,

$$y = \mathbf{H}x_0 = \mathbf{H}\boldsymbol{\Phi}\alpha_0 = \mathbf{F}\alpha_0 ,\qquad(13.2)$$

where the measurement vectors h_i are arranged as rows in a $m \times N$ matrix $\mathbf{H}$ (see Fig. 13.1), and x_0 has a sparse synthesis representation in $\boldsymbol{\Phi}$. This setup covers the special case of Shannon-type sampling where h_i are Diracs, magnetic resonance imaging where h_i are sines and y are the Fourier coefficients.

13.2.1 Incoherence and Sparsity

CS theory asserts that one can recover certain signals and images from far fewer measurements m than data samples N. Toward this goal, CS relies on two tenets:

■ *Sparsity (compressibility*, see Section 1.1.2): This reflects the fact that the information contained in a signal can be much smaller that its effective bandwidth. CS exploits explicitly the fact that the data are economically represented in some dictionary $\boldsymbol{\Phi}$ (assumed to be an orthobasis for the moment).

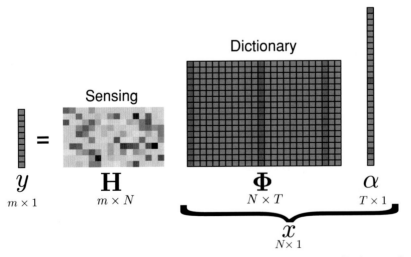

Figure 13.1. The compressed or compressive sensing paradigm. Each row of **H** is a question asked of the signal. (See *color plates*.)

■ *Incoherence between the sensing modality and* Φ: This extends the uncertainty principle between time and frequency, in the sense that signals that are sparse in Φ must be spread out in the domain in which they are acquired. That is, the sensing vectors are as different as possible from the sparsity atoms (and vice versa), and unlike the signal, the sensing vectors must have a dense representation in Φ.

As explained in Chapter 1 (see e.g., Section 1.1.2), transform coders exploit the fact that many signals have a sparse representation in a fixed basis, meaning that one can store only a small number of adaptively chosen transform coefficients without much loss. Typically, in data acquisition systems, the full N-sample signal x_0 is acquired; the complete set of transform coefficients $\Phi^T x_0$ is computed, and the largest coefficients are encoded and all others are discarded. The legitimate question is, then, why spend so much effort in acquiring the whole signal if we know that most of it will end up being thrown away?

CS is a protocol that shows that it is possible to sense and compress data simultaneously according to (13.2) without going through the intermediate stage of acquiring N samples. CS operates by directly acquiring just the important information about the signal x_0 without knowing it in advance. This is a distinctive property of CS entailing that the measurement process is not adaptive, in the sense that it will not depend on the explicit knowledge of the signal x_0.

In CS, we are interested in undersampled situations in which case $m \ll N$. But in this situation, we are facing fundamental questions:

(i) Is it possible to get accurate reconstruction ("decompression" or decoding) from a small number of measurements? If so, how many such measurements are necessary? If such a decoder exists, is it tractable in practice?

(ii) How does one design the sensing modality $\mathbf{H}$ to capture non-adaptively almost all the information of the signal?

(iii) Is it possible to have stability when we deviate (reasonably) from the idealized situation (e.g., compressible signals, presence of noise)?

In fact, in answering question 1, one is trying to solve an underdetermined system of linear equations. Traditional mathematical reasoning – in fact the fundamental theorem of linear algebra – tells us not to attempt this: there are more unknowns than equations. On the other hand, using a sparsity prior, the situation radically changes as there are some rigorous results showing that reconstructing x_0 from y is possible (in fact, it is accurate and sometimes even exact) by solving a convex program. A first answer has already appeared in Section 8.1.1, where from the bound equation (8.4), it can be deduced that a k-sparse signal (i.e., the effective support I of the signal of length N is of size $|I| = k < N$ and potentially $k \ll N$) can be reconstructed exactly from $m \geq 4k^2$ measurements by solving the basis pursuit (BP) problem (7.2). This worst-case bound is however too pessimistic in practice. The next sections will show that much better bounds can be achieved.

13.2.2 Incoherent Sensing and Sparse Signal Recovery

Suppose that $(\overline{\mathbf{H}}, \Phi)$ is a pair of orthobases. Restriction to orthobases is not a limitation: see Candès and Tao (2006); Candès and Romberg (2007). $\mathbf{H}$ is obtained by extracting m rows from $\overline{\mathbf{H}}$. Incoherence between the sensing system $\overline{\mathbf{H}}$ and the sparsifying one Φ is measured by their mutual coherence (Candès and Tao 2006; Candès and Romberg 2007):

$$\mu_{\overline{\mathbf{H}},\Phi} = \sqrt{N} \max_{i,j} |\langle h_i, \varphi_j \rangle| = \sqrt{N} \max_{i,j} |\mathbf{F}[i, j]| . \tag{13.3}$$

The lower $\mu_{\overline{\mathbf{H}},\Phi}$ is, the more incoherent $\overline{\mathbf{H}}$ and Φ. For example, if $\overline{\mathbf{H}}$ is the canonical basis (sampling with Diracs), and the signal is sparse in the Fourier basis Φ, then $\mu_{\overline{\mathbf{H}},\Phi} = 1$ attains its lower-bound. In words, the canonical and the Fourier basis are maximally incoherent. Another interesting example is when $\overline{\mathbf{H}}$ is the noiselet basis (Coifman et al. 2001). Noiselets are largely incoherent with many dictionaries including wavelets, the canonical and Fourier bases. This holds true in any dimension. Thus, for many signals and images of practical interest, which are known to be sparse in the wavelet domain, noiselets provide a near optimal measurement ensemble. Noiselets also come up with a fast transform algorithm requiring $O(N)$ operations. This is of a high practical value for implementing CS.

With the information from $m < N$ measurements, we would like to recover α_0, hence $x_0 = \Phi \alpha_0$. This could be achieved by solving

$$\min_{\alpha \in \mathbb{R}^N} \|\alpha\|_0 \quad \text{s.t.} \quad y = \mathbf{H}\Phi\alpha , \tag{13.4}$$

However, this is a a non-smooth non-convex (even combinatorial) problem. The CS decoder resorts to convex relaxation by substituting the ℓ_1-norm for the ℓ_0-pseudo norm (see the geometrical intuition behind this in Fig. 13.2). This yields the BP problem (7.2). We remind the reader that in Section 7.5.4, we have shown that this problem can be solved efficiently by proximal splitting algorithms.

The following result asserts that when x_0 is sufficiently sparse in Φ, and Φ and $\mathbf{H}$ are incoherent, the recovery via ℓ_1-minimization is provably exact. More precisely, fix a signal support I of size $|I| = k$. Select m measurements in the $\overline{\mathbf{H}}$ domain and a sign sequence on I uniformly at random. Assume that

$$m \geq C\mu_{\overline{\mathbf{H}},\Phi}^2 k \log N . \tag{13.5}$$

Then, with high probability, every vector α_0 supported on I with signs matching the chosen ones can be recovered exactly by solving BP (see equation (7.2)) (Candès and

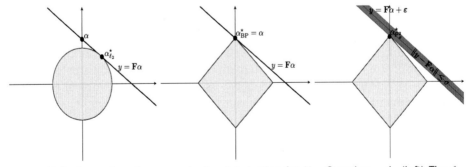

Figure 13.2. Geometry of recovery by ℓ_1-minimization for $N = 2$ and $m = 1$. (left) The ℓ_2-minimal solution is not sparse. (middle) The BP solution recovers the sparse solution exactly. (right) Solution of (P_2^σ) when noise is present in the measurements.

Romberg 2007). This result clearly establishes that fewer measurements are needed for incoherent systems. If $\mu_{\overline{\mathbf{H}},\Phi}$ attains its lower bound 1, only of the order of $k \log N$ measurements are needed to reconstruct exactly α_0 instead of N. In a nutshell, BP recovers the overwhelming majority of α_0 supported on I from measurements subsets of size m given by (13.5).

13.3 RIP-APPROACH OF COMPRESSED SENSING

13.3.1 Restricted Isometry Property

Let x_0 be k-sparse and suppose that the k locations of the non-zero entries in α_0 are known, then the simplified problem can be solved by least-squares provided $m \geq k$. This is in turn equivalent to imposing that any submatrix of k columns extracted from $\mathbf{F}$ is well-conditioned. This introduces the so-called restricted isometry property (RIP) (Candès and Tao 2005), which plays a fundamental role in the study of the recovery properties of compressed sensing. The RIP requires that there exists a $0 \geq \delta_k < 1$ such that for *all* k-sparse vectors $\alpha \in \mathbb{R}^N$, i.e. $\|\alpha\|_0 \leq k$,

$$(1 - \delta_k) \|\alpha\|^2 \leq \|\mathbf{F}\alpha\|^2 \leq (1 + \delta_k) \|\alpha\|^2 . \tag{13.6}$$

Variable δ_k is called the restricted isometry constant (RIC). A good k-order RIP matrix $\mathbf{F}$ is the one whose RIC δ_k is not too close to 1. In plain language, the matrix $\mathbf{F}$ approximately preserves the lengths of k-sparse vectors, implying that k-sparse vectors cannot be in the nullspace of $\mathbf{F}$. The RIP is also closely related to the incoherence property discussed above. Analysis of CS involving an asymmetric version of the RIP has been also proposed; see Foucart and Lai (2009); Blanchard et al. (2009).

Of course, the locations of the k non-zero entries in α_0 are not known in general. In such a setting, it is sufficient to require that $\delta_{2k} < 1$ to recover α_0 from y. Indeed, any feasible point of (13.4) takes the form $\alpha_0 + \zeta$, with $\zeta \in \ker(\mathbf{F}) \setminus \{0\}$. However, since $\mathbf{F}\zeta = 0$ and $\mathbf{F}$ satisfies the RIP of order $2k$, ζ is at least $(2k + 1)$-sparse. In turn, this implies that any $\alpha_0 + \zeta$ for $\zeta \neq 0$ is at least $(k + 1)$-sparse. That is, α_0 is the unique sparsest solution to (13.4). Hence, to recover k-sparse signals, the lower-bound in equation (13.6), which ensures that $\mathbf{F}$ is non-singular on the set of k-sparse signals, plays an important role. In fact, we will see that the RIP not only guarantees recovery by ℓ_1-minimization (exact for sparse and accurate for compressible signals), but also stability to noise.

13.3.2 Stability to Compressibility and Noise

For the CS to be widely applicable, the recovery process needs to be stable in the sense that small perturbations in the observed data should induce small perturbations in the reconstruction. Suppose now that the observed measurements are noisy according to equation (7.1), with $\|\varepsilon\| \leq \sigma$. Because of inaccurate measurements, CS proposes to solve the ℓ_1-regularized noise-aware variant (7.6). The latter can again be solved efficiently using the splitting methodology developed in Section 7.5.3.

Candès et al. (2006c) have shown that if $\mathbf{F}$ satisfies the RIP with a RIC $\delta_{2k} < \sqrt{2} - 1$, then the solution $\alpha^\star$ to equation (7.6) obeys

$$\|\alpha - \alpha^\star\| \leq \frac{C_1}{\sqrt{k}}\|\alpha - \alpha_{(k)}\|_1 + C_2\sigma , \qquad (13.7)$$

where $\alpha_{(k)}$ is the restriction of α to its k largest entries, $C_1 = 2\frac{1+(\sqrt{2}-1)\delta_{2k}}{1-(\sqrt{2}+1)\delta_{2k}}$ and $C_2 = \frac{4\sqrt{1+\delta_{2k}}}{1-(\sqrt{2}+1)\delta_{2k}}$. For instance, for $\delta_{2k} = 0.2, C_1 < 4.2$ and $C_2 < 8.5$; see Candès et al. (2006c). The preceding property is also known as the $\ell_2 - \ell_1$ instance optimality after Cohen et al. (2009).

This result is worth some comment. First, it says that the reconstruction error by ℓ_1-minimization is finite. Furthermore, the error is bounded by two terms. The first one is basically the approximation error that one would expect in the noiseless case if we knew exactly the locations of the nonzero coefficients, see Section 1.1.2. This error vanishes if the signal is strictly sparse. For compressible signals, the quality of the (nonadaptive) CS ℓ_1-decoder is within a factor of that of an oracle that knows the signal perfectly. The second error term is proportional to the noise size and predicts that the CS decoder will degrade reasonably as the noise increases. The preceding result is also fully deterministic and the same sensing matrix will work *uniformly* for all k-sparse signal with the proviso that it satisfies the RIP condition. In this sense, CS is a *universal* encoding strategy.

13.3.3 Designing Good Matrices: Random Sensing

If we are fortunate to be able to construct sensing matrices $\mathbf{H}$ such that $\mathbf{F}$ satisfies the RIP of order $2k$ with the appropriate RIC, then we are done. This is a matrix design problem which requires that equation (13.6) holds for all possible $\binom{T}{2k}$ $2k$-sparse vectors. This is where randomness and probability theory come into play.[1] Deterministic constructions of matrices satisfying the RIP are not as well developed as random ones, and only a few of them exist in the literature (DeVore 2007; Gurevich et al. 2008; Saligrama 2008).

It turns out that random constructions provide matrices obeying the RIP with overwhelming probability. We give here some useful examples and we do not delve into the technical details that are far from obvious. The interested reader may refer to Foucart and Rauhut (2013) for further details.

Suppose that the entries of $\mathbf{H}$ are independent and identically distributed (iid) Gaussian with mean zero and variance $1/m$. Then, with high probability, $\mathbf{F} = \mathbf{H}\boldsymbol{\Phi}$ (recall that $\boldsymbol{\Phi}$ is an orthobasis) satisfies the required RIP condition for equation (13.7) to hold provided that:

$$m \geq Ck\log(N/k) . \qquad (13.8)$$

The proof uses known concentration results about the singular values of Gaussian matrices. Sensing matrices whose columns are uniform on the unit sphere in $\mathbb{R}^m$, or whose entries are iid from a sub-Gaussian distribution (e.g., Bernoulli) with columns normalized to a unit norm, obey the RIP under equation (13.8). For pairs of orthobases, as in Section 13.2.2, where $\mathbf{H}$ was obtained by selecting at random m

rows from an orthobasis (e.g., Fourier) and then normalizing the columns to a unit ℓ_2-norm, the RIP holds with high probability (Candès and Tao 2006; Rudelson and Vershynin 2007) if

$$m \geq Ck(\log N)^4 . \tag{13.9}$$

This extends equation (13.5) to compressible signals and noisy measurements.

13.3.4 Sensing with Redundant Dictionaries

So far, we have considered that the signal x is sparse in some orthobasis $\mathbf{\Phi}$ $(T = N)$. But in many cases in practice, x is rather sparse in an overcomplete dictionary $\mathbf{\Phi}$ (i.e., $T > N$). To apply compressed sensing to such signals and maintain the theoretical guarantees of ℓ_1-minimization, we need to know how the combination of $\mathbf{H}$ and $\mathbf{\Phi}$ affects the RIP constant. This problem has been considered by Donoho (2006a); Rauhut et al. (2008); Ying and Zou (2009).

Let $\mu_{\mathbf{\Phi}}$ be the coherence of $\mathbf{\Phi}$ as defined in equation (8.3). In Rauhut et al. (2008), it was proved that the matrix $\mathbf{F} = \mathbf{H}\mathbf{\Phi}$, which is the composition of a random sensing matrix $\mathbf{H}$ and a sufficiently incoherent deterministic dictionary $\mathbf{\Phi}$, has a small RIC. Therefore, signals which are sparse in the redundant dictionary $\mathbf{\Phi}$ can be recovered by ℓ_1-minimization as above. More precisely, suppose that α is sufficiently sparse with

$$2 \|\alpha\|_0 = 2k \leq \mu_{\mathbf{\Phi}}^{-1}/16 + 1 ,$$

and $\mathbf{H}$ is a random matrix, whose entries are iid (e.g., Gaussian, Bernoulli, or any sub-Gaussian distribution), with normalized columns. Furthermore, assume that there is some constant C such that $m \geq Ck \log(N/k)$. Then, with a high probability, the RIC of $\mathbf{F}$ is

$$\delta_{2k} \leq 1/3 . \tag{13.10}$$

This upper bound is obviously less than $\sqrt{2} - 1$, as required for the recovery guarantee (13.7) to hold true.

13.4 RIP-LESS COMPRESSED SENSING

In the previous section, RIP-based recovery guarantees are uniform, in the sense that the recovery holds with high probability for all sufficiently sparse signals. There is another wave of work on RIP-less analysis of the recovery guarantees for CS. The claims are non-uniform, meaning that they hold for a fixed signal with high probability on the random sensing matrix. This line of approach improves on RIP-based bounds providing typically sharper constants. In the rest of this section, we will focus on the case where $\mathbf{H}$ is drawn from the standard Gaussian ensemble, i.e. the entries of $\mathbf{H}$ are iid Gaussian with zero-mean and unit variance. We also assume that $\mathbf{\Phi}$ is an orthobasis, and without loss of generality (rotation invariance of the Gaussian distribution), we take $\mathbf{\Phi} = \mathbf{I}$, i.e. the standard basis.

13.4.1 Noiseless Exact Recovery

Sufficient and Necessary Condition for Uniquness

Let us consider the BP problem, equation (7.2), with $\mathbf{F} = \mathbf{H}$. We introduce an important concept that will play a fundamental role in the following, called the descent cone associated with a function. The descent cone of a function F at $\alpha \in \text{dom}(F)$ is the conical hull of its sublevel set at α, i.e.

$$\mathbf{D}_F(\alpha) = \bigcup_{t \geq 0} \{\delta \in \mathbb{R}^N | F(\alpha + t\delta) \leq F(\alpha)\} .$$

The key observation is that a feasible point $\alpha^\star$ of problem (7.2) is its unique minimizer if, and only if,

$$\mathbf{D}_{\|\cdot\|_1}(\alpha^\star) \cap \ker(\mathbf{H}) = \{0\} . \tag{13.11}$$

In particular, α_0 is the unique solution to (7.2) if, and only if, condition (13.11) holds at $\alpha^\star = \alpha_0$. Indeed, problem (7.2) is equivalent to

$$\min_{\delta \in \ker(\mathbf{H})} \|\alpha^\star + \delta\|_1 .$$

Therefore, $\alpha^\star$ is the unique minimizer of (7.2) if, and only if, the ℓ_1 norm increases strictly whenever we move away from $\alpha^\star$ along $\ker(\mathbf{H})$. But this is precisely what is stated in condition (13.11)

Recovery Conditions based on Gaussian Width

As we supposed that $\mathbf{H}$ is a Gaussian measurement matrix, its nullspace is uniformly distributed among the set of $(N - m)$-dimensional subspaces of $\mathbb{R}^N$. The game now is to analyze when $\mathbf{H}$ satisfies condition (13.11), i.e. when the nullspace of $\mathbf{H}$ misses the descent cone $\mathbf{D}_{\|\cdot\|_1}(\alpha^\star)$. Gordon (1988) answered this question precisely by giving the probability that a uniformly random subspace intersects a subset of a cone. This probability depends on a summary parameter for convex cones called the *Gaussian width*. For a convex cone $\mathcal{C}$, its Gaussian witdh is defined as

$$w(\mathcal{C}) = \mathbb{E}\left(\sup_{z \in \mathcal{C} \cap \mathbb{S}^{N-1}} \langle z, Z \rangle \right)$$

where $\mathbb{S}^{N-1}$ is the unit sphere in $\mathbb{R}^N$, and the expectation is taken with respect to $Z \sim \mathcal{N}(0, \mathbf{I})$. Capitalizing on Gordon's result, Chandrasekaran et al. (2012) have shown that if

$$m \geq w\big(\mathbf{D}_{\|\cdot\|_1}(\alpha_0)\big)^2 + 1 , \tag{13.12}$$

then α_0 is the unique minimizer of (7.2) with high probability. It remains now to estimate $w(\mathbf{D}_{\|\cdot\|_1}(\alpha))$.

Using Jensen inequality and basic conjugacy rules (see Chapter 7 for definition of the Legendre-Fenchel conjugate), one can show that

$$
\begin{aligned}
w\big(D_{\|\cdot\|_1}(\alpha_0)\big)^2 &\leq \mathbb{E}\left(\left\|P_{D_{\|\cdot\|_1}(\alpha_0)}(Z)\right\|^2\right) \\
&= \mathbb{E}\left(\min_{u\in\bigcup_{t\geq 0} t\partial\|\cdot\|_1(\alpha_0)} \|Z-u\|^2\right) \\
&= \mathbb{E}\left(\inf_{t\geq 0}\min_{u\in t\partial\|\cdot\|_1(\alpha_0)} \|Z-u\|^2\right) \\
&= \mathbb{E}\left(\inf_{t\geq 0}\left\|Z - P_{t\partial\|\cdot\|_1(\alpha_0)}(Z)\right\|^2\right) .
\end{aligned}
\tag{13.13}
$$

Let I be the support of α_0, and $k = |I|$. Then

$$
\partial\|\cdot\|_1(\alpha_0) = \left\{u \in \mathbb{R}^N \big| u[i] = \mathrm{sign}(\alpha_0[i]), i \in I, \text{ and } |u[i]| \leq 1 \text{ otherwise}\right\}. \tag{13.14}
$$

Plugging the latter equation in the upper-bound of (13.13), and after some algebra, it can be shown that

$$
w\big(D_{\|\cdot\|_1}(\alpha_0)\big)^2 \leq 2k\log(N/k) + 5/4k ,
$$

see Chandrasekaran et al. (2012, Proposition 3.10). Thus

$$
m \geq 2k\log(N/k) + 5/4k + 1 \tag{13.15}
$$

is sufficient for α_0 to be recovered uniquely and exactly with high probability by solving (7.2). This bound may be compared to the RIP-based one in (13.8).

Statistical Dimension and Phase Transition

The bound deduced in (13.15) is a success condition ensuring exact recovery by solving (7.2). However, the failure condition remains an open question. On the other hand, it has been observed that (7.2) fails with high probability when the number of measurements is below a certain threshold that depends on the sparsity level. Clearly, solving (7.2) with random **H** exhibits a phase transition between success and failure as the number of measurements decreases. Thus it would be insightful to deliver reliable predictions about the quantitative aspects of the phase transition, and in particular the exact location and the width of the transition region.

The work of Amelunxen et al. (2014) is the first rigorous analysis that explains why phase transitions are ubiquitous in regularized linear inverse problems with random measurements such as (7.2). They also deliver reliable predictions about the quantitative aspects of the phase transition for exact noiseless recovery by solving for instance (7.2) from Gaussian measurements. This work relies on exact formulas from the field of conic integral geometry to check whether (13.11) if fullfilled or not with high probability. In this context, the general idea of using integral geometry is due to Donoho (2006); Donoho and Tanner (2009) who obtained an asymptotic upper bound, equivalent to (13.16), from polytope angle calculations.

Before stating the main result, we need to introduce another geometric quantity called the *statistical dimension* that arises from deep considerations in conic integral geometry. The statistical dimension canonically extends the linear dimension to convex cones. For convenience, we choose the following formulation that is often useful for calculating the statistical dimension of specific cones. The statistical dimension $\text{sdim}(\mathcal{C})$ of a closed convex cone $\mathcal{C}$ in $\mathbb{R}^N$ is

$$\text{sdim}(\mathcal{C}) = \mathbb{E}(\|P_{\mathcal{C}}(Z)\|^2),$$

the expectation is taken with respect to $Z \sim \mathcal{N}(0, \mathbf{I})$. The careful reader may have already identified the connection to the Gaussian width visible from equation (13.13). In fact, one has

$$w(\mathcal{C})^2 \leq \text{sdim}(\mathcal{C}) \leq w(\mathcal{C})^2 + 1 .$$

The lower-bound is that of (13.13), and the upper bound can be found in Amelunxen et al. (2014, Proposition 10.2). In plain words, the statistical dimension and the Gaussian width are essentially equivalent as summary parameters for cones.

Let us now apply this to the descent cone $D_{\|\cdot\|_1}(\alpha_0)$. In Amelunxen et al. (2014, Theorem II), the following result is proved. For a given tolerance $0 < \tau < 1$, the following holds

If $m \leq \text{sdim}\left(D_{\|\cdot\|_1}(\alpha_0)\right) - a_\tau \sqrt{N}$ (7.2) recovers α_0 with prob. $\leq \tau$

If $m \geq \text{sdim}\left(D_{\|\cdot\|_1}(\alpha_0)\right) + a_\tau \sqrt{N}$ (7.2) recovers α_0 with prob. $\geq 1 - \tau$

where $a_\tau = 4\sqrt{\log(4/\tau)}$. This result clearly establishes that we always encounter a phase transition when we use (7.2) to recover α_0 from the linear system (13.2) with Gaussian measurements. The transition occurs where m equals the statistical dimension of the descent cone. The width of the region from failure to success is of about $O(\sqrt{N})$ measurements.

It remains now to calculate $\text{sdim}(D_{\|\cdot\|_1}(\alpha_0))$. For this, we embark from (13.13) to get

$$\text{sdim}\left(D_{\|\cdot\|_1}(\alpha_0)\right) \leq \mathbb{E}\left(\inf_{t \geq 0} \left\|Z - P_{t\partial\|\cdot\|_1(\alpha_0)}(Z)\right\|^2\right)$$

$$\leq \inf_{t \geq 0} \mathbb{E}\left(\left\|Z - P_{t\partial\|\cdot\|_1(\alpha_0)}(Z)\right\|^2\right) ,$$

where Jensen's inequality was used once again to invert the inf and the expectation. Combining this with (13.14), it is easy to show that

$$\text{sdim}\left(D_{\|\cdot\|_1}(\alpha_0)\right) \leq \inf_{t \geq 0} k(1 + t^2) + 2(N - k) \int_t^{+\infty} (\tau - t)^2 \phi(\tau; 0, 1) d\tau , \qquad (13.16)$$

where we recall that $\phi(\tau; 0, 1)$ is the standard Gaussian pdf. The infimum is attained at $t^\star$, the unique positive root of

$$\int_t^{+\infty} (\tau/t - 1)\phi(\tau; 0, 1) d\tau = \frac{k}{2(N - k)} .$$

Though this estimate of the statistical dimension stems from an upper-bound estimate, its accuracy was shown in Amelunxen et al. (2014, Theorem 4.3), hence explaining why it works well in practice.

13.4.2 Stability to Noise

Let us now turn to the noisy measurements, equation (7.1), with $\|\varepsilon\| \leq \sigma$, and solve the ℓ_1-regularized noise-aware variant in equation (7.6). Observe that with this choice of $\|\varepsilon\|$, α_0 is a feasible point of (7.6). Assume again that condition (13.11) holds. Thus, for any minimizer $\alpha^\star$ of program (7.6), $\alpha^\star - \alpha_0 \in \mathrm{D}_{\|\cdot\|_1}(\alpha_0)$ by definition, and it follows from assumption (13.11) that $\mathbf{H}$ is injective at $\alpha^\star - \alpha_0$. In turn this leads to

$$\|\alpha^\star - \alpha_0\| \leq \|\mathbf{H}(\alpha^\star - \alpha_0)\|/\kappa_{\min} \leq 2\sigma/\kappa_{\min} ,$$

where $\kappa_{\min} = \inf_{\delta \in \mathrm{D}_{\|\cdot\|_1}(\alpha_0) \cap \mathbb{S}^{N-1}} \|\mathbf{H}\delta\|$, is the minimum singular value of $\mathbf{H}$ on the descent cone at α_0 (i.e. minimum conic singular value of $\mathbf{H}$). We stress the fact that by (13.11), $\kappa_{\min} > 0^2$. Using again the work of Gordon (1988) and concentration inequalities, see Tropp (2014), it can be shown that

$$\kappa_{\min} \geq \sqrt{m-1} - w\big(\mathrm{D}_{\|\cdot\|_1}(\alpha_0)\big) - \tau \geq \sqrt{m-1} - \sqrt{\mathrm{sdim}\big(\mathrm{D}_{\|\cdot\|_1}(\alpha_0)\big)} - \tau$$

with probability larger than $1 - \exp(-\tau^2/2)$. Piecing all this together, we have that

$$\|\alpha^\star - \alpha_0\| \leq 2\sigma/\kappa$$

with probability at least $1 - \exp\left(-\big(\sqrt{m-1} - w(\mathrm{D}_{\|\cdot\|_1}(\alpha_0)) - \kappa\big)^2/2\right)$ provided that

$$m \geq \big(w\big(\mathrm{D}_{\|\cdot\|_1}(\alpha_0)\big) + \kappa\big)^2 + 1 .$$

Compared to the bound (13.12) in the noiseless case, one can see that there is an overhead in the number of measurements which, as can be intuitively expected, increases as the recovery accuracy is lower.

13.4.3 Beyond Gaussian Measurements

The above results heavily hinge on the fact that $\mathbf{H}$ is standard Gaussian. For other measurement matrices, researchers use a variety of ad hoc techniques to study the recovery problem. In Tropp (2014), it was shown that sub-Gaussian sensing matrices exhibit behavior similar to the standard Gaussian measurement one. For the case of partial Fourier matrices, Candès and Plan (2011) used the "golfing scheme" introduced in Gross (2011) for noiseless and noisy sparse recovery. We will not elaborate more on these aspects that we believe are far beyond the scope of this chapter.

13.5 COMPRESSED SENSING IN SPACE SCIENCE

13.5.1 The Data Transfer Dilemma

The Herschel/Photodetector Array Camera and Spectrometer (PACS) mission of the European Space Agency (ESA)[3] was faced with a strenuous compression dilemma: it needed a compression rate equal to $\rho = 1/P$ with $P = 6$. The chosen solution consisted of averaging $P = 6$ consecutive images of a raster scan and transmitting the final average image. This approach leads unfortunately to a loss of resolution due to the high speed raster scanning.

In Bobin et al. (2008), the redundancy of raster scan data was emphasized: two consecutive images are almost the same image up to a small shift $\mathbf{t} = (t_1, t_2)$ (t_1 and t_2 are the translations along each direction). Then, jointly compressing/decompressing consecutive images of the same raster scan was proposed to alleviate the Herschel/PACS compression dilemma. The problem consists of recovering a single image x from P compressed and shifted noisy versions of it:

$$x_i = \mathbf{S}_{\mathbf{t}_i}(x) + \eta_i \quad \forall i \in \{1, \ldots, P\}, \tag{13.17}$$

where $\mathbf{S}_{\mathbf{t}_i}$ is a translation operator with a shift $\mathbf{t}_i$. The term η_i models instrumental noise or model imperfections. According to the compressed sensing paradigm, we observe

$$y_i = \mathbf{H}_i x_i \quad \forall i \in \{1, \ldots, P\}, \tag{13.18}$$

where the sampling matrices $(\mathbf{H}_i)_{\in \{1, \ldots, P\}}$ are such that their union spans $\mathbb{R}^N$. In this application, each sensing matrix $\mathbf{H}_i$ takes $m_i = \lfloor N/P \rfloor$ measurements such that the measurement subset extracted by $\mathbf{H}_i$ is disjoint from the other subsets taken by $\mathbf{H}_{j \neq i}$. Obviously, when there is no shift between consecutive images, this condition on the measurement subset ensures that the system of linear equations (13.18) is determined, and hence x can be reconstructed uniquely and stably from the measurements $(y_i)_{i=1, \ldots, P}$.

13.5.2 Compressed Sensing Paradigm

Following the compressed sensing rules, the decoding step amounts to solving the following optimization problem:

$$\min_{\alpha \in \mathbb{R}^T} \frac{1}{P} \sum_{i=1}^{P} \frac{1}{2} \left\| y_i - \mathbf{H}_i \mathbf{S}_{\mathbf{t}_i}(\boldsymbol{\Phi}\alpha) \right\|^2 + \lambda \left\| \alpha \right\|_1. \tag{13.19}$$

This problem has the same structure as equation (7.4) and can then be solved efficiently using the FB splitting algorithm or FISTA described respectively in Section 7.4.2 and Section 7.4.3. For intance, adapting the FB iteration (7.39) to equation (13.19), we get the recursion

$$\alpha^{(t+1)} = \text{SoftThresh}_{\mu_t \lambda} \left(\alpha^{(t)} + \mu_t \frac{1}{P} \sum_{i=1}^{P} \mathbf{\Phi}^{\text{T}} \mathbf{S}_{-\mathbf{t}_i} \left(\mathbf{H}_i^{\text{T}} \left(y_i - \mathbf{H}_i \mathbf{S}_{\mathbf{t}_i} \left(\mathbf{\Phi} \alpha^{(t)} \right) \right) \right) \right) \quad (13.20)$$

where $\mu_t \in (0, 2P/\sum_i \|\mathbf{H}_i\|^2 \|\mathbf{\Phi}\|^2)$. At each iteration, the sought after image is recon-
structed from the coefficients $\alpha^{(t)}$ as $x^{(t)} = \mathbf{\Phi} \alpha^{(t)}$. To accelerate this scheme, and following our discussion in Section 7.7.2, it was advocated by Bobin et al. (2008) to use a
sequence of thresholds $\lambda^{(t)}$ that decreases with the iteration number towards a final
value which is typically 2–3 times standard deviations of the noise. This allows us to
handle the noise properly.

Two approaches to solve the Herschel/PACS compression problem were
compared:

(i) The first, called MO6, consists of transmitting the average of $P = 6$ consecutive images.
(ii) The second approach uses the previously described compressed sensing
based solution. It consists of acquiring m compressed measurements according to equation (13.18) from $P = 6$ consecutive images of a raster scan. The
decoding step solves equation (13.19) using iteration (13.20).

In the following experiment, the sparsifying dictionary $\mathbf{\Phi}$ is the starlet transform
and the measurement matrices $\mathbf{H}_i$ are submatrices of the noiselet basis (Coifman
et al. 2001).

Figure 13.3 (top left) displays the original image x. In Fig. 13.3 (top right), we
show one of the $P = 6$ simulated observed images x_i including instrumental effects
(see Bobin et al. (2008) for details). The MO6 solution is shown on the bottom left
and the CS-based solution is shown on the bottom right of Fig. 13.3.

It was shown in Bobin et al. (2008) that compressed sensing provides a resolution
enhancement that can reach 30% of the full width at half maximum (FWHM) of the

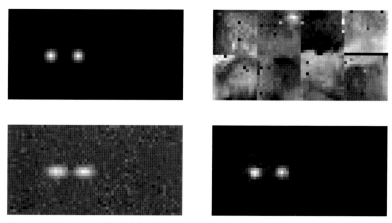

Figure 13.3. (top left) Original image. (top right) One of the $P = 6$ observed
noisy images. (bottom left) Mean of the 6 noisy images (see text for more
details). (bottom right) Reconstruction from noiselet-based CS measurements. The recursion equation (13.20) was used with 100 iterations.

instrument point spread function for a wide range of intensities of x. In summary, this experiment illustrates the reliability of the CS-based compression to deal with demanding, operational data compression needs. The efficiency of compressed sensing applied to the Herschel/PACS data compression relies also on the redundancy of the data: consecutive images of a raster scan are fairly shifted versions of a reference image. The good performance of CS is obtained by merging the information of consecutive images. The same *data fusion* scheme could be used to reconstruct with high accuracy wide sky areas from full raster scans. Based on this proof of concept, ESA has decided to study the CS with real Herschel data. Therefore, ESA has acquired a full data set without any compression, so the CS could be evaluated in realistic conditions, i.e. cosmic rays impact the detector, drift of the gain of the detector, non Gaussian noise, bad pixels, etc.

13.5.3 The Compressed Sampling ESA Herschel Study on NGC6946

Calibration observations of the galaxy NGC6946 were taken in fast scan mode (60 arcsec/s). The data set is made up of two cross scans in the blue band of

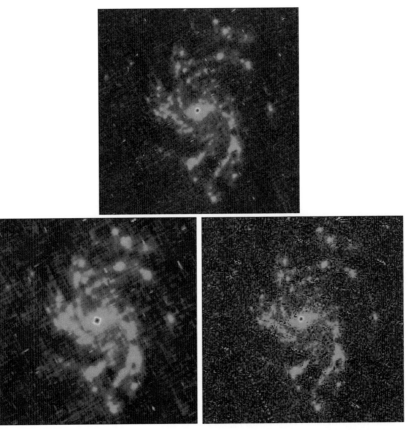

Figure 13.4. Map estimations of NGC 6946: top, reference map without any compression; bottom left, ESA pipeline using the averaging solution; and bottom right, CS solution. All maps have the same scale. (See *color plates*.)

Table 13.1. FWHM of sources in pixels in Figure 13.4 estimated using 2-dimensional Gaussian fits of four isolated sources randomly chosen from the map

FWHM (pixels)	Averaging	CS	Reference map
mean of 4 sources	4.30	3.27	3.15

approximately 60,000 frames each. Each frame has 256 pixels. The estimated map is made of 192×192 pixels of 3 arcsec each, resulting in a 10 arcmin^2 map. Because these acquired frames were uncompressed, it was possible to compress the data on the ground using both the averaging strategy and the CS, then to decompress the two images, and finally to compare them to the reconstructed image derived from the uncompressed data. Results are presented in Figure 13.4. The compression factor on the acquisition side is always 8, except for the reference map (Fig. 13.4 top) for which no compression is applied. Note that the reference map is not guaranteed to be the ground truth. In particular, it is affected by instrumental effects (i.e., noise, cosmic rays, etc.) as much as the other maps. However, it should be closer to the ground truth since it does not suffer from a loss of information due to compression.

Looking at Figure 13.4, the CS map is better resolved than the averaging map. This gain in resolution allows close sources to be better separated. This is supported by the quantitative results presented in Table 13.1, which gives the mean of the full width at half maximum (FWHM, in pixels) derived from Gaussian fits to four compact sources selected on the field. The gain in resolution is approximately 1 pixel, or 3 arcseconds. More details can be found in Barbey et al. (2011).

Hence, the compressed sensing theory can be successfully applied to real space data, taking into account all the instrumental effects. It was demonstrated that the various artifacts affecting the data can properly be handled in the CS framework (Barbey et al. 2011). CS and sparse recovery should definitely be considered as a useful technique for the design of future space missions such as TALC (Sauvage et al. 2014).

13.6 GUIDED NUMERICAL EXPERIMENTS

Here we use the `SplittingSolvers` toolbox described in Chapter 7, see Section 7.8. Refer to the accompanying software website (http://www.SparseSignalRecipes.info) for the code.

The goal in this experiment is to reveal the phase transition phenomeon in CS by estimating the probability that problem (7.2) succeeds as we vary the sparsity k of the unknown α_0 and the number m of Gaussian measurements. The script in the toolbox that reproduces the following experiment is `1D/Demos/testsCSPhaseTransition.m`. We consider a fixed ambient dimension $N = 100$, and we let $\boldsymbol{\Phi} = \mathbf{I}$ (i.e. $\mathbf{F} = \mathbf{H}$). For each pair (k, m), we generate a k-sparse vector x_0, and we draw m random measurements y, where $\mathbf{H} \in \mathbb{R}^{m \times N}$ has entries from an iid $\mathcal{N}(0, 1)$. We then solve (7.2). The result is depicted in Fig 13.5. The

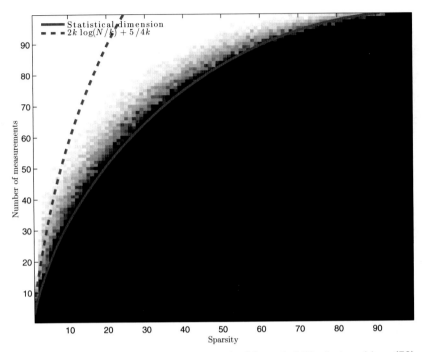

Figure 13.5. Phase transition phenomeon in CS: probability that problem (7.2) succeeds as we vary the sparsity k of the unknown x_0 and the number m of Gaussian measurements (ambient dimension is fixed to $N = 100$). The gray level represents certain success probability estimated from 50 independent trials (high is white and low is black).

gray level represents certain success probability estimated from 50 independent trials (high is white and low is black). It is seen that for a given sparsity level, (7.2) indeed almost always succeeds in recovering α_0 if m is sufficiently large, while the it almost always fails when m is fewer. One can also see that the two regimes are separated by a curve relating m to k (edge of the phase transition). In solid lines, we plotted the location of this threshold as theoretically predicted by the bound (13.15) and (13.16). The prediction of (13.16) coincides almost perfectly with the empirical 50% success.

In the second experiment, whose result is depicted in Fig 13.6, the goal is apply the CS paradigm to recovery of the $N = 512^2$ "Mondrian" painting image from 18% noiseless and noisy (SNR = 30 dB) Fourier measurements. The dictionary Φ is the orthogonal wavelet transform, and hence $\mathbf{F} = \mathbf{H}\Phi$ is a tight frame. In the noiseless case, the BP problem was again solved with Algorithm 30. In the noisy case, we used DR splitting to solve problem (7.6) since $\mathbf{F}$ is a tight frame, and primal-dual splitting (adapted from Algorithm 28) to solve problem (7.7). For (7.6), the radius of the ℓ_2-constraint was set to $\sigma = \sqrt{N}\sigma_\varepsilon$, and for (7.7) the constraint radius δ was set to λ. For Algorithm 26, the choice of the regularization parameter λ in (7.4) was done on a trial-test basis to get a residual error of σ. The results can be reproduced by running the script 2D/Demos/testsCSImplicitSynthesisMondrian2D.m.

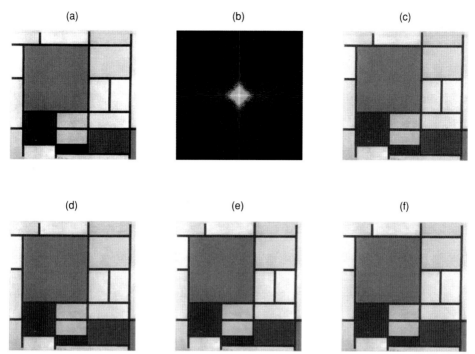

Figure 13.6. Recovery from CS Fourier measurements with the orthogonal wavelet sparsity basis. (a) Original 256 × 256 Mondrian image. (b) $m = 18\% \times 512^2$ noisy Fourier measurements (SNR = 30 dB). (c) Recovered by solving problem (7.4) using Algorithm 26, PSNR = 26.4 dB. (d) Recovered by solving problem (7.2) using Algorithm 30. (e) Recovered by solving problem (7.6) using (7.41), PSNR = 26.2 dB. (f) Recovered by solving problem (7.7) using primal-dual splitting, PSNR = 26.1 dB. Except for problem (7.2), which was solved with the noiseless measurements, all other algorithms were run on the noisy ones.

13.7 SUMMARY

In this chapter, we overviewed the essential ingredients of the compressed sensing theory as a paradigm for jointly sampling and compressing signals known to be sparse in some dictionary. By establishing a direct link between sampling and sparsity, compressed sensing is now beginning to have a huge impact in many scientific fields. We then discussed the recovery problem in compressed sensing, which is viewed as a linear inverse problem where the sparsity penalty is the ℓ_1 norm, and we gave sufficient conditions under which ℓ_1 minimization succeeds. We have seen that CS has been successfully applied to real space data, and can provide elegant solutions for future space missions.

Compressed sensing is currently one of the most active research areas in applied mathematics and signal processing. Despite the huge amount of work being published, many important questions remain to be investigated more deeply. Among them, we can think of proper ways of exploiting more structure in the signal (e.g., group sparsity, multiscale persistence, etc.) and understanding their theoretical and practical performance; figuring out deterministic constructions of sensing matrices (possibly for certain classes of signal and application) that have guarantees and practicality comparable to random ones; and finding tight sample complexity bounds for exact or approximate recovery in the sparsity analysis case. Many of these subjects have already started to attract interest. CS also holds great promise for some real world applications, and the space science one we discussed here confirms that CS can be a valuable solution under appropriate circumstances.

14

This Book's Take-Home Message

In this book, we have presented in detail how sparsity can be used to regularize a variety of inverse problems in signal, image, and more generally data processing. We have shown that sparse recovery involves four main ingredients that are the keys its its success. These ingredients are

- **The dictionary:** fixed dictionaries with fast analysis and synthesis operators, such as X-lets (including wavelets or curvelets described in Chapters 3, 5, 11, and 12), allow us to build very efficient algorithms, both in terms of computation time and of quality of the recovered solutions. We have seen in Chapter 8 that these fixed dictionaries can be gathered together to build a larger dictionary, but still using fast operators. To go beyond these fixed dictionaries, dictionary learning in Chapter 10 appears to be a promising paradigm to learn dictionaries adapted to the analyzed data. We showed its efficiency in astronomical image denoising and how it exceeds the performance of state-of-the-art denoising algorithms that use nonadaptive dictionaries.
- **The noise modeling:** having the right dictionary is only a part of the story and is not enough. In most inverse problems, one needs to disentangle the useful signal/information from the noise. This requires taking properly into account the noise behavior in the observed data. In a denoising setting, we have seen in Chapter 6 how this can be achieved for different kinds of noise models, such as Gaussian, Poisson, mixture of Gaussian and Poisson, and correlated noise, and can be used to derive the distribution of the coefficients and therefore to detect, with a given confidence level, significant coefficients that should be used to reconstruct the signal of interest.
- **The variational problem and minimization algorithm:** piecing together the first ingredient and the second one (i.e., regularization and data fidelity), solving the inverse problem at hand becomes solving a variational (optimization) problem. We have shown throughout the book how this can be achieved for several verse problems (e.g., Chapters 7, 8, and 9). To solve the obtained optimization problem, we described in Chapter 7 a very general class of optimization schemes, namely

proximal splitting algorithms, that are fast, are easy to implement, and enjoy prov-
able convergence.

■ **The choice of parameter(s):** variational formulation of inverse problems involves
parameters that must be chosen. For instance, in the penalized form, the choice of
the regularization parameter(s) is an very important and delicate issue. The practitioner scientist does not have to choose these parameters based on a tedious
trial-and-error approach, by running the algorithm many times with a range of
parameters. Furthermore, important decisions may have to be taken from the
obtained solution, and one definitively does not want to do this based on an ad-
hoc parameter. In Chapter 7, different approaches to perform this task in an automatic way are provided, some of them being very practical.

Finally, a very important aspect of sparsity is its relation to the compressed sensing
sampling theory. This is discussed in Chapter 13.

An distinctive aspect of this book is the availability of the code that has been used
to produce the book figures, following the philosophy of reproducible research.

To conclude this book on a beautiful scientific result in astronomical imaging,
where all the messages we have delivered have been carefully taken into account, we
show in Figure 14.1 a reconstructed image from LOFAR radio-interferometry data
of Cygnus A. LOFAR (the LOw Frequency ARray) is a giant radiotelescope with a

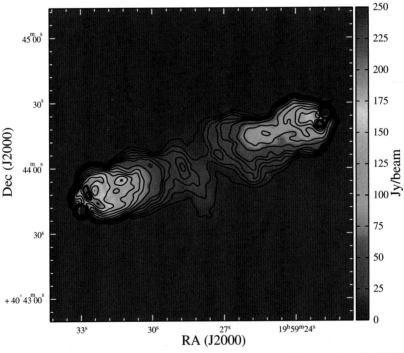

Figure 14.1. Color scale: reconstructed 512×512 image of Cygnus A at 151 MHz
(with resolution 2.8″ and a pixel size of 1″). Contour levels from a 327.5 MHz
Cyg A VLA image at 2.5″ angular resolution and a pixel size of 0.5″. Most of
the recovered features in the image were reconstructed using sparsity regularization corresponding to real structures observed at higher frequencies. (See *color
plates*.)

large antenna array comprising 25,000 elementary antennas grouped in 48 stations and distributed in different countries (the Netherlands, Germany, United Kingdom, France, Sweden and, soon, Poland). Cygnus A is one of the most powerful galaxies in the radio window. At a distance of 750 million light-years from Earth, it is considered to have a central black hole of 2.5 billion solar masses generating two symmetric jets, visible in radio on each side of the black hole. Radio-interferometers provide measurements in the Fourier domain, but without covering the whole domain. Sparse recovery allows to reconstruct the image with a resolution twice better than standard methods (Garsden et al. 2015), showing hotspot features and a much sharper reconstruction of the structures inside the lobes. These high-resolution details would be hard to believe because standard methods do not see show at all from the same data. But Cygnus A was also observed with another instrument, the Very Large Array (VLA), in another frequency band also with a resolution twice better than standard methods. Figure 14.1 shows that both images clearly present the same quality of details. The resolved structures inside the lobes, in the LOFAR image reconstructed using sparse recovery (color map), match the real structures observed at higher frequency and reconstructed with a standard method (contour), validating the capability of the method to reconstruct sources with high fidelity.

Notes

Chapter 1

1. The dictionary is supposed to be real. For a complex dictionary, $\boldsymbol{\Phi}^{\mathrm{T}}$ is to be replaced by the conjugate transpose (adjoint) $\boldsymbol{\Phi}^*$.

Chapter 2

1. Our normalization is such that these functions do not have a unit norm.

Chapter 3

1. In frame theory parlance, we would say that the UWT frame synthesis operator is not injective.
2. Its solution is not necessarily unique unless the system is over determined (i.e., the cardinal of the multiresolution support is greater than the number of samples in X).
3. This formula is exact in the orthogonal case. In the redundant case, it will be shown in Chapter 6 that this is the first iteration in an iterative denoising procedure.

Chapter 4

1. This integer wavelet transform is based on a symmetric, biorthogonal wavelet transform built from the interpolating Deslauriers-Dubuc scaling function where both the high-pass filter and its dual have 2 vanishing moments (Mallat 2008).
2. For discrete grayscale levels, the supremum is replaced by the pointwise maximum.
3. For discrete grayscale levels, the infimum is superseded by the pointwise minimum.
4. Reflection is essential here; see Serra (1982); Soille (2003). For a symmetric structuring element, the reflected version is the element itself.

Chapter 5

1. W_2^s is the Sobolev space of square integrable functions whose sth derivative is also square integrable.

Chapter 6

1. Rigorously speaking, $\boldsymbol{\Phi}$ should be a Parseval tight frame for this statement to hold.

Chapter 7

1. In the sense that there exists a bijection $\lambda \leftrightarrow \sigma \leftrightarrow \rho$ for which the three problems share the same solutions.
2. The latter statement is possible here because we are in a finite dimension.

3. We here choose one splitting of the functions J_1 and R_k, but other ones are possible, leading to slightly different forms of the primal-dual algorithm.

4. Again, here, we choose one particular splitting of the functions, but other ones are possible as well, leading to a different iteration.

5. This value must be multiplied by the ℓ_2 norm of each column of **F** if the latter is not normalized.

6. In the Gaussian case one could also think of replacing the data fidelity term in (7.62) by $(y - \cdot)^T \Sigma^{-1}(y - \cdot)$. This, however, would necessitate computing the inverse of Σ (which does not diagonalize necessarily easily, as for instance if the noise were stationary) and to store it. This can have a prohibitive computational cost.

Chapter 8

1. The Spark of a matrix is defined as its minimal number of linearly dependent columns, not to be confused with the rank.

2. For a complex dictionary, Φ^T is to be replaced by the adjoint Φ^*.

3. The objective (8.14) is not Lipschitz differentiable, but in practice the iteration still works for appropriately chosen μ.

4. The meaning of linear convergence is the one of the optimization literature.

5. Courtesy of GIP Cyceron, Caen, France.

Chapter 9

1. The adjectives *spectral* and *spatial* that characterize the dictionaries are not formal. Owing to the symmetry of the multichannel sparse decomposition problems, **A** and Φ have no formal difference. In practice and more particularly in multi/hyperspectral imaging, **A** will refer to the dictionary of physical spectra and Φ to the dictionary of image/signal waveforms. In the BSS problem, **A** is unknown.

2. The reasoning holds for $0 \le p \le 1$ from Section 7.6.1.

Chapter 10

1. With appropriate boundary conditions, of course.

Chapter 11

1. On a Cartesian grid, the slopes are equispaced, not the angles.

2. In fact, it should be ≈ 50 as can be read from Table 11.2.

Chapter 12

1. http://healpix.jpl.nasa.gov

2. The Mars Orbiter Laser Altimeter (MOLA) generated altimetry profiles used to create global topographic maps. The MOLA instrument stopped acquiring altimetry data on June 30, 2001, and after that operated in passive radiometry mode until the end of the Mars Global Surveyor mission. MOLA data sets are produced by the MOLA Science Team and archived by the PDS Geosciences Node.

3. The ETOPO5 data are credited to "Data Announcement 88-MGG-02, Digital relief of the Surface of the Earth. NOAA, National Geophysical Data Center, Boulder, Colorado, 1988".

4. Available from: http://www.nasa.gov/vision/earth/features/bmng_gallery_4.html

5. If X were to be vectorized by stacking the channels in a long column vector, **H** would be a block-diagonal matrix whose blocks are the circulant matrices $\mathbf{H}_{k_i}$.

6. An ΛCDM simulation at $z = 0$, which was calculated using 512^3 particles for the following cosmology: $\Omega_m = 0.3$, $\Omega_\Lambda = 0.7$, $H_o = 70$ kms^{-1} Mpc^{-1}, $\sigma_8 = 0.9$. The data cube provided is $479/2$ h^{-1} Mpc in length.

7. The WMAP data and mask we used here are available online at http://map.gsfc.nasa.gov/

8. astro.estec.esa.nl/Planck

Chapter 13

1. The probabilistic framework has already been used when the result (13.5) was stated.
2. Excluding the trivial case where α_0 is the unique minimizer of (7.6).
3. PACS was one of the three instruments on board ESA's Herschel Space Observatory. Herschel was a space telescope observing in the far infrared and submillimeter wavelength region. It was active from 2009 to 2013, and was the largest infrared telescope ever launched.

References

Abramovich, F., Benjamini, Y., Donoho, D., and Johnstone, I.: 2006, Adapting to unknown sparsity by controlling the false discovery rate, *Annals of Statistics* 34(2), 584–653

Abramowitz, M. and Stegun, I. A.: 1972, *Handbook of Mathematical Functions*, Dover Publications, New York

Abrial, P., Moudden, Y., Starck, J., Bobin, J., Fadili, M., Afeyan, B., and Nguyen, M.: 2007, Morphological component analysis and inpainting on the sphere: Application in physics and astrophysics, *Journal of Fourier Analysis and Applications* 13(6), 729–748

Abrial, P., Moudden, Y., Starck, J., Fadili, M. J., Delabrouille, J., and Nguyen, M.: 2008, CMB data analysis and sparsity, *Statistical Methodology* 5(4), 289–298

Achim, A., Bezerianos, A., and Tsakalides, P.: 2001, Novel Bayesian multiscale method for speckle removal in medical ultrasound images, *IEEE Transactions on Medical Imaging* 20(8), 772–783

Achim, A., Tsakalides, P., and Bezerianos, A.: 2003, SAR image denoising via Bayesian wavelet shrinkage based on heavy-tailed modeling, *IEEE Transactions on Geoscience and Remote Sensing* 41(8), 1773–1784

Acton, S. T., Mukherjee, D. P., Havlicek, J. P., and Bovik, A. C.: 2001, Oriented texture completion by AM-FM reaction-diffusion, *IEEE Transactions on Image Processing* 10(6), 885–896

Adelson, E., Simoncelli, E., and Hingorani, R.: 1987, Optimal image addition using the wavelet transform, *SPIE Visual Communication and Image Processing II* 845, 50–58

Afeyan, B., Won, K., Starck, J. L., Stevens, R., Mapoles, E., Johnson, M., and Haan, S.: 2006, MODEM: Morphological diversity extraction method to identify, classify and characterize surface defects of spherical ICF targets via AFM and phase shifting diffraction interferometry, in *Proceedings of the 17th Target Fabrication Meeting, San Diego, CA*, 1–5

Afonso, M. V., Bioucas-Dias, J. M., and Figueiredo, M. A.: 2011, An augmented Lagrangian approach to the constrained optimization formulation of imaging inverse problems, *Trans. Img. Proc.* 20(3), 681

Aharon, M., Elad, M., and Bruckstein, A.: 2006, K-SVD: An algorithm for designing overcomplete dictionaries for sparse representation, *IEEE Transactions on Signal Processing* 54(11), 4311–4322

Akaike, H.: 1970, Statistical predictor estimation, *Annals of the Institute of Statistical Mathematics* 22, 203–217

Amari, S. and Cardoso, J.-F.: 1997, Blind source separation – semiparametric statistical approach, *IEEE Transactions on Signal Processing* 45(11), 2692–2700

Amari, S.-I.: 1999, Superefficiency in blind source separation, *IEEE Transactions on Signal Processing* 47(4), 936–944

Amelunxen, D., Lotz, M., McCoy, M. B., and Tropp, J. A.: 2014, Living on the edge: A geometric theory of phase transitions in convex optimization, *IMA Journal of Information Inference* 3(3), 224

Anscombe, F.: 1948, The transformation of Poisson, binomial and negative-binomial data, *Biometrika* 15, 246–254

Antoine, J., Demanet, L., Jacques, L., and Vandergheynst, P.: 2002, Wavelets on the sphere: Implementation and approximation, *Applied and Computational Harmonic Analysis* 13, 177–200

Antoine, J. and Murenzi, R.: 1994, Two dimensional wavelet analysis in image processing, *Physicalia Magazine* 16, 105–134

Antoine, J.-P.: 1999, The 2-D wavelet transform, physical applications and generalizations, in J. van den Berg (ed.), *Wavelets in Physics*, Cambridge University Press, 23–76

Antoniadis, A., Bigot, J., and Sapatinas, T.: 2001, Wavelet estimators in nonparametric regression: A comparative simulation study, *Journal of Statistical Software* 6(6), 1–83

Antoniadis, A. and Fan, J.: 2001, Regularization of wavelet approximations, *Journal of the American Statistical Association* 96(455), 939–963

Antonini, M., Barlaud, M., Mathieu, P., and Daubechies, I.: 1992, Image coding using wavelet transform, *IEEE Transactions on Image Processing* 1, 205–220

Appleton, P. N., Siqueira, P. R., and Basart, J. P.: 1993, A morphological filter for removing cirrus-like emission from far-infrared extragalactic IRAS fields, *Astronomical Journal* 106, 1664–1678

Argyriou, A., Evgeniou, T., and Pontil, M.: 2008, Convex multi-task feature learning, *Machine Learning* 73(3), 243–272

Arivazhagan, S., Ganesan, L., and Kumar, T.: 2006, Texture classification using curvelet statistical and co-occurrence features, in *Proceedings of the 18th International Conference on Pattern Recognition (ICPR 2006)*, Vol. 2, 938–941

Arneodo, A., Argoul, F., Bacry, E., Elezgaray, J., and Muzy, J. F.: 1995, *Ondelettes, Multifractales et Turbulences*, Diderot, Arts et Sciences, Paris

Attouch, H., Bolte, J., and Svaiter, B.: 2013, Convergence of descent methods for semi-algebraic and tame problems: Proximal algorithms, forward–backward splitting, and regularized Gauss–Seidel methods, *Mathematical Programming* 137(1–2), 91

Atzeni, S. and ter Vehn, J. M.: 2004, *The Physics of Inertial Fusion*, Oxford University Press

Aubert, G. and Vese, L.: 1997, A variational method in image recovery, *SIAM Journal on Numerical Analysis* 34(5), 1948–1979

Aujol, J. and Chambolle, A.: 2005, Dual norms and image decomposition models, *International Journal of Computer Vision* 63(1), 85–104

Aujol, J., Gilboa, G., Chan, T., and Osher, S.: 2006, Structure and texture compression – modeling, algorithms, and parameter selection, *International Journal of Computer Vision* 67(1), 111–136

Aujol, J.-F., Aubert, G., Blanc-Féraud, L., and Chambolle, A.: 2005, Image decomposition into a bounded variation component and an oscillating component, *Journal of Mathematical Imaging and Vision* 22, 71–88

Averbuch, A., Coifman, R. R., Donoho, D. L., Israeli, M., and Waldén, J.: 2001, Fast slant stack: A notion of radon transform for data in a cartesian grid which is rapidly computible, algebraically exact, geometrically faithful and invertible, report, 2001 http://statweb .stanford.edu/~donoho/Reports/2001/FastSlantStack.pdf

Bach, F. R.: 2008, Consistency of the group lasso and multiple kernel learning, *Journal of Machine Learning Research* 9, 1179–1225

Balan, R.: 2007, Estimator for number of sources using minimum description length criterion for blind sparse source mixtures, in M. E. Davies, C. J. James, S. A. Abdallah, and M. D. Plumbley (eds.), *Independent Component Analysis and Signal Separation*, Vol. 4666 of *Lecture Notes in Computer Science*, Springer, 333–340

Bamberger, R. H. and Smith, M. J. T.: 1992, A filter bank for the directional decomposition of iimage: Theory and design, *IEEE Transactions on Image Processing* 40, 882

Baraniuk, R. G., Cevher, V., Duarte, M. F., and Hegde, C.: 2010, Model-based compressive sensing, *IEEE Transactions on Information Theory* 56, 1982

Barbey, N., Sauvage, M., Starck, J.-L., Ottensamer, R., and Chanial, P.: 2011, Feasibility and performances of compressed sensing and sparse map-making with Herschel/PACS data, *A&A* 527, A102

Bauschke, H. H. and Combettes, P. L.: 2011, *Convex Analysis and Monotone Operator Theory in Hilbert Spaces*, Springer-Verlag, New York

Beck, A. and Teboulle, M.: 2009, Fast iterative shrinkage-thresholding algorithm for linear inverse problems, *SIAM Journal on Imaging Sciences* 2, 183–202

Becker, S.: 2012, A quasi-newton proximal splitting method, in *In Advances in Neural Information Processing Systems (NIPS)*, Vol. 25, pp. 2627–2635

Becker, S., Bobin, J., and Candès, E.: 2011, NESTA: A fast and accurate first-order method for sparse recovery, *SIAM Journal of Imaging Sciences* 4, 1

Beckouche, S., Starck, J. L., and Fadili, J.: 2013, Astronomical image denoising using dictionary learning, *A&A* 556, A132

Bell, A. and Sejnowski, J.: 1997, The 'independent components' of natural scenes are edge filters, *Vision Research* 23(37), 3327–3338

Bell, A. and Sejnowski, T.: 1995, An information maximisation approach to blind separation and blind deconvolution, *Neural Computation* 7(6), 1129–1159

Belouchrani, A., Meraim, K. A., Cardoso, J.-F., and Moulines, E.: 1997, A blind source separation technique based on second order statistics, *IEEE Transactions on Signal Processing* 45(2), 434–444

Benjamini, Y. and Hochberg, Y.: 1995, Controlling the false discovery rate – a practical and powerful approach to multiple testing, *Journal of the Royal Statistical Society B* 57, 289–300

Benjamini, Y. and Yekutieli, Y.: 2001, The control of the false discovery rate in multiple testing under dependency, *Annals of Statistics* 29(4), 1165–1188

Bentley, P. and McDonnell, J.: 1994, Wavelet transforms: an introduction, *Electronics and Communication Engineering Journal* 6, 175–186

Bertalmío, M., Caselles, V., Haro, G., and Sapiro, G.: 2005, The state of the art of image and surface inpainting, in O. F. N. Paragios, Y. Chen (ed.), *Mathematical Models in Computer Vision: The Handbook*, Springer, 309–322

Bertalmío, M., Sapiro, G., Caselles, V., and Ballester, C.: 2000, Image inpainting, in *SIGGRAPH 2000*, Vol. 34, New Orleans, 417–424

Bertalmío, M., Vese, L., Sapiro, G., and Osher, S.: 2003, Simultaneous structure and texture image inpainting, *IEEE Transactions on Image Processing* 12(8), 882–889

Bickel, P. J., Ritov, Y., and Tsybakov, A.: 2009, Simultaneous analysis of lasso and Dantzig selector, *Annals of Statistics* 37, 1705–1732

Bijaoui, A. and Giudicelli, M.: 1991, Optimal image addition using the wavelet transform, *Experimental Astronomy* 1, 347–363

Bijaoui, A. and Jammal, G.: 2001, On the distribution of the wavelet coefficient for a Poisson noise, *Signal Processing* 81, 1789–1800

Bioucas-Dias, J.: 2006, Bayesian wavelet-based image deconvolution: A GEM algorithm exploiting a class of heavy-tailed priors, *IEEE Transactions on Image Processing* 15(4), 937–951

Bishop, C. M.: 2006, *Pattern Recognition and Machine Learning*, Springer

Blanc-Féraud, L. and Barlaud, M.: 1996, Edge preserving restoration of astrophysical images, *Vistas in Astronomy* 40, 531–538

Blanchard, J. D., Cartis, C., and Tanner, J.: 2009, The restricted isometry property and ℓ^Q-regularization: Phase transitions for sparse approximation, report. http://www.maths.ed.ac.uk/ERGO/pubs/ERGO-09-005.pdf

Blumensath, T. and Davies, M. E.: 2008, Iterative thresholding for sparse approximations, *Journal of Fourier Analysis and Applications* 14(5), 629–654

Bobin, J., Moudden, Y., Fadili, M. J., and Starck, J.-L.: 2009, Morphological diversity and sparsity for multichannel data restoration, *Journal of Mathematical Imaging and Vision* 33(2), 149–168

Bobin, J., Moudden, Y., Starck, J.-L., and Elad, M.: 2006, Morphological diversity and source separation, *IEEE Transactions on Signal Processing* 13(7), 409–412

Bobin, J., Moudden, Y., Starck, J. L., Fadili, M., and Aghanim, N.: 2008, SZ and CMB reconstruction using generalized morphological component analysis, *Statistical Methodology* 5(4), 307–317

Bobin, J., Starck, J.-L., Fadili, M. J., and Moudden, Y.: 2007a, Sparsity and morphological diversity in blind source separation, *IEEE Transactions on Image Processing* 16(11), 2662–2674

Bobin, J., Starck, J.-L., Fadili, M. J., Moudden, Y., and Donoho, D.: 2007b, Morphological component analysis: An adaptive thresholding strategy, *IEEE Transactions on Image Processing* 16(11), 2675–2681

Bobin, J., Starck, J.-L., Moudden, Y., and Fadili, M. J.: 2008, Blind source separation: The sparsity revolution, *Advances in Imaging and Electron Physics* 152, 221–306

Bobin, J., Starck, J.-L., and Ottensamer, R.: 2008, Compressed sensing in astronomy, *IEEE Journal of Selected Topics in Signal Processing* 2, 718–726

Bobin, J., Starck, J.-L., Rapin, J., and Larue, A.: 2014, Spare blind source separation for partially correlated sources. *IEEE International Conference on Image Processing (ICIP)*, pp. 6021–6025, 2014.

Bolte, J., Sabach, S., and Teboulle, M.: 2014, Proximal alternating linearized minimization for nonconvex and nonsmooth problems, *Mathematical Programming* 146(1–2), 459

Bonesky, T., Bredies, K., Lorenz, D., and Maass, P.: 2007, A generalized conditional gradient method for nonlinear operator equations with sparsity constraints, *Inverse Problems* 23, 2041–2058

Bredies, K. and Lorenz, D.: 2008, Linear convergence of iterative soft-thresholding, *Journal of Fourier Analysis and Applications* 14, 813–837

Bredies, K. and Lorenz, D. A.: 2009, Regularization with non-convex separable constraints, *Inverse Problems* 25(8), 085011

Breen, E., Jones, R., and Talbot, H.: 2000, Mathematical morphology: A useful set of tools for image analysis, *Statistics and Computing* 10, 105–120

Briceño-Arias, L. M. and Combettes, P. L.: 2011, A monotone+skew splitting model for composite monotone inclusions in duality, *SIAM Journal on Optimization* 21, 1230–1250

Briceño-Arias, L. M., Combettes, P. L., Pesquet, J.-C., and Pustelnik, N.: 2010, Proximal algorithms for multicomponent image recovery problems, *Journal of Mathematical Imaging and Vision* pp. 1–20

Brigger, P., Müller, F., Illgner, K., and Unser, M.: 1999, Centered pyramids, *IEEE Transactions on Image Processing* 8(9), 1254–1264

Bronstein, A., Bronstein, M., Zibulevsky, M., and Zeevi, Y.: 2005, Sparse ICA for blind separation of transmitted and reflected images, *International Journal of Imaging Science and Technology* 15/1, 84–91

Bruckstein, A., Donoho, D., and Elad, M.: 2009, From sparse solutions of systems of equations to sparse modeling of signals and images, *SIAM Review* 51(1), 34–81

Bruckstein, A. and Elad, M.: 2002, A generalized uncertainty principle and sparse representation in pairs of $\mathbf{r}^n$ bases, *IEEE Transactions on Information Theory* 48, 2558–2567

Buckheit, J. and Donoho, D.: 1995, Wavelab and reproducible research, in A. Antoniadis (ed.), *Wavelets and Statistics*, Springer, 53–81

Burt, P. and Adelson, A.: 1983, The Laplacian pyramid as a compact image code, *IEEE Transactions on Communications* 31, 532–540

Cai, T.: 1999, Adaptive wavelet estimation: A block thresholding and oracle inequality approach, *Annals of Statistics* 27, 898–924

Cai, T.: 2002, On block thresholding in wavelet regression: Adaptivity, block size, and threshold level, *Statistica Sinica* 12(4), 1241–1273

Calderbank, R., Daubechies, I., Sweldens, W., and Yeo, B.-L.: 1998, Wavelet transforms that map integers to integers, *Applied and Computational Harmonic Analysis* 5, 332–369

Candès, E., Demanet, L., Donoho, D., and Ying, L.: 2006a, Fast discrete curvelet transforms, *Multiscale Modeling and Simulation* 5(3), 861–899

Candès, E. and Donoho, D.: 1999, Ridgelets: The key to high dimensional intermittency?, *Philosophical Transactions of the Royal Society of London A* 357, 2495–2509

Candès, E. and Donoho, D.: 2001, Curvelets and curvilinear integrals, *Journal of Approximation Theory* 113, 59–90

Candès, E. and Donoho, D.: 2002, Recovering edges in ill-posed inverse problems: Optimality of curvelet frames, *Annals of Statistics* 30, 784–842

Candès, E. and Donoho, D.: 2004, New tight frames of curvelets and optimal representations of objects with piecewise C^2 singularities, *Communications on Pure and Applied Mathematics* 57(2), 219–266

Candès, E. and Guo, F.: 2002, New multiscale transforms, minimum total variation synthesis: Applications to edge-preserving image reconstruction, *Signal Processing* 82(11), 1519–1543

Candès, E. and Plan, Y.: 2009, Near-ideal model selection by L1 minimization, *Annals of Statistics* 25(5A), 2145–2177

Candès, E. and Romberg, J.: 2007, Sparsity and incoherence in compressive sampling, *Inverse Problems* 23, 969–985

Candès, E., Romberg, J., and Tao, T.: 2006b, Robust uncertainty principles: Exact signal reconstruction from highly incomplete frequency information, *IEEE Transactions on Information Theory* 52(2), 489–509

Candès, E., Romberg, J., and Tao, T.: 2006c, Stable signal recovery from incomplete and inaccurate measurements, *Communications on Pure and Applied Mathematics* 59(8), 1207–1223

Candès, E. and Tao, T.: 2005, Decoding by linear programming, *IEEE Transactions on Information Theory* 51(12), 4203–4215

Candès, E. and Tao, T.: 2006, Near optimal signal recovery from random projections: Universal encoding strategies?, *IEEE Transactions on Information Theory* 52, 5406–5425

Candès, E. and Tao, T.: 2007, The Dantzig selector: Statistical estimation when p is much larger than n, *Annals of Statistics* 35, 2392–2404

Candès, E. J.: 1999, Harmonic analysis of neural networks, *Applied and Computational Harmonic Analysis* 6, 197–218

Candès, E. J.: 2001, Ridgelets and the representation of mutilated Sobolev functions, *SIAM Journal on Mathematical Analysis* 33, 347–368

Candès, E. J. and Demanet, L.: 2003, Curvelets and Fourier integral operators, *Comptes Rendus de l'Académie des Sciences, Series I* 336, 395–398

Candès, E. J. and Demanet, L.: 2005, The curvelet representation of wave propagators is optimally sparse, *Communications on Pure and Applied Mathematics* 58(11), 1472–1528

Candès, E. J. and Plan, Y.: 2011, A probabilistic and RIPless theory of compressed sensing, *Information Theory, IEEE Transactions on* 57(11), 7235

Candès, E. J., Wakin, M. B., and Boyd, S. P.: 2008, Enhancing sparsity by reweighted L1 minimization, *Journal of Fourier Analysis and Applications* 14(5), 877–905

Cardoso, J. F.: 1997, Infomax and maximum likelihood for source separation, *IEEE Letters on Signal Processing* 4(4), 112–114

Cardoso, J.-F.: 1999, High-order contrasts for independent component analysis, *Neural Computation* 11(1), 157–192

Cardoso, J.-F.: 2003, Dependence, correlation and non-Gaussianity in independent component analysis, *Journal of Machine Learning Research* 4, 1177–1203

Carre, P., Helbert, D., and Andres, E.: 2003, 3D fast ridgelet transform, in *Proceedings of the IEEE International Conference on Image Processing*, Vol. 1, pp. 1021–1024

Cayón, L., Sanz, J. L., Martínez-González, E., Banday, A. J., Argüeso, F., Gallegos, J. E., Górski, K. M., and Hinshaw, G.: 2001, Spherical Mexican hat wavelet: An application to detect non-Gaussianity in the COBE-DMR maps, *Monthly Notices of the Royal Astronomical Society* 326, 1243–1248

CeCILL Free Software License, www.cecill.info/index.en.html

Chambolle, A.: 2004, An algorithm for total variation minimization and applications, *Journal of Mathematical Imaging and Vision* 20(1–2), 89–97

Chambolle, A. and Dossal, C.: 2014, *How to make sure the iterates of "FISTA" converges*, Technical report, HAL preprint

Chambolle, A. and Pock, T.: 2011, A first-order primal-dual algorithm for convex problems with applications to imaging, *J. Math. Imaging Vis.* 40(1), 120

Chan, T. F. and Shen, J. J.: 2005, *Image Processing and Analysis-Variational, PDE, Wavelet, and Stochastic Methods*, SIAM, Philadelphia

Chandrasekaran, V., Wakin, M., Baron, D., and Baraniuk, R.: 2004, Surflets : A sparse representation for multidimensional functions containing smooth discontinuities, *Information Theory, 2004. ISIT 2004. Proceedings. International Symposium on*

Chandrasekaran, V., Wakin, M., Baron, D., and Baraniuk, R.: 2009, Representation and compression of multidimensional piecewise functions using surflets, *IEEE Transactions on Information Theory* 55(1), 374

Chandrasekaran, V., Recht, B., Parrilo, P. A., and Willsky, A.: 2012, The convex geometry of linear inverse problems, *Foundations of Computational Mathematics* 12(6), 805

Charbonnier, P., Blanc-Féraud, L., Aubert, G., and Barlaud, M.: 1997, Deterministic edge-preserving regularization in computed imaging, *IEEE Transactions on Image Processing* 6, 298–311

Chartrand, R.: 2007, Exact reconstructions of sparse signals via nonconvex minimization, *IEEE Signal Processing Letters* 14, 707–710

Chartrand, R. and Staneva, V.: 2008, Restricted isometry properties and nonconvex compressive sensing, *Inverse Problems* 24(035020), 1–14

Chaux, C., Combettes, P., Pesquet, J.-C., and Wajs, V.: 2007, A variational formulation for frame based inverse problems, *Inverse Problems* 23, 1495–1518

Chaux, C., Duval, L., Benazza-Benyahia, A., and Pesquet, J.-C.: 2008, A nonlinear Stein based estimator for multichannel image denoising, *IEEE Transactions on Signal Processing* 56(8), 3855–3870

Chaux, C., Pesquet, J.-C., and Pustelnik, N.: 2009, Nested iterative algorithms for convex constrained image recovery problems, *SIAM Journal on Imaging Sciences* 2(2), 730–762

Chen, G. and Teboulle, M.: 1994, A proximal-based decomposition method for convex minimization problems, *Mathematial Programming* 64(1–3), 81

Chen, G. H.-G. and Rockafellar, R. T.: 1997, Convergence rates in forward–backward splitting, *SIAM Journal on Optimization* 7(2), 421–444

Chen, J. and Huo, X.: 2006, Theoretical results on sparse representations for multiple measurement vectors, *IEEE Transactions on Signal Processing* 54(12), 4634–4643

Chen, S. S., Donoho, D. L., and Saunders, M. A.: 1998, Atomic decomposition by basis pursuit, *SIAM Journal on Scientific Computing* 20(1), 33–61

Chen, Z. and Ning, R.: 2004, Breast volume denoising and noise characterization by 3D wavelet transform, *Computerized Medical Imaging and Graphics* 28(5), 235

Chesneau, C., Fadili, M. J., and Starck, J.-L.: 2010, Stein block thresholding for image denoising, *Applied and Computational Harmonic Analysis* 28(1), 67

Chesneau, C. and Hebiri, M.: 2008, Some theoretical results on the grouped variables Lasso, *Mathematical Methods of Statistics* 17(4), 317–326

Christensen, O.: 2002, *An Introduction to Frames and Riesz Bases*, Birkhäuser, Boston

Chui, C.: 1992, *Wavelet Analysis and Its Applications*, Academic Press, New York

Cichocki, A. and Amari, S.: 2002, Adaptive Blind Signal and Image Processing: Learning Algorithms and Applications, Wiley, New York

Cichocki, A., Zdunek, R., and Amari, S.-i.: 2007, Hierarchical ALS Algorithms for Nonnegative Matrix and 3D Tensor Factorization, in *Proceedings of ICA*, pp. 169–176, Springer

Cichocki, A., Zdunek, R., Phan, A. H., and Amari, S.-i.: 2009, *Nonnegative Matrix and Tensor Factorizations: Applications to Exploratory Multi-Way Data Analysis and Blind Source Separation*, John Wiley & Sons, Ltd

Claypoole, R., Davis, G., Sweldens, W., and Baraniuk, R.: 2003, Nonlinear wavelet transforms for image coding via lifting, *IEEE Transactions on Image Processing* 12(12), 1449–1459

Cohen, A.: 2003, *Numerical Analysis of Wavelet Methods*, Elsevier

Cohen, A., Dahmen, W., and DeVore, R.: 2009, Compressed sensing and best k-term approximation, *Journal of the American Mathematical Society* 22, 211–231

Cohen, A., Daubechies, I., and Feauveau, J.: 1992, Biorthogonal bases of compactly supported wavelets, *Communications in Pure and Applied Mathematics* 45, 485–560

Cohen, A., DeVore, R., Petrushev, P., and Xu, H.: 1999, Nonlinear approximation and the space $BV(R^2)$, *American Journal of Mathematics* 121, 587–628

Coifman, R. and Donoho, D.: 1995, Translation invariant de-noising, in A. Antoniadis and G. Oppenheim (eds.), *Wavelets and Statistics*, Springer-Verlag, 125–150

Coifman, R., Geshwind, F., and Meyer, Y.: 2001, Noiselets, *Applied and Computational Harmonic Analysis* 10(1), 27–44

Coifman, R., Meyer, Y., and Wickerhauser, M.: 1992, Wavelet analysis and signal processing, in M. Ruskai, G. Beylkin, R. Coifman, I. Daubechies, S. Mallat, Y. Meyer, and L. Raphael (eds.), *Wavelets and Their Applications*, Jones and Bartlett, 153–178

Coifman, R. and Wickerhauser, M.: 1992, Entropy-based algorithms for best basis selection, *IEEE Transactions on Information Theory* 38, 713–718

Combettes, P. and Pesquet, J.-C.: 2007a, A Douglas–Rachford splitting approach to nonsmooth convex variational signal recovery, *IEEE Journal of Selected Topics in Signal Processing* 1(2), 564–574

Combettes, P. L., Dũng, D., and Vũ, B. C.: 2010, Dualization of signal recovery problems, *Set-Valued and Variational Analysis* 18, 373

Combettes, P. L. and Pesquet, J.-C.: 2007b, Proximal thresholding algorithm for minimization over orthonormal bases, *SIAM Journal on Optimization* 18(4), 1351–1376

Combettes, P. L. and Pesquet, J.-C.: 2011, Fixed-point algorithms for inverse problems in science and engineering, in *Fixed-Point Algorithms for Inverse Problems in Science and Engineering*, Chapt. Proximal Splitting Methods in Signal Processing, pp. 185–212, Springer-Verlag

Combettes, P. L. and Pesquet, J.-C.: 2012, Primal-dual splitting algorithm for solving inclusions with mixtures of composite, Lipschitzian, and parallel-sum monotone operators, *Set-Valued and Variational Analysis* 20(2), 307

Combettes, P. L. and Vũ, B. C.: 2014, Variable metric forward-backward splitting with applications to monotone inclusions in duality, *Optimization* 63(9), 1289

Combettes, P. L. and Wajs, V. R.: 2005, Signal recovery by proximal forward-backward splitting, *Multiscale Modeling and Simulation* 4(4), 1168–1200

Comon, P.: 1994, Independent component analysis, a new concept?, *Signal Processing* 36(3), 287–314

Condat, L.: 2013, A generic first-order primal-dual method for convex optimization involving Lipschitzian, proximable and linear composite terms, *J. Optimization Theory and Applications* 158(2), 460

Cotter, S., Rao, B., Engan, K., and Kreutz-Delgado, K.: 2005, Sparse solutions to linear inverse problems with multiple measurement vectors, *IEEE Transactions on Signal Processing* 53, 2477–2488

Coupinot, G., Hecquet, J., Auriere, M., and Futaully, R.: 1992, Photometric analysis of astronomical images by the wavelet transform, *Astronomy and Astrophysics* 259, 701–710

Criminisi, A., Pérez, P., and Toyama, K.: 2004, Region filling and object removal by examplar-based image inpainting, *IEEE Transactions on Image Processing* 13(9), 1200–1212

Crittenden, R. G.: 2000, Igloo pixelations of the sky, *Astrophysical Letters and Communications* 37, 377–382

Curvelab: 2005, Second Generation Curvelet Toolbox, *Second Generation Curvelet Toolbox*, www.curvelet.org

Da Cunha, A. L., Zhou, J., and Do, M. N.: 2006, The nonsubsampled contourlet transform: Theory, design, and applications, *IEEE Transactions on Image Processing* 15(10), 3089

Dalalyan, A. and Tsybakov, A.: 2008, Aggregation by exponential weighting, sharp PAC-Bayesian bounds and sparsity, *Machine Learning* 72(1–2), 39–61

Dalalyan, A. and Tsybakov, A.: 2009, Sparse regression learning by aggregation and Langevin Monte-Carlo, in *22th Annual Conference on Learning Theory, COLT*

Darmois, G.: 1953, Analyse générale des liaisons stochastiques, *Revue de l'Institut International de Statistique/Review of the International Statistical Institute* 21, 2–8

Daubechies, I.: 1988, Orthogonal bases of compactly supported wavelets, *Communications in Pure and Applied Mathematics* 41, 909–996

Daubechies, I.: 1992, *Ten Lectures on Wavelets*, SIAM, Society for Industrial and Applied Mathematics

Daubechies, I., Defrise, M., and Mol, C. D.: 2004, An iterative thresholding algorithm for linear inverse problems with a sparsity constraint, *Communications on Pure and Applied Mathematics* 57, 1413–1541

Daubechies, I., DeVore, R., Fornasier, M., and Gütürk, C. S.: 2010, Iteratively reweighted least squares minimization for sparse recovery, *Communications on Pure and Applied Mathematics* 63(1), 1

Daubechies, I., Fornasier, M., and Loris, I.: 2008, Accelerated projected gradient method for linear inverse problems with sparsity constraints, *Journal of Fourier Analysis and Applications* 14(5–6), 764–792

Daubechies, I., Guskov, I., Schröder, P., and Sweldens, W.: 1999, Wavelets on irregular point sets, *Philosophical Transactions of the Royal Society of London A* 357, 2397–2413

Daubechies, I. and Sweldens, W.: 1998, Factoring wavelet transforms into lifting steps, *Journal of Fourier Analysis and Applications* 4, 245–267

Davenport, M., Duarte, M., Eldar, Y., and Kutyniok, G.: 2012, Compressed sensing: Theory and applications, in *Compressed Sensing: Theory and Applications*, Chapt. Introduction to Compressed Sensing, pp. 1–68, Cambridge University Press

Davies, M.: 2004, Identifiability issues in noisy ICA, *IEEE Signal Processing Letters* 11, 470–473

Delabrouille, J., Cardoso, J.-F., Le Jeune, M., Betoule, M., Fay, G., and Guilloux, F.: 2009, A full sky, low foreground, high resolution CMB map from WMAP, *A&A* 493, 835

Deledalle, C., Vaiter, S., Fadili, M., and Peyré, G.: 2014, Stein Unbiased GrAdient estimator of the Risk (SUGAR) for multiple parameter selection, *SIAM Journal of Imaging Sciences* 7(4), 2448

Deledalle, C.-A., Vaiter, S., Peyré, G., Fadili, J., and Dossal, C.: 2012, Proximal splitting derivatives for risk estimation, in *Journal of Physics: Conference Series 386 012003*, IOP Publishing

Demanet, L.: 2006, *Curvelets, Wave Atoms, and Wave Equations*, Ph.D. thesis, California Institute of Technology

Demanet, L., Song, B., and Chan, T.: 2003, *Image inpainting by correspondence maps: A deterministic approach*, Report 03–40, UCLA CAM

Demanet, L. and Ying, L.: 2005, Curvelets and wave atoms for mirror-extended images, in *Wavelets XII Conference*, San Diego

Demanet, L. and Ying, L.: 2007, Wave atoms and sparsity of oscillatory patterns, *Applied and Computational Harmonic Analysis* 23(3), 368–387

den Berg, E. V., Schmidt, M., Friedlander, M. P., and Murphy, K.: 2008, *Group sparsity via linear time projection*, Technical Report TR-2008–09, Department of Computer Science, University of British Columbia

DeVore, R.: 2007, Deterministic constructions of compressed sensing matrices, *Journal of Complexity* 23, 918–925

Dima, A., Scholz, M., and Obermayer, K.: 1999, Semiautomatic quality determination of 3D confocal microscope scans of neuronal cells denoised by 3D wavelet shrinkage, in H. H. Szu (ed.), *Society of Photo-Optical Instrumentation Engineers (SPIE) Conference Series*, Vol. 3723, pp. 446–457

Do, M. and Vetterli, M.: 2003a, Framing pyramids, *IEEE Transactions on Image Processing* 51(9), 2329–2342

Do, M. N. and Vetterli, M.: 2003b, Contourlets, in J. Stoeckler and G. V. Welland (eds.), *Beyond Wavelets*, Academic Press

Do, M. N. and Vetterli, M.: 2003c, The finite ridgelet transform for image representation, *IEEE Transactions on Image Processing* 12(1), 16–28

Do, M. and Vetterli, M.: 2005, The contourlet transform: An efficient directional multiresolution image representation., *IEEE Transactions on Image Processing* 14(12), 2091–2106

Donoho, D.: 1995a, De-noising by soft-thresholding, *IEEE Transactions on Information Theory* 41(3), 613–627

Donoho, D.: 1995b, Nonlinear solution of inverse problems by wavelet-vaguelette decomposition, *Applied and Computational Harmonic Analysis* 2, 101–126

Donoho, D.: 1999, Wedgelets: Nearly minimax estimation of edges, *Annals of Statistics* 27(3), 859

Donoho, D.: 2000, Nonlinear pyramid transforms based on median-interpolation, *SIAM Journal on Mathematical Analysis* 60, 1137–1156

Donoho, D.: 2006a, Compressed sensing, *IEEE Transactions on Information Theory* 52(4), 1289–1306

Donoho, D.: 2006b, For most large underdetermined systems of linear equations, the minimal ℓ_1 solution is also the sparsest solution, *Communications on Pure and Applied Mathematics* 59(7), 907–934

Donoho, D. and Duncan, M.: 2000, Digital curvelet transform: strategy, implementation and experiments, in H. Szu, M. Vetterli, W. Campbell, and J. Buss (eds.), *Aerosense 2000, Wavelet Applications VII*, Vol. 4056, SPIE, 12–29

Donoho, D. and Elad, M.: 2003, Optimally sparse representation in general (non-orthogonal) dictionaries via ℓ^1 minimization, *Proceedings of the National Academy of Sciences* 100, 2197–2202

Donoho, D., Elad, M., and Temlyakov, V.: 2006, Stable recovery of sparse overcomplete representations in the presence of noise, *IEEE Transactions on Information Theory* 52(1), 6–18

Donoho, D. and Flesia, A.: 2002, Digital ridgelet transform based on true ridge functions, in J. Schmeidler and G. Welland (eds.), *Beyond Wavelets*, Academic Press

Donoho, D. and Huo, X.: 2001a, Lecture notes in computational science and engineering, *Lecture Notes in Computational Science and Engineering*, Chapt. Beamlets and Multiscale Image Analysis, Springer

Donoho, D. and Huo, X.: 2001b, Uncertainty principles and ideal atomic decomposition, *IEEE Transactions on Information Theory* 47(7), 2845–2862

Donoho, D. and Johnstone, I.: 1994, Ideal spatial adaptation via wavelet shrinkage, *Biometrika* 81, 425–455

Donoho, D. and Johnstone, I.: 1995, Adapting to unknown smoothness via wavelet shrinkage, *Journal of the American Statistical Association* 90, 1200–1224

Donoho, D., Johnstone, I., Kerkyacharian, G., and Picard, D.: 1995, Wavelet shrinkage: Asymptopia?, *Journal of the Royal Statistical Society Series B* 57, 301–369

Donoho, D. and Levi, O.: 2002, Fast X-ray and beamlet transforms for three-dimensional data, in D. Rockmore and D. Healy (eds.), *Modern Signal Processing*, pp. 79–116

Donoho, D., Levi, O., Starck, J.-L., and Martínez, V.: 2002, Multiscale geometric analysis for 3-D catalogues, in J.-L. Starck and F. Murtagh (eds.), *SPIE Conference on Astronomical Telescopes and Instrumentation: Astronomical Data Analysis II, Waikoloa, Hawaii, 22–28 August*, Vol. 4847, SPIE

Donoho, D. and Tanner, J.: 2005, Neighborliness of randomly-projected simplices in high dimensions, *Proceedings of the National Academy of Sciences* 27(102), 9452–9457

Donoho, D., Tsaig, Y., Drori, I., and Starck, J.-L.: 2012, Sparse solution of underdetermined linear equations by stagewise orthogonal matching pursuit, *IEEE Transactions on Information Theory* 58, 1094

Donoho, D. L.: 2006, High-dimensional centrally symmetric polytopes with neighborliness proportional to dimension, *Discrete and Computational Geometry* 35(4), 617–652

Donoho, D. L. and Huo, X.: 2001, Beamlets and multiscale image analysis, *Multiscale and Multiresolution Methods, Lecture Notes in Computational Science and Engineering* 20, 149

Donoho, D. L. and Jin, J.: 2006, Asymptotic minimaxity of false discovery rate thresholding for sparse exponential data, *Annals of Statistics* 34(6), 2980–3018

Donoho, D. L. and Tanner, J.: 2009, Counting faces of randomly projected polytopes when the projection radically lowers dimension, *J. Amer. Math. Soc.* 22(1), 1

Doroshkevich, A. G., Naselsky, P. D., Verkhodanov, O. V., Novikov, D. I., Turchaninov, V. I., Novikov, I. D., Christensen, P. R., and Chiang, L.-Y.: 2005, Gauss-Legendre sky pixelization (GLESP) scheme for CMB maps, *International Journal of Modern Physics D* 14(2), 275–290

Dossal, C., Kachour, M., Fadili, M. J., Peyré, G., and Chesneau, C.: 2013, The degrees of freedom of the Lasso for general design matrix, *Statistica Sinica* 23, 809

Douma, H. and de Hoop, M. V.: 2007, Leading-order seismic imaging using curvelets, *Geophysics* 72, S231–S248

Duchi, J., Shalev-Shwartz, S., Singer, Y., and Chandra, T.: 2008, Efficient projection onto L1 ball for learning in high dimension, in *ICML '08: Proceedings of the 25th International Conference on Machine Learning*, 272–279

Dupé, F.-X., Fadili, J. M., and Starck, J.-L.: 2011, Linear inverse problems with various noise models and mixed regularizations, in *1st International Workshop on New Computational Methods for Inverse Problems*, Paris

Dupé, F.-X., Fadili, M., and Starck, J.-L.: 2009, A proximal iteration for deconvolving Poisson noisy images using sparse representations, *IEEE Transactions on Image Processing* 18(2), 310–321

Durand, S.: 2007, M-band filtering and nonredundant directional wavelets, *Applied and Computational Harmonic Analysis* 22(1), 124–139

Durand, S., Fadili, J., and Nikolova, M.: 2010, Multiplicative noise removal using l1 fidelity on frame coefficients, *Journal of Mathematical Imaging and Vision* 36(3), 201

Durand, S. and Froment, J.: 2003, Reconstruction of wavelet coefficients using total variation minimization, *SIAM Journal on Scientific Computing* 24(5), 1754–1767

Dutilleux, P.: 1987, An implementation of the "algorithme à trous" to compute the wavelet transform, in J. Combes, A. Grossmann, and P. Tchamitchian (eds.), *Wavelets: Time-Frequency Methods and Phase-Space*, Springer-Verlag, 298–304

Easley, G., Labate, D., and Lim, W.-Q.: 2008, Sparse directional image representation using the discrete shearlet transform, *Appl. Comput. Harmon. Anal.* 25, 25

Eckstein, J.: 1989, *Splitting methods for monotone operators with application to parallel optimization*, Ph.D. thesis, MIT

Eckstein, J. and Bertsekas, D. P.: 1992, On the Douglas-Rachford splitting method and the proximal point algorithm for maximal monotone operators, *Mathematical Programming* 55(3), 293

Efros, A. A. and Leung, T. K.: 1999, Texture synthesis by non-parametric sampling, in *IEEE International Conference on Computer Vision*, Vol. 2, Kerkyra, Greece, 1033–1038

Elad, M.: 2006, Why simple shrinkage is still relevant for redundant representations, *IEEE Transactions on Information Theory* 52(12), 5559–5569

Elad, M. and Aharon, M.: 2006, Image denoising via sparse and redundant representations over learned dictionaries, *IEEE Transactions on Image Processing* 15(12), 3736

Elad, M., Milanfar, P., and Rubinstein, R.: 2007, Analysis versus synthesis in signal priors, *Inverse Problems* 23(3), 947–968

Elad, M., Starck, J.-L., Donoho, D., and Querre, P.: 2005, Simultaneous cartoon and texture image inpainting using morphological component analysis (MCA), *Applied and Computational Harmonic Analysis* 19, 340–358

Elad, M. and Yavneh, I.: 2009, A plurality of sparse representations is better than the sparsest one alone, *IEEE Transactions on Information Theory* 55(10), 4701

Eldar, Y. C. and Mishali, M.: 2009, Robust recovery of signals from a structured union of subspaces, *IEEE Transactions on Information Theory* 55, 5302

Engan, K., Aase, S. O., and Husoy, J. H.: 1999, Method of optimal directions for frame design, in *Proceedings of ICASSP '99*, pp. 2443–2446, IEEE Computer Society, Washington, DC

Fadili, J. M., Starck, J.-L., Elad, M., and Donoho, D.: 2010, Mcalab: Reproducible research in signal and image decomposition and inpainting, *IEEE Computing in Science and Engineering* 12(1), 44

Fadili, M. J., Bobin, J., Moudden, Y., and Starck, J.-L.: 2009a, Erratum to "Morphological diversity and sparsity for multichannel data restoration," *Journal of Mathematical Imaging and Vision* 33, 149–168

Fadili, M. J. and Boubchir, L.: 2005, Analytical form for a Bayesian wavelet estimator of images using the Bessel k form densities, *IEEE Transactions on Image Processing* 14(2), 231–240

Fadili, M. J. and Bullmore, E.: 2005, Penalized partially linear models using sparse representations with an application to fMRI time series, *IEEE Transactions on Signal Processing* 53(9), 3436–3448

Fadili, M. J. and Starck, J.-L.: 2005, EM algorithm for sparse representation-based image inpainting, in *IEEE ICIP'05*, Vol. 2, Genoa, Italy, 61–63

Fadili, M. J. and Starck, J.-L.: 2006, Sparse representation-based image deconvolution by iterative thresholding, in F. Murtagh and J.-L. Starck (eds.), *Proceedings of Astronomical Data Analysis IV*, Marseille, France

Fadili, M. J. and Starck, J.-L.: 2009, Monotone operator splitting for fast sparse solutions of inverse problems, *SIAM Journal on Imaging Sciences* pp. 2005–2006

Fadili, M. J., Starck, J.-L., and Boubchir, L.: 2007, Morphological diversity and sparse image denoising, in *IEEE ICASSP'07*, Vol. I, Honolulu, Hawaii, 589–592

Fadili, M. J., Starck, J.-L., and Murtagh, F.: 2009b, Inpainting and zooming using sparse representations, *The Computer Journal* 52, 64–79

Fan, J.: 1997, Comments on "Wavelets in statistics: A review," by A. Antoniadis, *Journal of the Italian Statistical Society* 6, 131–138

Faÿ, G. and Guilloux, F.: 2011, Consistency of a needlet spectral estimator on the sphere, *Statistical Inference for Stochastic Processes* 14(47–71)

Faÿ, G., Guilloux, F., Betoule, M., Cardoso, J.-F., Delabrouille, J., and Le Jeune, M.: 2008, CMB power spectrum estimation using wavelets, *Physics Review D* 78(8), 083013

Feauveau, J.: 1990, *Analyse multirésolution par ondelettes non-orthogonales et bancs de filtres numériques*, Ph.D. thesis, Université Paris Sud

Fernandes, F., van Spaendonck, R., and Burrus, S.: 2003, A new framework for complex wavelet transforms, *IEEE Transactions on Signal Processing* 51(7), 1825–1837

Fernandes, F., Wakin, M., and Baraniuk, R.: 2004, Non-redundant, linear-phase, semi-orthogonal, directional complex wavelets, in *Proceedings of IEEE Conference on Acoustics, Speech and Signal Processing*

Feuer, A. and Nemirovsky, A.: 2003, On sparse representation in pairs of bases, *IEEE Transactions on Information Theory* 49(6), 1579–1581

Field, D.: 1999, Wavelets, vision and the statistics of natural scenes, *Philosophical Transactions of the Royal Society of London A* 357, 2527–2542

Figueiredo, M., Bioucas-Dias, J. L., and Nowak, R.: 2007, Majorization–minimization algorithms for wavelet-based image restoration, *IEEE Transactions on Image Processing* 16(12), 2980–2881

Figueiredo, M. and Nowak, R.: 2003, An EM algorithm for wavelet-based image restoration, *IEEE Transactions on Image Processing* 12(8), 906–916

Figueiredo, M., Nowak, R., and Wright, S.: 2007b, Gradient projection for sparse reconstruction: Application to compressed sensing and other inverse problems, *IEEE Journal of Selected Topics in Signal Processing* 1(4), 586–597

Fortin, M. and Glowinski, R.: 1983, *Augmented Lagrangian Methods: Applications to the Numerical Solution of Boundary-Value Problems*, Elsevier Science Publishers, Amsterdam

Foucart, S. and Lai, M.-J.: 2009, Sparsest solutions of underdetermined linear systems via ℓ_q-minimization for $0 < q \leq 1$, *Applied and Computational Harmonic Analysis* 26(3), 395–407

Foucart, S. and Rauhut, H.: 2013, *A Mathematical Introduction to Compressive Sensing*, Birkhäuser series in applied and numerical harmonic analysis, Birkhäuser

Freeden, W. and Schneider, F.: 1998, Regularization wavelets and multiresolution, *Inverse Problems* 14, 225–243

Freeden, W. and Windheuser, U.: 1997, Combined spherical harmonics and wavelet expansion – a future concept in Earth's gravitational potential determination, *Applied and Computational Harmonic Analysis* 4, 1–37

Fryźlewicz, P. and Nason, G. P.: 2004, A Haar-Fisz algorithm for Poisson intensity estimation, *Journal of Computational and Graphical Statistics* 13, 621–638

Fuchs, J.-J.: 2004, On sparse representations in arbitrary redundant bases, *IEEE Transactions on Information Theory* 50(6), 1341–1344

Gabay, D.: 1983, Applications of the method of multipliers to variational inequalities, in M. Fortin and R. Glowinski (eds.), *Augmented Lagrangian Methods: Applications to the Numerical Solution of Boundary-Value Problems*, North-Holland Publishing Company, Amsterdam

Gabay, D. and Mercier, B.: 1976, A dual algorithm for the solution of nonlinear variational problems via finite element approximation, *Computers & Mathematics with Applications* 2(1), 17

Gabor, D.: 1946, Theory of communications, *Journal of the IEE (London)* 93(III), 429–457,

Gao, H.-Y.: 1998, Wavelet shrinkage denoising using the non-negative garrote, *Journal of Computational and Graphical Statistics* 7, 469–488

Gao, H.-Y. and Bruce, A.: 1997, Waveshrink with firm shrinkage, *Statistica Sinica* 7, 855–874

Garsden, H., Girard, J. N., Starck, J. L., Corbel, S., Tasse, C., Woiselle, A., McKean, J. P., van Amesfoort, A. S., Anderson, J., Avruch, I. M., Beck, R., Bentum, M. J., Best, P., Breitling, F., Broderick, J., Brüggen, M., Butcher, H. R., Ciardi, B., de Gasperin, F., de Geus, E., de Vos, M., Duscha, S., Eislöffel, J., Engels, D., Falcke, H., Fallows, R. A., Fender, R., Ferrari, C., Frieswijk, W., Garrett, M. A., Grießmeier, J., Gunst, A. W., Hassall, T. E., Heald, G., Hoeft, M., Hörandel, J., van der Horst, A., Juette, E., Karastergiou, A., Kondratiev, V. I., Kramer, M., Kuniyoshi, M., Kuper, G., Mann, G., Markoff, S., McFadden, R., McKay-Bukowski, D., Mulcahy, D. D., Munk, H., Norden, M. J., Orru, E., Paas, H., Pandey-Pommier, M., Pandey, V. N., Pietka, G., Pizzo, R., Polatidis, A. G., Renting, A., Röttgering, H., Rowlinson, A., Schwarz, D., Sluman, J., Smirnov, O., Stappers, B. W., Steinmetz, M., Stewart, A., Swinbank, J., Tagger, M., Tang, Y., Tasse, C., Thoudam, S., Toribio, C., Vermeulen, R., Vocks, C., van Weeren, R. J., Wijnholds, S. J., Wise, M. W., Wucknitz, O., Yatawatta, S., Zarka, P., and Zensus, A.: 2015, LOFAR sparse image reconstruction, *A&A* 575, A90

Geman, D. and Reynolds, G.: 1992, Constrained restoration and the recovery of discontinuities, *IEEE Transactions on Pattern Analysis and Machine Intelligence* 14, 367–383

Geman, D., Reynolds, G., and Yang, C.: 1993, Stochastic algorithms for restricted image spaces and experiments in deblurring, in A. J. R. Chellappa (ed.), *Markov Random Fields Theory and Applications*, Academic Press, 39–68

Genovesio, A. and Olivo-Marin, J.-C.: 2003, Tracking fluorescent spots in biological video microscopy, in J.-A. Conchello, C. Cogswell, and T. Wilson (eds.), *Three-Dimensional and Multidimensional Microscopy: Image Acquisition and Processing X*, Vol. 4964, SPIE, 98–105

Georgiev, P. G., Theis, F., and Cichocki, A.: 2005, Sparse component analysis and blind source separation of underdetermined mixtures, *IEEE Transactions on Neural Networks* 16(4), 992–996

Giryes, R., Elad, M., and Eldar, Y.: 2011, The projected GSURE for automatic parameter tuning in iterative shrinkage methods, *Applied and Computational Harmonic Analysis* 30(3), 407

Glowinski, R. and Tallec, P. L.: 1989, *Augmented Lagrangian and Operator-Splitting Methods in Nonlinear Mechanics*, SIAM

Goldstein, T. and Osher, S.: 2009, The split Bregman method for l1-regularized problems, *SIAM J. Imaging Sci.* 2, 323

Gordon, Y.: 1988, On milman's inequality and random subspaces which escape through a mesh in R^n, in *Geometric Aspects of Functional Analysis*, Vol. 1317 of *Lecture Notes in Math.*, pp. 84–106, Springer, Berlin

Gorodnitsky, I. F. and Rao, B. D.: 1997, Sparse signal reconstructions from limited data using focuss: A re-weighted minimum norm algorithm, *IEEE Trans. Signal Process.* 45(3), 600

Górski, K. M., Hivon, E., Banday, A. J., Wandelt, B. D., Hansen, F. K., Reinecke, M., and Bartelmann, M.: 2005, HEALPix: A framework for high-resolution discretization and fast analysis of data distributed on the sphere, *Astrophysical Journal* 622, 759–771

Goupillaud, P., Grossmann, A., and Morlet, J.: 1985, Cycle-octave and related transforms in seismic signal analysis, *Geoexploration* 23, 85–102

Goutsias, J. and Heijmans, H.: 2000, Nonlinear multiresolution signal decomposition schemes. Part 1: Morphological pyramids, *IEEE Transactions on Image Processing* 9, 1862–1876

Gribonval, R. and Nielsen, M.: 2003, Sparse representations in unions of bases, *IEEE Transactions on Information Theory* 49(12), 3320–3325

Gribonval, R. and Nielsen, M.: 2008, Beyond sparsity: Recovering structured representations by 1-minimization and greedy algorithms. Application to the analysis of sparse underdetermined ICA, *Journal of Advances in Computational Mathematics* 28, 23–41

Gribonval, R., Rauhut, H., Schnass, K., and Vandergheynst, P.: 2008, Atoms of all channels, unite! Average case analysis of multi-channel sparse recovery using greedy algorithms, *Journal of Fourier Analysis and Applications* 14(5), 655–687

Gross, D.: 2011, Recovering low-rank matrices from few coefficients in any basis, *Information Theory, IEEE Transactions on* 57(3), 1548

Grossmann, A., Kronland-Martinet, R., and Morlet, J.: 1989, Reading and understanding the continuous wavelet transform, in J. Combes, A. Grossmann, and P. Tchamitchian (eds.), *Wavelets: Time-Frequency Methods and Phase-Space*, Springer-Verlag, 2–20

Grossmann, A. and Morlet, J.: 1984, Decomposition of Hardy functions into square integrable wavelets of constant shape, *SIAM Journal on Mathematical Analysis* 15, 723–736

Guo, C., Zhu, S., and Wu, Y.: 2003, A mathematical theory of primal sketch and sketchability, in *Proceedings of the Ninth IEEE International Conference on Computer Vision (ICCV)*, Nice, France

Guo, K., Kutyniok, G., and Labate, D.: 2006, Sparse multidimensional representations using anisotropic dilation and shear operators, in G. Chen and M. J. Lai (eds.), *Wavelets und Splines*, Nashboro Press, Nashville, pp. 189–201

Guo, K. and Labate, D.: 2007, Optimally sparse multidimensional representation using shearlets, *SIAM Journal on Mathematical Analysis* 39(1), 298

Guo, K., Labate, D., Lim, W.-Q., Weiss, G., and Wilson, E.: 2004, Wavelets with composite dilations, *Electronic research announcements of the American Mathematical Society* 10(9), 78

Gurevich, S., Hadani, R., and Sochen, N.: 2008, On some deterministic dictionaries supporting sparsity, *Journal of Fourier Analysis and Applications* 14, 859–876

Haar, A.: 1910, Zur Theorie der orthogonalen Funktionensysteme, *Mathematische Annalen* 69, 331–371

Hale, E. T., Yin, W., and Zhang, Y.: 2008, Fixed-point continuation for l1-minimization: Methodology and convergence, *SIAM Journal on Optimization* 19, 1107–1130

Hall, P., Kerkyacharian, G., and Picard, D.: 1998, Block threshold rules for curve estimation using kernel and wavelet methods, *Annals of Statistics* 26(3), 922–942

Hall, P., Kerkyacharian, G., and Picard, D.: 1999, On the minimax optimality of block thresh-olded wavelet estimators, *Staistica Sinica* 9, 33–50

Han, B., Kutyniok, G., and Shen, Z.: 2011, Adaptive multiresolution analysis structures and shearlet systems, *SIAM Journal of Numerical Analysis* 49, 1921

Härdle, W., Kerkyacharian, G., Picard, D., and Tsybakov, A. B.: 1998, *Wavelets, Approximation and Statistical Applications*, Lecture Notes in Statistics, Springer, New York

Heavens, A. F. and Taylor, A. N.: 1995, A spherical harmonic analysis of redshift space, *MNRAS* 275, 483

Heijmans, H. and Goutsias, J.: 2000, Multiresolution signal decomposition schemes. Part 2: Morphological wavelets, *IEEE Transactions on Image Processing* 9, 1897–1913

Heijmans, H., Pesquet-Popescu, B., and Piella, G.: 2005, Building nonredundant adaptive wavelets by update lifting, *Applied and Computational Harmonic Analysis* 18(3), 252–281

Heijmans, H., Piella, G., and Pesquet-Popescu, B.: 2006, Adaptive wavelets for image compres-sion using update lifting: Quantization and error analysis, *International Journal of Wavelets, Multiresolution and Information Processing* 4(1), 41–63

Hennenfent, G. and Herrmann, F.: 2006, Seismic denoising with nonuniformly sampled curvelets, *IEEE Computing in Science and Engineering* 8(3), 16–25

Herrity, K. K., Gilbert, A. C., and Tropp, J. A.: 2006, Sparse approximation via iterative thresh-olding, in *IEEE Conference on Acoustics, Speech and Signal Processing*, Vol. 3, 624–627

Herrmann, F. and Hennenfent, G.: 2008, Non-parametric seismic data recovery with curvelet frames, *Geophysical Journal International* 173(1), 233

Herrmann, F. J., Moghaddam, P. P., and Stolk, C. C.: 2008, Sparsity- and continuity-promoting seismic image recovery with curvelet frames, *Applied and Computational Harmonic Anal-ysis* 24, 150–173

Holschneider, M.: 1996, Wavelet analysis on the sphere, *Journal of Mathematical Physics* 37(8), 4156–4165

Holschneider, M., Kronland-Martinet, R., Morlet, J., and Tchamitchian, P.: 1989, A real-time algorithm for signal analysis with the help of the wavelet transform, in *Wavelets: Time-Frequency Methods and Phase-Space*, Springer-Verlag, 286–297

Huang, L. and Bijaoui, A.: 1991, Astronomical image data compression by morphological skeleton transformation, *Experimental Astronomy* 1, 311–327

Huber, P.: 1981, *Robust Statistics*, Wiley

Hyvärinen, A. and Hoyer, P.: 2001, A two-layer sparse coding model learns simple and complex cell receptive fields and topography from natural images, *Vision Research* 41, 2413–2433

Hyvärinen, A., Karhunen, J., and Oja, E.: 2001, *Independent Component Analysis*, Wiley, New York

Ichir, M. and Djafari, A.: 2006, Hidden Markov models for wavelet-based blind source sepa-ration, *IEEE Transactions on Image Processing* 15(7), 1887–1899

Jacques, L., Hammond, D. K., and Fadili, M. J.: 2009, Dequantizing compressed sensing, *IEEE Transactions on Signal Processing*, ArXiv preprint

Jalobeanu, A.: 2001, *Modèles, estimation bayèsienne et algorithmes pour la déconvolution d'images satellitaires et aériennes, Ph.D. thesis*, Université de Nice Sophia Antipolis

Jansen, M. and Bultheel, A.: 1998, Multiple wavelet threshold estimation by generalized cross validation for data with correlated noise, *IEEE Transactions on Image Processing* 8(7), 947–953

Jansen, M., Malfait, M., and Bultheel, A.: 1997, Generalized cross validation for wavelet thresh-olding, *Signal Processing* 56(1), 33–44

Jeng, F. and Woods, J.: 1991, Compound Gauss-Markov random fields for image estimation, *IEEE Transactions on Signal Processing* 39, 683–697

Jia, J. and Tang, C.-K.: 2005, Tensor voting for image correction by global and local intensity alignment, *IEEE Transactions on Pattern Analysis and Machine Intelligence* 27(1), 36–50

Jin, J., Starck, J.-L., Donoho, D., Aghanim, N., and Forni, O.: 2005, Cosmological non-Gaussian signatures detection: Comparison of statistical tests, *EURASIP Journal* 15, 2470–2485

Jobson, D. J., Rahman, Z., and Woodell, G. A.: 1997, Properties and performance of a center/surround retinex, *IEEE Transactions on Image Processing* 6(3), 451–462

Johnstone, I.: 1999, Wavelets and the theory of non-parametric function estimation, *Philosophical Transactions of the Royal Society of London A* 357, 2475–2494

Johnstone, I.: 2002, Function estimation and Gaussian sequence models, *Unpublished manuscript* 2(5.3), 2, Draft of monograph

Johnstone, I.: 2004, Wavelet deconvolution in a periodic setting, *Journal of the Royal Statistical Society B* 66(3), 547–573

Johnstone, I. M. and Silverman, B. W.: 1997, Wavelet threshold estimators for data with correlated noise, *Journal of the Royal Statistical Society B.* 59, 319–351

Jourjine, A., Rickard, S., and Yilmaz, O.: 2000, Blind separation of disjoint orthogonal signals: Demixing n sources from 2 mixtures., *ICASSP '00, IEEE International Conference on Acoustics, Speech, and Signal Processing* 5, 2985–2988

Juditsky, A., Rigollet, P., and Tsybakov, A. B.: 2008, Learning by mirror averaging, *Annals of Statistics* 36, 2183–2206

Karlovitz, L.: 1970, Construction of nearest points in the ℓ^p, p even and ℓ^1 norms, *Journal of Approximation Theory* 3, 123–127

Khalifa, J., Mallat, S., and Rougé, B.: 2003, Deconvolution by thresholding in mirror wavelet bases, *IEEE Transactions on Image Processing* 12(4), 446–457

Kim, Y., Kim, J., and Kim, Y.: 2006, Blockwise sparse regression, *Statistica Sinica* 16(2), 375–390

Kingsbury, N.: 1998, The dual-tree complex wavelet transform: A new efficient tool for image restoration and enhancement, in *Proceedings of European Signal Processing Conference*, 319–322

Kingsbury, N.: 1999, Shift invariant properties of the dual-tree complex wavelet transform, in *Proceedings of IEEE Conference on Acoustics, Speech and Signal Processing*

Kingsbury, N.: 2001, Complex wavelets for shift invariant analysis and filtering of signals, *Applied and Computational Harmonic Analysis* 10(3), 234

Kolaczyk, E.: 1997, Nonparametric estimation of gamma-ray burst intensities using Haar wavelets, *Astrophysical Journal* 483, 340–349

Kolaczyk, E. and Dixon, D.: 2000, Nonparametric estimation of intensity maps using Haar wavelets and Poisson noise characteristics, *Astrophysical Journal* 534, 490–505

Koldovsky, Z. and Tichavsky, P.: 2006, Methods of fair comparison of performance of linear ICA techniques in presence of additive noise, in *Proceedings of IEEE International Conference on Acoustics, Speech, and Signal Processing*, Vol. 5

Koldovsky, Z., Tichavsky, P., and Oja, E.: 2006, Efficient variant of algorithm FastICA for Independent Component Analysis attaining the Cramér-Rao lower bound, *IEEE Transactions on Neural Networks* 17, 1265–1277

Komodakis, N. and Pesquet, J.-C.: 2015, Playing with duality: An overview of recent primal-dual approaches for solving large-scale optimization problems, arXiv preprint arXiv:1406.5429

Korostelev, A. P. and Tsybakov, A. B.: 1993, *Minimax Theory of Image Reconstruction*, Vol. 82 of *Lecture Notes in Statistics*, Springer-Verlag, New York

Kreutz-Delgado, K., Murray, J., Rao, B., Engan, K., Lee, T., and Sejnowski, T.: 2003, Dictionary learning algorithms for sparse representation, *Neural Computation* 15(2), 349–396

Kunszt, P. Z., Szalay, A. S., and Thakar, A. R.: 2001, The hierarchical triangular mesh, in A. J. Banday, S. Zaroubi, and M. Bartelmann (eds.), *Mining the Sky*, Helix Books, 631–637

Kutyniok, G. and Lim, W.-Q.: 2011, Compactly supported shearlets are optimally sparse, *Journal of Approximation Theory* 163(11), 1564

Kutyniok, G., Lim, W.-Q., and Reisenhofer, R.: 2014, Shearlab 3d: Faithful digital shearlet transforms based on compactly supported shearlets, *arXiv preprint arXiv:1402.5670*

Kutyniok, G. and Sauer, T.: 2009, Adaptive directional subdivision schemes and shearlet multiresolution analysis, *SIAM Journal of Mathematical Analysis* 41, 1436

Kutyniok, G. et al.: 2012a, *Shearlets: Multiscale Analysis for Multivariate Data*, Springer Science & Business Media

Kutyniok, G., Shahram, M., and Zhuang, X.: 2012b, Shearlab: A rational design of a digital parabolic scaling algorithm, *SIAM Journal of Imaging Sciences* 5, 1291

Labate, D., Lim, W.-Q., Kutyniok, G., and Weiss, G.: 2005, Sparse multidimensional representation using shearlets, in *Wavelets XI*, Vol. 5914, SPIE, 254–262

Lambert, P., Pires, S., Ballot, J., García, R., Starck, J.-L., and Turck-Chièze, S.: 2006, Curvelet analysis of asteroseismic data. I. Method description and application to simulated sun-like stars, *A&A* 454, 1021–1027

Lange, K.: 2004, *Optimization*, Springer Texts in Statistics, Springer-Verlag, New York

Lanusse, F., Paykari, P., Starck, J.-L., Sureau, F., Bobin, J., and Rassat, A.: 2014, PRISM: Recovery of the primordial spectrum from Planck data, *A&A* 571, L1

Lanusse, F., Rassat, A., and Starck, J.-L.: 2012, Spherical 3D isotropic wavelets, *A&A* 540, A92

Le Pennec, E. and Mallat, S.: 2005, Sparse geometric image representations with bandelets, *IEEE Transactions on Image Processing* 14(4), 423–438

Lee, J. D., Sun, Y., and Saunders, M.: 2014, Proximal newton-type methods for minimizing convex objective functions in composite form, *SIAM Journal on Optimization* 24(3), 1420

Lee, T.-W., Girolami, M., Bell, A. J., and Sejnowski, T. J.: 2000, A unifying information-theoretic framework for independent component analysis, *Computers and Mathematics with Applications* 39(11), 1–21

Leistedt, B. and McEwen, J. D.: 2012, Exact wavelets on the ball, *IEEE Transactions on Signal Processing* 60, 6257

Lemaréchal, C. and Hiriart-Urruty, J.-B.: 1996, *Convex Analysis and Minimization Algorithms I and II*, Springer, 2nd edition

Lemoine, D.: 1994, The discrete Bessel transform algorithm, *Journal of Chemical Physics* 101, 3936

Lewicki, M. S. and Sejnowski, T. J.: 2000, Learning overcomplete representations, *Neural Computation* 12(2), 337–365

Li, Y., Amari, S., Cichocki, A., Ho, D., and Xie, S.: 2006, Underdetermined blind source separation based on sparse representation, *IEEE Transactions on Signal Processing* 54, 423–437

Liang, J., Fadili, M., and Peyré, G.: 2014, Local linear convergence of forward–backward under partial smoothness, in *In Advances in Neural Information Processing Systems (NIPS)*

Lieu, L. H. and Vese, L. A.: 2008, Image restoration and decomposition via bounded total variation and negative Hilbert-Sobolev spaces, *Applied Mathematics and Optimization* 58(2), 167–193

Lim, W.-Q.: 2010, The discrete shearlet transform: A new directional transform and compactly supported shearlet frames, *IEEE Transactions on Image Processing* 19, 1166

Lim, W.-Q.: 2013, Nonseparable shearlet transform, *IEEE Transactions on Image Processing* 22(5), 2056–2065

Lindl, J.: 1997, *Inertial Confinement Fusion: The Quest for Ignition and Energy Gain Using Indirect Drive*, AIP, American Institute of Physics Press

Lions, P.-L. and Mercier, B.: 1979, Splitting algorithms for the sum of two nonlinear operators, *SIAM Journal on Numerical Analysis* 16, 964–979

Littlewood, J. and Paley, R.: 1931, Theorems on Fourier series and power series, *Journal of the London Mathematical Society* 6(20), 230–233

Lounici, K., Pontil, M., Tsybakov, A. B., and van de Geer, S.: 2009, Taking advantage of sparsity in multi-task learning, in *22th Annual Conference on Learning Theory, COLT*

Louys, M., Starck, J.-L., Mei, S., Bonnarel, F., and Murtagh, F.: 1999, Astronomical image compression, *A&A, Supplement Series* 136, 579–590

Lu, Y. and Do, M.: 2003, Crips-contourlets: A critical sampled directional multiresolution image representation, in *Wavelet X*, SPIE

Lu, Y. and Do, M.: 2007, Multidimensional directional filter banks and surfacelets, *IEEE Transactions on Image Processing* 16(4), 918

Lu, Y. and Do, M. N.: 2005, 3-D directional filter banks and surfacelets, in *Proceedings of SPIE Conference on Wavelet Applications in Signal and Image Processing XI, San Diego*

Luisier, F., Blu, T., and Unser, M.: 2007, A new SURE approach to image denoising: Inter-scale orthonormal wavelet thresholding, *IEEE Transactions on Image Processing* 16(3), 593–606

Lustig, M., Donoho, D. L., and Pauly, J. M.: 2007, Sparse MRI: The application of compressed sensing for rapid MR imaging, *Magnetic Resonance in Medicine* 58(6), 1182–1195

Ma, J. and Hussaini, M.: 2007, Three-dimensional curvelets for coherent vortex analysis of turbulence, *Appl. Phys. Letters* 91(184101)

Mairal, J., Bach, F., Ponce, J., and Sapiro, G.: 2010, Online learning for matrix factorization and sparse coding, *Journal of Machine Learning Research* 11, 19

Mairal, J., Elad, M., and Sapiro, G.: 2008, Sparse representation for color image restoration, *IEEE Transactions on Image Processing* 17, 53–69

Malgouyres, F.: 2002a, Mathematical analysis of a model which combines total variation and wavelet for image restoration, *Journal of Information Processeses* 2(1), 1–10

Malgouyres, F.: 2002b, Minimizing the total variation under a general convex constraint for image restoration, *IEEE Transactions on Image Processing* 11(12), 1450–1456

Malioutov, D., Çetin, M., and Willsky, A. S.: 2005, A sparse signal reconstruction perspective for source localization with sensor arrays, *IEEE Transactions on Image Processing* 53(8), 3010–3022

Mallat, S.: 1989, A theory for multiresolution signal decomposition: The wavelet representation, *IEEE Transactions on Pattern Analysis and Machine Intelligence* 11, 674–693

Mallat, S.: 2008, *A Wavelet Tour of Signal Processing, The Sparse Way*, Academic Press, 3rd edition

Mallat, S.: 2009, Geometrical grouplets, *Applied and Computational Harmonic Analysis* 26(2), 161–180

Mallat, S. and Peyré, G.: 2008, Orthogonal bandlet bases for geometric images approximation, *Communications on Pure and Applied Mathematics* 61(9), 1173–1212

Mallat, S. and Zhang, Z.: 1993, Matching pursuits with time-frequency dictionaries, *IEEE Transactions on Signal Processing* 41(12), 3397–3415

Marinucci, D., Pietrobon, D., Balbi, A., Baldi, P., Cabella, P., Kerkyacharian, G., Natoli, P., Picard, D., and Vittorio, N.: 2008, Spherical needlets for cosmic microwave background data analysis, *Monthly Notices of the Royal Astronomical Society* 383, 539–545

Martinet, B.: 1972, Détermination approchée d'un point fixe d'une application pseudo-contractante, *Comptes Rendus de l'Académie des Sciences de Paris* 1274, 163–165

Masnou, S. and Morel, J.: 1998, Level lines based disocclusion, in *IEEE International Conference on Image Processing*, Vol. III, 259–263

Masnou, S. and Morel, J.: 2002, Disocclusion: A variational approach using level lines, *IEEE Transactions on Image Processing* 11(2), 68–76

Matheron, G.: 1967, *Elements pour une Théorie des Milieux Poreux*, Masson

Matheron, G.: 1975, *Random Sets and Integral Geometry*, Wiley

Matus, F. and Flusser, J.: 1993, Image representations via a finite Radon transform, *IEEE Transactions on Pattern Analysis and Machine Intelligence* 15(10), 996–1006

McEwen, J. D., Hobson, M. P., Mortlock, D. J., and Lasenby, A. N.: 2007, Fast directional continuous spherical wavelet transform algorithms, *Signal Processing, IEEE Transactions on* 55(2), 520

McEwen, J. D., Vielva, P., Wiaux, Y., Barreiro, R. B., Cayon, L., Hobson, M. P., Lasenby, A. N., Martinez-Gonzalez, E., and Sanz, J. L.: 2007, Cosmological applications of a wavelet analysis on the sphere, *Journal of Fourier Analysis and Applications* 13, 495–510

McEwen, J. D. and Wiaux, Y.: 2011, A novel sampling theorem on the sphere, *IEEE Transactions on Signal Processing* 59, 5876

Meier, L., van de Geer, S., and Bühlmann, P.: 2008, The group Lasso for logistic regression, *Journal of the Royal Statistical Society B* 70(1), 53–71

Meinshausen, N. and Bühlmann, P.: 2006, High-dimensional graphs and variable selection with the Lasso, *Annals of Statistics* 34(3), 1436–1462

Meneveau, C.: 1991, Analysis of turbulence in the orthonormal wavelet representation, *Journal of Fluid Mechanics* 232, 469–520

Meyer, F., Averbuch, A., and Coifman, R.: 2002, Multilayered image representation: Application to image compression, *IEEE Transactions on Image Processing* 11, 1072–1080

Meyer, Y.: 1993, *Wavelets: Algorithms and Applications*, SIAM, Philadelphia

Meyer, Y.: 2002, Oscillating patterns in image processing and non linear evolution equations, *University Lecture Series, American Mathematical Society* 22

Miettinen, K.: 1999, *Nonlinear Multiobjective Optimization*, Kluwer, Boston

Miller, C. J., Genovese, C., Nichol, R. C., Wasserman, L., Connolly, A., Reichart, D., Hopkins, A., Schneider, J., and Moore, A.: 2001, Controlling the false-discovery rate in astrophysical data analysis, *Astronomical Journal* 122, 3492–3505

Moreau, J.-J.: 1962, Fonctions convexes duales et points proximaux dans un espace hilbertien, *Comptes Rendus de l'Académie des Sciences Série A Mathématiques* 255, 2897–2899

Moreau, J.-J.: 1963, Propriétés des applications "prox," *Comptes Rendus de l'Académie des Sciences Série A Mathématiques* 256, 1069–1071

Moreau, J.-J.: 1965, Proximité et dualité dans un espace hilbertien, *Bulletin de la Société Mathématique de France* 93, 273–299

Moudden, Y., Cardoso, J.-F., Starck, J.-L., and Delabrouille, J.: 2005, Blind component separation in wavelet space: Application to CMB analysis, *EURASIP Journal on Applied Signal Processing* 15, 2437–2454

Murenzi, R.: 1988, Wavelet transforms associated with the n-dimensional Euclidean group with dilations: Signal in more than one dimension, in A. G. J.M. Combes and P. Tchamitchian (eds.), *Wavelets: Time-Frequency Methods and Phase Space*, Springer-Verlag

Murtagh, F.: 2005, *Correspondence Analysis and Data Coding with R and Java*, Chapman & Hall/CRC Press

Murtagh, F. and Starck, J.: 2008, Wavelet and curvelet moments for image classification: Application to aggregate mixture grading, *Pattern Recognition Letters* 29, 1557–1564

Murtagh, F., Starck, J.-L., and Bijaoui, A.: 1995, Image restoration with noise suppression using a multiresolution support, *A&A, Supplement Series* 112, 179–189

Nadal, J.-P. and Parga, N.: 1994, Non-linear neurons in the low-noise limit: A factorial code maximises information transfer, *Network* 4, 295–312

Nam, S., Davies, M. E., Elad, M., and Gribonval, R.: 2013, The cosparse analysis model and algorithms, *Applied and Computational Harmonic Analysis* 34(1), 30

Needell, D. and Tropp, J. A.: 2008, CoSaMP: Iterative signal recovery from incomplete and inaccurate samples, *Applied and Computational Harmonic Analysis* 6, 301–321

Needell, D. and Vershynin, R.: 2010, Signal recovery from incomplete and inaccurate measurements via regularized orthogonal matching pursuit, *IEEE Journal of Selected Topics in Signal Processing* 4, 310–316

Neelamani, R., Choi, H., and Baraniuk, R. G.: 2004, ForWard: Fourier-wavelet regularized deconvolution for ill-conditioned systems, *IEEE Transactions on Signal Processing* 52(2), 418–433

Negahban, S. and Wainwright, M. J.: 2009, *Simultaneous support recovery in high dimensions: Benefits and perils of block ℓ_1/ℓ_∞-regularization*, Technical Report 774, UC Berkeley

Negi, P. and Labate, D.: 2012, 3-d discrete shearlet transform and video processing, *Image Processing, IEEE Transactions on* 21(6), 2944

Nemirovsky, A. S. and Yudin, D. B.: 1983, *Problem Complexity and Method Efficiency in Optimization*, John Wiley & Sons, New York

Nesterov, Y.: 1983, A method for solving the convex programming problem with convergence rate $o(1/k^2)$, *Doklady Akademii Nauk SSSR (DAN SSSR) Proceedings of the USSR Academy of Sciences* 269(3), 543

Nesterov, Y.: 2005, Smooth minimization of non-smooth functions, *Mathematical Programming* 103(1, Ser. A), 127–152

Nesterov, Y.: 2007, *Gradient methods for minimizing composite objective function*, CORE Discussion Papers 2007076, Université Catholique de Louvain, Center for Operations Research and Econometrics (CORE)

Ngolè Mboula, F. M., Starck, J.-L., Ronayette, S., Okumura, K., and Amiaux, J.: 2015, Super-resolution method using sparse regularization for point-spread function recovery, *A&A* 575, A86

Nia, X. S. and Huo, X.: 2009, Another look at Huber's estimator: A new minimax estimator in regression with stochastically bounded noise, *Journal of Statistical Planning and Inference* 139(2), 503–515

Nikolova, M.: 2000, Local strong homogeneity of a regularized estimator, *SIAM Journal on Applied Mathematics* 61(2), 633–658

Nowak, R. and Baraniuk, R.: 1999, Wavelet-domain filtering for photon imaging systems, *IEEE Transactions on Image Processing* 8, 666–678

Olshausen, B. and Field, D.: 1996a, Sparse coding with an overcomplete basis set: A strategy employed by V1?, *Vision Research.* 37, 3311–3325

Olshausen, B. A. and Field, D. J.: 1996b, Emergence of simple-cell receptive-field properties by learning a sparse code for natural images, *Nature* 381(6583), 607–609

Osborne, M. R., Presnell, B., and Turlach, B. A.: 2000, A new approach to variable selection in least squares problems, *IMA Journal of Numerical Analysis* 20(3), 389–403

Papoulis, A.: 1984, *Probability, Random Variables, and Stochastic Processes*, McGraw-Hill

Paykari, P., Lanusse, F., Starck, J.-L., Sureau, F., and Bobin, J.: 2014, PRISM: Sparse recovery of the primordial power spectrum, *A&A* 566, A77

Pearlmutter, B. and Parra, L.: 1997, Maximum likelihood blind source separation: A context-sensitive generalization of ICA, *Advances in Neural Information Processing Systems* 9, 613–619

Peng, G.-J. and Hwang, W.-L.: 2014, Reweighted and adaptive morphology separation, *SIAM Journal on Imaging Sciences* 7(4), 2078

Peyré, G., Fadili, M. J., and Starck, J.-L.: 2007, Learning adapted dictionaries for geometry and texture separation, in *Wavelet XII*, SPIE, San Diego

Peyré, G., Fadili, M. J., and Starck, J.-L.: 2010, Learning the morphological diversity, *SIAM Journal of Imaging Sciences* 3(3), 646

Peyré, G. and Mallat, S.: 2007, A review of bandlet methods for geometrical image representation, *Numerical Algorithms* 44(3), 205–234

Pham, D.-T., Garrat, P., and Jutten, C.: 1992, Separation of a mixture of independent sources through a maximum likelihood approach, in *Proceedings of EUSIPCO*, 771–774

Piella, G. and Heijmans, H.: 2002, Adaptive lifting schemes with perfect reconstruction, *IEEE Transactions on Image Processing* 50(7), 1620–1630

Pizurica, A., Philips, W., Lemahieu, I., and Achenoy, M.: 2002, Joint inter- and intrascale statistical model for Bayesian wavelet-based image denoising, *IEEE Transactions on Image Processing* 11(5), 545–557

Portilla, J., Strela, V., Wainwright, M., and Simoncelli, E.: 2003, Image denoising using scale mixtures of Gaussians in the wavelet domain, *IEEE Transactions on Image Processing* 12(11), 1338–1351

Raguet, H., Fadili, M. J., and Peyré, G.: 2013, A generalized forward-backward splitting, *SIAM Journal on Imaging Sciences* 6(3), 1199

Ramlau, R. and Teschke, G.: 2006, A projection iteration for nonlinear operator equations with sparsity constraints, *Numerische Mathematik* 104, 177–203

Ramlau, R., Teschke, G., and Zhariy, M.: 2008, A compressive Landweber iteration for solving ill-posed inverse problems, *Inverse Problems* 24(6), 065013

Rane, S., Bertalmio, M., and Sapiro, G.: 2002, Structure and texture filling-in of missing image blocks for wireless transmission and compression applications, *IEEE Transactions on Image Processing* 12(3), 296–303

Rapin, J., Bobin, J., Larue, A., and Starck, J.-L.: 2012, Robust non-negative matrix factorization for multispectral data with sparse prior, *Proceedings of ADA7*, Cargese, France

Rapin, J., Bobin, J., Larue, A., and Starck, J.-L.: 2013a, Sparse and non-negative BSS for noisy data, *IEEE Transactions on Signal Processing* 61, 5620

Rapin, J., Bobin, J., Larue, A., and Starck, J.-L.: 2013b, Sparse redundant formulations and non-negativity in blind source separation, in *Proceedings of EUSIPCO*, Marrakech, Morocco

Rapin, J., Bobin, J., Larue, A., and Starck, J.-L.: 2013c, Sparse regularizations and non-negativity in BSS, in *Proceedings of SPARS*, Lausanne, Switzerland

Rapin, J., Bobin, J., Larue, A., and Starck, J.-L.: 2014, NMF with sparse regularizations in transformed domains, *SIAM Journal on Imaging Sciences* 7(4), 2020

Rassat, A. and Refregier, A.: 2012, 3D spherical analysis of baryon acoustic oscillations, *AA* 540, A115

Rauhut, H., Schass, K., and Vandergheynst, P.: 2008, Compressed sensing and redundant dictionaries, *IEEE Transactions on Information Theory* 54(5), 2210–2219

Remi, K., Evans, A., and Pike, G.: 1999, MRI simulation-based evaluation of image-processing and classification methods, *IEEE Transactions on Medical Imaging* 18(11), 1085

Rice Wavelet Toolbox, Wavelet transform toolbox, *Wavelet Transform Toolbox*, www.dsp.rice.edu/software/rwt.shtml

Rioul, O. and Duhamel, P.: 1992, Fast algorithms for discrete and continuous wavelet transforms, *IEEE Transactions on Information Theory* 2(38), 569–586

Rockafellar, R.: 1970, *Convex Analysis*, Princeton University Press

Romberg, J., Wakin, M., and Baraniuk, R.: 2002, Multiscale wedgelet image analysis: Fast decompositions and modeling, in *IEEE International Conference on Image Processing 2002*, Vol. 3, pp. 585–588

Rubinstein, R., Peleg, T., and Elad, M.: 2013, Analysis k-svd: A dictionary-learning algorithm for the analysis sparse model, *IEEE Trans. on Signal Processing* 61(3), 661

Rudelson, M. and Vershynin, R.: 2007, On sparse reconstruction from Fourier and Gaussian measurements, *Communications on Pure and Applied Mathematics* 61(8), 1025–1045

Rudin, L., Osher, S., and Fatemi, E.: 1992, Nonlinear total variation noise removal algorithm, *Physica D* 60, 259–268

Rusanovskyy, D. and Egiazarian, K.: 2005, Video denoising algorithm in sliding 3D DCT domain, *Lecture Notes in Computer Science* 37(08), 618

Saevarsson, B., Sveinsson, J., and Benediktsson, J.: 2003, Speckle reduction of SAR images using adaptive curvelet domain, in *Proceedings of the IEEE International Conference on Geoscience and Remote Sensing Symposium, IGARSS '03*, Vol. 6, 4083–4085

Saligrama, V.: 2008, *Deterministic Designs with Deterministic Guarantees: Toeplitz Compressed Sensing Matrices, Sequence Designs and System Identification*, ArXiv preprint

Sardy, S., Antoniadis, A., and Tseng, P.: 2004, Automatic smoothing with wavelets for a wide class of distributions, *Journal of Computational and Graphical Statistics* 13(2), 399–421

Sardy, S., Bruce, A., and Tseng, P.: 2000, Block coordinate relaxation methods for nonparametric wavelet denoising, *Journal of Computational and Graphical Statistics* 9(2), 361–379

Sauvage, M., Chanial, P., Durand, G. A., Rodriguez, L. R., Starck, J.-L., Ronayette, S., Aussel, H., Minier, V., Motte, F., Pantin, E. J., Sureau, F., and Terrisse, R.: 2014, The science case and data processing strategy for the Thinned Aperture Light Collector (TALC): A project for a 20m far-infrared space telescope, in *Society of Photo-Optical Instrumentation Engineers (SPIE) Conference Series*, Vol. 9143 of *Society of Photo-Optical Instrumentation Engineers (SPIE) Conference Series*, p. 1

Scargle, P.: 1993, Wavelet methods in astronomical time series analysis, in O. Lessi (ed.), *Applications of Time Series Analysis in Astronomy and Meteorology*, University of Padua

Schmitt, J., Starck, J. L., Casandjian, J. M., Fadili, J., and Grenier, I.: 2010, Poisson denoising on the sphere: application to the Fermi gamma ray space telescope, *A&A* 517, A26+

Schmitt, J., Starck, J. L., Casandjian, J. M., Fadili, J., and Grenier, I.: 2012, Multichannel Poisson denoising and deconvolution on the sphere: application to the Fermi Gamma-ray Space Telescope, *A&A* 546, A114

Schröder, P. and Sweldens, W.: 1995, Spherical wavelets: Efficiently representing functions on the sphere, *SIGGRAPH 95, Computer Graphics Proceedings*, 161–172

Schwarz, G.: 1978, Estimating the dimension of a model, *Annals of Statistics* 6, 461–464

Selesnick, I.: 2004, The double-density dual-tree DWT, *IEEE Transactions on Image Processing* 52(5), 1304

Selesnick, I. and Figueiredo, M.: 2009, Signal restoration with overcomplete wavelet transforms: Comparison of analysis and synthesis priors, in *SPIE Conference on Signal and Image Processing: Wavelet Applications in Signal and Image Processing XIII*

Selesnick, I., Kingsbury, N. G., and Baraniuk, R. G.: 2005, The dual-tree complex wavelet transform – a coherent framework for multiscale signal and image processing, *Signal Processing Magazine* 22(6), 123–151

Selesnick, I. and Li, K. 2003, Video denoising using 2D and 3D dual-tree complex wavelet transforms, in *Proceedings of SPIE Conference on Wavelet Applications in Signal and Image Processing X*

Sendur, L. and Selesnick, I.: 2002a, Bivariate shrinkage functions for wavelet-based denoising exploiting interscale dependency, *IEEE Transactions on Signal Processing* 50(11), 2744–2756

Sendur, L. and Selesnik, I.: 2002b, Biavariate shrinkage with local variance estimation, *IEEE Signal Processing Letters* 9(12), 438–441

Serra, J.: 1982, *Image Analysis and Mathematical Morphology*, Academic Press

Shannon, C.: 1948, A mathematical theory for communication, *Bell System Technical Journal* 27, 379–423

Shensa, M.: 1992, Discrete wavelet transforms: Wedding the à trous and Mallat algorithms, *IEEE Transactions on Signal Processing* 40, 2464–2482

Simoncelli, E., Freeman, W., Adelson, E., and Heeger, D.: 1992, Shiftable multi-scale transforms, *IEEE Transactions on Information Theory* 38(2), 587–607

Simoncelli, E. and Olshausen, B.: 2001, Natural image statistics and neural representation, *Annual Review of Neuroscience* 24, 1193–1216

Slezak, E., de Lapparent, V., and Bijaoui, A.: 1993, Objective detection of voids and high density structures in the first CfA redshift survey slice, *Astrophysical Journal* 409, 517–529

Smith, M. and Barnwell, T.: 1988, Exact reconstruction technique for tree structured subband coders, *IEEE Transactions on Acoustics, Speech, and Signal Processing* 34, 434–441

Smoot, G. F., Bennett, C. L., Kogut, A., Wright, E. L., Aymon, J., Boggess, N. W., Cheng, E. S., de Amici, G., Gulkis, S., Hauser, M. G., Hinshaw, G., Jackson, P. D., Janssen, M., Kaita, E., Kelsall, T., Keegstra, P., Lineweaver, C., Loewenstein, K., Lubin, P., Mather, J., Meyer, S. S., Moseley, S. H., Murdock, T., Rokke, L., Silverberg, R. F., Tenorio, L., Weiss, R., and Wilkinson, D. T.: 1992, Structure in the COBE differential microwave radiometer first-year maps, *Astrophysical Journal Letters* 396, L1–L5

Soille, P.: 2003, *Morphological Image Analysis*, Springer

Starck, J., Martinez, V., Donoho, D., Levi, O., Querre, P., and Saar, E.: 2005a, Analysis of the spatial distribution of galaxies by multiscale methods, *Eurasip Journal on Applied Signal Processing* 15, 2455

Starck, J.-L.: 2002, Nonlinear multiscale transforms, in T. Barth, T. Chan, and R. Haimes (eds.), *Multiscale and Multiresolution Methods*, Springer, 239–278

Starck, J.-L., Aghanim, N., and Forni, O.: 2004a, Detecting cosmological non-Gaussian signatures by multi-scale methods, *A&A* 416, 9–17

Starck, J.-L. and Bijaoui, A.: 1994, Filtering and deconvolution by the wavelet transform, *Signal Processing* 35, 195–211

Starck, J.-L., Bijaoui, A., Lopez, B., and Perrier, C.: 1994, Image reconstruction by the wavelet transform applied to aperture synthesis, *A&A* 283, 349–360

Starck, J.-L., Bijaoui, A., and Murtagh, F.: 1995, Multiresolution support applied to image filtering and deconvolution, *CVGIP: Graphical Models and Image Processing* 57, 420–431

Starck, J.-L., Candès, E., and Donoho, D.: 2002, The curvelet transform for image denoising, *IEEE Transactions on Image Processing* 11(6), 131–141

Starck, J.-L., Candès, E., and Donoho, D.: 2003a, Astronomical image representation by the curvelet tansform, *A&A* 398, 785–800

Starck, J.-L., Donoho, D. L., and Candès, E. J.: 2001, Very high quality image restoration by combining wavelets and curvelets, in *Wavelets: Applications in Signal and Image Processing IX*, Vol. 4478, SPIE, 9–19

Starck, J.-L., Elad, M., and Donoho, D.: 2004, Redundant multiscale transforms and their application for morphological component analysis, *Advances in Imaging and Electron Physics* 132

Starck, J.-L., Elad, M., and Donoho, D.: 2005, Image decomposition via the combination of sparse representation and a variational approach, *IEEE Transactions on Image Processing* 14(10), 1570–1582

Starck, J.-L., Fadili, J., and Murtagh, F.: 2007, The undecimated wavelet decomposition and its reconstruction, *IEEE Transactions on Image Processing* 16, 297–309

Starck, J.-L., Fadili, J. M., Digel, S., Zhang, B., and Chiang, J.: 2009, Source detection using a 3D sparse representation: Application to the Fermi gamma-ray space telescope, *AA* 504, 641

Starck, J.-L., Fadili, M. J., and Rassat, A.: 2013, Low-ℓ CMB analysis and inpainting, *A&A* 550, A15

Starck, J.-L., Martinez, V., Donoho, D., Levi, O., Querre, P., and Saar, E.: 2005c, Analysis of the spatial distribution of galaxies by multiscale methods, *EURASIP Journal on Applied Signal Processing* 15, 2455–2469

Starck, J.-L., Moudden, Y., Abrial, P., and Nguyen, M.: 2006, Wavelets, ridgelets and curvelets on the sphere, *A&A* 446, 1191–1204

Starck, J.-L. and Murtagh, F.: 1994, Image restoration with noise suppression using the wavelet transform, *A&A* 288, 343–348

Starck, J.-L. and Murtagh, F.: 2006, *Astronomical Image and Data Analysis*, Springer, 2nd edition

Starck, J.-L., Murtagh, F., and Bertero, M.: 2011, Starlet transform in astronomical data processing, *Handbook of Mathematical Methods in Imaging*, Springer, pp. 1489–1531

Starck, J.-L., Murtagh, F., and Bijaoui, A.: 1998, *Image Processing and Data Analysis: The Multiscale Approach*, Cambridge University Press

Starck, J.-L., Murtagh, F., Candès, E., and Donoho, D.: 2003b, Gray and color image contrast enhancement by the curvelet transform, *IEEE Transactions on Image Processing* 12(6), 706–717

Starck, J.-L., Murtagh, F., and Fadili, M.: 2010, *Sparse Image and Signal Processing*, Cambridge University Press

Starck, J.-L., Murtagh, F., Pirenne, B., and Albrecht, M.: 1996, Astronomical image compression based on noise suppression, *Publications of the Astronomical Society of the Pacific* 108, 446–455

Starck, J.-L., Nguyen, M., and Murtagh, F.: 2003c, Wavelets and curvelets for image deconvolution: A combined approach, *Signal Processing* 83(10), 2279–2283

Steidl, G., Weickert, J., Brox, T., Mrázek, P., and Welk, M.: 2004, On the equivalence of soft wavelet shrinkage, total variation diffusion, total variation regularization, and SIDEs, *SIAM Journal on Numerical Analysis* 42(2), 686–713

Stein, C.: 1981, Estimation of the mean of a multivariate normal distribution, *Annals of Statistics* 9, 1135–1151

Stollnitz, E., DeRose, T., and Salesin, D.: 1995, Wavelets for computer graphics: A primer, Part 1, *IEEE Computer Graphics and Applications*, 76–84

Stoschek, A.: 2003, *Compression of optical readout biomolecular sensory data*, US Patent 6580831

Sweldens, W.: 1997, The lifting scheme: A construction of second generation wavelets, *SIAM Journal on Mathematical Analysis* 29, 511–546

Sweldens, W. and Schröder, P.: 1996, Building your own wavelets at home, in *Wavelets in Computer Graphics*, ACM Special Interest Group on Computer Graphics, SIGGRAPH course notes, 15–87

Tegmark, M.: 1996, An icosahedron-based method for pixelizing the celestial sphere, *Astrophysical Journal Letters* 470, L81–L84

Tenorio, L., Jaffe, A. H., Hanany, S., and Lineweaver, C. H.: 1999, Applications of wavelets to the analysis of Cosmic Microwave Background maps, *Monthly Notices of the Royal Astronomical Society* 310, 823–834

Tibshirani, R.: 1996, Regression shrinkage and selection via the Lasso, *Journal of the Royal Statistical Society* 58(1), 267–288

Tikhonov, A.: 1963, Solution of incorrectly formulated problems and the regularization method, *English translation of Doklady Akademii Nauk SSSR* 151, 501–504

Timmermann, K. E. and Nowak, R.: 1999, Multiscale modeling and estimation of Poisson processes with applications to photon-limited imaging, *IEEE Transactions on Signal Processing* 46, 886–902

Tropp, J.: 2006a, Algorithms for simultaneous sparse approximation. Part II: Convex relaxation, *Signal Processing* 86(589–602)

Tropp, J.: 2014, Convex recovery of a structured signal from independent random linear measurements, in *Sampling Theory, a Renaissance*, Birkhäuser

Tropp, J. and Gilbert, A.: 2007, Signal recovery from partial information via orthogonal matching pursuit, *IEEE Transactions on Information Theory* 53(12), 4655–4666

Tropp, T.: 2006b, Just relax: Convex programming methods for subset selection and sparse approximation, *IEEE Transactions on Information Theory* 52(3), 1030–1051

Tseng, P.: 1991, Applications of a splitting algorithm to decomposition in convex programming and variational inequalities, *SIAM Journal on Control and Optimization* 29(1), 119–138

Tseng, P.: 1997, Alternating projection-proximal methods for convex programming and variational inequalities, *SIAM Journal on Optimization* 7(4), 951

Tseng, P.: 2001, Convergence of a block coordinate descent method for nondifferentiable minimizations, *Journal of Optimization Theory and Applications* 109(3), 457–494

Tseng, P.: 2008, On accelerated proximal gradient methods for convex-concave optimization, preprint

Unser, M.: 1999, Splines: A perfect fit for signal and image processing, *IEEE Signal Processing Magazine* 16(6), 22–38

Unser, M., Aldroubi, A., and Eden, M.: 1993, The L_2-polynomial spline pyramid, *IEEE Transactions on Pattern Analysis and Machine Intelligence* 15(4), 364–379

Vaiter, S., Deledalle, C.-A., Peyré, G., Dossal, C., and Fadili, J.: 2013, Local behavior of sparse analysis regularization: Applications to risk estimation, *Applied and Computational Harmonic Analysis* 35(3), 433

Vaiter, S., Peyré, G., Dossal, C., and Fadili, M. J.: 2013, Robust sparse analysis regularization, *IEEE Transactions on Information Theory* 59(4), 2001

Van De Ville, D., Blu, T., and Unser, M.: 2005, Isotropic polyharmonic B-Splines: Scaling functions and wavelets, *IEEE Transactions on Image Processing* 14(11), 1798–1813

Van Den Berg, E. and Friedlander, M. P.: 2008, Probing the Pareto frontier for basis pursuit solutions, *SIAM Journal on Scientific Computing* 31(2), 890–912

van den Dries, L. and Miller, C.: 1996, Geometric categories and o-minimal structures, *Duke Mathematical Journal* 84(2), 497

van Spaendonck, R., Blu, T., Baraniuk, R., and Vetterli, M.: 2003, Orthogonal Hilbert transform filter banks and wavelets, in *IEEE Conference on Acoustics, Speech and Signal Processing*, Vol. 6, 505–508

Velisavljevic, V., Beferull-Lozano, B., Vetterli, M., and Dragotti, P.: 2006, Directionlets: Anisotropic multi-directional representation with separable filtering, *IEEE Transactions on Image Processing* 15(7), 1916–1933

Vese, L. and Osher, S.: 2003, Modeling textures with total variation minimization and oscillating patterns in image processing, *Journal of Scientific Computing* 19, 553–577

Vetterli, M.: 1986, Filter banks allowing perfect reconstruction, *Signal Processing* 10(3), 219–244

Vielva, P., Martínez-González, E., Barreiro, R. B., Sanz, J. L., and Cayón, L.: 2004, Detection of non-Gaussianity in the Wilkinson Microwave Anisotropy Probe first-year data using spherical wavelets, *Astrophysical Journal* 609, 22–34

Vielva, P., Wiaux, Y., Martínez-González, E., and Vandergheynst, P.: 2006, Steerable wavelet analysis of CMB structures alignment, *New Astronomy Review* 50, 880–888

Vincent, E.: 2007, Complex nonconvex lp norm minimization for underdetermined source separation, in M. E. Davies, C. J. James, S. A. Abdallah, and M. D. Plumbley (eds.), *Independent Component Analysis and Signal Separation*, Vol. 4666 of *Lecture Notes in Computer Science*, Springer, 430–437

Vincent, E., Gribonval, R., and Févotte, C.: 2006, Performance measurement in blind audio source separation, *IEEE Transactions on Audio, Speech & Language Processing* 14(4), 1462

Vonesch, C., Ramani, S., and Unser, M.: 2008, Recursive risk estimation for non-linear image deconvolution with a wavelet-domain sparsity constraint, in *ICIP*, pp. 665–668, IEEE

Vonesch, C. and Unser, M.: 2007, A fast iterative thresholding algorithm for wavelet-regularized deconvolution, *Proceedings of IEEE International Symposium on Biomedical Imaging, ISBI*

Vũ, B.: 2013, A splitting algorithm for dual monotone inclusions involving cocoercive operators, *Advances in Computational Mathematics* 38(3), 667

Wainwright, M. J.: 2009, Sharp thresholds for high-dimensional and noisy sparsity recovery using ℓ_1-constrained quadratic programming (lasso), *IEEE Transactions on Information Theory* 55(5), 2183–2202

Wavelab 802: 2001, Wavelab toolbox, *WaveLab Toolbox*, www-stat.stanford.edu/~wavelab

Weaver, J. B., Yansun, X., Healy, D. M., and Cromwell, L. D.: 1991, Filtering noise from images with wavelet transforms, *Magnetic Resonance in Medicine* 21(2), 288–295

White, R. A. and Stemwedel, S. W.: 1992, The quadrilateralized spherical cube and quad-tree for all sky data, in D. M. Worrall, C. Biemesderfer, and J. Barnes (eds.), *Astronomical Data Analysis Software and Systems I*, Vol. 25 of *Astronomical Society of the Pacific Conference Series*, 379–381

Wiaux, Y., Jacques, L., Vielva, P., and Vandergheynst, P.: 2006, Fast directional correlation on the sphere with steerable filters, *Astrophysical Journal* 652, 820–832

Wiaux, Y., McEwen, J. D., Vandergheynst, P., and Blanc, O.: 2008, Exact reconstruction with directional wavelets on the sphere, *Monthly Notices of the Royal Astronomical Society* 388, 770–788

Wiaux, Y., McEwen, J. D., and Vielva, P.: 2007, Complex data processing: Fast wavelet analysis on the sphere, *Journal of Fourier Analysis and Applications* 13, 477–493

Willet, R. and Nowak, R.: 2007, Multiscale Poisson intensity and density estimation, *IEEE Transactions on Information Theory* 53(9), 3171–3187

Willett, R. M. and Nowak, R. D.: 2003, Platelets: A multiscale approach for recovering edges and surfaces in photon-limited medical imaging, *IEEE Transactions on Medical Imaging* 22(3), 332–350

Woiselle, A., Starck, J., and Fadili, M.: 2010, 3d curvelet transforms and astronomical data restoration, *ACHA* 28(2), 171

Woiselle, A., Starck, J., and Fadili, M.: 2011, 3-D Data denoising and inpainting with the low-redundancy fast curvelet transform, *Journal of Mathematical Imaging and Vision* 39(2), 121

Wright, S., Nowak, R., and Figueiredo, M.: 2009, Sparse reconstruction by separable approximation, *IEEE Transactions on Signal Processing* 57, 2479–2493

Xiao, L. and Zhang, T.: 2013, A proximal-gradient homotopy method for the sparse least-squares problem, *SIAM Journal on Optimization* 23(1062–1091)

Yaghoobi Vaighan, M., Nam, S., Gribonval, R., and Davies, M. E.: 2013, Constrained overcomplete analysis operator learning for cosparse signal modelling, *IEEE Transactions on Signal Processing* 61(9), 2341

Yamada, I.: 2001, The hybrid steepest descent method for the variational inequality problem over the intersection of fixed point sets of nonexpansive mappings, in D. Butnariu, Y. Censor, and S. Reich (eds.), *Inherently Parallel Algorithms in Feasibility and Optimization and Their Applications*, Elsevier, pp. 473–504

Ying, L., Demanet, L., and Candès, E.: 2005, 3D discrete curvelet transform, in *Wavelets XI Conference*, San Diego

Ying, L. and Zou, Y. M.: 2009, Linear transformations and restricted isometry property, *CoRR* abs/0901.0541

Yu, G., Mallat, S., and Bacry, E.: 2008, Audio denoising by time-frequency block thresholding, *IEEE Transactions on Signal Processing* 56(5), 1830–1839

Yuan, M. and Lin, Y.: 2006, Model selection and estimation in regression with grouped variables, *Journal of the Royal Statistical Society B* 68(1), 49–67

Zdunek, R. and Cichocki, A.: 2007, Blind image separation using nonnegative matrix factorization with Gibbs smoothing, in *Proceedings of ICONIP*, pp. 519–528

Zhang, B., Fadili, M., and Starck, J.-L.: 2008a, Fast Poisson noise removal by biorthogonal Haar domain hypothesis testing, *Statistical Methodology* 5(4), 387–396

Zhang, B., Fadili, M. J., and Starck, J.-L.: 2008b, Wavelets, ridgelets and curvelets for Poisson noise removal, *IEEE Transactions on Image Processing* 17(7), 1093–1108

Zhang, Z., Huang, W., Zhang, J., Yu, H., and Lu, Y.: 2006, Digital image watermark algorithm in the curvelet domain, in *Proceedings of the International Conference on Intelligent Information Hiding and Multimedia Signal Processing (IIH-MSP'06)*, 105–108

Zhi-Oei Liang, P. C. L.: 2000, *Principles of Magnetic Resonance Imaging*, IEEE Press

Zibulevski, M.: 2003, Blind source separation with relative Newton method, *Proceedings of ICA, Independent Component Analysis, 2003*, 897–902

Zibulevsky, M. and Pearlmutter, B.: 2001, Blind source separation by sparse decomposition in a signal dictionary, *Neural Computation* 13, 863–882

Zou, H., Hastie, T., and Tibshirani, R.: 2007, On the "degrees of freedom" of the Lasso, *Annals of Statistics* 35, 2173–2192

Index

Printed in the United States
by Baker & Taylor Publisher Services